FOREIGN AFFAIRS

Other books by the National Society of Film Critics

Produced and Abandoned:
The Best Films You've Never Seen
The Movie Star
Movie Comedy
Film 73/74
Film 72/73
Film 71/72
Film 70/71
Film 69/70
Film 68/69
Film 67/68

FOREIGN AFFAIRS

THE NATIONAL SOCIETY OF FILM CRITICS'
VIDEO GUIDE TO FOREIGN FILMS

edited by
KATHY SCHULZ HUFFHINES

Mercury House, Incorporated
San Francisco

Published in the United States by
Mercury House
San Francisco, California

Printed on acid-free paper
Manufactured in the United States of America

Library of Congress Cataloging-in-Publication Data

Foreign affairs : the national society of film critics' video guide to foreign
films / edited by Kathy Schulz Huffhines.
    p.   cm.
  Includes index.
  ISBN 1–56279–016–1
  1. Foreign films — United States — Reviews.   2. Video recordings —
Reviews.   I. Huffhines, Kathy Schulz.
PN1995.9.F67F68   1991
791.43'75 — dc20   91–9960
                                                                        CIP

CONTENTS

Kathy Schulz Huffhines, 1943–91   xv

Introduction   xvii

The First Wave, 1920–45   1

Denmark: Carl Dreyer
- Retrospective, *Andrew Sarris*   4
- Gertrud (1964), *Andrew Sarris*   5
- Vampyr (1932), *Pauline Kael*   6

England: Michael Powell
- Retrospective, *Carrie Rickey*   7

England: Charles Crichton
- The Lavender Hill Mob (1951), *Pauline Kael*   10

England: Alfred Hitchcock
- Sabotage (1936), *Michael Sragow*   10

England: David Lean
- Oliver Twist (1948); Hobson's Choice (1954),
  Michael Sragow   11

England: Carol Reed
- The Fallen Idol (1948), *Michael Sragow*   12

France: Max Ophuls
- The Earrings of Madame de . . . (1953),
  Pauline Kael   13

France: Jean Renoir
- Retrospective, *Jay Carr*   16

France: Jean Vigo
- L'Atalante (1934), *Terrence Rafferty*   21
- Zéro de Conduite (1933), *John Powers*   26

France: Marcel Carné
- Bizarre, Bizarre (1937), *Peter Rainer*   26
- Children of Paradise (1945), *Pauline Kael*   29

France: René Clair
- À Nous la Liberté (1931), *Pauline Kael*   29

France: Henri-Georges Clouzot
- The Raven (1943); The Wages of Fear (1953), *Michael Sragow*   30

France: Jean Cocteau
- Orpheus (1949), *Michael Sragow*   31

France: Julien Duvivier
- Pépé le Moko (1937), *Pauline Kael*   32

France: Georges Franju
- Judex (1963), *David Ansen*   33

France: Marcel Pagnol
- The Baker's Wife (1938), *Pauline Kael*   33

Germany: Fritz Lang
- Metropolis (1927); M (1931), *Morris Dickstein*   34

Germany: F. W. Murnau
- Nosferatu (1922), *Pauline Kael*   36

Germany: G. W. Pabst
- Pandora's Box (1928), *Jay Carr*   37

Germany: Josef von Sternberg
- The Blue Angel (1929), *Pauline Kael*   38

Germany: Robert Wiene
- The Cabinet of Dr. Caligari (1919), *Pauline Kael*   39

Italy's Big Four
- Visconti, Rossellini, Antonioni, Fellini, *Andrew Sarris*   40

Italy: Michelangelo Antonioni
- L'Avventura (1960), *Pauline Kael*   44
- Red Desert (1964), *Jonathan Rosenbaum*   46
- The Passenger (1975), *John Powers*   46

Italy: Federico Fellini
- Nights of Cabiria (1957), *Andrew Sarris*   47
- La Strada (1954), *Morris Dickstein*   53

Italy: Roberto Rossellini
- Open City (1945), *Pauline Kael*   54
- Paisan (1946), *Pauline Kael*   55

■ General della Rovere (1959), *Pauline Kael*   55

Italy: Luchino Visconti

■ The Leopard (1963), *Michael Sragow*   56
■ La Terra Trema (1947), *Pauline Kael*   62

Italy: Vittorio De Sica

■ Shoeshine (1947), *Pauline Kael*   63
■ The Bicycle Thief (1949),
   Michael Wilmington   65
■ Umberto D. (1952), *Michael Sragow*   65

Japan: Kon Ichikawa

■ Odd Obsession (1959), *Pauline Kael*   66
■ The Makioka Sisters (1985), *Michael Sragow*   69

Japan: Akira Kurosawa

■ The Seven Samurai (1954), *Dave Kehr*   75
■ Kagemusha (1980), *Morris Dickstein*   79
■ Stray Dog (1949), *Kevin Thomas*   82
■ High and Low (1963), *Kevin Thomas*   83

Japan: Kenji Mizoguchi

■ The Life of Oharu (1952),
   Jonathan Rosenbaum   84
■ Ugetsu (1954), *Pauline Kael*   87
■ Sansho the Bailiff (1954), *Michael Sragow*   88

Japan: Yasujiro Ozu

■ Tokyo Story (1953), *John Powers*   89
■ Floating Weeds (1959), *Michael Wilmington*   93

Soviet Union: Sergei Eisenstein

■ Alexander Nevsky (1938),
   Kathy Schulz Huffhines   93
■ Potemkin (1925), *Andrew Sarris*   97

Soviet Union: Alexander Dovzhenko

■ Earth (1930), *Pauline Kael*   98

Soviet Union: Vsevolod Pudovkin

■ Mother (1926), *Pauline Kael*   98

Spain: Luis Buñuel

■ Retrospective, *Morris Dickstein*   99
■ The Discreet Charm of the Bourgeoisie (1972),
   Jonathan Rosenbaum   102

Sweden: Ingmar Bergman

■ Retrospective, *Richard Corliss*   108

■ The Silence (1963); Persona (1966),
Morris Dickstein   113

The Second Wave, 1945–65   121

Lindsay Anderson
■ This Sporting Life (1962), *Judith Crist*   123
■ If . . . (1968), *Richard Schickel*   125

Bernardo Bertolucci
■ Last Tango in Paris (1972), *Pauline Kael*   127
■ The Last Emperor (1987), *Peter Rainer*   135
■ The Conformist (1970), *Pauline Kael*   138

John Boorman
■ Hope and Glory (1987), *David Ansen*   139
■ Point Blank (1967), *John Powers*   141

Robert Bresson
■ Diary of a Country Priest (1950); Mouchette (1967),
Henry Sheehan   142

Claude Chabrol
■ The Cousins (1959), *Pauline Kael*   147
■ Landru (1963), *Kevin Thomas*   151
■ Story of Women (1988), *Henry Sheehan*   152

Milos Forman
■ Loves of a Blonde (1965), *Judith Crist*   157
■ The Firemen's Ball (1968),
Michael Wilmington   158

Jean-Luc Godard
■ Retrospective, *Armond White*   159

Sergio Leone
■ Once upon a Time in the West (1969),
Dave Kehr   164
■ The Good, the Bad, and the Ugly (1967),
Dave Kehr   169

Joseph Losey
■ The Servant (1963), *Andrew Sarris*   169
■ Accident (1967), *Charles Champlin*   172

Louis Malle
■ Murmur of the Heart (1971), *Michael Sragow*   174
■ Au Revoir les Enfants (1987), *Peter Rainer*   177
■ Zazie dans le Métro (1960), *Pauline Kael*   181

Jean-Pierre Melville
■ Bob le Flambeur (1955), *Stephen Schiff*   181
■ Le Doulos (1962), *Kathy Schulz Huffhines*   187
■ Les Enfants Terribles (1949), *Pauline Kael*   188

Nikita Mikhalkov
■ An Unfinished Piece for a Player Piano (1977),
Sheila Benson   188

■ A Slave of Love (1984), *Michael Wilmington*   191

Sergei Paradjanov

■ Overview, *Jonathan Rosenbaum*   191

Pier Paolo Pasolini

■ Overview, *Jonathan Rosenbaum*   192

Roman Polanski   ■ Repulsion (1965), *Bruce Williamson*   194

■ Knife in the Water (1961), *Michael Sragow*   196

Satyajit Ray   ■ The Home and the World (1984), *Peter Rainer*   196

■ Pather Panchali (1955), *Pauline Kael*   200

■ Aparajito (1957), *Pauline Kael*   201

■ The World of Apu (1959), *Pauline Kael*   201

Alain Resnais   ■ Night and Fog (1955), *Kevin Thomas*   202

■ Hiroshima, Mon Amour (1959), *Andrew Sarris*   203

■ Providence (1977), *Richard T. Jameson*   204

Tony Richardson

■ The Entertainer (1960), *Michael Sragow*   207

■ Look Back in Anger (1958),
Michael Wilmington   211

Jacques Rivette   ■ The Nun (1966), *Dave Kehr*   211

■ Paris Belongs to Us (1960),
Jonathan Rosenbaum   213

Eric Rohmer   ■ My Night at Maud's (1968), *Richard Schickel*   214

■ Boyfriends and Girlfriends (1988),
Terrence Rafferty   216

Francesco Rosi   ■ Three Brothers (1981), *Kathy Schulz Huffhines*   219

■ Christ Stopped at Eboli (1979), *Michael Sragow*   222

Carlos Saura   ■ Cria! (1975), *Richard T. Jameson*   223

■ Carmen (1983), *Jay Carr*   225

John Schlesinger

■ Billy Liar (1963), *Judith Crist*   225

■ Sunday Bloody Sunday (1971), *Pauline Kael*   227

Andrei Tarkovsky

■ Retrospective, *Jay Carr*   228

Jacques Tati   ■ Parade (1973), *Jonathan Rosenbaum*   231

Bertrand Tavernier

■ Coup de Torchon (1981), *Dave Kehr*   237

■ Life and Nothing But (1989),
Kathy Schulz Huffhines   241

François Truffaut

■ Retrospective, *Terrence Rafferty*   243

Agnès Varda ■ Vagabond (1985), *Julie Salamon* 249
■ Cleo from 5 to 7 (1962), *Pauline Kael* 251
Andrzej Wajda ■ Man of Marble (1976), *Stephen Schiff* 251
■ Kanal (1956), *Michael Wilmington* 255

The Third Wave, 1965–90 **257**

Percy Adlon ■ Céleste (1981), *David Ansen* 259
■ Sugarbaby (1984), *Michael Wilmington* 260
Pedro Almodóvar
■ Retrospective, *Carrie Rickey* 262
Jean-Jacques Beineix
■ Diva (1981), *Stephen Schiff* 265
■ Betty Blue (1986), *Andrew Sarris* 270
Bertrand Blier
■ Get Out Your Handkerchiefs (1978),
David Denby 271
■ Beau Père (1981), *Kathy Schulz Huffhines* 275
■ Going Places (1974), *Pauline Kael* 281
David Cronenberg
■ Scanners (1981), *Kenneth Turan* 282
■ Dead Ringers (1988), *Dave Kehr* 284
Rainer Werner Fassbinder
■ The Marriage of Maria Braun (1978),
Richard T. Jameson 286
■ Berlin Alexanderplatz (1980), *Andrew Sarris* 289
Bill Forsyth ■ Local Hero (1983), *David Denby* 291
■ Gregory's Girl (1981), *Kathy Schulz Huffhines* 294
Stephen Frears ■ My Beautiful Laundrette (1985), *John Powers* 294
■ Prick Up Your Ears (1987), *Peter Rainer* 298
Peter Greenaway
■ The Draughtsman's Contract (1982),
John Powers 302
■ The Cook, the Thief, His Wife and Her Lover (1989),
Andrew Sarris 303
Werner Herzog ■ Aguirre, the Wrath of God (1972), *David Ansen* 304
■ The Enigma of Kaspar Hauser (1974),
Charles Champlin 307

Shohei Imamura

■ The Pornographers (1966), *J. Hoberman*   309

■ Eijanaika (1981), *Dave Kehr*   311

Juzo Itami   ■ Tampopo (1986), *Richard Schickel*   315

■ A Taxing Woman (1987), *Jay Carr*   317

Neil Jordan   ■ Mona Lisa (1986), *David Denby*   319

■ The Company of Wolves (1984),
Michael Wilmington   322

Emir Kusturica   ■ When Father Was Away on Business (1985),
Jay Carr   322

■ Time of the Gypsies (1989),
Kathy Schulz Huffhines   324

Maurice Pialat   ■ Loulou (1980), *Andrew Sarris*   325

■ À Nos Amours (1983), *Henry Sheehan*   327

■ Under Satan's Sun (1987), *John Powers*   329

Paolo and Vittorio Taviani

■ Padre Padrone (1977), *David Ansen*   330

■ The Night of the Shooting Stars (1981),
Pauline Kael   332

Paul Verhoeven

■ The Fourth Man (1983), *David Ansen*   338

Peter Weir   ■ Picnic at Hanging Rock (1975),
Richard T. Jameson   339

■ Gallipoli (1981), *Bruce Williamson*   343

Wim Wenders   ■ Retrospective, *Stephen Schiff*   344

■ Wings of Desire (1987), *Jay Carr*   349

The Next Wave   353

African Films: Souleymane Cisse

■ Yeelen (Brightness) (1987), *Jonathan Rosenbaum*   354

African Films: Idrissa Ouedraogo

■ Yaaba (1989), *Armond White*   355

Theo Angelopoulos

■ Retrospective, *Michael Wilmington*   358

Jane Campion   ■ Sweetie (1989), *Hal Hinson*   364

Atom Egoyan   ■ Speaking Parts (1989); Family Viewing (1987),
J. Hoberman   367

Fifth Generation Chinese Films: Tian Zhuangzhuang

■ The Horse Thief (1987), *Jonathan Rosenbaum*   369

Fifth Generation Chinese Films: Zhang Yimou
    ■ Red Sorghum (1988), *Kathy Schulz Huffhines*   373
Hong Kong Films: Tsui Hark
    ■ Peking Opera Blues (1986), *J. Hoberman*   375
Hong Kong Films: Stanley Kwan
    ■ Rouge (1987), *John Powers*   377
Hong Kong Films: John Woo
    ■ A Better Tomorrow (1986), *John Powers*   377
International Coproductions: Nikita Mikhalkov
    ■ Dark Eyes (1987), *Jay Carr*   378
Japanimation: Hiroaki Yoshida
    ■ Twilight of the Cockroaches (1987),
        Carrie Rickey   380
Aki Kaurismäki   ■ Retrospective, *J. Hoberman*   382
Mira Nair   ■ Salaam Bombay (1988), *Armond White*   386

Recommended from England   389

Jon Amiel   ■ The Singing Detective (1986), *Jay Carr*   390
Kenneth Branagh
    ■ Henry V (1989), *Joseph Gelmis*   392
Alex Cox   ■ Sid and Nancy (1986), *Owen Gleiberman*   394
Terrence Davies   ■ Distant Voices, Still Lives (1988),
        Jonathan Rosenbaum   400
David Hare   ■ Wetherby (1985), *Roger Ebert*   404
David Leland   ■ Wish You Were Here (1987), *Hal Hinson*   405
John Mackenzie   ■ The Long Good Friday (1980), *Michael Sragow*   409
Peter Medak   ■ The Krays (1990), *Kathy Schulz Huffhines*   412
Chris Menges   ■ A World Apart (1988), *Owen Gleiberman*   414
Pat O'Connor   ■ Cal (1984), *Kathy Schulz Huffhines*   418

Recommended from France   421

Claude Berri   ■ Jean de Florette (1986), *Richard Schickel*   422
Claire Denis   ■ Chocolat (1988), *Armond White*   424
Diane Kurys   ■ Entre Nous (1983), *Gary Arnold*   426
Claude Lanzmann
    ■ Shoah (1985), *J. Hoberman*   430
Patrice Leconte   ■ Monsieur Hire (1989), *Henry Sheehan*   436
Chris Marker   ■ Sans Soleil (1982), *Henry Sheehan*   438

Marcel Ophuls ■ Hotel Terminus: The Life and Times of Klaus Barbie
(1987), *Stuart Klawans*   442
Jean-Paul Rappeneau
■ Cyrano de Bergerac (1990), *Peter Travers*   446
Jean-Charles Tacchella
■ Cousin, Cousine (1975), *Charles Champlin*   447

Recommended from Elsewhere in West and East Europe   451

Bille August ■ Pelle the Conqueror (1987), *Jay Carr*   452
Gabriel Axel ■ Babette's Feast (1987), *Richard Schickel*   454
Costa-Gavras ■ Z (1969), *Judith Crist*   456
Doris Dörrie ■ Men . . . (1985), *Julie Salamon*   458
Victor Erice ■ The Spirit of the Beehive (1976), *David Ansen*   460
Lasse Hallstrom ■ My Life as a Dog (1985), *Sheila Benson*   463
Ermanno Olmi ■ The Tree of Wooden Clogs (1978),
Andrew Sarris   465
Wolfgang Petersen
■ Das Boot (1981), *Kenneth Turan*   468
Edgar Reitz ■ Heimat (1983), *Michael Wilmington*   470
Jerzy Skolimowski
■ Moonlighting (1982), *John Powers*   473
Istvan Szabo ■ Mephisto (1981), *Michael Wilmington*   476
Giuseppe Tornatore
■ Cinema Paradiso (1988), *Peter Travers*   479

Recommended from the Soviet Union   481

Tengiz Abuladze
■ Repentance (1987), *Sheila Benson*   482
Alexei Gherman ■ My Friend Ivan Lapshin (1986), *Sheila Benson*   484
Vitaly Kanevski ■ Freeze, Die, Come to Life (1990),
Kathy Schulz Huffhines   487
Pavel Lounguine
■ Taxi Blues (1990), *Jay Carr*   489
Vasily Pichul ■ Little Vera (1988), *Stuart Klawans*   491

Recommended from South America   495

Suzana Amaral ■ Hour of the Star (1985), *John Powers*   496
Hector Babenco ■ Pixote (1981), *Pauline Kael*   497

Bruno Barreto ■ Dona Flor and Her Two Husbands (1977),
  Gary Arnold   502

Maria-Luisa Bemberg
  ■ Camila (1984), *Carrie Rickey*   504

Carlos Diegues ■ Bye Bye Brazil (1980), *Roger Ebert*   506

Ruy Guerra ■ Opera do Malandro (1986),
  Michael Wilmington   507

Gregory Nava ■ El Norte (1983), *Kathleen Carroll*   509

Euzhan Palcy ■ Sugar Cane Alley (1983), *Henry Sheehan*   511

Luis Puenzo ■ The Official Story (1985), *Richard Schickel*   513

Recommended from Australia   515

Bruce Beresford ■ Breaker Morant (1980), *Kenneth Turan*   516

Paul Cox ■ Man of Flowers (1984), *Richard T. Jameson*   518

George Miller ■ The Road Warrior (1981), *Richard T. Jameson*   521

Carl Schultz ■ Careful, He Might Hear You (1983), *Jay Carr*   524

Nadia Tass ■ Malcolm (1986), *Sheila Benson*   526

About the Contributors   529

Mail-Order Video Rental and Sales Companies   535

Permissions   539

Index of Directors   546

Index of Actors   550

Index of Films   557

About the Editor   567

KATHY SCHULZ HUFFHINES, 1943–91

Who could have dreamed that this book would be Kathy Huffhines's epitaph? Three hours after she Federal Expressed the photos for it, a 200-year-old oak tree fell over, crushed the roof of the car in which she was riding, and sent her into a coma she never came out of. Until what was literally that last day, she had spent six hectic months zestfully producing this book while working full-time at her job as film critic of the *Detroit Free Press*. She laughingly described *Foreign Affairs* as a triumph of nagging—a view that any editor who ever tried to extract copy from forty writers by fax, phone, and letter will appreciate.

Because I was close to her, thus making my remarks suspect, I probably should go easy on praising her astuteness, her considerable critical and writing ability, the sharp, bright, buoyant spirit that shone from her work and her life, the respect she had for genuineness of feeling, and the high value she placed on humor. She was graceful, airy, witty, irresistibly eccentric, full of brains and heart and integrity, and she had the shiniest hair! Let me just add that when I read her reviews of *Beau Père* (included in this book), *Kagemusha*, and *Tootsie*, I knew she was in the right business. Her last year was the best year of her life, in large part because she felt secure in the knowledge that at the *Detroit Free Press* she had found a congenial home and a large, receptive audience after years of paying dues. She was a rising star.

I will not try to reproduce the acknowledgments that Kathy intended to write, but I know she planned to heap praise on Michael Sragow, film critic of the *San Francisco Examiner*, who edited the previous National Society of Film Critics anthology, *Produced and Abandoned*. This book would never have taken shape as expeditiously as it did without him. He never said no. Kathy also intended to thank Peter Moore for his ready assistance in answering numerous factual questions and Zipporah Collins for steadfast and diligent handling of the editorial production of the book.

Finally a word about Kathy's two role models—her aunt, Frances Moffat, who for years covered society for the *San Francisco Examiner* and *San Francisco Chronicle,* and Pauline Kael, who needs no introduction here. In one of those unforeseen convergences in which life abounds, Frances Moffat can gaze down on the office of this book's publisher from her home on Telegraph Hill. And Kathy's happiest moment with the book came in June when she visited Pauline Kael and came away feeling Pauline thought she had done OK. As for me, I miss her more than I can say.

—Jay Carr

INTRODUCTION

A few blocks from where you live sit three hundred of the best foreign films ever made, available at a video rental store. If you go to specialty shops or mail-order video rental companies, there's even more at your zip-code fingertips: rare, early, hard-to-find titles; movies from countries that don't get enormous shelf space at your local outlet; movies so unavailable previously that they're missing from the best-known books about the great foreign directors. Look at it as an extension to your living room—a high-tech version of André Malraux's Museum Without Walls.

If you're interested in, say, Jean Renoir, his *Grand Illusion* and *The Rules of the Game* are likely to be nearby. Specialty video outlets can give you access to *La Chienne* (1931), *Boudu Saved from Drowning* (1932), *Madame Bovary* (1934), *The Crime of Monsieur Lange* (1935), *La Marseillaise* (1937), *La Bête Humaine* (1938), *A Day in the Country* (1946), *The River* (1951), *The Golden Coach* (1952), *Elena and Her Men* (1956), *French Can-Can* (1956), *Picnic on the Grass* (1959), *The Elusive Corporal* (1962), and *The Little Theater of Jean Renoir* (1969). You can even see Renoir's star-struck wife, Catherine Hessling, the woman who got him into the movie game, by renting the two silent shorts she starred in: *The Little Match Girl* (1928) and *The Charleston* (1927).

It goes without saying that these films are at their best when they're respected as film and projected on a big screen. Even though the ranks of repertory theaters are thinning, every city still offers opportunities to see these movies in theaters or at libraries, schools, and clubs. The best way to use this book is to go for big-screen experiences whenever possible and fill in with the new small-screen options.

But there's a lot to be said for a video age that gives people in any city, no matter how small, immediate access to twenty-nine films by Ingmar Bergman, twenty by Akira Kurosawa, twenty by Luis Buñuel, fifteen by Roberto Rossellini, ten by Wim Wenders, seven by Pedro

Almodóvar. If you liked Claude Berri's 1986 version of Marcel Pagnol's *Jean de Florette* and *Manon of the Spring,* this is the first time anyone anywhere can go immediately to the nine films written and/or directed by Pagnol himself between 1931 and 1954.

This book was compiled to help guide you through today's rapidly expanding availability of foreign films. The first four chapters pinpoint key directors in four waves of international filmmaking, highlighting the most important directing careers that began between 1920–45; 1945–65; 1965–85; and a "next wave" of directors or schools of filmmaking currently gaining international attention. The last six chapters recommend additional films from the countries that—so far—have elicited the greatest worldwide interest.

Key directors are covered through retrospectives or in-depth reviews supported by shorter capsule reviews and additional recommendations in the chapter introductions. Who are they? What are their movies about? What are their styles? The retrospectives answer those questions over the course of a career; the longer reviews answer the same questions by looking at one or more of the director's best movies in depth.

"The first thirty meters of *Zéro de Conduite* establish Jean Vigo's reputation as a great director," François Truffaut said in his essay on Vigo in *The Films of My Life.* "It is sometimes claimed that a man's character is formed between the age of seven and twelve. In the same way, it can also be said that a film director's entire career can be assessed from the first fifty meters of film he has shot.

"The essence of the man will be contained in that early footage and he will remain essentially true to himself from then on, though he may do better work (masterpieces) or lesser work (failures). The whole of Orson Welles is contained in the first reel of *Citizen Kane,* the whole of Buñuel in *Un Chien Andalou.*"

It's our hope to find "the whole" of directors like Yasujiro Ozu, Bille August, Pedro Almodóvar, or Jane Campion by taking a long look at one of their best movies: Ozu's *The Tokyo Story,* August's *Pelle the Conqueror,* Almodóvar's *Women on the Verge of a Nervous Breakdown,* Campion's *Sweetie.*

We think all four of these movies are accessible and artistic. But that's an editorial "we." Some group members would say that any fan of Ozu films is too enamored of Those Obscure Objects of Desire. Some group members would say that any fan of *Pelle the Conqueror* is too enamored of Cinematic Paradiso. But, as foreign film enthusiasts will quickly recognize, this is a book that takes in the full range—Obscure Objects of Desire to Cinematic Paradiso and all stops between.

The pieces in the book were written by members of the National Society of Film Critics—a group of thirty-seven writers from major general-interest publications: mainstream newspapers like the *Los Angeles Times* and the *Washington Post;* alternative weeklies like the *Village Voice* and the *Chicago Reader;* magazines like *Time, Newsweek,* the *New Yorker,* and *Film Comment;* quarterlies like *Partisan Review.*

"Key" directors were chosen by the editor; or by book committee members Jay Carr, Richard Jameson, Peter Rainer, Michael Sragow, and Michael Wilmington; or by the urgent appeals of several other National Society of Film Critics members. Because of space limitations, directors who aren't covered by retrospectives are covered by at least one longer review, one shorter review, and additional recommendations in the chapter introductions.

Through these coverage combinations, we list each "key" director's top two to five films available on video. This book lists only recommended films; it doesn't represent mixed or negative reactions. Directors with fewer than two recommended films available on cassette are included in the later chapters organized by country. Many good films aren't mentioned at all. If you want to read about them, tell our publisher that you'd like to see an expanded edition.

We have included a handful of films that are being considered for cassette release but will not be available on video by this book's publication date. Those entries are listed as Video Requests. Otherwise, you'll be able to find any title in this book at a local video rental chain or at one of the mail-order video rental or sales companies listed on page 534.

Kathy Schulz Huffhines

THE FIRST WAVE, 1920–45

Movies began as a global art, narrowed to centers in Europe and America between 1940 and 1980, and once again are going global. In this chapter, we indicate the countries of origin (alphabetically) to emphasize the worldwide nature of important moviemaking in the first eras of silent and sound film — most notably with extended surveys of directors from France, Italy, and Japan. The section on France also includes brief reviews indicating the importance of such directors as René Clair, Henri-Georges

Opposite page: scene from *L'Atalante*.

Clouzot, Jean Cocteau, Julien Duvivier, Georges Franju, and Marcel Pagnol.

England is represented by a retrospective on Michael Powell—the filmmaker whose work might be least familiar—and brief reviews pointing out some earlier, less well-known, more atmospherically British movies by Charles Crichton, Alfred Hitchcock, David Lean, and Carol Reed.

Russian filmmaking is covered by an extended section on Sergei Eisenstein and brief reviews of films by Alexander Dovzhenko and Vsevolod Pudovkin; German filmmaking is surveyed by a longer look at Fritz Lang's two best early movies and briefer pieces indicating the importance of F. W. Murnau, G. W. Pabst, Josef von Sternberg, and Robert Wiene.

For directors with multiple coverage, the retrospectives run first, then the chronologically ordered longer reviews offering an in-depth look at themes and styles, then the shorter reviews. For instance: Buñuel is covered by Morris Dickstein's retrospective, then Jonathan Rosenbaum's review of *The Discreet Charm of the Bourgeoisie*. Kurosawa is covered by Dave Kehr's review of *The Seven Samurai,* one of Kurosawa's best earlier films; then by Morris Dickstein's review of *Kagemusha,* considered by some the best of Kurosawa's late style; then by Kevin Thomas's reviews guiding fans to two of Kurosawa's best lesser-known movies available on videocassette.

Italian directors Rossellini, Visconti, De Sica, Antonioni, and Fellini—whose careers began in the early 1940s but whose most important films came out from the late forties to the early sixties—are included here to make the point that the French New Wave was really a second wave that built on the achievements of filmmaking around the world from the twenties to the fifties—particularly their French fathers and Italian neorealist older brothers.

Other recommended foreign-language titles available on video are:

Marcel Carné: *Le Jour Se Lève* (1939), *Les Visiteurs du Soir* (1942)

René Clair: *The Italian Straw Hat* (1928), *Sous les Toits de Paris* (1929), *Le Million* (1931)

Henri-Georges Clouzot: *Jenny Lamour* (1947), *Manon* (1948), *Diabolique* (1955)

Jean Cocteau: *Blood of a Poet* (1930), *Beauty and the Beast* (1946)

Julien Duvivier: *Poil de Carotte* (1932), *Panique* (1946)

Georges Franju: *Eyes without a Face* (1959)

Max Ophuls: *Liebelei* (1932), *La Ronde* (1950), *Le Plaisir* (1951), *Lola Montès* (1955)

Marcel Pagnol: screenwriter: *Marius* (1931), *Fanny* (1932); screenwriter-director: *Cesar* (1936), *Harvest* (1937), *The Well-Digger's Daughter* (1941)

Jean Vigo: *À Propos de Nice* (1929)

Fritz Lang: *Spiders* (1919), *Dr. Mabuse, the Gambler* (1922), *Spies* (1928)

F. W. Murnau: *The Last Laugh* (1924), *Faust* (1926), *Sunrise* (1927), *Tabu* (1931)

G. W. Pabst: *Joyless Street* (1925), *Diary of a Lost Girl* (1929), *Kameradschaft* (1931), *The Threepenny Opera* (1931)

Josef von Sternberg: *Docks of New York* (1928), *Morocco* (1930), *Anatahan* (1953)

Michelangelo Antonioni: *Il Grido* (1957), *Eclipse* (1966), *Blow-Up* (1966)

Federico Fellini: *The White Sheik* (1951), *I Vitelloni* (1953), *La Dolce Vita* (1961), *8½* (1963)

Roberto Rossellini: *Germany Year Zero* (1947), *Stromboli* (1949)

Luchino Visconti: *Ossessione* (1942), *Bellissima* (1951), *Senso* (1954), *Death in Venice* (1971)

Vittorio De Sica: *Miracle in Milan* (1951), *The Garden of the Finzi-Continis* (1971)

Akira Kurosawa: *Ikiru* (1952), *The Hidden Fortress* (1958), *Yojimbo* (1961), *Ran* (1985)

Kon Ichikawa: *The Burmese Harp* (1956), *Fires on the Plain* (1959), *Tokyo Olympiad* (1965)

Kenji Mizoguchi: *The Sisters of the Gion* (1936), *The Story of the Last Chrysanthemum* (1939)

Yasujiro Ozu: *Late Spring* (1949), *Early Summer* (1951)

Alexander Dovzhenko: *Zvenigora* (1928)

Sergei Eisenstein: *Strike* (1924), *Ten Days That Shook the World* (1927), *Ivan the Terrible* (Part One, 1947)(Part Two, 1956)

Vsevolod Pudovkin: *End of St. Petersburg* (1927)

Denmark: Carl Dreyer

■

RETROSPECTIVE

Carl Theodor Dreyer, a man always out of season, now belongs to the agelessness of art. He died in March 1968 in Denmark at the age of seventy-nine. All in all, fourteen features and five documentaries constitute the legacy of half a century of Dreyer's desperately personal filmmaking. No fewer than nine of his features were silent movies commissioned and delivered in the decade between 1918 and 1928, and culminating in his most celebrated achievement, *The Passion of Joan of Arc*, with Marie Falconetti. Thirty years later Godard paid tribute to Dreyer by cross-cutting Karina's tears with Falconetti's within his own Passion of a prostitute, *My Life to Live*.

Unfortunately, Dreyer's Passion did not end with *Joan of Arc*. It was only beginning. The intervals of activity in the next forty years speak for themselves: *Vampyr* (1932), *Day of Wrath* (1943), *Two People* (1945), *Ordet* (1955), and *Gertrud* (1965). Along the way Dreyer acquired admirers, but not backers. His talking films were stronger in the long haul than in the short run. *Day of Wrath* ran for only one week at the Little Carnegie despite raves from Archer Winsten and the late James Agee. *Vampyr* never achieved the vogue of such inferior horror films as James Whale's *Frankenstein* and Tod Browning's *Dracula*. *Gertrud* concluded Dreyer's career on a note of critical scandal and commercial disaster. His difficulties with financiers made such intransigent individualists as Buñuel and Stroheim seem like Dale Carnegies by comparison. Buñuel and Stroheim could at least promise the titillation of shock and sacrilege; Dreyer, like Bresson, could offer nothing but austerity and eternity.

Dreyer was never so much ahead of his time as out of his time. No critic ever described him as "modern." *The Passion of Joan of Arc* seemed backward in its period, not only because it was a silent movie released in the midst of talkies with all the self-consciousness of an "art" film but also because Dreyer's enormous close-ups lacked the structural dynamism of Eisenstein's dialectical montage in *Potemkin* and *October*. *Day of Wrath* struck most critics of its time as too slowly paced for the demands of film art. The sin of *Gertrud* was that it dared to be deliberately slow and stately in an era in which film critics worshipped the cinematic virtuosity of elongated television commercials. For

Dreyer, unfortunately, there were no shortcuts or even jump-cuts to eternity.

Dreyer was never as interested in jazzy film techniques as in the subtlest feelings that could be expressed through the human face by a staring camera. He was therefore less a dramatist than a portraitist, but a portraitist gifted with a metaphysical urgency and implacability. His gallery of witches, bigots, persecutors, sensualists, and perverts never became a rogues' gallery, simply because Dreyer saw the torments of his characters in terms of a world still governed by God. For Carl Theodor Dreyer, man, not the medium, was the message.

—*Andrew Sarris*

Denmark: Carl Dreyer

■

GERTRUD (1964)

Gertrud is a sternly beautiful work of art with none of the fashionable flabbiness of second-chance sentimentality exemplified most vividly in Monica Vitti's compassionate caress of Gabriele Ferzetti in the final, ultimate blank-wall composition of *L'Avventura*. Dreyer has lived long enough to know that you live only once and that all decisions are paid in full to eternity. Some critics have attacked Gertrud herself as a Hedda Gabler character, consumed by her destructive demands for perfection in others. The difference between the two, however, is the difference between a genuine idealism, however intolerant, and foolish fantasizing. Dreyer did not create the character of Gertrud; he has "merely" adapted a play to the screen. Yet no mere adaptation could capture the lyrical intensity and lucid interiority of this film. Dreyer has poured his soul into the luminous light into which the actors float on an ever so subtly and ever so slowly moving camera. "But this isn't cinema!" snort the registered academicians with their kindergarten notions of kinetics. How can you have cinema when two people sit and talk on a couch as their life drifts imperceptibly out of their grasp? The academicians are right of course. Dreyer simply isn't cinema. Cinema is Dreyer.

That wildly beating heart struggling against its mortal coils, that fierce resignation one encounters in characters who realize too late that love is the only meaningful issue of life, the only consolation of memory. Admittedly there is something cold and merciless and implacable in Dreyer's vision of life, and the *Mensch*-munch audience may be put off by the film's intolerant attitude toward inadequacy. The whining of Herzog is more in the mode than the settled solitude of Gertrud, but Dreyer should not be tagged as an elitist. He grasps and treasures what he has held despite his tortured awareness of what he has lost. The tenacity of his art is summed up in the ceremonial style Gertrud maintains to the last flickering light of her life, to the last conversation on a couch, to the last warm, human encounter before the meaningless mists of eternity enshroud her. *Gertrud* is the kind of masterpiece that deepens with time because it has already aged in the heart of a great artist.

—*Andrew Sarris*

Denmark: Carl Dreyer

■

VAMPYR (1932)

Most vampire movies are so silly that this film by Carl Dreyer — a great vampire film — hardly belongs to the genre. Dreyer preys upon our subconscious fears. Dread and obsession are the film's substance, and its mood is evocative, dreamy, spectral. Death hovers over everyone. The cast is headed by Julian West (the movie name of Nicolas de Gunzburg), with Henriette Gérard as the vampire, and Rena Mandel and Sybille Schmitz as her potential victims. The incomparable photographic effects are the work of Rudolph Maté. Movie lovers may cherish what appears to be Dreyer's homage to Cocteau — the use of the little heart from *The Blood of a Poet.* (Roger Vadim's 1960 exercise in supernatural chic, *Blood and Roses*, is based on the same story by Sheridan Le Fanu that Dreyer used.)

—*Pauline Kael*

England: Michael Powell

■

RETROSPECTIVE

British filmmaker Michael Powell, who died February 19, 1990, in London at eighty-four, was a dapper, mustachioed man who had the courtly manners of an Oxford don.

You never would have pegged this tweedy gent for the director of that Wagnerian magic carpet ride *The Thief of Baghdad* (1940) or the creator of *Black Narcissus* (1947), surely the only genteel movie ever made about the erotic fantasies of nuns.

Powell's colleague Richard Attenborough saluted him in London on Tuesday, saying, "Of his generation, he was unquestionably the most innovative and creatively brilliant filmmaker this country ever boasted." Note that Powell's "generation" of Britons includes Alfred Hitchcock, Alexander Korda, and David Lean.

In New York, Martin Scorsese cited Powell's "great influence on my work," and called him "one of the giants of world cinema."

Why all the fuss? Michael Powell was not a filmmaker; he was a deity worshiped by cinephiles everywhere. He had a unique vision, and his films—even those shot on sound stages—boast an almost palpable sense of place.

In Britain, where he made virtually all of his thirty-odd features, Powell was a rogue surrealist among the realists. He exploited the inherent dreaminess of the medium, matter-of-factly defending his approach with "Of course, all films are surrealist. They are making something that looks like the real world but isn't."

Powell, born in 1905 in Bekesbourne, Kent, was roughly the same age as the infant medium of film. Though trained as a banker, he opted for a career in film and in the late 1920s toiled as a photographer on Hitchcock projects. Powell's earliest produced screenplays were for *Caste* (1930) and *Hotel Splendide* (1932), "quota quickies" hastily made to boost Britain's domestic film industry.

After a string of such quickies, Powell made his mark as a writer-director with the quirky, shot-on-location film *Edge of the World* (1937), a mystical, folkloric account of villagers in Scotland's Shetland Isles. It was named best foreign film by the New York Film Critics Circle.

The turning point in Powell's career came in 1938 when Korda, an émigré Hungarian, introduced his countryman Emeric Pressburger to the director. The unlikely marriage of the bohemian Briton and peppery Hungarian produced England's greatest films. With the exception of *The Thief of Baghdad,* a fantasy Powell directed with Ludwig Berger and Tim Whelan in 1940, and *Peeping Tom,* a notorious Powell thriller made in 1959, his best work was in collaboration with Pressburger.

Though the credits read, "written, produced, and directed by Michael Powell and Emeric Pressburger," it was generally understood that Pressburger invented the stories and wrote them in fractured English and that Powell polished the scripts and directed the films.

Their first collaboration, the U-boat melodrama *The Spy in Black* (1938), meditated on the German national character, a theme that would emerge in subsequent Powell-Pressburger films. Their movies suggested that there were good Germans and bad, a provocative subject for patriotic Englishmen on the eve of World War II.

Reflecting the relationship of their filmmakers, Powell-Pressburger films were dialogues between a Northern European and a Central European. Their legendary *The 49th Parallel* (1940) — about Nazi spies in Canada — and *The Life and Death of Colonel Blimp* (1943) — about the forty-year friendship between a British and a German soldier — were startling accounts of how British gentlemanliness might be crushed by Teutonic "total war."

The 49th Parallel earned Pressburger an Oscar for "best screen story." *Colonel Blimp* earned both men the contempt of Prime Minister Winston Churchill, who found the film starring Roger Livesey, Anton Walbrook, and Deborah Kerr "too critical" of the English military. Friends warned Powell off *Blimp,* telling him that if he made it "the old man (Churchill) will be very cross, and you'll never get a knighthood."

Powell never did.

Also during wartime, he and Pressburger made the enchanted romance *I Know Where I'm Going* (1945), starring Livesey as a Scottish laird and Wendy Hiller as a headstrong woman determined to marry a millionaire. The film's lilting look at the Scottish landscape and people presaged *Local Hero* by forty years.

Stairway to Heaven (1946) earned Powell and Pressburger international acclaim. This realistic/fantastic account of a wounded World War II pilot (David Niven) shows him in limbo between death and life, pleading before a heavenly tribunal to let him live so that he can marry

Kim Hunter, a WAC. The fighter-pilot sequences are fantasylike, the heavenly scenes as realistic as a British bureau of licenses.

Where *Stairway to Heaven* was a matter of life or death, *Black Narcissus* (1946) was a matter of faith or flesh. This breathtakingly beautiful color film set in the Himalayas (but shot in England) stars Kerr as the sister superior in an order of nuns dispatched to run a mountain-top infirmary in a converted brothel. As in all Powell-Pressburger films, the personality of the place possesses the souls of its inhabitants.

And, of course, there is *The Red Shoes* (1948), which stars Moira Shearer as the ballerina who must choose between love or work. Inspired by the Hans Christian Andersen fairy tale, *The Red Shoes* is most haunting.

Though Powell would continue to make movies through the 1970s, his baroque sensibility was at odds with the prevailing British taste for realism. At first he was dismissed for such films as his adaptation of Offenbach's *The Tales of Hoffmann* (1951), which was called "a spectacular failure." Like most of his films, its mood of romanticism vs. pessimism seems modern.

Powell was virtually forgotten in this country until 1980, when the Museum of Modern Art in New York hosted a retrospective of "The Films of Powell and Pressburger." Championed by Scorsese, Francis Coppola, and George Lucas, Powell was rediscovered.

Shortly after the death of his wife, Frances Reidy, in 1983, Powell attended the premiere for Coppola's *One from the Heart* at Radio City Music Hall in New York. Asked by a reporter if he had any regrets, the seventy-seven-year-old Powell replied, "Thirty-five years ago I made a movie about the incompatibility of love and work called *The Red Shoes*. I regret that I didn't believe its message."

The following year Powell married Thelma Schoonmaker, Oscar-winning editor of *Raging Bull* and other Scorsese films. He bloomed, wrote two volumes of his memoirs (the first was published in 1987, the year before Pressburger died) and talked about possible film projects. Last seen by the same reporter a year ago, Powell was optimistic, conceding that perhaps love and work were compatible after all.

Like the end of his best movies, the last years of Powell's life were a triumph of romance over pessimism.

— *Carrie Rickey*

England: Charles Crichton

■

THE LAVENDER HILL MOB (1951)

As the prim, innocuous civil servant with a hidden spark of nonconformity, Alec Guinness carries out a dream of larcenous glory: robbing the Bank of England. A man who steals three million in gold bullion may be permitted to coin a word: Guinness describes his gleaming-eyed, bowler-hatted little man as the "fubsy" type, and he's an image of Everyman. T. E. B. Clarke's script, Charles Crichton's direction, and Georges Auric's music contribute to what is probably the most nearly perfect fubsy comedy of all time. It's a minor classic, a charmer. Stanley Holloway is the genteel, artistic accomplice; Alfie Bass and Sidney James the professional assistants; and one of the beneficiaries of Guinness's wrongdoing is a bit player, Audrey Hepburn.

—Pauline Kael

England: Alfred Hitchcock

■

SABOTAGE (1936)

Eric Rohmer, Claude Chabrol, and François Truffaut dismissed it; Graham Greene praised it. Alfred Hitchcock's 1936 *Sabotage* could be described as a Hitchcock film for people who don't like Hitchcock films—although many Hitchcock cultists like it, too. This spare, harrowing adaptation of Joseph Conrad's *The Secret Agent* is the most character-oriented and emotionally daring of the director's early thrillers. It's about espionage as shabby-genteel terrorism. Oscar Homolka and Sylvia Sidney are touchingly incongruous as man and wife—Mr. and Mrs. Verloc, who manage an East London movie theater and care for Mrs. Verloc's younger brother, Stevie (Desmond Tester). The young, pretty, sensitive Mrs. Verloc has married for the security her husband provides Stevie and herself. That's why it's so heartbreaking and ironic that the deceptively phlegmatic Mr. Verloc is a saboteur.

A Scotland Yard investigator (John Loder) takes a cover job at the green-grocer's next to the movie theater and ends up falling in love with Mrs. Verloc. But *Sabotage* is an antiromantic suspense film. In the United States it was called *A Woman Alone,* and for once an American title is apt—Mrs. Verloc learns just how nightmarish a marriage of compromise can be. The movie deserves to be seen fresh, without having its surprises revealed and then analyzed to death. Hitchcock creates an atmosphere of booby-trapped claustrophobia: the characters release their secret hatreds and ambitions in terrifying spasms and explosions. The killings don't offer audiences the usual cathartic genre thrills; instead, they deepen our identification with Mrs. Verloc. This film is as wrenching as it is eruptive. Hitchcock never went further beyond pop than he did in *Sabotage.*

—*Michael Sragow*

England: David Lean
■

OLIVER TWIST (1948)
HOBSON'S CHOICE (1954)

Since David Lean is best known as the master of the Anglo-American superproduction, it may come as a surprise that the best double bill you could see in an extensive salute to the British director is a pair of black-and-white beauties. His 1948 *Oliver Twist* is the epitome of bravura visual storytelling. From the movie's stormy prologue to its climactic rooftop chase, Lean propels Dickens's tale of a crime-buffeted orphan with stylized sequences that connect in electric arcs. He surrounds his limpid, poignant Oliver, John Howard Davies, with a terrifying and delightful rogues' gallery, including Robert Newton as Bill Sikes and a young Anthony Newley as the Artful Dodger. The movie's influence on Carol Reed's great movie musical *Oliver!* is evident when Alec Guinness, a magnificently scurvy Fagin, transforms a pickpocketing lesson into a comic ballet.

The musical side of Lean's talent comes to the fore in his delightful 1954 adaptation of Harold Brighouse's play *Hobson's Choice,* in which a turn-of-the-century male-chauvinist shoe-store owner (Charles

Laughton) gets his comeuppance at the hands of his eldest daughter (Brenda de Banzie) and his most gifted shoemaker (John Mills). Lean creates humorous cadenzas by linking his camera movements and the soundtrack music. The wonderfully zesty performers — at times, Mills suggests Chaplin — give the material (which had been filmed twice before) a vaudevillian lift. Seeing this double bill, you realize what a shame it is that Lean has never directed a full-fledged musical comedy.

—Michael Sragow

England: Carol Reed

■

THE FALLEN IDOL (1948)

Carol Reed's *The Fallen Idol,* written by Graham Greene from his short story "The Basement Room," is a psychological thriller with subtleties and tensions that at times recall Henry James's "The Turn of the Screw." The central figure is a lonely boy named Felipe (Bobby Henrey), an ambassador's son living in a sprawling London embassy; the story hinges on his hero worship for the butler, Baines (Ralph Richardson), an unhappily married man in love with an embassy secretary named Julie (Michelle Morgan). The villain is Mrs. Baines (Sonia Dresdel), whom Greene described as "thin, menacing, dusty." Her life-denying decision to hang on to Baines at all costs — and Baines's dreams of escape — traps Felipe in a tissue of lies.

This vintage (1948) suspense film is remarkably tender; it gains a fluid emotionality from the shifts in Felipe's heart. With an absent father and a mother ailing far away from home, Felipe clings to Baines as his life raft. Baines is a decent, playful, alternately bluff and decorous sort, with a genuine fondness for the boy. The moviemakers have an uncanny feeling — expressed in both dialogue and camera angles — for how a child gets through the same events as adults yet experiences them completely differently. In one wistful sequence, Baines and Julie steal some time for each other when they take Felipe to the zoo; the viewer is torn between sympathy for the furtive lovers and for the boy, who badly needs companionship. In *The Fallen Idol,* childhood and adulthood travel on parallel tracks connected by catastrophe.

—Michael Sragow

France: Max Ophuls

■

THE EARRINGS OF MADAME DE . . . (1953)

Madame de, a shallow, narcissistic beauty, has no more feeling for her husband than for his gifts: she sells the diamond earrings he gave her rather than confess her extravagance and debts. Later, when she falls in love with Baron Donati, he presents her with the same pair of earrings and they become a token of life itself. Once she has experienced love she cannot live without it: she sacrifices her pride and honor to wear the jewels, she fondles them as if they were parts of her lover's body. Deprived of the earrings and of the lover, she sickens . . . unto death.

This tragedy of love, which begins in careless flirtation and passes from romance, to passion, to desperation, is, ironically, set among an aristocracy that seems too superficial and sophisticated to take love tragically. Yet the passion that develops in this silly, vain, idle society woman not only consumes her but is strong enough to destroy three lives.

The novella and the movie could scarcely be more unlike: the austere, almost mathematical style of Louise de Vilmorin becomes the framework, the logic underneath Ophuls's lush, romantic treatment. In *La Ronde* he had used Schnitzler's plot structure but changed the substance from a cynical view of sex as the plane where all social classes are joined and leveled (venereal disease is transmitted from one couple to another in this wry roundelay) — to a more general treatment of the failures of love. For Ophuls *La Ronde* became the world itself — a spinning carousel of romance, beauty, desire, passion, experience, regret. Although he uses the passage of the earrings as a plot motif in the same way that Louise de Vilmorin had, he deepens and enlarges the whole conception by the creation of a world in such flux that the earrings themselves become the only stable, recurrent element — and they, as they move through many hands, mean something different in each pair of hands, and something fatally different for Madame de because of the different hands they have passed through. It may not be accidental that the film suggests de Maupassant: between *La Ronde* and *The Earrings of Madame de . . .* Ophuls had worked (rather unsuccessfully) on three de Maupassant stories which emerged as *Le Plaisir.*

In these earlier films he had also worked with Danielle Darrieux; perhaps he was helping to develop the exquisite sensibility she brings to Madame de — the finest performance of her career. Her deepening powers as an actress (a development rare among screen actresses, and particularly rare among those who began, as she did, as a little sex kitten) make her seem even more beautiful now than in the memorable *Mayerling* — almost twenty years earlier — when, too, she had played with Charles Boyer. The performances by Danielle Darrieux, Charles Boyer, and Vittorio De Sica are impeccable — ensemble playing of the smoothness usually said to be achieved only by years of repertory work.

However, seeing the film, audiences are hardly aware of the performances. A novelist may catch us up in his flow of words; Ophuls catches us up in the restless flow of his images — and because he does not use the abrupt cuts of "montage" so much as the moving camera, the gliding rhythm of his films is romantic, seductive, and, at times, almost hypnotic. James Mason once teased Ophuls with the jingle: "A shot that does not call for tracks is agony for poor dear Max." The virtuosity of his camera technique enables him to present complex, many-layered material so fast that we may be charmed and dazzled by his audacity and hardly aware of how much he is telling us. It is no empty exercise in decor when Madame de and the Baron dance in what appears to be a continuous movement from ball to ball. How much we learn about their luxurious lives, the social forms of their society, and the change in their attitudes toward each other! By the end, they have been caught in the dance; the trappings of romance have become the trap of love.

The director moves so fast that the suggestions, the feelings, must be caught on the wing; Ophuls will not linger, nor will he *tell* us anything. We may see Madame de as a sort of Anna Karenina in reverse: Anna gets her lover but she finds her life shallow and empty; Madame de's life has been so shallow and empty she cannot get her lover. She is destroyed, finally, by the fact that women do not have the same sense of honor that men do, nor the same sense of pride. When, out of love for the Baron, she thoughtlessly lies, how could she know that he would take her lies as proof that she did not really love him? What he thinks dishonorable is merely unimportant to her. She places love before honor (what woman does not?) and neither her husband nor her lover can forgive her. She cannot undo the simple mistakes that have ruined her; life rushes by and the camera moves inexorably.

The very beauty of *The Earrings of Madame de . . .* is often used against it: the sensuous camerawork, the extraordinary romantic atmosphere, the gowns, the balls, the staircases, the chandeliers, the polished, epigrammatic dialogue, the preoccupation with honor are all regarded as evidence of lack of substance. Ophuls's reputation has suffered from the critics' disinclination to accept an artist for what he can do—for what he loves—and their effort to castigate him for not being a different *type* of artist. Style—great personal style—is so rare in moviemaking that critics might be expected to clap their hands when they see it; but, in the modern world, style has become a target, and because Ophuls's style is linked to lovely ladies in glittering costumes in period decor, socially minded critics have charged him with being trivial and decadent. Lindsay Anderson, not too surprisingly, found him "uncommitted, unconcerned with profundities" (Anderson's *Every Day Except Christmas* is committed all right, but is it really so profound?) and, in his rather condescending review of *The Earrings of Madame de . . .* in *Sight and Sound,* he suggested that "a less sophisticated climate might perhaps help; what a pity he is not, after all, coming to make a film in England." It's a bit like telling Boucher or Watteau or Fragonard that he should abandon his pink chalk and paint real people in real working-class situations.

The evocation of a vanished elegance—the nostalgic fin de siècle grace of Ophuls's work—was perhaps a *necessary* setting for the nuances of love that were his theme. If his characters lived crudely, if their levels of awareness were not so high, their emotions not so refined, they would not be so vulnerable, nor so able to perceive and express their feelings. By removing love from the real world of ugliness and incoherence and vulgarity, Ophuls was able to distill the essences of love. Perhaps he cast this loving look backward to an idealized time when men could concentrate on the refinements of human experience because in his own period such delicate perceptions were as remote as the Greek pursuit of perfection.

Born Max Oppenheimer in Germany in 1902 (he changed his name because of family opposition to his stage career) he worked as an actor and then directed more than two hundred plays before he turned to movies in 1930. His first film success, *Liebelei,* came in 1932; because he was Jewish, his name was removed from the credits. The years that might have been his artistic maturity were, instead, a series of projects that didn't materialize or, if started, couldn't be completed. He managed to make a few movies—in Italy, in France, in Holland; he became a French citizen; then, after the fall of France, he went to Switzerland, and from there to the United States, where, after humiliating experiences on such films as *Vendetta*, he made *Letters from an Unknown Woman, Caught*, and *The Reckless Moment*. In 1950 in France he finally got back to his own type of material with *La Ronde*; the flight from Hitler and the chaos of the war had lost him eighteen years. Working feverishly, with a bad heart, he had only a few years left—he died in 1957. No wonder the master of ceremonies of *La Ronde* says, "J'adore le passé"; the past of Ophuls's films is the period just before he was born. There was little in his own lifetime for which he could have been expected to feel nostalgia. Perhaps the darting, swirling, tracking camerawork for which he is famous is an expression of the evanescence of all beauty—it must be swooped down on, followed. It will quickly disappear.

—Pauline Kael

France: Jean Renoir
■

RETROSPECTIVE

The films of Jean Renoir never land heavy on the eye or the spirit. There are no conquering heroes in them. Identifying profoundly with uncertainty and frailty, Renoir became the poet of chaos theory. He humanized it long before existentialism and physics got their hands on it. Physically ungainly—and keenly aware of it—he costumed himself as a galumphing bear for his ringmaster's role in his masterpiece, *The Rules of the Game* (1939). In that film, he uses bumptiousness and forced garrulousness to conceal feelings he can scarcely contain at the spectacle of a chateauful of people he loves all looking for love in the wrong places. The sensibility—in contrast to the lumpish envelope that contains it—is delicate, observant, embracing, never unaware of the problematic nature of life.

So gently affirmative are Renoir's films that one is taken aback to read that he once described life as a tissue of disappointments. There's always a heartful of pain in Renoir, but it never weighs his films down. It's as if they have tempo markings—*allegro, vivace, prestissimo. The Rules of the Game* is like Feydeau (Renoir used one of his sex farces for his first sound film, *On Purge Bébé*), but less vulgar, more cultivated, more ironic, more improvisatory, more deeply felt. The country house party scamperings are anything but a game. They're played for keeps. And the only rule is that there are no rules. Yet *The Rules of the Game* never succumbs to cynicism; it's filled with a respect, bordering on humility, for the desperation and emotional nakedness of people whipsawed by their needs—the exquisitely considerate *arriviste* of a marquis, his combative mistress, his heedlessly romantic wife, an aviator who loves her, a charming drone of a friend, a stern steward, a pert chambermaid, a foxlike poacher who works his way inside the henhouse, all the modish types spilling from the bedrooms.

It's this regard for the integrity of emotion that forbids Renoir from ever feeling contempt for any of his characters. Renoir is film's answer to Mozart—the slow movements of the great piano concertos, the haunting minor-key tonalities of his next-to-last symphony, the smiling tolerance of *Cosi fan tutte,* the piercing wistfulness of *The Marriage of Figaro.* Like Mozart, Renoir was inspired by Beaumarchais, linked to a culture where elegance was held in esteem. Unlike Mozart, he was not a creature of the court and the coffeehouse. Like his famous painter father, Pierre Auguste, Jean Renoir was of the atelier, a craftsman. "Art is making," his father told him, and he listened. He didn't have to be told that the heart has its reasons, or that to understand is to forgive. What he understood best of all was what the world called weakness.

Human relations became the real subject of Renoir's films, even though that wasn't his intention at the start. He married his father's last model, who took the stage name Catherine Hessling. He saw himself as a potter, only leaving his kiln to make his wife a star. His first film was *Une Vie sans Joie,* made in 1924, later retitled and rereleased as *Catherine.* Neither that nor his second vehicle for her, *La Fille de l'Eau* (1924), were successes. Renoir's films stemmed literally, if not figuratively, from his father's paintings, many of which he sold to finance the films. "Every sale seemed a betrayal," he wrote, possibly recalling almost going broke to finance his biggest Hessling spectacular, *Nana* (1926).

That encounter with Zola—*Nana* was the most opulent of Renoir's silents—was heavily influenced by Erich Von Stroheim's *Foolish Wives* and in it Hessling's doll-like ferocity made its biggest impression. Her *Charleston* (1927) and *The Little Match Girl* (1928) amount to little more than curios. Still, material and motifs that Renoir later refined show up in these early efforts. The impressionistic water imagery in *La Fille de l'Eau* reached its apotheosis in *The River* (1950), in which Renoir's serenity matched that of India, where the film was shot. And the voyeuristic way in which Hessling's shivering match girl rubs frost off a restaurant window to watch the well-to-do dine presages Renoir's affecting way of avoiding cliché in the seminal *La Chienne* (1931), where he has duped clerk Michel Simon watch numbed through a rain-streaked window as his mistress pulls the man she really loves into bed.

La Chienne, France's first sound film shot on location and Renoir's first hit, was a milestone film—as well as remaining a surprisingly entertaining one, wearing its years lightly. Renoir entered filmmaking to please his wife, then became hooked by it. When he was offered the chance to direct *La Chienne,* he took it and directed another woman (Janie Marese) in its leading role, even though his wife had threatened to leave him because of it—and did. The breakup squared with his essentially pessimistic view of life. For Renoir, the story of the hen-pecked clerk and Sunday painter who naively falls in love with a prostitute named Lulu and is victimized by her and her pimp reso-nated provocatively on several levels.

Opening with the kind of puppet show prologue he was to return to in his last film, *Le Petit Théâtre de Jean Renoir* (1971), he proclaims that he's giving us neither a social drama nor a comedy of manners. "It has no moral whatever," he says, "and proves nothing at all. The characters are neither heroes nor villains, but plain people like you and me." In its compassionate detachment, the film seems to foreshadow *Rules of the Game.* But Renoir has a few psychic scores to settle, and the film has bite. Finding in the shambling Michel Simon a surrogate self, he presents the clerk as too cultivated for his milieu, and proceeds to depict with tart comedy every tone of his bad marriage—first with a shrewish wife, then with a grabby streetwalker.

Clearly, Renoir also entered this film with strong—and in some ways conflicted—feelings about the role of art (his father's and his own) and about his own role in relation to his father's art and his guilt in selling it. It's impossible not to speculate upon the sources of the timid clerk's rage when he discovers that Lulu, in order to support her pimp, has uncaringly sold the paintings he gave her. Much as Renoir was to move toward serenity and nostalgia in later years, he remained open to degrees of pain and feeling that were alien to his father's canvases, which were filled with freshness and vigor, but never the hesitations and ambivalences in his son's films.

Both women who wrong the Renoir surrogate die in *La Chienne,* but Renoir emerges purged, with a more lightly sophisticated view of the fate of art. In an airy epilogue in which Simon-Renoir, turned *clochard,* blithely exchanges art for money, he says goodbye to a painting being driven off in a millionaire's roadster and hello to day-to-day expediency. What he's really saying hello to is the world of film. *La Chienne* — remade by Fritz Lang as *Scarlet Street* with Edward G. Robinson — marks Renoir's commitment to an art form that was to enable him to emerge from his father's shadow.

After filming Renoir's *Night at the Crossroads* with his brother, Pierre Renoir, as Inspector Maigret, Renoir made *Boudu Saved from Drowning* (1932), with Simon as the tramp fished from the Seine and threatened with civilization (this film, too, inspired a Hollywood remake, Paul Mazursky's *Down and Out in Beverly Hills*). Even more warmly steeped in everyday Parisian atmosphere than *La Chienne* with its Montmartre scenes — and all the stronger for it — *Boudu* ends with a burst of pure anarchist impulse close to Renoir's pacifist heart. In it, Boudu escapes the encumbrances of the bourgeois life heaped upon him, faking his drowning, then pulling himself out of the Seine yet again, relishing his freedom. That full-circle pan, in which we share Boudu's sense of reliberation, was to return in *French Can-Can* (1955), with impresario Jean Gabin this time serving as the figure escaping that tied-down feeling.

Although Renoir made two overt Popular Front films, the best of them was covert, *La Crime de Monsieur Lange* (1935), in which his benign impulses toward his actors proved to be the factor that carried the film past the pitfalls of agitprop. Like the best Renoir films, it's a great milieu piece — with a male-run print shop and female-run laundry sitting across a cramped courtyard in affectionate solidarity that ripens into something more when the laundry's proprietress becomes the protector of the man who unwittingly sets in motion a seizure of the print shop by its workers after its evil capitalist boss goes too far in exploiting him. Will the printer, who becomes a hit author with his escapist fantasies about a character named Arizona Jim, get away with murder? The film ends with the audience serving as jury. And Renoir's warmth and humanity extend to the villainous capitalist, Batala, played by Jules Berry with the disarming charm of a boulevardier.

It was Renoir's seizing upon the chance to employ Erich Von Stroheim, his *Foolish Wives* mentor, that made *La Grande Illusion* (1937) the great film it became. Hailed as an antiwar film, with its story of

French soldiers escaping a German prison camp during World War I, it became much more than a simple square-off of social classes. When Marcel Dalio also signed on, joining Jean Gabin's vital working-class type as a Jewish banker's son also fleeing the crumbling old aristocratic milieu represented by the prison and breaking away to new beginnings, further richness was added to the social tapestry. But mostly the film belongs to Von Stroheim and Pierre Fresnay, linked by their roots in the aristocracy and finding those links stronger than the national boundaries that came much later in the history of their respective families.

The melancholy nobility of the imminently extinct similarly informs *The Rules of the Game* (1939), which predictably flopped and wasn't recognized as the masterpiece it is until after the war. Renoir's refusal to moralize — or to designate a star and bring his restless camera to rest on him or her — wasn't what the mass audience craved. Working as much from intuition as from programmatic intent, Renoir's country houseparty all too successfully captures the ephemeral life of a generous and gracious but decadent society dancing on the brink of war. The film's whiff of war is conveyed in a now classic scene in which the aristocrats slaughter birds and rabbits during a shoot — presaging the film's climactic incident of poignantly absurd human sacrifice.

Renoir later said he wanted a certain disorder, wanted to tell a light story about a world dancing on a volcano. His indirection, his refusal to become explicit, is the reason the film remains so hauntingly resonant. Most other directors would simply have satirized characters a bit too given to the heartless mechanics of social games. Renoir went further. Years later, in a documentary filmed by Jacques Rivette, Renoir congratulated Marcel Dalio for his play of emotions during the scene where the Marquis de la Chesnaye, an eccentric collector, unveils an elaborate mechanical orchestra to amuse his guests. "The combination of humility and pride, success and doubt, on the edge of so many things, nothing definite — it was my best shot," Renoir says.

Later, using color film, Renoir the apostle of contemporary lyric realism turned to artifice, reduced his scale, turned backward in time. In *The Golden Coach* (1953) and *French Can-Can* (1955), with their remarkably similar stories of women turning their backs on love for careers as artists, Renoir seemed determined to recreate his father's sunlit visual world — but with greater detachment. It's as if he took his early thirties disappointment in his first wife — and his renewed belief in art — one step too far. In the fable-like *Golden Coach,* set in an imagined Peru, actress Anna Magnani rejects suitors representing domesticity, passion, and power. Ditto for dancer Françoise Arnoul in *French Can-Can,* with its idealized Moulin Rouge milieu. *Elena and Her Men* (1956), starring Ingrid Bergman as a Belle Epoque Juno who also wreaks amatory havoc, allows her to succumb to love, but otherwise is just as sumptuous—and Olympian—as *The Golden Coach* and *French Can-Can.* Like Orson Welles, furtively longing for a bygone world in *Citizen Kane,* and then not so furtively longing for it in *The Magnificent Ambersons,* Renoir unmistakably genuflects to the world of his youth in this trilogy.

But in all Renoir's films, you find at the core the spirit of his warm, sympathetic, melancholy Octave in *Rules of the Game.* He wanted to be an orchestral conductor, but the world never warmed to him, says Renoir-Octave, who affably falls in with the world's perception of him as a failure. Yet Octave, the outwardly clumsy, inwardly suave seducer, is—like the man inhabiting him—the figure most sensitive to the feelings of the others and their mercurial mood shifts. Although Renoir's touch is always gentle, he won't let Octave off the hook, yanks him from diversionary buffoonery to sobering self-awareness. Subtle, prismatic, acute, infinitely embracing, *Rules of the Game* is one of the century's undisputed masterworks. Renoir thought he was reworking Beaumarchais and de Musset, but *Rules of the Game*—right down to its figure of the little poacher bringing mischievous nature indoors— seems kin to Shakespeare's *Midsummer Night's Dream.* It's a sublime comedy of the mutability of human feelings that manages, without ever becoming sentimental, to turn into a celebration of humankind.

—*Jay Carr*

France: Jean Vigo

■

L'ATALANTE (1934)

Jean Vigo, who died in 1934 at the age of twenty-nine, was one of the greatest artists in the history of the movies, and probably the most tantalizing. His body of work consists of a pair of short documentaries, a forty-seven-minute fiction film (*Zero for Conduct*), and one full-length feature—all told, less than three hours of finished film. The feature, *L'Atalante,* was released in Paris in September, 1934 (just three weeks before Vigo's death), in a version the filmmaker had never seen: the distributor had cut the movie by almost a third, added a mediocre popular song, and then, for good measure, retitled the picture *Le Chaland Qui Passe,* after the new tune. *L'Atalante* was largely restored in 1940, but it has retained over the years the aura of something fragile and patched up, and that quality of seeming slightly damaged is perhaps what has made it for many viewers an object of special devotion: it's a movie that people see again and again, and love in ways they find difficult to explain. Now *L'Atalante* has been given another major renovation. This version, prepared by Pierre Philippe and Jean-Louis Bompoint, adds about nine minutes of footage not included in the previous reconstruction, and the restorers discovered in the archives of the British Film Institute a pristine nitrate print of a cut of the movie which obviously preceded the distributor's intervention; *L'Atalante* now looks and sounds better than ever. (The prints that have been circulating for the last fifty years are uniformly atrocious.) Thanks to Philippe and Bompoint, we can see all the lucid beauties of Boris Kaufman's cinematography, rather than have to struggle to imagine them, and hear Maurice Jaubert's lovely score without distortion; we can even make out the dialogue, which in previous prints was often just a low rumble of undifferentiated sound. But the best thing about this shiny new *L'Atalante* is that, for all the restorers' diligence, the film is still messy, imperfect, defiantly incomplete. Like everything Vigo did, like his frustratingly brief career, *L'Atalante* is an unfinished product, unsuitable for framing: even in its current spruced-up condition, it's essentially a collection of inspired fragments, the sketchbook of an artist whose imagination was, and will forever remain, gloriously immature.

This movie was, in part, Vigo's attempt to "grow up" as a filmmaker—to make a conventional commercial picture. His previous film, *Zero for Conduct,* about a revolt in a boys' boarding school, was a celebration of the pure freedom of children's imaginations, a stirring expression of resistance to the forces of authority and order—to anything that would impose discipline on the diverse, unruly energy of play. *Zero for Conduct* isn't constructed like an ordinary movie; Vigo evidently considered the discipline of narrative a form of repression, too, and his indifference to it has a lot to do with why *Zero for Conduct* still seems, fifty-seven years later, like one of the few truly subversive movies ever made. And the French censors—as alert to insubordination as the dwarf headmaster and the malevolent instructors who rule the world of Vigo's schoolboys—banned the movie from public exhibition. For *L'Atalante*, Vigo agreed to work within the constraints of a simple and apparently innocuous story (from an original scenario by an undistinguished writer named Jean Guinée). Jean (Jean Dasté), the captain of a river barge named *L'Atalante*, marries Juliette (Dita Parlo), a girl from one of the villages on the barge's route. As the newlyweds travel down the river, Juliette becomes increasingly restless and disenchanted; she has escaped from her village, but all she's seeing of the world is riverbanks, the inside of cramped cabins, and her husband and his odd crew—a rambunctious old salt called Père Jules (Michel Simon) and a quiet cabin boy (Louis Lefèvre). Bored and impatient, she sneaks off to see the sights of Paris, but when she returns to the place where the barge was docked she discovers that Jean has shoved off without her. She wanders on the shore, he drifts downstream on the boat, and the separation makes them both miserable. Finally, they find each other again; life resumes its intended course.

The miracle of *L'Atalante* is that Vigo keeps breaking free of the story's ordained course: he's incapable of simply riding that dull, even current and making only the scheduled stops. He treats the story the way a jazz musician treats a popular song, improvising on the melody by plunging into its carefully sequenced chords and predictable rhythms and taking them apart to see what they're made of: he hits notes that we had never dreamed were there but that seem, once we've heard them, pure and essential, like pearls dredged from far beneath the smooth, lulling flow of the song. In one of the film's most sublime sequences, Jean, aching from the absence of Juliette, dives off the barge into the river because his bride once told him that you see the face of the one you love when you look under the surface of the water. Jean has tried the trick a couple of times before, jokingly and unsuccessfully, but this time—now that he is abandoned, mad with grief, reckless—he sees her: luminous in her wedding dress, and laughing with an unforced, innocent joy that looks like the sweetest of invitations, the promise of every kind of pleasure. The floating images of Juliette superimposed on Jean's desperate, searching face are reminders of some of our earlier views of her, and especially of a ghostly image of the bride in her white dress walking slowly along the top of the barge as it glides down the river at twilight: in the underwater sequence, Jean seems, at last, to be seeing his wife the way Vigo has seen her from the start — as an ordinary woman who becomes radiant when she is looked at with desire. This sequence tells us most of what we need to know about Vigo's eroticized approach to the art of moviemaking: he forgets his orders, immerses himself in the ordinary beauties of the sensual world, and summons up visions that shine with the possibilities of earthly pleasure.

The other key to Vigo is his attraction to chaos, clutter, sheer profusion — a quality that is, in a sense, just another side of his eroticism. The toys and gadgets and bric-a-brac that fill his movies are played with and caressed by the camera with such loving attention that they seem like fetishes. And there are so *many* of them — so many objects to divert us from the implacable responsibilities of living, so many beautiful distractions. Père Jules's cabin, overrun by cats and jammed with bizarre mementos that are the residue of a full and gleefully disorderly life, is the image not only of its inhabitant but also of its creator. This museum of useless things — with which, in a long and brilliantly sustained sequence, the old sailor enchants Juliette — is Vigo's world in miniature, a place where something to tickle the imagination or to stir memories or simply to gaze at in wonder is always ready to hand. And the character itself, as it is conceived by Vigo and played by the magnificently peculiar Simon, is the presiding spirit of the movie: Père Jules is a comic metaphor for the diversity of the world's riches; he is, in his demented, random way, a living encyclopedia. At one point, he gets excited, and all sorts of strange stuff bubbles out of him, with startling alacrity: Indian war whoops, bullfighting moves, snippets of songs and dances from Russia, Africa, the Orient. (He takes us around the world in about eighty seconds.) His body is covered with crudely drawn tattoos, and in one of the most welcome of the newly restored shots he amuses Juliette by making a face tattooed on his belly appear to smoke by putting a cigarette in his navel. Père Jules is, of course, a child, both splendid and monstrous, and there is, too, something profoundly childlike about the way the character is conceived: only a very innocent eye could see this crazy old drifter as the epitome of worldly experience.

Vigo may have been trying, with some part of himself, to make a "normal" movie — one conventional enough, at least, to get past the censors and into the commercial cinemas — but *L'Atalante* shows how hopelessly, wonderfully unsuited he was to popular moviemaking. His storytelling is still casual, almost perfunctory: the narrative will slow to a languorous drift, then abruptly begin chugging forward, then stop to give us a long look at some unanticipated marvel off in the distance, then lurch irritably ahead again. And his approach to composition and editing is so personal that audiences expecting an ordinary movie might become disoriented: shots are taken from unexpected angles, are held longer than usual, are juxtaposed with other shots in unprecedented ways. Vigo was helplessly original; he seems at times to be speaking a different language from other filmmakers. (On seeing Vigo's work for the first time, James Agee wrote, "It is as if he had invented the wheel.") He is the most playful and the least rigid of the great film artists; he had the liveliest eye, and perhaps the freest imagination. Everything he shows us looks mysteriously new, full of possibilities, and so encourages us to linger on it, investigate it, dream it, have our way with it.

In a sense, the restorers' work on *L'Atalante* springs from impulses like those — from the feeling, evoked at virtually every moment in Vigo's films, that there's something more for us to discover. The latest version of *L'Atalante* is new only in the sense that this movie has always seemed new; it isn't changed in any fundamental way. The footage added by Philippe and Bompoint is just extra stuff, beautiful and inessential and thus fully in keeping with the movie's expansive spirit. They've given us a few more glittery things to hoard in our imagination and fondle in our memories when life gets a little dull. In Jean Vigo's movies, greater profusion only creates stronger desire: his images seduce us with the promise of a larger, richer world and unbounded freedom to roam in it — the promise, that is, of endless stimulation, inexhaustible sensations. There can be no definitive *L'Atalante,* because the world of Vigo's films subverts the very idea of definition. This extraordinary movie will always elude our attempts to grasp it and keep it in its place: we'll never see everything in Père Jules's cabin; the image of the woman in the water disperses when we try to embrace it, then forms itself again and leads us on.

— *Terrence Rafferty*

France: Jean Vigo

■

ZÉRO DE CONDUITE (1933)

The most instinctively radical of all great filmmakers, Jean Vigo once proclaimed that "the camera is not an airpump for creating vacuums." He practiced what he preached in this forty-seven-minute film about a repressive boarding school as seen through the eyes of its students. Veering between the gritty and the baldly surreal, Vigo captures the boys' rough, yet honorable dealings with each other, their affection for the one fun-loving teacher (who makes comic-strip drawings come to life in the classroom), and their contempt for the headmaster (portrayed as a midget) and his skulking hatchet man; the boys' hatred for authority and craving for freedom leads them to a minirevolution against the school and its governors. The director Jacques Rivette once wrote that Vigo "suggests an incessant improvisation of the universe, a perpetual and calm and self-assured creation of the world," and *Zéro de Conduite* does invent life afresh, never more unforgettably than in the boys' ecstatic procession amidst a blizzard of feathers. Flagrantly subversive—the authorities banned it for twelve years—Vigo's first fiction film is an ode to fierce joy, ending with kids on a roof reaching for the sky, a lyrical finale that celebrates the liberating genius of childhood and offers this director's vision of how we all should try to live.

—John Powers

France: Marcel Carné

■

BIZARRE, BIZARRE (1937)

Marcel Carné's *Bizarre, Bizarre* (also known as *Drôle de Drame*), written by the poet Jacques Prévert from a novel by J. Clouston, is a whirling, joyful farce, as exquisitely designed as a precision timepiece. It's both elegantly sophisticated and antic. Everything is in motion, everyone has some secret to conceal. The wacky geometry of this movie can make your head reel.

As the film opens, Archibald, the vicar of Bedford (Louis Jouvet), is denouncing the immoral pleasures of detective novelist Felix Chapel's oeuvre to his captive flock. (No one has ever set eyes on the mysterious Chapel.) Down the aisle saunters the vicar's cousin, Irwin Molyneaux (Michel Simon), a rumply botanist (his latest work: *The Mimesis of Mimosas*). We're so primed for farce that we know right away who Felix Chapel must be. When the vicar invites himself over to the Molyneaux house for dinner that night, the botanist's wife (Françoise Rosay) — no friend of the vicar's — hides out in the kitchen. The vicar suspects something's up and, like "the man who came to dinner," decides to stay on. What to do? The wife can't hide in the kitchen forever, and Molyneaux suspects that, with the vicar around, his secret will be discovered. (The vicar's raised eyebrow at the sight of Eva, the maid, suggests he'll be there for a while.) Mrs. Molyneaux is smuggled out of the house by Eva, but the spying vicar interprets the subsequent moonlit garden tête-à-tête between Eva and Irwin as proof that she's been murdered by her husband. Irwin soon skedaddles and before long, all of England is thirsty for the "murderer's" blood. He hides out with his wife in a Limehouse flophouse that's right out of *Broken Blossoms* — fugitives of their own misfired ruse.

Meanwhile, back at the maison, Eva's adoring milkman boyfriend (Jean-Pierre Aumont looking like a sprightly young Olivier) is suspected of being an accomplice to the "murder." The most incriminating bit of evidence: a kitchen filled with milk bottles. The vicar, fearful lest Scotland Yard find in the Molyneaux guest room a misplaced cheesecake photo addressed to him, sneaks back into the house at night to find it first. Creeping through the mimosas, he's dressed to the hilt in his foolproof disguise: kilts and dark glasses.

Irwin Molyneaux has another problem. The magazine that regularly printed his Felix Chapel episodes is now only buying Molyneaux murder stories. So he must investigate himself by impersonating Felix Chapel. But the real source of his ideas — the milkman, as we discover — is locked up, and Eva, their go-between, is angry at both of them. Left alone in Limehouse, Mrs. Molyneaux has a run-in with the notorious "slaughterhouse terror" William Kramps, the animal lover who murders butchers (Jean-Louis Barrault, at his most sunken-cheeked). The run-in turns rapidly into a romantic tryst. Kramps, overjoyed at his new-found love, confronts "Chapel" at the Molyneaux residence and, informed by the beleaguered botanist of his disguise, rejoices by drunkenly escorting Irwin back to Limehouse to meet his new girlfriend.

And so on. A flowchart of this movie's plotting would resemble a visual diagram of the Los Angeles freeway system, but Carné keeps everything lucid and spinning in midair. It's hard to believe he was only twenty-eight when he directed this film, his second. (Before becoming a director, he was an assistant to René Clair and Jacques Feyder.) Even though the script is a tightly structured farce, it allows for Carné's youthful exuberance.

The team of Carné-Prévert didn't look back to this style again; the following year, they rolled in the fog for *Port of Shadows* and ushered in a period of poetic realism that reached its fullest expression in the fatalistic *Le Jour Se Lève* (1939). Carné and Prévert were among the few film artists who managed to work in France during World War II without collaborating with Vichy. *Children of Paradise,* begun in 1943 but not completed until 1945, is their masterpiece: the contrapuntal plotting of *Bizarre, Bizarre;* the moodiness of their subsequent three films; the fairy-tale poetry of *Les Visiteurs du Soir* (1942) — all combined to create a work of Balzacian richness.

Bizarre, Bizarre is a trifle by comparison, but it's a wonderful trifle. It's one of the most neglected French classics from the thirties. At the end of the movie, a bunch of rabble-rousers pursues the latest murder suspects. As they yell their way out of a courtyard, leaving behind a little boy, there's a perfect lyric touch: An old man, one of the rabble, saunters back into view and takes the child's hand. Together they walk off to join the others and suddenly, all that hollering is diffused.

The plotting isn't the only contrapuntal element in the movie — the actors are used contrapuntally too. The imperious Louis Jouvel's high forehead and cat's eyes give him the look of a sci-fi Tartuffe; Michel Simon could be Orgon (except that Barrault is the one who tries to cuckold him). Françoise Rosay has the impressive dowager bulk and the klutzy flirtatiousness of a Margaret Dumont. And Jean-Louis Barrault — thin and skittish as a spider — is so poetically intense that he's comic. The difference in these actors' styles gives *Bizarre, Bizarre* a fractured unity — their disparities cohere. The movie even offers — as a sidelight — a gentle burlesque of Edwardian manners. If the young Max Ophuls had teamed with Georges Feydeau at the Mack Sennett studios, the result might have been something like *Bizarre, Bizarre.*

—*Peter Rainer*

France: Marcel Carné

■

CHILDREN OF PARADISE (1945)

This lushly romantic creation, directed by Marcel Carné and written by Jacques Prévert, is a one-of-a-kind film, a sumptuous epic about the relations between theater and life. At first, it may seem a romance set in the Paris of Balzac; it turns into a comparison of dramatic modes — it includes at least five kinds of theatrical performance. And, encompassing these, it is a film poem on the nature and varieties of love — sacred and profane, selfless and possessive. It was made during the Occupation, and it is said that the starving extras made away with some of the banquets before they could be photographed. With Jean-Louis Barrault as the soulful mime Deburau (the Pierrot — Barrault sucks in his cheeks so much that he sometimes suggests Dietrich); the incomparable Arletty as Garance; Pierre Brasseur as the Shakespearean actor Lemaître (the Harlequin); Louis Salou as the count; Marcel Herrand as the philosophical murderer; Pierre Renoir as the ragpicker-informer; and Maria Casarès, who has the unrewarding role of the theater manager's daughter, who marries Deburau and becomes the mother of an abominable offspring. (The child is pure Hollywood.) **(Video request.)**

— Pauline Kael

France: René Clair

■

À NOUS LA LIBERTÉ (1931)

René Clair's imaginative social satire on the mechanization of modern life begins with a man (Raymond Cordy) who escapes from prison and builds a phonogaph-record business with an assembly line that's as regimented as the prison. This factory owner is modelled on Charles Pathé, who said of his phonograph-cinema empire, "Only the armaments industry made profits like ours." The tycoon's pal from his prison days is a softhearted "little man" (Henri Marchand) — the underdog embodiment of a free, humanistic spirit. Beautifully made, the picture has elegantly futuristic sets by Lazare Meerson, and Georges Périnal's cinematography has a simplified, formal perfection; the whole film is paced to Georges Auric's memorable score—one of the earliest (yet best) film scores ever written. Clair's directing demonstrates that sound pictures can be as fluid as silents were, and this picture is rightly considered a classic. Yet it isn't as entertaining as his earlier (silent) *The Italian Straw Hat* or his later *Le Million;* the scenario (which he wrote) turns a little too carefree and ironic—the film grows dull. *À Nous la Liberté* was obviously the source of some of the ideas in Chaplin's 1936 *Modern Times;* the producing company filed suit against Chaplin for copyright infringement, but Clair had the suit dropped, saying that "All of us flow" from Chaplin, and "I am honored if he was inspired by my film."

—Pauline Kael

France: Henri-Georges Clouzot
■

THE RAVEN (1943)
THE WAGES OF FEAR (1953)

Two bracingly cynical Henri-Georges Clouzot thrillers, 1943's *The Raven* (*Le Corbeau*) and 1953's *The Wages of Fear* (*Le Salaire de la Peur*) register in today's sentimental movie climate like welcome gusts of profane air.

Both movies are as up to the minute as CNN's "Headline News." In the first, Pierre Fresnay plays a small-town doctor who's accused, by a poison-pen artist called the Raven, not just of having an affair with a psychiatrist's wife but also of performing abortions. When it comes to obstetric close calls, Fresnay prefers to save the mother. In *The Wages of Fear,* a monstrous oil fire breaks out at a well owned by an American company in South America. To ignite a counter-blaze, an oil honcho hires four down-and-outers (Yves Montand, Charles Vanel, Peter Van Eyck, Folco Lulli) to drive trucks loaded with nitro across rough country.

The Raven is a surgical critique of provincial life; it's distinguished by sardonic masterstrokes, such as a scandal letter floating from a church spire down to an aghast congregation. *The Wages of Fear,* on the other hand, is a harrowing epic. From the first shot—a boy toying with battling insects—to the final unexpected cataclysm, Clouzot's incisive, unvarnished viciousness is mesmerizing. His world isn't merely dog-eat-dog but beetle-eat-beetle: *No Exit* staged on mobile time bombs.

—*Michael Sragow*

France: Jean Cocteau
∎

ORPHEUS (1949)

In nineties movies such as *Flatliners* and *Ghost*—fantasies that ache to be moral and reassuring—death allows spirits to confront and solve the problems that haunted them in life. In *Orpheus,* Jean Cocteau's superb modern version of the Greek myth, death isn't so easy. The inscrutable administrators and envoys of the afterlife, including the slim, severe Princess (played by Maria Casarès), follow their own rules. That's what makes the netherworld attractive to the poet Orphée (Jean Marais), who seeks a fresh source of inspiration. The attraction is mutual: the Princess, who is destined to be the Death of Orphée, develops a crush on the poet, going so far as to kill his wife, Eurydice (Marie Déa). The movie is about how the Princess's right-hand man, Heurtebise (François Périer), and the Death-smitten Orphée enter "the Zone" that exists on the other side of mirrors and try to restore Eurydice to life.

The movie has an eerie seamlessness: emotionally and visually it's a modulated, lyrical tremble. Mounting the film in 1949 (twenty-three years after the premiere of his stage play), Cocteau joined his own romantic melancholy to the dislocations of the time. Francis Steegmuller, in his biography of Cocteau, lists the film's late-forties ingredients, from the post-Liberation tribunals echoed in the Zone to the motorcycle policemen Cocteau saw as Death's special agents and the "protobeatniks" he transformed into bacchantes. The enveloping magic of Cocteau's work is in many ways beyond explication. He manages both to explore and to preserve the mysteries of mortality.

He makes you believe in a twilight world where Death can face a fate worse than itself.

—*Michael Sragow*

France: Julien Duvivier

■

PÉPÉ LE MOKO (1937)

Superb entertainment. A classic romantic melodrama of the thirties, and one of the most compelling of all the fatalistic French screen romances, yet seen by few Americans because it was remade in Hollywood two years later as *Algiers,* starring Charles Boyer and "introducing" Hedy Lamarr. *Algiers* was so closely copied from *Pépé le Moko* that look-alikes were cast in many of the roles, and some sequences were followed shot by shot. But *Algiers* is glamorous pop that doesn't compare to the original, directed by Julien Duvivier and starring Jean Gabin as the gangster who finds love but can't find his freedom. No one who saw *Pépé* is likely to forget the scene in which the homesick-for-Paris Gabin looks at a Métro ticket and recites the names of the stations. Ironically, Duvivier had hoped to make an American-style gangster film and had drawn some of his characters from *Scarface.* With Mireille Balin, Marcel Dalio, Gaston Modot, Gabriel Gabrio, Line Noro, Saturnin Fabre, and Charpin. The script by Henri Jeanson is based on a novel by Ashelbé (Henri La Barthe), at one time commissioner of the Paris police. (The American version was remade as the musical *Casbah* in 1948).

—*Pauline Kael*

France: Georges Franju

■

JUDEX (1963)

Now if this isn't an ideal summer movie, what is? Inspired by the silent film serials of Louis Feuillade, it's the French equivalent of a Batman adventure — but with Art Nouveau trappings. Judex, the hero, is a vision from childhood — dressed in a black cloak and mask, he's the Avenger of evil deeds. But director Georges Franju, who sets his film in 1914, doesn't play his melodrama for camp. He presents his Manichean world straight, in stately, moon-lit images, that recreate the atmosphere of a more naive world where Good triumphs and Evil is punished. A wonderful entertainment, dramatically simple but visually sumptuous, with doves flying out of capes and hooded figures scurrying across rooftops. Franju's films, which have been compared to Cocteau's, are rarely seen in America. One of his elegant chillers, *Eyes without a Face,* did pop up on the bottom half of a horror double bill, dubbed and retitled *The Horror Chamber of Doctor Faustus.*

— *David Ansen*

France: Marcel Pagnol

■

THE BAKER'S WIFE (1938)

The village baker (Raimu) cannot work because he laments his wife's departure with a stupid, sexy shepherd; the villagers, who want their bread, organize to bring her back. Raimu's baker is an acting classic — a true tragicomic hero — and it's easy to agree with Orson Welles, who cited this comedy as proof that "a story and an actor, both superb," can result in "a perfect movie" even if the direction and the editing are not "cinematic." Marcel Pagnol, a playwright who turned scenarist and then writer-director, adapted this classic of cuckoldry from Jean Giono's *Jean le Bleu* and directed it very simply. With Ginette Leclerc (who can pout with her mouth open) as the wife; Charpin; and Charles Moulin.

— *Pauline Kael*

Germany: Fritz Lang

■

METROPOLIS (1927)
M (1931)

With its brilliantly futuristic sets, its stylized acting, great special effects, and absurd allegorical story, Fritz Lang's *Metropolis* uses the techniques of German expressionism to create an indelible work of science fiction as social parable. Inspired by his first view of the Manhattan skyline from the New York harbor, Lang uses architecture and the machine to portray the mixture of modernity and misery, high style and squalor in the contemporary city. The 1920s were marked by a sense of social crisis, especially in Germany, where war and inflation had left the economy in ruins, and the powerful forces of capital and labor faced each other across a divide that threatened to end in violence and chaos. But with the work of the Bauhaus in Germany, Le Corbusier in France, the constructivists in Russia, it was also a period of rich innovation in the application of architectural ideas to urban life. *Metropolis,* set in the year 2000, is one such advanced design, but Lang's stunning visual conception far outstrips the simplistic social ideas he developed with his wife, the scenarist Thea von Harbou.

Metropolis gives us a vertical city, clean-lined, geometrical, with the pleasure gardens and command posts of the rich up high, the machines of the worker-slaves below ground, the workers' homes still further down, and the abandoned catacombs of an ancient city far beneath them. When the boss's son, Freder, falls in love with Maria, a worker's daughter, he descends into the pit and finds out for the first time how the workers live and toil. He sees their bodies literally integrated into the machine for ten-hour shifts, virtual human sacrifices to Moloch, a pitilessly devouring pagan god. Meanwhile Maria preaches a gospel of love, peace, and redemption to groups of workers who gather secretly in the catacombs like the early Christians. When Freder's father learns of these "plots," he calls upon Rotwang, a mad scientist (played demonically by Lang's favorite actor, Rudolf Klein-Rogge), to create a robot-double of Maria to incite the workers to a self-destructive uprising. In a few minutes of classic terror, the deformed, impotent Rotwang stalks Maria with a flashlight in the catacombs, then uses her to create the robot, a scene echoed in many later sci-fi films such as *The*

Bride of Frankenstein. In a virtuoso performance, Brigitte Helm plays both the angelic Maria and her leering, abandoned, shamelessly sexual double, who spouts Marxist slogans at the gullible workers and lures them towards anarchy.

Long before René Clair and Charlie Chaplin satirized the assembly line in *À Nous la Liberté* and *Modern Times,* Lang's film dramatized the condition of workers bound to the machine and warned of future discontent and revolution. The love story shows how the "heart" can mediate between the "head" and the "hand," but Lang and von Harbou are unable to conceive of the workers as anything *but* hands, downtrodden masses, or frenzied rioters, easily manipulated, already robots except for their physical limitations. Though the film concludes with a Christian scene of reconciliation, with boss and worker shaking hands in front of a cathedral, its conception of society remains strictly sentimental, melioristic, and hierarchical, for all the streamlined modernity of its grand visual design.

■

The same sense of hierarchy, the same fear of anarchy, is translated into psychological terms in *M,* the other great film of Lang's German period. In this thriller based on the actual case of a child-murderer in Düsseldorf, the vertical city also becomes the vertical psyche as Peter Lorre plays the pudgy, harmless-looking Beckert who, time and again, is overcome by a powerful compulsion to kill. Lang's work was marked by a deep streak of fatalism and paranoia, which was all too closely related to the social ferment of the period. He had made his reputation with quasi-mythical films about master criminals and spies, as played by Klein-Rogge in *Dr. Mabuse the Gambler* and *Spies,* men who manipulate appearances and conspire to take over the city, the world. In *M,* as in his later American films, Lang naturalized this vision, showing us gangs of real criminals and a killer who is himself a victim, dominated by his own tyrannical urges. In his final speech before a kangaroo court of ordinary crooks who have captured him, Lorre agonizingly evokes the forces that stalk him, that compel him to kill, just as he disrupts and terrifies the city as a whole. This is a film about the horror within.

To show how people's lives are dominated by powers outside their control, Lang repeatedly emphasizes scenes of off-screen action that mysteriously define what we see in the frame. All of Lorre's violence is committed out of sight; he himself comes only slowly into view as the film proceeds. He looks gentle, kinky, decadent, anything but murderous, wearing the mask of the strange but ineffectual man. Lang first hints menacingly at what he will soon do, then provides oblique evidence of what he's already done: a mother's wistful cry for her missing daughter, an untouched setting at the table, the stray balloon that Beckert bought for the young girl (whose name, Beckmann, resembles his own).

Again and again, the ordinary criminals' lives are disrupted by the forces of the Law, hunting for Beckert. He is identified at his "trial" by a blind beggar who recognizes his whistling, who reaches in and grasps his shoulder from outside the frame. Thwarted by the same kind of invisible force, these "judges" fall back when the Law arrives to break up the trial. When the criminals are closing in on Beckert, we see him scurrying through the streets like a rat in a maze, and when he takes refuge in a warehouse he is lost in shadows yet they close in on him methodically. The entrapped killer becomes another victim, as he has been all along, pursued from within and without. The *Murderer among Us*, the film's original title, is also the murderer inside us, the force of the irrational, the instinctive, the obsessional, over which we have so little real influence. Head, hand, and heart are even further apart than they were in the stratified society of *Metropolis*. Combining abnormal psychology with a police procedural drama, Freud with crime documentary, Lang—working in the last troubled years of the Weimar republic—gives his paranoid vision its most realistic framework, something Hollywood would also demand during his twenty years of filmmaking in America.

—*Morris Dickstein*

Germany: F. W. Murnau
■

NOSFERATU (1922)

Directed by F. W. Murnau, the original, superbly loathsome German version of Bram Stoker's novel *Dracula* is a concentrated essay in horror fantasy, full of weird, macabre camera effects. Though ludicrous at times (every horror film seems to become absurd after the passage of years, and many before—yet the horror remains), this first important film of the vampire genre has more spectral atmosphere, more ingenuity, and more imaginative ghoulish ghastliness than any of its successors. The movie often seems more closely related to demonic painting than to the later, rather rigid vampire-movie genre. Because Murnau concentrated on scenes of suggestive and horrible beauty and didn't make the narrative line very clear, those who have had little contact with bloodsuckers may be helped by a bit of outline. Henrik Galeen's adaptation of the novel changes the setting from Victorian England to Bremen in 1938. A real-estate agent in Bremen sends his young, recently married clerk to the Carpathian woods to settle some property matters at the castle of Nosferatu (the Vampire). An emaciated skeleton of a man with a rodent face, Nosferatu spends his days in his coffin, his nights sucking blood. The clerk, though weakened by the nightly loss of blood, escapes and returns to his wife. But Nosferatu follows: he boards a sailing ship for Bremen and, incarnating and carrying pestilence, he infects the whole crew. The phantom ship reaches Bremen, and Nosferatu meets the wife, who, knowing that vampires cannot survive the dawn, surrenders herself to him. As the morning sun breaks into her bedroom, Nosferatu dissolves. The influence of this film can be seen in movies as disparate as Bergman's *The Magician* (the opening sequences of the coach) and Godard's *Alphaville* (the use of negative film). With Max Schreck as Nosferatu. (In 1978, Werner Herzog made *Nosferatu the Vampyre,* in homage to Murnau's film.)

—*Pauline Kael*

Germany: G. W. Pabst

■

PANDORA'S BOX (1928)

Henri Langlois's revivals of the 1928 *Pandora's Box* — cut to 110 minutes from its original 140 — at the Cinémathèque initiated the Louise Brooks cult. It was a stroke of casting genius for the German director G. W. Pabst to change his mind about hiring Marlene Dietrich for the role of the man-eating Lulu and to cast Brooks — the sturdy, bouncy, corn-fed dancer from Kansas. The point of the Frank Wedekind plays on which the film is based is that Lulu's destructive sensuality is instinctual, not calculated. To be effective, she must be an innocent. Pabst understood this; flapper Brooks, with her black helmet of bobbed hair and her exuberant freedom of movement, seems a force of nature, not a performer, even during her comic scene when she throws a backstage tantrum. The sexual energy moves in torrents under Pabst's imaginative editing. On the strength of this performance alone, Brooks will be remembered as one of film's great femmes fatales.

—*Jay Carr*

Germany: Josef von Sternberg

■

THE BLUE ANGEL (1929)

The director, Josef von Sternberg, had been working in Hollywood for more than fifteen years when he went to Germany, at Emil Jannings's request, to direct this film; he had directed Jannings in *The Last Command,* one of the two American silent films that had won Jannings the Academy Award in 1927–28, and Jannings wanted him to guide his first sound film. They set in motion the Marlene Dietrich myth that was eventually to surpass their fame. Adapted from Heinrich Mann's novel *Professor Unrath,* this film deals with the breakdown of an authoritarian personality. Jannings plays the inhibited, tyrannical high-school instructor who is prudishly indignant about his students' visiting Lola Lola (Dietrich), the singer at the Blue Angel; he goes to the cafe to put a stop to it and instead succumbs to her callous, impassive sexuality. Dietrich's Lola Lola is a rather coarse, plump young beauty; as she sings "Falling in Love Again," her smoldering voice and sadistic indifference suggest sex without romance, love, or sentiment. The pedant becomes her husband, her slave, her stooge; he travels with the cafe troupe, hawking dirty pictures of his wife. Dietrich is extraordinary, and *The Blue Angel* is a movie you can admire sequence by sequence, because it's made in an imaginative, atmospheric style, yet you may feel that you don't really like it on an emotional level; the sexual humiliation gets very heavy in the scenes in which the teacher, now a clown, returns to his home town and to his old classroom.

With Hans Albers. Songs by Friedrich Hollaender (later Frederick Hollander).

—Pauline Kael

Germany: Robert Wiene

■

THE CABINET OF DR. CALIGARI (1919)

The audience, confined in the madman's universe, sees what the madman sees: distorted perspectives, eerie painted lights and shadows, an angular, warped world of fears and menace. The sets are used expressionistically to convey the madman's thoughts, to intensify the characters' emotions, and to emphasize the meanings of the action. This film is so entrenched in the "masterpiece" classification that a few cautionary remarks should be added, lest your initial reaction be disappointment: you may be delighted that the flats express something, because most of the actors don't; you may find that the decor, which is highly experimental in terms of space and distance but is derivative from the stage use of expressionism, is a monotonous zigzag (too many hooks and no fish). *Caligari,* the most complete essay in the decor of delirium, is one of the most famous films of all time, and it was considered a radical advance in film technique, yet it is rarely imitated—and you'll know why. Werner Krauss is the nightmare image of a psychoanalyst—the hypnotist Caligari—with, in his cabinet, the somnambulist Cesare, played by the extraordinary tall, thin, young Conrad Veidt. The cast also includes Lil Dagover, and Friedrich Feher as the student-inmate. Produced by Erich Pommer; directed by Robert Wiene. The scenario by Carl Mayer and Hans Janowitz was originally intended as an attack on irrational authority, but the meanings got turned around; the art direction is the work of three painters—Hermann Warm, Walter Reiman, and Walter Röhrig. The Nazis labelled the film "degenerate art." Eisenstein, who, in his own way, agreed, called it "this barbaric carnival of the destruction of the healthy human infancy of our art." (A 1962 American film used the same title, but has no other connection with the original.)

—Pauline Kael

Visconti, Rossellini, Antonioni, Fellini

▪

ITALY'S BIG FOUR

Of the 118 directors now involved in the industrial renaissance of Italian filmmaking only four—Luchino Visconti, Roberto Rossellini, Michelangelo Antonioni, and Federico Fellini—seem destined for more than the immortality of a footnote. The significant history of the Italian cinema can be encompassed within their career spans even though Italian filmmakers were producing ambitious spectacles before Griffith's *Birth of a Nation* in 1915.

Because of freakish distribution problems, Visconti's *Ossessione* (1942) and Rossellini's *Open City* (1946) have been separately honored as the midwives of neorealism, an overdefined movement that in its time and place simply marked the rejection of the sanctimonious conventions of Fascism. The Italian cinema before *Ossessione* is a mountain of spaghetti, some of it reasonably tasteful, most of it too starchy for anything but home consumption. Mussolini came to power more than a decade before Hitler, and the crucially formative years of the twenties found Murnau, Lang, Pabst, and lesser German directors evolving their techniques under the relatively protective aegis of the Weimar Republic while their Italian colleagues were marking time under Il Duce's balcony.

Visconti at sixty-four, Rossellini at fifty-four, Antonioni at forty-eight, and Fellini at forty-one seem reasonably safe from the creeping standardization that has afflicted so many of their once-promising colleagues. One might except the late Curzio Malaparte, whose one film, *Strange Deception,* lent the Italian cinema intellectual prestige at a crucial point in its postwar development; and on another level of deception, a special note must be devoted to the inflated reputation of Vittorio De Sica in the early fifties.

If Visconti and Rossellini invented neorealism in *Ossessione* and *Open City* and then invested it with the ultimate profundity of *La Terra Trema* and *Paisan,* De Sica milked it dry with *Shoeshine* and *The Bicycle Thief.* Lacking an insight into the real world, De Sica relied instead on tricks of pathos that he had learned too well as an actor. It is unlikely that any of the Big Four would have made *The Bicycle Thief* in the De Sica–Zavattini manner. Visconti would have catapulted his victim into the Roman underworld, where social corruption and a sense of personal dignity would transform the wronged laborer into a professional bicycle thief. Rossellini's character, heroically transfigured by God during the search, would return home with the awareness that his integrity as a human being was more important than any material object. Antonioni's hero, realizing the futility of his isolated existence in an impersonal society, would ride the recovered bicycle off an embankment in a quasi-suicidal gesture. After some bizarre experiences, Fellini's protagonist would find his bicycle only to have it stolen again the next day, but the hapless victim would come up smiling at the hope radiated by a little girl playing a harmonica.

All four directors have diverged from the literal path of neorealism, which was never anything more than the *Stalinallee* of social realism. In Visconti's work there has always been an unreconciled tension between a Marxian vision of society and an operatic conception of character. *Rocco and His Brothers* is comparable in its contradictions to what might have come out of a Verdi-Brecht adaptation of *The Brothers Karamazov*. The unity of the family in *Rocco* is destroyed partly because of the urban pressures of Milan on the rural mystique of the depressed South, partly because of the inhumanly Christlike sanctity of Rocco, partly because of the destructive intervention of a willful prostitute, and partly because of the fratricidal destiny of the brothers. The disturbing homosexual overtones of *Rocco* (and *Ossessione*) reflect additional conflicts with which the director must cope.

Throughout his career Visconti has been haunted by the image of the destructive woman. In the sublime cinema of Mizoguchi and Ophuls, most notably in *Ugetsu* and *Lola Montès*, woman is presented as the Redeemer of men but for Visconti she is man's Nemesis. The females in *Ossessione, Senso, White Nights, Bellissima,* and *Rocco* wreak their havoc not through spidery machinations but through a psychic force that the male can neither resist nor overcome. It follows almost logically that Visconti is the best director of actresses in the world, and the performances of Clara Calamai (*Ossessione*), Anna Magnani (*Bellissima*), Alida Valli (*Senso*), Maria Schell (*White Nights*), and Annie Girardot (*Rocco*) are among the most memorable creations of the cinema.

Roberto Rossellini had directed three obscure wartime films—*La Nave Bianca, Un Pilote Ritorna, L'Uomo Della Croce*—before he emerged on the world scene with his neorealistic classics *Open City, Paisan,* and *Germany Year Zero.* Then he went into a Magnani-Cocteau period with *The Miracle, The Human Voice,* and *The Infernal Machine* before the advent of Ingrid Bergman in *Stromboli, Europa 51 (The Greatest Love), Strangers, Joan at the Stake,* and *Fear.* During his Bergman period he also directed *Flowers of St. Francis, Dov'È la Liberta,* an episode in *The Seven Deadly Sins* ("Envy"), and *We Are the Women* (with Bergman). Except for the brilliant, scandal-provoking documentary *India,* Rossellini was off the screen for five years before making his comeback with *General Della Rovere,* a patriotic success followed by *Era Notte a Roma,* Stendhal's *Vanina Vanini,* and *Viva Italia!*

The most Catholic of all directors, Rossellini has always been obsessed by the inner miracles of human personality. In his oddly stylized treatment of the Honegger-Claudel *Joan at the Stake,* Rossellini sends Ingrid Bergman awkwardly soaring into heaven, a fitting climax to his cinematic conversion of the actress into a saint. Rossellini has confronted death as a metaphysical experience with none of the histrionics of Visconti, the despair of Antonioni, the emotional causality of Fellini. The final death images of Magnani in *Open City,* the partisans in *Paisan,* the prostitute in *Europa 51* and De Sica in *General Della Rovere* possess a formal dignity unique in world cinema. However, like most mystics, Rossellini sacrifices fact for truth, and the ambiguities of the human condition often elude him. With Chaplin and Buñuel, he stands apart from the other artists of his time, irritating, inimitable, and indispensable.

Next to Resnais, Antonioni is the most abstract filmmaker in the world today. The director envisages the world as a chessboard on which the kings and queens, the knights and bishops of old have been replaced by pawns whose moves are hopelessly confused by the application of obsolete rules. His first film, *Cronaca di un Amore,* focuses on two lovers who are parted by the accidental deaths of a friend and a husband, deaths willed but not executed by the couple. Ever since, Antonioni has been preoccupied with the shadow of guilt that hovers over human relationships before the police arrive. No director in history has been as fascinated by the moral repercussions of suicides and fatal accidents. Hitchcock and Buñuel have derived dark humor from this casuistic problem that apparently torments Antonioni.

However, Antonioni's films before *L'Avventura — Cronaca di un Amore, La Signora Senza Camelia, Le Amiche, I Vinti, Il Grido —* were concerned also with problems arising from class distinctions and economic calculations. (The key to the director's treatment of the relationship between men and women is stated by a character in *Le Amiche:* "Every woman who lives with a man to whom she is superior is unhappy.") *L'Avventura* and *La Notte* derive their maddening rhythm from the idea that the duration of time drains away human emotions, and their distinctive visual shape from the suggestion that spatial forms create psychological barriers. The unique aesthetic developed by Antonioni has led him to abandon the lower and middle classes, where lives are constricted by necessity, and to concentrate on the idle rich, who have the time to torture each other.

Fellini is the only one of the four with a flair for comedy, amply projected in his first two films, *Variety Lights* (codirected with Alberto Lattuada) and *The White Sheik*. In a more somber vein, *Vitelloni, La Strada,* and *Cabiria* are all bathed in a tragicomic lyricism that is intensely personal and reflects Fellini's compassion for the rejects of the modern world. After this impressive trilogy Fellini undertook *La Dolce Vita* to provide a Dantean vision of the modern world as viewed from the top instead of the bottom. Unfortunately there is more to a great film than a great conception, and Fellini has enlarged his material without expanding his ideas. Consequently the film is as bloated as the fish that terminates the orgy sequence.

However, it can be argued that in terms of social impact *La Dolce Vita* is the most important film ever made. This does not imply a correlation with artistic merit, since by the standard of impact *Uncle Tom's Cabin* is superior to *Moby Dick*. The fantastic popularity of *La Dolce Vita* may be summed up in the beggar's comment in Buñuel's *Viridiana:* "One must sin before one can repent." Without being consciously hypocritical, Fellini has dramatized the fundamental injustice of social morality. The poor creatures abandoned by Antonioni to their lives of necessity flock to *La Dolce Vita* to share Fellini's disgust with the sweet life, but the spectacle of corruption fills them with envy for the options of the hero. Confident of their ultimate righteousness, many spectators would like to slide along the infernal surfaces of fur and chrome before regaining their moral footing. If *La Dolce Vita* contributes to an awareness of the hypocrisy of so-called social morality, which denies to the peasants and the proles the sweet Faustian decisions of the Kennedys and the Rockefellers, the film may be forgiven for its intellectual and formal failures.

Although their aspiration often exceeds their sensibility, the Big Four act as the conscience of the Italian film industry. As a national bloc, their most serious challengers active today are the French Big Five of Renoir, Bresson, Resnais, Truffaut, and Godard. It would be difficult to find more than ten active directors from the rest of the world on the same artistic plane. At this moment the Big Four are critically fashionable, but just a few years ago their films were being hissed and booed on three continents, and a few years from now they will probably be downgraded again. This absurd oscillation of critical judgments is caused largely by the haphazard system of distribution and revival in practice today. If there is such a thing as ultimate judgment, only time will tell if the Big Four are the wave of the future or the last gasp of the past.

—Andrew Sarris

Italy: Michelangelo Antonioni
■
L'AVVENTURA (1960)

It had begun to look as if only those with a fresh eye—working in poverty and inexperience and in underdeveloped countries, discovering the medium for themselves—could do anything new and important (like the Apu Trilogy). The future of movies seemed to lie with filmmakers who didn't know that it had all been done before. For those with great traditions behind them, the only field to explore seemed to be comedy—and "black" comedy at that—or, at least, works which suggest black comedy: *Eroica, Kagi, Breathless, The Cousins, Smiles of a Summer Night, The Seventh Seal.*

L'Avventura is, easily, the film of the year, because Antonioni, by making his movie about this very problem—depleted modern man—demonstrated that the possibilities for serious, cultivated, personal expression in the film medium were not yet exhausted. *L'Avventura* is a study of the human condition at the higher social and economic levels, a study of adjusted, compromising man—afflicted by short memory, thin remorse, easy betrayal. The characters are passive as if postanalytic, active only in trying to discharge their anxiety—sex is their sole means of contact and communication. Too shallow to be truly lonely, they are people trying to escape their boredom in each other and finding it there. They become reconciled to life only by resignation. Claudia, the only one capable of love, is defeated like the rest; her love turns to pity.

It's a barren view of life, but it's a *view*. Perhaps compassion is reserved for the lives of the poor: the corruption of innocence is tragic in *Shoeshine;* the intransigence of defeated man is noble in *Umberto D.;* hope and gullibility are the saving grace of *Cabiria.* But modern artists cannot view themselves (or us) tragically: rightly or wrongly, we feel that we defeat ourselves—when were we innocent? when are we noble? how can we be "taken in"? Antonioni's subject, the fall (that is to say, the exposure) of a rich, handsome, gifted man is treated accumulatively and analytically—an oblique, tangential view of love and society, a view not raised to the plane of despair. In its melancholy *L'Avventura* suggests Chekhov. Because it is subtle and ascetic, yet laborious in revealing its meanings, it suggests the Henry James who chewed more than he bit off. And perhaps because the characters use sex destructively as a momentary blackout, as a means of escaping self-awareness by humiliating someone else, it suggests D. H. Lawrence. Most of all, I think, it suggests the Virginia Woolf of *The Waves:* the mood of *L'Avventura* is "Disparate are we." Antonioni is an avowed Marxist—but from this film I think we can say that although he may believe in the socialist criticism of society, he has no faith in the socialist solution. When you think it over, probably more of us than would care to admit it feel the same way. A terrible calm hangs over everything in the movie; Antonioni's space is a kind of vacuum in which people are aimlessly moving—searchers and lost are all the same, disparate, without goals or joy.

For those who can take movies or leave them alone, *La Dolce Vita* is obviously the film of the year: audiences can enjoy its "vice" (the name they give their own fantasies when somebody else acts them out) and they can hold up their hands in horror (peeking through the fingers) at all that wicked decadence and all those orgies.

—*PaulineKael*

Italy: Michelangelo Antonioni

•

RED DESERT (1964)

Michelangelo Antonioni's first feature in color remains a watermark for using colors creatively, expressionistically, and beautifully; to get the precise hues he wanted, Antonioni had entire fields painted. A newly struck and restored print of the film makes clear why audiences were so excited a quarter of a century ago by his innovations, which include not only expressive uses of color for moods and subtle thematic coding but striking uses of editing as well. This film comes at the tail end of his most fertile period, immediately after his remarkable trilogy consisting of *L'Avventura, La Notte,* and *L'Eclisse; Red Desert* may not be quite as good as the first and last of these, but the ecological concerns of this film look a lot more prescient today than they did at the time. Monica Vitti plays an extreme neurotic married to industrialist Richard Harris, and Antonioni does eerie, memorable work with the industrial shapes and colors that surround her, which are shown alternately as threatening and beautiful; she walks through a science fiction lunar landscape spotted with structures that are both disorienting and full of possibilities. Like any self-respecting Antonioni heroine, she's looking for love and meaning—more specifically, for ways of adjusting to new forms of life—and mainly finding sex. But the film's most spellbinding sequence depicts a pantheistic, utopian fantasy of innocence, which she recounts to her ailing son.

—*Jonathan Rosenbaum*

Italy: Michelangelo Antonioni

•

THE PASSENGER (1975)

Moving from the breathtaking austerity of the Sahara to the goofy grandeur of a Gaudí mansion in Barcelona, Michelangelo Antonioni's last great movie is also the last word on the modern idea of tourism. Jack Nicholson plays David Locke, a successful TV journalist who's grown sick of his career, his past, his Westernness; he dreams of learning what's on "the other side of that window" — the world beyond himself. Finding a friend's corpse in a North African hotel bed, he takes on the dead man's identity; it turns out he's turned himself into a gunrunner, who winds up in Spain with a beautiful woman (*Last Tango in Paris*'s Maria Schneider) and is pursued by figures from the old identity he's fleeing and the new one he's taken on. While this may sound like the stuff of an international thriller (which, in a loose sense, it is), Antonioni's true subject is how our lives are shaped by our habitual, fragmentary ways of seeing — be it journalistic "objectivity," the imperialist confidence of the Westerner in the Third World, or simply our familiar style of confronting the world each day. Antonioni wants to push beyond such blinkered perceptions of life, to open the world anew. And everything comes together in one of the few miraculous shots in the history of movies, a seven-minute tracking shot which begins with Locke lying in a hotel bed and winds up answering the question of what lies on "the other side of the window." An eerie, Eastern serenity pervades the entire scene — all the hero's subjective pangs have been refined away and we're left with the mysterious calm of a world that lies beyond the feeble history of its passengers. One of the most beautiful and mysterious movies of the seventies.

—John Powers

Italy: Federico Fellini

■

NIGHTS OF CABIRIA (1957)

Cabiria (*Le Notti di Cabiria*), with its titular evocation of D'Annunzio and the epic tradition of early Italian films, is the name of a shabby prostitute in Federico Fellini's parable on the human condition. Attired in a sleeveless, zebra-striped blouse, a moth-eaten fur stole, and grotesquely inappropriate bobby socks, Giulietta Masina's Cabiria impishly burlesques her ancient calling and then poignantly transcends it in a burst of tragic irony. The film ends on a note of high pathos, comparable to the finest moments of Chaplin, as Miss Masina's final close-up sums up one of the most resourceful performances in screen history.

The plot of *Cabiria* consists of five events in the heroine's life, each event logically related to the development of her character. The film opens with Cabiria running across a lonely field with her lover. The camera remains distant from the apparently carefree couple. The two figures are framed against a bleak, gray-lit landscape, its pastoral simplicity marred by telephone poles and distant housing developments. The absence of mood music and expository dialogue creates some of the sinister tension of the first sequences in *Great Expectations*. The suspense heightens as Cabiria stops at the edge of a stream and gaily swings her handbag in an ever-widening arc while her lover furtively glances about. Suddenly Cabiria's escort seizes her handbag, shoves her into the stream, and runs off, never to be seen again.

This one episode establishes the pattern of Cabiria's life from illusion to disillusion. In the early scenes the loud, vulgar, ungainly aspects of Cabiria's personality are emphasized. She is literally dragged from the stream and absurdly handled like a sack of soggy potatoes. Her rescue and the inept artificial respiration that follows deny her even the dignity of a disaster. The audience is almost invited to laugh at her plight, but the physical discomfort of the situation — her young rescuers shivering in their bathing suits, Cabiria almost collapsing as she calls her lover and tries to escape from her nightmarish predicament — kills the laughter her appearance would normally arouse. At this point in the film it is not clear what mood Fellini is trying to achieve. His manner is cold and impersonal.

Cabiria soon resumes the nightly routine of her existence with her circle of prostitutes, dope peddlers, and procurers on the Via Borghese. Here Fellini does not glamorize Cabiria's profession. Actually, prostitutes are merely another tribe in the confederation of wanderers and outcasts, wastrels and opportunists, with whose irregular patterns of living Fellini has been concerned throughout his distinguished career. In his first film, *The White Sheik,* Fellini satirized the bumbling artisans of the Italian comic strips. (Giulietta Masina appeared briefly here as a whimsical lady of the evening.) *I Vitelloni* dramatized the aimless existence of young loafers in a resort town; *Il Bidone* examined the machinations of confidence men; *La Strada* was an odyssey of itinerant circus performers. In each instance Fellini approached his untidy characters on a plane of universal meaning.

By casting the diminutive, clown-visaged, essentially sexless Giulietta Masina as his prostitute, Fellini has automatically divorced himself from the currently fashionable exploitation of lurid themes. His treatment is neither sensual nor sentimental. By depicting Cabiria's spirited recovery from her ludicrous betrayal, Fellini indicates his concern with the indestructibility of his heroine, and by implication, of the human spirit generally. We sense that Cabiria's dunking in the stream is not her first setback, and Fellini quickly insures that it shall not be her last.

Cabiria jauntily plies her wares in a more fashionable part of Rome, where she witnesses a violent argument between a famous actor (Amedeo Nazzari) and his glamorous mistress (Dorian Gray). After the mistress stalks away, the actor curtly summons Cabiria to his car. They drive to a nightclub, and from there to his palatial villa. Cabiria stands up in the actor's convertible and waves to more elegant prostitutes in the neighborhood to display her good fortune.

When they arrive at the villa, Cabiria is overwhelmed by the splendor around her. The actor solemnly plays Beethoven's Fifth Symphony on his phonograph and confides to Cabiria that he is fond of this music. The actor and Cabiria are at emotional cross-purposes in this situation, but both are equally silly in their poses. There is something unpleasant in the actor's condescension to Cabiria; he seems to have no desire to make love to her, and his reluctance to do so curiously reaffirms Cabiria's stylized, somewhat unreal personality.

The actor's disaffected mistress returns unexpectedly; the actor hastily conceals Cabiria in his sumptuous bathroom, where she spends the night while the actor and his first desire renew their relationship. Cabiria is surreptitiously released the next morning. As the actor quietly leads her through the bedroom, Cabiria looks wistfully over her shoulder at the girl sleeping contentedly. The pathos of the situation is intensified when Cabiria attempts to return the money the actor gives her. Her gesture is clearly intended to make the actor recognize her as a human being, and like every other such gesture in her life, it fails.

As it turns out, this is the funniest episode in the film. The pace is leisurely as Miss Masina runs through her bag of low-comedy tricks. She collides with glass doors, grapples with endless curtains, scales heavily carpeted stairs with the hunched-forward determination of an Alpine skier, and grimaces at every new situation with the knowingly pursed lips of a fishwife at an art gallery. Her defeat here is less of a downfall than a pratfall, and the entire sequence seems gratuitous until the total symmetry of the film is perceived.

Suddenly God enters Cabiria's life in the guise of a miracle-seeking procession to a shrine of the Virgin Mary. Here Fellini divides his attention between Cabiria, who prays for the intangible miracle of a new life, and a crippled procurer and dope peddler, who has come to have his limbs healed. In a brilliantly composed and edited passage, Cabiria and the procurer alternately struggle through a milling, hysterical crowd of penitents to reach the altar. At the edge of one overhead shot, an elaborate loudspeaker subtly mocks the spontaneity of the occasion. The forward motion of the scene accelerates until the procurer throws away his crutches and collapses, writhing and threshing briefly on the floor before Fellini tastefully fades out the scene.

Fellini's treatment of this episode is crucial to an understanding of his general position. Although he does not believe in the more obvious manifestations of the miraculous (he was the author of Rossellini's controversial work, *The Miracle*), Fellini does not indulge in De Sica's sly anticlericalism. The problem for Fellini is one of individual faith rather than social responsibility. The emotional power of the religious spectacle he creates suggests that God is sanctioned by man's need for faith, possibly even that God was created by man to supply hope for a better life. Fellini never spells out his personal commitments, but he seems to accept the Church as part of the furniture of his environment. There are indications in *Cabiria* as well as in *La Strada* that Fellini is more kindly disposed to the humanistic influences within the Church than to its authoritarian dogmas. A mendicant friar whom Cabiria meets on a lonely road has a greater impact on her soul than all the elaborate machinery of the miracle festival. However, like Cabiria and Gelsomina, and the nun in *La Strada,* who shares Gelsomina's sense of rootlessness, the friar is something of an outcast in the eyes of the Church. To accept the universality of these people as Fellini apparently does, it is necessary to consider the notion that in some sense we are all outcasts in our moments of loneliness and in the individual paths we follow to our salvation. In any event, by stressing the pugnacity and indestructibility of Cabiria, Fellini comes closer to creating a viable symbol of humanity than does De Sica with his whining protagonist in *The Bicycle Thief.*

Although Fellini has a limited degree of compassion for his band of stragglers, he never ignores the probabilities of their existence. When Cabiria attempts to regenerate herself, Fellini rewards her efforts with the most disastrous experience of her life. After denouncing her companions for remaining unchanged after their pious invocations to the Madonna, Cabiria temporarily abandons her profession and visits a tawdry music hall, where a hypnotist recruits her for his act. Cabiria is quickly thrust into a romantic fantasy before a boorish audience. She gracefully dances with an imaginary lover whom the hypnotist calls Oscar as the orchestra plays a tinny version of "The Merry Widow Waltz." After picking some imaginary flowers, Cabiria relives her youthful innocence, which is symbolically evoked by her memory of her long black hair. In a breathtaking scene of dramatic recall, Cabiria worriedly asks Oscar if he really loves her and is not just deceiving her. She is then snapped out of her trance to find herself an object of derision and ridicule.

Outside, a shy young man (François Périer) tells her that he was moved by the purity of her memories, and the final movement of the film starts slowly toward its preordained conclusion. After a series of meetings, Cabiria's suspicions are lulled by the apparent guilelessness of her admirer, whose name, by what he claims to be a fateful coincidence, is Oscar. Even after Cabiria reveals her profession, he asks her to marry him. On the day they are to leave for the country to be married, he lures her to the edge of a cliff overlooking the sea. Lacking the courage to push Cabiria to her death, he leaves her clawing the ground in grief-stricken revulsion against her fate while he ignobly picks up the handbag she has dropped at his feet and runs and stumbles through the forest.

Cabiria rises eventually and slowly makes her way to the road, Fellini's perennial symbol of life. There a group of adolescents light-heartedly serenading each other include Cabiria in their merry circle. A young girl smilingly greets Cabiria, whose tears are suddenly illuminated by her smile as the camera closes in on her face, slightly turned, slowly moving forward toward an unconditional acceptance of life. At that final moment Cabiria is in a state of secular grace, innocent and inviolate despite all the deceptions that have been practiced upon her.

In *Cabiria* one sees the familiar landmarks of the anarchic subworld of Fellini's imagination. Empty fields, roads, and streets set off by solitary travelers and distant buildings convey an image of the world as a lonely desert populated by insubstantial De Chirico figures vainly striding toward mathematically improbable intersections of humanity. In such a world, social theories are meaningless, since society itself seems to exist beyond the horizon of any given individual. Personal relationships, however tenuous, achieve an exaggerated intensity, and the mystiques of romantic illusion and religious faith become the indispensable components of existence. This would be a forbiddingly dismal view of life if Fellini did not provide compensations with a rich sense of humor and a perceptive eye for colorful detail. Fellini does not merely assert that life is worth living under the worst circumstances, he demonstrates the strange joys that flourish in the midst of loneliness and suffering. Without this demonstration *Cabiria* would be an unbearably sadistic experience.

Fellini's work since *The White Sheik* has been a continuous adventure in symbolism within the framework of unusually complex plots. Yet Fellini's technique does not lend itself to what we are accustomed to in the way of symbolic imagery. He does not give surfaces or objects any special gloss or lighting to emphasize their significance. There are never any meaningful shadows in a Fellini film, or any unusual contrasts between sunlight and darkness. His shots, day or night, fall into a neutral zone of grayness.

It might be argued that Fellini does not need to construct bizarre images, since such oddities abound in the Italian landscape. Italian religious festivals, for example, outdo Orson Welles in their addiction to grotesque shock effects. However, no matter how colorful the paraphernalia of Italian Catholicism may be, prop symbolism is only a small part of Fellini's achievement. It is in the symbolism and dreamlike quality of experience itself that Fellini excels. Here the lonely streets and fields serve their main function. What are Fellini's unforgettable images? The young men walking slowly on a deserted beach in *I Vitelloni;* Gelsomina marching behind three musicians in *La Strada;* Cabiria dancing on a stage suddenly detached from the audience — these are his magical moments.

It is odd to think of Fellini following in the footsteps of the neorealists, but it would be an error to consider his work completely apart from their influence. Indeed, it is the realism in Fellini's technique that enriches his symbols. He does not prettify reality although he tends to control it somewhat more than his predecessors. He does not shrink from dirt or grime or the garish ugliness of stage makeup. Indeed, like most neorealists, Fellini seems more at ease with settings of poverty and moderate means than with citadels of luxury. His cheap, noisy music hall in *Cabiria* seems more authentic than the plush, unusually quiet nightclub. Cabiria's drab house seems less of a caricature than the actor's incredibly palatial villa. It is not a question of visual reality but one of camera treatment. Fellini looks at the poorer settings objectively, picking out their most characteristic elements. However, the luxurious settings are viewed satirically and only their most ridiculous features are emphasized.

Similarly, in *Cabiria* at least, the upper-class people—the actor and his mistress—are seen mechanically from the viewpoint of a lowly wide-eyed prostitute. Fellini's unwillingness to study a wider range of social strata does not imply an inability to do so. Still, with all its merits, *Cabiria* may represent the point at which Fellini's concern with the stragglers of society begins to yield diminishing returns. Somehow *Cabiria* does not have the feel of greatness that *I Vitelloni* communicates. In *I Vitelloni* every character counts for something and every incident advances toward a common truth. *Cabiria* is too much of a one-woman show, with Giulietta Masina's heroine achieving a sublime illumination while all the other characters linger in the darkness of deception and irresolution. Like *La Strada*, Fellini's other near-masterpiece, *Cabiria* has some of the limitations of an acting vehicle that sometimes loses its way on the road of life and forks out into the bypaths of a virtuoso performance.

—*Andrew Sarris*

Italy: Federico Fellini
.

LA STRADA (1954)

Fellini's greatest film is at once a road movie, a circus film, an offbeat love story, and a spiritual parable. Giulietta Masina, Fellini's wife, gives a magical performance as the childlike waif who is bought and mistreated by Anthony Quinn, a brutal circus strongman. A third important character is The Fool, a tightrope walker played by Richard Basehart, who is as airy and spiritual as Quinn is earthy and coarse. Masina falls in love with Quinn, despite his abuse and neglect, but when he kills The Fool her wits begin to wander and eventually, terrified, he abandons her. Five years later, when he hears of her death, he is stricken by something—belated love, remorse, a sense of bereavement — perhaps the first feelings he's ever had for another person. The "road" of the title is finally a metaphor, for the film is about his spiritual redemption into the human community.

— *Morris Dickstein*

Italy: Roberto Rossellini

■

OPEN CITY (1945)

Roberto Rossellini burst upon the world with this film, made just after the Allies took Rome. The fame of his brutal, melodramatic account of the underground resistance to the Nazi occupation rests on its extraordinary immediacy and its rough, documentary look; at its most startling, it seems "caught" rather than staged. Many Americans, used to slick war films, reacted to it as if it actually were caught, documentary footage, and mistook the great Anna Magnani and Aldo Fabrizi, Maria Michi, and the other actors for nonprofessionals — this despite such stock elements as a rapacious lesbian Gestapo agent and a Hollywood-and-Vine-type Gestapo chief. The plot devices are often opportunistic, but there's a unifying fervor: shot on odds and ends of film stock, with fluctuating electricity, and showing people who a few weeks before had been part of the events, the movie gave us a cross section of a city under terrible stress. When the initial $25,000 that Rossellini had raised was used up, he and Magnani sold their clothes; Maria Michi, who had hidden men like Togliatti — and the scriptwriter, Sergio Amidei — in her flat, now provided the flat for some of the sequences. Federico Fellini assisted Amidei on the script.

— *Pauline Kael*

Italy: Roberto Rossellini

■

PAISAN (1946)

Roberto Rossellini made this episodic film after his breakthrough with *Open City* the year before. Each of the six parts has a story and deals with an aspect of the war that had just ended. The present-tense semidocumentary visual style is innovative, the content less so. Some of the stories have a tidy O. Henry finish, and there's a lot of sentimentality, though the film gives the impression of being loose and open. The script by Federico Fellini and Rossellini was based on stories they and others had written. (The Florence episode is by Vasco Pratolini, who isn't credited.) With Maria Michi and Gar Moore in the Roman episode, and Dots M. Johnson as the black soldier in Naples. Cinematography by Otello Martelli.

—Pauline Kael

Italy: Roberto Rossellini

■

GENERAL DELLA ROVERE (1959)

Vittorio De Sica has perhaps his greatest role in this otherwise mediocre film, directed by Roberto Rossellini. It is set in Genoa in 1943. De Sica is a small-time swindler with a classic con man's grand manner; the Germans induce him to impersonate a Resistance general whom they have inadvertently shot and send him to a political prison, where he is supposed to ferret out information for them. But the petty, self-loathing crook, experiencing for the first time the respect and admiration—even the awe—of other men, becomes as courageous as the fighter he impersonates. The mask has molded the man, and the Nazis must destroy their own creation. De Sica is superb; we watch his evolution from worm to Il Generale with utter astonishment and delight. At its most original, the film is a shockingly funny black comedy: the con man, battered and bleeding from torture, weeps sentimentally over a photograph of the real Generale's children—a scene as excruciatingly comic as the surreal torture scenes in *Bend Sinister*, Nabokov's novel about the Nazis. But this film, made on a slender budget and shot and edited in six weeks, is—surprisingly—too long; the director doesn't seem to have discovered his best material until it was too late to pull the story together. The compositions, the groupings of actors, the ideas, and the milieu are like a reprise of the neorealist *Open City* (1945). The rawness and immediacy are gone, though; the faces are actorish, and the sets are obviously sets. With Hannes Messemer, Sandra Milo, Giovanna Ralli, Anne Vernon. From a script by Sergio Amidei, Diego Fabbri, Indro Montanelli, and Rossellini.

—Pauline Kael

Italy: Luchino Visconti
■
THE LEOPARD (1963)

Seeing Burt Lancaster in his grandest role—Prince Fabrizio di Salina, the title character in Luchino Visconti's 1963 film *The Leopard*—is, at first, a shock. For most of four decades Lancaster's image has been that of a wily buccaneer. But here he is, giving the performance of his career as a philosophical 1860s Sicilian aristocrat facing down Garibaldi's revolution. And just as the Prince holds his family together through strength of will, Lancaster holds Visconti's crowning achievement together, not with his usual volatility but with an impassioned, ramrod intelligence. When the Prince flashes the toothy Lancaster grin, it's tightly wired; when the star's bouncing swagger breaks through, it gives a jolt of spring-driven energy to the Prince's proper gait. Fabrizio, the Leopard, is a man who checks his spontaneity and filters his passions. But Lancaster creates a character who's as physically expressive as any of his men of action. His ruddy hair, furry mustache, and mutton-chop sideburns frame the strong square cut of his face, and his formal vested clothes accent the long, proud line of his posture. When Lancaster's bold, magnificent Prince paces in and out of his opulent quarters, with their tapestries and damasks, he cuts through the movie's marvelous, overstuffed atmosphere like an upholsterer's knife.

The Leopard is the culmination of Lancaster's career rather than its contradiction. Ever since he made his debut as the doomed boxer in the 1946 movie of Hemingway's *The Killers,* he has seasoned his beefcake with a romantic melancholy. And in films like *The Flame and the Arrow* (in which he plays an Italian peasant) his braggadocio has rippled with as much wit as muscle. Like Kirk Douglas, Lancaster became a star in the late forties by embodying a Depression kid's get-ahead drive tempered by the Second World War. His richest roles were both avid and anguished; his tough army sergeant in *From Here to Eternity* may have been a cocky, take-charge guy, but he was also a protector of the weak, particularly of the obsessed bugler Robert E. Lee Prewitt. The son of a New York City postal worker, Lancaster was a circus acrobat (nicknamed "Mr. Teeth and Muscles") and a floor-walker in the lingerie department of a Marshall Field's store before he took up acting. With this hardscrabble background, it's no wonder that his performances are often double-edged: they depict the glory of making it in the world, and the toll the world takes in private feelings.

From John Huston to Sam Peckinpah, Lancaster has collaborated with some of the most adventurous, "masculine" American directors, and in recent years he's won thunderous acclaim for his work in Louis Malle's *Atlantic City* and Lamont Johnson's *Cattle Annie and Little Britches.* Still, few of the characters he's portrayed have released everything that's in him (not even his showboat turns in *Elmer Gantry* and *The Rainmaker*). Astonishingly, the one moviemaker who fully realized Lancaster's complexity on film was an equally complicated, superficially opposite personality — the homosexual Marxist aristocrat Luchino Visconti. In *The Leopard,* Lancaster channels his animal grace and exploits a quality that Norman Mailer once alluded to: his ability to suggest self-creation. This extraordinary movie is, along with *Lawrence of Arabia,* the most successful cinematic attempt to interpret spectacular historical events through one person's consciousness.

The rerelease of *The Leopard* gives Boston a chance to live up to the reputation it's had since the Bogey and Bergman revivals — as a moviegoing city that supports the best of films. The "uncut" version now on view is slightly shorter than the original 1963 Italian print, but it's the one that Visconti had hoped would reach international release, and it's been reprocessed to approximate cinematographer Giuseppe Rotunno's gold-tinged, russet palette. Appropriately, it was first screened in America last Easter: *The Leopard* is about the decline of the Sicilian aristocracy, but the story behind the movie is a tale of resurrection. The original novel by Giuseppe Tomasi di Lampedusa, which became one of the literary events of the late fifties, nearly fell into obscurity. Tomasi di Lampedusa was himself a Sicilian prince who for most of his adult life had contemplated writing a novel about his great-grandfather. He was nearing sixty before he even started, and he died before the work could be published. Only through the efforts of Giorgio Bassani (the author of *The Garden of the Finzi-Continis,* another tale of a lost aristocratic class) did *The Leopard,* which takes its name from the central figure on the Lampedusa coat of arms, reach print—and turn into an international bestseller.

Visconti was drawn to the novel's aristocratic hero and to its vision of Italy's persecuted southern wasteland (a subject he'd treated before in *La Terra Trema* and *Rocco and His Brothers*). But despite the book's commercial success, he was able to arrange financing through 20th Century-Fox only if he agreed to cast an American star. Visconti's version won the Golden Palm at Cannes in 1963. However, Fox studio executives, laboring under the financial burden of *Cleopatra* (and, according to David Ehrenstein's *Film Comment* account, *unaware* that Visconti had made a foreign-language film), ordered a brutal reediting and redubbing for the British and American release. Twenty years later a Fox employee, Natasha Arnoldi, suggested that the studio strike a new, complete print of *The Leopard* (which had survived intact in Rome), whereupon it became the talk of Los Angeles's Filmex festival. But it reopened in LA too late to capitalize on that sensation, and when it premiered in New York, only Vincent Canby and Pauline Kael bothered to rereview it. Surprisingly, Lancaster's performance improves when an Italian actor reads his lines; since we're not confused by Lancaster's distinctive American accent, we can concentrate on his physicality. The neglect of this film is a tragedy, because the reconstructed *Leopard* is Luchino Visconti's masterpiece—graceful, lucid, and seductive.

"Sometimes, as with Lampedusa, a single novel, coming late in life, seems less the practice of an art than a distillation of years of human experience." What Anthony Burgess wrote about the novel in 1967 also applies to Visconti's movie and to Lancaster's performance. Using all the skills he has acquired as a stage director of Chekhov, Shakespeare, and Verdi and as a moviemaker, Visconti extols the luxury of the aristocrats' estates even as he reveals the hairline cracks behind the tapestries. He was a virtuoso of the languorous sexy gesture and the sultry camera placement: the simple heave of a bosom in a bodice makes one yearn to catch each muffled heartbeat. Visconti was also the master of the poetically charged landscape, and here he captures the scraggly Sicilian countryside in all its sweaty, burnt-sienna beauty. The film builds on the contrast between the heat and dust outside and the rich, decaying life within. As it opens, the camera is sidling through the sweltering afternoon into the Prince's palazzo as the family says its rosary. And a dead soldier is found in the garden—an omen of the family's destiny.

The Prince is the one man in his clan who's retained the feudal virtues: he's in command whether hunting in the field with his vassals or chatting in the parlor with contessas and priests. He also knows when to be pragmatic. When Garibaldi's popular revolution threatens not only to unite the two kingdoms of Italy but also to overthrow the traditional ruling class, the Prince uses his wealth and influence to preserve his family's standing. In the end, under the constitutional monarchy of Victor Emmanuel II, the aristos *and* the Garibaldini lose out to the land-grabbing, Mafia-ridden middle class. Only by endorsing the machinations of his opportunistic nephew, Tancredi (Alain Delon), does the Leopard save the House of Salina's pride. "If we want everything to stay as it is, everything must change," declares Tancredi, who in the course of the film shifts his allegiance from Garibaldi's redshirts to Victor Emmanuel's bluecoats; he's merely being shrewd and politically correct. Tancredi's marriage to Angelica (Claudia Cardinale), the gorgeous daughter of a social-climbing mayor (Paolo Stoppa), firmly allies the Salinas with the now-powerful bourgeoisie. The aristocracy, though, will never again be viewed as a heavenly elite. The Prince foresees the fate of his class—and he knows he cannot escape.

For all the sumptuous, even lighthearted ease of its presentation, *The Leopard* is constructed dialectically, uncovering the contradictions within the old state of things and the new. The Prince rides to his mistress with the family priest without recognizing the need for confession: surrounded by representations of classical deities, studying the heavenly bodies through his telescopes, he's a demigod himself. (The priest even admits as much when explaining the Prince to some peasants.) Fabrizio's dedication to aristocratic form goes beyond the sad particulars of his family; in his view, only Tancredi is aristocratic material. "Maybe a young man as distinguished, discriminating, and fascinating as Tancredi cannot be produced without ancestors who ran through a half dozen fortunes," says the Prince. He appreciates the modesty and culture of his own daughter, Concetta (Lucilla Morlacchi), yet he realizes that Angelica, with her full-bodied sensuality, and fortune, is a better match for Tancredi. And though he sees Angelica for what she is (a hot-blooded charmer at play in the fields of the lords), he too is drawn to her, as she is to him.

Prince Fabrizio may defend the feudal aristocrats as proper rulers of his native Sicily, but he also declares that all Sicilians, ruler and peasant alike, are doomed by their apocalypse of a homeland. In his most eloquent speech, the epitome of Tomasi di Lampedusa's wisdom, he explains his Sicilian perspective to a representative of King Victor Emmanuel II (who hopes the Prince will join the government): "Sleep is what Sicilians want, and they will always hate anyone who tries to wake them, even in order to bring them the most wonderful of gifts. All our expression, even the most violent, is really wish fulfillment: our sensuality is a hankering for oblivion, our shooting and knifing a hankering for death, even the sweetness of our sherbets is a hankering for voluptuous immobility, that is, for death again." The beleaguered history of Sicily ("for 2500 years a colony") as well as its "violence of landscape, cruelty of climate, continual tension in everything," have caused its citizens to settle into "torpor." And yet, the Sicilians "never want to improve, for the simple reason that they think themselves perfect; their vanity is stronger than their misery."

For the first two-thirds of the movie, Visconti uses the cinematic equivalent of the detached first-person: though there's little subjective camera, the Leopard is the center of nearly every scene, and even when he isn't, Visconti's distance from the action matches his champion's. The street fighting that breaks out when Garibaldi reaches Sicily is presented in one self-contained sequence, without inflated derring-do. And the heroism is a matter not of conquest but of preserving sensibility—the movie becomes lyrical only when evoking the aristocrats' personal world of wonders. Visconti's camera virtually partners the prancing Tancredi when he's still the focus of Concetta's dreams; and when the family makes its annual late-summer trek to a palace in Donnafugata, the town Angelica's father rules, the moviemaking takes on the warmth we associate with Jean Renoir (Visconti's mentor). But their sentimental journey has uneasy undertones: sitting in their high wooden pews in church, smothered with dust from the road and with incense, they look like spirits of the dead.

Visconti and his collaborators hew close to Tomasi di Lampedusa's narrative, with only minor differences in emphasis. Visconti chooses to highlight the Sicilian masses' unrest in order to point up that the feudal lords "*had* to go" — and that the Mafia and bourgeoisie will prove to be just as oppressive. And he trusts his own staging expertise and Lancaster's dynamism to convey Tomasi di Lampedusa's interior narration. (Visconti and his four cowriters, including longtime collaborator Suso Cecchi d'Amico, also do a remarkable job of transposing the Prince's private thoughts into dialogue.) But the director's greatest inspiration is to use the novel's climactic setpiece — the ball that introduces Angelica into high society — as a grand summation; it takes up the film's final hour, suggesting everything that Tomasi di Lampedusa spelled out in his concluding chapters. Throughout the movie, Lancaster dominates the frame with his sculptured, imperious presence. By the time we arrive at the grand ball, Visconti is gliding effortlessly into the Prince's mind; everything we see is refracted through his sensibility. As he watches the dancers trip from room to room, the entire palace becomes a single interwoven memory. In a collaborative peak between actor and director, Lancaster's Prince becomes transparent.

Earlier, the Prince had displayed a rueful self-awareness when he judged Victor Emmanuel's envoy to be an honest man and let his thoughts and feelings flow: rebels and reformers try to teach aristocrats "good manners," he said, "but they won't succeed — because we think we are gods." Now, at the Ponteleone ball, his sense of mortality catches up with him and strips him; he can't help expressing his fear and desire. Tancredi aside, the Salina family is uneasy about the arrival of Angelica and her bumptious father (though she becomes the belle of the ball). But what upsets Prince Fabrizio even more is the quavering senescence of his own class. The aging nobles are too easily impressed by the pompous boasts and sentimental flourishes of the bourgeois colonel who's fired on Garibaldi. Their children have even less fiber. Seeing a roomful of giddy girls, the Prince observes that intermarriage among cousins hasn't improved the race; he compares them to chattering monkeys who will soon climb up the chandeliers and show off their behinds.

The combination of lavishness and decadence exhausts him. He catches his breath in a library; Greuze's *Death of a Just Man* hangs on the wall, and he studies every detail as he puffs on a cigar. Angelica shakes the Prince out of his doldrums when she (with the jealous Tancredi looking on) asks him to dance. The Prince waltzes with the rigid elegance of a music-box figurine, but he can't conceal the tortured longing he feels when his eyes meet Angelica's. Although the girl is smitten with him, he cannot return to youth. And the older members of his class have matured into corruption. He sheds a tear, alone, in a tiny room next to dozens of chamber pots, and walks home by himself. Worried and humbled, he kneels before a passing priest. Shots ring out; King Victor Emmanuel's soldiers have executed some Garibaldi renegades. Tancredi, riding back in the carriage with the dozing priest, barely flinches as he hugs Angelica to his side. Still kneeling, Don Fabrizio looks up at the morning star. Calm, thoughtful, he asks out loud, "When will you give me an appointment less ephemeral in your region of perennial certitude?"

The vividness and poignance and odd, lush urgency of *The Leopard* stem from its intensely mixed feelings about the death of the feudal ruling class. Lancaster's Prince, so full of sad wisdom about his place in the world that he must look for hope in the stars, is not merely a sympathetic representative of that class; he's the aristocracy's apotheosis. Out of all the violence and aggression of centuries has come a man who's decent, vital, disinterested — but he hasn't come in time to justify the class's continued rule. Seeing this movie, you feel Fitzgerald was right: the rich are very different from you and me — and the European rich are even more different. But when Prince Fabrizio faces both social obsolescence and his own death, he joins the rest of humanity in being unable to harness history. At the end of Visconti's previous epic, *Rocco and His Brothers,* Rocco moaned, "Everything's falling to bits!" *The Leopard* is an elegy perched atop oblivion. But if there is a posterity, this film will live on in it.

—*Michael Sragow*

Italy: Luchino Visconti

■

LA TERRA TREMA (1947)

Luchino Visconti's neorealist tragedy, set among the exploited Sicilian fishermen, is long and full of political clichés, and yet in its solemnity and beauty it achieves a true epic vision. The film is lyrical yet austere, and it's beautifully proportioned. It may be the best boring movie ever made: although you might have to get up and stretch a few times, you're not likely to want to leave. Filmed on location in Aci-Trezza, Sicily. Director of photography, G. R. Aldo; camera operator, Gianni di Venanzo. The assistant directors were Francesco Rosi and Franco Zeffirelli. The script is by Visconti.

—Pauline Kael

Italy: Vittorio De Sica
■

SHOESHINE (1947)

When *Shoeshine* opened in 1947, I went to see it alone after one of those terrible lovers' quarrels that leave one in a state of incomprehensible despair. I came out of the theater, tears streaming, and overheard the petulant voice of a college girl complaining to her boyfriend, "Well I don't see what was so special about that movie." I walked up the street, crying blindly, no longer certain whether my tears were for the tragedy on the screen, the hopelessness I felt for myself, or the alienation I felt from those who could not experience the radiance of *Shoeshine*. For if people cannot feel *Shoeshine*, what *can* they feel? My identification with those two lost boys had become so strong that I did not feel simply a mixture of pity and disgust toward this dissatisfied customer but an intensified hopelessness about everything . . . Later I learned that the man with whom I had quarreled had gone the same night and had also emerged in tears. Yet our tears for each other, and for *Shoeshine*, did not bring us together. Life, as *Shoeshine* demonstrates, is too complex for facile endings.

Shoeshine was not conceived in the patterns of romance or melodrama; it is one of those rare works of art which seem to emerge from the welter of human experience without smoothing away the raw edges, or losing what most movies lose—the sense of confusion and accident in human affairs. James Agee's immediate response to the film was, "*Shoeshine* is about as beautiful, moving, and heartening a film as you are ever likely to see." A few months later he retracted his evaluation of it as a work of art and wrote that it was not a completed work of art but "the raw or at best the roughed-out materials of art." I think he should have trusted his initial response: the greatness of

Shoeshine is in that feeling we get of human emotions that have not been worked-over and worked-into something (a pattern? a structure?) and cannot really be comprised in such a structure. We receive something more naked, something that pours out of the screen.

Orson Welles paid tribute to this quality of the film when he said in 1960, "In handling a camera I feel that I have no peer. But what De Sica can do, that I can't do. I ran his *Shoeshine* again recently and the camera disappeared, the screen disappeared; it was just life . . ."

When *Shoeshine* came to this country, *Life* magazine wrote, "New Italian film will shock the world . . . will act on U.S. audiences like a punch in the stomach." But few Americans felt that punch in the stomach. Perhaps like the college girl they need to be hit by an actual fist before they can feel. Or, perhaps, to take a more charitable view of humanity, they feared the pain of the film. Just about everybody has heard of *Shoeshine* — it is one of the greatest and most famous films of all time — but how many people have actually seen it? They didn't even go to see it in Italy. As De Sica has said, "*Shoeshine* was a disaster for the producer. It cost less than a million lire but in Italy few people saw it as it was released at a time when the first American films were reappearing . . ." Perhaps in the U.S. people stayed away because it was advertised as a social protest picture — which is a little like advertising *Hamlet* as a political study about a struggle for power.

Shoeshine has a sweetness and a simplicity that suggest greatness of feeling, and this is so rare in film works that to cite a comparison one searches beyond the medium — if Mozart had written an opera set in poverty, it might have had this kind of painful beauty. *Shoeshine,* written by Cesare Zavattini, is a social protest film that rises above its purpose. It is a lyric study of how two boys (Rinaldo Smordoni [Giuseppe] became a baker; Franco Interlenghi [Pasquale] became a film star) betrayed by society betray each other and themselves. The two young shoeshine boys who sustain their friendship and dreams amid the apathy of postwar Rome are destroyed by their own weaknesses and desires when sent to prison for black-marketeering. This tragic study of the corruption of innocence is intense, compassionate, and above all, humane.

— Pauline Kael

Italy: Vittorio De Sica
■

THE BICYCLE THIEF (1949)

Vittorio De Sica's neorealist masterpiece, about an impoverished young Roman's search for his stolen bicycle—an odyssey through the city's lower depths which becomes (without a trace of contrivance) the pursuit of a lost sense of manhood, one's soul—and, by extension, a defeated nation's quest for self-respect and self-reliance. One of the movies that shatters you, if you see it at a young, idealistic age.

—*Michael Wilmington*

Italy: Vittorio De Sica
■

UMBERTO D. (1952)

In 1952, the screenwriter Cesare Zavattini, who had already collaborated with Vittorio De Sica on a succession of classics (the best known is *The Bicycle Thief*), declared that he hoped to create a movie so full of "truly significant and revealing" details that it would seem like "ninety minutes in the daily life of mankind." The same year, De Sica and Zavattini came as close as anyone ever has to achieving this goal. Their eruptively moving *Umberto D.,* the story of a debt-ridden retired civil servant who's forced from his home by a cruel landlady, is neorealism at its peak. The movie brings to mind a line from Tolstoy: "Ivan Ilyich's life had been most simple and most ordinary and therefore most terrible."

On the surface, *Umberto D.* simply follows the title character, played with a tattered bourgeois hauteur by the retired professor Carlo Battisti, as he and his dog wander through Rome in a futile search for money and fellowship. But De Sica and Zavattini turn mundane rituals into eloquent presentations of character. The movie starts with its only panoramic scene: elderly men demand an increase in their pensions. (The sequence is echoed later in a dog pound.) De Sica tightens his focus so unerringly that the final shot—Umberto D. playing fetch, trying to win back his dog's alienated affections—is a prodigious expression of modern man's aloneness. De Sica made a handful of wonderful movies, but *Umberto D.* is his masterpiece.

—*Michael Sragow*

Japan: Kon Ichikawa

■

ODD OBSESSION (1959)

Among the good films ignored or ludicrously misinterpreted by the critics is, currently, the Japanese film *Kagi*, or *Odd Obsession,* a beautifully stylized and highly original piece of filmmaking—perverse in the best sense of the word, and worked out with such finesse that each turn of the screw tightens the whole comic structure. As a treatment of sexual opportunism, it's a bit reminiscent of *Double Indemnity,* but it's infinitely more complex. The opening plunges us into the seat of the material. A young doctor, sensual and handsome, smug with sexual prowess, tells us that his patient, an aging man, is losing his virility. And the old man bends over and bares his buttocks—to take an injection. But the old man doesn't get enough charge from the injection, so he induces the young doctor, who is his daughter's suitor, to make love to his wife. By observing them, by artificially making himself jealous, the old man is able to raise his spirits a bit.

The comedy, of course, and a peculiar kind of black human comedy it is, is that the wife, superbly played by Machiko Kyo, is the traditional, obedient Japanese wife—and she cooperates in her husband's plan. She is so obedient and cooperative that, once aroused by the young doctor, she literally kills her old husband with kindness—she excites him to death. The ambiguities are malicious and ironic: the old man's death is both a perfect suicide and a perfect murder. And all four characters are observed so coldly, so dispassionately that each new evidence of corruption thickens the cream of the jest.

The title *Kagi*—the key—fits the Tanizaki novel, but does not fit the film, which might better be called the keyhole. Everybody is spying on everybody else, and although each conceals his motives and actions, nobody is fooled. The screen is *our* keyhole, and we are the voyeurs who can see them all peeking at each other. When the old man takes obscene pictures of his wife, he gives them to the young man to develop. The young man shows them to his fiancée, the daughter, whose reaction is that she can do anything her mother can do.

But a further layer of irony is that she *can't*. For the film is also a withering satire on the Westernized modern Japanese girl. The mother — mysterious, soft, subtle — uses her traditional obedience for her own purposes. She never says what she thinks about anything — when she starts a diary she puts down romantic hypocrisy worthy of a schoolgirl — and she is infinitely desirable. The daughter, a college student who explains what is going on quite explicitly, is just as corrupt as her mother, but has no interest or appeal to her parents or even to her fiancé. In her sweaters and skirts, and with her forthright speech, she is sexually available but completely unattractive. When she tells her father that nothing so simple as adultery is being practiced by her mother and the young doctor, she seems simply ludicrous; her mother can lower her eyes and murmur distractedly about the terrible things she is asked to do — and excite any man to want to try out a few.

The director, Kon Ichikawa, is probably the most important new young Japanese director. His study of obsessive expiation, *The Burmese Harp*, was subjected to a brutal, hack editing job, and has reached only a small audience in this country; *Enjo* (1958), based on Mishima's novel about a great crime, the young Zen Buddhist burning the Golden Pavilion, has not yet played here. (An earlier film of Ichikawa's — a puppet version of a Kabuki dance — was destroyed by MacArthur's aides because, according to Japanese film historian Donald Richie, they regarded Kabuki as feudalistic. What did they think MacArthur was?)

Kagi, made in 1959, took a special prize at the Cannes Festival in 1960 (the other special prize went to *L'Avventura*). *Kagi* was given "Special commendation for 'audacity of its subject and its plastic qualities.'" I've indicated the audacity of the subject; let me say something about the film's plastic qualities. It is photographed in color, with dark blue tones predominating, and with an especially pale soft pinkish white for flesh tones. I don't think I've ever seen a movie that gave such a feeling of flesh. Machiko Kyo, with her soft, sloping shoulders, her rhythmic little paddling walk, is like some ancient erotic fantasy that is more suggestive than anything Hollywood has ever thought up. In what other movie does one see the delicate little hairs on a woman's legs? In what other movie is flesh itself not merely the surface of desire but totally erotic? By contrast, the daughter, like the exposed, sun-tanned healthy American girl, is an erotic joke — she is aware, liberated, passionate, and, as in our Hollywood movies, the man's only sexual objective is to get *into* her and have done with it. With Machiko Kyo the *outside* is also erotic substance.

Ichikawa's cold, objective camera observes the calculations and designs, the careful maneuvers in lives that are fundamentally driven and obsessive; and there's deadly humor in the contrast between what the characters pretend they're interested in and what they actually care about.

Kagi is conceived at a level of sophistication that accepts pornography as a fact of life which, like other facts of life, can be treated in art. The subject matter is pornography, but the movie is not pornographic. It's a polite, almost clinical comedy about moral and sexual corruption. It even satirizes the clinical aspects of sex. Modern medicine, with its injections, its pills, its rejuvenating drugs, adds to the macabre side of the comedy. For *Kagi* has nothing to do with love: the characters are concerned with erotic pleasure, and medicine is viewed as the means of prolonging the possibilities of this pleasure. So there is particular humor in having the doctors who have been hastening the old man's death with their hypodermics try to place the blame for his death on the chiropractor who has been working on his muscles. They have all known what they were doing, just as the four principals all know, and even the servant and the nurse. The film has an absurd ending that seems almost tacked on (it isn't in the book); if it ended with the three survivors sitting together, and with Machiko Kyo reading her diary aloud, it could be a perfect no-exit situation, and the movie would have no major defects or even weaknesses.

Reading the reviews, you'd think that no American movie critic had even so much as heard of that combination of increasing lust and diminishing potency which destroys the dignity of old age for almost all men; you'd think they never behaved like silly, dirty old men. Japanese films in modern settings have a hard time with the art-house audience: perhaps the Americans who make up the foreign-film audience are still too bomb-scarred to accept the fact that business goes on as usual in Japan. In *Kagi* the beds — where a good part of the action takes place — are Western-style beds, and when the people ply each other with liquor, it's not saki, it's Hennessy. *Kagi* is the first Japanese comedy that has even had a chance in the art houses: if the judgments of incompetent critics keep people from seeing it, when will we get another? Crowther finds the husband of *Kagi* "a strictly unwholesome type." Let's put it this way: if you've never gotten a bit weary of the classical Western sex position, and if you've never wanted to keep the light on during intercourse, then you probably won't enjoy *Kagi*. But if you caught your breath at the Lady Wakasa sequences in *Ugetsu*, if you gasped when Masayuki Mori looked at Machiko Kyo and cried out, "I never dreamed such pleasures existed!" then make haste for *Kagi*.

—*Pauline Kael*

Japan: Kon Ichikawa
■

THE MAKIOKA SISTERS (1985)

The Makioka Sisters has one of the most gorgeous and evocative precredit sequences I've ever seen: a family gathering in 1938 Kyoto, when the cherry blossoms are at their peak. The bluffs of bright pink flowers softened by spring rain, framing vistavisions of hills and valleys, are like schoolbook memories of Japan brought to life by a light-fingered poet. And as the Makiokas, aristocrats from Osaka, sit in their tea room with a view, their ceremonious beauty matches the allure of all outdoors. This movie's instant aura of nostalgia is deliberate. Dressed in their festive kimonos, the Makiokas have taken this trip as a magic act of continuity with their past. We soon realize that elsewhere in their lives history has barged in and broken their spell.

The eldest of the four sisters, Tsuruko (Keiko Kishi), admits that the reason her husband, Tatsuo (Juzo Itami), didn't come is that there's no cherry blossom in his blood. Teinosuke (Koji Ishizaka), the husband of the second eldest, Sachiko (Yoshiko Sakuma), admires the way the mouth of the third sister, Yukiko (Sayuri Yoshinaga) forms an O—an oddly sensual observation that ripples through the group's politesse like a pebble in a rock pond. Yukiko is unmarried—her latest suitor has been disqualified because of his mother's mental illness—even though she has an irresistible coy demureness that drives her brother-in-law Teinosuke crazy, and in her floral white robe she's like a hothouse orchid. Taeiko (Yuko Kotegawa), the youngest sister, may wear the brightest kimono of them all, a great golden cocoon with swirling butterflies, but she's no Mademoiselle Butterfly. She's a rebel who's trying to pursue a dollmaking career and sorely wants her late father's legacy to help out. According to tradition, she can't marry until Yukiko does, and she can't be awarded her inheritance until she is married. The discussions climax when Sachiko, arguing for her younger sister, hops over to Tsuruko's place setting and exchanges "Yes!" "No!" "Yes!" "No!" "Yes!" "No!" in verbal ping-pong diplomacy. When the rain halts, peace returns, and the Makiokas move outside, where they adorn even the luscious Kyoto countryside. Westernized onlookers gawk at their dignified yet effervescent loveliness. So, of course, do we.

The Makioka Sisters is an unassuming masterpiece. With the most forthright and beguiling artistry, director Kon Ichikawa revives the vanished world of a proud Japanese merchant family; then, with tones of irony and lamentation, he lets it fade away like a midsummer night's dream recollected in the dead of winter. Ichikawa draws an abundance of characters and emotion-charged situations from the celebrated novel by Junichiro Tanizaki. But this modern master doesn't cram his movie with incidents (he ignores the most "cinematic" one, a devastating flood). Instead, he fills it with essences. The Makioka Sisters has the pull of grand soap opera, but in its tragicomic delicacy, it resembles a Japanese Chekhov.

It's hard to find an American film parallel to this movie, because our end-of-an-era dramas highlight historical cataclysms. When you think of cosseted upper-class women brought down to earth in our culture, all that comes to mind are the Southern belles forced to dirty their hems in Gone with the Wind. War rages through the Orient in the background of The Makioka Sisters, but the image you get of the aging Japanese body politic is of small family cells, only loosely connected. Ichikawa focuses on the ritualistic details of the Makiokas' family life, which to contemporary audiences everywhere — including Japan — must be a source of both aesthetic awe and ticky comedy. This is a movie in which a woman is mildly reprimanded for having a squeaky obi. One Makioka is so taken with another sister's bare shoulder that, after powdering it, she kisses it. And all the small touches add up. We see the cohesive power of the Makiokas' decorative femininity — how these prefeminist women manipulate it to their advantage, and how perilous it is for Taeko to break away.

The four sisters are the daughters of a long-dead tycoon, one of the top three shipbuilders in Japan. The other main characters, the husbands, never feel fully at home in the family traditions, even though they've taken on the Makioka name. The family's way of life has been frozen at the point of the father's death—perhaps even (Tatsuo complains) before. And Tatsuo and Teinosuke, the businessmen husbands, who are at best only corporals of industry, can't live up to the legend of old man Makioka. The sisters (including, to some extent, Tsuruko) resent Tatsuo in particular for selling out a large family holding and keeping a tight fist on the legacies. But he's just an earnest bureaucrat working for a banking company. And his brother-in-law, Teinosuke, heads the clothing division of a department store—an occupation that comes in handy when he must explain to wife Sachiko what he's been doing caressing his sister-in-law, Yukiko. The men must face the pressures both of traditional caste and status and of industrial bureaucracies—the pressures of modern Japan. Except for Taeko, the Makioka sisters try to hold these Westernizing pressures to the periphery of their lives.

But they can't escape twentieth-century fate, which in the course of the movie makes more than one appointment in Osaka. Even the highest-born families are now prey to the leveling power of the press, as the Makiokas find out when the impatient Taeko runs away with a jeweler's son and the event gets reported in the newspaper—what's worse, with Yukiko's name instead of Taeko's. (Tatsuo demands a retraction, which doesn't improve matters.) Taeko is retrieved before she can marry the boy, and she breaks up with him later anyway. She becomes a liberated woman before her time as she tries to turn her dollmaking into a business. Meanwhile, Yukiko, despite her "tarnished" name, goes from one ceremonial marriage interview, or *miai,* to the next. These *miai* define the film's ironic/elegiac tone. Yukiko meets several horrible mutations of ancient patriarchy and modern wealth and officialdom: my favorite is a fishery technician who can speak only of the importance of breeding freshwater fish. Yet these scenes are never strident. They're made deft and romantic by Yukiko's presence—she's the incarnation of a prewar Japanese grace. Yukiko can be a pain, insisting on intricate conditions for her hand: pre-premarital agreements. But her suitors forgive her when they see that she's born and bred to be displayed at *miai. The Makioka Sisters* gives off a flickering image of a female aristocracy in its final flower. Ichikawa's vision works like a magic box, interleaving tableaux of Japan's eternal beauty with flashes of the faster, cruder, more cynical way of life threatening to snuff it out.

When Ichikawa made such classic adaptations as *Kagi* (also from a Tanizaki novel) and *Fires on the Plain,* he and his longtime cowriter, wife Natto Wada, would live with the original material for weeks, bringing the screenplay along (he once said) as one would a child or a puppy. Written by Ichikawa with Shinya Hadaka, *The Makioka Sisters* has the same hard-won organic quality. Ichikawa had wanted to film the book for thirty-five years (two other directors beat him to it), but now he says he's glad he waited, because now he has humility. Perhaps, too, as a young man he wouldn't have had the understanding of time that binds the film together: the past and present beat at the core of the story with the diastolic/systolic rhythm of the human heart. Hack dramatists would take an incident like the newspaper scandal and withhold it from the audience in order to tease the drama along into a trumped-up climax. Ichikawa builds the revelations of the scandal gradually, with acute psychological intent, so that we feel the shock of the bold newspaper type and the family's residue of guilt long before the ramifications become clear. And when he flashes to the aftermath, he dramatizes it completely, so that every long-harbored family resentment spills out. That's when Yukiko and Taeko break with tradition and choose to stay with the younger Sachiko and Teinosuke rather than Tsuruko and Tatsuo. The flashbacks set off reverberations: we understand why, when an elderly aunt suggests that the younger sisters should move back, Taeko shakes with rage.

Ichikawa's script manages to keep the narrative as graceful and intriguing as it is dense. You're always feeling pings of recognition. Underneath the screenplay's hieratic surface is a sense of character that's fluid and dynamic. At one point or another, everyone "gets caught in the act," whether it's Yukiko flashing Teinosuke some leg or Taeko sizing up a photographer friend while her sisters think she's still involved with the jeweler's son. The film doesn't move as simply as it first seems — it oscillates, in one-step-forward, two-steps-backward fashion. By the end, Taeko is living with a bartender and working as a seamstress; the older sisters have reached complicated understandings with their husbands; and Yukiko, retiring but tenacious, has found her match. But when Sachiko tells Taeko that "nothing has changed," in a sense she's right. Whether they're rebelling against tradition or struggling to fulfill it, they're all measuring their lives by the ideals of their past.

Ichikawa's compression, and his disdain for conventional explication, can be disconcerting: when Sachiko calls for "some B" and receives a hypodermic shot with a wince, I had to go back to Tanizaki's novel to discover that "Beri-Beri was in the air of the Kobe-Osaka district and every year from summer into autumn the whole family came down with it. The vitamin injection had become a family institution." Yet seeing Sachiko so abruptly and cruelly take her medicine adds a level of comic mystery to the sisters' brushes with modernity. Elements of uncertainty keep tumbling into the drama. The Makiokas' brusque treatment of their servants, for example, offers broad satirical relief, but it also suggests how their aristocratic bauble of a lifestyle rests on stooping shoulders.

Ichikawa's dramatic and visual instincts combine in a glittering, seamless display of old-fashioned yet up-to-the-minute artistry. Audie Bock, in her splendid overview *Japanese Film Directors,* voices the minor reservation that "parts of the film become a kimono show." I think the entire movie is a cinematic kimono — yards of material cunningly folded into a harmonious whole, overflowing with diverse colors, embroidered with fine touches. Bock refers mainly to a scene that sounds a keynote for the film: it starts surrealistically, with rows of Japanese lanterns bobbing against pitch blackness, and the camera swoops down as if in wonderment at one breathtaking kimono after another — echoing the admiration of Tsuruko, who's been laying out these family heirlooms, these grand designs of the past, in anticipation of Yukiko's wedding. The last Ichikawa film I saw, *An Actor's Revenge,* was in part a tribute to Japanese theater's legacy to the movies. In *The Makioka Sisters,* Ichikawa celebrates the aesthetic glory of a privileged class who make their everyday life into a work of theater. Occasionally, the dropping of a red-lined cape with the family crest functions as the falling of a curtain. Ichikawa uses every skill available to film and theater directors with an almost invisible virtuosity. Most of his compositions have the formal balance we'd associate with veteran directors, but he'll also slip in a vertiginous off-angle shot, as when Yukiko must handle that strange new creature the telephone; throughout, his subtle camera movements and insinuating editing ensure that we notice her around the edges. And the formal patterning of Ichikawa's staging pays off subliminally. In perhaps the most moving sequence, Tatsuo learns that his wife, Tsuruko, who has become the empress of the family, has agreed to leave the ancestral home in Osaka and move to Tokyo so he can accept a promotion — and in a panic of happiness, this big man makes skittery lobsterlike motions with his arms before falling to his knees to thank her. It's a wonderful instant, and afterward we realize how skillfully it's been prepared. We always seem to see Tatsuo lowering his head in the ancestral house, as if it were built too small for him. In the earlier scene of the newspaper scandal, the family grouped around him in judgment; after outrageous blustering to his wife, he skulked around like a stage villain until he was sure his in-laws had left, and only then did he apologize. We see Tatsuo's triumph in the same room — from a different angle. Ichikawa may have removed the novel's literal flood, but he gives us an emotional one.

After this film, Ichikawa must be reckoned one of the masters of color in the cinema. He's designed the movie so that the burnished interiors of the sisters' homes provide a tawny frame in which the women shimmer like flowers in a still life. When Yukiko comes to a nobleman's estate to meet the suitor of her dreams, the camera moves outside — we witness the measured dignity of the Makiokas' group posture through a window, as the decorative and natural beauties of Japan merge in a moment of pure filmmaking bliss. Ichikawa isn't afraid to break with the overall design by using color in vivid associational splashes. He punctuates the cresting of Taeko's dollmaking career with a brilliant azure cloudscape — and gets a delayed reaction when, near the end, Sachiko visits Taeko on a grimy waterfront and finds her wearing a sky-blue sweater.

Contemporary kimono designer Nobuo Nakamura recently echoed Sachiko when he told the *Boston Herald*, "In nature, everything is always moving, changing. But even dramatic changes, like the leaves of a tree turning color and then falling to the ground, do not really change the tree itself. It still retains the same shape and function." In this film, that's Ichikawa's philosophy too. He's worked in the spirit best suited to the material — a spirit of inventive conservatism. Ichikawa ran out of money before he could score the film, so he and his sound recorder ran the Largo from Handel's *Xerxes* through a synthesizer and then added a guitar. This desperate stroke works; it even adds to the film's universality. *The Makioka Sisters* is one of the most accessible of all the great Japanese films, a work of spirited imagination and translucent, meditative grandeur.

— Michael Sragow

Japan: Akira Kurosawa

■

THE SEVEN SAMURAI (1954)

In Europe, the wide reissue of classic films accounts for a fair portion of the movie business, but in America it's very unusual for a film both old and foreign — as is Akira Kurosawa's 1954 *The Seven Samurai* — to be revived at commercial theaters. What makes *The Seven Samurai* viable as a commercial reissue — where virtually any other classic Japanese film would not be — is its special relationship to American films and American audiences. From its opening shot of silhouetted horsemen galloping across a horizon line, Kurosawa's film announces its sources. The setting may be a sixteenth-century Japan convulsed by civil war, but those wide-open, lawless spaces are immediately recognizable as those of the Hollywood West.

Kurosawa has made no secret of his debt to the western in general and John Ford in particular: the small farming village of *The Seven Samurai,* nestled between mountain and plain, might be the Tombstone of *My Darling Clementine.* The marauding brigands who wait in the woods could be the vicious Clantons of Ford's film, and the seven samurai hired by the villagers for their defense could be the band of deputies, saloon girls, and alcoholic hangers-on assembled by Henry Fonda's Wyatt Earp. There is, no doubt, a broad and general resemblance between the American western and the Japanese samurai film — in terms of the themes both genres treat, and in the historical setting they choose for their work — but in *The Seven Samurai* the correspondences are strict and specific. We recognize the rules of the game that Kurosawa is playing in *The Seven Samurai,* where in a more arcanely Japanese samurai film such as Hideo Gosha's *Bandits vs. Samurai Squadron,* we do not.

Like Ford in his westerns, Kurosawa organizes the action of *The Seven Samurai* around three different elements: the civilized (the villagers), the savage (the brigands), and those who live in between (Ford's soldiers and lawmen, Kurosawa's samurai), defending civilization by savage, violent means. (This three-point, triangular structure is, of course, also something personal to Kurosawa; it pops up in different contexts throughout his work, most decisively in *Kagemusha.*) By placing his samurai in the same mediating position as Ford's lawmen, Kurosawa is self-consciously breaking with the traditions of the samurai genre, in which the samurai represent civilization at its most refined, entrenched, and aristocratic. The heroes of Kurosawa's film are masterless samurai, no longer attached to a royal house (and hence, I believe, no longer entitled to be called samurai — masterless samurai are called *ronin*). Both Ford's lawmen and Kurosawa's samurai are profoundly marginal figures, prevented from fully entering society by the possession of the same skills they must employ in upholding it. But where Ford in his middle-period films searches constantly for ways to reintegrate the lawman into society (before resolving, in his late work, that such a reconciliation is impossible), Kurosawa in *The Seven Samurai* emphasizes the unbridgeable differences between the villagers and their hired defenders. Though the townspeople and the samurai can fight in temporary alliance, they can never fight for the same goals: the villagers fight for home and family, the samurai for professional honor. The only society allowed to the samurai is their own; if civilization has no place for them, they must make a place of their own. The formation of the samurai's separate, self-enclosed society — the professional group — is the subject of some of the finest passages in Kurosawa's film: once a suitable father has been found, in the form of the veteran warrior Kambei (Takashi Shimura), the other members of the family fall into place, down to a wifely companion for Kambei (Shichiroji, an old comrade-in-arms played by the comedian Daisuke Kato), a dutiful son (the apprentice Katsushiro, played by Ko Kimura), and a black sheep (Toshiro Mifune's drunken, playful Kikuchiyo). The remaining samurai are distributed like the Three Graces — Wisdom (Yoshio Inaba's Gorobei), Skill (Seiji Miyaguchi's ace swordsman Kyuzo), and Hope (the incurably optimistic Heihachi, played by Minoru Chiaki). As schematic as this arrangement may sound, Kurosawa never lets it solidify; there is no flat sense of allegory here, but rather an open vision of different talents and attributes brought into harmony. To distinguish between the members of the group, Kurosawa gives each a defining gesture, much as Walt Disney differentiated his seven dwarfs: Kambei's reflective rubbing of his scalp, Kikuchiyo's leaps and whoops, Katsushiro's imploring eyes, etc. This, too, is classic Hollywood shorthand technique, in which a ritual gesture completely subsumes a character's psychology. And there is a pleasure in its repetition: each time Kambei scratches his head, he is reasserting the strength and constancy of his character. The gesture never changes, and neither does he. He is permanent, and in this one movement we know him and trust him.

At least one-quarter of *The Seven Samurai* is devoted to the relations between the townspeople and the professional group. Kurosawa seems to be looking for a stable, workable relationship, but he rejects each possibility in turn; there is always a dissonance, a contradiction, between the two groups. The samurai take charge of fortifying the village and training the farmers to fight, yet because they are, in the end, mere employees of the villagers, they are never in a position of genuine authority. The samurai tell themselves that they are fighting on behalf of the poor and helpless, but the cozy paternalism of this relationship is undermined by the suggestion that the farmers have been holding out — that they have secret reserves of rice and sake they refuse to share with their protectors. Two of the samurai have ties to the villagers — Katsushiro, who falls in love with a village girl, and Kikuchiyo, who is revealed to be a farmer's son — yet neither of these bonds is allowed to endure. By insisting so strongly on the absolute separation of the groups, Kurosawa departs radically from the western archetype: the lawmen can no longer derive their values from the community, as they did in Ford and Hawks, but must now define those values for themselves. This sense of moral isolation — fresh and startling in the genre context of 1954 — eventually became Kurosawa's gift to the American western, his way of giving back as much as he took. Even before *The Seven Samurai* was officially remade as a western (John Sturges's 1960 *The Magnificent Seven*), Kurosawa's variation had been incorporated in the genre, giving rise to the series of "professional" westerns that runs from Hawks's optimistic *Rio Bravo* to the final cynicism of Sergio Leone.

Separation is also the subject of Kurosawa's *mise-en-scène*. Using both the foreground-background separation of deep-focus shots and the flattening, abstracting effect of telephoto lenses, Kurosawa puts a sense of unbridgeable space in nearly all of his shots. Even in what should be the most intimate and open scenes among the samurai themselves, Kurosawa arranges his compositions in distinct, rigid planes, placing one or two figures in the extreme foreground, two or three more in a row in the middle, the balance lined up in the background (this will also be the design applied to the burial mound at the film's conclusion). The primary visual motif is one of boundaries: the natural boundaries formed around the village by the mountains, woods, and flooded rice fields, the man-made boundaries of fences, stockades, and doorways. The extreme formality of Kurosawa's compositions also emphasizes the boundaries of the frame; there is only occasionally a sense of off-screen space, as if nothing existed beyond the limits of the camera's eye. The world of *The Seven Samurai* is carefully delineated, compartmentalized; not only are the characters isolated in their separate groups, but in separate spaces.

The compartmentalization reflects Kurosawa's theme, but it also works (more originally, I think) in organizing the film emotionally — in building its suspense and narrative power. Three hours pass between the announcement of the brigands' attack and its arrival — an impossibly long time to keep the audience waiting for a single event. But where most filmmakers would try to fill the interval with minor flurries of action, Kurosawa gives us only two: Kambei's rescue of a child (which comes quite early in the film) and the guerrilla foray into the brigands' camp (which comes quite late). These incidents are so widely spaced (misplaced, even, in terms of conventional rhythm) that they don't serve at all to support the structure of crest and valley, crest and valley that the long form usually depends on. Instead, Kurosawa sticks to a strict linearity: the narrative has been divided (compartmentalized?) into discrete acts (the posing of the threat, the recruitment of the samurai, the fortification of the village, the battle), separated not by strongly marked climaxes but by slow and subtle transitions. The rigorous chopping, dividing, and underlining of space is the only constant factor through these transitions: no matter what the characters may be doing, the visual style is bearing down on them, forcing them further into immobility, isolation, entrapment. The suspense builds visually, subliminally, until we long for the final battle with its promise of release.

The battle in the rain is the most celebrated passage in Kurosawa's work, justly famous for its overwhelming physicality — the sense of force and texture, of sensual immersion, produced by staging the sequence in the mud and confusion of a fierce storm. But the rain also accomplishes something else — it fills in the spaces that Kurosawa has so carefully carved off, creating a continuity, an even density, from foreground to background. The rain begins the night before the battle, during the greatest moment of divisiveness between the townspeople and the samurai — the confrontation over Kikuchiyo's right to love a village girl. By forcing the two groups to fight more closely together, the rain closes this gap during the battle. And suddenly, all the other boundaries are broken open: as part of their strategy, the samurai allow some of the brigands to cross the fortifications (cut off from support, they can be killed more easily in the village square) and the camera loses its fixity and formality, panning wildly to follow details of action within the struggle. It is an ineffable moment of freedom, and of course it cannot last.

For his epilogue, Kurosawa returns to divided space. The surviving samurai are seen in one shot, standing still before the graves of those who fell; the villagers are seen in another, singing and moving in unison as they plant the new rice crop. There probably isn't a more plangent moment in all of Kurosawa's work than this juxtaposition of two different spaces, two different tempos, two different worlds. They are separated only by a cut, but they are separated forever.

—Dave Kehr

Japan: Akira Kurosawa

■

KAGEMUSHA (1980)

At the 1981 New York Film Festival, the single most animating event was the arrival of a new film, *Kagemusha,* by Akira Kurosawa, a mesmerizing work head and shoulders above anything else shown. (It is also the first film he has been able to make in Japan in ten years.) When the seventy-year-old director, looking surprisingly youthful and fit, came out on the stage to introduce the movie he was greeted with a long standing ovation, a gesture of spontaneous homage for a whole career. But I wonder how many in the audience actually expected *Kagemusha* (*The Shadow Warrior*) to be the extraordinary masterpiece it certainly is. If *Kagemusha* belongs to any film genre, it most resembles the medieval costume epics Hollywood used to love, marzipan movies like *Ivanhoe* and *Knights of the Round Table.* What Kurosawa has achieved is what Bresson tried and failed to do in his *Lancelot of the Lake:* to probe more deeply into the nature of such spectacles, which depend so heavily on ritualistic forms and the play of appearances. *Kagemusha* is a film about the power of images and appearances; it takes place in a historical setting, but implicitly it is also a film about the cinema itself.

At the center of *Kagemusha* is Shingen, a famous sixteenth-century warlord and military tactician, and a thief who strikingly resembles him and learns to impersonate him. Shingen is shot by a sniper on the eve of his greatest triumph and eventually dies, but the elders of his clan use the "shadow warrior" as his surrogate for nearly three years. (Both parts are played by the same actor.) At first it seems that the image of Shingen alone is enough to keep up morale in the clan and terrify its enemies. In formal councils and in the flickering light of battle, the round, bald head and scraggly beard of the chief's double take on an iconic luminescence. The thief is a prickly, rambunctious person, and he resists immuring himself in the stiff public identity of the old lord. He most enjoys playing with the chief's grandson, who first sees through him but then grows deeply attached to him.

Over the years, however, the spirit of the old lord seems to settle on the imposter; when he breaks his silence and speaks in council, his cautious approach is very much in line with Shingen's military views. But when he is publicly found out and Shingen's hotheaded son takes over the clan, the result is military disaster—a catastrophe foreseen and feared long ago by the old lord. During this climactic battle we mainly watch not the warriors but the faces of the elders and generals, no longer impassive as the icon had been, but reflecting every twist and turn of the clan's terrible decimation. Though cast out by the clan, the thief too watches in horror, like the last incarnation of the clan's former grandeur. It seems that more than the public aura of Shingen had lived on in his shadow. Something of his real presence survived in the thief, as it did not in the flesh-and-blood son he had always rejected. This identification is stressed from the very opening scene, the only one which shows the chief and the shadow together, when Shingen admits that he too is a thief and a scoundrel, though on a larger scale.

So great is the formality and remoteness of this story that even as I retell it I find myself falling into the stately language of legend. *Kagemusha* is first of all a spectacle, lush and opulent in the meticulous details of costume and battle but austere and formal in its cinematic technique. Shingen's nickname is "the mountain," and he is known for the awesome immobility of his strategic approach. When the thief echoes him in council he simply tells the army not to move, and this is precisely how Kurosawa often uses the camera. It's not farfetched, then, to see *Kagemusha* not only as a comment on the parallel between charismatic public images and cinematic images but a more particular parable about Kurosawa's relation to the Japanese film studios, which have thwarted all his plans for the past decade. The leaderless clan, beset by hungry rivals, courts destruction when an impulsive new generation violates the old lord's conservative testament, and only the despised outcast preserves a residue of his spirit. As the action unfolds and the battles rage, the helpless generals who have set it in motion sit on the sidelines on folding seats not unlike directors' chairs, and we see these decisive events only as shadows that play across their grim features. This is a movie with a "cast of thousands," the most expensive ever made in Japan, but at key moments the mass of actors remain off-camera and we intuit their fate only through its oblique personal reflection.

Shingen dies in a moment of delirium, imagining that he was about to conquer the holy city of Kyoto, his lifelong dream. But the movie is really more about his shadow, an unruly, rebellious man snatched from the jaws of death, a man of irreverent humor who would rather be a thief than a chief—who actually sees little difference between the two, but who hates to lose his freedom and identity by becoming an actor, a performer. *Kagemusha* shows how this man gradually, unwillingly, comes to play a great role, and attaches himself to a larger cause he scarcely understands, which eventually proves itself unworthy of him. The movie is about the power of images but also ultimately about the limits of that power, the insubstantiality of all shadows and shadow warriors, who do battle in a world of appearances. Like Shakespeare's *Tempest, Kagemusha* is a testamentary work, an extended reflection not only on film and on history but also on death, which concludes with a tapestry of carnage that resembles Picasso's *Guernica.* Yet old men ride into battle tranquil with the certainty of death. Kurosawa, the most Shakespearean of directors, seems to be saying with Prospero that the world is finally an "insubstantial pageant" and "these our actors, / As I foretold you, were all spirits and / Are melted into air, into thin air."

—*Morris Dickstein*

Japan: Akira Kurosawa

■

STRAY DOG (1949)

Akira Kurosawa's *Stray Dog* is like seeing *The Bicycle Thief,* the De Sica masterpiece, for the first time.

Both films were made in 1949, both deal with the difficult postwar periods of two defeated nations, and both reflect the bold response of two great directors to a new freedom of expression, long suppressed by the police state.

Just as the laborer loses the bicycle that is essential to his job of plastering up posters around Rome, the young detective has his service pistol stolen from him in a crowded Tokyo bus.

Murakami's search for his .38 Colt automatic to save face soon becomes a necessity when it falls into the hands of a killer—a "stray dog" that has turned into a mad dog.

The closer Murakami gets to his man the more he finds he has in common with him. Both had their packs stolen when they were soldiers, but only one of them gave up and turned to a life of crime as a result.

In a scene that sums up the film's theme, veteran detective Sato tells Murakami to leave speculations about the forces that have shaped the killer's character to the sociologists, that their job is only to get him before he kills again. To dwell upon the disgrace of World War II is useless, implies Kurosawa: we must set our house in order by ourselves, and we need men like Murakami to do it.

In style, *Stray Dog* is the visual equivalent of a Raymond Chandler detective story. As Murakami's search for his pistol becomes a quest for identity and, by extension, that of a nation, Kurosawa examines Tokyo the way Chandler did L.A. In a series of overlapping shots the camera follows the detective through Tokyo's poverty-ridden streets for one entire reel without dialogue. Equally superb is the acting by Toshiro Mifune as Murakami, Takashi Shimura as Sato, and Keiko Awaji as the killer's girl friend.

Today Kurosawa remains the moralist. In *The Bad Sleep Well* he showed that extensive corruption has accompanied Japan's return to prosperity. In his latest film, *High and Low,* his hero (Mifune, as usual) will have to choose between wealth and power and the fate of his kidnapped child—a decision that may give the film the same kind of impact as *Stray Dog.*

—*Kevin Thomas*

Japan: Akira Kurosawa

■

HIGH AND LOW (1963)

High on a hill above Yokohama, Kingo Gondo, a shoe manufacturer, looks down from his expensive home at the ugly port city below. He has just arranged a fifty-million-yen loan in order to gain control of his corporation when the phone rings and a kidnapper demands the very same amount in ransom for his only son. That the kidnapper has taken the son of Gondo's chauffeur by mistake only makes the situation worse — must Gondo face financial ruin in order to save the life of another man's child?

Gondo's decision and how it affects his life and the lives of those around him is revealed in Akira Kurosawa's *High and Low.*

Entertainment as well as art, it has uniformly excellent performances by a cast consisting mostly of Kurosawa "regulars" and has extraordinary camera work. Indeed, the photography alone could serve as a primer in film technique.

High and Low, however, is remarkable in many ways. Most importantly, it reverses the trend toward increasing pessimism that has characterized the director's recent work and indicates a return to the humanist themes of his early pictures. This does not mean that Kurosawa is merely repeating past successes: to the contrary, he is one of the few great directors to emerge after the end of the war who have been able to keep up with the times. While Roberto Rossellini is still fighting World War II, Kurosawa has become a provocative commentator on the prosperous society of present-day Japan.

Ed McBain's 87th Precinct mystery, *King's Ransom,* furthermore, has provided an ideal starting point for Kurosawa's study of a man who must measure the extent of his responsibility to others. In fact, *High and Low* represents the best reason for making a movie of a novel: the use of someone else's story to express a director's own ideas.

Structurally, the film is quite a departure for Kurosawa. As soon as Gondo, played by Toshiro Mifune, comes to his decision, he literally drops out of the picture until almost the end. Kurosawa then concentrates on the police search for the kidnapper. The camera itself replaces the familiar, dominating figure of Mifune as it restlessly probes the crowded slums and amusement areas of Yokohama in sequences reminiscent of *Stray Dog* and *Ikuru.*

Unconventional and controversial (in Japan Kurosawa has been criticized for justifying the unnecessarily dangerous way his police bait the criminal), *High and Low* is an exciting attempt to break new ground.

—*Kevin Thomas*

Japan: Kenji Mizoguchi
■

THE LIFE OF OHARU (1952)

The early 1700s. Oharu Okui, a fifty-year-old street prostitute, enters a temple and gazes upon the idols, remembering her past life: Kyoto, 1686. The beautiful young daughter of a samurai serving at the Imperial Palace, she is stopped on her way to the temple by Katsunosuke, a page, who calls her to an unexpected meeting with Lord Kibukozi; upon arrival she discovers the proposed meeting to be an invention of Katsunosuke designed to give him a chance to declare his love for her. After feigning indifference, she responds to his passion; the two are caught, the latter beheaded for his violation of the social code, and Oharu and her parents are exiled to the country. A servant of Lord Matsudaira from Edo arrives in Kyoto searching for a concubine who matches his master's precise physical specifications, to bear him a son; returning empty-handed, he chances upon Oharu and successfully bargains for her with her parents, despite her objections. After bearing Matsudaira a son, she is banished by his clan for "draining the Lord's energy"; her father, pushed into debt by this sudden action, forces her to work as a courtesan in Shimabara, where she is eventually dismissed for being too proud. Next she is hired as a maid by a wealthy merchant, who sends her away after learning about (and taking advantage of) her past as a courtesan and incurring his aging wife's wrathful jealousy. A brief period of happy marriage to a fan-maker is cut short when Oharu's husband is killed by thieves; housed in a Buddhist convent, she prepares to become a nun until she is expelled after persuading a clerk, Bunkichi, to give her free dress material and seducing his employer, Yakichi, when the latter comes to collect payment. She joins Bunkichi, who has also been dismissed, but the latter is quickly caught by Yakichi for stealing his gold. Reduced to begging, she is taken in by two lower-class prostitutes and shortly joins their profession, where she is mocked for her age and ugliness. Back in the temple recalling her past, she collapses in despair, and is visited at her sickbed by her mother, who informs her that her father has died and that her son has just succeeded the recently deceased Lord Matsudaira, so that Oharu can now go to live with him. But upon arrival at Edo, she is informed that her behaviour has been "the shame of the clan" and permitted only to catch a secret glimpse of her son. Back to street-begging, Oharu passes a pagoda, bows briefly, and continues on her way.

According to scriptwriter Yoda Yoshikata, Mizoguchi's ambitions for *The Life of Oharu* were largely stimulated by the prize accorded to Kurosawa, a relative newcomer, for *Rashomon* at Venice in 1951. The bet paid off, and *Oharu* was awarded the Silver Lion at Venice in 1952, thereby inaugurating Mizoguchi's international reputation at the age of fifty-six, four years before his death. Differing substantially from Saikaku's novel—a looser collection of episodes narrated by an elderly nun recalling her decline from a promising youth, and ending with a scene of a prostitute entering a temple and hallucinating the faces of former lovers in the idols there—*Oharu*'s script gravitates round the feudal persecutions of one woman. It appears that Mizoguchi was something of a Stroheim on the set—requiring that the garden of Kyoto's Koetsu temple be "rebuilt" instead of using the nearly identical original location, and firing his assistant, Uchikawa Seichiro, when the latter complained about making last-minute changes in the positions of the studio-built houses for the scene of Bunkichi's arrest. Intransigence of this sort seems borne out by the relentless polemical thrust of *Oharu*, which quite likely comprises the most powerful feminist protest ever recorded on film. (It may not be entirely accidental that Kinuyo Tanaka, the extraordinary actress playing Oharu, went on to become the first woman director in Japan the following year.) Eschewing the elements of fantasy and myth that figure in his subsequent period films (excepting only *Chikamatsu Monogatari,* which it resembles in other respects), *Oharu* combines the form of the picaresque novel with much of the social analysis common to Mizoguchi's "contemporary" geisha films. Above all, it is a *materialist* analysis—a depiction of woman treated, traded, valued, degraded, and discarded as material object: the inspection of Kyoto's "most beautiful" women by Matsudaira's servant (delineated in one lengthy tracking shot), periodically checking the details of his model drawing against the "specimens" offered; the remarkable subplot of the vulgar big-spender at the Shimabara brothel, who throws fistfuls of coins to watch the courtesans fight and scramble—valuing Oharu "highest" because she refuses to participate, and then purchasing her as a consequence—and cackling "Money is everything," before being unveiled as a counterfeiter; the black comedy in the wealthy merchant's home about the wife's loss of her hair, her spiteful cutting of Oharu's, and Oharu's revenge of getting a kitten to make off with the former's wig. The obi (sash) that Oharu's husband is clutching when he is killed is subsequently discarded in a strip tease where she "pays" Yakichi for his material by throwing it at him, offering her body at the same time. The pagoda that she acknowledges in the final shot, visually echoing the shape of her hat, implies her equivalence to an object, while the camera remaining on the pagoda after she has left the frame—like its lingering on the ground of Kibukozi's garden after she and Katsunosuke leave on their lovers' tryst, or on a tree in the courtyard during the flight of the uncovered counterfeiter—suggests that all these things will outlast her. The predilection of French critics for linking Mizoguchi with Murnau seems largely dictated by this sense of fatality, expressed equally by striking high-angle shots, a fairly constant use of the diagonal line, and the movement between the "sympathy" and autonomy of several extended camera movements in relation to Oharu: her endless flight of despair through the woods after reading Katsunosuke's parting message to her; her nocturnal street walk in the opening shot—repeated near the film's close—as an axis round which things happen, which closely resembles the City Woman's walk in *Sunrise.* But quite apart from the visual rendering of Oharu's condition and fate—a "statement" that is made no less contemporary by the beauty and density of its period detail—one must also consider Ichiro Saito's prodigious musical score. From the solo instrument accompanying Oharu and her parents' departure from Kyoto to the percussive wooden blocks punctuating the grunts of the men carrying Matsudaira's servant there; from Oharu's discovery of an old courtesan singing in a broken voice to her later recapitulation of the same song, in comparable circumstances; from the dead silence when she sees her son passing on the road as a child to the throbbing, harp-like arpeggios that accompany her brief glimpse of him as a man—*Oharu*'s soundtrack achieves a rare diversity of effect that never deviates from the film's sustained emotional and narrative rigour. By the time we reach the choral passage over the closing shot, we have arrived at a sublime tabula rasa that perfectly complements the one we see on the screen: as with the closing shots of *Queen Christina* and *Les Bonnes Femmes,* it is a coda that tells us nothing and, by doing so, expresses everything.

—*Jonathan Rosenbaum*

Japan: Kenji Mizoguchi

■

UGETSU (1954)

This subtle, violent yet magical film is one of the most amazing of the Japanese movies that played American art houses after the international success of *Rashomon* in 1951. The director, Kenji Mizoguchi, handles the narrative in two styles: barbaric sequences dealing with greed and civil war that seem realistic except that the characters are deliberately animalistic and are symbolically acting out the bestial side of man; and highly stylized sequences dealing with the aesthetic, luxurious, and romantic modes of life. When the hero (Masayuki Mori), a grunting peasant potter, develops self-awareness and becomes an artist, the meanings multiply. The film is upsetting and unspeakably cruel at times, and then so suggestive and haunting that it's confounding. When, in the midst of serene elegance, the phantom Lady Wakasa (Machiko Kyo) offers the potter-artist rarefied sensual delights, you know how he feels as he cries, "I never imagined such pleasures existed!" Heavy going in spots, but with marvelous passages that are worth a bit of patience. With Kinuyo Tanaka as the potter's wife.

—*Pauline Kael*

Japan: Kenji Mizoguchi

■

SANSHO THE BAILIFF (1954)

Kenji Mizoguchi's 1954 masterpiece, *Sansho the Bailiff,* is a heartbreaking medieval fable with modern political and psychological undertones. It may seem odd for Mizoguchi to name the movie for its villain—the ruthless overseer of a private slave camp—instead of for its antihero, the late-blooming Zushio. But the choice reflects the director's tragic vision. The film is about virtue tortured, altered, and emerging only partially triumphant. Zushio's statesman father, exiled because he shielded his peasants from a military draft, taught his son that "without mercy, a man is like a beast." When kidnappers separate Zushio and his sister Anju from their mother—the siblings are sold into slavery, the mother into prostitution—the boy can't hold on to his father's ideals. In Sansho's inferno, Zushio becomes a barbarian. Like the worst concentration-camp Kapo, he willingly executes Sansho's order to brand attempted escapees on the forehead.

The first half hour, which depicts the downfall of Zushio's father and the dispersal of his family, is a cascade of flashbacks and present-tense action. (Kinuyo Tanaka brings a tremulous eloquence to the role of the mother—she's the movie's emotional center as much as the father is its conscience.) The most striking shot is of the family walking through a field of long grass and reeds, the flora floating above their heads like an army's plumes; the most devastating shot is of the mother and nurse being thrown into a boat while the children are seized on shore. Once Zushio and Anju arrive at Sansho's slave camp, the volatile lyricism gives way to a steady, cumulative power. It's as if Mizoguchi is saying, sadly, this is how the world works.

The movie explores the strength and the tenuousness of family bonds in scenes that are freshets of pure feeling. In Mizoguchi, as in Faulkner, the past isn't dead—in Faulkner's words, "It's not even past." Near the end, when Sansho sees a newly freed and elevated Zushio, the bailiff exclaims: "It's like a fairy tale. A slave becoming a governor!" But in this fairy tale no one lives happily ever after. Terrifying and cathartic, *Sansho the Bailiff* is a morality play without easy moralism.

—*Michael Sragow*

Japan: Yasujiro Ozu

■

TOKYO STORY (1953)

I was nineteen when I saw my first movie by Yasujiro Ozu — *Early Summer,* I think it was — and I'll never forget railing against its simple story line, emotional restraint, and resolute lack of the rebel energy I adored in Jean-Luc Godard and Sam Peckinpah. I wondered how anyone could make a movie so damned quiet. Two decades later, Ozu is one of the handful of directors whose work I love passionately. It's not that his movies changed, for he died in 1963, seven years before I'd ever seen one. But after years of watching overblown movies and discovering my own limitations, I came to see the beauty in Ozu's deceptively simple tales of marriage and loneliness, disappointment and death. No artist shows more respect for simple decency or looks on ordinary life with more tenderness.

Ozu made his first great movies during the 1930s, when he became a master of the so-called *shomin-geki* (drama of the common people), which focused on the economic hardships faced by ordinary folks. Yet his concerns were always more spiritual than material and, starting with his 1949 masterpiece *Late Spring,* he began to refine his vision of reality in a series of exquisite movies that were cowritten with the same man (Kogo Noda), used the same stock of actors (most notably, Ozu-surrogate Chishu Ryu), adopted the same minimalist style, and returned, almost ritualistically, to the same elemental stories of frailty and loss — troubled marriages, deaths in the family, aging fathers marrying off their daughters, insoluble tensions between parents and children, the collapse of Japanese family life under the weight of postwar modernization. Critics often joke that it's impossible to tell these late movies apart, and there's justice to the quip; the film I hated at nineteen may well have been *The End of Summer* and not *Early Summer* — they have the same plot. But Ozu didn't rehearse the same stories from a failure of imagination, but out of fidelity to the world he knew and loved. Like Barbara Pym writing of spinsters and vicars, or Cézanne painting Mt. Ste.–Victoire over and over — discovering new shades of light as he sought to perfect his own artistic vision — Ozu returned to middle-class family life again and again, teasing out fresh meanings from threadbare situations, honing his style to the vanishing point of absolute simplicity.

This stylistic spareness and the insistent domesticity of his themes have gotten him labelled the "most Japanese" of directors—a tag I mistrust, since Japan is a country that embraces both tea ceremonies and Mitsubishi. Be that as it may, Ozu's Japaneseness doesn't make his movies imposing or difficult for Western viewers; on the contrary, his work confirms the paradox that nothing is more universal than the particular. A fine case in point is *Tokyo Story* (1952), his most famous movie, whose story would hit home anywhere in the world: it begins with parents visiting their children, and ends with children mourning the death of a parent.

When we first see Shukishi Hirayama (Chishu Ryu) and wife Tomi (Chiyeko Higashiyama), an elderly couple from the town of Onomichi, they're excited about visiting their grown-up children in Tokyo. But the reality of the trip is frustrating for everyone. Busy and selfish, the kids find their folks a burden and quickly ship them off to a spa; for their part, the parents are discouraged to learn that their son lives in a dingy suburb—he's not the prosperous doctor they imagined—and that their daughter, a beautician, is no longer a nice person. In fact, they're only treated with due respect by their son's young widow Noriko (Setsuko Hara), who takes off work to show them the sights, serves them special foods and *sake*, sees their visit as a blessing instead of an annoyance. Although Noriko has a generosity that their natural son and daughter lack, Ozu characteristically doesn't pass a harsh judgment on the Hirayama children's selfishness—they're flawed, not evil. (And they are frustrated by their own saucy, self-absorbed kids.) When their mother becomes critically ill, they rush to Onomichi filled with genuine grief and regret at not having been kind enough to her, one of them ruefully quoting the proverb, "Be kind to your parents when they are alive—filial piety cannot extend beyond the grave." Still, these people are who they are, and once they've done their duty as they've seen it, they race back to Tokyo, again leaving Noriko to behave with the appropriate grave generosity.

At one point, the Hirayamas' youngest daughter Kyoko, who still lives at home, begins to complain about her siblings' lack of proper respect for the dead. "Isn't life disappointing?" she says, and Noriko smiles bravely and gives her a simple, direct reply: "Yes, it is." There may be no purer distillation of Ozu's notion of life than this brief exchange. Like all of his movies, *Tokyo Story* is filled with disappointments: children not living up to their parents' dreams or their own dreams of themselves as good children; middle-aged men whose careers aren't as grand as they hoped; kindly young women condemned to loneliness because their husbands were killed in the war; old men left alone after decades of marriage. For Ozu, loss, failure, and disappointment lie at the very heart of life. But so, too, does learning to live with their pain. In his first great film, 1932's funny, poignant *I Was Born But . . .* , two young boys are angry and humiliated to see their father bowing and scraping before his boss, but eventually come to accept the fact that some men (including their father) are destined to be clerks and not great men. This doesn't mean that life's not worth living, only that it often can't live up to our hopes and expectations.

It's in the American character to rebel against such an idea of acceptance, which seems not so much bracing philosophy as defeatist passivity—we believe in doing something to make things better. Ozu does, too, and clearly loves Noriko for her scrupulous kindness, born of her pain at losing her husband. Yet, as *Tokyo Story* makes obvious, solitude and disillusionment are woven into the recurring pattern of life and cannot be escaped, only accepted and gone beyond. What's at issue here isn't the wry acceptance of human foibles found in, say, *Annie Hall* or *Broadcast News,* but something closer to Buddhist calm or the stoicism of Seneca. Always compassionate, Ozu knows that such a philosophical approach to life's hardships is almost impossible to maintain, and he never looks down on those who fail; his movies are filled with characters who seek consolation in drink—which Ozu, himself a committed drinker, thought a perfectly acceptable response to the human condition.

Nothing expresses Ozu's vision more clearly than the clear-eyed minimalism so evident in *Tokyo Story.* Not only does he refuse bravura performances and high-powered stories (plot bored him, he said), but he strips his visual style to the bone, avoiding all obtrusive editing devices (fades, dissolves, etc.) and keeping his camera remarkably static (it moves only twice in *Tokyo Story*'s 139 minutes). Far from thrusting us into the action, Ozu deliberately keeps us distant, shooting every scene at midrange with the camera always at the same height, about three feet from the floor—eye level for one sitting on a mat known as a *tatami.* In shot after shot, the Hirayamas are framed by doorways, windows, sliding screens, rectangular patterns on the wall, and Ozu often keeps the film rolling even after the characters have walked out of a scene, leaving an empty room (after all, the world exists independently of his characters and extends beyond the screen).

What underlies his style—which itself has the force of ritual—is a profound faith in the power of the image; like Carl Theodor Dreyer and Robert Bresson (two directors with whom he's usually linked), Ozu assumes that the camera can reveal the truth of the world and that viewers will recognize that it's done so. By paring away the irrelevant flash and fluff that pads most movies, he hopes to lay bare the human essence of his story—as Bresson once wrote, you have to drain the pond to catch the fish. And by keeping us distant, having us take the action in from our *tatami,* he hopes to create a properly contemplative, sanity-inducing attitude toward what we're seeing, be it the quiet beauty of Mrs. Hirayama walking along a hilltop with her grandson, or her husband's lonely silhouette when all the children have gone away. His minimalism is a moral statement. The irony of Ozu's style is that its simplicity and restraint make his movies far more moving than works designed to wallop us emotionally. While *Beaches* or *Awakenings* put all their emotions up on the screen—the actors do all your feeling for you—*Tokyo Story* breaks our hearts with all the things it *isn't* showing us. Everything is nuanced, delicate; the way a man sips his *sake* says as much about his soul as any soliloquy. (Ozu was famous for doing ten or twenty takes of the simplest actions.) The movie makes us feel Mr. Hirayama's solitude not by giving him dramatic outbursts, but with a lingering shot of empty train tracks that encapsulates the whole film—his trip to Tokyo with his wife, Noriko's return to her small Tokyo apartment, the forlorn eloquence of iron bars stretching into the distance with no life upon them. Precisely because it lets the viewer do the feeling, this shot of train tracks may be the most heartwrenching moment in *Tokyo Story.*

Just before that shot, the widowed Noriko and Mr. Hirayama sit talking. He gives her his dead wife's watch as a keepsake and, praising her unwavering kindness, urges her to remarry. She insists, perversely, that she's actually quite selfish; we know she'll never remarry. It's a classic Ozu scene, not only in its pairing of an old man and a young woman, but in its absolute generosity of spirit. Watching them talk, we know that both are condemned to a future of loneliness—Mrs. Hirayama's watch counting the hours—but we also know they will live through it with decency and grace and good humor, sometimes drinking too much in sadness or falling into depression, but never losing their love for what's wonderful in life, the elegance of a sunrise, the kindness of strangers, the memories of whom and what they've lost. Under Ozu's gentle gaze, their ordinary heroism takes on a luminous beauty that may not transcend life's bleakness, but goes a long way toward redeeming it.

—John Powers

Japan: Yasujiro Ozu

■

FLOATING WEEDS (1959)

Yasujiro Ozu's late remake of his silent classic: about a travelling theatrical troupe and its interactions with the provincials of a small town, where their leader, many years ago, fathered an illegitimate child. The mood is the late Ozu mood: immaculately serene, quietly poignant; the color camera work is magnificent.

—Michael Wilmington

Soviet Union: Sergei Eisenstein

■

ALEXANDER NEVSKY (1938)

Sergei Eisenstein picked up a camera, then he picked up a pen. In *Potemkin* (1925), he made the first film acclaimed as a masterpiece around the world. Then he defined the theory linking its inspiration in Marxist dialectics to what he saw as the nature of film itself: "Conflict! Collision!" he said in *Film Forum*.

Film, he said, exists in space as "conflicts within the frame: conflict of graphic direction, conflict of scale, conflict of volumes, conflict of masses, conflict of depths." It exists in time as "conflicts of close shots and long shots; pieces of darkness and pieces of lightness; pieces resolved in volume with pieces resolved in area."

Even in his way of writing about those theories, Eisenstein was clearly gripped by the thrill of conflict. "Linkage: Pudovkin! Collision: Eisenstein!" he wrote, explaining how fellow filmmaker Vsevolod Pudovkin kept trying to persuade him that framing and editing are based on harmony until Eisenstein argued him down. "Not long ago we had another talk," Eisenstein says with pleasure later in the chapter. "Today he agrees with my point of view!"

Even when Eisenstein thinks about light, he thinks: conflict! "Lighting is the collision between a stream of light and an obstacle, like the impact of a stream from a fire hose striking a concrete object, or of the wind buffeting a human figure." Where light is, can sound be far behind? "Let us not forget," he continued, "that soon we shall face another and less simple problem in counterpoint: the conflict in the sound film of acoustics and optics."

So it's not surprising that Eisenstein made one of the great battle movies of all time when he made *Alexander Nevsky* (1938). Putting his theories of framing and editing into artful practice, he was also devising a strategic solution for his political conflicts with Stalin.

Nevsky opens with fisherman prince Alexander (Nikolai Cherkassov) confronting the Mongol warlord who wants to hire him as a mercenary. Nevsky says no. "We'll get him later," he suggests. "First, the Germans." That probably seemed like savvy politics when Eisenstein was writing and filming in 1938. But by the time the movie was released, Stalin had signed the nonaggression pact with Hitler.

Eisenstein was trying to get back on the state's A-list of directors after falling into disfavor for malingering too long in America and Mexico. Upon his return, he made *Bezhin Meadow* (1937), a film Stalin considered too religious. So the movie about victorious Russians and defeated Teutonic knights seemed like a good idea. It survived the setback of the nonaggression pact when Stalin soft-pedaled its anti-German elements and emphasized its pro-Russian historical elements.

Born from conflict, enduring conflict, epitomizing a film theory based on conflict, it's about conflict. There are scenes that form an introduction and epilogue, but, basically, it's one battle — the Battle on the Ice of Lake Chudskoe in 1242. If the Odessa steps sequence in *Potemkin* is a microcosm of Eisenstein's theory, *Alexander Nevsky* is the macrocosm. Between the two films, Eisenstein's writings, which originally emphasized editing, took more and more notice of framing. But both films artfully frame and edit oppositions to create every sequence.

The movements between massed events, like the crowd's panic on the Odessa Steps, and individual events, like the woman with shattered eyeglasses, may be quicker in the earlier film than in the symphonically alternating designs of the later one. But both draw on the same core of ideas.

Eisenstein's genius is his talent for realizing those ideas. Other filmmakers could take his follow-the-dots directions for making a film and come up with a bad movie. Eisenstein had the eye that let him do what he talked about and make it work. Fifty years later, you can see why his battle choreography has been borrowed by so many later filmmakers — most notably Kurosawa.

The central battle is a symphony of struggle in five movements.

The German Advance: As the battle begins, white-cloaked Teutonic knights are spread out along a high horizon line, moving toward the dark clumps of Russian peasants in homespun tunics, their rough-hewn staves planted vertically at their sides. As the Germans advance, the horizon seems to be coming down on the Russians — as if their own landscape were engulfing them. Punctuated by midshots of hand-to-hand combat, the Germans, in their orderly lines and impersonal, tin-bucket helmets, are frightening and overwhelming as they relentlessly take up all the space below the horizon.

The Russian Counterattack: The shambling Russians pour out of the foreground, hacking away with staves and axes. Many midshots of hand-to-hand combat, and lots more of Eisenstein's favorites: diagonals. For the ultimate in conflict and collision, you can't beat slanting lines cutting the screen and sweeping first to the left, then to the right. Prole power to the max, with individual Russkies emerging as heroes — particularly peasant suitors Vasya and Gavrilo, who've made a bet that the most valiant can marry the girl they both love. When a Russian Brunnhilde throws him a stave the size of an oak tree, Vasya gulps a bucketful of water to get in the mood, then swings his phone pole, bashing Teutonic helmets and sweeping away arcs of enemies.

The German Retreat: As they fall back, the Germans stop in a line with their horses, kneel, raise their banners, point a bristling row of spears toward the Russians, and launch flights of arrows from the crossbows positioned behind the protective front line. As the massed Russian army rides down against the Germans, Alexander and the German leader meet in one-on-one combat, ending when the metal horns on the German's helmet are lopped off and he's dragged to a sledge as a captive. The Russians, who've taken over the horizon line, ride down in hurtling diagonals. Reversing the opening shots, they chase the white knights into deep center screen, their point of origin.

The Drowning: Long before World War II's Leningrad, Eisenstein was telling the Germans the Russian landscape would beat them. As the lake's ice cracks diagonally across the frame, single German soldiers fall in; the whole line disappears; hands grab at floating chunks of ice; and a single white cape is dragged underwater as the elaborate metal gear takes a whole army down to their death.

The Aftermath: An ice floe carrying wounded and dying bodies drifts downstream to the left as if disappearing in a river of time — or as if the pull of history were wiping out the names of the men who gave their lives. As Russian women holding torches come to search for survivors, the mezzo-soprano voice of Mother Russia sings the most touching melody in Sergei Prokofiev's score:

> *If you died for Russia as a brave man dies*
> *I will plant a kiss on your eyes*
> *To the gallant youth who remains alive*
> *I will be the true, true wife.*

That Prokofiev score, long considered among the best pieces of film music ever composed, was a collaborative effort. Every night, Prokofiev looked at the rushes. The next morning, according to Eisenstein's notebooks, "on the dot of 11:55 A.M. I knew that a small, dark blue automobile would come through the gates of the film studio. Sergei Prokofiev would get out of the car. And in his hands would be the next piece of music for *Alexander Nevsky.*"

In some cases, Prokofiev's compositions underscore the visual design, with diagonal violin melodies repeating the flight of arrows. In others, ripping chase music or anxious drum beats recreate the emotions of the battle's advances and setbacks. Throughout, the score stops for the aural counterpoint of clanking German swords or clunking Russian staves — or for the silence that adds poignancy to anticipation, anxiety, death. It's the union of Eisenstein's visual design and Prokofiev's aural design that makes *Nevsky* the mother of all montages.

— *Kathy Schulz Huffhines*

Soviet Union: Sergei Eisenstein

■

POTEMKIN (1925)

Eisenstein's silent *Potemkin* galvanized a whole generation of film aesthetes with the revolutionary battle cry of *"montage!"* The influential pioneering of America's D. W. Griffith notwithstanding, Russia's Eisenstein and *Potemkin* became synonymous with an elevation of the editing process to the status of a dynamic stylistic imperative. It was not so much the content of a shot that mattered—that was merely "theater." What mattered was the dialectical collision of two shots that created, between them, an ideological synthesis—one that could be conveniently associated with the theories of Marx and Engels. Or as film historian Eric Rhode once summarized this dictum: "Two plus Two equals Five."

Potemkin is still regarded by many arts historians as one of the greatest—if not indeed *the* greatest—motion pictures ever made. But the mystique of montage has been reduced over the years from an imperative to an option. Modern movie aestheticians have begun to pay more attention to the *content* of shots, even in *Potemkin*.

The videocassette version of *Potemkin* just released by Corinth has a score by Dimitri Shostakovich, adapted in the seventies from themes from his symphonies. It is more lyrical but less rousing than the famous Meisel score added in Germany in the twenties (and used in the TV version shown in the U.S. by PBS).

Eisenstein's account of a successful mutiny by the sailors on the battle cruiser *Potemkin* during the otherwise aborted 1905 uprising against the czar is perhaps most famous today for its Odessa Steps sequence, in which a line of cossacks marches inexorably forward and downward, firing at unarmed terrified civilians in its path. But the complete movie constitutes a "must" acquisition for any individual or institution even remotely involved with movie history and movie scholarship.

—Andrew Sarris

Soviet Union: Alexander Dovzhenko

■

EARTH (1930)

The specific subject is collectivization, but Dovzhenko's masterwork is a passionate lyric on the continuity of man, death, and nature. The theme is perhaps most startlingly expressed in a sequence about a man who has just celebrated the arrival of a tractor. He starts to dance — for sheer love of life — on his way home, and as he dances in the middle of the moonlit road he is suddenly struck by a bullet. (In the fifties, it was voted one of the ten greatest films of all time by an international group of critics.)

—Pauline Kael

Soviet Union: Vsevolod Pudovkin

■

MOTHER (1926)

Frequently selected by critics as one of the greatest films of all time. Pudovkin's masterpiece, based on Maxim Gorky's novel, which is set during the 1905 revolution, is not overtly political; it gives an epic sense of that revolution through the emotions of the participants, and sweeps one along by its fervor and a brilliant and varied use of the medium. Vera Baranovskaya plays the mother who is tricked by the police into betraying her son (Nikolai Batalov). Pudovkin (unusual among the great Russian directors for his interest in acting) himself plays the officer who interrogates her.

—Pauline Kael

Spain: Luis Buñuel

■

RETROSPECTIVE

Luis Buñuel, the great film director who died in late July 1983 at the age of 83, went to school with the Jesuits in his native Spain, but came of age in the exhilarating cultural milieu of Paris in the twenties. "A religious education and surrealism have marked me for life," he once said.

His early films, *Un Chien Andalou,* made with Salvador Dali in 1928, and *L'Age d'Or,* his 1930 masterpiece, were shock treatments applied as much to the sentimental conventions of narrative cinema as to the prudish inhibitions of the bourgeoisie. Behind the rebelliousness and anticlericalism, the intellectuals had their own piety: a facile synthesis of Marx and Freud as anarchists of the spirit and liberators of the psyche. Buñuel went further.

His mocking humor and prankish irreverence were grounded in a fantastic intuition for powerful images. Everyone remembers the razor neatly slicing the eyeball in *Un Chien Andalou.* Was there ever a shot more obscene than Lya Lys sucking dreamily on the toe of a marble statue in *L'Age d'Or?*

Abandoning straightforward narrative as a form of artistic repression, the surrealists conspired to allow the unconscious to speak directly — through images, dreams, and fantasies. Freud was fascinated by Buñuel's early work, but the new naturalism of the sound era and the economics of the Depression, with its demand for escapist entertainment, made surrealism untenable. Fritz Lang was castigated for introducing a symbol into his first Hollywood movie, but it took Buñuel much longer to adapt his vision to the exigencies of commercial filmmaking.

During the thirties and forties Buñuel did everything but direct movies — dubbing, producing, working in the film department at the Museum of Modern Art. Then after a twenty-year hiatus came *Los Olvidados* in 1950, a masterfully brutal portrait of slum youths in Mexico City. In this harshly fatalistic film, Buñuel explores a world of savage cruelty — the meanest character is a blind beggar, a great believer in law and order — that includes but transcends all sociological categories.

In the tradition of Freud and the surrealists, Buñuel saw his people less as victims of their environment than as pawns of their own murderous and sado-masochistic fantasy lives. In later films he learned to take this with grim amusement and, finally, with serene detachment. His fascination with ugliness and violence was almost stereotypically Spanish.

In his third masterpiece, *Viridiana,* which marked his brief return to Spain in 1961, he shows us a scrofulous pack of beggars who take over a respectable household and enact a blasphemous parody of the Last Supper, with the music of *The Messiah* booming in the background. Vile, filthy, and deliriously destructive, these quintessential objects of Christian charity are no candidates for sainthood or progressive amelioration.

Buñuel's was an art of deliberate incongruity and coolly insolent free association. True to his first films, he learned to insert dream and fantasy sequences into otherwise realistic stories. Like Hitchcock, he detested the fraudulence of theatrical emoting. He taught actors to flatten their performances into enigmatic masks while he was projecting their psychic abysses directly on the screen. Only Genet, a much lusher temperament, surpassed him in exploring his characters' baroque fantasies. But where Genet wrote to excite himself, Buñuel affected the iron detachment of a surgeon, probing and slicing into psychic tissue.

In the film criticism he wrote in the twenties, Buñuel was fond of using medical images. He preferred Buster Keaton's blank natural grace to the mannered expressionism of an Emil Jannings, and described Keaton as "an eminent specialist in the treatment of all sentimental disorders."

He once recommended examining films under a microscope and said of one Hollywood screenplay that it was "riddled with melodramatic germs, infected throughout with sentimental typhus compounded by romantic and naturalistic bacilli." Keaton's *College,* on the other hand, was a film that had "the cool beauty of a bathroom."

As any Freudian could tell us, there's no contradiction between Buñuel's crisp, clean, antiseptic sensibility and his obsessive interest in all forms of degradation and corruption. One of his key themes was the testing of an inhuman purity or beauty in the fleshpots of the world.

In *Mexican Bus Ride* (1951) a dense tropical jungle sprouts in the back of a rickety bus and a young man, whose wedding night has been interrupted by an errand of mercy, makes glorious love to a blond fellow-passenger. In *El* (1952) Buñuel's protagonist is a middle-aged religious fanatic, long celibate, who is wracked by insane anxiety over the faithfulness of his new wife. In *Viridiana* a young novice, summoned from a convent, endures the advances of her lascivious uncle — she reminds him of his late wife — and, after his suicide, an assortment of would-be seducers. She exchanges her unworldly perfection for a sardonic knowledge of life in its mixed and uncertain condition. In *Belle de Jour* (1967), his most formally perfect, most immaculate-looking film, Buñuel examines the secret life of a far-from-ordinary housewife, the sado-masochistic fantasies that underlie the glacial beauty of Catherine Deneuve, who spends her afternoons in a high-class brothel.

Amazingly, there was never anything sordid about Buñuel's studies in obsession and corruption. In his old age Buñuel achieved the ironic distance on his own ideas that is the autumnal sign of great artistry.

After *Viridiana* he turned from the scabrous underclass to make elegant fables about the ludicrous rituals of middle-class life — the dinner-parties and infidelities that keep boredom from the door. At the same time his bitter anger gave way to a witty raillery that joined the young surrealist to the old man who had seen everything and had become the effortless master of his craft.

Like the Italian directors after neorealism — and perhaps inspired directly by *L'Avventura* — Buñuel became the chronicler of an age of affluence and ennui, not as sociology but as parable.

Sometimes his fables didn't jell, their associations seemed arbitrary and eccentric. The more willful incongruities in films like *The Exterminating Angel* (1962) and *The Discreet Charm of the Bourgeoisie* (1972) feel like bare ideas or threadbare conceits. But all in all Buñuel had the grandest old age an artist could wish for: a whole new career in his sixties and seventies, ten uniquely personal films between *Viridiana* and *That Obscure Object of Desire* (1977) that made him seem the youngest, most vital spirit in films, as well as a precious, long-suppressed link to the avant-garde of the twenties.

Somehow Buñuel became famous and successful without growing dull, pompous, and official. He made his peace with realistic storytelling without yielding an inch to well-rounded characters, laws of probability, or sentimental melodrama infected by "romantic and naturalistic bacilli."

Religion, sex, and class were the keystones of his work, but he neither eulogized the poor nor underestimated the powerful, the rich, and the pious. He graduated from a simple *épater le bourgeois,* an easy blasphemy and obscenity, to subtler allegories that humanized his adversaries and showed that he too had felt the discreet charms of the bourgeoisie.

He was an atheist in dialogue with God, a lapsed believer who portrayed the cruelty and irrationality of life without a trace of false consolation but with innumerable moments of aberrant pleasure and dark laughter.

—*Morris Dickstein*

Spain: Luis Buñuel
■

THE DISCREET CHARM OF THE BOURGEOISIE (1972)

"Once upon a time . . ." begins *Un Chien Andalou,* in mockery of a narrative form that it seeks to obliterate, and from this title onward, Buñuel's cinema largely comprises a search for an alternative form to contain his passions. After dispensing with plot entirely in *Un Chien Andalou, L'Age d'Or,* and *Las Hurdes,* his first three films, and remaining inactive as a director for the next fifteen years (1932–47), Buñuel has been wrestling ever since with the problem of reconciling his surrealistic and anarchistic reflexes to the logic of storylines. How does a sworn enemy of the bourgeoisie keep his identity while devoting himself to bourgeois forms in a bourgeois industry? Either by subverting these forms or by trying to adjust them to his own purposes; and much of the tension in Buñuel's work has come from the play between these two possibilities.

Buñuel can always tell a tale when he wants to, but the better part of his brilliance lies elsewhere. One never finds in his work that grace and economy of narration, that sheer pleasure in exposition, which informs the opening sequences of *Greed, La Règle du Jeu, The Magnificent Ambersons, Rear Window, Sansho Dayu,* and *Au Hasard, Balthazar.* On the contrary, Buñuel's usual impulse is to interrupt a narrative line whenever he can find an adequate excuse for doing so—a joke, ironic detail, or startling juxtaposition that deflects the plot's energies in another direction. A typical "Buñuel touch"—the "Last Supper" pose assumed by the beggars in *Viridiana*—has only a parenthetical relation to the action, however significant it may be thematically. And lengthier intrusions, like the dream sequences in *Los Olvidados,* tend to detach themselves from their surroundings as independent interludes, anecdotes, or parables. For the greater part of his career, Buñuel's genius has mainly expressed itself in marginal notations and insertions. To my knowledge, his only previous attempt at an open narrative structure since 1932 has been *La Voie Lactée*—a picaresque religious (and antireligious) pageant, much indebted to Godard's *Weekend,* which came uncomfortably close to being all notations and no text, like a string of Sunday school jokes.

If *Le Charme Discret de la Bourgeoisie* registers as the funniest Buñuel film since *L'Age d'Or,* probably the most relaxed *and* controlled film he has ever made, and arguably the first contemporary, global masterpiece to have come from France in the seventies, this is chiefly because he has arrived at a form that covers his full range, permits him to say anything—a form that literally and figuratively lets him get away with murder. One cannot exactly call his new work a bolt from the blue. But its remarkable achievement is to weld together an assortment of his favourite themes, images, and parlour tricks into a discourse that is essentially new. Luring us into the deceptive charms of narrative as well as those of his characters, he undermines the stability of both attractions by turning interruption into the basis of his art, keeping us aloft on the sheer exuberance of his amusement.

Seven years ago, Noël Burch observed that in *Le Journal d'une Femme de Chambre,* Buñuel had at last discovered Form—a taste and talent for plastic composition and a "musical" sense of the durations of shots and the "articulations between sequences"; more generally, "a rigorous compartmentalization of the sequences, each of which follows its own carefully worked out, autonomous curve" ("Two Cinemas," *Moviegoer* No. 3, Summer 1966). *Belle de Jour* reconfirmed this discovery, but *Le Charme Discret* announces still another step forward: at the age of seventy-two, Buñuel has finally achieved Style.

Six friends—three men and three women—want to have a meal together, but something keeps going wrong. Four of them arrive at the Sénéchals' country house for dinner, and are told by Mme. Sénéchal that they've come a day early; repairing to a local restaurant, they discover that the manager has just died, his corpse laid out in an adjoining room — how can they eat *there*? — so they plan a future lunch date. But each successive engagement is torpedoed: either M. and Mme. Sénéchal (Jean-Pierre Cassel and Stéphane Audran) are too busy making love to greet their guests, or the cavalry suddenly shows up at dinnertime between maneuvers, or the police raid the premises and arrest everyone. Don Raphael Acosta (Fernando Rey), Ambassador of Miranda — a mythical, campy South American republic resembling several countries, particularly Spain — arranges a secret rendezvous in his flat with Mme. Thévenot (Delphine Seyrig), but M. Thévenot (Paul Frankeur) turns up at an inopportune moment. The three ladies — Mmes. Sénéchal and Thévenot and the latter's younger sister, Florence (Bulle Ogier) — meet for tea, and the waiter regretfully announces that the kitchen is out of tea, coffee, alcohol, and everything else they try to order. Still other attempted get-togethers and disasters turn out to be dreams, or dreams of dreams. At one dinner party, the guests find themselves sitting on a stage before a restive audience, prompted with lines; another ends with Don Raphael, after a political quarrel, shooting his host; still another concludes with an unidentified group of men breaking in and machine-gunning the lot of them.

At three separate points in the film, including the final sequence, we see all six characters walking wordlessly down a road, somewhere between an unstated starting place and an equally mysterious destination — an image suggesting the continuation both of their class and of the picaresque narrative tradition that propels them forward. Yet if the previous paragraph reads like a plot summary, it is deceptive. The nature and extent of Buñuel's interruptions guarantee the virtual absence of continuous plot. But we remain transfixed as though we were watching one: the sustained charm and glamour of the six characters fool us, much as they fool themselves. Their myths, behaviour, and appearance — a seductive, illusory surface — carry us (and them) through the film with a sense of unbroken continuity and logic, a consistency that the rest of the universe and nature itself seem to rail against helplessly. Despite every attempt at annihilation, the myths of the bourgeoisie and of conventional narrative survive and prevail, a certainty that Buñuel reconciles himself to by regarding it as the funniest thing in the world.

Interruptions, of course, are a central fact about modern life; as I write this in a friend's apartment, the phone has been ringing about once every two paragraphs. Using this sort of comic annoyance as a structural tool, Buñuel can shoot as many arrows as he wants into our complacencies about narrative, the characters' complacencies about themselves. He exercises this principle of disruption in a multitude of ways, in matters large and small: in the opening scene at the Sénéchals' house, Florence's dopey, indifferent, comic-strip face drifts irrelevantly into the foreground of a shot while other characters chatter about something else behind her, and similar displacements of emphasis abound everywhere.

Take the last attempted dinner. It begins with a red herring which leads us to suspect poisoning ("I prepared the soup with herbs from the garden"); the conversation is broken off for a cruel exchange with the maid about her age and broken engagement; and while M. Sénéchal demonstrates the correct method of carving lamb, Florence stubbornly insists on pursuing her deadpan astrological profile of Don Raphael. After the gang breaks in to shoot them all, our sense of their total demise—a Godardian image of overlapping corpses—is interrupted when we realize that Don Raphael has hidden under the dinner table, and is reaching for a piece of lamb. Still crouching under the table, he bites savagely into the meat—a comic-terrifying reminder of the dream in *Los Olvidados*—and is finished off by a final blast of gunfire. Lest we suppose that this is the last possible interruption, we next see Don Raphael waking up from his nightmare. He gets out of bed, goes into the kitchen, and opens the refrigerator to take out a plate of veal.

Every dream and interpolated story in the film carries some threat, knowledge, or certainty of death—the central fact that all six characters ignore, and their charm and elegance seek to camouflage. Ghosts of murder victims and other phantoms of guilt parade through these inserted tales, but the discreet style of the bourgeoisie, boxing them in dreams and dinner anecdotes, holds them forever in check. To some extent, Buñuel shares this discretion in his failure to allude to his native Spain even once in the dialogue, although the pomp and brutality of the Franco regime are frequently evoked. (The recurrent gag of a siren, jet plane, or another disturbance covering up a political declaration—a device familiar from Godard's *Made in USA*—acknowledges this sort of suppression.) But the secret of Buñuel's achieved style is balance, and for that he must lean more on irony—an expedient tactic of the bourgeoisie—than on the aggressions of the rebel classes; when he sought imbalance in *L'Age d'Or,* the revolutionary forces had the upper edge. An essential part of his method is to pitch the dialogue and acting somewhere between naturalism and parody, so that no gag is merely a gag, and each commonplace line or gesture becomes a potential gag. Absurdity and elegance, charm and hypocrisy become indistinguishably fused.

Another form of resolution is hinted at in the treatment of a secondary character, Monsignor Dufour (Julien Bertheau), a bishop who is hired by the Sénéchals as a gardener ("You've heard of worker-priests? There are worker-bishops too!"), and figures as clergy-in-residence at many of the abortive dinner parties. Late in the film, he is brought to the bed of an impoverished, dying man — a gardener himself — by an old woman who asserts that she's hated Jesus Christ since she was a little girl, and promises to tell him why when she returns from delivering carrots. Dufour then proceeds to attend to the dying gardener, who confesses to having poisoned the bishop's wealthy parents when Dufour was a child. Dufour kindly and dutifully gives him absolution, then lifts up a nearby rifle and shoots the man through the skull. Thus Buñuel appears to arrive at the conclusion that Catholicism, far from being the natural opponent of surrealism, is the ultimate expression of it; and it seems strangely appropriate that after this scene both the bishop and the old woman with her promised explanation are abruptly dropped from the film, as though they've suddenly cancelled each other out.

■

Writing in 1962, Andrew Sarris remarked that Buñuel's "camera has always viewed his characters from a middle distance, too close for cosmic groupings and too far away for self-identification." The singular achievement of Buñuel's crystallised style is to allow both these viewpoints to function — to let us keep our distance from the characters while repeatedly recognising our own behaviour in them. Cryptic throwaway lines, illogically repeated motifs, and displacements in space and time give the film some of the abstractness of *Marienbad,* yet the richness of concretely observed social behaviour is often comparable to that in *La Règle du Jeu.* A similar mixture was potentially at work in *The Exterminating Angel* — the obvious companion-film to *Le Charme Discret,* with its guests unable to leave a room *after* finishing dinner. But despite a brilliant script, the uneven execution left too much of the conception unrealized.

Undoubtedly a great deal of credit for the dialogue of *Le Charme Discret* should go to Jean-Claude Carrière, who has worked on the scripts of all Buñuel's French films since *Le Journal d'une Femme de Chambre:* the precise banality of the small talk has a withering accuracy. Even more impressive is the way that Buñuel and Carrière have managed to weave in enough contemporary phenomena to make the film as up-to-date — and as surrealistic, in its crazy-quilt juxtapositions — as the latest global newspaper. Vietnam, Mao, Women's Lib, various forms of political corruption, and international drug trafficking are all touched upon in witty and apt allusions. Fernando Rey unloading smuggled heroin from his diplomatic pouch is a hip reference to *The French Connection,* and much of the rest of the film works as a parody of icons and stances in modern cinema.

Florence's neuroticism — as evidenced by her loathing of cellos and her "Euclid complex" — lampoons Ogier's role in *L'Amour Fou;* Audran's stiff elegance and country house hark back to *La Femme Infidèle;* while Seyrig's frozen, irrelevant smiles on every occasion are a comic variation of her ambiguous *Marienbad* expressions. And as I've already suggested, Godard has become a crucial reference point in late Buñuel — not only in the parodies and allusions, but also in the use of an open form to accommodate these and other intrusions, the tendency to keep shifting the center of attention.

A few years ago, Godard remarked of *Belle de Jour* that Buñuel seemed to be playing the cinema the way Bach played the organ. The happy news of *Le Charme Discret* is that while most of the serious French cinema at present — Godard included — seems to be hard at work performing painful duties, the Old Master is still playing — effortlessly, freely, without fluffing a note.

—Jonathan Rosenbaum

Sweden: Ingmar Bergman

■

RETROSPECTIVE

Times surely have changed. Why, in my day, sonny, you couldn't open a film magazine without reading some highbrow critic's solution to the latest Ingmar Bergman conundrum. Would Death have beaten Bobby Fischer at chess? What did it mean if God was a spider (*Through a Glass, Darkly*), or indifferent to man's prayers (*Winter Light*), or not there at all (*The Silence*)? Was the relationship of Art (Liv Ullmann) and Humanity (Bibi Andersson) symbiotic or parasitic in *Persona*? Why did the morally constipated characters in Bergman's films always wear glasses, and how come so many of them had the surname Vergerus? Back then, we all took ourselves, the cinema, and Bergman much more seriously. Andrew Sarris wrote a long analysis of *The Seventh Seal* for *Film Culture* and, upon completion, came down with choking spells. That sort of thing doesn't happen when you're writing about *Tootsie*.

For a lot of us—well, for me and a few other premature geezers—the discovery of Ingmar Bergman in the late fifties was as exciting as the arrival of the Beatles would be a few years later. Suddenly we could see the difference between *movies* and *film,* between the Hollywood product we assimilated like so many White Tower hamburgers and the *haute cuisine* food-for-thought of European cinema. Bergman was an exhilarating night school: he showed the Silent Generation that films could be considered with the seriousness previously reserved for the poems of Wallace Stevens. Long before structuralism hit film academe, Bergman provided "texts" to be explicated only by readings in literature and psychology. You could get a liberal education trying to find appropriate references to even the jolliest of his films: Marivaux (not Molière) for *Smiles of a Summer Night,* Casals for *All These Women,* Shaw for *The Devil's Eye.* I remember looking at Sarris's program notes for a Bergman retrospective in which he alluded to Ernst Lubitsch's *Heaven Can Wait* as one analogue for *The Devil's Eye,* and thinking, "Compare Bergman to a Hollywood director? Never!"

"Never" came soon enough—in the next decade—as Sarris and Pauline Kael and Robin Wood offered strong arguments for the legitimacy of the American cinema. Old Hollywood was a yawning unconscious open to almost any interpretation, as art, entertainment, or industry; New Hollywood was throwing off its training wheels to become every bit as sophisticated and salacious as the toppled gods of Europe. Though all three of those seminal critics continued to address Bergman films with measures of enthusiasm and respect, not many of their followers did. Compare Bergman to Lubitsch or Ford or Hitchcock or Hawks, and his concerns seemed too ethereal, his *mise-en-scène* too stodgy, the problems his films posed simultaneously too tough and too easy to solve, like a British-style crossword. In the rush to embrace the physical and dump the metaphysical, all the art-house European filmmakers suffered. And Bergman, as the most prominent, suffered the most.

Fashions in celebrity move, not with a steady pendulum swing, but with the ricochet of a drunken jaywalker. So it's hard to predict whether Bergman will again be hot, either with the release of his domestic epic *Fanny and Alexander,* or in the next few years, or posthumously. At the moment, prospects don't look good. The Zeitgeist has turned away from him and his kind of films. The Strained Seriousness of High Hollywood and Old Europe may reassert itself at Oscar time, with *Gandhi* knighted for its plodding nobility, but at the box office and in the critical columns Strained Frivolousness reigns. Ask today's brightest American directors to pick a mentor, and they would choose Walt Disney or Hitchcock or even Harvey Kurtzman over Bergman.

And why not? American masters for American filmmakers, even if the elect are limited to manipulators of Masscult. Bergman's solemnity, his insularity, his *largo* pacing, his insistence that viewers work for their pleasure, all are aspects of a temperament foreign in every way to the passionate proficiency of the new Hollywood technocrats. When Bergman is cited in a movie these days, it is in a mixed spirit of homage and parody; and it comes from filmmakers (Woody Allen, Monty Python) working from an older sensibility, one that grew up with a subtitle squint in the eyes and the linger of cappuccino in the nostrils. To see Death stalk a modern suburban dinner party in *Monty Python's The Meaning of Life* is to realize that satire can also function as nostalgia for the avant-garde of one's youth.

■

Is it that same upscale nostalgia, on the part of authors and editors, that fuels the scholarly engine of Bergman books? In the face of popular indifference toward their subject — indeed, toward the notion of serious film studies — they keep coming: Vlada Petric's symposium on Bergman and dreams, Lise-Lone Marker and Frederick J. Marker's study of Bergman's extensive and crucial theater work, Paisley Livingston's analysis of Bergman as social critic, Peter Cowie's biography of the filmmaker. This last book — brisk, thorough, fastidious — is catnip to the unregenerate Bergmaniac. By detailing the seismic rumbles of Bergman's not-so-private life, with five wives and at least three longtime colleague-mistresses enlivening the story, Cowie gives the Bergman viewer evidence of what he has always suspected: that the films are a species of emotional autobiography, in tone if not in content. Look at Bergman's forty-year, forty-film career, and divide by conquest.

The Harriet Period. "There's never been a girl in Swedish films who radiated more uninhibited erotic charm," says Bergman of Harriet Andersson (in *Bergman on Bergman,* a conversation, with Swedish critics Stig Björkman, Torsten Manns, and Jonas Sima, that runs a close second to *Hitchcock/Truffaut* as insider chat, and surpasses the earlier colloquy for access to the filmmaker's spirit). Bergman had cast Andersson, just turning twenty, as the wanton lead in *Summer with Monika,* and he tumbled to her charms as quickly as the film's hero. "I was no little infatuated with Harriet," Bergman recalls merrily. "Oh yes, we took our time when trying out costumes!" They stayed together for three years.

Bergman has noted that the mood of his scripts often complements his own disposition while writing them — that the gay and wise *Smiles of a Summer Night,* for example, was composed during a period of black depression. If this is so, Bergman must have been ecstatic with Harriet. *Monika,* despite a midfilm lovers' idyll, is as brooding and sultry as the sky before an August rainstorm; and the strong, splendid Harriet is renounced for her character's amorality. Their next film, *The Naked Night* (*Sawdust and Tinsel* in Britain, and *Clowns' Twilight* in Swedish), would be Bergman's most merciless screed on human companionship until *The Silence* a decade later. He cites E. A. Dupont's silent film *Variety* as his model, but *The Naked Night* is even more starkly Teutonic. The circus-performer couple at the film's core must slog through life on pity instead of love, and the only character with a poetic vision is a clown who dreams of finding warmth and solace in his wife's womb. The Harriet films suggest that, as much as he was attracted to her robust sexuality, the parson's son needed to distance himself from it — to punish himself and her for the uncomplicatedness of young lust.

The Bibi Period. "Just take a girl like Bibi Andersson. You can never get *her* to do anything she doesn't want to!" Another teenage Andersson came into Bergman's life in 1954; she played a tiny role in *Smiles of a Summer Night*. And starting with *The Seventh Seal*, Bibi incarnated the careless optimism of youth that Bergman now chose to allow into his films. She could cozen a smile out of craggy old Victor Sjöström in *Wild Strawberries* and, with the help of flashbacks, reconcile him to life and death. She was a merry maid in *The Magician* and a rebellious mother-to-be in *Brink of Life*. The later Bibi Andersson — the mature actress of *Persona, The Touch,* and *Scenes from a Marriage* — would provide self-criticism for these young women. A frown would cross her sunny features, and then a cynical rictus. But in 1955–58, the great years that brought Bergman to international acclaim, Bibi sat alone on the "healthy" side of the filmmaker's weighted scales, and then jumped gaily off, friskily eluding the swinging scythe.

The Käbi Period. Käbi Laretei was not an actress; she was a wife, Bergman's fourth, and the first he might consider an artistic equal. A renowned pianist, Käbi would have an important influence on her new husband's films. These are the chamber plays: the "God trilogy," with few characters, desolate settings, and scenarios that enclose the actors like an adult fist around a child's finger. To perform these rituals of a dying faith, Bergman employed three of his strongest actresses: Harriet Andersson, with a burning intelligence behind her dark, feral eyes, in *Through a Glass, Darkly;* Ingrid Thulin, the aristocratic avatar of worldly-wise common sense in his fifties films, now daring to play homely, tortured women whose only expression of self-love is self-abuse, in *Winter Light* and *The Silence;* and Gunnel Lindblom, dark-skinned, flashing-eyed, rangy and powerful, as a pathetic parishioner in *Winter Light* and Thulin's sulfurously sexy sister in *The Silence*.

As a vacation treat after the trilogy, Bergman made a color comedy, *All These Women,* based on an anecdote of Käbi's; but its mood of airy burlesque soon turned flat and sour as curdled *sorbet*. The word at the time (1964) was that the seven actresses who starred in the film as the mistresses of a randy cellist were all former mistresses of Bergman's: among them, Harriet and Bibi Andersson and the magnificent comedienne Eva Dahlbeck, who had brought her Lombardian grace to a half dozen Bergman films of the fifties. Considering how poorly all these women are used, one would like to think the rumor was false.

The Liv Period. Liv Ullmann accompanied Bergman through some of his most harrowing and beautiful films, and through the years that revealed the first cracks in the statuary of his reputation. Some say Ullmann wielded the chisel. She has been attacked for choosing to appear in perhaps the most meretricious handful of English-language movies made by a major actress in the seventies; her autobiography earned sniggers, her good deeds sighs. Recently David Denby criticized Ullmann for lacking "that saving grace of any actress, a sense of humor." He may be right; certainly her characters lack it. But, after her smashing debut in *Persona* (1966), Ullmann was cast by Bergman as the harried housewife—harried by her husband's demons (*Hour of the Wolf*) or her own (*Face to Face*), ravaged by the onset of war (*Shame*) or fascism (*The Serpent's Egg*), crippled by remembrance and remorse (*The Passion of Anna*), gutted by the rapier masochism of family life (*Cries and Whispers, Scenes from a Marriage*)—and, withal, trying heroically to cope, like Irene Dunne in an Ibsen role. Not a lot of laughs for any actress to mine there.

And yet there is in Liv Ullmann a softness—something that wants to surrender—not evident in other Bergman heroines. Harriet Andersson went mad in *Through a Glass, Darkly,* but she *fought* that madness. Bibi Andersson developed, against her brighter instincts, an arsenal of invective. Lindblom and Thulin were two more tigresses of the spirit. Ullmann's beauty—her Technicolor blue eyes framed by white, almost translucent skin—is passive, childlike, more traditionally feminine. And her strength as an actress is to find the black hole of desperation in the "average" woman. It was her and Bergman's rotten luck that they chose to investigate The Old Woman just as a new one was emerging in Western consciousness—one closer to the fiery goddesses of Bergman's, and our, youth.

■

Now, just before he turns sixty-five (on July 14), Bergman has offered what he promises/threatens (which side are you on?) to be his last film. In a way, *Fanny and Alexander* represents a conciliatory move by Bergman toward the appetites of the new movie audience: it is airy and bawdy in its first part, spooky and magical toward the end. It means to send viewers away happy and a bit misty-eyed. And for the remaining Bergman stalwarts, it offers a concordance of referents to his earlier films. (I do wish that *Fanny and Alexander* had reunited some of the director's favorite actresses of days gone by. There are roles here that would have been perfect for Dahlbeck, Thulin, Lindblom, and Bibi Andersson. As it is, the lead roles are played mostly by Bergman's B team.) Its three-hour running time begs the moviegoers' indulgence—but who deserves that indulgence more than Bergman? No contemporary filmmaker has tried as hard, aimed as high, made as many challenging works of art.

If *Fanny and Alexander* restores Bergman's cachet, good for him. If it doesn't, bad for the churls. In any case, the new film is just an exclamation point to the career of this solemn Swede, who has earned our respect and gratitude for wrestling with God, art, and fickle us.

—*Richard Corliss*

Sweden: Ingmar Bergman
■

THE SILENCE (1963)
PERSONA (1966)

Ingmar Bergman first appeared on the international scene as the metaphysician and mythmaker of *The Seventh Seal* and *The Magician,* the fabulist of *Wild Strawberries* and *The Virgin Spring.* I was nineteen and twenty when I first saw these films, soon after they were made, and they enthralled me with their combination of Gothic virtuosity, full of tricks and showmanship, and austere existential brooding.

It was that earnest, troubled time of life when we're given to musing about all the ultimate questions—love, death, and the meaning of life: Woody Allen territory—and Bergman's films of this period, full of allegory and spectacle, must have fueled thousands of impassioned late-night undergraduate arguments.

In the next few years we found the self-lacerating religious concerns of *Through a Glass, Darkly,* and *Winter Light* somewhat less attractive, but still it seemed that no filmmaker since Dreyer had used the medium as a vehicle for such sustained reflection on matters of life and death.

No one today thinks of Bergman, as we did then, as a thinker rather than a storyteller. Existentialism, which we drank in with such *angst* and exhilaration, has long since faded into a literary remnant of the postwar years, especially on the Left Bank. Even in the early sixties, despite the persistence of Bresson and the puckish anticlericalism of

Buñuel, religious and spiritual themes were giving way to the social and political issues that would mark the latter part of the decade. The meaning of life was going out of fashion. The supernatural element was disappearing even from the *look* of Bergman's work, which under the hand of Sven Nykvist was taking on far more muted and naturalistic tones.

The stark contrasts in *The Seventh Seal* and *The Magician* were giving way to the subtle gray shadings of *The Silence*. Still stylized to some extent, this was a fable set in a mysterious city in which people speak a strange language. But it was also a chamber film involving "real" people, in a contemporary setting, locked in a suffocatingly intense psychological combat.

Centering on women again as he had in the early fifties, Bergman shifted from questions of faith to the desperate needs of individual selves in obscure but powerfully anguished personal relationships. Eschewing the lightness and liveliness of his romantic dramas of the fifties, Bergman infuses a story of love and need with the existential bleakness of his more metaphysical films.

Besides the ache of an immediate personal reality, *The Silence* included many touches that would be crucial for Bergman's later films: a tormented sexuality; a conflict between two women (sisters, it seems, yet also lovers); an exceptional isolation of the characters, emphasized by constant close-ups and nearly empty spaces, so that the film at times becomes a tableau of writhing bodies and implacable, contending faces; and finally, despite the tight enclosure of this airless setting, a topical element that appears in the tanks which rumble through the alien streets, apparently as preparations for war or self-defense.

All this is brought home by the enveloping "silence" of the film: the mysterious language that surrounds the characters, the dead spaces between them even when they can talk to each other, and the wordless, unsatisfying language of the body that they take refuge in for want of anything else that feels solid and real.

It is not hard to see how *The Silence* was a rehearsal for *Persona*, Bergman's most profound yet also his most formally innovative film. The terminal illness of Ingrid Thulin becomes the nervous breakdown of Liv Ullmann, while the atmospheric silence of the first film becomes her actual muteness — her adamant resistance to the roles of actress, mother, and wife which she's been playing.

Persona was the first and greatest of Bergman's psychological masterpieces of the sixties and seventies, though the historical dimension is still present, for the rolling tanks of *The Silence* have become the Vietnam and Holocaust images of the later film, including the famous picture of the Jewish boy surrendering to the Gestapo in the Polish ghetto, who must remind us of Liv Ullmann's abandoned son, whose photo she tears up.

In *The Silence* there is still a residue of metaphors and Gothic symbols in the old Bergman manner — the alien, unidentified country, the unbearable heat, the couple making violent love at the cabaret, the almost-deserted hotel, the kindly but fantastic porter, the company of performing midgets who seem to be the only other guests.

In *Persona* these are replaced by an equally austere but rigorously realistic situation, a sanitarium, the doctor's country house, yet also several brief framing sequences, filled with quick images and cinematic references, that have no direct relation to the story itself but instead draw attention to the film as a film, including, at one point, a shot of the camera and crew filming one of the last scenes.

Just as Liv Ullmann has suddenly become acutely conscious of the roles she plays, both as an actress and as a person, Bergman is determined to make us directly aware of the performances we are watching, even the strips of film and carbon lamps bringing them to us. He puts us inside the proscenium, looking up at the glaring lights, as the masklike face of the actress goes dumb during a performance of *Electra*. He places us inside her nurse's mind as Ullmann goes from a case to be treated, distantly and objectively, to an invasive consciousness that cannot be set aside, that blurs the boundaries between self and other, reality and hallucination.

Eventually the nurse (played by Bibi Andersson), who was at first so crisp and businesslike, sees her own defenses break down just as her patient's had, and comes frighteningly to see her own behavior as a series of performances detached from who and what she is. The underpinnings of her separate identity begin to come apart, along with the neat, comfortable plans she has made for her life. Revealing the little details of her past, exposing herself to the contingencies of the present, she shatters the unquestioning routine on which she has predicated her future.

As Sister Alma has feared from the beginning, Elisabet Vogler's ability to withhold herself shows just how strong she is: the nurse, the "normal" woman, begins to come apart as she hurls herself at her gifted patient's impregnable silence.

Relaxed yet growing voluble and excited, for she is talking to the first person who has really listened to her, Alma gradually becomes the patient herself, awash in a kind of transference, hysterically frustrated by the silent withholding of analysis. She grows convinced that the actress is merely studying her, observing her with the same professional detachment she herself had tried to sustain.

The boundaries of her life, the borders of her mind, begin to crumble. The actress's story begins to leak into her own, as Bergman gives us several scenes which may be "real" or, more likely, may be Alma's fantasies, or even Elisabet's. "Bergman's film," writes Susan Sontag, "profoundly upsetting, at moments terrifying, relates the horror of the dissolution of personality."

In *The Silence* the two women were sharply distinct types, and the main tension between them was sexual. Ester, a translator, played by Ingrid Thulin, was hard-edged, severe, and intellectual, while Anna (Gunnel Lindblom), was a kind of Tennessee Williams type, sultry, steamy, intensely feminine.

Ester's eroticism is perverse, unrequited, and dooms her to a lonely death. Her field is language, but there is little here that she can communicate, for language fails her in this alien territory, which is also the country of the dying. Anna's sexuality is little more than a desperate heat, like the choking atmosphere around her. Casually seductive with her young son, she cannot deal with the other woman except to throw her sexuality and hatred in her face, and show her how much she rejects and detests her. When she abandons the dying woman, we feel that she too, the survivor, is coming to a miserable end.

The tension between the two women is never explained or resolved, never worked through, and Bergman makes it particularly opaque by filtering the action through the eyes of Anna's son, to whom everything about the adult world is magical and fascinating. It's as if Bergman's pessimism about sex and love forces him to retreat to a prelapsarian viewpoint, a kind of wonderment at the strangeness and unhappiness of it all.

Unlike the two women, always at cross-purposes, who always seem so much alone, the boy has somehow managed to enjoy himself, in part by spending time with marginal characters like the playful porter and the frisky midgets. This world has room to breathe only at the edges.

The Silence is a powerful movie but not a wholly successful one. It is too unremittingly anguished, obscure, grim, and private — a child's-eye vision of utter vacancy and misery. *Persona* is no less difficult a film, but it is perfectly coherent, and uses the close encounters between two women to deal with a different subject—not our sexual but our social identities. The child's point of view is shunted to the frame: the boy we see at the beginning and the end caressing the enlarged, blurry images of the two women. (Perhaps he is Elisabet's neglected child, perhaps Alma's aborted child.)

The women, far from being schematically different from each other, are all too similar. Instead of distinct selves, the movie tells us, we all have multiple, overlapping selves, which we cover over with a social personality, a mask, a face. *Persona* above all is a film about faces, but also about the haunting gap between our faces and who we feel we really are.

Elisabet has experienced a kind of vertigo on the stage, a sudden identity crisis. According to her doctor, she has found everything she does and says a lie, a performance, a form of "seeming" rather than "being." In an audacious speech we hear twice, once with the camera on Elisabet's face, the second time with the camera moving in on her own, Alma describes Elisabet's attraction to motherhood in the same terms—as a role she plays, an expansion of her emotional range, combined with a revulsion from her actual child, who, despite her rejection, has developed "a strange and violent love" for her.

By making Elisabet an actress, and by making us constantly aware of the mechanics of filmmaking, Bergman uses acting and filmmaking as metaphors for our roles in life and our relations with each other. As a primly starched professional, and as the fiancée of a man she doesn't really love, Alma too is playing a part which, as she feas, robs her of inner unity and true identity. "Can we really be two people?" she asks herself.

As she loosens up with her patient, she reveals to her (and us) what she has till now suppressed, her long, hopeless love affair with a married man, the impromptu orgy on the beach with two adolescent boys, when the sex was so good, and then the abortion that followed, which still makes her feel queasy and bereaved.

Alma is digging down, as in a therapeutic situation, exposing things she didn't know she knew, or had tried to keep herself from taking seriously. But facing these things—and then feeling patronized by Elisabet—leaves her with nowhere to turn. As the skin of her personality breaks down, grows porous, she first becomes violent with Elisabet, then begins to merge with her, to dissolve into her. At a key moment, in fact, their faces actually lock together on the screen, a visual trick that works well because it's only the last of a daring series of doubling effects we have already seen.

These give *Persona* its distinctive signature and they memorably visualize its theme. Initially, *Persona* is a tour-de-force of dialogues between a speaking voice and a listening face—a beautiful symmetry between a wordless performance and one which is all words. But as the women grow closer, the film becomes an endlessly varied arrangement of two faces on a screen.

After Alma opens herself to Elisabet, she slides inexorably towards *becoming* Elisabet, first "hearing" her voice, whispering words she herself repeats, then "seeing" her come into her room at night, ghostlike, shadowy, caressing her face as if it were her own. Her fantasy becomes ours as well: we "see" her with Elisabet's husband, first protesting, then acting out all the emotions she projects on the other woman, who stands by watching, as if separated by a sheet of glass, on a different part of the picture plane. Bergman gives a new meaning to "composing in depth."

As Alma disintegrates, their two faces become the movie. In Alma's twice-told speech to Elisabet, the camera each time moves in on a face itself divided, half in light, half in shadow, until the brighter halves of both faces merge in a harsh and rigid composite. It would be hard to think of a more remarkable moment in any Bergman film. Now neither woman is quite real, as Bergman will remind us by showing once again that we are watching a movie, by retreating from the story to the frame.

Persona cannot be said to have a resolution, except to return the two women to the daylight world, where the fiction of personality holds sway, and to return the viewer to the Brechtian-Pirandellian frame of self-conscious moviemaking.

Though the fictive Elisabet seemed less deeply affected than the other woman, Alma has forced her to speak, if only a few words, and by the end she is mouthing Alma's own words. Eventually she will return to the stage.

But we never learn how the two women will fare on the smaller stage of their lives, for they have no real existence outside the compass of the movie—we don't think of them as going on. Their shells have been broken, ours too, in a way that can never fully be restored, only filled in and mended.

Like them, we have had our separateness violated, our illusion of completeness and self-sufficiency. Having peered behind the mask, we can never quite put it back into place.

—Morris Dickstein

THE SECOND WAVE, 1945–65

When Jean-Luc Godard, François Truffaut (and Chabrol, Malle, Resnais, Rivette, Rohmer, Tavernier, and Varda) jump-cut their way to the elliptical, spontaneous movie-making that was both more realistic and more rambunctiously stylized than what had gone before, they were called the New Wave. In fact, they were building on the directors mentioned in the first chapter and on the immediate French precursors included here as part of their movement: Jean-Pierre Melville's poetic gangsters,

---

Opposite page: scene from *Jules and Jim.*

Jacques Tati's celebration of eccentricity in a regimented world, Robert Bresson's luminous spiritual realism.

In England, Tony Richardson, John Schlesinger, and Lindsay Anderson looked into the kitchen sink and saw England itself in movies like *The Entertainer, Billy Liar,* and *If . . . .* Investigating the real world with more acerbic style, Joseph Losey's claustrophobic American thrillers took on deeper resonances through his association with Harold Pinter in two early sixties movies: *The Servant* and *Accident.* John Boorman, considered in David Thomson's influential *Biographical Dictionary of Film* as "the most important British director functioning today," justified the early enthusiasm for films like *Point Blank* with his marvelous 1987 film, *Hope and Glory.*

In Italy, Francesco Rosi began with the documentary realism of *Salvatore Giuliano,* moved toward popular realism, then toward the more lyrical style of his films from the late seventies and eighties. Bernardo Bertolucci's essential subject and style sprang full-grown in the early films that forecast his ongoing preoccupation with tensions between real life and the beauty of images.

In Russia, Andrei Tarkovsky and Sergei Paradjanov had a harder time eluding Soviet censors to pursue their spiritual, symbolic themes than Nikita Mikhalkov did pursuing literary themes. In Poland, Andrzej Wajda's career, beginning in the fifties, took up the theme of national menace — while Roman Polanski's career, beginning in the sixties, took up the theme of psychic menace.

India's Satyajit Ray and Spain's Carlos Saura are two more examples of the worldwide New Wave — directors who built on earlier generations to create their own styles of poetic realism. It's no accident that their best films — Ray's Apu Trilogy and Saura's *Cria!* — center, like Truffaut's *The 400 Blows,* on children.

Other recommended titles available on video are:
Lindsay Anderson: *O Lucky Man!* (1973)
Bernardo Bertolucci: *Before the Revolution* (1964), *The Spider's Stratagem* (1970)
Robert Bresson: *Pickpocket* (1959)
Claude Chabrol: *Le Beau Serge* (1958), *Les Biches* (English title: *Bad Girls*) (1969), *Wedding in Blood* (1973)
Sergio Leone: *A Fistful of Dollars* (1964), *Once Upon a Time in America* (1984)
Joseph Losey: *The Boy with Green Hair* (1948)

Louis Malle: *The Lovers* (1959), *Elevator to the Gallows* (alternative title: *Frantic*)(1964)

Nikita Mikhalkov: *Oblomov* (1980)

Roman Polanski: early shorts—*Two Men and a Wardrobe* (1958), *Mammals* (1963), *The Fat and the Lean* (1964); *Cul de Sac* (1966)

Satyajit Ray: *Two Daughters* (1961), *Devi* (1962), *Distant Thunder* (1974)

Alain Resnais: *Last Year at Marienbad* (1961), *Muriel* (1961), *Mon Oncle d'Amérique* (1980)

Tony Richardson: *Tom Jones* (1963)

Eric Rohmer: *Claire's Knee* (1971), *Chloe in the Afternoon* (1972), *Pauline at the Beach* (1983)

Francesco Rosi: *Lucky Luciano* (1973), *Bizet's Carmen* (1984)

Carlos Saura: *The Garden of Delights* (1970), *Blood Wedding* (1981), *El Amor Brujo* (1987)

John Schlesinger: *A Kind of Loving* (1962), *Darling* (1965)

Bertrand Tavernier: *The Clockmaker* (1975), *A Sunday in the Country* (1984), *The Passion of Beatrice* (1988)

Andrzej Wajda: *Kanal* (1956), *Ashes and Diamonds* (1958), *Birch Wood* (1971), *Danton* (1982)

Lindsay Anderson

■

THIS SPORTING LIFE (1962)

A desolate animal cry of anguish rises in solitary screaming crescendo and is suddenly overwhelmed, lost in the jungle screeching of the stadium crowds. Thus *This Sporting Life,* a brilliantly ruthless portrait of a professional football player and his brutish world.

But the portrait created by Richard Harris in Karel Reisz's production is a universal one, going far beyond the confines of its British factory town and seedy sportsmanship to epitomize the beast-man, whose all too human hungering for love can be translated only into terms of explosive violence. It is a total portrait of the avid animal who meets frustration only briefly with bewilderment and ultimately with destructive force, of the tragedy of the unreasoning man, unable to cope with a subtlety of soul.

Mr. Harris's Frank Machin is not the schemer of *Room at the Top* or the groping drifter of *Saturday Night and Sunday Morning*. His scope is focused: "You see something you want and you go out and get it. It's as simple as that." Thus it has been with his literally smashing success on the football field, in his getting all he wants his money to buy, in his gauging his career and sustaining its battering and shattering rewards. But faced with a woman who does not, who ultimately cannot, love him, he faces destruction of the animalism that has sustained him as the unthinking, crashing, smashing force on the football field.

It is a fascinating duel — for indeed the plot of this movie is secondary, since it is basically a chronicle of a man's self-examination. It devolves into a duel between the demanding man and the strangely distant widow who yields her home, her pride, her body — but never her heart. There is a smile, a happy moment with her children, a brief second of self-revelation — but the man's hunger, expressed always with a fierce and frightening violence, and the woman's almost somnolent introversion, cut each episode short. These are closed lives bound by some strange compulsiveness that is instantly recognizable as a groping of the spirit, a reaching toward the heart that even the brute and the somnambulist experience. Theirs is an unmagnificent obsession, degrading and doomed.

But it is searing and enthralling as its course is followed in David Storey's taut, terse screenplay and Lindsay Anderson's direction which suggest rather than specify, provide the mood and the setting and leave the characters to make their mark upon us.

Mr. Harris, a black-haired giant who is a remarkable young physical blend of Marlon Brando and Trevor Howard, bristles with the ego and impatience of the man aware of his physical superiority. He warms with naïveté and childish charm at his success, bellows in befuddlement at the quicker brains and more venal men about him and can but scream with anguish at his final loss.

And yet he is not all brute. There is a decency in his rejection of his patron's wife, albeit a decency combined with an awareness of her contempt; he is without illusion about the sportsmanship of the sporting life; he is abject with a basic realization of his own destructiveness. He gives in the best terms he knows and it is the rejection, incomprehensible and absolute, that destroys him. All this Mr. Harris captures in his stunning performance.

As the widow, Rachel Roberts provides a memorable mixture of a woman afraid to open her heart, ashamed of yielding in female or feminine ways, ultimately refusing to surrender. She creates a complex creature, one that defies both a final analysis and our sympathy and yet stimulates them both.

In this, his first feature film, Mr. Anderson has woven a detailed fabric with harsh impressionistic photography and a hard and stunningly realistic soundtrack. The grotesque almost battlefield ferocity of the playing field and infantilism of the locker rooms, the scheming unhealthy sideviews of team sponsors and fans, are all point and counterpoint in an ugly world — and a shockingly familiar one.

It is not a pleasant film, raw in its exposition, blood-spattered, mud-streaked, unsparing in details. Some characterizations and motivations are incomplete, some transitions abrupt and unsatisfying. But certainly Mr. Harris's portrait of a present-day hairy ape, a man very much of our time, the physical hero struck dumb before the spirit, stands without rival, an unforgettable figure within a powerful and impressive frame.

—Judith Crist

Lindsay Anderson
■
IF . . . (1968)

If . . . reminds me of a hornet. According to aerodynamic theory, any creature so woefully misdesigned is not supposed to be able to fly at all, and according to such theories of movie construction as I hold, a mixture of film moods and methods like *If* . . . shouldn't be able to get off the ground either. But it does — angry, tough, and full of sting.

It begins as if it is going to be just another in that long line of nastinesses about English public school life — perhaps more sharply observed than most, a little more intense in its feeling about these institutions and the boys trapped in them. Along toward the middle, however, it becomes clear that grimly humorous realism is only a small part of director Lindsay Anderson's intention. Without warning or explanation he modulates into the fantasies of escape, rebellion, and destruction shared by the school's three least tractable scholars.

By the end of the film they—and we—have shared in fancy the charms of a ferociously eager cafe hostess, disrupted the school's annual military maneuvers by using real bullets, and staged a full-scale bloody guerrilla attack on the Founder's Day exercises. And we have been smoothly but forcibly transported from our traditional position of coolly objective observers of human behavior into experiencing what it is like to live again inside the skin of an adolescent. One is reminded how very sweaty and feverish it is in there, difficult to breathe because the space is crowded with dusty cartons of conventional wisdom left there by careless adults and the fantasy a kid manufactures for himself out of misapprehension and undischarged imaginative energy.

Anderson has called his film a "vision," and like all good visions there is nothing escapist or comforting about it. It will, I am sure, puzzle and anger a good many people. Many will observe that Anderson has borrowed much of his style from Jean-Luc Godard. Like the Frenchman, he divides his film into sections—each introduced with a title—and, of course, his casual unexplained leaps from reality to unreality are right out of Godard's film can. But he, too, does it well, and he forces our close attention and strong emotional response with the technique.

Nevertheless, and it's greatly to his credit, he is an Englishman. Which means that he shares with his country's best novelists and filmmakers a taste for characterizations—both of people and institutions—which has never been one of Godard's strong points. Godard's people are nearly always abstractions, intellectual constructs, designed to help him illustrate philosophical theories. Anderson, by contrast, is a former documentarian who can reveal the public school's character simply by letting his camera prowl its corridors and rooms, precisely and economically presenting the evidence of its seedy and irrelevant traditionalism. He is equally good at personifying a lonely new boy, a fatuous faculty member, a sadistic upperclassman with a glance or a shard of dialogue.

A public school boy himself, Mr. Anderson has obviously thought hard about what happens when unformed adolescents come into conflict with rigidly formed institutions. The result is that his film is *felt*. I stress the point because youth is a terribly attractive subject for moviemakers today, and one sees so many films (Hall Bartlett's *Changes* and Jacques Demy's *The Model Shop* are two recent examples) that do nothing with it beyond taking an attitude of rather squishy, patronizing tolerance for youthful angst. Anderson alone transforms psychological and sociological data into a passionate personal statement. He really remembers what it was like growing up absurd.

Some may object more strenuously than I have to Anderson's use of borrowed avant-garde techniques to revitalize material that is excessively familiar. As I said at the outset, the overall design of *If...*, considered with scientific detachment, is quite disconcerting. Sometimes, indeed, one feels as if he is about to turn black and blue from the pounding and jarring administered by Anderson and a very gifted group of young actors as they endlessly shift their emotional gears. But one does not so much attend this movie as submit to it.

—Richard Schickel

Bernardo Bertolucci
■

LAST TANGO IN PARIS (1972)

Bernardo Bertolucci's *Last Tango in Paris* was presented for the first time on the closing night of the New York Film Festival, October 14, 1972; that date should become a landmark in movie history comparable to May 29, 1913 — the night *Le Sacre du Printemps* was first performed — in music history. There was no riot, and no one threw anything at the screen, but I think it's fair to say that the audience was in a state of shock, because *Last Tango in Paris* has the same kind of hypnotic excitement as the *Sacre,* the same primitive force, and the same thrusting, jabbing eroticism. The movie breakthrough has finally come. Exploitation films have been supplying mechanized sex — sex as physical stimulant but without any passion or emotional violence. The sex in *Last Tango in Paris* expresses the characters' drives. Marlon Brando, as Paul, is working out his aggression on Jeanne (Maria Schneider), and the physical menace of sexuality that is emotionally charged is such a departure from everything we've come to expect at the movies that there was something almost like fear in the atmosphere of the party in the lobby that followed the screening. Carried along by the sustained excitement of the movie, the audience had given Bertolucci an ovation, but afterward, as individuals, they were quiet. This must be the most powerfully erotic movie ever made, and it may turn out to be the most liberating movie ever made, and so it's probably only natural that an audience, anticipating a voluptuous feast from the man who made *The Conformist,* and confronted with this unexpected sexuality and the new realism it requires of the actors, should go into shock. Bertolucci and Brando have altered the face of an art form. Who was prepared for that?

Many of us had expected eroticism to come to the movies, and some of us had even guessed that it might come from Bertolucci, because he seemed to have the elegance and the richness and the sensuality to make lushly erotic movies. But I think those of us who had speculated about erotic movies had tended to think of them in terms of Terry Southern's deliriously comic novel on the subject, *Blue Movie;* we had expected *artistic* blue movies, talented directors taking over from the *Schlockmeisters* and making sophisticated voyeuristic fantasies that would be gorgeous fun — a real turn-on. What nobody had talked about was a sex film that would churn up everybody's emotions. Bertolucci shows his masterly elegance in *Last Tango in Paris,* but he also reveals a master's substance.

The script (which Bertolucci wrote with Franco Arcalli) is in French and English; it centers on a man's attempt to separate sex from everything else. When his wife commits suicide, Paul, an American living in Paris, tries to get away from his life. He goes to look at an empty flat and meets Jeanne, who is also looking at it. They have sex in an empty room, without knowing anything about each other — not even first names. He rents the flat, and for three days they meet there. She wants to know who he is, but he insists that sex is all that matters. We see both of them (as they don't see each other) in their normal lives — Paul back at the flophouse-hotel his wife owned, Jeanne with her mother, the widow of a colonel, and with her adoring fiancé (Jean-Pierre Léaud), a TV director, who is relentlessly shooting a sixteen-millimeter film about her, a film that is to end in a week with their wedding. Mostly, we see Paul and Jeanne together in the flat as they act out his fantasy of ignorant armies clashing by night, and it *is* warfare — sexual aggression and retreat and battles joined.

The necessity for isolation from the world is, of course, his, not hers. But his life floods in. He brings into this isolation chamber his sexual anger, his glorying in his prowess, and his need to debase her and himself. He demands total subservience to his sexual wishes; this enslavement is for him the sexual truth, the real thing, sex without phoniness. And she is so erotically sensitized by the rounds of love-making that she believes him. He goads her and tests her until when he asks if she's ready to eat vomit as a proof of love, she is, and gratefully. He plays out the American male tough-guy sex role — insisting on his power in bed, because that is all the "truth" he knows.

What they go through together in their pressure cooker is an intensified, speeded-up history of the sex relationships of the dominating men and the adoring women who have provided the key sex model of the past few decades — the model that is collapsing. They don't know each other, but their sex isn't "primitive" or "pure"; Paul is the same old Paul, and Jeanne, we gradually see, is also Jeanne, the colonel's daughter. They bring their cultural hangups into sex, so it's the same poisoned sex Strindberg wrote about: a battle of unequally matched partners, asserting whatever dominance they can, seizing any advantage. Inside the flat, his male physical strength and the mythology he has built on it are the primary facts. He pushes his morose, romantic insanity to its limits; he burns through the sickness that his wife's suicide has brought on — the self-doubts, the need to prove himself and torment himself. After three days, his wife is laid out for burial, and he is ready to resume his identity. He gives up the flat: he wants to live normally again, and he wants to love Jeanne as a *person*. But Paul is forty-five, Jeanne is twenty. She lends herself to an orgiastic madness, shares it, and then tries to shake it off — as many another woman has, after a night or a twenty years' night. When they meet in the outside world, Jeanne sees Paul as a washed-up middle-aged man — a man who runs a flophouse.

Much of the movie is American in spirit. Brando's Paul (a former actor and journalist who has been living off his French wife) is like a drunk with a literary turn of mind. He bellows his contempt for hypocrisies and orthodoxies; he keeps trying to shove them all back down other people's throats. His profane humor and self-loathing self-centeredness and street "wisdom" are in the style of the American hardboiled fiction aimed at the masculine-fantasy market, sometimes by writers (often good ones, too) who believe in more than a little of it. Bertolucci has a remarkably unbiased intelligence. Part of the convulsive effect of *Last Tango in Paris* is that we are drawn to Paul's view of society and yet we can't help seeing him as a self-dramatizing, self-pitying clown. Paul believes that his animal noises are more honest than words, and that his obscene vision of things is the way things really are; he's often convincing. After Paul and Jeanne have left the flat, he chases her and persuades her to have a drink at a ballroom holding a tango contest. When we see him drunkenly sprawling on the floor among the bitch-chic mannequin-dancers and then baring his bottom to the woman official who asks him to leave, our mixed emotions may be like those some of us experienced when we watched Norman Mailer put himself in an indefensible position against Gore Vidal on the Dick Cavett show, justifying all the people who were fed up with him. Brando's Paul carries a yoke of masculine pride and aggression across his broad back; he's weighed down by it and hung on it. When Paul is on all fours barking like a crazy man-dog to scare off a Bible salesman who has come to the flat, he may — to the few who saw Mailer's *Wild 90* — be highly reminiscent of Mailer on his hands and knees barking at a German shepherd to provoke it. (This scene was deleted from *Last Tango in Paris* by the director after the New York Film Festival showing.) But Brando's barking extends the terms of his character and the movie, while we are disgusted with Mailer for needing to prove himself by teasing an unwilling accomplice, and his barking throws us outside the terms of his movie.

Realism with the terror of actual experience still alive on the screen — that's what Bertolucci and Brando achieve. It's what Mailer has been trying to get at in his disastrous, ruinously expensive films. He was right about what was needed but hopelessly wrong in how he went about getting it. He tried to pull a new realism out of himself onto film, without a script, depending wholly on improvisation, and he sought to bypass the self-consciousness and fakery of a man acting himself by improvising within a fictional construct — as a gangster in *Wild 90,* as an Irish cop in *Beyond the Law* (the best of them), and as a famous director who is also a possible presidential candidate in *Maidstone.* In movies, Mailer tried to will a work of art into existence without going through the steps of making it, and his theory of film, a rationale for this willing, sounds plausible until you see the movies, which are like Mailer's shambling bouts of public misbehavior, such as that Cavett show. His movies trusted to inspiration and were stranded when it didn't come. Bertolucci builds a structure that supports improvisation. Everything is prepared, but everything is subject to change, and the whole film is alive with a sense of discovery. Bertolucci builds the characters "on what the actors are in themselves. I never ask them to interpret something preexistent, except for dialogue — and even that changes a lot." For Bertolucci, the actors "make the characters." And Brando knows how to improvise: it isn't just Brando improvising, it's Brando improvising as Paul. This is certainly similar to what Mailer was trying to do as the gangster and the cop and the movie director, but when Mailer improvises, he expresses only a bit of himself. When Brando improvises within Bertolucci's structure, his full art is realized. His performance is not like Mailer's acting but like Mailer's best writing: intuitive, rapt, princely. On the screen, Brando is our genius as Mailer is our genius in literature. Paul is Rojack's expatriate-failure brother, and Brando goes all the way with him.

We all know that movie actors often merge with their roles in a way that stage actors don't, quite, but Brando did it even on the stage. I was in New York when he played his famous small role in *Truckline Café* in 1946; arriving late at a performance, and seated in the center of the second row, I looked up and saw what I thought was an actor having a seizure onstage. Embarrassed for him, I lowered my eyes, and it wasn't until the young man who'd brought me grabbed my arm and said "Watch this guy!" that I realized he was *acting.* I think a lot of people will make my old mistake when they see Brando's performance as Paul; I think some may prefer to make this mistake, so they won't have to recognize how deep down he goes and what he dredges up. Expressing a character's sexuality makes new demands on an actor, and Brando has no trick accent to play with this time, and no putty on his face. It's perfectly apparent that the role was conceived for Brando, using elements of his past as integral parts of the character. Bertolucci wasn't surprised by what Brando did; he was ready to use what Brando brought to the role. And when Brando is a full creative presence on the screen, the realism transcends the simulated actuality of any known style of *cinéma vérité,* because his surface accuracy expresses what's going on underneath. He's an actor: when he shows you something, he lets you know what it means. The torture of seeing Brando—at his worst—in *A Countess from Hong Kong* was that it was a *reductio ad absurdum* of the wastefulness and emasculation (for both sexes) of Hollywood acting; Chaplin, the director, obviously allowed no participation, and Brando was like a miserably obedient soldier going through drill. When you're nothing but an inductee, you have no choice. The excitement of Brando's performance here is in the revelation of how creative screen acting can be. At the simplest level, Brando, by his inflections and rhythms, the right American obscenities, and perhaps an improvised monologue, makes the dialogue his own and makes Paul an authentic American abroad, in a way that an Italian writer-director simply couldn't do without the actor's help. At a more complex level, he helps Bertolucci discover the movie in the process of shooting it, and that's what makes moviemaking an art. What Mailer never understood was that his *macho* thing prevented flexibility and that in terms of his own personality he *couldn't* improvise — he was consciously acting. And he couldn't allow others to improvise, because he was always challenging them to come up with something. Using the tactics he himself compared to "a commando raid on the nature of reality," he was putting a gun to their heads. Lacking the background of a director, he reduced the art of film to the one element of acting, and in his confusion of "existential" acting with improvisation he expected "danger" to be a spur. But acting involves the joy of self-discovery, and to improvise, as actors mean it, is the most instinctive, creative part of acting — to bring out and give form to what you didn't know you had in you; it's the surprise, the "magic" in acting. A director has to be supportive for an actor to feel both secure enough and free enough to reach into himself. Brando here, always listening to an inner voice, must have a direct pipeline to the mystery of character.

Bertolucci has an extravagant gift for sequences that are like arias, and he has given Brando some scenes that really sing. In one, Paul visits his dead wife's lover (Massimo Girotti), who also lives in the run-down hotel, and the two men, in identical bathrobes (gifts from the dead woman), sit side by side and talk. The scene is miraculously basic — a primal scene that has just been discovered. In another, Brando rages at his dead wife, laid out in a bed of flowers, and then, in an excess of tenderness, tries to wipe away the cosmetic mask that defaces her. He has become the least fussy actor. There is nothing extra, no flourishes in these scenes. He purifies the characterization beyond all that: he brings the character a unity of soul. Paul feels so "real" and the character is brought so close that a new dimension in screen acting has been reached. I think that if the actor were anyone but Brando many of us would lower our eyes in confusion.

His first sex act has a boldness that had the audience gasping, and the gasp was caused — in part — by our awareness that this was Marlon Brando doing it, not an unknown actor. In the flat, he wears the white T-shirt of Stanley Kowalski, and he still has the big shoulders and thick-muscled arms. Photographed looking down, he is still tender and poetic; photographed looking up, he is ravaged, like the man in the Francis Bacon painting under the film's opening titles. We are watching *Brando* throughout this movie, with all the feedback that that implies, and his willingness to run the full course with a study of the aggression in masculine sexuality and how the physical strength of men lends credence to the insanity that grows out of it gives the film a larger, tragic dignity. If Brando knows this hell, why should we pretend we don't?

The colors in this movie are late-afternoon orange-beige-browns and pink—the pink of flesh drained of blood, corpse pink. They are so delicately modulated (Vittorio Storaro was the cinematographer, as he was on *The Conformist*) that romance and rot are one; the lyric extravagance of the music (by Gato Barbieri) heightens this effect. Outside the flat, the gray buildings and the noise are certainly modern Paris, and yet the city seems muted. Bertolucci uses a feedback of his own—the feedback of old movies—to enrich the imagery and associations. In substance, this is his most American film, yet the shadow of Michel Simon seems to hover over Brando, and the ambience is a tribute to the early crime-of-passion films of Jean Renoir, especially *La Chienne* and *La Bête Humaine*. Léaud, as Tom, the young director, is used as an affectionate takeoff on Godard, and the movie that Tom is shooting about Jeanne, his runaway bride, echoes Jean Vigo's *L'Atalante*. Bertolucci's soft focus recalls the thirties films, with their lyrically kind eye for every variety of passion; Marcel Carné comes to mind, as well as the masters who influenced Bertolucci's technique—von Sternberg (the controlled lighting) and Max Ophuls (the tracking camera). The film is utterly beautiful to look at. The virtuosity of Bertolucci's gliding camera style is such that he can show you the hype of the tango-contest scene (with its own echo of *The Conformist*) by stylizing it (the automaton-dancers do wildly fake head turns) and still make it work. He uses the other actors for their associations, too—Girotti, of course, the star of so many Italian films, including *Senso* and *Ossessione,* Visconti's version of *The Postman Always Rings Twice,* and, as Paul's mother-in-law, Maria Michi, the young girl who betrays her lover in *Open City.* As a maid in the hotel (part of a weak, diversionary subplot that is soon dispensed with), Catherine Allegret, with her heart-shaped mouth in a full, childishly beautiful face, is an aching, sweet reminder of her mother, Simone Signoret, in her *Casque d'Or* days. Bertolucci draws upon the movie background of this movie because movies are as active in him as direct experience—perhaps more active, since they may color everything else. Movies are a past we share, and, whether we recognize them or not, the copious associations are at work in the film and we feel them. As Jeanne, Maria Schneider, who has never had a major role before, is like a bouquet of Renoir's screen heroines and his father's models. She carries the whole history of movie passion in her long legs and baby face.

Maria Schneider's freshness — Jeanne's ingenuous corrupt innocence — gives the film a special radiance. When she lifts her wedding dress to her waist, smiling coquettishly as she exposes her pubic hair, she's in a great film tradition of irresistibly naughty girls. She has a movie face — open to the camera, and yet no more concerned about it than a plant or a kitten. When she speaks in English, she sounds like Leslie Caron in *An American in Paris,* and she often looks like a plump-cheeked Jane Fonda in her *Barbarella* days. The role is said to have been conceived for Dominique Sanda, who couldn't play it, because she was pregnant, but surely it has been reconceived. With Sanda, a tigress, this sexual battle might have ended in a draw. But the pliable, softly unprincipled Jeanne of Maria Schneider must be the winner: it is the soft ones who defeat men and walk away, consciencelessly. A Strindberg heroine would still be in that flat, battling, or in another flat, battling. But Jeanne is like the adorably sensual bitch-heroines of French films of the twenties and thirties — both shallow and wise. These girls know how to take care of themselves; they know who No. 1 is. Brando's Paul, the essentially naive outsider, the romantic, is no match for a French bourgeois girl.

Because of legal technicalities, the film must open in Italy before it opens in this country, and so *Last Tango in Paris* is not scheduled to play here until January. There are certain to be detractors, for this movie represents too much of a change for people to accept it easily or gracefully. They'll grab at aesthetic flaws — a florid speech or an oddball scene — in order to dismiss it. Though Americans seem to have lost the capacity for being scandalized, and the Festival audience has probably lost the cultural confidence to admit to being scandalized, it might have been easier on some if they could have thrown things. I've tried to describe the impact of a film that has made the strongest impression on me in almost twenty years of reviewing. This is a movie people will be arguing about, I think, for as long as there are movies. They'll argue about how it is intended, as they argue again now about *The Dance of Death.* It is a movie you can't get out of your system, and I think it will make some people very angry and disgust others. I don't believe that there's *anyone* whose feelings can be totally resolved about the sex scenes and the social attitudes in this film. For the very young, it could be as antipathetic as *L'Avventura* was at first—more so, because it's closer, more realistic, and more emotionally violent. It could embarrass them, and even frighten them. For adults, it's like seeing pieces of your life, and so, of course, you can't resolve your feelings about it— our feelings about life are never resolved. Besides, the biology that is the basis of the "tango" remains.

—*Pauline Kael*

Bernardo Bertolucci

■

THE LAST EMPEROR (1987)

As a film artist, Bernardo Bertolucci is such a voluptuary that the subject of his new film, *The Last Emperor,* sounds almost too ecstatically good to be true, too rich. With close to 90 of its 160 minutes set inside China's Forbidden City, this epic about Pu Yi, the last imperial ruler of China, has enough grand-scale exotica to keep Bertolucci—and us— in a constant delirium.

When this film really sings, it's as if Bertolucci had tapped the wellspring of cinema and, ecstatic, discovered the eroticism at its essence. Not that *The Last Emperor* is *Last Tango in Paris.* There's almost no overt eroticism in the film, but Bertolucci's ardor for the deep and sensual look of things fills every frame. He's a true pantheist; his bodyscapes and landscapes have the same vibrant, fervid lyricism.

Pu Yi was three when, in 1908, he was installed as Lord of Ten Thousand Years by his great aunt, the Lucretia Borgia–like empress dowager Tzu Hsi, who died within two days. (She's like a cross between Dickens's Miss Havisham and Jabba the Hut.) Forced to abdicate four years later with the first Republic of Sun Yat-Sen, Pu Yi remained locked inside the Forbidden City in the center of Beijing for twelve years—a figurehead deity surrounded by servants and eunuchs and a fortune in annual allowance.

The sequences inside the Forbidden City have the luster of fairy-tale enchantments, with the reds and violets and yellows glowing like pages from an illuminated manuscript. When little Pu Yi first enters his throne room in the Hall of Supreme Harmony, with its immense carved stone Buddhas and golden dragons, it's as if he had gusted into a Manchu Oz. The dying empress on her giant bed at the far end of the hall has a fetid, decayed luxuriousness.

The weight of the ancient hangs in every corner of this city — a most extraordinary prison. Pu Yi rules it in a kind of cuckoo charade. His eunuchs and attendants kowtow to his every whim; his bedroom, the scene of his wedding night to seventeen-year-old Wan Jung (Joan Chen), is lined top to bottom with small golden Buddhas. (On that unconsummated first night, invisible courtesans remove the couple's clothes layer by layer; the sheer *sound* of fabric against fabric has never seemed so erotic.)

With virtually no contact to the world outside the city's walls, except for the presence of his Scottish tutor (played by Peter O'Toole in all his brittle, storky magnificence), Pu Yi seems as illusory as a hologram inside a make-believe castle. He's a figment of a dynasty that no longer has any worldly function except a symbolic one, and even that is shorn away when Pu Yi, in 1924, is ordered by a warlord's troops to quit the Imperial Palace in an hour.

The abruptness of Pu Yi's exile is preceded by some of Bertolucci's most sweeping and caressing camera work. He turns us into voluptuaries, too; we're ripe for the acres and acres of sweet, liquid, legend-toned opulence that glides before our eyes. This is more than a triumph of production values. What you get from the Forbidden City sequences is something like a whiff from the center of the mystery. Working in a culture completely alien to him, Bertolucci raids it for its resonances. He *embraces* its unknowability.

If you've read any of Pu Yi's childhood diaries, published as *The Last Manchu,* you can see how Bertolucci has used the text as a fairy-tale source book. He's not interested in making a historical tract. What excites him, what has always excited him, is the spooky dualism of personality. An early film, *Partner,* was derived from Dostoevsky's *The Double.* In *The Conformist,* Jean-Louis Trintignant tried to normalize himself behind a mask of fascist aristocracy; in *Last Tango in Paris,* Marlon Brando's Paul, in his sexual trysts, tried to erase himself into anonymity.

Pu Yi is an extension of this effacement. He's a "deity" and yet he is all too insignificantly mortal. He's a living relic of a vanished dynasty. Exiled from the palace to Tientsin, where he carries on like a Western playboy and calls himself Henry, and then to Manchuria, where the Japanese set him up as a puppet ruler, he tries to regain his emperorship. Pu Yi is like one-half of a split image trying to once again become whole. Instead, captured by the communists after World War II, sent for nine years to a Maoist "reeducation" camp, he spends his last years as a gardener in the Botanical Gardens of Beijing: an ordinary citizen. His anonymity is complete. He has become the Ultimate Conformist. He also seems wholly human for the first time — happy.

The largeness of this story resides in Pu Yi's insignificance against the vast, rolling backdrop of history. It's a mock ironic epic with something of a Kafka kick to it. But Bertolucci is also in love with finality and fatalism — it's no accident that two of his films begin with *Last* — and that limits his emotional involvement with Pu Yi. For all its delectations, *The Last Emperor* is a cool experience in many ways. (The convention of having Chinese characters for the most part speak English also undercuts the exotica.)

The emotion in this film comes through in the opulent visionary tableaux, which are as astonishing as anything ever put on film. But Pu Yi is distanced from us, and Bertolucci is content to keep his distance. He begins the film in the reeducation camp, and flashes back, just so we know how Pu Yi will end up — the film is one long inexorable slide into enforced anonymity. Bertolucci uses the foreignness of the culture to license his own hands-off approach to Pu Yi.

There's no attempt at a psychological portrait; it's as if Pu Yi was a concoction of fabulists, a creature prepsychological, presexual, hence timeless. And so we don't get more than the nuances of what it must have been like to grow up friendless, treated as a god; we don't get the dislocations of Pu Yi's life outside the palace, only his mania for imperial restoration. John Lone's performance is striking, mesmerizing, but it's essentially a series of almost Kabuki-style postures and congealments of mood. (Its closest equivalent is probably Nikolai Cherkassov's Ivan in Eisenstein's *Ivan the Terrible,* a film which, in its frieze-frozen audacity, has had its influence on this one.)

It's also surprising that the man who made *1900,* which concluded with a grand-scale peasants' hoedown under a giant red flag, declined to bring out more of the political flavor of Pu Yi's story. Maoism, like the factionalism that preceded it, is treated as so much show-trial pageantry. Particularly in its second half, the movie becomes a bit too edgy and truncated for the ceremoniousness that preceded it. (This may be because the theatrical version is one hour and twenty minutes shorter than its projected "video" cut.)

The political machinations of the Japanese are presented flash-card-style, and Pu Yi's Manchurian ancestry never quite comes into focus for us. You'd have a tough time figuring it out from this movie, but the Chinese considered the Manchu alien rulers, which must have made Pu Yi feel like an internal exile in his own country even before he abdicated.

And yet, the film does work up a rising wave of emotion at the end, when Pu Yi, now an old man, reenters the Imperial Palace and sneaks back onto his golden throne. He's reconnected to his childhood: the double-image has finally joined. I thought back to little Pu Yi scampering through a billowing golden curtain to the thousands awaiting his coronation; racing as a teenager across the city's tile embankments, unable to escape his confinement. The black jest of Pu Yi's story is the confinement that was his curse was also the key to his glory, for only by being closed off from the world could he pretend godliness.

I had thought the operative image in *The Last Emperor* was Pu Yi standing, expelled, before the great crimson doors of his palace, his eyes blanked by sunglasses. I'm left instead with the image of the old emperor once again in his throne. For Bertolucci, Pu Yi's implacability isn't something to be delved into; the mystery *is* the man. In the end, that mysteriousness takes on the dimensions of a deep and sad and ancient story, and our distance from this man becomes both infinite and infinitesimal.

—*Peter Rainer*

Bernardo Bertolucci

■

THE CONFORMIST (1970)

Bernardo Bertolucci wrote and directed this extraordinarily rich adaptation of the Alberto Moravia novel about an upper-class follower of Mussolini. It's set principally in 1938. Bertolucci's view isn't so much a reconstruction of the past as an infusion from it; the film cost only $750,000—Bertolucci brought together the decor and architecture surviving from that modernistic period and gave it all unity. Jean-Louis Trintignant, who conveys the mechanisms of thought through tension, the way Bogart did, is the aristocratic fascist—an intelligent coward who sacrifices everything he cares about because he wants the safety of normality. Stefania Sandrelli is his deliciously corrupt, empty-headed wife, and Dominique Sanda, with her swollen lips and tiger eyes, is the lesbian he would like to run away with. The film succeeds least with its psychosexual approach to the fascist protagonist, but if the ideas don't touch the imagination, the film's sensuous texture does. It's a triumph of feeling and of style—lyrical, flowing, velvety style, so operatic that you come away with sequences in your head like arias. With Pierre Clémenti as the chauffeur, Gastone Moschin as Manganiello, and Enzo Tarascio as the antifascist professor (who resembles Godard). Cinematography by Vittorio Storaro.

—Pauline Kael

John Boorman

■

HOPE AND GLORY (1987)

The subversive thesis of John Boorman's *Hope and Glory* is this: *war is a lark.* This exhilarating memory film, based on Boorman's boyhood recollections of the London blitz, offers a child's-eye view of the war at home. For eight-year-old Bill (Sebastian Rice Edwards), September 3, 1939, marked the beginning of a grand adventure in which his dull suburban street was transformed into a chaotic playground with fireworks displayed at night and, by day, riotous looting parties in the rubble with his gang of prepubescent confederates. For his fifteen-year-old sister Dawn (Sammi Davis), the war is an aphrodisiac. The threat of death makes her hormones run wild, propelling her out for late-night trysts with her new Canadian soldier boyfriend. And even for their mother, Grace (Sarah Miles), for all her complaints about having to raise three kids while Dad serves his country, the blitz is strangely liberating. She finds she prefers not sharing her bed with Clive (David Hayman) every night; independence suits her spirit and frees her to enjoy the companionship of her husband's best friend Mac (Derrick O'Connor), the man she always wanted to marry.

Many filmmakers, confronted with their own family history, grow solemn and self-indulgent. Certainly one might have expected from the director of *Deliverance, Excalibur,* and *The Emerald Forest,* something dark, violent, and mythic. But autobiography has liberated Boorman's comic spirit. Turning the pious clichés of World War II melodrama on their heads, Boorman has made his most dizzyingly funny movie, an anarchic celebration of family. The warmth that exudes from these turbulent recollections isn't a sentimental heat but a joyful one: Boorman's eyes see the foibles and betrayals of adult life, the casual savagery of children, and forgive all. It's an idyll set amidst urban rubble.

In the film's final third, the idyll moves to a more conventionally idyllic setting. The family house is destroyed by fire — it's an accident, not a bomb — and Grace, Bill, six-year-old Sue (Geraldine Muir), and the now pregnant Dawn take refuge at the Thames-side cottage of crotchety Grandfather George (a magnificently irascible Ian Bannen), a patriarch overrun by women. By then the film has built up such a head of steam — whirling from one delirious anecdote to the next, effortlessly careering from farce to the brink of horror — that one momentarily fears a letdown. Not to worry: this pastoral segment is as crowded and inventive as the rest, right on up to the grand joke that caps the tale. *Hope and Glory's* stylistic assurance is breathtaking: it conveys the illusion of having flowed, effortlessly whole, direct from Boorman's memory onto the screen.

His actors all seem to understand perfectly the tenor of the jest. Young Rice Edwards, who'd never acted before, has a grave diffidence that sets him apart from most child actors: watchful and introverted, he's believable as a boy who'll grow into an artist. And Sammi Davis, a mass of reckless, contradictory adolescent feelings, is a deliciously rebellious Dawn. The adults, true to the child's-eye view, have a slightly bigger-than-life quality: Sarah Miles, sometimes hopelessly mannered in the past, has never been so good, and Susan Wooldridge is fine as Mac's straying wife. In a hilarious bit part, Gerald James plays the headmaster at Bill's school, a Welsh tyrant who, in Bill's very personal mythology of the war, is the true image of the enemy.

In England, where *Hope and Glory* has already opened, audiences who lived through the war have been writing Boorman letters describing similar experiences, expressing amazement that he'd captured a reality long buried under the official mythology. But some are offended by the jovial tone. "Actually, it's not so much older people as younger," explains Boorman, in Manhattan for the film's debut at the

New York Film Festival. "They feel that it's somehow flippant and sacrilegious to suggest that war can be fun in any way or that people in the midst of a war could have moments of levity and deep pleasure. That seems deeply shocking to some people." Boorman chuckles: "But I can't really imagine people seeing this movie going off and starting a war."

Does *Hope and Glory,* his most personal film, mark a sea change in the director's career, a mellowing? It would seem so: the two projects he's thinking of next—one set in Russia, the other a contemporary London social story designed for Sean Connery—are both comedies. "Somehow I don't have the stomach anymore for the films I used to make." He laughs mischievously: "I suppose I've turned soft."

—David Ansen

John Boorman
■

POINT BLANK (1967)

When John Boorman's thriller first appeared in 1967, critics praised it but also called it show-offy, even pretentious. Almost a quarter century later, it has the authority of a minor classic. Lee Marvin plays Walker, the first of the questing heroes who dominate Boorman's work; in fact, he's an antihero, a thuggish loner with a vendetta against the criminal organization that left him to die and cheated him of his money. As Walker murders his way up the organization ladder demanding his money, he gradually discovers that crime (and by extension all business) is no longer the province of individuals but of faceless corporations—everybody he meets claims that he has to see somebody higher. Nobody takes responsibility, the organization runs everything, paranoia is king. This idea alone makes *Point Blank* one of the prophetic sixties movies, but what's initially most striking is Boorman's stylistic inventiveness. With a cartoonist's sense of graphic possibility, he plays Marvin's battering-ram physicality off the heartless architecture that surrounds him, producing scenes as memorably witty as those in any crime film: at one point, Walker gets a guy to confess by ramming and ramming his car against the concrete support of a freeway overpass.

Boorman was the first director to capture the alienated allure of contemporary L.A., its cement riverbed, its glittering highrises that show you nothing, its luxurious hillside houses with their Hockney-esque swimming pools and spiritual emptiness — the only signs of life are the noises made by radios and blenders. Obviously influenced by the French New Wave, Boorman's way of shooting the modern city itself influenced countless other directors (you can see it in *Performance's* picture of London); I only wish subsequent directors could've captured the ferocity he gives to Walker's relationship to his love interest Angie Dickinson. Its high point comes when she smacks Walker for what must be a full thirty seconds, before collapsing in exhaustion and fury at his absolute impassivity. Nifty character work by Carroll O'Connor, Keenan Wynn, and the reliably unreliable John Vernon.

—*John Powers*

Robert Bresson
■

DIARY OF A COUNTRY PRIEST (1950)
MOUCHETTE (1967)

In these times of adornment and commercial fecundity, Bresson almost invites obscurity. If we are to go along with his wishes and discount *Les Affaires Publiques,* which he made in 1934, he has made only thirteen films beginning with 1943's *Les Anges du Peche* up through 1983's *L'Argent* (at age eighty-four, he may yet still add to the total), and those films, concerned as they are with grace and redemption, and filmed in a style of austere restraint, have hardly been the type to create public excitement. Yet despite the surface difficulties of his works, and the apparent inability of distributors to come up with decently manufactured prints and videotaped copies of his films, Bresson has enjoyed a relatively widespread appreciation, even popularity.

Because cinema deals insistently with the concrete, the actual, and the specific, Bresson's quest for the airy substance that animates life's shadowplay is not only far from recondite, but easily apprehended by any viewer with a soupçon of sympathy. In fact, Bresson's two adaptations of novels by Georges Bernanos — 1950's *Diary of a Country Priest*

(*Journal d'un Curé de Campagne*) and 1967's *Mouchette* (both available on video) — despite their stories of spiritual desperation and even despair, reveal a generous and openhanded approach to character and understanding, a filmmaker far more kindly disposed towards his characters and audience than generally admitted.

Diary of a Country Priest, Bresson's third film by his own counting, marked a considerable refinement of his style, particularly in its treatment of personality. Bresson has little use for the glib explanations of dramatic psychology: as he sees it, human behavior results from forces far deeper and less fathomable than are explicable by mere cause and effect, a scheme that discounts too much of what is profound and elevates too much trivia. Divine forces empower men and women, yet not in a deterministic way. If floods of divinity shape a soul, it is left to each person to shape the way those waters course, the same way a river bank can direct its flow to marry with the ocean or to evaporate in a sere desert. For Bresson, the problem is allowing that plan to emerge from its modern camouflage.

To eliminate the distractions of psychology's flummery, Bresson put severe restrictions on his actors beginning around the time of *Diary*. Its players — impersonating a sick young priest, a local squire and his troubled household, an atheistic doctor, a worldly monsignor, and various villagers — reject the usual assortment of gestures and intonations for what, at first glance at least, appears to be a flattened out and deliberately inexpressive approach. Blank faces are often inscrutable, matter-of-fact line readings flirt with monotone, and motions across sets and landscapes are deliberate and modest. Yet, for all that, the performances that emerge are ultimately devastating and transparent in their revelations.

One help to the audience in the face of this stylization is the reading of the priest's diary which accompanies and even explains the simultaneous action, planting a convenient window into the soul of the troubled young priest of Ambricourt, a muddy and chilled French village. Frail and otherworldly in the face of his parishioners' hardy bitterness, the priest (Claude Laydu) and his devotions and spiritual certainties are regarded with a mixture of indifference and derision; one particularly angelic-looking little girl in the priest's communion class spends her time thinking up ways to humiliate him by inviting his confidence and then betraying it.

And the priest is an inviting figure for such cruel pranks. Dedicated to his devotions and prayer in that self-abnegating way often found in the French Catholic Church, the priest is embarked on a process of self-inflicted physical punishment. Racked by pain that centers in his stomach and often on the verge of passing out from even the most minor exertions, he stubbornly restricts his diet to hard bits of bread soaked in the cheapest red wine, a practice of self-denial that unintendedly leads the villagers to regard him as a self-indulgent tippler. Likewise, his attempts to reach out to the locals and involve them in church activities — vague plans for a youth club and the like — are dismissed by superiors and parishioners alike as entirely unworkable.

However, the priest is far from ineffective; in fact, as it develops, *Diary of a Country Priest* becomes a study in effectiveness, in the troubling consequences of priestly intervention, and in the need to act despite those consequences. It is a diagram, both corporal and spiritual, of the intersection of human action and divine order. The priest is drawn into the sphere of the local nobleman (Jean Riveyre) both by the vestiges of social hierarchy and by the troubled imprecations of his daughter (Nicole Ladmiral), his governess/lover (Nicole Maurey), and his wife (Marie-Monique Arkell).

An encounter with the countess forms the central dynamic of the film. Grieving to the point of hatred for both God and man, the wealthy woman has been in an extended and enervating mourning for her long-dead son. The priest, well enough acquainted with mercy to know that it is a harsh and stiff-backed virtue, challenges the twisted residue of her sorrows, holding up her self-indulgence and growing resentments as walls that will eventually separate her from her son for eternity.

The encounter propels the countess towards a spiritual resurgence, but one accompanied by an earthly setback, and the priest is once again misunderstood and misinterpreted, his one success seemingly foredoomed to bring down more failure, more indifference. Even his own death begins to overcome him just as his spiritual agonies deepen. At one point, he protests to his journal that he is unable to pray.

However, in the same entry, he also acknowledges that to God, the effort to pray is the same as prayer, and he never confuses God's will with any possible short-circuiting of his own individual free will. If he is to die, that is up to God; but how he lives in the meantime is up to him. Thus, his rejection of doctors both temporal and spiritual is not a surrender, in the sense that he becomes completely passive in the face of the divine, but that he asserts the right to choose his own path.

Because this issue of free will is often overlooked — sometimes it seems deliberately — Bresson has been accused of being a Jansenist, a believer in a seventeenth-century heresy. And while it is true that Bernanos, who supplied the source material for *Diary* and *Mouchette,* did subscribe to some Jansenist-associated beliefs (particularly that God might bestow grace on people unequipped or unable to deal with the blessings), Bresson does not. He has always insisted that Bernanos's two books provided him with *raw* material, and nothing else. In fact, Maurice Pialat's recent *Under the Sun of Satan,* with its self-scourging priest, is a far more thematically faithful adaptation of a Bernanos work than anything Bresson ever did.

Much has also been made of the way that Bresson likes to film close-ups of minute human actions, householding details that appear subordinate, or even irrelevant, to the main import of a scene. Although this has been described as his way of introducing transcendence, it is not all that likely that Bresson feels a need to transcend the world. It is, after all, in the Bressonian world, God's creation, and a way to know God by knowing his works.

In fact, these ongoing and often lengthy depictions of hands at work are depictions, not of immanence of transcendence, but of human agency, of individually directed labor within a divinely ordered universe. This expression of man's will is at the core of Bresson's work and gives meaning to those who surrender it to a divine plan. Desire is a spur, direction is a conclusion.

Mouchette, on the surface the most dispiriting of Bresson's films and certainly the grimmest, opens with hands at work fashioning bird traps. Soon after, one bird will die and another will be freed as a result of another set of hands in one of Bresson's most compressed and evocative demonstrations of action and consequence. For salvation is not a matter of individual effort or knowledge in Bresson's Catholic world, but a result of the communion of souls right here on earth; *Mouchette* is a disturbing and heart-rending, but completely unsentimental, rendering of the failure of that communion.

Using a nonprofessional cast headed by Nadine Nortier, and employing the most heretofore extreme usage of stripped-down performance, Bresson recounts the last day or so of Mouchette, a village girl, the daughter of the local bootlegger and a dying mother, another misunderstood soul, a virgin regarded as a slut. An outcast by station and by action (she pelts her classmates with dirt even after she is victimized by an insensitive music teacher), Mouchette is most often ignored, but frequently abused.

When Mouchette visits a traveling carnival, she enjoys one of her few respites from pain when she climbs into a bumper car and careers around the track, alternately whooshing past and banging into what, under better circumstances, would be her friends. A perfect embodiment of her condition—she mans the steering wheel of a vehicle which resists direction—the happiness serves only to throw her suffering into starker relief.

In the discussion of his spiritual concerns, it is easy to overlook that Bresson is a master delineator of French village life, and if his rural characters often seem unnaturally sour, they should be viewed in the context of French filmmaking that tends to soften and sentimentalize, and thus trivialize, them. Among the townspeople in *Mouchette* are Arsene, the local poacher, and Mathieu, the local gamewarden. Locked in a ceaseless contest for, if not supremacy, then advantage, they exemplify the specious moral equilibrium of the village, where every propriety hides an indifference, where every kindness disguises contempt. In their acquiescence to relativism, these two ostensible combatants need one another, and in the middle of one midnight life-and-death struggle, they collapse in mutual laughter, unable to complete a charade which, taken seriously, would result in one's death.

This moral tolerance, however, is tantamount to a sin in Bresson's moral universe, and a poor and even horrendous substitute for real mercy. For when Arsene leaves Mathieu and stumbles off into the night and one of his cabins, he encounters Mouchette, wandering lost. When she confesses she was on her way to warn him—a fellow outcast, she naively thinks—that Mathieu was after him, Arsene takes the offer of help for an invitation to abuse and, in the middle of the courtesies he assigns equals, he rapes Mouchette.

To complete Bresson's recapitulation of the misleadingly generous and evilly tolerant social arrangement between Arsene and Mathieu, the gamekeeper and his wife will, again within the context of apparent courtesy, offer Mouchette recrimination and accusation. They push the poorly educated, nearly unloved, and not-too-bright girl further away from the succor they are divinely charged to provide, and which should be institutionally available. Of all the absences in the film, the absence of churchly intervention is the most acute.

When Mouchette finally dies, wrapped in a shroud conveniently provided by yet another damned courtesy, Bresson regards the sin with a broken heart, but a broken heart that keeps its distance. He has shown Mouchette, in a few simple acts, as a young woman capable of love and affection, of care and sudden intimations of happiness. But the immortality that ran in her veins has been dammed up by the people around her, prevented from flowing to her heart. And Bresson will waste no false and easy sympathy on her, avoiding the traps of sentimentality that ensnared the people who could really have helped her.

For all the austerity, the stylistic provocations of acting and detail, what Bresson leaves you with at the end of his films is a profound sense of humanity, a sense that is more acute because of his appreciation for something greater that invests it. You do not have to subscribe to his theology — as I do not — to be moved by his creations, as long as you admit to his own humanity.

—*Henry Sheehan*

Claude Chabrol

▪

THE COUSINS (1959)

The Cousins was so badly received in this country that my liking it may seem merely perverse, so let me take it up in some detail. Perhaps the best introduction to this skillful, complex film is through the American critics who kept people from seeing it. The ineffable Bosley Crowther wrote in the *New York Times* that it "has about the most dismal and defeatist solution for the problem it presents — the problem of youthful disillusion — of any picture we have ever seen. . . . M. Chabrol is the gloomiest and most despairing of the new creative French directors. His attitude is ridden with a sense of defeat and ruin." Youthful disillusion is a fact and that is how *The Cousins* treats it. The movie doesn't offer any solution because it doesn't pose any problem. Robert Hatch wrote in the *Nation:*

The latest of the "New Wave" French imports is *The Cousins,* a country mouse–city mouse story that dips into the lives and affairs of today's Paris student bohemia. The picture is written and directed by Claude Chabrol, but I had the feeling that it was an exercise in self-expression thrown together by the characters themselves. It is just such a story as these bright, aimless, superficially tough, and perilously debauched boys and girls might consider profound and moving.

Time put it down more coolly in a single-paragraph review that distorted the plot and missed the point:

> *The Cousins* . . . is a fairly clever, mildly depressing study of France's I-got-it-beat generation. Made for $160,000 by a twenty-seven-year-old film critic named Claude Chabrol, the film offers a switch on the story of the city mouse (Jean-Claude Brialy) and the country mouse (Gérard Blain). In this case the city mouse is really a rat. Enrolled in law school, he seldom attends classes, spends his time shacking up with "can't-say-no" girls, arranging for abortions, curing one hangover and planning the next. When the country cousin, a nice boy but not too bright in school, comes to live with him, the rat nibbles away at the country boy's time, his girl friend (Juliette Mayniel), and his will to work. In the end, the country cousin fails his examinations and the city cousin casually shoots him dead with a gun he didn't know was loaded. And that, the moral would seem to be, is one way to keep 'em down on the farm after they've seen Paree.

The critical term "depressing," like "gloomiest and most despairing," almost guarantees that readers will stay away.

Time's reviewer may not have been briefed on the Catholic background of *The Cousins,* or may have thought that its kind of religiosity would not be inspirational enough for American audiences. After all, it was *Time* that cautioned the public that if they went to see *Diary of a Country Priest* — surely the one great religious film of recent years — they "might be grateful for a resident theologian in the lobby." Yet *Time,* in its laudatory review of *The Hoodlum Priest,* indulges in a piece of upbeat theology that might confuse anyone. *Time* describes what happens when the priest tells the condemned convict about Christ's love, and, according to *Time:*

> Suddenly, wonderfully, a new dimension of reality surrounds and penetrates the scene: the dimension of divine love. Like an

impossible hope it flickers in his heart. In this hope the condemned man and his audience are so intensely interfused and mutually identified . . . that the spectator not only shares the victim's agony in the gas chamber but may even, at one transcendent moment in this film, feel himself dead in the dead man, feel the dead man living in himself. The experience is extraordinary—nothing less than an illusion of immortality.

The Cousins, oddly enough, is about just such an interchange—but with a complete loss of hope. The hero, who is, of course, the *city* cousin, knows that he is *dead* in the dead man. Why did American reviewers consider the honest, plodding, unimaginative, provincial cousin the hero? Possibly identification—they have certainly behaved like country innocents about *The Cousins.* What is exciting about its content is precisely the oblique view we get of the decadent, bizarre, rich young nihilist—the dissipating cynic who is the antithesis of all bourgeois virtues. It is he, not his hardworking, conscientious, romantic, and idealistic cousin, who has moral force, and it is *his* character that is relevant to the actual world. The only certainties in his life are promiscuity and vice, but he recognizes them for what they are and he has established a code of behavior—it might even be construed as a code of honor.

The Cousins has the most remarkable collection of faces in recent films: in every shot there is someone to look at. And there are the remarkable principals: the suave Jean-Claude Brialy as the city cousin—we first see him made up like Toulouse-Lautrec in his Japanese-gentleman photographs; Gérard Blain in the difficult role of the country boy; and a new young actress, Juliette Mayniel, who has the most astonishingly beautiful cat-eyes since Michele Morgan in her trenchcoat and beret came out of the fog of *Port of Shadows.*

As a production, *The Cousins* glitters as if it were terribly expensive. It contains some of the best orgies on film, and every scene is smooth and elegant. Perhaps it is Chabrol's almost extravagant command of the medium—the fluency of movement and the total subordination of the large cast to their roles and milieu—that made Americans less sympathetic than they have been toward unpolished, rough, uncontrolled work. In the film society and art-house audiences, awkwardness and pretension are often associated with film art, and there seems to be almost an appetite for filmic inadequacy—which looks like proof of sincerity and good intentions. How else can one explain the enthusiasm for that feeble refugee from a surrealist short—the union-suited devil of *Black Orpheus?* You may like or dislike *The Cousins* but you certainly won't feel that the director is an amateur to whom you should be charitable.

The sensationalism and glossy stylishness of *The Cousins* suggests commercial film making at its most proficient. As a critic, Chabrol is identified with his studies of Hitchcock. He particularly admires *Strangers on a Train,* which, as you may recall, also suggested a peculiar role transference between two men—Farley Granger and Robert Walker—and dealt with a particularly corrupt social climate of extreme wealth and extreme perversity. Chabrol is the showman of the New Wave, but he is also a moralist who uses the dissolute milieu of student life for a serious, though chic, purpose. The students are products of the post-Nazi world, and in one disturbing sequence, the city cousin interrupts a wild party he is giving to stage an extraordinary ritual: with Wagner on the hi-fi, he puts on an SS officer's hat and walks among his drunken guests with a lighted candelabrum, as he recites in German what sounds like a mawkish parody of German romantic poetry.

The older characters are, ironically, misleading or treacherous or disgusting. There is, for example, a kindly bookseller, whom, at first, one might take to be the chorus, as he counsels the country boy to stick to his studies and stay away from the nasty sophisticates. But his advice is dated and it won't work. The others—the procurer, and the Italian industrialist—are obsessed by sexual desires they can't satisfy. The students abhor the industrialist because he is an old-fashioned kind of lecher who wants to buy his way into the company of youth. The students are, within their own terms, honest in the way they take their pleasure: *The Cousins,* more than any other film I can think of, deserves to be called *The Lost Generation,* with all the glamour and romance, the easy sophistication and quick desperation that the title suggests.

Chabrol shows that the old concepts of romance are inadequate to a world of sexual ambiguities, and he shows that, from the point of view of the bright and gifted, and in our world—where the present, as much as the future—is uncertain—a country cousin who plods to make good and get ahead must be a little dull witted. Perhaps that country boy is not really so honest as he seems: his diligence, his sobriety, all his antique virtues may be just a self-deceiving defense against the facts of modern life. The heroine, who almost thinks she loves him, realizes that this is just an intellectual and aesthetic response; she would like to be able to believe in a pure, sweet, and enduring love. It would be so much prettier than the truth about herself. The others treat him with a gentle nostalgia—as toward a figure from the past.

—*Pauline Kael*

Claude Chabrol

■

LANDRU (1963)

In a quaint kiosk in the Luxembourg Gardens in Paris the band starts playing "Fascination." The park is full of beautiful women wearing exquisite period costumes. Each is carrying different flowers—Michele Morgan, one perfect pink rose; Danielle Darrieux, a bunch of violets. The atmosphere suggests *Gigi*, but the hero of *Landru* (English title: *Bluebeard*) is thanking heaven for lonely women, not little girls.

All of these lovely ladies have answered an ad placed by the infamous Henri-Desire Landru, who was guillotined in 1922 for murdering eleven women. Charles Denner expertly plays the short little criminal with a shiny bald pate and a wicked-looking beard that he loves to stroke.

According to director Claude Chabrol and his scenarist, Françoise Sagan, Landru was more a businessman with a large family to support than a monster. He suffered financial reverses and approached his new work with efficiency. His base of operations was a small country house inherited from his first victim (played by Mlle. Darrieux), who remarked before her sudden death that her kitchen stove was inadequate (but not for what Landru had in mind).

Like Chaplin in *Monsieur Verdoux*, Chabrol saw the comic possibilities in this grisly true-life tale, and he has created a very funny film, reminiscent of *Kind Hearts and Coronets*. Actually, the art nouveau interiors and costumes, in extraordinary color, would be reason enough for seeing the picture.

Chabrol uses color symbolically, especially red. He shows a close-up, for example, of a bright red gladiolus, and Landru remarks "I like fragility," as he strokes Catherine Rouvel's neck. Later, Landru holds out his cupped hands filled with berries to an eager elderly victim-to-be. After she has eaten them we see her juice-stained face.

Despite his stylish success in handling horror, Chabrol has made two artistic errors, neither of which is serious enough to spoil the show. First, he frequently intercuts World War I newsreels to draw an artificial parallel between the slaughter on the western front and Landru's murders in the quiet countryside. This pointless, redundant device provides neither satisfactory justification, motivation, nor explanation for Landru's crimes and serves only to undercut the comic effect by blatantly reminding us of this Bluebeard's monstrousness, which Chabrol and his cameraman, Jean Rabier, show us throughout the film in more subtle ways.

Second, Chabrol ends the picture with a long court trial which has a serious tone that conflicts with the macabre comedy that has gone before.

Still, *Landru* is satisfying and boasts an excellent cast, which also includes Hildegarde Neff as another attractive victim and Stéphane Audran as the criminal's devoted mistress.

—Kevin Thomas

Claude Chabrol

■

STORY OF WOMEN (1988)

We have been missing Claude Chabrol in this country. For years the director of *The Cousins, Les Bonnes Femmes, Les Biches, La Femme Infidèle, This Man Must Die, Le Boucher, La Rupture, Juste avant la Nuit, Wedding in Blood,* and *Une Partie de Plaisir*—what an extraordinary list of accomplishments!—has been embargoed from American theaters. It has been ten years since his last commercial American release—1978's *Violette*—and the only signs of his productive life here have been brief, one-shot appearances at film festivals. Now we have *Story of Women.* It is quite simply the masterpiece that shows Chabrol has been growing and changing, modifying his fundamental concerns and refining his already elevated technique, but retaining his extraordinary combination of psychological insight and formal control.

Isabelle Huppert stars as Marie, a young provincial mother living out the dull deprivation that followed France's defeat by the Nazis. Dutifully fulfilling her obligations to her children, she also refuses to completely quell a fun-loving, if restive, nature: "I'm still young, you know," she tells her seven-year-old son as she prepares to leave him and his younger sister for an evening of stolen fun at the shabby neighborhood bistro. One day, however, one of Marie's girlfriends tells her she is the victim of an unwanted pregnancy. Marie quickly volunteers an old remedy, and, with soapy water and a long rubber tube, performs a rudimentary, but effective, abortion. It is not long before the news of Marie's facility has spread, and almost before she knows it, Marie is prospering from a steady clientele of pregnant women.

Marie's business invariably leads her into friendship with a prostitute, and the young woman's increasingly sharp business sense again leads her into a profitable venture, renting out a small bedroom in her flat for the horizontal trade. Everything would be going fine, but for Marie's husband, Paul (François Cluzet), a repatriated prisoner of war who, upon his return to hearth and home, has been greeted with, at best, indifference, and, more often, outright hostility. There is no question of Marie allowing Paul to sleep with her; from his first night home, Marie—whose business is only just getting off the ground—makes it clear that the idea repulses her, and that she has broken her nuptial chains forever. But while Paul, who has trouble getting work, can understand his wife's drive to earn money, and even tolerate her intolerance, he cannot stand it when she starts an affair with a local gigolo and small-time informer (Nils Tavernier). That pushes Paul too far, a dangerous move in a climate poisoned by the failure of one of Marie's operations, a failure that has led to a death, a suicide, and the orphaning of a large family of children.

Marie seems a perfect subject for judgment, but Chabrol is a curious kind of a judge. Rather than address Marie's condition from an omniscient point of view, the director constantly shifts from one character's view of Marie to another's. For example, the first sign of Marie's indifference to her own children's feelings—a casual remark that her daughter, her second child, is beautiful, because she "got it right the second time"—is described from her son's angle. A quick-reaction shot of the boy hearing his mother's offhand cruelty in hurt wonder, followed by a shot that depicts her looming dominance in his eyes, quickly emphasizes Marie's almost monstrous insensitivity and the price her victims — handcuffed to her by bonds of family, marriage, and love — pay for it.

Of course, using a child's tear-filled eyes as an indicator of a mother's bad character is a fairly cheap way of manipulating an audience, and if it were the only move that Chabrol made, it would not bear much scrutiny. But this is only the opening salvo in a bombardment of shifts. The most complex and subtle involves Paul, Marie's husband. When he first shows up after being freed by the Nazis, Marie discovers him lounging on their bed after she returns home with the kids from a shopping trip. From her side, he appears malevolent, resentful, and dangerous. It seems he has not been in the house for ten minutes before he has packed the kids off to their curtained-off nook of the tiny, cramped apartment and is forcing Marie to fondle him with violent intimacy.

So Marie's abhorrence appears not only natural, but politically correct. After all, Paul has returned to her like a longtime john to a hooker. But gradually Chabrol reveals more and more about Paul, including his essential gentleness, his despair at his country's subjugation, and his love for his children. And from revealing more of Paul's nature, Chabrol proceeds to describing Marie's actions as Paul sees them. Far from being the consequences of a liberated personality, Marie's actions begin to seem motivated by an infantile appetite for pleasure and cruelty. Marie's transformation from friendly therapist to calculating abortionist is well suited to the exigencies of times when women cheat on their imprisoned husbands with their husbands' scourges. Thus Marie suddenly changes from freedom fighter to jailer.

These reversals in perception never stop, and work both as overarching constructions through the entire film, and within each individual scene. In one sequence — which for sheer generous understanding and social insight I can only compare to Jean Renoir — Chabrol encapsulates his entire approach. Marie's most pathetic client is a poor woman driven to the brink of suicide by the knowledge she is carrying another baby. Her life, wracked by constant poverty and the daily drudgery of scrounging for survival, is already hopelessly complicated by the large brood she already has, and another pregnancy — the sickness and weakness culminating in another mouth to feed — is too much for her. Her husband discovers her in the barn trying to drink poison, and, moved by her desperation, tells his wife about the townswoman he has heard about who might solve their problem.

Marie handles the operation casually, turning over most of the work to a maid she has employed. But this time, perhaps because the woman's insides have been damaged by her attempted suicide, the mother as well as the foetus dies. In agony, the husband soon follows, throwing himself under the wheels of a train.

Chabrol treats this highly melodramatic material (which is based on true wartime incidents, by the way) with cold realism leading up to a confrontation between Marie and her victim's sister-in-law. Advancing on Marie's home with two children in tow, the sister greets Marie's kids playing in a wet courtyard with a kind of sardonic sympathy, and then confronts the abortionist in her lair. Although as written the scene is a right-to-lifer's dream diatribe, Chabrol has set up the meeting as a judicious weigh-in. The vengeance-minded sister finds Marie all dressed up and on her way out. Chabrol shoots the gussied-up Marie from a slightly elevated angle, so that Marie appears somewhat small, even childlike. Here Marie, on the verge of a moral condemnation, seems ever the offspring of circumstance, blundering innocently through a forest of conflicting demands. For all the reasonableness of the sister's anger at both Marie's actions and her apparent lack of understanding of their consequences (Marie stubbornly resists the notion that she might have anything to do with the tragedy), Marie does not come off the convicted criminal. And when the scene ends, both women depart with an air of self-justification.

However, although *Story of Women* resists condemnation, it does not refrain from any assessment of guilt. After all, the context for the unfolding action is that creature of institutionalized moral equivocation, Vichy France. While maintaining a pretense of independence, the France Marie and her compatriots inhabit is clearly a Nazi domain, and just as Paul can no longer function in such a society, clinging to memories and illusions, Marie's eagerness to throw off the chains of the past lead her to embrace a newly repressive future. In fact, although Marie's life appears to be improved, she has merely traded in one form of exploitation for another.

Chabrol is probably the cinema's most consistent feminist, having made overt notice of male dominance at least as far back as 1960's *Les Bonnes Femmes*. In that film, Parisian shopgirls found that every instinct they had for pleasure could be perverted by society into a lever of exploitation, even to the point of murder. And although Marie has enriched herself by performing abortions and letting out a room to prostitutes, she has essentially become a different sort of handmaiden.

Her services allow Frenchwomen to serve the sexual appetites of Nazi conquerors, yet still maintain the pretense that they are faithful to their vanquished, and symbolically castrated, husbands.

Marie's insistence on living out the illusion of her freedom finally provides her undoing. When her husband catches her lying on their nuptial bed with her lover, he is finally moved to inform on her, not to the Nazis, but to the Vichy authorities. This act enables French men to perform a ritualistic resuscitation of their national honor in sexual terms. Marie, who has defied convention and acted as a free individual, yet at the same time so conveniently served even darker forces than she has overcome, will pay the price of a whole sex's betrayal. The abortions provide a likely excuse for Marie to be disposed of in the most drastic way.

This is social criticism of the highest order, and there right at the heart of it is a sublime moment that combines Chabrol's political sympathies and psychological acuity. After spending her ill-gotten gain on improved housing and food for her family, Marie spends her profits realizing her dream of becoming a singer by enrolling in singing lessons. As Chabrol shows her walking to her tutor's home, the camera tracks down a street, slightly ahead of Marie, as if leading her on. It accompanies her to the front door, and then, after she enters, tracks back along the wall, past the tiled designs under a window, and then up the window to a high angle that, facing downward through the pane, captures Marie as she stands by her teacher's piano and begins to sing the scales. Again, Marie is made to look the innocent child, dwarfed by a towering camera that emphasizes the essential harmlessness of her ambition. Yet the frames of the window hem her in, tracing a trap that her own society sets for those whose grasp exceeds the reach that has been foreordained for them. And even beyond that, Marie stands somewhat obscured behind glass and curtain, somehow beyond the reach of our own judgment, just barely comprehensible to our discernment.

—*Henry Sheehan*

Milos Forman

■

LOVES OF A BLONDE (1965)

The Fourth New York Film Festival got off to a fine start last night with Milos Forman's *The Loves of a Blonde*. Beyond providing us with the best opening-night festival fare to date, this hilarious and touching Czech comedy sets a fast and sparkling pace for the films to follow.

Once again we are left to marvel at the peculiar ability of Czech filmmakers to find universal truths in the simplest situations, to discern both the humor and the heartbreak in the human comedy and to translate them to film with a sharp but compassionate eye.

Mr. Forman is shrewdly aware of the foolish hearts and simple minds at hand, but fondness and understanding make comedy rather than condescension the touchstone of his realism. And realism it is, an unabashedly forthright view of young people in all their vulnerability, their foibles, their frailties, and their essential romanticism, disguised though it may be in all the messy-haired amorality and yeh-yeh-yeh accoutrements that seem to be the same the whole world over.

His blonde, Andula, snub-nosed, Bardot-haired and not very bright, is all for love—and regardless of how her encounters with an errant cyclist or a much-married game warden or a parent-ridden pianist turn out, she can always come up with a breathlessly romantic version for the benefit of her confidante at the factory-workers' hostel in which she lives.

To solve the drastic shortage of males and keep his factory girls happy, the plant manager has arranged for a detachment of soldiers to be stationed in the provincial town. At a dance to celebrate their arrival, Andula loses her heart (and more) to Milda, the orchestra's piano player, a smooth operator from Prague, who can cope with country girls a bit more easily than he can manipulate window shades or city maids. Andula, alas, takes him up on his suggestion that she come up and see him some time in the city, and she learns to her sorrow that even big-time operators come complete with nagging mamas and henpecked papas. But it still makes a good story for the girls at the hostel.

Mr. Forman's eye for detail and gift for finding hilarity in the humblest of happenings make Andula almost secondary to his story. The evening-long attempts of three middle-aged soldiers to brace themselves to pick up Andula and two friends at the dance, the gaucheries of would-be Lotharios, the put-on pruderies of avid females, and the romantic fiasco and fizzle that ensue provide the highest of comedy—matched only by a subsequent sequence in which Milda's parents—and Milda—find themselves in the family bed with a blonde on their hands.

The young director's affection for his folk does not keep him from a clear-eyed view of their banality, whether it's in a quick glance at the television screen before which Milda's parents drowse, a close-up of a soldier frenziedly removing his wedding ring in preparation for philandering, a glimpse at the factory manager's paternalistic smuggery in pairing off two completely frustrated people, or a study of the hostel housemother lecturing her girls on purity.

The directorial talent suggested in Mr. Forman's first film, *Black Peter,* comes to full flower in this second one; despite the attention to minutiae, the film never flags and the canvas is crowded with beautiful portraits of perhaps unbeautiful but very real and very appealing people.

The Loves of a Blonde will soon be in general release. The pleasure will be yours.

—*Judith Crist*

Milos Forman

■

THE FIREMEN'S BALL (1968)

Milos Forman's hilarious deadpan comedy about a provincial firemen's ball descending into utter chaos: The party is a shambles, the dying guest of honor is ignored, and, nearby, an old man's house burns to the ground. Forman captures the ghastly air of these celebrations with such wry, exaggerated perfection that he nearly provoked a national incident: Czechoslovakia's firemen threatened a national strike.

—*Michael Wilmington*

Jean-Luc Godard

■

RETROSPECTIVE

At any public screening of a Jean-Luc Godard film it is inevitable that someone will walk out. This is not surprising because Godard's movies represent such a challenge to conventional methods of filmmaking and film watching that casual viewers can become irritated, perplexed, *angry* at the very things that make a Godard film exciting—his innovative editing, his celebrations of color, his emphasis on sound and music, his attention to compositional graphics, his modern impatience with the nonessentials of plot, and the undetermined psychology of his very contemporary characters.

Yet viewers keep coming. Each new generation of college students and postadolescent hipsters latches onto Godard's uniqueness. This has made *Breathless* (1959), Godard's first feature film, a perennial item in the fading repertory cinema. Young movie lovers seek it out as the source/guidebook/fashion catalog of their own cool detachment from the sentimentality and hypocrisy of the world—despite the fact that the sensibility *Breathless* preserves has virtually vanished from contemporary film culture.

Breathless remains respected in an era that has largely forgotten the French New Wave's lively explorations of the fundaments of film language. This, perhaps, explains the American critical community's failure to rally a defense for the seriousness of Godard's art during the 1985 *Hail, Mary!* controversy. It might also be the reason *Breathless* remains so fresh and seems more invigorating than the many movies it influenced (the best of them: *Bonnie and Clyde, Chinatown, Pretty Poison, Last Tango in Paris, Stranger Than Paradise, Drugstore Cowboy*). Seeing *Breathless* more than thirty years after its premiere remains a difficult, inspiring, and rewarding activity.

It is an adventure made from the clash of ideologies and the revolution in Western pop culture. Telling a simple love story between a French hood, Michel (Jean-Paul Belmondo), and an American girl, Patricia (Jean Seberg), living in Paris, Godard brings in the general cultural ferment of the time. He addresses the clichés of male-female difference; the hate-fascination of Franco-American political and cultural relations; the tension between post–World War II morality and prewar sentiment; and—the foremost counterpoint—movies contrasted with real life.

All those themes remain important throughout the almost three dozen (so far) features of Godard's career, but no more so than in their first consolidation in *Breathless*. That's because the love-of-opposites theme uses a dialectic that is crucial to Godard's means of expression. A former student of ethnography, the Swiss-born Godard first entered film as a critic (for *Cahiers du Cinéma* during the 1950s), and both backgrounds are evident in the way he advances new ideas in relation to existing ones. Formal intellectual rigor defined his "dramatic" style as seen in *Breathless*'s heady set of playful and meaningful contrasts.

It is Michel's adoration of American archetypes—especially the model of manhood he distills from Humphrey Bogart iconography—that illustrates Godard's most profound insight. The distance between one's social condition and personal identity—a fit that no longer fit—defined a generation's unease and the disaffection of the modern era.

That Godard got this much from the movies (and lay the tragedy of it at America's feet—personified by Seberg's betrayal of Belmondo) proved a new way of looking at cinema. He gave pop culture, but film especially, a philosophical glamor and weight. *Breathless* established the modernist sensibility in film. It gave legitimacy to the previously disreputable practice of taking movie myths to heart in one's own life. Godard, using the skeleton of the American B-movie gangster genre (which he returned to in later masterpieces *Band of Outsiders* and *Made in USA*) was able to call up a viewer's naive affection for movies from their subconscious.

Godard's radical move was to consciously use the awareness of film style and history to address the issues and experiences relevant to everyday life. At one level every one of Godard's movies is about movies, but he always plays with film form as a way of giving greater immediacy to real life. Film style was the language of his poetry and *Breathless* employed a new syntax. Inventor of the jump-cut (making an ellipsis within consecutive action), restorer of the inter-title, manipulator of the hand-held "random" camera, exploiter of real time ("Cinema is truth twenty-four times a second"), Godard created a new cultural archetype in *Breathless*. He proved that films that took unabashed pleasure in their form, style, and historical antecedents would not simply be esoteric but could be lively, substantive, quizzical, brilliant, and warm.

Godard has made many amazing statements, but one applies to his entire career like an article of faith: "Everything remains to be done." None of the other New Wave directors have so consistently challenged cinematic orthodoxy and no filmmaker from the fifties has moved into the nineties with the magisterial technique and palpable creative excitement that Godard showed in *Nouvelle Vague* (for which the National Society of Film Critics voted a special citation).

The intellectual integrity of Godard's work is based so deeply in the philosophy and structure of film that his movies have never been coopted by the bourgeois sentimentality of "art cinema" as happened with the other New Wave directors. Godard demands sophistication of his viewers, but not like a pedagogue; his thirst for beauty and his reflexive wit are charmingly coercive — derived from the shared experience of movie culture. This has not changed during the last decade — his films remain vital and innovative — but movie culture has lost its zeal for experimentation. Extraordinary features such as *Hail, Mary!*, *Detective, King Lear,* and *Nouvelle Vague* have scarcely been seen, but they should be. Godard keeps blazing new trails. Here are some signposts on that infinite road:

Alphaville (1965), Godard's sci-fi experiment, was the most influential movie of that genre next to Kubrick's *2001.* Adapting the French B-movie Lemmy Caution serials (starring Eddie Constantine, the expatriate American actor), Godard depicted the future in terms of film noir paranoia. In a soulless world taken over by technology, fascism rules over any emotion, any art. Detective-hero Caution stands in for Godard, representing the principles recognized as the caring, educated humanism of our day. Godard combines an Aldous Huxley–type presentiment to the then-new sociological perceptions of Marshall McLuhan. When Caution attempts to flee the totalitarian zone of this future world and save Natacha von Braun (Anna Karina), a robot with feelings, Godard achieved a striking blend of chivalrous legend and Murnau's *Nosferatu.* The mythology has been reprised in the plots of Robert Altman's *The Long Goodbye* and Ridley Scott's *Blade Runner.*

Contempt (1963) represents Godard's only concession to mainstream filmmaking by adapting the Alberto Moravia novel *Il Diprezzo* for producers Carlo Ponti and Joseph E. Levine. About infidelity among the international filmmaking set, its screenwriter and his wife, Paul and Camille (Michel Piccoli and Brigitte Bardot), bicker due to interference from producer Prokosch (Jack Palance). The soap opera premise is used on a serene, modernist meditation on filmmaking and sexual love. The opening scene—Bardot nude, spread across the Cinemascope screen, asking Piccoli which of her physical features he likes best—announces the issues of filmic representation and the erotic/emotional confusions of love. Godard also added a role for legendary German director Fritz Lang, here playing a pontificating filmmaker adapting Homer's *Odyssey*. Each character represents a level of inquiry on sex, love, power, and creativity. Because he is more poet than pedant, Godard counters the verbal emphasis with nearly overwhelming visual and sensual beauty—Georges Delerue's evocative score became a major element in Annie-Marie Mieville's short, *The Book of Mary*, which accompanies *Hail, Mary!*

Masculine-Feminine (1966), Godard's survey of postadolescent Left Bank students, distilled the aching differences between boys and girls. Paul (Jean-Pierre Léaud of *The 400 Blows* in his first grown-up and still finest performance) meets Madeline (Chantal Goya), a would-be rock singer, and is hopelessly smitten—even when her interest cools off. Their battle of the sexes is related to the era's most pressing politics: Vietnam, civil rights, urban violence, militant rock 'n' roll. A tangential episode features an interview with Miss 19 Consumer Product, a pageant winner who forever illustrates the naiveté, self-absorption, and baffling innocence of youth. Love, Godard observes, is the tragic force that ends that idyll.

My Life to Live (1963), divided into fifteen segments that tell the story of the rise and fall of a Parisian call girl, was intended to be a detached, sociological analysis. Instead, Godard's emotions and artistry got in the way. He created a sedulous, moody tribute to the actress who plays the part, Anna Karina, his wife at the time. The theme of prostitution as capitalism's designated social role for women (reprised in Godard's 1980 *Sauve Qui Peut/La Vie*) is expanded by Karina's presence into an illustration of the exploitation inherent in the filmmaking collaboration between a director and actress.

Karina's character is Nana—an anagram of her own name as well as a reference to Zola's heroine and Jean Renoir's 1928 silent film starring his own wife, Catherine Hessling. Despite his attempts to put a cold, formal structure between himself and his wife, Godard's own regard breaks through in two memorable scenes. When Nana goes to the movies, Godard intercuts her with the on-screen tears of Falconetti as Carl Dreyer's Joan of Arc. Later as Nana listens to a reading of Poe's "The Oval Portrait," Godard himself interjects: "This is our story,

Anna, the artist painting a picture of his wife." Essay and autobiography combine to transcend genre; Karina herself transcends her other screen appearances, and Raoul Coutard's sharp black-and-white photography is a ravishing asset.

Weekend (1968) is the cumulative work of the first phase of Godard's career. In *Weekend,* a married couple, Roland and Corrine (Jean Yanne and Mireille Darc) leave their city apartment to visit—and murder—the wife's parents in the country, hoping to collect on their will. En route, the couple encounter the breakdown of society through the many different characters they meet (including Lewis Carroll, God, and Saint-Just). It's a surreal road movie and the highlight is a long traffic jam filmed in one uninterrupted shot (nearly fifteen minutes). The automobile—the signal possession of the bourgeoisie—represents the mindset and values of each owner, and Godard's massive traffic bottleneck becomes an amazing, frightening metaphor for a chaotic world, the end of civilization as we know it.

Hail, Mary! (1985) is a surprisingly respectful, spiritual movie. If *Weekend* was the end of an unprecedented cinematic joyride, Godard returned in the eighties with an astonishing set of films as brilliantly melancholic as the sixties films were brilliantly gay. Here, Godard (raised a Calvinist) treats the basic tenet of Christianity more quizzically than reverently. In this premise, Mary (Myriem Roussel) loves to play basketball and works in her father's gas station; her boyfriend Joseph (Thierry Rode) drives a cab; and the Angel Gabriel (Philippe Lacoste) flies in on a plane to announce the great event.

It's an intellectual's Christmas pageant, a lyrical hypothesis on sex and love, faith and divinity. God's miracles from The Creation to the Virgin Birth are seen through the wonderment that always preoccupied Godard: the mystery that binds men to women and is itself an archetype of worship and religious practice.

Hail, Mary! is the sign of life—a pledge of faith (in movies, if not in God)—that literal-minded fans missed in Godard's recent films where he displayed his devotion to art in the midst of spiritual despair. Films like *Passion, First Name: Carmen, Detective,* even the very moving *Sauve Qui Peut/La Vie* were the preparation for the renewed vitality that return to Godard's art with *Hail, Mary!*'s radiant sense of possibility.

—Armond White

Sergio Leone
■

ONCE UPON A TIME IN THE WEST (1969)

Nineteen-sixty-nine wasn't a good year for the western. Between John Wayne's self-parodying performance as an aging sheriff in *True Grit* and the new definition of the outlaw provided by Peter Fonda and Dennis Hopper in *Easy Rider,* the noble old genre seemed just about exhausted. All that remained was for Sam Peckinpah's *The Wild Bunch* to come along and — after one last spasm of apocalyptic action — give it a proper burial. This wasn't the time for an ambitious Italian filmmaker to be setting out on an epic that would be at once the grandest tribute the genre had ever received and a penetrating criticism of it. When Sergio Leone's *Once upon a Time in the West* was released, it was an instant failure, and just as instantly was cut by twenty-four minutes. But despite the fact that the crippled American version no longer made even rudimentary narrative sense, the film's reputation has grown steadily in the last fifteen years. Various "restored" versions have surfaced at the film societies and revival houses over the years, but none until now has been definitive. The Wilmette-based distributor Films Incorporated has just issued a superb new thirty-five-millimeter print of the 168-minute European cut; though stories persist in buff circles of even more "complete" versions, this is likely to be as close as we will ever come to *Once upon a Time in the West* as Leone intended it.

And it is a masterpiece, a film that springs entirely from other films — from American westerns as seen by Europeans — and yet assumes an emotional texture every bit as varied and full-bodied as a film taken from lived experience. There's nothing secondhand in it: it's as if Leone had been able to inhabit this landscape that never existed, as if for him the movie West were a place as real as Athens or Rome. Christopher Frayling, in his excellent study *Spaghetti Westerns,* demonstrates how the Italian westerns of the sixties grew out of the mythological epics that had been an integral part of the Italian industry since its beginnings in the 1900s — for Leone, the idea of a western "myth" isn't just a critical construction, but something with a literal force, something that shares the same imaginative dimension with the myth of Hercules. Most of the American antiwesterns that followed in the wake of *The Wild Bunch* were concerned with debunking the myth of the West — with demonstrating how far the movie West departed from the sordid, brutal, and crushingly dull reality documented in the historical records. But all of these films—among them *Soldier Blue, Dirty Little Billy,* the absurdist variation of *Little Big Man*—seemed profoundly beside the point: myth can't be attacked by reality, because our belief in myth is very different from our belief in facts—it's a belief in something we already know to be untrue. Leone is the only western director to have realized that myth must be attacked from within—attacked in mythic terms. And because, as a European—an outsider—he can accept the myth untroubled by its problematic links to historical reality, he is uniquely qualified to bring it closer to reality—to restore those elements, chiefly the hard face of capitalism, that the other versions of the myth have left out. In Leone's hands, capitalism itself becomes a mythic force, as much a part of the landscape (it's embodied here by the building of a railroad across the desert) as the horses or mountain ranges. In criticizing the myth—in filling in the economic relationships American westerns have skipped over—Leone expands and enriches it, which is what the best criticism does.

For his framework, Leone chose the western's foundation plot, the most grandiose of the genre's variations and the one upon which John Ford built his masterworks. A corner of the wilderness is turned into a city, a civilization is created—but by whom and at what cost? For Ford, the founder was often a lone hero (Henry Fonda in *My Darling Clementine,* John Wayne in *The Man Who Shot Liberty Valance*); Leone imagines four founders, no one of whom could have done the job alone, but who, bound together in the mysterious relationship that is the film's true subject, succeed in bringing something forth. All four are stock figures, characters distilled from a thousand half-remembered movies: Jill McBain (Claudia Cardinale) is a New Orleans whore who has come out West in hopes of beginning a new life as a wife to a widowed rancher; but when she arrives at Sweetwater farm, she finds that her husband and his three children have been murdered by bandits. Cheyenne (Jason Robards) is the local outlaw, seemingly as much an institution around the town of Flagstone as the mayor; he has his own sense of decency, and when he's accused of the killing, he rides out to Sweetwater to tell Jill it wasn't him. The real killer is Frank (Henry Fonda), a sadistic gunslinger who works removing "small obstacles" for the railroad, whose silver path is heading straight toward Sweetwater. Frank is being pursued by an enigmatic figure known only by a nickname, Harmonica (Charles Bronson); to find Frank and exact his vengeance, Harmonica must pass through Sweetwater, too.

The four characters are arranged in an increasingly strained relationship to society: at the center is Jill, associated with the family and sexuality (a mother and a whore, she is a synthesis of the roles the western allots to women). Cheyenne is outside the law, but defined by his relationship to it; as a professional bandit, he has his own role to play in the primitive western economy. Frank, though an outlaw, has been adopted by a society that has a temporary need for his services; his methods are savage, but he is working for the spread of civilization. At the furthest remove is Harmonica, a man whose only social tie is his hatred for Frank. Leone treats him as a ghostly figure—when Frank asks him who he is, he answers with the names of men Frank has killed—who lives not only beyond the law, but seemingly beyond the laws of time and space. Harmonica is never seen entering a set: he is always already present, hiding in the shadows or standing just beyond the frame line, waiting to enter the action at its crucial point. Ennio Morricone's score (itself a masterpiece of movie music) assigns a different theme to each of the four main characters. The music defines and, in some way, idealizes them, freezing each character in his essential traits and rhythms (reportedly, Leone played the music on the set, asking his actors to mold their performances to it; the relationship of music and character is certainly unusually tight, almost operatic). No longer stock figures, they are archetypes, each identified with a distinct moral stance, and each linked to the others because of that distinction: together, they form a closed set, a mythological universe. Standing apart, and perhaps above them, is Morton (Gabriele Ferzetti), the crippled boss of the railroad who directs its construction from within his private parlor car. Morton is the prime mover who brings the static relationship to life, forcing the four main characters to come together and to break apart, to form alliances and enmities in response to his actions. Though he himself has lost the use of his legs, Morton is Leone's embodiment of motion in all of its senses—as narrative impetus, as social progress, as rampaging capitalism. He is not a simple heavy, in the western tradition of the slimy eastern banker; he knows that he will die before his railroad reaches the Pacific, but he presses on, possessed by his dream. It is Morton's itch— an inseparable blend of profit motive and pure idealism—that underlies all the action of *Once upon a Time in the West;* he is the element of change introduced into the static mythological system, the element that will both animate it and bring it to its end.

The body of the film follows the relationships among the four main characters through nearly all of their possible permutations. Cheyenne throws in with Jill because she's a whore and makes good coffee (two qualities that remind him of his mother); Harmonica joins Jill when he finds out why her husband was killed — his farm sits on the only water supply within a hundred miles of desert, and the railroad needs water for its engines. By staying with Jill, Harmonica knows that he'll draw Frank out. But this configuration doesn't hold. Kidnapped by Frank, Jill offers to ally herself with him in exchange for her life. Frank arranges a rigged auction that will give him Sweetwater at an absurdly low price, but at the last minute Harmonica enters with a bid of $5,000 — money he's raised by turning Cheyenne in for a reward. In the film's most perverse twist, Harmonica joins up with Frank to save him from an ambush prepared by Frank's own men (who have been paid off by Morton to get rid of him); Harmonica, after all, wants the pleasure of killing Frank himself — at the right moment and in the right way.

Leone's style, both narrative and visual, is built on bold contrasts. Extreme long shots, often marked by an exaggerated depth of field (at one point, Leone holds in perfect focus both a single bolt on the roof of a train car and a mountain range thirty or forty miles in the distance), are abruptly broken by the massive close-ups — two gigantic eyes that fill the wide Panavision frame — that were the trademark of his Clint Eastwood films. In much the same way, Leone uses trivial details (Jill making coffee) to lead into epic panoramas (Jill serving coffee to members of the construction crew that has just brought the railroad to the threshold of her house), or align lowbrow burlesque with the loftiest tragic sentiments. Space, time, scale, and tone are all fluid elements, which can be expanded or contracted at will. And yet these transformations aren't arbitrary, decorative touches; they are closely tied to the central themes of change and movement. The film opens with a celebrated sequence in which three gunmen (Jack Elam, Woody Strode, and Al Mulock) wait in a broken-down frontier train station for the arrival of Harmonica, whom they have been assigned to kill. The train is late, and the minutes stretch out: Elam keeps himself entertained by trapping a fly in the barrel of his gun; Strode stands under a leaky water tower, letting the slow drips accumulate in the brim of his hat until he has enough to take a drink. The sequence goes on and on (it must occupy nearly two reels of screen time) until the train arrives and it ends in a brief flurry of action. The aesthetic of the opening sequence is one of absolute realism — an insistence on showing everything — but as the film progresses, the action becomes more and more elliptic; by the end, entire scenes — as crucial to the plot as Cheyenne's escape from jail and his brush with Morton's men — are skipped over with the barest acknowledgment. It's as if time has contracted as the film has gone on, growing smaller and less commodious, and indeed it has: the arrival of the train has changed the relationship of time and space, turning the far into the near, turning a day's ride into an hour's. Morton's train devours time, collapses space: the coordinates of the old West no longer hold, and the frozen time of myth gives way to the bustling time of machines.

As the train approaches Sweetwater, Harmonica at last approaches his goal. Frank can no longer ignore the mysterious stranger who has shattered all his plans; in the end, nothing matters to him but finding out what he wants. They meet for a duel in the shadow of Sweetwater; the train crews are just over the hill. As they prepare to draw, there is one final expansion of time — one final burst of the "old" time. The sequence is extraordinary: Harmonica stares into Frank's eyes, and with the force of his stare, he seems to project the memory that is filling his mind — the memory of his first meeting with Frank, when he was a boy. Frank receives the images, seeing them as Harmonica sees them — it's a dual flashback, a fused memory. A shot is fired, and it's over.

With this killing, the central relationship is broken: the main characters are now free to move away, as if the mythic time that bound them together had been shattered, and they could now move into Morton's time, the new time. The train begins to move, pulling up to the open ground in front of Sweetwater, which has now become a station and soon will become a town. The Panavision frame, so achingly empty at the beginning of the film, is now full to bursting with men, machinery, buildings. It's Jill's city — Jill's civilization — and the camera follows her as she moves into the crowd of men, carrying a pot of the coffee that first endeared her to Cheyenne. There isn't any room for the survivor of a gunfight in this image of teeming domesticity, and as the camera continues to move — past the chugging locomotive and down to the end of the tracks, where the wilderness takes over again — it catches the figure of a lone rider, moving away. In the continuity of this final sequence, Leone balances a beginning and an ending, a settling and an escape, a celebration and a profound mourning. It is one of the most complex images in the history of the western, and certainly one of the most beautiful.

—Dave Kehr

Sergio Leone
■

THE GOOD, THE BAD, AND THE UGLY (1967)

Sergio Leone's comic, cynical, inexplicably moving epic spaghetti western, in which all human motivation has been reduced to greed— it's just a matter of degree between The Good (Clint Eastwood), The Bad (Lee Van Cleef), and The Ugly (Eli Wallach). Leone's famous close-ups—the "two beeg eyes"—are matched by his masterfully composed long shots, which keep his crafty protagonists in the subversive foreground of a massively absurd American Civil War. Though ordained from the beginning, the three-way showdown that climaxes the film is tense and thoroughly astonishing.

—Dave Kehr

Joseph Losey
■

THE SERVANT (1963)

The Servant is the first work in Joseph Losey's tortured career to bear his personal signature from the first frame to the last. Since Losey has always displayed a tendency to invest his most conventional projects with personal and social overtones of a perverse nature, it is hard to believe that he would collaborate with Harold Pinter on a trivial melodrama patterned after *Kind Lady* or *The Green Bay Tree*. Yet some critics have objected to the slackening of tension in the second half of the film as if they were back on Angel Street. Part of the confusion may be caused by the preciseness and fluidity of Losey's camera style. It's too beautiful to be anything but melodrama, our dreary realists would argue. But it must be remembered that Losey was an admirer of Brecht long before such admiration was either fashionable or feasible, and that if he is any kind of realist at all, he is a symbolic realist. Still, no matter how symbolic you get, if the psychology is false, the sociology is equally false. Where many critics have gone wrong is in assuming a psychology for the Losey-Pinter characters in accordance with the preconceptions of a genre. If Dirk Bogarde's Servant is immediately identified as half Mephistopheles and half Machiavelli out to corrupt James Fox's innocent Master, half Faust and half Dorian Gray, then we are no longer in the realm of the why but of the how. Intellectual irony gives way to formal allegory, and the turns of the plot transcend the turns of the screw.

Now let's stop and think a moment. Why would a Brechtian-Marxist like Losey be unduly concerned over the possible corruption of an upper-class Englishman by his servant? The answer is that Losey is not particularly interested in this aspect of the plot. What must have interested Losey from the beginning was the opportunity provided by Robin Maugham's conventional novel of decadence to dissect British class society within a controlled frame. By concentrating on four characters — master, servant, master's fiancée, servant's mistress — Losey could establish all the necessary lines of communication between classes and then snarl them up with insolence and ignoblesse oblige. One critic has asked why the servant undertakes to undermine his master. The servant's references are in order. He doesn't do this as a hobby. What's his motivation? Well, "motivation" is a kind of Sammy Glick script-conference word left over from Hollywood's traumatic experience with the talkies. What is Hamlet's motivation? If we knew for sure, perhaps *Hamlet* would not fail so dismally as a straightforward revenge play. Too much slackness in the second half, you know.

There is one staggering episode in *The Servant* that provides the key to all the motivations. It is the famous restaurant scene with the snatches of bullying conversations from three unrelated couples. This is not an extraneous sample of Pinter's virtuosity for comedy relief. It is the evocation of power as the dominant passion of a collapsing class society. Why, then, does the servant take over his master? Simply because someone has to take over someone else. Every relationship — indeed, every conversation — is a power struggle. Lacking a plan, the servant has to improvise. Each nastiness, like Hitler's, leads to unexpected gains, and the process continues until the servant is as corrupted by power as the master is corrupted by sloth. The servant goes too far. He is fired, then rehired. Chaos. Utter perversion. Then, finally, a fine house where everyone once knew his place has been converted into a seedy brothel where everyone now knows his vice — in short, Losey's vision of contemporary England.

The ensemble acting is extraordinary. Dirk Bogarde gives the performance of his life with a skillful blend of charm, rascality, and uncertainty. Sarah Miles exudes sex as a rousing stimulus rather than a rhetorical symbol, and no one since the early days of Joan Greenwood has been more delectably suspicious of her own sensuality. Wendy Craig is uncommonly expert in the difficult role of the upper-class character with too much character and not enough facade to play the chess game to the bitter end. In the most difficult part, James Fox manages his upper but not higher role without a trace of caricature or condescension.

The Servant is undeniably the most exciting movie of the year so far. There is some overelaboration of Losey's circular camera movements that trace the shape of his deterministic conceptions, and there is also some leakage of meaning through hysteria. It must be acknowledged, if only on the most sublime level of moviemaking, that Losey lacks the unified vision of a Renoir in *The Rules of the Game.* Nevertheless *The Servant* is a genuinely shocking experience for audiences with the imagination to understand the dimensions of the shock. In years to come *The Servant* may be cited as a prophetic work marking the decline and fall of our last cherished illusions about ourselves and our alleged civilization.

—*Andrew Sarris*

Joseph Losey

■

ACCIDENT (1967)

Life proceeds by silence as well as by speech, by what does not happen
not less than by what does, by noises and objects, by what is thought
and not said, said and not meant, by innuendo and half-truth, evasion
and ambiguity.

The old stage and screen conventions of explicit plots and neat and
tidy exposition were born of various necessities, but they are seen to be
very limiting devices for conveying the complexities and subtleties of
human relationships.

The recent excitement about films has been that they have tried,
often brilliantly, to get at a good deal more than gross events, to suggest
states of being which are beyond or below speech, to show the textures
of our age of affluent anxiety.

The triumph, almost the miracle, of Joseph Losey's *Accident* is that
the tense and tangled relationships of several sophisticated men and
women clustered around Oxford emerge through understatement and
eloquent silence, through noises, geography, and objects, and through
a camera which lingers thoughtfully over the places people have been,
like an intelligence reluctant to move on until it has savored the
implications of what it has just seen. Harold Pinter's dialogue is, as
always, sparse and oblique but it is unusually revealing.

It is a film incessantly aware of sounds. A clock ticks, just audible, in
the musty quiet of the faculty reading room, and what is implied is the
suffocating sterility of the moment and perhaps of the life.

The picture opens in silence broken only by the faint sounds of the
English countryside in the hours past midnight. Beyond the noiseless
and businesslike titles, we watch a Georgian house, dark and presumably asleep. A low drone becomes identifiable as the sound of a fast-
approaching car. There are, just off camera, the sounds of a skid, a
fearful screech, a pause, a shattering crash, silence.

A light goes on in the house, a man hurries from the front door
toward the road. And the spell of implication, if it can be called that, is
already so strong that it seems sure the man knows whom he will find
in the wreckage. (He does.)

In simple terms, Pinter's screenplay (from a novel by Nicholas
Mosley) is of the catalytic, catastrophic effect on several lives of the

arrival of a new and beautiful Austrian student (Jacqueline Sassard) at Oxford. The accident is not the beginning but almost the conclusion of the story, which now goes in flashbacks.

Dirk Bogarde is her tutor, Stanley Baker his old friend, and fellow don Michael York another of Bogarde's students. (All three performances are not less than stunning, instances of that rare occasion when acting, as craft, becomes invisible.) The men are thrown into a muted rivalry for the girl, who, like a catalyst, is herself curiously inert and passive. For Bogarde overwhelmingly and for Baker, the confrontation is (in James Joyce's usage) an epiphany, a summoning in the blood that reveals deeper dissatisfactions and fears.

The film's longest episode is of a day-long and finally drunken gathering at that Georgian house of Bogarde's: the three men, the girl, Bogarde's very pregnant wife (Vivien Merchant) all on hand. Rarely has a surface of such polite affability—very funny in places—been shown to conceal so many lusts, longings, jealousies, and fears.

Like Antonioni, Pinter (who as actor has a short, vivid bit as a TV executive in the film) and Losey have a remarkable sense of place and character and their interaction, and proved it memorably in *The Servant*. The dank cloisters and eroded carvings of Oxford catch a sense of timelessness which is both asset and liability to the university. The incredible green loveliness of the countryside, caught in rare sunlight, becomes counterpoint to the dark mood.

The characters emerge with unusual swiftness: Bogarde's chill apprehensions of middle age, his sense of entrapment and of inadequate assertiveness; York's youthful aristocratic arrogance, tinged equally with naïveté and cruelty; Baker's worldlier charm and strength (he is also a novelist and TV panelist) but his sense, too, of a certain unfulfillment.

At the end, the girl has left, the boy is dead (in the accident); Baker, who has had her as his mistress, has lost her; Bogarde picks up the pieces of a life shown to be hollow at its center.

(John Dankworth's wispy, fragmented score, mostly for two harps, is just right.)

We finish, as we began, looking at the Georgian house, although now in the sunstruck afternoon. There is again the low drone of an approaching car, a screech, a pause, a shattering crash, silence. Another accident? More, I think, a reminder that the soul hears echoes of its own.

Accident, no accident, is a breathtaking piece of virtuoso filmmaking, at once naturalistic and poetic, speaking volumes with incredible economy. It is not, it may be, so much moving as compelling and thought-provoking. Yet, like that echoing crash, it seems likely to recur in the silences of those who see it.

— *Charles Champlin*

Louis Malle

■

MURMUR OF THE HEART (1971)

Murmur of the Heart, Louis Malle's comic masterpiece, is the most American of great French films. Its Gallic knowingness is carbonated with a Yankee-flavored fizz. The soundtrack is filled with jazz by Charlie Parker and Sidney Bechet (the teenage hero is an aficionado of the music); America's pop invasion, too, crops up in the images, in the form of Brando and Bogart movie posters.

And Malle's free-for-all view of upper-middle-class family life has the spontaneity and rambunctiousness that Americans pride themselves on. Even though it depicts psychologically charged material— including incest—that would normally resist comic handling, Malle gives the whole shebang a crackpot symmetry worthy of American screwball comedy at its peak.

Furthermore, Malle's setting of his story in 1954 Dijon, during the French downfall at Dien Bien Phu, brings home parallels to the middle-class rebelliousness that broke out here during the Vietnam War. When teenagers rag their elders for their support of French colonialism, Malle captures the combination of righteous outrage over a corrupt status quo and sarcastic goading of the generation in power that also permeated suburban households in our Vietnam era.

The move to remedy this film's neglect couldn't come at a better time. The movie world has become so timid that even a mild Freudian whimsy like Woody Allen's "Oedipus Wrecks" episode in *New York Stories* has been welcomed in sophisticated quarters with a sigh of relief.

The far more daring, astonishingly confident *Murmur of the Heart* could be called "Oedipus Gloriosus." With sweet, disarming brazenness, it takes the Oedipus complex out of the realm of analysis and returns it to the world of art.

Malle doesn't resort to the stylization and ethnic stereotypes that reduce "Oedipus Wrecks" to an extended Jewish mother joke. The atmosphere in *Murmur of the Heart* is realistic; what makes it seductive and hilarious as well are the warmth and unexpected eccentricity of the moviemaker's observations.

Malle's fourteen-year-old hero, Laurent (played by Benoit Ferreux), has a taste for Camus that upsets his Catholic schoolteachers, and a yen for jazz that helps him bebop to a different drummer. Malle and Ferreux offer an unusually full and individualized characterization of the sort of unformed figure who can stymie dramatic artists—a boy whose yearnings, sensitivity, and fantasies outstrip his personality.

The whole movie is built on Laurent's inchoate nature and the way it makes him, as his adoring mother says, "unpredictable." Without setting him too far apart from the other children in his class, or from his frolicsome two brothers (Thomas, played by Ferreux's real-life brother, Fabien, and Marc, played by Marc Winocourt), Malle gets across how Laurent's imagination imbues him with more vulnerability, awareness, and also more charisma than the others.

A lot of Laurent's distinctiveness comes out in the writing: Malle gives him lines that are replete with deadpan derision, and Ferreux delivers them with innocent insouciance—as though he's the first to discover the pleasures of the put-down. He's as funny when collecting for the wounded in Indochina and urging a recalcitrant record-shop owner (from whom he's just shoplifted) to donate money "for France" as he is when outraging propriety-obsessed mothers at a spa by telling them their daughters are all lesbians, and that one of their sons told him so.

But just as much of Laurent's infectious quality comes from his off-kilter visual impression. His gangling, thin-legged coltish look doesn't quite keep pace with the determined-to-be-cool expressions that steal across his shrewd, observant, sometimes bemused face.

Laurent and his brothers—the older, even slyer, equally tousled Thomas and the experienced, lewdly impish-looking Marc—mesh with their mother, Clara (Lea Massari), more than they do with their father, Dr. Charles Chevalier (Daniel Gelin), a gynecologist. The movie rebuts the "Father Knows Best" caricatures that have pervaded bourgeois pop culture everywhere by showing that the rest of the family knows Father's limitations all too well.

The name Dr. Chevalier, with its reference to the lowest rank of the French Legion of Honor, mocks upper-middle-class social aspirations. (Malle also includes a jocular scene of the family watching Maurice Chevalier on TV.) Still, the father isn't an ignoble man. He's just complacent beyond his years. His sons' exuberance amuses him and wears him out; he's allowed the easy intimacy he once had with his wife to fade. But he's genially robust when he brags about eating and drinking like a traveling salesman during a trip to Paris.

With the vibrant Massari giving one of the great performances of the seventies, Clara is the character who, along with Laurent, dominates the household and the film. This passionate Italian, who grew up in a political family in a villa designed by Michelangelo, says she fell for Chevalier because with a beard he looked like Garibaldi. She's got a voracious appetite for sensual pleasure and anarchistic freedom. She can't help treating her sons as playmates; she lets them filch her money.

When Laurent first discovers that Clara has a lover, he's stricken. He runs to his father, who shoos him out of the office before he can say anything. With his heart and mind in turmoil, he's further confused when his brothers pay for his initiation into sex with a friendly, compliant prostitute and then, in a drunken prank, pull him off prematurely.

The murmur of the heart of the title is literally the heart murmur that Laurent develops after a bout of scarlet fever. Metaphorically it stands for the way that a sensitive adolescent's life can seem to skip a beat.

Laurent and Clara move ever closer to each other during his convalescence, and when they go off together to a health spa, where they share close quarters, they turn from mother and son, or even friends, to soul-mates. She recognizes his frustration as he comes on to a couple of pretty young patients, while he gets nearer than he wants to one of her liaisons.

For mother and son, their inebriated celebration of Bastille Day becomes a time of emotional liberation. They make love in the least incestuous incest scene imaginable. There's no Bertolucci-like portentousness; Malle doesn't treat it as a taboo. He ties it too closely to the dreams and needs of a drunken, amorous teenager and a drunken, amorous woman. Rather than set off damaging psychic depth charges, the experience gives Laurent a virility shot. Almost immediately afterward, he goes on the night prowl for those two girls, and gets lucky with one of them.

That's true to the extroverted spirit of the whole movie, which both ridicules the limitations of bourgeois life, particularly its clannishness and cliquishness, and turns them inside out. The home-as-castle conservatism of the father has joined with the fervor of the mother to give these guys a springboard resilience. When the kids carry on like spoiled brats, playing "spinach tennis" when their parents are away or rolling up the rugs for a party, they aren't just being fresh—they're filling the house with fresh air.

They aren't as mindlessly self-centered as the kids who throw similar party scenes in American movies like *Risky Business*—they can discuss Camus, and they pride themselves on their powers of artistic connoisseurship (their best gag centers on a fake Corot).

Although Malle has said that this movie isn't strictly autobiographical, the sensibility of the film is in keeping with the zesty wit and curiosity of the adolescent heroes. Even the supporting parts are beautifully sketched, like the youthful snob Hubert (François Werner), who thinks it's worldly for him to defend colonialism. And Ricardo Aronovich's cinematography has an exultant bloom.

Above all else, the movie boasts the high spirits to match its high intelligence. The rerelease of *Murmur of the Heart* doesn't mark a historic restoration—the film that's opening now is the same one that opened eighteen years ago. But it is a restorative film. In today's movie scene, it registers more like a roar than a murmur.

—*Michael Sragow*

Louis Malle
■

AU REVOIR LES ENFANTS (1987)

In Louis Malle's great *Au Revoir les Enfants,* based on incidents from his own childhood, there doesn't seem to be any blockage between his feelings and what we see on the screen. The simplicity of his technique is such that, after almost thirty years as a moviemaker, he doesn't need the usual director's tricks to tell a story anymore.

As a result, you may feel, watching Malle's new film, that his direct, unfussy immediacy is perhaps closer to the truth of experience than movies have ever come before. And because his subject—an eleven-year-old boy's recognition of the horrors of the adult world—is such a resonant one, the final effect of Malle's bracing, unencumbered directness is overwhelming. Rarely have audiences' tears been more honestly wrung.

Malle has explained in interviews that the real-life experiences behind this film were his motivation for becoming a film director, that he wanted to make the film as his first but felt he could do the subject justice only now. (It's the first film he's directed in France in ten years.)

This probably explains why *Au Revoir les Enfants,* set in a provincial Catholic boarding school at the end of World War II, seems like a culmination of the themes Malle has dealt with in the past in movies like *Lacombe, Lucien* and *Murmur of the Heart.* Everything comes together in this film: bourgeois japery, Catholicism, mother love, guilt, and collaboration. And yet we never feel as if we're watching a compendium. Rather, we appear to be tapping into the source of Malle's inspiration. It's easy to understand why Malle considers this story the archetype for his artistry.

At the beginning of the film, eleven-year-old Julien (Gaspard Manesse) and his older brother, François (Stanislas Carre de Malberg), say goodbye to their mother after the Christmas holidays and take the train back to boarding school. There, a new boy, Jean Bonnet (Raphael Fejto), one of three new arrivals, is quartered in Julien's dormitory. Julien and his classmates don't make things easy for Bonnet—they taunt him at recess, call him "Easter Bonnet." The pranks have the usual cruel harmlessness of a boys' club initiation, but Bonnet doesn't seem at all interested in being initiated.

He's a loner in a special, unexpressed sort of way, a way that begins to seem exotic to Julien. Like his classmates, Julien is an upper-class kid with a smart sense of privilege; he's a pint-size custodian of his own good fortune. But Bonnet's sense of inner privilege seems more rooted—there's something else besides money at work here.

At first Julien resents Bonnet, who effortlessly challenges his academic superiority: Bonnet is a math whiz, a voracious reader—he's even an adept pianist. But there's nothing show-offy about Bonnet, and that probably rankles Julien most of all. In his boy's view of things, Bonnet is snubbing him by so matter-of-factly expressing his talents.

It's as if Bonnet didn't care enough about his competition to flaunt his gifts.

Malle structures the movie as a kind of boy's-book detective story, but with an adult's perspective. Gradually it becomes clear to Julien that Bonnet, along with the two older new students, are Jews in hiding from the Gestapo. (Bonnet's real surname is Kippelstein.) Julien holds onto his little secret for a while, as if to warm himself with it. When he finally tips Bonnet off that he knows, the boys tussle, and the subject is never brought up again. Bonnet's remoteness, which the other children interpret as snobbishness, has a blanked-out, stupefied quality; he's trying to understand his intimate inclusion in the war's vast machinery of hate.

One reason Julien never brings up Bonnet's Jewishness again is that he doesn't really know what to *do* with the revelation. He knows nothing of the horrors lying in wait for the Jews, only that they are, somehow, marked as undesirables.

In one scene near the end, when Julien and Bonnet have become tentative, mutually respectful friends, Julien reads to Bonnet a hot passage from a contraband copy of *Arabian Nights*. For Julien, Bonnet's Jewishness is part of the same fantasy-world exotica. When Bonnet joins Julien and his mother and brother for dinner during parents' visiting day, Julien toys out loud with the misbegotten notion that his family may have a Jewish aunt. He's tickled by the subterfuge of being Jewish.

In that same restaurant scene, Malle stages a confrontation between some Vichy collaborators and an old gentleman, a regular customer eating alone at the table across from Julien who turns out to be Jewish. The collaborators are shouted down by the patrons, even by a table of German soldiers.

The sequence, like several other confrontations with "the enemy" in the film, has a deliberate clumsiness. The French collaborators are so primed to accommodate the Germans that they've become walking parodies of their captors: The Germans scoff at their absurdity. All the military maneuvers that intrude on the boys' cloistered world have the same dumb play-act frightfulness, as if the war outside were simply a more cumbersome, adult version of the school's color wars.

Julien is obviously meant to be Malle as a young boy, but the characterization is free of the moody nostalgia that tenderizes most artists' self-portraits. Gaspard Manesse is an extraordinary little actor, and his face is ideal for the role: You can see how his features are being shaped by his intelligence. There's an acuity, a principled defiance, in his look.

And a touch of vanity, too. When he clucks to himself in amazement, "I'm the only one in this school who thinks of death," we can laugh at his fatuousness. The true terror of death hasn't even hit him yet: he's just being fancy and self-absorbed.

Julien hints early on that he wants to become a priest, and one suspects it's because the Catholic Church appeals to his sense of privileged pomp. But also, it appeals to his decency, the same decency that eventually comes out in his friendship with Bonnet.

In one of the most remarkable scenes in the film, the school's headmaster, Father Jean (Philippe Morier-Genoud), delivers a sermon to the boys' assembled families, derived from St. Paul, about the necessity for Christian charity. (Some of the well-to-do parents storm out, feeling under attack.) Julien has absorbed the enlightenments of his teachers; it's no accident that the priests of *this* school chose to hide the Jews.

There's another remarkable scene in the film where the priests show Chaplin's silent short *The Immigrant* to the kids, with a live piano and violin accompaniment. The sequence goes on for a long time — too long, I thought at first. But Malle is right to keep the scene going. It's the only time in the film when all the boys' hopes, and the priests', are raised at once. It's the only time we see them unified by a common purity of feeling, and you want the moment to last forever, because you know it can't. It's the only time we see Bonnet laugh — this same boy who, later, when asked by Julien whether he's ever afraid, replies, "All the time."

This scene carries over into the rest of the film like a piano chord held by a pedal until it gradually fades away. The sequence fades into the terror of the final moments, when the Gestapo moves in. Malle is summoning up a nightmare for us piece by piece; the linkage of events has a nauseating inevitability. We can see in Julien's stricken, benumbed face that he will never forget what he is seeing, that he will spend his whole life trying to comprehend its horror. *Au Revoir les Enfants* is Malle's attempt to comprehend, and it's an epitaph, too. It ranks with the greatest films to come out of France since the war that spawned its sad story.

— Peter Rainer

Louis Malle

■

ZAZIE DANS LE MÉTRO (1960)

Movies are said to be an international language, but sometimes a film that is popular in one country finds only a small audience in another. This anarchistic, impudent comedy (From Raymond Queneau's novel), a great success in France in 1960, was hardly heard of in the United States. The film, which is like a Mack Sennett two-reeler running wild, seemed to be peculiarly disturbing for American critics and audiences alike. To Americans, *Zazie* seemed to go too far—to be almost demonic in its inventiveness, like a joke that gets so complicated you can't time your laughs comfortably. The editing, which is very fast, may be too clever; some critics have suggested that for Americans this comedy sets off some kind of freakish, fantastic anxiety. Putting it as squarely as possible, Bosley Crowther wrote in the *Times:* "There is something not quite innocent or healthy about this film." Yet it's like *Alice in Wonderland:* Zazie (Catherine Demongeot) is a foul-mouthed little cynic, age eleven, who comes to Paris for a weekend with her uncle (Philippe Noiret), a female impersonator, and nobody and nothing are quite what they seem. Louis Malle, who directed, includes satirical allusions to *La Dolce Vita* and other films, and a parody of his own *The Lovers.* Many of the modern styles in film editing, which were generally thought to derive from Alain Resnais or Richard Lester, have an earlier source in *Zazie.*

—Pauline Kael

Jean-Pierre Melville

■

BOB LE FLAMBEUR (1955)

Montmartre, in Paris, isn't just a district. It's a geographical joke, a cautionary tale, a moral metaphor made of plazas and trees and crooked little houses. At the top, the church known as Sacré Coeur casts its aura of snowy rectitude, but the streets of Montmartre wind downhill from there. And they end at Pigalle, home of strip shows and streetwalkers, nightclubs and bars. Between that chilly heaven and that seductive hell live the artists, or so tradition has it—the ones who are supposed to navigate moral ascents and descents. And there, too, according to *Bob le Flambeur,* lives Bob Montagné (Roger Duchesne), in a roomy apartment with a grand view of Sacré Coeur—and a slot machine hidden in the closet.

Flambeur means "gambler," and Bob is the king of gamblers. In his Bogie-style Stetson and trenchcoat, he rules the dawn, wandering from one Pigalle bar to the next, greeting his gangland courtiers, rolling dice here and anteing up there: known and welcome wherever bets are placed. Bob pulled his last big robbery years ago (at the Rimbaud bank, the movie giggles). He did time for it, and now he's friendly with cops as well as robbers. Everyone knows Bob would never squeal about a job, or encourage a risky one. Everyone knows he hates pimps, and everyone knows he can be relied on to give advice or help you out of a jam. His protégé, Polo (Daniel Cauchy), takes a lot of ribbing for trying to emulate Bob, but no one blames him. Suave and silver-haired, Bob does everything right: he understands how to enter a room, how to order a drink, and how to ask a lady to dance. The paradox of Montmartre is Bob's paradox, too: he's a moral hood, an outlaw with the rigorous ethics of a monk.

Made in 1955, but released in the United States in 1982 for the first time, Jean-Pierre Melville's wonderful *Bob le Flambeur* begins by entrancing us. We're in Pigalle, at dawn, and Melville's in love with the way the dawn looks to someone who's been up all night. The neon signs blink out, and a street-cleaning truck taxis through a square. A charwoman rushes off to work, an American sailor invites a pretty young French girl for a motorcycle ride, and in the bars, a lone vibes player toys with the movie's melancholy theme. The cinematographer, Henri Decaë, had made his debut on Melville's first feature, *Le Silence de la Mer* (1947), and would go on to be one of the finest cinematographers of the New Wave, but by 1955, he was already a master. Using Tri-X black-and-white film, he creates a gambler's world of pewter skies and glassy streets; his grays are woolly and his whites soft, and his black tones have a sexy obsidian luster. The cruel shadows in the American gangster movies and film noirs that Melville admired have turned sleek and glamorous here; the music is jazzy, but with a French twinkle. In fact, Melville's entire approach to the gangster picture was peculiarly, deliciously French. When American directors (many of them German immigrants) made crime movies, they drew chilling portraits of a corrupt urban world, but Melville was a movie nut who'd fallen in love with that world, who found the creepy alleys inviting, and the hard-bitten loneliness of Bogie and Alan Ladd enviable. His Paris nightworld is as strange and luminous as Brassai's, but it doesn't have Brassai's hothouse evil: here the cops are intelligent and the hoods jaunty, lovable, even avuncular. Shooting runty buildings from down low, so they'd seem taller, Melville tried to make Paris look like New York. And the harsh angles American filmmakers used to jar audiences with have been set aright; Melville's angles may be odd, but they're soothing and balanced, and his sudden close-ups reassure. Light, funny, and romantic, *Bob le Flambeur* is the American crime movie no American could have made: it turns the mean streets into a fairyland.

Like Bob Montagné, Jean-Pierre Melville affected American Stetsons and raincoats, and like Bob, he gradually came to be regarded as a father figure. Born Jean-Pierre Grumbach, in 1917 (he renamed himself after his favorite American author), he was an Alsatian Jew, and a film buff almost from birth. At the age of five, he already owned a projector, and at the age of six, he acquired a hand-cranked camera; at seven, he made his first movie, and he kept making them throughout his teens. In 1937, he was drafted; when he reentered civilian life in 1945, after stints in the French, English, and Gaullist armies, he immediately set out to join the French film industry. No one would hire him. So he formed his own production company and made a short subject, *Vingt-quatre Heures de la Vie d'un Clown.* The movie was a minor success, but Melville was still refused a union card (and hence any chance of a job). In 1947, he made his first feature anyway: *Le Silence de la Mer,* from a Vencors short story. He had obtained neither the rights to the story nor a production permit — he was unstoppable.

Le Silence de la Mer was about a French girl who falls in love with the aristocratic Wehrmacht officer billeted in her home; told without dialogue (the girl's uncle provides voice-over narration), it's a forbiddingly austere work, set in the sort of cramped, stifling rooms that would become a Melville trademark. Scarcely anyone saw it, but Robert Bresson did. (Melville would later say, "I sometimes read, 'Melville is being Bressonian.' . . . I'm sorry, but it's Bresson who has always been Melvillian.") And Jean Cocteau saw it, too; in 1949, he asked Melville to direct the screen adaptation of his play *Les Enfants Terribles,* a spooky, claustrophobic study of incest, disorder, and sexual violence. *Les Enfants Terribles* remains Melville's best-known film (it's one of the very few that can be seen in this country), but it wasn't until 1955 and *Bob le Flambeur* that the director hit his stride. He would go on to make a series of brilliantly stylized gangster films—*Le Doulos* (1962), *Le Deuxième Souffle* (1966), *Le Samourai* (1967), *L'Armée des Ombres* (1969), and so forth—starring such big-name French actors as Jean-Paul Belmondo and Alain Delon. By the time he died in 1973, of cancer, he had achieved not a place in the French mainstream but a cultish glory: he had become known as the father of the French New Wave.

Not that Melville actually spawned the New Wave, or even shared its enthusiasms. Like the young critics who would later become the New Wave directors—Truffaut, Godard, Chabrol, and the others—Melville adored American movies, but his favorite auteurs were the glossy, classical directors the young French critics despised, especially William Wyler and Robert Wise. And though Melville's unshakable independence—his ability simply to tramp out into the streets of Paris with a cameraman and a few actors and make a movie—inspired the New Wave directors, Melville himself hated the shaggy spontaneity of their early films. According to Melville's protégé, the German director Volker Schlöndorff, "he was terribly sarcastic when discussing the amateurish style of the New Wave filmmakers. . . . He kept up a friendly relationship with many of them—especially Godard and Chabrol, who visited him often—but they would drive him to the brink of despair when they disregarded his freely offered advice. He believed in certain rules and followed them precisely. Every shot could be shot only *one* way; anything else was 'wrong.' Exacting and pedantic, he measured who had to look left or right, and, even more so, the precise angle, whether over the shoulder or not, etc. Hand-held cameras, under- and over-exposures, and zoom shots he considered cheap tricks, a sign of incompetence—or even worse."

But Melville's influence on the most important early New Wave film, Godard's *Breathless,* is unmistakable. He even appears in it, as the celebrity who tells Jean Seberg it's his ambition to become immortal and then to die. Bob Montagné is mentioned in passing, and in that famous moment when Godard's gangster, Poiccard (Jean-Paul Belmondo), looks at a poster, fingers his lip, and sighs, "Bogie," Godard pays homage not just to a great American prototype but also to the scene in *Bob le Flambeur* when Bob looks into a mirror, sees his Bogie-like image reflected back at him, and remarks, "Good-looking crook."

But *Bob le Flambeur* has none of the psychological probing, the literary references, the pessimism, or the profundity of *Breathless*. Written by Melville with Auguste le Breton, who wrote *Rififi*, it's a caper movie, and a racy, elegant exercise in style. You don't see into Bob, the way you see into Poiccard, and that's only partly because Roger Duchesne is not the actor Belmondo is. A husky, world-weary sort who had enjoyed minor success in French films of the thirties, Duchesne doesn't penetrate his character because he doesn't have to: Melville understood that his audience would know Bob intimately almost from the moment he walked on screen. Duchesne needed only to fill the part—to look good in a raincoat, to cock his eyebrow, to seem tough when circumstances warranted, and to soften up when a pal needed sympathy or a lady was in distress. If Belmondo's Poiccard is a crook who wants to live a Bogart movie, Duchesne's Bob is a crook who can't help living one. He's a French imitation, but he seems an original, because he has the placid grace and integrity of a man who's completely unself-conscious. Bob never reflects, never worries, never doubts. He simply stays up all night and gambles. He does what a Bob Montagné would do.

Bob le Flambeur is about what happens when its hero goes out of character. A bit down on his luck, Bob enlists his sweet-tempered pal Roger (André Garet, who looks a lot like Edwin Newman) to help him rob the plush Deauville casino: it's an impossible heist, but it could set them up for life. We sense the scheme is doomed, however, when Roger makes Bob promise not to gamble until the job's been carried off. Bob agrees, and almost immediately he starts making mistakes. He trusts an untried kid, Polo, who inadvertently betrays him. Worse, he lets a woman into his life, a sensual, insouciant teenager (Isabelle Corey) who's slowly drifting toward prostitution. And in the end, only one thing can save him: a return to his true nature—a mad bout of obsessive gambling.

In filming *Bob le Flambeur,* Melville thought he was creating a moral cinema. "A man of the cinema must choose between the way of the documentarian and that of the moralist," he said. "I have chosen the latter. I have a fear of aesthetics and, personally, prefer ethics." Above all, he admired the ethical explorations of the American western. "I have transposed them and placed them in the underworld," he declared. And it's true that the central topic of the great westerns is morality: in a lawless wilderness, they ask, what are manliness and heroism, goodness and justice? In classic westerns like *Ride the High*

Country, The Wild Bunch, The Searchers, The Tin Star, and *The Far Country,* we watch how men grapple with these questions, and how they shiver from the clash of the moral forces inside them. But Bob doesn't shiver, doesn't grapple, doesn't question. He's an icon, and he has the code of ethics proper to an icon. He's a big tipper. He's generous to his friends when they need dinner or a loan. He's gentle with women, and, like many a gumshoe and many a cowboy, he prizes his independence from them (and here, as in so many American genre pictures, women are betrayers, easily overpowering the men who surrender to them). In fact, he doesn't trust alliances of any sort; being a loner is part of his code. In a typical exchange, the wily, likable police inspector (Guy Decomble) explains his friendship with Bob. Montagné, he says, saved his life once, knocking the inspector out of a gunman's line of fire. Why? The inspector isn't sure. Maybe because Bob knew the inspector was unarmed. Or maybe just to keep the gunman from getting the maximum sentence.

That certainly *sounds* ethical, but its very vagueness exposes the way Melville has misread his own work. Bob is loyal, brave, and honorable, and Solomonic in his wisdom, but he never makes the sort of clear, shattering choices—between friendship and family, for instance, or between righteousness and justice, or between the mob and the law— that deepen the great westerns. The ethics of *Bob le Flambeur* carry no more weight than Bob's costumes; in this movie, style is morality. And perhaps that's the only morality a rigid fatalist like Melville could believe in. Fate controls nearly all his characters, from Bob, with his commitment to a heist he suspects is doomed, to Alain Delon's cold-hearted gunman in *Le Samourai,* marching toward a violent death because he knows it's his destiny. And to Melville, the fate of a gangster-movie hero is inseparable from his style or his morality: it's part of the form he occupies, just as his Cadillac and his chivalrous manners are. A man has no choice; if he's in a gangster picture, he looks a certain way, behaves a certain way, and dies a certain way. Genre is destiny—and ethics. In fact, Melville's films express a philosophy that only a Frenchman could have dreamed up—and only a movie-mad Frenchman at that: it's genre existentialism.

Now I don't think genre existentialism is capable of producing moral profundities, but in Melville's hands, it certainly produces enchantment. I'd go back to see *Bob le Flambeur* again for the soundtrack alone. Eddie Barclay and Jean Boyer's music is full of emotional layers: bright accordion passages float by as if from a passing carnival (or a Fellini movie); themes disappear into a thicket of film noir strings only to reemerge as swirls of cocktail piano; in one scene, while Polo scurries past Pigalle's various nightclubs, we hear colliding snatches of hot jazz and rhumba music—it's like a Charles Ives miniature. This isn't just a crime movie, it's a little art object; you want to touch it, to hold it in your hand. And if it isn't quite a great film, it's an inspiring one. *Bob le Flambeur* makes you feel the way the New Wave directors must have felt watching it—as though anybody who loved movies with all his heart could take a camera out into the streets and capture the mysterious beauty waiting there.

— *Stephen Schiff*

Jean-Pierre Melville

■

LE DOULOS (1962)

Bob le Flambeur celebrates the debonair romanticism of an aging gambler's mist-and-neon ideals—halfway between the lofty trams scaling Montmartre and the garish bars of Pigalle, Melville's *Le Doulos* (*The Stoolie*) celebrates the tougher romanticism of the sly hood played by Jean-Paul Belmondo. As a lithe, double-dealing gangster trying to stay one step ahead of the game of life, Belmondo equals his role as the amoral, Bogart-imitating hood in Godard's *Breathless*.

Knowing existence is shifty, Belmondo's Silien responds with his own shape-shifting. A friend of criminals and cops, he's both a thief and a squealer, a seller of safecracking tools and a guy who eludes police interrogation by feigned friendliness and feigned threats. Melville's story shocks you with its sudden twists: chummy scenes that turn out to be murder scenes; a flirtation that turns out to be information extortion. In the biggest twist at the end of the movie, a simple phone call is the world's suavest good-bye and a simple glance in the mirror is the ultimate in foolhardy, heroic, deadly, death-defying self-definition as you discover that the director himself has been a stoolie and that life itself is the real double-crosser.

— *Kathy Schulz Huffhines*

Jean-Pierre Melville

■

LES ENFANTS TERRIBLES (1949)

The director, Jean-Pierre Melville, expands Cocteau's novel about the shared disorder and confused narcissism of a brother and sister into a baroque tragicomedy. The movie glides along, gathering intensity, as the characters move—compulsively, as in a dream—toward self-destruction. With Nicole Stéphane, fiercely elegant as the dominating Elisabeth; Edouard Dermithe as Paul; Renée Cosima as Dargelos and Agatha; Jacques Bernard as Gérard. Almost voluptuous in its evocation of temperament and atmosphere, this film was shot, on a shoestring, in "real" settings—the director's flat, the lobby of the *Petit Journal,* the stage of the Théâtre Pigalle. When Melville was ill, Cocteau directed the summer beach scene in Montmorency, under snow. Cocteau also provides cryptic, emblematic narration. The music (Bach-Vivaldi) is one of the rare effective film usages of great music. (Melville appeared in *Breathless* as the celebrity being interviewed.) Cinematography by Henri Decaë.

—Pauline Kael

Nikita Mikhalkov

■

AN UNFINISHED PIECE
FOR A PLAYER PIANO (1977)

More filmed Chekhov? Another collection of doomed gentlefolk, forever on their way nowhere. Desuetude, pathos, decay: is this something we need now?

Ah, but Nikita Mikhalkov's *An Unfinished Piece for a Player Piano* is great and definitive Chekhov, so tenderly funny and beautiful that it leaves a stain on your memory like raspberries on a linen napkin. A lyrical film, in which actors, screenplay, and production are knit into a consummate whole, *Unfinished Piece* reinforces Mikhalkov's place as one of the world's great younger directors, as if that fact needed reinforcing after *Slave of Love* and *Oblomov*.

Mikhalkov, with coadapter Alexander Adabashian, has combined several short stories with Chekhov's early play *Platonov* and moved the action forward about thirty-five years. This places its aristocrats somewhere around 1910 where, if they listened attentively, they might pick up rumbles of the revolution to come. (Adabashian, besides being cowriter, also is listed as one of the film's two art directors; certainly a rare pairing of credits.)

It takes a little careful attention just at the beginning to puzzle out the relationships, but we get the characters sorted out at the country estate of a general's widow, the stunningly beautiful and lively Anna Petrovna (Antonia Shuranova). She is full of contrasts, an elegant woman who whistles like a sailor, a languid, amusing hostess whom one suitor admiringly describes as "emancipated with a vengeance. Kiss her arm and you get a whiff of gunpowder."

Anna Petrovna's weekend guests include her tall, blond-bearded stepson, Sergei (Yuri Bogatyrev), so enthralled with her that he calls her Maman. Sergei is something of a booby, which makes the fact that the ravishing Sophia has recently married him all the more astonishing. (Sophia is Elena Solovei of *Slave of Love* and *Oblomov*.)

On the premises is Dr. Triletsky (director Mikhalkov), a handsome, frightened man, uneasy in his profession, who covers his panic with wicked social behavior and brandy.

With the arrival of the crass landowner Pavel Shcherbuk, to whom noble birth and a pure race are bywords, a quartet of actors from *Oblomov* has been assembled. The portly Oleg Tabakov, so endearing in the title role of Oblomov, is a winner here as the aristocrat you love to hate. As Shcherbuk attempts to kiss her hand, Sophia and her husband explain proudly that they consider this demeaning, since Shcherbuk would not kiss a man's hand. Shcherbuk is stopped only briefly. A moment later he turns unexpectedly, seizes her hand and kisses it, laughing uproariously at her shocked reaction. It is like social rape.

Among the other arrivals are Platonov (Alexander Kalaigin), the village schoolteacher, a mordant, self-satisfied man about to turn thirty-five, and his silly goose of a wife (Eugenia Glushenko), innocent and adoring in her foolish, candy-box straw hat.

The estate may be falling upon bad times, yet to our eyes it is still spectacular. True, one of the remaining servants has to fish one of the splendid wicker chairs out of the pond, muttering angrily, "These nobles, they're worse than the peasants," yet the total effect is seductive—the house itself with its bare, high-ceilinged, scrubbed wooden porch, white linen curtains and unglazed pots of field flowers; the women in white lace drifts of dresses, the men in rumpled white linen suits, playing dangerous games of "forfeits" in the late-afternoon glow.

Romantic entanglements begin to surface, two of them centering around the schoolteacher Platonov. The most crucial is his rekindled ardor for the luminous Sophia, his love when they were idealistic students, she an actress, he a young poet. She is crushed, after she finally recognizes him, to discover the extent to which he has become stifled and suburban. On his part, he cannot believe she has settled for this mental pygmy, Sergei.

The film becomes a *Midsummer Night's Dream* of romantic encounters, brilliantly funny, wickedly revealing. Mikhalkov's camera flows around these dalliances with the ease of an Ophuls, with the same breathtaking beauty that set Mikhalkov's other films apart so distinctively.

Sardonic, insightful, and tender by turns, Chekhov-Mikhalkov have an eye for characters with unexpected reserves of strength or endearing quirks. Stepson Sergei is most certainly a fool, yet how can you resist him as he cries ecstatically to his beautiful wife: "Voltaire, you, and Maman—my life is complete."

Mikhalkov is not intimidated by the deepest level of Chekhovian intent, the famous *Cherry Orchard* stage direction which calls for "A distant sound . . . coming from the sky as it were, the sound of a snapping string, mournfully dying away." The film's magical sound is a yearning chord—used once, twice—which seems to fill the screen and then subside. Its second sound is exquisitely realistic: Bjoerling (standing in for Caruso), singing "Una furtiva lacrima" over the last moments, carrying them upward with the music.

At the film's end, as farcical melodrama turns into a touching demonstration of the strength of pure love, the weekend party assembles itself in the pink, misty dawn. "Nothing will change," Anna Petrovna mutters, a true enough prediction for this crowd. A glowing sun rises, yet surely for them it is a sun whose heat is vastly diminished.

But its rays are enough to wake the young boy who has been part of this group, yet aloof from it, a rail-thin youngster clearly intended to be the Russia of the future. He wakes and turns away from the light to sleep, leaving you to study his thin, bare shoulders, wondering if they are strong enough for the upheaval to come.

— Sheila Benson

Nikita Mikhalkov
■

A SLAVE OF LOVE (1984)

Nikita Mikhalkov's affectionate and sarcastic portrayal of the earliest prerevolutionary years of Soviet filmmaking. It's a movie on movies that really seethes with life and color: whirling, blazing, impish.

— Michael Wilmington

Sergei Paradjanov
■

OVERVIEW

We've encountered most of the visionary work of Sergei Paradjanov (1924–1990) at the rate of one film per decade; imagine what our perception of Van Gogh would be like if we saw only one of his paintings once every ten years. Fortunately, three of Paradjanov's films — perhaps his finest — are now available on video.

Born to poor Armenian peasants in Tbilisi, Georgia, he studied film with Eisenstein in the midforties and made all his early films in Ukrainian; roughly the first half of his work has never been exported. Our first glimpse of his genius comes in the ravishing *Shadows of Our Forgotten Ancestors* (1964), the film that also started his difficulties with Soviet authorities when he refused to dub the dialogue into Russian. Mystically pantheistic and lyrically exuberant, this love story about a rural woodsman in the Carpathians is a mixture of paganism, ritual, poetry, and dance driven by rapturous camera movements.

Returning to Tbilisi after nineteen years in Kiev, Paradjanov found all his projects blocked until he went to Armenia and made his second masterpiece, *Sayat Nova* (1968), about the celebrated Armenian poet, troubadour, and folk philosopher. Mainly shot in frontal tableaux bursting with juicy colors, this radical, enigmatic, erotic film was banned for two years and released only after another director recut it, but it still survives as Paradjanov's purest poetic work.

Arrested on multiple and mainly trumped-up charges (including "homosexual coercion") in 1973 and again in 1982, Paradjanov was forbidden to work for eleven years until he made *The Legend of Suram Fortress* in 1984, a medieval Georgian tale that resumes the ethnographic-ecstatic mode of his earlier work in yet another style. Finally allowed to travel to the West for the first time in 1988, this wizened Mr. Natural was able to make only one more feature before he died a couple of years later.

—*Jonathan Rosenbaum*

Pier Paolo Pasolini

▪

OVERVIEW

The critical neglect in the U.S. suffered by an Italian filmmaker as important as Pier Paolo Pasolini (1922–75) undoubtedly stems in part from the fact that he was in equal measure a Christian, a Marxist, and a homosexual—not to mention an intellectual who was fully aware of the contradictions inherent in being all of these things at once. It isn't surprising that the serious attempts in his work to reconcile these three identities often created a scandal—compounded by the fact that roughly half his features were adaptations of classics in world literature. But what is often overlooked is the degree to which this poet, novelist, theorist, and essay writer remained in the forefront of modern European cinema throughout his career. The mentor of Bernardo Bertolucci and the favorite living director of Sergei Paradjanov, he remains a vital and challenging figure whose collected works—including, paradoxically, his movies set in the remote past—constitute a dramatic and persuasive vision of the contemporary world.

Fortunately, most of Pasolini's major work is available on video, including all of the features described below. Beginning in film as a scriptwriter (on such films as Fellini's *Nights of Cabiria*), he started out in *Accatone* (*The Scrounger,* 1961) as a radical stepson of neorealism by adapting one of his own novels, *A Violent Life*—a passionate account of a pimp living in Pigneto, a squalid suburb of Rome where Pasolini had himself lived during the forties. Inspired by the frescoes of Masaccio and Giotto, Pasolini gives notice at the outset that his intention isn't merely to reproduce life as he sees it, but to render it with a sense of poetry and gravity that can only be described as religious.

Indeed, he first attained worldwide notoriety with his stark and unconventional *The Gospel According to St. Matthew* (1964), available on video in both dubbed and subtitled versions, which retells the story of Christ to the strains of Bach, Mozart, Prokofiev, Webern, African music, American blues and spirituals, and Russian revolutionary songs. His next feature, *Hawks and Sparrows* (1964)—a comic free-form essay in the form of a picaresque journey taken by an old friar (Toto) and a young novice (Pasolini regular Ninetto Davoli), accompanied by a talking raven—provides both an excellent introduction to Pasolini's work and one of his finest inventions. A delightful, provocative adventure that is set alternatively—and at times simultaneously—in the year 1200 and the present, it is the only film that comes to mind which starts off with singing credits, and it clearly gives the lie to any suspicions that Pasolini's underlying seriousness was uninflected by any sense of fun or wit.

Beginning in the ancient past and ending in the present, Pasolini's powerful *Oedipus Rex* (1967) may well be the strongest of all his classical adaptations, although his subsequent encounters with Greek tragedy, both completed in 1970—a *Medea* featuring the only film performance of Maria Callas (in a nonsinging part), and *Notes for an African Oresteia,* a short feature with an original score by Gato Barbieri—should also be noted.

The controversial and pungent *Teorema* (*Theorem,* 1968) probably remains the most influential of all of Pasolini's films. It grew out of notes for a verse tragedy that also yielded a novel written partially in verse, and it describes the arrival of a divine visitor (Terence Stamp) in a contemporary bourgeois household, his subsequent seduction of all four family members and the maid (Massimo Girotti, Silvano Mangano, Anne Wiazemsky, Andrès José Cruz Soublette, and Laura Betti), and the subsequent traumas and convulsions created by his no less mysterious departure.

Significantly, *Teorema* was Pasolini's last feature with a contemporary setting. Loathing everything that the modern world had become, he turned next in his acclaimed "trilogy of life" to a celebration of guiltless paganism in other eras, beginning with an erotic *Decameron* (1970), continuing with the scatological *Canterbury Tales* (1971), and ending with his very carnal and sensuous *Arabian Nights* (1974). He then concluded his career, before being brutally murdered, with his most extreme film, *Salo* (1975), an adaptation of *The 120 Days of Sodom* that transposes the Marquis de Sade's eighteenth-century novel to fascist Italy in 1944. As Pasolini described his intentions in a self-interview, "Aside from the metaphor of the sexual relationships (obligatory and ugly), which the tolerance of consumeristic power imposes on us nowadays, all the sex in *Salo* (and there is an enormous quantity of it) is also a metaphor for the relationship between power and those who are subjected to it."

—Jonathan Rosenbaum

Roman Polanski
■

REPULSION (1965)

Repulsion more than lives up to its title. It also affords grisly evidence that thirty-two-year-old Polish director Roman Polanski, who won fame with *Knife in the Water,* is no slash-in-the-pan wonder boy but an imaginative and perverse master of the dark art of menace. Polanski's first English-language film, *Repulsion,* at first glance looks like a case study of a fragile psychopath. At second glance, or as often as a moviegoer can bear to peek through his knotted fingers, it is a Gothic horror story, a classic chiller of the *Psycho* school and approximately twice as persuasive.

The heroine, played with exquisite, deadly grace by Catherine Deneuve—the radiant waif of *Umbrellas of Cherbourg*—is a French manicurist working in London. Her days pass among the minimal terrors of a de luxe beauty salon where she helps refinish the surfaces of wealthy, parchment-faced matrons. In the street outside lies a world of hot-mouthed males whose attentions send her into panicky flight.

Every night in bed she waits, staring, petrified, until her uninhibited sister (Yvonne Furneaux) and a married lover come home to curdle a young girl's blood with their noisy nocturnal diversions.

The crisis point is reached when the lovers leave for a holiday in Italy, abandoning the sexually repressed girl to her fantasies. And never has the inch-by-inch descent into total madness been more startlingly recreated on film. Slowly, Polanski assembles the fragments of a nightmare mosaic. A man's undershirt, a razor, and a skinned rabbit on a platter become objects of dread. An oppressive silence is broken only by the buzzing of flies, dropping water, a ticking clock. Rooms change shape, the mere flip of a light switch creates fissures in the walls, a phantom ravisher begins to stalk the tiny flat.

Each grey morning, while the laughter of nuns echoes from a nearby courtyard, it becomes clearer that awful deeds are imminent. One day the girl takes a rabbit's severed head to work in her purse. The real and the unreal merge, and soon her human victims appear. The first is a suitor (John Fraser) whose conventional acts of gallantry lead to a gruesome end. Later an indignant landlord (played with mordant, bumbling humor by Patrick Wymark) comes to collect his rent and lingers to try his luck. Right up to the grisly climax, the audience seldom wonders what will happen, but endures agonies as to how and when.

In this simplified sexual interpretation of psychosis, no attempt is made to explain behavior except through the familiar device of a family portrait in which one sister stands aloof and stricken, while the other lies draped seductively over her father's knees. Writer-director Polanski nonetheless makes his fair murderess seem authentically tragic, herself the most pitiable victim of the evil she does. Whether such a film finally serves any purpose other than to scare people silly remains doubtful, yet in the long tradition of cinematic shockers, *Repulsion* looms as a work of monstrous art.

— *Bruce Williamson*

Roman Polanski

■

KNIFE IN THE WATER (1961)

Roman Polanski's *Knife in the Water,* made when he was twenty-eight, is the work of a wunderkind who grew up fast: it has the low-key wryness and technical assurance you expect from directors twice as old. This prickly, sinister, three-character movie — set mostly during a daylong sailboat journey on the lakes of Mazury, in Poland — is an unpredictable fusion of psychological drama and unromantic comedy.

When a well-off husband and wife (Leon Niemczyk, Jolanta Umecka) take on a student hitchhiker (Zygmunt Malanowicz) as a deckhand, sexual tension and masculine rivalry add fire to built-in class jealousies. Using all his worldliness and expertise, Niemczyk, a successful sports reporter, bullies both the buxom young Umecka and the woefully unseaworthy Malanowicz.

But *Knife in the Water* never becomes a triangle or crime-of-passion movie, even when the husband's two victims have sex. The film is about people trying to transcend a gnawing recognition of their limitations. Shortly before they couple, the wife tells the student, "You're just the same. Only younger by half, weaker, and twice as stupid." Polanski maintains a cool tone that still seems contemporary; no one leaves the water unscathed.

— *Michael Sragow*

Satyajit Ray

■

THE HOME AND THE WORLD (1984)

The imagery in the new Satyajit Ray film, *The Home and the World,* set in 1907 during the British partitioning of Bengal, has a deep-toned beauty that's suffused with the ancient. The yellows are the color of holy-book parchment, the greens and reds and blues in the drawing rooms and bedrooms seem burnished by time: they stand out with the clarity of fairy-tale illuminations. The colors in this movie seem drawn from an India that is slowly slipping from our eyes, and yet it is this India — this antiquity — that gives the imagery its extraordinary, mystical resonance. The glow comes from deep inside.

More than any other director, Satyajit Ray is aware of the talismanic power in the ordinary. It's not just the people in his film who carry mythic overtones; so do the objects — the chairs, tables, rugs, clothing. They carry an emotional weight out of all proportion to their placement on screen. A mystical collusion exists between the people in *The Home and the World* and the ornamental finery with which they surround themselves. Bimila (Swatilekha Chatterjee), the young wife of an East Bengal maharajah (Victor Banerjee), moves with the slow and sensual, fated sweep of ritual; when she opens her closet and runs her fingers through her saris, she's dipping into a magic box, and her dark hands blend with the burnished golds and reds like oil paints.

Married to Banerjee's Nikhil for ten years, Bimala is a traditional Indian wife, satisfied in her ritualized seclusion from the outside world (purdah). Since her arranged wedding, she has never moved beyond her husband's quarters in the country estate where he is landlord; she has never mixed with his friends or associates. Bimala is pampered, but she doesn't have the plush narcissism of a housebound queen. She's ample, yet ethereal, and her face is suffused with the beauty of the classic Indian heroines. Nikhil adores her; a Hindu and a liberal, he encourages her to learn to speak and sing English, meet his friends, move about the estate. The movie is adapted from a 1919 Rabindranath Tagore novel, and Nikhil incarnates one of the great poet-philosopher's credos: "The broad mind is not afraid of accepting truth from all sources." Nikhil accepts those sources as a privilege of life.

When Sandip (Soumitra Chatterjee), a college friend of Nikhil's, arrives at the estate, Nikhil arranges for him to meet his wife for the first time, after only hearing her praises sung for ten years. Sandip is a political firebrand who stirs audiences with his ringing, cadenced speeches denouncing the British colonial policy of divide and rule that will split Bengal into two rival administrative units of Hindus and Moslems. He leads his followers in the cheer "Hail, Motherland!" and promotes the boycotting of foreign-made goods among the estate's poverty-stricken Moslem tenants — even though no adequate, cheaply priced Indian substitutes for these goods exist. (That's one of many reasons why Nikhil opposes Sandip's tactics.)

Nikhil's motivation in introducing Sandip to Bimala is, on the surface, impeccable: He wants his wife to break out of purdah. But we sense Nikhil's deeper motive. How can he be sure his wife truly loves him if she has never been exposed to other men? He prizes Bimala, but the unreality of his situation gnaws at him; he suspects his bliss may be counterfeit. And so he introduces Bimala to Sandip even though (or, rather, precisely because) Sandip is a galvanizing presence and a known womanizer. Sandip is everything Nikhil believes himself not to be.

Is Nikhil also unconsciously inflaming some private urge for self-destruction here? Perhaps, and that possibility gives the movie a darker psychological tone. But if Nikhil's selflessness is tinged with masochism, it also has an element of awe. There's a dazzle in his eyes as he introduces Bimala to Sandip: To be preferred by his wife in the face of such temptation will surely send him into a state of grace. Nikhil is looking for both confirmation and benediction in his marriage.

Ray shows us Bimala's unfolding entrancement with the outside world, which, to Nikhil's despair, comes to be personified by Sandip. Bimala watches Sandip's torch-lighted orations through a lattice, her face striped in shadow, and she's stirred — without fully realizing it. Even though Ray is spiritually, and politically, in sympathy with Nikhil (as Tagore also was), he doesn't deny Bimala's wonder. When she walks for the first time through the doors that lead into another part of the estate, where Sandip awaits, Ray shows us her passage in a slight slow motion that mythologizes the moment; the hallway, with its gimcrack ornamentation, seems bright and candied, like a gingerbread house.

It's a child's storybook tableau, and because we perceive the passage through Bimala's wonderstruck eyes, the tableau is entirely appropriate. Ray moves us through the film with a trenchancy that makes each scene a revelation. The Tagore novel was written in a diary format, with each of the principals contributing his or her story in sections. Ray achieves a similar result on film by shifting the film's viewpoint among the three players, so that we indulge the sympathies of each in turn. The actors are so extraordinary that the sympathy never wavers. Their melancholy is almost a state of grace. With their great generosity, Swatilekha Chatterjee and Victor Banerjee (Dr. Aziz in *A Passage to India*) and Soumitra Chatterjee (a Ray veteran) are the ideal actors for Ray, who is among the most humanely compassionate — humanely *fair* — of directors.

So was Jean Renoir, who encouraged Ray as a young man about to embark on his first film: *Pather Panchali.* Renoir's oft-quoted response to those who asked him why his movies never contained villains was: "Everyone has his reasons." And so it is with Ray as well. It would have been easy to portray Sandip as a viper, but Ray understands his posturings (which is not the same thing as endorsing them). We see how Sandip bedazzles Bimala and, in so doing, bedazzles himself—the mark of a true narcissist.

We also see through him, with such clarity that he achieves the clownish poignance of a posturer who, finally, cannot live up to his own fantasy image. He's right to appeal to Indian nationalism but wrong (and obnoxiously self-serving) in his methods. When the poor reject his plea to stop buying foreign goods, he resorts to terrorism: sinking boats, torching crops. Because Nikhil is Sandip's friend, the poor, with their ancient, enraged faces, believe he is equally responsible. Sandip puts his friend's life in danger, but neither he nor the poor understand Nikhil's true gambit. Nikhil can't even ask Sandip to leave, because he knows his wife (or his wife's heart: same thing) would follow. His life is bound up totally with his love for his wife, and he demonstrates this in a final act of supreme romanticism—which is, of course, an act of supreme folly.

Like so many of Ray's films, *The Home and the World* can be viewed as a meditation on the mysteries of women. When Bimala is together with Sandip and Nikhil for the first time, Sandip flatters her with high-flown prattle about women's intuition. And yet Ray is in awe of women himself. For him, women are ineffably linked to the pull of the past; they glow with an aureole of antiquity. Ray shows us India as a palimpsest—the past is everywhere in the present. And women personify this past-in-the-presentness; they emblematize Ray's vision of life.

When she's viewed in this way, it's not surprising that Bimala, as simple as she appears, is nevertheless resonant with mystery. Sandip, with his virile beard and hortatory beguilements, is the male as posturer—the man whose mystery turns out to be that he has no mystery. Nikhil, on the other hand, has a fine-drawn beauty and a highly delicate sensitivity, as if his soul were embossed with gold leaf. In the movie's terms, he has a feminized spirituality (for Ray, that phrase would be redundant). Nikhil has the "women's intuition" that Sandip applauds in Bimala, and what he intuits about his wife drives him to despair.

At the end, Nikhil and Bimala face each other with an intensity that appears to merge them. They are more than husband and wife at this point; they're soulmates in the most transcendent of senses. When he leaves her in the night to meet the furious mobs, Bimala's soul is halved, and in the final harrowing close-ups of her ruined face, each slight shift is like a rent in the heavens. This is a major movie by one of the world's major artists.

—Peter Rainer

Satyajit Ray
■

PATHER PANCHALI (1955)

This first film (variously translated as *Song of the Road, The Lament of the Path,* etc.) by the masterly Satyajit Ray—possibly the most unembarrassed and natural of directors—is a quiet reverie about the life of an impoverished Brahman family in a Bengali village. Beautiful, sometimes funny, and full of love, it brought a new vision of India to the screen. Though the central characters are the boy Apu (who is born near the beginning) and his mother and father and sister, the character who makes the strongest impression on you may be the ancient, parasitic, storytelling relative, played by the eighty-year-old Chunibala, a performer who apparently enjoyed coming back into the limelight after thirty years of obscurity—her wages paid for the narcotics she used daily. As "auntie," she is so remarkably likable that you may find the relationship between her and the mother, who is trying to feed her children and worries about how much the old lady eats, very painful. Ray continued the story of Apu in *Aparajito* and *Apur Sansar* (*The World of Apu*), and the three films, all based on a novel by B. B. Bandapaddhay, became known as the Apu Trilogy. (Robin Wood's study, *The Apu Trilogy,* does the films justice.) Cinematography by Subrata Mitra; music by Ravi Shankar.

—Pauline Kael

Satyajit Ray

■

APARAJITO (1957)

The central film of Satyajit Ray's great Apu Trilogy is transitional in structure, rather than dramatic, but it's full of insights and revelations. Ray takes the broken family of *Pather Panchali* from its medieval village life to the modern streets of Benares and follows the boy Apu in his encounter with the school system, and, later, when he has left his mother, with the intellectual life at the University of Calcutta. (There is a luminous moment when Apu recites a poem in a classroom—you understand how it is that art survives in the midst of poverty.) The film chronicles the emergence of modern industrial India, showing it to be not a primitive society but a corrupted society. However, Apu himself embodies Ray's belief that individuals need not become corrupt. Music by Ravi Shankar.

—Pauline Kael

Satyajit Ray

■

THE WORLD OF APU (1959)

Satyajit Ray's protagonist, Apu, whose consciousness developed from the village life of *Pather Panchali* and the university in *Aparajito,* marries the exquisite Sharmila Tagore and grows beyond self-consciousness. Rich and contemplative, and a great, convincing affirmation. The full-grown Apu is played by the remarkable Soumitra Chatterjee, who starred in several other Ray films. Music by Ravi Shankar.

—Pauline Kael

Alain Resnais
■

NIGHT AND FOG (1955)

"This is not a film of reminiscence nor of hatred but of disquietude."

—Jean Cayrol, narrator of *Night and Fog.*

Time must be the ultimate judge of Alain Resnais's avant-garde feature films. Yet regardless of how the stream-of-consciousness of *Hiroshima Mon Amour* or the abstractness of *Last Year at Marienbad* holds up with the passing of the years, he will always be remembered for his thirty-one-minute *Night and Fog,* perhaps the most profound documentary on the Nazi concentration camps ever made. More timely than ever, this remarkable, award-winning movie is surely a landmark in film history. As evidence of Resnais's genius, it is more immediately convincing than any of his other films.

For what Resnais has accomplished is to wrest a work of art from the most terrible instance of man's inhumanity to man in history. He has put an aesthetic distance between the view and the subject that makes it possible to understand the pain of watching shot after shot of the victims of starvation and torture, yet feel the full significance of the insane slaughter. He achieves this by creating a structure of images whose complexity—and yes, beauty—anticipates his later films.

Throughout, the movie is composed of almost constant counterpoint—between voice and music, sound and image, still and motion pictures, black and white and color, past and present, living and dead. *Night and Fog*—the title was a term used by Hitler to describe the fate of certain persons who were to disappear into the night and fog without a trace even of their burial places—begins in the present and in color. As the camera tracks over Auschwitz today in its peaceful dereliction, the narrator begins to tell the story of the purpose, construction, and operation of the camps—a guided tour that is soon interrupted with flashbacks of marching soldiers and of Jews being herded into freight cars.

From here on, Resnais shifts between past and present. The color camera shows us more and more of Auschwitz—rows of rusty cremation furnaces looking as harmless as abandoned bakery ovens, barren laboratories for monstrous experiments, dilapidated barracks—intercutting these leisurely sequences with film clips showing the actual victims in the same settings.

At the beginning of the film, the beautiful, green fields of springtime and the crumbling structures themselves give us a reassuring sense that all this evil is past, but by the end — as Resnais piles on images of mute horror — our feelings have been reversed: Auschwitz's present appearance of decay now seems dangerously deceptive. We are left convinced that it could happen all over again.

In the making of this brief movie, which was based on Olga Wormser and Henry Michel's *The Tragedy of the Deportations,* Resnais had many assistants who were to work with him again and who were to become distinguished in their own right. The eloquent yet matter-of-fact narration was written and spoken by poet and novelist Jean Cayrol, a camp survivor who wrote the script for Resnais's most recent picture, *Muriel.*

One of the assistant directors was Chris Marker, a *cinéma-vérité* pioneer. (Editor's note: Marker is discussed in the chapter "Recommended from France" in this book.)

— *Kevin Thomas*

Alain Resnais

■

HIROSHIMA, MON AMOUR (1959)

When *Hiroshima, Mon Amour* electrified audiences at the 1959 Cannes Film Festival, Resnais became one of the brightest lights of the *nouvelle vague.* When I saw the movie in New York in 1960, its themes of loss and memory struck home with me with special force because I was still mourning my dead brother. Now, more than a quarter of a century later, watching it on videocassette, I must confess that it is not quite as stylistically startling nor emotionally explosive as it was back in the early sixties. But it remains a landmark of world cinema in many other ways.

The literary influence of author Marguerite Duras seems more pronounced now than it did back then. By now we have become more familiar with the one basic story Duras keeps retelling — of a young girl seduced at an early age and traumatically affected by a doomed, impossible love. But in 1960 many American art-house viewers were more affected by the movie's evocation of the horror of Hiroshima in the first part of the story than by the seemingly endless night of *amour* and the contemplation of *amour* that followed. On the surface, the politics of the movie seemed modishly leftist in the ironic French manner, but the major theme for Resnais — then and later — was memory and forgetfulness. His was a materialistic view of a world in which the mystical faith necessary for narrative is totally absent. That is why — then and now — the "plot" of *Hiroshima, Mon Amour* seems to backtrack, flash-forward, and otherwise meander so much.

As an artist, Resnais functions in the eternal present — since the images of people and places from the past exist only in the minds of present-day characters. Once we forget, we kill our beloved once and for all. The one-night liaison of a French actress and a Japanese architect was hot stuff in 1960 at a time when the Production Code still frowned on miscegenation. Even today Emmanuele Riva's unabashed sensuality projects the kind of grown-up "Continental" behavior that served for many of us years ago as a repudiation of Hollywood's coyness and evasiveness on the subject.

Ultimately, *Hiroshima, Mon Amour* is more an essay than a story. It is made up of many jagged fragments of memory and history that, for a time at least, made up a beautiful jigsaw puzzle. Anyone even remotely interested in the sheer art of the cinema cannot afford to pass up this work of exquisite taste and craftsmanship.

—Andrew Sarris

Alain Resnais

■

PROVIDENCE (1977)

Alain Resnais has been one of the art-house heavies since the turn of the sixties. Not one of the semipopular heavies, like Bergman, Truffaut, or Fellini, the filmmakers who can take pretty much for granted that their latest work is going to be bought by an American distributor and funneled into the major U.S. outlets without much delay. But a theoretical heavy, the kind of guy critics and buffs keep looking to to change the face of the art. Because he did that, once upon a time.

Hiroshima, Mon Amour (1959) and *Last Year at Marienbad* (1961) rewrote most of the going rules for treating time and memory, and levels of imaginative and objective reality, in the cinema. Indeed, time and memory virtually became Resnais's overriding subjects, through which he proceeded to approach problems of historical and political conscience and themes of personal guilt.

Resnais's impact was not confined to art-theater audiences and the little magazines. Other filmmakers were paying attention too — for Resnais's style was intoxicating, his technical command daunting — and even genre movies like *Point Blank* (the John Boorman-Lee Marvin gangster picture) began to reflect the influence.

Before the influences started showing up, Resnais's star had begun to descend. While his films were highly sensuous in an abstract way, they lacked the vigor, the cheekiness of his contemporaries Truffaut and Godard, the sense of commingled life- and movie-energy even art-house audiences respond to most readily and lastingly.

Providence is Resnais's newest film and his first in English. In it, the director is up to nothing new, which may be why the film comes to us with such a vehemently negative set of reviews from the East. Yet the nothing new, as filtered through a highly self-aware sensibility and two of the most lushly listenable instruments in the English-speaking cinema, has yielded an eminently pleasurable, very classy entertainment, for this viewer at least.

The camera, borne on a tide of tastefully epic film music, moves toward an ivy-shrouded gate and a plaque reading "PROVIDENCE," then lifts and pushes into the dim nocturnal precincts of an English estate. Above a side door, a light burns. In an antique bedchamber, a withered hand reaches for a wineglass, knocks it to the floor, and slams repeatedly onto the nighttable, each concussion accompanied by a "Damn! Damn! Damn! Damn!"

A helicopter passes between two cathedral towers. An old man, dressed in rags and literally covered with gray fur, scurries through underbrush as a machine gun–toting army patrol scours the woods. Dirk Bogarde turns to us in a bright courtroom and chirps, "Surely the facts are not in dispute!"

It is probably at that point that you either begin to delight in *Providence* or think about gathering up your overcoat and scuttling for the door. If you stay, you will learn (and I hate to reveal it in advance, so witty is the gradual disclosure) that the only "real" phenomenon on view, the agent of Providence, is a cancerous old English novelist (John Gielgud) whose rectal agonies and copiously bitter memories keep him awake on the night before his seventy-eighth birthday, trying out scenes, characters, situations for the novel he may not survive to write.

The leading characters are modeled on his offspring, in-laws, ghosts of the present and the past; but finally, they are all really modeled on the novelist himself. As his voice occasionally supplants one character's while an on-screen Bogarde or Ellen Burstyn or David Warner mouths the words, so do his personal quirks and guilts and desires take temporary residence in one corporeal host or another, frequently carrying on a dialogue among themselves.

This is a game (as *Marienbad* was a game), for the novelist and for Resnais, in which the rules are made up as we go along, and often recognized only after being broken and revised. It's a game that tells us a lot about the nature of human aspiration and the ways we delude, flatter, lacerate, rearm, and console ourselves. The characters play it in this movie, and Resnais, very genially, plays it in making this movie.

He has never played it more self-consciously. His movie materials gleefully percolate with Pirandellian richness: the sonorous self-parody of Gielgud's and Bogarde's readings; Gielgud's image as the Honored Artist; Bogarde's career iconography as tortured twit with a legacy of sexual queasiness; Warner's holy-geek heritage from *Morgan!* (the script is by *Morgan!* writer David Mercer); and by all means Miklos Rozsa's (here, knowingly) pompous orchestration.

Resnais so clearly enjoys sweeping along Rozsa's melodious line, listening to Sir John make night music of the fondest four-letter words in the language, showcasing the precision with which Bogarde does a puffy imitation of his former sleek self and then redeems the caricature as a wounded, hurtfully adaptable human being. "Aren't these guys marvelous?" the director seems to ask, as a connoisseur of fellow craftsmen; and as a vulnerable human being himself, "Isn't style brave?"

If you think you might enjoy seeing some immensely talented artists taking their pretentious public identities and making artful existential play out of them, get to *Providence* fast.

—*Richard T. Jameson*

Tony Richardson

■

THE ENTERTAINER (1960)

Hair parted in the middle and flared back in wavelets, smile fractured by a gap between two front teeth, face whitened, lips pursed, and eyebrows blackened—like an invisible man with features outlined by Etch-a-Sketch—Laurence Olivier's Archie Rice, the third-rate music hall song-and-dance comedian who's the title character of *The Entertainer* (1960), is a harrowing embodiment of the divided, decaying spirit of England at midcentury.

Olivier is at his mesmerizing peak in director Tony Richardson's volatile, gripping, heart-rending movie; Olivier himself preferred it to his and Richardson's original stage production of John Osborne's play. The greatest classical actor of our time was never more low-down and poetic, more brilliant and blatant, more graceful and crude, more eruptive and restrained than in this modern role.

Olivier turns the portrayal of a mediocrity into a feat. Even Archie's junky song-and-dance routines become fascinating failures—at first, Olivier gives them a loose-hipped bounce that falls just a few beats short of being as quirky and likable as Ray Bolger's.

But, amazingly, his performance doesn't come off as a stunt. It illuminates Osborne's acid text with excruciating elegance. The divisions that Olivier builds into both his physical makeup and his mindset reflect the breakdowns in the character's world. He tries to prolong the music-hall tradition—a tradition founded on a code of honor between a star and his fans—by goosing it, mocking it, making it play at any cost for a vaudeville/burlesque audience that moved on to other things (radio, TV, rock 'n' roll) and couldn't care less.

The white gloves he wears onstage give him a disconcerting resemblance to an animated character by Disney. However, there's nothing innocent or cartoonish about Archie.

He hopes he comes off as the Spirit of Music Hall Past, overflowing with warmth and humanity. He knows he's more like the Spirit of Music Hall to Come—a strutting skeleton. To Richardson and Osborne (who cowrote the script, with Nigel Kneale, from Osborne's play), Archie's downfall is tied to that of an England also reeling from a combination of outmoded traditions, shaky foundations, and unsatisfied appetites.

Archie, who struggles to keep a tacky nudie show going at a coastal resort town, represents both the last gasp and the final corruption of music hall theatrics, which, as Osborne wrote in a prefatory note to the published play, "was truly a folk art." Archie's father, Billy (Roger Livesey), was the sort of entertainer who could seem to be just like the people in the audience — "only," as he puts it, "more like them than they are themselves."

When Billy performs for his social club, you see that he and his fans hold an unshakable belief in the Empire and their own place in it. They still cheer a song that protests the dismantling of the Royal Navy. Although Osborne doesn't sentimentalize the old man, he respects the elder Rice's spirit and humanity; Billy's romantic courtliness and old-fashioned nationalism are true expressions of fraternity — and of what used to be called "national character."

When Archie's daughter, Jean, asks Billy if he's been to Archie's show, Billy remarks that audiences don't want "human beings" any more. Archie, when he's performing, isn't a human being — he's a deliberate parody of a human being. But Richardson and Osborne see Archie's dirty frivolity as something bred, in part, by his audiences. Archie may be what they deserve. That's why there's such a lingering air of menace when he signs off with "You've been a good audience. Very good. A very good audience. Let me know where you're working tomorrow night — and I'll come and see you."

Archie's condition resembles the dislocation we all feel when the soundtrack that's playing in our heads doesn't jibe with the action surrounding us. But as a performer, Archie can't accept that gap. He's on the firing line — and, unlike Billy, he has no laurels to fall back on. Archie's not a nostalgic presence; he resorts to cheesy lewdness. And just to keep going, he sacrifices his dignity, his family, and any hope he has of pure and simple gratification.

Joel Gray's demonic emcee in *Cabaret* owes something to Olivier's Rice, and so may Steve Martin's sheet-music salesman in *Pennies from Heaven*. But none has rivaled Olivier at expressing the nuances of hollowness, the intensity of a limited man's anguish.

Onstage Archie survives — barely — on his reflexes. Offstage he's more like the performer's alter ego than a full-bodied son, husband, or father. He manages to gull his kids by always acting the inveterate comedian; he gets by with his touchingly tipsy second wife, Phoebe (Brenda DeBanzie), because she thinks he's funny.

In one cold-blooded scene, Archie admits to Jean that her mother caught him in bed with Phoebe, resulting in divorce and remarriage. And he proves he's still a skirt-chaser when he beds a runner-up in a beauty-queen contest (played by Shirley Anne Field). Mostly, he wants her parents to bankroll a new show. Yet he flirts with the idea of marrying the young woman, without telling her he has a family.

For years, maybe decades, Archie has been living off the top of his head. The movie picks up on him as he drifts toward oblivion. To sensible Jean (Joan Plowright), a social worker, he seems to be lost in a fantasy land; his weaker, more impressionable son, Frank (Alan Bates), thinks that Archie faces reality every day on the dying music-hall stage. The other son, Mick (Albert Finney), is forced to face the reality of the outside world: He's sent to fight in Suez. And it's only Mick's incarceration and death that get to Archie, momentarily.

Midway through, Archie tells Jean that "the most moving thing he ever heard" was an immense American black woman singing "about Jesus or something" at a bar: "You knew somehow in your heart that it didn't matter how much you kick people, the real people, how much you despise them, if they can stand up and make a pure, just natural noise, like that. . . . If I'd done one thing as good as that in my whole life, I'd have been all right."

The movie builds to the moment when he hears that Mick has died—and in a moment both moving and horrible, tries to belt out a bluesy gospel song. He can't summon up the purity; he can't summon up the soul.

Archie's confusion and bitterness resemble that of any man who's had his buttresses torn from him. So does his destructive power, which comes from self-loathing turned inside out. He makes everyone around him feel defenseless: His entire household has a bunker mentality. And his egomania defines them all. Billy gives him glory by association. Jean is his confessor, Frank his servant. Archie is officially bankrupt—that's why Phoebe, who works at Woolworth's, has to sign all his checks. What's worse, Archie is emotionally bankrupt. He overdraws on everyone—especially Phoebe.

It's proof of Osborne's artistry that Phoebe, an artless, sometimes infuriating woman who recalls the mangy-minded, nay-saying mother of Osborne's autobiography (*A Better Class of Person*), becomes a poignant figure. In a moment of grace, she buys a cake to celebrate Mick's expected return; when Billy unthinkingly takes a slice of it, the action is, as Olivier once called it, a "violation."

Under Richardson's direction, the superb actors surrounding Olivier never let Archie's friends and family come off as supporting players in his life. DeBanzie manages to be both thickheaded and haunting as Phoebe. You can see the hurt and the unthinking stubbornness in her face when Archie brushes her off; when she sings a sentimental song—"Oh the boy I love, he's up in the gallery"—her thin voice exudes the innocence that Archie will never recover.

Finney, in a cameo, has galvanizing eyes that contrast (in the mind) with Olivier's flashy yet dead ones. And Livesey's presence as Billy is as comforting as Olivier's Archie is abrasive. His distinctive, dulcet speaking voice—both furry and nippy—matches up with his mustache. Livesey doesn't soften the old boy up; when he slices Phoebe's cake, he's just a thoughtless old coot.

Richardson's work in the kitchen-sink and ratty stage milieus has a surprising beauty: He knows just when to hold Olivier in close-up (as in a bout of postcoital emptiness) and when to pull back (as when he tries to belt out that spiritual). In the most theatrical scenes, his staging is filled with surprising strokes that come at you without warning— like the instant when Archie takes a disastrous phone call and his chorus girls turn into a Greek chorus. And with cinematographer Oswald Morris, Richardson captures the sadness of the seaside, the faded glamour underneath the big theater's seediness.

Even for moviegoers whose artistic experience of spiritual fatigue dates back no farther than Jackson Browne's *Running on Empty, The Entertainer* will provide a potent expression of confusion and despair. What's most astonishing about the movie is that Archie—an exploiter, opportunist, and deserved failure—is nonetheless able to wring tears.

In art, intense expressions of even the most sombre emotions can be revitalizing. *The Entertainer* is about life-in-death, but you'll feel far more alive walking out of it than you did walking in.

—*Michael Sragow*

Tony Richardson

■

LOOK BACK IN ANGER (1958)

A good, well-cast film transcription of one of the most exciting and influential British plays of the fifties: John Osborne's howl of protest against contemporary life and ossified traditions, through the vitriolic eloquence of his violently disillusioned Jimmy Porter (Richard Burton) — whose rants at life have a grand scale and bitterness. The film, while not stagey, may be a little film-ey; director Tony Richardson pushes the locations too hard to let us relax into them.

— *Michael Wilmington*

Jacques Rivette

■

THE NUN (1966)

Though based on a 1760 novel by Denis Diderot, Jacques Rivette's long-unseen *The Nun* reflects very much the year of its making, 1966. Here is a film full of the creative energy and experimental spirit of the French New Wave, then achieving its pinnacle with the work of Rivette and his contemporaries, including François Truffaut, Jean-Luc Godard, and Claude Chabrol.

And here is a film full of cold anger and frustration, conveying the full extent of the mounting resentment against a too rigid social structure that would soon erupt — for Diderot, with the revolution of 1789; for Rivette, with the near revolution of 1968.

Because the image of that repressive social structure is provided by the Catholic Church, and in particular the eighteenth-century convents that functioned as holding pens for the unwanted, unmarried daughters of the privileged classes, *The Nun* has amassed a history of censorship problems. Diderot's novel was not published until after the revolution, in 1796, and Rivette's film was banned for two years by the Gaullist government.

Rivette's heroine, the stoic, eternally victimized Suzanne, is the daughter of a bourgeois family who has been installed in a convent because no money remains to give her a dowry; she is also, we later discover, spiritually compromising, being the product of an extramarital dalliance by her mother. Suzanne is thus a double threat to her society: as a woman with no place in the economic order, and as the value-carrier of an anarchic, romantic passion the age cannot tolerate.

Suzanne's experience moves from the extreme of an exceedingly harsh, self-punishing existence of a highly devout order to the sticky sensualism of a more liberal convent, where the nuns decorate their habits with lace and the mother superior takes an interest in Suzanne that goes beyond the state of her soul. This seemingly more liberated world is, Suzanne discovers, merely another kind of trap, where she once again finds herself the prisoner of other people's desires.

Cast as Suzanne is Anna Karina, the placid, classically beautiful former model who was then Godard's wife and favorite leading lady; she brings to the film a modern edge of flinty individualism but also an ancient sense of resignation and ultimate acceptance of her fate—a sad wisdom that ties her to the heroines of Kenji Mizoguchi, the Japanese director who was here Rivette's acknowledged inspiration.

At a time when Godard was furiously restructuring film form through editing, Rivette turned to the theater for his stylistic model, preferring to shoot in long, continuous takes that created a stable, restricting, stagelike space around his actors. At the same time, the religious ritual that Rivette observes so closely in *The Nun* becomes a kind of theatrical performance, a pattern of exaggerated gestures that reflects and gives vent to the tightly suppressed hysteria of the characters.

This artificial quality is reinforced by Rivette's daring use of sound—a different, one-note aural theme (twittering birds, howling wind, clanging bells) laid over each sequence that, while ostensibly bringing in an off-screen world, actually serves to underline the isolation of the dramatic space, turning even the exterior sequences into synthetic constructs.

There is a fundamental tension here—between a stolid, almost stodgy realism of space and an undermining artificiality of performance and incident—that Rivette would explore more systematically in his subsequent films, including the masterful *Celine and Julie Go Boating* (1973) and the recent *Gang of Four*. Rivette's films remain situated on the border between extreme naturalism and pure myth, where the everyday dissolves imperceptibly into the irrational and unknowable.

—Dave Kehr

Jacques Rivette

■

PARIS BELONGS TO US (1960)

Ironically, the epigram that opens *Paris Belongs to Us* (1960), Jacques Rivette's haunting first feature, is "Paris belongs to no one." Both of these opposing sentiments apply to this early French New Wave feature about Paris bohemian life, shot on a shoestring by one of the best of the *Cahiers du Cinéma* critics, with a little help from his friends. (François Truffaut and Claude Chabrol coproduced; the latter, along with Jean-Luc Godard, Jacques Demy, and Rivette himself, put in cameo appearances.) A shy Sorbonne student (Betty Schneider) becomes involved with an independent theater group rehearsing Shakespeare's *Pericles,* and sets out to find the "apocalyptic" guitar music for the production recorded by a Spanish exile who committed suicide. She moves through a labyrinthine, claustrophobic, and troubled world inhabited by political refugees (including an American victim of the McCarthy witch hunts), artists, and intellectuals, many of whom allude to a possible worldwide conspiracy that she seeks to uncover. Whether this conspiracy is real or a paranoid fantasy, it seems to lead to the same unsettling consequences in this obsessive and somber metaphysical thriller. This is the first New Wave picture to quote from another movie—the visionary Tower of Babel sequence from Fritz Lang's *Metropolis*—and the Lang reference certainly matches the film's sense of impending doom. Yet the innocence and sincerity of the heroine and the idealism of the theater group have a luminous poignancy; Paris *does* seem to belong to them for a brief spell. A lyrical feeling for the place and period (Paris in the late fifties) is indelibly captured. With Gianni Esposito, Françoise Prevost, and Jean-Claude Brialy.

—Jonathan Rosenbaum

Eric Rohmer

■

MY NIGHT AT MAUD'S (1968)

"There is," says critic Andrew Sarris, "no greater spectacle in the cinema than a man and a woman talking away their share of eternity together." I happened to read that passage just before seeing *My Night at Maud's,* and it seems to me that at the very least its director, Eric Rohmer, brilliantly proves Sarris's proposition. In so doing, he flies in the face of the prevailing film aesthetic, which offers such warm comfort to all those directors who have been gouging away at our eyeballs with all the very latest instruments of visual torture.

Mr. Rohmer's idea of a really big eye trip is a glimpse in black and white of some rather ordinary scenery passing by outside a car window and his notion of a hot editing technique is to use a reverse angle right where you'd expect to find a reverse angle. Mostly his people just sit around and talk, unaided by Shavian or even Mankiewiczian wit. What they talk around and about is a self-confessed mediocrity (Jean-Louis Trintignant) who takes his minuscule adventures of mind and spirit with desperate seriousness. An engineer working for a large firm in a small town, he is deep into calculus and Pascal, the remarkably dull sermons offered down at the local cathedral and, most important, Jansenism, the theological doctrine that denies free will in favor of predestination. A friend, for devious reasons, introduces him to the lady of the title, and Trintignant passes a couple of ambivalent days with her, fearful that she will upset his conviction that he is pre-destined to marry a blonde he has glimpsed (but not met) at the cathedral.

Turns out, by God (the phrase is used literally), that he *was* supposed to marry the blonde and that, indeed, she was more closely inter-woven into his destiny than anyone suspected and that in the end things work out just as nicely as one hopes they will if Jansen was right. But the details of the story, if one can so dignify the skeleton over which Rohmer has stretched his movie, are of less consequence than the remarkable manner in which these ordinarily pretentious, faintly foolish, incredibly *verbal* people compel our attention — the shifting of a glance or of a position in a chair becomes an event as important as, say, a murder or a cavalry charge in an ordinary movie.

How soberly involved everyone is! How comic is the care with which they examine themselves and each other about their motives and the effect their small statements and actions are having! In particular, how moving it is to watch Trintignant prove himself one of the master screen actors of our time as he studies the life flowing past him to see if it proves or disproves the theories he has been toying with. Years ago D. W. Griffith perceived that one of the unique qualities of the movie camera was its ability to "photograph thought," a quality that has not been, by and large, adequately pursued in films of late but which is the principal aim of Rohmer, who is fortunate indeed to have found in Trintignant and friends (François Fabien, Marie-Christine Barrault, Antoine Vitez) actors who can give him some thoughts to shoot.

I doubt that any major American actors would risk such quiet roles in so quiet a picture, and I doubt that, in our present overheated climate, a man like Rohmer could obtain backing for a project containing so little action, so little "youth appeal." Is there, in fact, an American producer who understands that eroticism can be intellectual, may involve neither coupling nor stripping? Is there one who would risk a satire on the modern demi-intellectual's insistence on analyzing everything to death that you do not begin to laugh at until after you have left the theater and the lovely absurdity of the whole enterprise begins ticking like a time bomb in your brain? Is there one who would risk a dollar on a man whose style can only be described as classic formalism? I doubt it. Which means that if you value these virtues, you're going to have to read a lot of subtitles in order to rediscover them.

Still, *My Night at Maud's* has found a surprisingly large audience in New York among the thoughtfully silent minority, and I'm sure there exist elsewhere enough people of similar bent to give this dry, delicate, elegant novella of a film the audience it deserves.

—*Richard Schickel*

Eric Rohmer

■

BOYFRIENDS AND GIRLFRIENDS (1988)

Eric Rohmer's latest movie, *Boyfriends and Girlfriends* (*L'Ami de Mon Amie*), could hardly be more insubstantial. It's a light romantic comedy in which four completely unremarkable young people — two women, two men — reshuffle their affections so that, after the usual misunderstandings, hesitations, and temporary disappointments, each winds up with the "right" partner in the end. And nearly all the action takes place in the most banal setting imaginable: a modern community in the suburbs of Paris — Cergy-Pontoise, a self-contained development of high-rise housing, sleek office buildings, pristine recreational areas, and cozy, overdesigned clusters of shops and cafes. Cergy-Pontoise isn't a futuristic horror. It's a parody of a town, a calculated and slightly ridiculous attempt to create a happy, secure community out of nothing at all, but the people who live there don't mind: they look very content as they stroll, in bright, crisp sports clothes, through the spotless town square, or windsurf on the lake amid the splashing and the jagged laughter of children. The town is a middle-class playground, perfectly ahistorical: it suggests neither the heavy, weary Old World nor an especially brave new one. Rohmer didn't invent Cergy-Pontoise — it actually exists — but the place has the wispy, unreal quality of an abstraction, one of those literary never-never lands designed to allow young lovers to find each other. It's a bland utopia, a bourgeois Forest of Arden.

Boyfriends and Girlfriends is fluff of a rarefied order. The movie is so rigorous and elegant and extreme that it seems, finally, to be about its own weightlessness — not so much a thin romantic comedy as a comic meditation on the thinness of romance. It's a French intellectual's beach-party movie: fluff degree zero. Yet, for all its formality and self-consciousness, the film isn't lifeless. It's artificial without being oppressive — a graceful, friendly abstraction. Like all of Rohmer's movies, *Boyfriends and Girlfriends* unfolds slowly. The characters walk around, chat about this and that, tease each other a little, argue amiably, eat a couple of meals, bump into each other on street corners; as we watch their aimless daily routines we're wondering just who these people are and what, if anything, is going to happen. The beauty of Rohmer's best films is that his characters seem to be wondering the same thing: they're in a state of expectancy, waiting for some half-imagined significance to emerge from their everyday selves, and trying to decide whether there's anything they can do to speed the process along. They, and we, discover that in Rohmer's world meaning takes its sweet time and turns up in unexpected forms. *Boyfriends and Girlfriends* is essentially the same leisurely comedy of self-knowledge that Rohmer has been making for nearly twenty years — since *My Night at Maud's* — but this time he treats his themes with a frivolous, casual, almost dismissive air. The young lovers of Cergy-Pontoise aren't as introspective or as driven as Rohmer's usual protagonists, and they suffer only minor spiritual agonies in the course of selecting their mates. Blanche (Emmanuelle Chaulet), a direct, uncomplicated girl who lacks confidence and blushes when she has to tell a lie, develops a crush on a passive lady-killer named Alexandre (François-Eric Gendron); her best friend, Léa (Sophie Renoir), who's willful and a bit devious, lives with a good-natured windsurfing enthusiast named Fabien (Eric Viellard). By the end of the movie, Blanche has paired off with Fabien, and Léa with Alexandre, and not for any very profound reasons: Blanche and Fabian simply feel comfortable together, and Léa and Alexandre enjoy each other's little games. The women have a few stabs of guilt about poaching on each other's territory, but their qualms don't seriously threaten the suburban idyll. The final arrangement of things seems so natural, so effortlessly right, that no one's inclined to complain or feel betrayed. The lovers shrug and accept their happiness.

The cheerful superficiality of *Boyfriends and Girlfriends* — its relative lack of moral tension and emotional complexity — is a bit of a surprise, especially since this film concludes the six-part cycle of Comedies and Proverbs, which Rohmer began, in 1980, with *The Aviator's Wife.* If we were expecting some great summing-up, a true resolution, this movie isn't it. The real climax of the series turns out to have been the fifth film, called *Summer* in this country. Its original title, *Le Rayon Vert,* means *The Green Ray,* and refers to a rare visual phenomenon that, according to Jules Verne, occurs the instant after the sun has dropped below the horizon. In this amazing film, which followed the two weakest and most contrived of the Comedies and Proverbs — *Pauline at the Beach* and *Full Moon in Paris* — Rohmer relaxed his customary iron control over the narrative: the movie was made in an on-the-run documentary style, in sixteen-millimeter and with direct sound, and the dialogue, usually chiselled and epigrammatic in his movies, was largely improvised by the actors. It's as if Rohmer knew that the time had come for him to subject himself to the kinds of uncertainties and anxieties that he had always been content merely to observe. In *Summer* he's exploring, a little nervously, hoping that something will emerge from the mess of daily improvisations, wondering if anything will *happen* as he follows his restless heroine from one French vacation to another. Of all Rohmer's films, this one comes closest to being a self-portrait. Delphine (Marie Rivière) is a slim, dark, delicate-featured depressive. Since breaking up with her boyfriend, she has become cautious, conservative, almost pathologically wary. Her response to everything is refusal: she's a vegetarian, she flees from men who approach her, she won't even admit, after two years, that her love affair is over. Rohmer, whose art is based on refusal—he quietly declines to indulge in the ordinary, vulgar pleasures that movies provide so easily—understands her very well. The movie has the tentative, irresolute rhythm of its heroine's search for a place where she can feel at ease on her long French summer holiday. This woman is comically, absurdly, infuriatingly incapable of enjoying herself: she goes somewhere, gets disgusted with it, returns to Paris, takes off for someplace new, and is unhappy everywhere. Her idea of vacation reading is *The Idiot*. She drives us crazy, but she's in real pain, the mundane, annoying, debilitating kind that won't go away yet isn't spectacular enough to win much sympathy—like a migraine. When relief comes, it's sudden, arbitrary, a stroke of luck or grace. While Delphine is waiting for a train in Biarritz to take her back to Paris after another vacation fiasco, she decides, impulsively, to tag along with a pleasant young man on his way to the coastal town of Saint-Jean-de-Luz. She surprises herself, and us, with her boldness: after all her self-imposed restrictions, this act has the force of a reckless break with her old self, or perhaps a return to a freer, more spontaneous relationship to experience. In Saint-Jean-de-Luz, she's rewarded: watching the sun go down, she sees the green ray, which, according to Verne, enables its viewer to "see clearly into his own heart and the hearts of others." She cries "Yes!" and clutches her gentle companion. This is one of the purest moments of happiness in recent movies: we feel that Rohmer, along with his heroine, has finally found a way to release himself, to be at ease with the accidents, the scary contingencies, of the natural world.

Summer is a great film. *Boyfriends and Girlfriends* isn't, and isn't meant to be. It's the afterglow of the green ray: though the film was fully scripted by Rohmer, its mood is relaxed, blissfully inconsequential. His suburban characters are too young and too protected to have suffered much or to have developed very complex responses to experience, and they live in an inglorious environment of commercial artifice, but Rohmer finds real beauty in both the people and the setting. He takes pleasure in the cleanness and brightness of this world, in the contented buzz of shoppers and office workers and Sunday picnickers, in the forthright way his characters pursue their comforts. This is, of course, an intellectual's dream of simplicity and unself-consciousness; there's no condescension in it, though. Rohmer even allows himself to indulge in some of the conventions of popular French comedy. (Not that the movie is likely to be confused with abject crowd-pleasers of the *Cousin, Cousine* variety.) In a way, this picture is a perfect conclusion to the Comedies and Proverbs series. Its ease is unexpected, a green bolt from the blue: as Rohmer has often suggested, the end of our self-explorations is something we didn't know we had been waiting for. *Boyfriends and Girlfriends* looks accidental, but its lovely insubstantiality is hard-won.

— Terrence Rafferty

Francesco Rosi

■

THREE BROTHERS (1981)

"Ever since I left Naples, I have felt like an emigrant," director Francesco Rosi told an interviewer. "I am part of that dispersal which has uprooted the people of the South from their culture, their origins, their mental and emotional foundations. In my film, one of the brothers says, 'What is the tragedy of the emigrant? It's that he always misses the earth under his feet.' I've felt that way for years."

Rosi's *Three Brothers* makes us all feel like emigrants. The three brothers who return to Italy's South for their mother's funeral are the fragmented parts of Rosi, Italy, and our century. When at the end of the film they cry for their dead mother, we cry, too, for what we've all lost.

Like Rosi himself, the brothers had to leave home to find work. Fifty-year-old Raffaele (Philippe Noiret) is a judge in Rome. Forty-year-old Rocco (Vittorio Mezogiorno) teaches teen delinquents in Naples. Thirty-year-old Niccolo works in Turin's Fiat factory. Back in their hometown, village life and the work of farming were part of the same world. But in Italy's cities, there are no links between the lawmakers and the workers. Raffaele receives death threats from terrorists. Niccolo, a union activist, organizes violent rallies. Rocco defuses trouble between the Naples police and the kids in his reformatory.

None of the brothers has the solid family life his parents knew, and there's something out of tempo about each of them — something too static in Raffaele's sagging, portly face and in the quiet corridors of the Roman courts; something too demanding and hurried in Niccolo's arrogantly handsome features; something too dreamy in Rocco's way of drifting through the kids' dormitories, his gentle face hidden behind glasses.

But once they're home, the Southern countryside draws them into its harmony of movement and stillness. Like other recent Italian films (the Taviani's *Padre, Padrone;* Olmi's *Tree of Wooden Clogs;* Rosi's own *Eboli*), this film is so driven to capture the feeling of the earth beneath your feet that it pushes beyond ordinary ways of framing and editing to an astonishing expressiveness. Taken together, these Italian films about the land are closer to cinematic poetry than the current films of any other country.

As the movie opens, the father, Donato (Charles Vanel), is on his way to send his sons the telegram: MOTHER DEAD. Passing old farmhouses that cling to the hillsides like the scrubby brush he's walking through, he's suddenly overcome by a vision of his wife a few days before she died. The camera tracks quickly as we see the two of them chasing a rabbit along a row of bushes. Then, when they've made the catch, there's a sudden stillness; and, with a gently spectral smile, Donato's wife releases the rabbit, saying, "It was afraid of dying." She vanishes, reappears on a distant hill, still smiling and waving farewell in slow motion; then she's gone forever.

There's something hauntingly natural in the rhythm of moving and ceasing to move that's present throughout the film in Rosi's harmonies of editing and in the deep spaces of his still shots. The three brothers return home. Slowly, like three strangers, they explain their lives to each other. Then, at some point in the day, each finds a moment of perfect stillness that connects him to his past. Raffaele goes to see his old nurse and is led back through the courtyard gates to the decaying fig tree deep in her garden. Niccolo, visiting his old girlfriend, sees through receding doorways the marriage bed that might have been his.

Rocco loses himself in the church whose music had been one of his mother's greatest pleasures.

This is a movie that's pushing for big images in its picture of nature as a holy trinity: nurse, lover, church. And in its picture of the brothers as a kind of father, son, and holy ghost in their respective love of order, passion for change, and longing for reconciliation. The schematic symbolism isn't overpowering, though, because of the way Rosi makes it work through details and quiet harmonies.

As the whole film moves in rhythms of day and night, the brothers find themselves most completely when each slips into a dream of the future. Of the three, Rocco is the only one who has had a strong memory of their mother, of the day in the forties when she sheltered him against her skirts as a lone American tank rolled over the fields and an Italian-American leapt out of the tank, kissed the earth and shouted, "Paisano! I'm one of you! War is over!" It's when Rocco dreams that we feel the mother is most alive in his longing for a day when the war between the judges and outlaws, the state and its citizens, the old and the new will be over.

But it's the grandfather and granddaughter whose lives extend so deeply into the past and future that they touch the countryside around them. The grandfather is the fourth dreamer. In his dream, he goes back to the open field where his wedding was celebrated and the afternoon at the ocean when his wife, digging her arms and legs into the sand, lost and found her wedding ring. When we see him later in the abandoned fields and empty courtyard that should be filled with his children and grandchildren, we think of the hopes that didn't come true and realize how much he has lost. Then the camera moves in on Vanel's ninety-year-old face, as gently eroded by the sun and wind as the land itself, and we think of how much is still there.

The features are enduring and sustaining, something his granddaughter Marta instinctively reaches out to touch. And, at the heart of the movie's deepest frames, she finds her way to the softly glowing grain loft in the recesses above the room where her grandmother's body lies, slipping into its kernels the way her grandmother dug into the sand on her wedding day. At the movie's end, Donato slips his wife's wedding ring next to his own: for him, the circle has closed. But the wedding earrings are willed to the granddaughter. They shine with a light as soft and promising as the golden reflections of the grain loft, and they will go with Marta on a journey into the future.

—*Kathy Schulz Huffhines*

Francesco Rosi

■

CHRIST STOPPED AT EBOLI (1979)

In 1935, the antifascist writer, doctor, and painter Carlo Levi was exiled to the arid Lucania region of southern Italy, about which he wrote, "Christ never came this far, nor did time, nor the individual soul, nor hope, nor the relation of cause to effect, nor reason nor history." The people Levi encountered there were superstitious, passionate, and selfless.

In the 1979 film adaptation of Levi's memoir, *Christ Stopped at Eboli*, the director, Francesco Rosi, tells the story of Levi's growing bond with the citizens of this Mediterranean equivalent of Siberia. Gian-Maria Volonte projects an astounding degree of empathy and intelligence in the role of Levi. This warm, quizzical character doesn't sentimentalize Lucania's people; he loves them. His unpatronizing respect for their customs and beliefs throws urban audiences off balance. We may be spooked by the tradition of displaying funeral ribbons as decorations, or charmed by the notion that unbaptized children who die haunt the world as playful gnomes, and then shocked when Levi's cleaning woman (the formidable Irene Papas) appears to welcome a slap he gives her either as a sign of sexual attention or as a show of absolute force.

The movie expresses the inexorable rhythm of the peasants' lives. For them, time exists not as a measure for transacting business, not even as an expression of the seasons, but as a drop in the well of eternity. Pasqualino de Santis's photography captures the changeability of barren landscapes; you feel yourself "reading" every shifting dune and passing cloud as a harbinger or an omen. *Christ Stopped at Eboli* is a secular miracle.

—*Michael Sragow*

Carlos Saura

■

CRIA! (1975)

One of the most harrowing scenes in the cinema occurs at the beginning of Ingmar Bergman's *Cries and Whispers* when Harriet Andersson wakes in the middle of the night to find herself strangling, plunging with shocking suddenness toward the death she has lived with so long. As it happens, death is to be deferred a while longer; but for one awful moment it is in the room, a palpable presence, photographable in the face of the woman who sees it.

Carlos Saura's *Cria!* contains a comparable sequence. Geraldine Chaplin lies writhing on a bed, the covers thrown back, her skin stretched paper-taut. She seems to catch the camera's eye, and chokes out a rueful confession: "It's all a lie. Nothing exists. I've been fooled. I'm afraid. I don't want to die." But she already has, long before the film began.

The Bergman scene (if I remember rightly) was a single, integral closeup of Andersson in the blue dimness of that eternal Bergman night. Saura's scene takes place in the light of day and begins with a terrible, disarming casualness: Ana Torrent, as the second of Chaplin's three daughters, comes down a hall, sees a maid, her arms full of clean linen, phoning the doctor, and moves undetained into her mother's room. The camera—as in so much of the film—is in her service; Saura intercuts freely between her and Chaplin, so that when Chaplin speaks into the camera's eye she is delivering an admonition, a veritable commission, to Ana at the same time she seems to address us directly; and Ana, looking at the dying woman, gazes at us also.

Death is a constant presence throughout *Cria!*—the overriding fact of life—but only during this sequence, actually a memory of Ana's, is its horror explicitly confronted. Even here, the horror is mediated; we are not along in confronting the skull. It is the child who sees, sees definitively: Ana Torrent, the prodigy from Victor Erice's *Spirit of the Beehive,* with her calm face and black, sad, bright engulfing eyes. It is Ana who learns from her mother that death is what life is all about, and accepts it with an awesome serenity. If "it's all a lie" and "nothing exists," then there can be no nightmares—only dreams of phantoms and friendly vampires. Certain knowledge, even of the horrible, lends a sense of order and security, which a child's predilection for myth and ritual turns into a game for the highest stakes, and Saura's benign (but entirely unsentimental) sensibility renders into art.

"Story" doesn't dominate *Cria!,* although before the film is over we have been made privy to the essential history of several generations of Ana's family, their friends, lovers, and servants, their place in the social and imaginative scheme of their nation. The film begins with the camera roaming about a dark interior, discovering the pajama-clad Ana silently descending the stair as the murmur of clandestine lovers comes muffled through a door and, overall, the piano music of a dead woman sounds. A moment later the murmurs have changed to cries of alarm. The man, Ana's father, has succumbed to a heart attack and the mistress, flashing a startled look at the child who shouldn't be in the downstairs hall, has fled into the early morning light.

The meaning of this exchanged glance, and of another over the father's bier, will retroactively change at several points in the film. (Ana has her own solemn, bizarrely comic explanation of why her father died.) But the intensely private atmosphere, charged with guilts old and new, with longing and frustration, and also with an indomitable will to "explore," is never really lifted, no matter how hard well-meaning adults try to impose their bankrupt rationality on Ana and her sisters. Ana's explorations, her weighing of human experience, remain uncompromised. Within Saura's carefully balanced narrative she is the world and yet separate from the mundane, like the house and garden — which remain the film's main location — cloistered in modern Madrid by walls and trees. Ana can stand in that garden and see herself atop the high roof of the house, yet when her second self leaps, the camera — and the film — soars.

Cria! plays stylistic games of its own with time and space — cutting, for instance, from Geraldine Chaplin as the mother, in the past, to Ana Torrent as Ana in the present, who is then panned off-screen to be replaced by Chaplin as Ana grown into the adult commentator on her own childhood. The shifting layers of reality include "real," present-tense experience, memory, dream, daydream, mirror reflection, play-acting (a luminous, joyous, troubling scene: Ana and her sisters affecting adult flirtatiousness while dancing, then putting on adult wigs and makeup and reenacting their parents' quarrels). But it is never a flashy film; Saura's touch is seasoned, assured, deeply humane. He is worthy of the eight-year-old actress who inspired the movie in the first place, without whom it would never have been made: Ana Torrent, who, having fixed us with her gaze, must never blink; for we would probably disappear.

— Richard T. Jameson

Carlos Saura
■
CARMEN (1983)

Dance is at the heart of this flamenco *Carmen.* Carlos Saura (who began his career photographing dancers) and choreographer Antonio Gades yank the story into the present, restoring the character of Carmen's husband, present in the Prosper Mérimée original, but absent in Bizet's opera. Here he's a dope dealer just sprung from jail. But the real heat, the sexual fireworks, lie in the insinuating rhythms and foot-stamping rehearsal sequences on the studio floor, especially when fiercely controlled Christina Hoyos squares off against the panther-like Carmen of Laura Del Sol.

— Jay Carr

John Schlesinger
■
BILLY LIAR (1963)

Billy Liar is a teenage Walter Mitty—and the stuff that adolescent dreams are made on in this British film is universal and funny and ironic. It strikes close to home and all but the dreamer strikes close to the heart.

Billy despises his family, a frustratedly bullying father, a fond and despairing mother, a gabbling grandmother, and detests his job as clerk in an undertaking parlor; he has small liking even for the two girls to whom he has become simultaneously engaged. But Billy has a dream world, an all-embracing one, that makes life more than possible until the fateful Saturday of the story.

The dream world includes, first of all, Ambrosia, a country full of heroes (all of them Billy) and political crises (all of them solved by Billy) and progressive reforms (all instituted by Billy), ruled, of course, by Billy, with Liz, his real-life dream girl, as his consort. But Ambrosia is for relaxed escape in solitude. For momentary needs, Billy can suddenly turn a machine gun on his tormentors or toss a hand grenade at his loathed employer; he can promptly provide himself with substitute parents, strictly upper-U, swilling champagne and sharing his contempt for the world; and if his conscience twinges about his theft of some office petty cash, Billy sees himself whiling away the years in prison writing a best-selling exposé of conditions that wins him fame, fortune, and reduction of sentence.

On the Saturday of the tale, Billy has dire need of his dreams: his father has just about "bloody well had him"; his employer has begun an open discussion about the petty cash; both fiancées are demanding ownership of the one engagement ring, and Liz, lovely footloose Liz, is briefly in town to challenge his inertia.

Billy is, in fact, surrounded by assassins, by the gritty ordinary demands of life that destroy procrastinating dreams — and the machine guns and hand grenades lose their efficacy in the face of his grandmother's sudden illness, his fiancées' meeting head-on, Liz's demand that he escape with her to London, his father's final fury, and his mother's inarticulate despair.

Suddenly the gaiety, the youthful insouciance and recklessness, is gone; fantasy becomes a mesh of ugly and childish lies, and boyish contempt is laid bare in all its self-centered cruelty.

The switch of mood is sudden; Billy's charm is gone and his humiliation rouses no compassion, for there is an ambiguity in Billy's ultimate decision against escape. Unlike Keith Waterhouse's novel, the screenplay, which he wrote with Willis Hall, gives us no indication of whether it is a sudden intimation of humanity and manliness or whether it is only Ambrosia-inspired inertia that brings him back to the semidetached house that is his home.

It is the sudden change of mood and the ambiguity of the ending that flaws an otherwise excellent human comedy. The performances are flawless, from Tom Courtenay's boyishly fey Billy to Mona Washbourne's restrained and touching mother, Ethel Griffies's maundering grandmother, and Leonard Rossiter's macabrely progressive undertaker (plastic coffins are the coming thing: "No use living in one style and dying in another"). The fiancées are superb, Helen Fraser as the

prudish domestic-minded Barbara ("Are you all right, Billy?" she asks
as his hand touches her knee) and Gwendolyn Watts as the shrewish
Rita ("I'm going to get that rotten ring back and I'm going to meet your
rotten mother and your rotten father and your rotten grandmother—
we're engaged whether you like it or not," she assures her backward
lover). And Julie Christie, as the ardent and independent Liz, is just too
lovely to be as true as she is.

There's vigor, high comedy, dry wit, and subtlety in *Billy Liar*. And it
presents to us an adolescent nonhero whose dreams, alas, are far more
likable than his reality.

—Judith Crist

John Schlesinger
■

SUNDAY BLOODY SUNDAY (1971)

John Schlesinger directed this complex, remarkably modulated
English movie about three Londoners and the breakup of two love
affairs, from a delicate, pungent screenplay by Penelope Gilliatt, and it
may be his finest work. It's an unusual film—perhaps a classic. A
homosexual doctor in his forties, played by Peter Finch, and an
employment counsellor in her thirties, played by Glenda Jackson, are
both in love with a boyish, successful kinetic sculptor, played by
Murray Head, who casually divides his time and affections between
them. He has no special sexual preferences and doesn't understand
what upsets the two older people about sharing him, since he loves
them both. The film is a curious sort of plea on behalf of human
frailty—it asks for sympathy for the nonheroes of life who make the
best deal they can. People can receive solace from it—it's the most
sophisticated weeper ever made. There is perhaps a little too *much*
sensibility; compassion is featured. "People can manage on very little,"
the doctor says to relatives of an incapacitated patient. "Too late to start
again," a sad, heavy-lidded woman who looks like Virginia Woolf says
of her miserable marriage. Schlesinger has a gift for pacing and the
energy to bring all the elements of a movie together, but he uses his
technique so that it's just about impossible for you to have any reaction

that he hasn't decreed you should. The film is full of planted insights; you can practically count the watts in the illuminations. With Peggy Ashcroft, Vivian Pickles, Tony Britton, and Maurice Denham. Cinematography by Billy Williams.

—Pauline Kael

Andrei Tarkovsky

■

RETROSPECTIVE

When expatriate Russian film director Andrei Tarkovsky died in Paris in December 1986, he left a legacy of seven films. The number is not great. Had Tarkovsky not been cut down by cancer, he might have doubled his output. He was only fifty-four. Yet it would be a mistake to think that Tarkovsky died unfulfilled. Although his difficulties with Soviet authorities often meant years between films, his place as a profound artist of world cinema is assured. He achieved the only kind of success that matters to an artist: he specified a world, in a unique cinematic vocabulary.

In *My Name is Ivan* (1962), Tarkovsky's second film, and first to be shown in the West, are present all the elements that Tarkovsky was to plumb and reshape in films to come. In young Ivan, a boy orphaned by war, who fiercely turns to spying against the Germans, Tarkovsky introduced the child as innocent and seer, an important part of his last film, *The Sacrifice* (1968). Tarkovsky's feel for the particulars of landscape and texture are present, as is his almost mystical invocation of water imagery—constant in films to come. Tarkovsky's repeated uses of fire, birds, mirrors, and levitating bodies bordered on the shamanistic. Yet Tarkovsky was no pantheist, or twentieth-century searcher after myth. He was a Christian with an Eastern cast to his thought. He decried what he saw as a falling away from spirituality in pursuit of shallow materialistic imperatives.

Such blindness can only lead to disaster, in Tarkovsky's view. In *The Sacrifice,* a dense, poetic parable that was unique among last year's films in its ability to equal the reach and greatness of literature, it does just that. A retired actor looks on horrified as the world he hopes to pass on to his young son is consumed by atomic holocaust. He tries to retrieve it in a sort of Faustian bargain with God, employing the offices of a good witch.' *The Mirror* (1974), the most overtly autobiographical of Tarkovsky's films, begins with images of a mute boy, who anticipates the boy in *The Sacrifice*. Like the protagonist of *My Name Is Ivan*, a sort of aura hovers over him as his story unfolds, fracturing conventional narrative form, blending past and present into an interior world where conventional constructs evaporate into meaninglessness.

Although no contemporary Russian director can match Tarkovsky's feel for the particulars of landscape—no mere sentimentalizing of birch trees here—Tarkovsky's landscapes were interior. That was their strength, their integrity, their uniqueness. That's also what guaranteed him a difficult time with the commissars, who operated out of the traditional Soviet bureaucratic distrust of anything abstract, much less the idiosyncratic individualism Tarkovsky's films expressed. Even when they were about supposedly safe subjects—Russian heroism in World War II (*My Name is Ivan*) and the commemoration of a people's artist (*Andrei Rublev*)—they turned into psychic autobiographies.

Andrei Rublev (1966) represents the sort of tug-of-war undergone by so many Soviet artists of integrity—Shostakovich in music, Pasternak in literature, to name only two. Possibly the commissars thought they were getting Soviet realism in the story of a fifteenth-century icon painter able, after a series of discouragements and bouts with pessimism, to wrench beauty from the brutality surrounding him. Few observers in the West—where Tarkovsky has always been most highly regarded—were able to read it as anything but an allegory of the artist's struggle. Yet it would be doing a great injustice to Tarkovsky's work to see it as nothing more than simple allegory. Even in such lesser works as his two science-fiction films, *Solaris* (1971) and *Stalker* (1979), he quickly got away from the particulars of the respective novels from which they stemmed to focus instead on the internal worlds of the characters.

If there is any message in Tarkovsky's work, it is that life is an internal affair, played out in one's soul, not in public. The implications of that belief were enough to ensure muted enthusiasm for his work on the part of Soviet officialdom. Tarkovsky's last two films, *Nostalgia* (1983) and *The Sacrifice* (1986), are deeply felt testaments. In the first, the parallels are obvious between Tarkovsky and the film's protagonist—a Russian scholar who goes to Italy to retrace the steps of an eighteenth-century Russian composer who visited the same place, then returned home to die. What's made most manifest in the flashbacks, and water symbolism, and gorgeous but doleful landscapes, is the agony of the exile and the foreboding hitched to a sense of impending death.

One scene in *Nostalgia* shows a book of poetry going up in flames after a translation of it is read. It can be seen as a comment on the impossibility of bridging languages and cultures. Poetry was of prime importance to Tarkovsky, who sought to work at the level of those he called the poets in cinema—Bresson, Mizoguchi, Dovzhenko, Bergman, Buñuel, Kurosawa. Tarkovsky's own father, Arseny Tarkovsky, is a well-known lyric poet. In *The Mirror,* the elder Tarkovsky reads his poems. In *Nostalgia,* his are the poems that go up in flames after being translated. So concerned was Tarkovsky about the purity of his images that he deliberately became sparing to the point of austerity in his use of color, which he felt interfered with viewers' ability to immerse themselves in the netherworlds he was determined to bring to the screen with a hermetic lyricism all his own. The color in *The Sacrifice* is slate-gray, lichenlike.

In 1984, Tarkovsky chose to stay in the West permanently after the Soviet government refused to allow him a visa extension. He and his family lived in Florence, then in West Berlin, then Paris. Last year his fifteen-year-old son, Andrei, nicknamed Andrushka, journeyed to Cannes to accept the Jury Prize for *The Sacrifice* in place of his father, who, undergoing chemotherapy, was too ill to travel and later had to cancel an appearance at Dartmouth College, where Telluride Film Festival founders Bill and Stella Pence scheduled the first Tarkovsky retrospective in the United States. The appearance of the pale, soft-voiced Andrushka, whose voice could barely be heard, was a vindication for his father. Tarkovsky, who knew he was dying when he made *The Sacrifice,* dedicated it "with hope and confidence" to his son, after having dedicated *Nostalgia* to his mother. It was the final public expression of a nobility of spirit rare in contemporary art and almost without parallel in contemporary cinema.

—*Jay Carr*

Jacques Tati

■

PARADE (1973)

Jacques Tati's last feature, *Parade,* is about as unpretentious as a film can get. One of the first films to have been shot mostly in video (on a shoestring budget for Swedish TV), it's a music-hall and circus show featuring juggling, music, gags, pantomime, minor acrobatics, and various forms of audience participation. Though it might seem a natural for TV—and in fact has been shown on TV, as well as theatrically, in Europe—it has never been broadcast in this country. Most critics who have seen it, including many passionate Tati fans, regard it as minor and inconsequential.

I don't wish to argue that *Parade* is a work of undiscovered depths, any more than Tati's other half dozen features are. The paradoxical thing about all of his films is that what you see (and hear) is what you get; like Poe's purloined letter, it's all there, right on the surface— if we are alert enough to observe what is happening right in front of us. But thanks to a lifetime of bad training in watching movies and TV, we often can't be that alert. *Parade* is devoted to showing us how we could be.

Sometimes the most radical and profound ideas turn out to be very simple. Some of the most radical and profound ideas in *Parade* are at least as old as Brueghel, although they're a good deal fresher and considerably more advanced than those in any of the commercial features released this year. A few of these ideas can be represented in simple sentences, all of them having to do with the nature of spectacle, and all of them saying pretty much the same thing:

There is no such thing as an interruption.

There is no such thing as "backstage."

At no point does life end and "the show" begin—or vice versa.

Amateurs and nobodies—that is to say, ordinary people—are every bit as important, as interesting, and as entertaining as professionals and stars.

Poetry always takes root in mundane yet unlikely places, and it is taking place all around us, at every moment.

Simple ideas, and in the film they're all expressed exclusively in terms of light entertainment; yet sixteen years after *Parade*'s release, they remain elusive, difficult, complex, and highly subversive in relation to most notions about the art of spectacle that circulate today. Worse yet, they are often expressed in terms that are unfashionable, in relation to either 1973 or the present.

When a European rock band performs in the film, for instance, it is the unhippest hippie band imaginable, at least by our own standards, and when we see some of the youths in the bleachers clap and dance to the music, we become painfully aware of Tati's remoteness from that segment of his audience (he was in his midsixties when he made *Parade*). Even in *Playtime* (1967), Tati's supreme masterpiece, the gaucheness and lack of stylishness of the leading female character, a young American tourist, represents a stumbling block for many viewers.

One of our besetting limitations in relation to art is that we tend to distrust pretension, yet at the same time we're wary of taking entertainment seriously if it doesn't wear art with a capital *A* on its sleeve. Tati's refusal — or inability — to make movies that were fashionable or conventionally slick didn't prevent his first three features — *Jour de Fête* (1949), *Mr. Hulot's Holiday* (1953), and *Mon Oncle* (1958) — from becoming worldwide hits, each bigger than the last. All three films were highly original and eccentric expressions — in their loose and unconventional attitude toward narrative, in their peculiar handling of humor, in their satirical comments on the periods and milieus in which they were made, in the sorts of characters and behavior they focused on, and in their unique employments of sound, pacing, editing, and framing. Yet the truth of Tati's observations was so immediately recognizable to the general public that none of these idiosyncrasies stood in the way of commercial success.

But when Tati made his most ambitious, accomplished, and expensive movie, *Playtime,* the public wasn't ready for it. In an attempt to sabotage the centrality of Hulot, the character Tati had created and played in his two previous features, in *Playtime* Tati created a series of false Hulots — characters who resembled Hulot from a distance — which deliberately and productively confused both on-screen characters and the audience. But the public only wanted more of their hero Hulot, not a mechanism demonstrating that everyone else — on the screen and in the audience — was equally funny and important.

From then on, Tati's career operated under a shadow that persists to this day — not merely because of the box-office failure of *Playtime,* which landed him in bankruptcy, but also because it had become painfully clear that Tati's vision threatened the politics of spectacle as we know it. The democratic, nonelitist idea that three dozen characters can all be on-screen at once and can all be equally worthy of interest—which is central to the hour-long climactic sequence in *Playtime* devoted to the opening of a restaurant, conceivably the most richly orchestrated piece of *mise en scène* in the history of cinema—sabotages not only the star system, but principles of storytelling, dramaturgy, composition, foreground and background, and moral and social hierarchies central to other movies. And indeed, the immediate consequence of this crisis was that Tati was forced to make a conscious regression in his next film (*Traffic*)—bringing back Hulot as a more central character in a simpler and more conventional story—in order to continue making movies at all.

I can speak of Tati's intentions with some confidence because I was privileged to have worked for him on an unrealized feature called *Confusion* in 1972, the year after *Traffic* was released. Tati was trapped in the paradox of being loved all over the world for his creation, a character he had grown to detest; it was Hulot who stood in the way of Tati's desire to grow as a filmmaker. This is not to say that Tati had ceased to be a performer; our four- and five-hour work sessions were dominated by his impromptu performances (and my so-called job as "script consultant" consisted of responding to those performances). But it is equally important to note that, for him, the role of performer and the role of spectator were inseparably linked.

He had started out as an athlete and amateur comic whose routines, based on what he saw and heard, led to an extended stint in music halls, and all his movies were vast frescoes of observations that became inventions only when he tried to duplicate and/or develop them. Having lunch with Tati in a bistro mainly consisted of sitting next to him in front of the spectacle of everyday life, which he was constantly reacting to and mimicking; "scripting" a film sequence, for him, mainly consisted of remembering such moments and translating them into shots—duplicating with his body and voice everything that one would see and hear. A purely intuitive rather than intellectual process, based less on words than on sounds and images, it equated acting with watching and watching with acting to such a degree that it dissolved the usual distinctions between the two.

Parade's title appears over a drumroll, in the form of a multicolored marquee in the night sky above a circus building, and the camera pulls back from this building before cutting to a closer shot of people filing in. Then the first "gag" occurs—a detail so slight that by conventional standards it hardly qualifies as a gag at all, although it is quintessential Tati: a teenager in line picks up a striped, cone-shaped road marker on the pavement and dons it like a dunce cap; his date laughs, finds another road marker, and does the same thing.

At least three basic Tatiesque principles are set forth in this passing detail. There is the notion of bricolage, or the appropriation of impersonal objects for personal use that enables people to reshape and reclaim their environment, an idea central to Tati's work (the restaurant sequence in *Playtime* formulates it on an epic scale), which reaches its distilled essence throughout *Parade,* both offstage and on. (Tati, one should note, directed all the stage acts himself, altering in some instances the performers' usual props, costumes, and gestures, such as getting the jugglers to juggle with paintbrushes — another good example of bricolage.)

Then there is the offhand inflection and punctuation of the gag, making it a slightly disorienting moment of strangeness in the midst of normality rather than the conventional setup followed by a payoff. As a consequence, the dunce-cap gag is more likely to make us smile than laugh; but the cumulative effect of dozens of such underplayed gags is to make reality itself seem both slightly off-kilter and alive with comic possibilities.

Finally, one should note that at the very outset, Tati is placing spectators rather than performers in the primary creative role. The "parade" begins before the audience even enters the theater, as is fully apparent in the brightly colored, festive, and flamboyant clothes worn by the hippies in the audience as well as the props carried by many of the younger kids. The implication is that Tati's democratic aesthetics are more than just a matter of everything and everyone in a shot being worthy of close attention. They also function on a temporal plane — every shot and moment is worthy of close attention, and a moment without a fully articulated gag is not necessarily inferior to a moment with one, because the spectator's imagination is unleashed by the mere possibility that one might occur.

One of the kids, a little boy wearing a gun and holster, stops briefly inside the lobby to adjust his gear, and briefly makes eye contact with a little girl before each of them is dragged off in opposite directions by his or her respective parent. These are the same two children who will literally take over the movie in the epilogue, entering the empty stage and playing with various props as they try to reproduce the acts they have seen. They are also seen periodically in the bleachers throughout the show, and their responses to the show and each other are accorded at least as much attention as any of the acts.

The movie lingers over a good many other preliminaries before the circus actually begins: people drifting to their seats, musicians tuning up, carpenters and painters working on props. The fact that these activities are as important as what follows dawns on us only gradually. When the opening trumpet fanfare is played by two clowns in the bleachers, many spectators are still arriving, and the camera seems so distracted by such details that we come to accept the fanfare, the following introduction of performers, and a subsequent drum fanfare as part of the preliminaries, too. Even when Tati himself strolls onstage in a top hat and is greeted by applause, the camera abruptly sweeps past him to settle on the front rows in the bleachers, where the little girl is clearly bored out of her wits, and the little boy, while applauding in the row ahead, is looking at the girl, not at Tati.

When Tati, the official master of ceremonies, begins to speak, it is in a multilingual, seminonsensical patter. But then the camera cuts away from him again to focus on the drifting trajectories of a wandering toddler, proceeds out into the lobby to linger on a latecomer checking his motorcycle helmet at the cloakroom, remains with the befuddled female attendant surrounded by a sea of other helmets, then proceeds down a hallway to the comic entrances and exits of a hockey player and a violinist. When the camera finally returns to the auditorium, it is to the bleachers, where another motorcyclist is asked by the woman seated behind him to remove his helmet so she can see better—but his decompressed hair creates even more of an obstruction. Finally we get to see the musicians playing onstage, but from an oblique overhead angle that includes the stage rigging.

Even when the camera spends more time on the stage, the physical borders of spectacle and audience are broken down through a variety of means. The painters and carpenters working on props are frequently visible and even prominent as spectators during some of the acts. (Only much later, when a painter starts competing with an onstage magician in performing card tricks, and when several of the painters start juggling with their paintbrushes, does it become fully apparent that these characters are "performers" rather than "extras.") An onstage row of fake bleachers containing black-and-white cutouts of spectators is integrated into some of the acts; this effect is undermined in turn when real spectators are later glimpsed in the same spot, or when fake spectators are glimpsed in the actual bleachers. Time and space often become mutable, but the premise as well as the illusion of a show taking place in real time and on a single stage is rigorously maintained.

Among the acts included are many of Tati's most famous music-hall pantomimes, depicting a football game, a fisherman, a tennis match, a tennis player circa 1900, and a horseback rider. The continuity between these solo routines and Tati's directorial style is that both appeal to a spectator's imagination through a panoply of subtle suggestions. (Reviewing one of Tati's mime performances in 1936, Colette wrote, "He has created at the same time the player, the ball and the racket; the boxer and his opponent; the bicycle and its rider. His powers of suggestion are those of a great artist.")

While it might seem from the foregoing that Tati somehow undercuts the performers (himself included) in order to glorify the spectators, he actually treats them all with respect. His directorial sleight of hand keeps bringing the audience into the act, but never in such a way that it betrays or impugns the talents of the performers. It is the ideology of spectacle and its attendant hierarchies that he is out to dismantle — not the pleasures of spectacle itself, which he is in fact inclined to spread around liberally and democratically, emphasizing its continuities with everyday life.

A central aspect of *Parade,* more contemporary and more in tune with advanced filmmaking than its other qualities, is its complex interaction between nonfiction and fiction, chance and programming — a dialectical approach followed with comparable fruitfulness in such films as Jacques Rivette's *Out 1,* Orson Welles's *F for Fake,* Chris Marker's *Sans Soleil,* Françoise Romand's *Mix-Up,* Claude Lanzmann's *Shoah,* Joris Ivens and Marceline Loridan's *A Story of the Wind,* and the most recent works of Peter Thompson and Leslie Thornton.

Tati began by shooting with an audience in the circus building for three days, using four video cameras. Then he spent twelve days in a studio reshooting portions of the stage acts in thirty-five millimeter. Thus he wound up with a film that combines spontaneous *and* planned material on video with planned material on film, and although the visual definition in the studio-filmed portions is noticeably sharper, the mixture of materials is so deft in other respects that it is generally impossible to separate the documentary segments from the fictional details. The sole exception to this is the film's epilogue and pièce de résistance, in which the boy and girl are left alone with the stage props after the show has ended; Tati shot two hours of improvised play with several video cameras, then extracted the few minutes that are used in the film.

The studio shooting of *Playtime,* which entailed the construction of an entire city set, precluded such experimentation—the only real location used in the film is the exterior of Orly airport—but some early forays into documentary can be found in certain sequences of *Traffic,* detailing the behavior and habits of various drivers, which are so gracefully threaded into the rest that they register as a continuation of the fiction rather than a departure from it.

Expanding this technique considerably, *Parade* creates a privileged zone of its own in which the free play between fiction and nonfiction becomes an open space to breathe in. It is a utopian space where equality reigns between spectators and performers, children and adults, foreground and background, entertainment and everyday life, reality and imagination—an evening's light diversion that, if taken seriously, as it was meant to be, could profitably crumble the very ground beneath our feet.

—Jonathan Rosenbaum

Bertrand Tavernier

■

COUP DE TORCHON (1981)

Black comedy is a badly abused term these days—it can mean anything from Mel Brooks's Nazi jokes to the campy horror of *The Texas Chainsaw Massacre,* and generally settles on anything that combines slapstick and dead bodies. But black humor in its more elevated sense, as practiced by Swift, Kafka, Waugh, is very rare in the movies; there is Howard Hawks's *Scarface,* Jacques Becker's *Goupi Mains Rouges,* George Romero's *Dawn of the Dead,* and not much else (though I think I'd add an obscure British film I'm fond of, Dick Clement's *A Severed Head*). Death, violence, and moral corruption aren't just slapstick props in these films, but agonizingly real presences, and their comedy isn't a release from horror but a confrontation with it. Laughter can often be a defense, a way of shunting aside disturbing emotions, of reducing horror to triviality. But in these films, humor and horror exist side by side; they play on the very thin line that separates a laugh from a scream, touching the hysteria common to both. To laugh is to give yourself up to the irrational as much as to scream; it is an irrational, emotional, convulsive response to an irrational situation. The best black humor makes us feel the horror, and if we laugh instead of shudder, it's only because the artist has nudged us that way. The slighter and subtler the nudge the better, and in Bertrand Tavernier's *Coup de Torchon,* the nudge is so slight that it's almost imperceptible. Tavernier has placed his film exactly on the dividing line; it demands a deep complexity of response, with its ambiguity filtered from levels of theme to character to style to audience reaction. It's a black comedy of the richest kind: a film that teeters on the edge.

The film is dark and sometimes despairing, yet it's a surprisingly warm movie. If there's one characteristic that runs through the stylistic diversity of Tavernier's work, it's his closeness to his characters; he takes an evident delight in observing the patterns and quirks of their behavior from up close, never allowing his visual ideas (which range from the high baroque of *The Judge and the Assassin* and *Death Watch* to the classic simplicity of *Spoiled Children*) to come between them and the audience. And Tavernier prefers a certain kind of actor—best represented by Philippe Noiret, who has appeared in five of his films— who hasn't been seen much lately: a classical, open-faced kind of actor, who declines the Method priorities of "being" in favor of a more theatrical "showing," a concentration on an absolute clarity of gesture and diction, more directly addressed to the audience. In *Coup de Torchon,* Noiret is Lucien Cordier, the cowardly, corrupt, hopelessly ineffectual police chief of Bourkassa, a small village in the colonial French West Africa of 1938. Huguette, Cordier's wife (Stéphane Audran), is carrying on a barely concealed affair with her live-in boyfriend, Nono (French pop singer Eddy Mitchell); she tells Cordier he's her brother, and she might be telling the truth. Cordier has a mistress, Rose (Isabelle Huppert, in a very lively, funny performance), but when he hears her husband beating her in the street, he can hardly stir himself to have a look. But his real problem is Le Peron, the local pimp (Jean-Pierre Marielle), who has bribed Cordier so many times that he has a line of credit; Le Peron insults Cordier constantly and shoves him around, while Cordier meekly puts each new offense on the tab. But when Cordier finds Le Peron and his sidekick engaged in a new kind of sport—taking target practice on the bodies of plague victims cast into the river—it is, finally, too much. He takes the bribe but travels to district headquarters to ask his superior, Chavasson (Guy Marchand), what to do. Chavasson's advice is to kick them back twice as hard as they kicked him. It's good advice: Cordier returns to town and murders both men in cold blood.

Tavernier doesn't signal any obvious change in Cordier's character: he's still the same affable, easygoing loser after the murder as before (which is why, in part, he's able to get away with it). But something has changed deep inside: Cordier's sense of right and wrong, dormant for so long in this sunbaked climate, has been revived. Suddenly, he feels the need to act morally—to do something decisive to redeem the debased world around him—yet if the need is clear the methods are not. Most of Tavernier's films are built around one of two basic situations—passive, observant characters who are brought to realize the need for action (*The Clockmaker, Death Watch, Spoiled Children*), or characters who are already in a position of power but are struck by the suspicion that their actions are useless, their methods immoral, or their goals unclear (*Let Joy Reign Supreme, The Judge and the Assassin, A Week's Vacation*). *Coup de Torchon* combines these two plots: Cordier's moral awakening is followed by a moral paralysis, the crippling realization that doing right entails a great deal of doing wrong. Cordier's first killing has a social justification behind its personal motivation—he has murdered two men who have humiliated him, but he has also rid the town of two thugs. The second killing—the execution of his mistress's brutish husband—has a greater element of personal satisfaction; by the end, he is killing only to cover his own tracks.

Throughout the film, Noiret's personal performance is so rumpled, relaxed, and witty—there aren't many actors as instantly likable as he is—that it becomes harder and harder to reconcile the character with his acts. A kind of shadow character emerges behind Noiret, a different Cordier who is haunted by black thoughts and deep despair, and who may have been driven mad by those thoughts. This other Cordier, as morbidly romantic as a figure out of Poe, appears only rarely; it's a tribute to Tavernier's skills as a rhetorician that he emerges as clearly as he does, defined only by the implications of fleeting acts and fleeting expressions. It's as if the film had two fully developed protagonists, both inhabiting the same body, and it's impossible to tell from moment to moment which Cordier is on the screen. By splitting his protagonist, Tavernier deliberately knocks his film off-kilter. There's no moral center (either positive or negative) for the audience to focus on, no reliable point of view that the audience can simply share. Even the images fail to provide stability and certainty: instead of using balanced, formal compositions and the traditional logic of angle, reverse-angle editing, Tavernier covers many of his scenes in single long takes filmed with a hand-held camera. This isn't the jittery, ragged hand-held familiar from documentaries and the old Warhol films, but an eerily elegant, free-floating effect made possible by the new gyroscopic Steadicam mounts. It's unusual to see a filmmaker so readily turning new technology to personal, expressive ends, rather than simply use it to punch up his style; the Steadicam here is used to describe a world in constant flux, in which the always evolving, unbordered image is no easier to pin down than the moral certainties of the plot. The Steadicam does provide a point of view, but it is a profoundly fluid, slippery one. Nothing in this world is anchored, not even the camera.

Coup de Torchon is based on *Pop. 1280,* a novel by the neglected American writer Jim Thompson (the book, unfortunately, has long been out of print). Thompson's novel was set in the deep South, but Tavernier's transfer of the action to colonial Africa preserves the setting in its essentials, and possibly adds some new themes (the setting is further unsettled by the approaching war with Germany). The fundamental division in this world is, of course, the division of race; once the majority of the population has been defined as nonhuman (Cordier and his police superior have a long argument over the differences between blacks and cows), morality no longer exists — you can't commit a crime against an animal. Bourkassa, as designed by veteran set decorator Alexandre Trauner (his career goes back to *The Children of Paradise,* and beyond) and photographed by Pierre William Glenn, is a village of glaring primary colors, madly jumbled together. The only visual constant is the yellow heat of the sun, which blends with the dry, yellowed earth. Everything seems to run backward here — the river isn't a source of life, but a cemetery — and many of the gags hang on this sense of reversal. In a movie seen from behind a bed-sheet screen, an officer crisply salutes with his left hand; a priest, replacing a termite-worn cross, enthusiastically recrucifies a statue of Jesus by nailing him to a new mount. When the twin brother of the murdered pimp shows up in town, no one seems very surprised: dead men are regular visitors in this neighborhood. Is Cordier really reacting against this upside-down world, or is he just another product of it? In this inverted context, it seems only natural that the town coward is also the local hero — that cravenness is courage and spinelessness is strength.

Tavernier is often attracted to didactic formats (sometimes literally—the heroine of *A Week's Vacation* is a schoolteacher, and teachers appear in both *Spoiled Children* and *Coup de Torchon*), yet he always ends by subverting them: teachers and pupils exchange roles, or the lesson turns out to be that there isn't any lesson. Didacticism is a closed form, but Tavernier's content is open—he's the enemy of pat conclusions, final judgments. When he applies a closed form to an open thematic, the form inevitably snaps, and that snap—the spillover of unresolvable problems, unanswerable questions—is nowhere more satisfying in his work than in *Coup de Torchon*. During the film's last half hour, the violence contained in Cordier breaks out, infecting the other characters, and the narrative breaks down, fragmenting into shorter scenes and harsher transitions. The sanitizing operation implied by the title (it translates literally as "stroke of the towel"—wiping up) has left more grime than before. Yet it is still too simple to say that the lesson of *Coup de Torchon* is that violence inevitably fails, and that nothing can be done about the evil in the world. Cordier has unquestionably accomplished some good through his actions, and in a way they have purified him. He is a better man at the end of the film, more aware, more compassionate, more involved. He's a monster with a lofty soul.

—*Dave Kehr*

Bertrand Tavernier

■

LIFE AND NOTHING BUT (1989)

On a broad canvas painted in constantly shifting shades of blue-gray and brown, life emerges from the aftermath of World War I in Bertrand Tavernier's rich, deeply satisfying meditation *Life and Nothing But.* Along with *A Sunday in the Country,* it's Tavernier at his best because he's found deeper ways to patiently draw warmth from a moment in history, a group of characters, and a landscape that at first are hidden under a cold fog of uncertainty.

On the hillsides where France lost 1.5 million men, Major Dellaplane (Philippe Noiret) is in charge of 350,000 missing-in-action cases. Alice (Pascale Vignal), a young schoolteacher from the provinces, bicycles into his territory looking for her lost fiancé. Irene (Sabine Azema), an aristocratic Parisian, arrives in a chauffeured touring car to insist on a top-priority investigation of her husband's whereabouts.

Under the drizzly, slate-gray skies of northern France, where unexploded shells still hide in muddy fields, both women think they may have traced their men to the train full of corpses in a tunnel buried by German mines. Looking for people who may be dead or alive, Alice and Irene try to pick their way through the borderland between the past and the future, the end of the war and the beginning of peace.

So is Dellaplane, who saves his most bitter cynicism for his additional assignment—to find the body of a single Unknown Soldier to be placed under the Arc de Triomphe. Out of 350,000, he's supposed to choose one. He's supposed to be the magician who changes several hundred thousand symbols of anonymous devastation into one symbol of anonymous courage—who changes all the things his country wants to forget into the one thing it wants to remember.

While an artist commissioned to sculpt the monument to a village's dead scurries around the train excavation site looking for inspiration, Dellaplane knows the most sadly fitting monument is the mud that's slid down to bury the men in the tunnel. Or the pathetic personal belongings—photos, Bibles, cups—dug from the wreckage and picked over by families who don't know whether their sons, brothers, and husbands are dead or alive.

In the end, Alice, Irene, and Dellaplane find they also have to choose between death and life. It's right that Vignal's Alice—vivid, fervent, too young to have had her hopes crushed—moves most quickly through the strongest outward signs of grief and reawakening.

It's right that Noiret's Dellaplane moves most slowly and sadly toward his choice. The actor who looks like a softly eroded farm field is a walking expression of cynicism weathered into melancholy, then into a gentle, humane patience. After seven films with Tavernier, the director's alter ego has found his most touching distillation in this role that won Noiret his first French Oscar for Best Actor. Most of all, though, it's right that Azema's Irene is the catalyst for Dellaplane's choice. Refined, high-strung, demanding and unbending, her pride conceals the greatest passion. Her journey, the most secretive, is also the most intense. It's Azema's presence in both *A Sunday in the Country* and *Life and Nothing But* that makes them Tavernier's best.

The director has said that he modeled the Irene-Dellaplane relationship on thirties comedies matching Katharine Hepburn's thoroughbred eccentricity with Cary Grant's bumbling reticence. Tavernier's reworking matches Azema's high-strung breeding and ardent spirit with Noiret's seasoned tolerance and compassionate resignation.

As they move toward each other, the film's muted, misty slates and sepias turn into richer shades of sky-blue and earth-brown. His long shots of people framed by a war-torn world turn into close-ups of faces radiating hopes for a newer, better world.

Tavernier is from the same generation as the French New Wave directors epitomized by François Truffaut. Where their films are iconoclastic and personal, Tavernier's are classic, historical, panoramic, collective. Truffaut's best movies were like fresh springs of emotion. Tavernier's *A Sunday in the Country* and *Life and Nothing But* are the stately rivers of understanding that took a longer time to find their director's broadest, deepest talent for suggesting that life and nothing but is always a matter of love and nothing but. **(Video request.)**

—Kathy Schulz Huffhines

François Truffaut
■

RETROSPECTIVE

François Truffaut, who died in October 1984, at the age of fifty-two, was first a critic and then a filmmaker. As a filmmaker, he was at his best in historical films, like *Jules and Jim, The Wild Child,* and *The Story of Adèle H.* As a critic, he did his most passionate writing in obituaries for directors he loved. A tone of retrospection, of elegy, came easily to him. The period films are made poignant by his wholly distinctive editing style: rapid, fleeting, episodic, a series of intense moments that often appear to have been cut off prematurely, before we can surrender to the illusion of their dramatic immediacy—vignettes linked only by matter-of-fact narrations whose effect is strangely melancholy, interpreting and mediating, and thus reminding us that the lives we're watching are long over. These pictures are moving in the way discovered letters and journals are, intimate and remote in equal measure:

we follow the traces of once vital passions. In his writings on film, Truffaut was always looking for such traces in the work of his favorite directors, scanning even the most apparently opaque Hollywood surfaces for the features of the artists behind them. (This is the essence of the "auteur theory," which Truffaut championed in Cahiers du Cinéma in the fifties.) What interested him was the personality of the filmmaker, and his criticism often reads like a peculiar form of biography—as if every director's body of work were the journal of a life, as if every individual movie were a letter addressed to him. Truffaut's articles, and especially his obituaries, express a profound desire for identification with their subjects, coupled with an ironic awareness that they can be no more than sympathetic commentaries, voice-overs.

In the course of his erratic career, Truffaut left elements of autobiography, signs of himself, everywhere, and in a variety of forms. His works include the explicitly autobiographical Antoine Doinel series of films (The 400 Blows, the "Antoine and Colette" episode of Love at Twenty, Stolen Kisses, Bed and Board, and Love on the Run); three movies (The Wild Child, Day for Night, and The Green Room) in which he played an important character himself, and others in which he did Hitchcocklike cameos; a memorable appearance as a UFO expert in Spielberg's Close Encounters of the Third Kind; innumerable interviews; a large handful of graceful, very personal prefaces, mostly to editions of his own screenplays and to the work of his mentor, the critic André Bazin; the text of his extensive conversations with Alfred Hitchcock, known here as Hitchcock/Truffaut; and his own selection of his critical writings from the midfifties through the midseventies, The Films in My Life. Truffaut clearly wanted members of his audience to be able to evoke him as they watched his films—for him this direct contact between the filmmaker and the moviegoer was the essence, the real experience, of the movies. He once characterized the films of Jean Renoir, the director he most admired, as "conversations," and the body of Renoir's work as "thirty-five natural and alive films, modest and sincere, as simple as saying hello."

Truffaut's descriptions of his own early moviegoing, in the forties, are lyrical and finely detailed, almost reverent, with a kind of awe at the feelings these movies stirred in him. In his introduction to one of Bazin's collections, Truffaut wrote about the first movie he could remember seeing, Abel Gance's Paradis Perdu: "The coincidence between the situation of the characters in the film and that of the spectators was such that the entire audience wept, hundreds of handkerchiefs piercing the darkness with little points of white. Never again was I to feel such an emotional unanimity in response to a film." The movies were for Truffaut what the radiant femme fatale Catherine was for Jules and Jim, what Lieutenant Pinson was for Adèle Hugo, what water and sunlight were for Victor, the wild boy of Aveyron—the first great experience, the one that seems to embody all the world's secrets, the moment to which our imaginations are ceaselessly returning. Truffaut's idea of cinema was of a sacred, magical instrument that transmitted to him, across great distances, the voices of great men; and too frequently, both in his criticism and—more damagingly—in his films, he made the mistake of believing that the greatness of cinema could be found in the properties of the instrument itself rather than in the quality of the voice or the magnitude of the emotional response. When he grilled Hitchcock for fifty hours on the secrets of his technique, when he tried his hand at his own "Hitchcock films" (*The Bride Wore Black* and *Mississippi Mermaid*), and when, at the end of his career, he began to turn out smooth and utterly impersonal exercises in classical style, like *The Last Métro* and *The Woman Next Door,* Truffaut was perhaps conducting experiments on the source of the cinema's grace—hoping, with a seminarian's uneasy faith, that it could be found in perfectly imitated forms, precise invocations.

His youthful passion for moviegoing may have dwindled, over time, to a mythic notion of "cinema," but Truffaut's best movies were also triumphant vindications of that passion—proof that a full and sympathetic response to movies, or literature, can be the means to a complex understanding of experience. The exhilarating early scenes of *Jules and Jim,* in which the two young intellectuals of 1912 argue about literature, experiment with love, and discover Catherine, their feminine ideal, are the work of an artist who knows that exuberance, that playful and profound rapture. What makes the movie so unsettling is that Truffaut also knows (just two years after *The 400 Blows* and the rest of the first crop of New Wave films had seemed to reinvent the rules of the game for cinema) the fading of that spirit, the messy accumulation of experience that blurs the clear outline of the ideal. The movie's buoyant, helter-skelter rhythms stop abruptly with the outbreak of the First World War, and from then on the narrative proceeds by way of long leaps in time, the characters losing sight of each other for gaps of weeks, even months; and every time we pick them up again we read their faces closely (Why does Jules look so wan and small, swaddled in his bulky sweater? Why has Catherine's mouth set that way?) to fill in the gaps, to figure out how these people got so tired from living up to their younger selves. The beauty, the real wisdom, of *Jules and Jim* is that the disillusionment of its characters—their painfully protracted awareness of failure—doesn't diminish the value of their moral experiment.

If you see *Jules and Jim* at the right age—in college—you may feel the way Truffaut did when he saw *Paradis Perdu* as a child, overwhelmed by the possibilities of movies, or the way he felt later on while watching Renoir's films, as if he were engaged in a lively, intimate conversation; what we hear in *Jules and Jim,* though, isn't a master's voice but that of a brilliant and generous student. Perhaps better than any other filmmaker, Truffaut conveys the thrill of *learning,* and the wide range of emotion in *Jules and Jim* reflects the range of its director's long apprenticeship in the movies: from his childhood discovery of their power, to the more articulate appreciation of the young critic, to the anxious joy of making movies of his own, of hearing for the first time that mysterious language spoken in his own voice. This excitement, strangely, doesn't come across so forcefully in the autobiographical Antoine Doinel pictures that followed *The 400 Blows,* or in his movies about movies, like the Hitchcock pastiches and *Day for Night.* Maybe he needed the distance of history to be able to express himself freely; maybe he worked best when the very making of the movie was a process of learning, when he could immerse himself in the effort of understanding and re-creating a past age. Or maybe Truffaut, with his double perspective of filmmaker and critic, the iconoclastic New Wave pioneer and the reverent *auteur* theorist (who gave the heading *The Big Secret* to his writings on directors who began in the silent era), brought to his historical films his deepest and most complex sense of himself: that his own passions, his most spirited inventions would someday—like those of his characters and of his cinematic masters—be things of the past, objects of study.

Truffaut's habit of retrospection, the melancholy that invaded *Jules and Jim,* was more pronounced in his later films, as he became (in technical terms, at least) less the adventurous student and more the confident master. The madness of Adèle Hugo, the heroine of Truffaut's last masterpiece, is kin to the romantic folly of Jules and Jim, but the style of the film is hermetic, perfectly controlled: the love affair that is Adèle's obsession is over before the story begins, and *The Story of Adèle H.,* with sympathy and irony, traces her attempt to turn her passion into a myth, to immortalize herself as her father, Victor Hugo, immortalized her drowned sister, Léopoldine. "Despite my youth," she says, in voice-over, as we watch the beautiful nineteen-year-old Isabelle Adjani writing in her journal, "I sometimes feel I am in the autumn of my life." Near the end, as she glides through the streets of Barbados in a long, dark cloak, Adèle seems truly disembodied, and the narrator, over a still photograph of her grave, tells us that she spent the last forty years of her life in a clinic, writing her journals in a secret language.

In his final appearance on the screen, Truffaut played the lead in the morbid, unpleasant *The Green Room.* His character, Julien Davenne, is a man obsessed with preserving the memory of his dead wife and of all his compatriots killed in the First World War; he works for a newspaper no one reads anymore, and is a genius at obituaries. Davenne's behavior is outrageous, but we can't read any irony in Truffaut's face or hear it in the voice of the film. And in the movies that followed *The Green Room* the author's voice isn't audible at all—as if he had finally drowned in the imperious language of his masters. The sight of Truffaut, as Davenne, yearning for a reunion with his beloved dead is unnerving: it's an extension of the ideas in *Adèle H.,* and it's consistent—as an extreme consequence—with some of the traces of personality he scattered through his work. But a portrait of the artist based on this image would be a distortion—a death mask, more obituary than true biography. *Jules and Jim,* for all its elegiac consciousness of youthful spirits' eventual exhaustion, taught a generation of movie lovers and moviemakers that the process was more important than the end, that the give-and-take vitality of conversation was everything—that the giddy, briefly magical convergence of Jules and Jim and Catherine mattered more than Jules's ultimate solitude. Everything converged for Truffaut in the middle of his career as a director with *The Wild Child,* his most beautiful film and his fullest revelation of himself.

The Wild Child, set in 1798, is based on the writings of Jean Itard, a French doctor who tried to educate a "wild boy" found in the forest of Aveyron. Truffaut cast himself as Itard, and the scientist's earnest, rational eighteenth-century spirit dominates the film, as if it had taken possession of the director: the movie is lucid and serenely paced, composed primarily of medium and long shots in elegant, plain black and white, the narrative thread provided by Truffaut's voice-over reading of Itard's precisely worded observations of his humane experiments with the wild boy. The only "effect" is an archaic one: the repeated use of an iris—a device that isolates a detail in a kind of cameo within an otherwise darkened frame—as a transition between scenes. (In order to avoid the impersonal look of effects created in the laboratory, Truffaut's cinematographer, Nestor Almendros, actually searched for, and found, an iris that had been used in the silent era. "The iris of the silent film," Almendros has written, "had the quality, now lost, of a handmade thing.") The homage to the early days of movies isn't arbitrary: this film about an experiment in education, the attempt to teach an inarticulate boy to speak, is suffused with Truffaut's radiant love for the movies' beginnings, when everything was being done for the first time, when the language was learned.

The movie, filmed eight years after *Jules and Jim* and eight years before *The Green Room,* has a miraculous kind of balance: between freedom and control, originality and homage, the discovery of new experience and the contemplation of the past—between the boy Victor's mysterious ecstasy as he opens his mouth to drink in the falling rain and the supremely rational pleasure of Itard as he stands by the window and records the progress of the lessons, his journal bathed in the clear light of the eighteenth century. In this film, Truffaut gives us an image of himself as both master and student, the image that contains all we need to know of him. The story of *The Wild Child* is just an episode artfully isolated from the lives of Itard and the wild boy: the film doesn't tell us how Victor came to be abandoned in the forest (the truth was never known), and it doesn't tell us, either, that Victor lived almost thirty years longer without ever coming close to mastering verbal communication. At the end, when Victor returns to Itard's house after a brief attempt at escape, Truffaut just irises out on the wild boy's youthful, intelligent, troubled face suspended within the surrounding blackness of the frame as he ascends the stairs.

— Terrence Rafferty

Agnès Varda

■

VAGABOND (1985)

The blunt power of *Vagabond* grabs hold right from the beginning. Discordant music jars the pastoral calm of the golden-lighted French countryside. A field hand unearths the body of a woman, her face lightly caked with mud so that she looks like a plaster mannequin.

Two *gendarmes* appear on the scene. A little flustered, they consult. "A natural death," they finally decide.

This ironic conclusion is one of French director and screen writer Agnès Varda's many deft touches as she pulls us into the death and final weeks of an eighteen-year-old dropout who called herself Mona. As created by Ms. Varda and played by the haunting young actress Sandrine Bonnaire, Mona becomes the mesmerizing symbol of homelessness, leading a life the *gendarmes* would think most decidedly "unnatural."

I say symbol because we come to know Mona only through people she bumped into during her brief days on the road. Rather than a fully realized character, she becomes a fantasy for some — the ultimate free spirit — and an object of pity or revulsion for others — the repository of their shame and guilt. "She scares me because she repels me," says a young man who leaves her retching in a train station. "I should have done something for her," says a woman professor, who picked up Mona hitchhiking, fed her, and let her sleep in her car. "I don't even know her name."

Director Varda, one of the pioneers of the French New Wave that began in 1959, has directed and written ten films, including three documentaries. Although *Vagabond* moves with the artistic flow of fiction, Ms. Varda has taken an unsentimental, quasi-documentary approach, as she weaves into the narrative interviews with those who met Mona.

In some ways, Mona is really a foil for the witnesses to the last weeks of her enigmatic life, a way for them to voice their hopes, fears, bigotry, lost dreams. And that is the film's power, because it connects us with the way we find ourselves in life reacting to people lying stinking on the street, begging for change or simply staring into space. We step over them, feed them, or weep helplessly for them depending upon a variety of things, including how much room for compassion we happen to have in store on a particular day.

When Mona briefly hooks up with a middle-aged hippie, a former philosophy student who lives on a goat farm with his wife and baby, he reminisces with the drifter about his days as a goatherd on the road. "Not the same," she says. With the goats, a wife, "It's like a moving house." Finally, though, the philosopher-farmer gets fed up with Mona's utter aimlessness, her refusal to conform to his particular mode of rebellion and work the land. Exasperated, he says, "That's not wandering. It's withering."

Yolanda, a rich lady's maid saddled with an ungrateful bum of a boyfriend, gazes longingly at the sight of Mona sleeping in the arms of another trespassing vagabond. The hapless Yolanda repeatedly sighs over the memory of this scene, which for her becomes the ultimate in romantic love. Ms. Varda wrests even another small twist from this interlude, as Mona and her friend eat beans from cans, huddle together under blankets and chain-smoke. "Usually it doesn't last two days with me," Mona tells him earnestly. After she's gone, he says: "I thought she was a homebody. The staying kind."

The facts we have about Mona are few: She went to high school, was a secretary, has no family. She has a sense of humor; she puns a lot. Ms. Varda has used Ms. Bonnaire's hollow-eyed beauty powerfully. Traipsing across a field jauntily lugging her backpack, a cigarette hanging out of her mouth, Mona is the picture of freedom. There's something compelling in her defiant spirit, as when a woman who has given her some food and champagne asks her why she's dropped out and Mona takes a slug of bubbly from the bottle: "Champagne on the road tastes better," she says. Later, though, when she is cold, dirty, sick, her eyes go blank. She becomes the walking dead.

Mona seems like a throwback to the anomic youth of Jean Luc-Godard's *Breathless*, someone for whom aimlessness itself has become the only response to an aimless society. Yet Ms. Varda isn't on a crusade. Mona isn't set up to be a hero or a victim, nor are the people who make up "society" monolithic in their response to her. Some are kind, some cruel, some indifferent. They are human. And, through this tough, memorable film, Ms. Varda reaches for our humanity with a force that very few movies can muster.

—*Julie Salamon*

Agnès Varda

■

CLEO FROM 5 TO 7 (1962)

One of the few films directed by a woman in which the viewer can sense a difference. The story is about the moods of a beautiful, chic popular singer (Corinne Marchand) during the two hours she waits to find out if she has cancer. Childish and fearful, she consults her horoscope and goes to a fortuneteller; she buys a hat; she rehearses a song; she cries. And throughout, the writer-director, Agnès Varda, sustains an unsentimental yet subjective tone that is almost unique in the history of movies. Cinematography by Jean Rabier; editing by Janine Verneau; music by Michel Legrand (who also plays a part). With Antoine Bourseiller, Dorothée Blanck, and Dominique Davray.

—Pauline Kael

Andrzej Wajda

■

MAN OF MARBLE (1976)

The films that come to us from Eastern Europe bear the wounds of repression: holes in the dialogue, inexplicable plot leaps, missing scenes. In fact, gaps and contradictions are the least of it; repression bleeds into the very aesthetics of these movies, into the look of each shot and gesture. We're accustomed to thinking of Eastern European films as drizzly, *angst*-ridden studies of drizzly, *angst*-ridden people; repression has made them taciturn and sullen—or else, as in the case of Miklos Jancso, furiously pictorial, as if a long-suppressed scream had burst forth in the violence of soldiers, pounding hooves, and vast, wintry landscapes. Occasionally, however, repression cuts into an artist and his work in a manner that's almost sculptural: by carving away everything but the urgency and the anger, repression can turn a good artist into a great one. I think we've seen this in the case of Carlos Saura, whose dark, glittering fables are unimaginable outside the claustrophobic world of Franco's Spain. And now there is *Man of*

Marble (1977), a restless, uneven, beautiful work by the Polish director Andrzej Wajda (pronounced An-jay Vy-da), who in the fifties commanded the world's attention with *Kanal* (1956) and *Ashes and Diamonds* (1958). Thirteen years in the making, and nearly three hours long, *Man of Marble* is not as tidy as the earlier Wajda films. It sprawls and stumbles and irritates, and its goals often outstrip its means. But it is also quite moving, and in an unexpected way: one is touched not by its story or its characters but by the seething spirit underneath, the spirit of an artist struggling to say what mustn't be said, to show what mustn't be shown.

Man of Marble is monumentally ambitious; it borrows the structures of *Citizen Kane* and then uses them to evoke the entire history of Poland since 1950. On one level, this is the story of Agnieszka (Krystyna Janda), a tense, willful young movie director who wants to make a film about the rise and fall of a Polish "model worker" of the fifties, Mateusz Birkut. Birkut, it seems, had made a name for himself by devising a five-man method of bricklaying and using it to lay thirty thousand bricks in a single shift—this, apparently, was postwar Poland's idea of a media event. Filmed and publicized, his bricklaying performance had made Birkut a national figure, but sometime before the Stalinist government of Boleslaw Beirut gave way to the reformist government of Wladyslaw Gomulka, his face had disappeared from posters, and his name from the annals of Polish heroism. Beginning, as *Citizen Kane* does, with a deftly satirical newsreel about the hero's life, *Man of Marble* follows Agnieszka's obsessive investigation into the real story of Birkut. Stymied by her sponsor's reluctance to obtain classified material for her—and eventually by his outright refusal to let her make the film—Agnieszka bulls ahead, interviewing Birkut's best friend, his boss, his wife, even the secret police agent who had once hounded him. Most of them, of course, would rather keep quiet. (Indeed, Birkut's story is never really completed in the version of *Man of Marble* available to us: before its enormously successful Polish debut in 1977, the censors removed a crucial reference to Birkut's death in the Gdansk workers' riots of 1970—the very riots that resulted in the downfall of Gomulka's government.) Birkut's story unfolds in flashbacks: we watch him through the eyes of his former comrades, and, like Welles, Wajda provides enough nuance and detail to let us judge the storytellers along with their stories. But for Birkut, there is no "Rosebud"; he seems to have been a rather simple man, an idealist who sincerely thought his construction technique would result in greater productivity — eventually in a cozy little home for every worker in Poland. How could he know that other workers would find the prodigious productivity standards he's set more burdensome than inspiring; or that his very innocence and energy would mark him as a dangerous man when the tides of official opinion shifted? In the end, it isn't Birkut whose depths seem unfathomable, it's Poland. Instead of the history of a man, we unexpectedly find ourselves caught up in the history of a society — a history as murky and twisted as the inner life of Charles Foster Kane.

To Americans, of course, the dissection of a society is probably not as thrilling as the dissection of a great man. We're all individualists here, all intoxicated by the belief that men create history and bend the world to their wills; the theology of individual ambition has become our state religion. But in Eastern Europe, the state itself is the dominant religion. The state bends men to *its* will, creates personalities in its own image, and, when that image changes, destroys those who can't change with it. In the Poland that Wajda paints, one must be as canny as a con man to survive; one must watch for signals, for shifts in tone and emphasis; one must endorse the right propaganda. Public life comes to seem an endless game of cat and mouse, and woe to the innocent peasant who, like Birkut, becomes a pawn without even knowing he's playing. Jerzy Radziwilowicz, who portrays Birkut with a sort of incandescent naïveté, is like a homelier Gary Cooper — or rather, like a Gary Cooper who's awakened to find Gérard Depardieu's nose jammed onto his face. Big and sincere and sexy, with a child's wet, excitable eyes, this Polish Mr. Deeds is clearly a manufactured hero — in fact, his bricklaying feat turns out to have been staged by an ambitious young filmmaker who needed a star for his propaganda film *Architects of Our Happiness*. In a wonderfully sardonic sequence, we watch as Birkut is fed enormous quantities of sausage and steak, then shaved, clipped, and perfumed by a squadron of barbers, and finally released to his bricklaying — a task performed to the accompaniment of a radio announcer, an enthusiastic crowd, and even a miserably oom-pah-ing band. But living in the public eye proves perilous. When Birkut demonstrates his new method to workers in a remove province, someone hands him a red-hot brick, and his hands are horribly burned. Birkut's best friend is framed for this sabotage, and Birkut protests — rather too loudly for his own good. As he righteously pursues the issue all the way to Warsaw, we gradually become aware of watchful eyes and clandestine murmurs. *Man of Marble*'s story and characters may feel a bit distant, but the movie is never dull. It's a tale of intrigue — the daily intrigue of the life of a reluctant Polish hero — and it twists and turns like a spy novel.

So, in fact, does Wajda: his style is a perfect distillation of the tricky game that is survival in Poland. Wajda's camera feints, winks, jabs, and then drops back, as if to avoid reprisal, and beneath nearly every shot, one can feel the turbulent energy of an artist reining in his rage. In fact, Wajda's ferocity occasionally breaks loose to invade the screen; characters suddenly loom above us in low-angle shots, or turn to stare belligerently into the camera; scenes about Polish bureaucracy take place in corridors that have been stretched into endless tunnels by Wajda's wide-angle lens. The eclectic wit that bubbles through this film should lay the drizzly reputation of the Polish cinema to rest, at least for a decent interval. In a brilliant twenty-minute sequence, Wajda re-creates portions of *Architects of Our Happiness,* including the requisite denunciation of degenerate capitalist artists (like Henry Moore) and a parade in which monstrous effigies of Truman, Eisenhower, and MacArthur lope by to the jeers of the happy throng. And when Agnieszka visits Birkut's old friend Witek, who has now straightened up and become the high muckamuck of a proud new steel foundry, he keeps interrupting her questions to praise his mill and his machinery, in hopes that she'll give up on Birkut and make a nice, neat propaganda film about the wonders of Poland's steel industry — whereupon Wajda inserts his own little hooray-for-steel movie, in response, no doubt, to similar encounters of his own.

At the heart of this jittery, high-strung film is a jittery, high-strung performance — that of Krystyna Janda, the rangy blonde who plays Agnieszka. Dressed in a uniform of bell-bottom jeans, denim jacket, and yards of scarf, Janda gulps on cigarettes, twists her lanky frame into impossible positions, chews on her lips; her headlong walk is like a cartoon of youthful determination, and Wajda slyly mocks this abrasive Hope of the Future by setting her crew scurrying to keep up with her, dragging equipment and rolling their eyes in exasperation. Watching Janda, in fact, is rather startling; one realizes how rare such a characterization is in American movies, where actresses are generally confined to playing a narrow range of sexual ideals. In an American *Man of Marble,* Agnieszka would probably be portrayed by Jane Fonda, and as we wondered whether she'd get her film made, we'd also be wondering whom she'd sleep with. For better or for worse, Wajda evinces no attitude whatsoever about Agnieszka's sexuality; she's not pretty and she's not ugly, and we are left to our own conclusions. All of which feels, if not exactly refreshing, at least exotic. Censorship comes in many forms: there is censorship by government and censorship by the marketplace. Even in Eastern Europe, it seems, a filmmaker may take liberties that the stern code of Hollywood forbids.

—Stephen Schiff

Andrzej Wajda

■

KANAL (1956)

John Simon once declared this portrayal of the collapse of the 1944 Warsaw uprising against the Nazis one of the dozen or so finest films of all time and a true vision of hell. Was that because most of the movie takes place in a sewer? The movie comes from Wajda's graphically exciting sixties black-and-white period; it has the claustrophobic intensity and steadily mounting suspense of the best fifties war films. Wajda's partisans wander through the city's dank underground, while gunfire rakes the sunlit streets above; freedom seems a chimera to which they desperately cling.

—Michael Wilmington

THE THIRD WAVE, 1965–90

Push the edge of the second wave's envelope of funkiness, freakiness, irony, and self-conscious stylization and you get the third wave of international directors — starting with Germany's Rainer Werner Fassbinder, Werner Herzog, and Wim Wenders in the mid-sixties. The German New Wave brought Fassbinder, gangster stylist of melodrama and politics; Herzog, friend of dwarfs and enemy of empire builders; and Wenders, the road movie existentialist whose films have grown the most.

Opposite page: scene from *Get Out Your Handkerchiefs*.

In France, gnarly funkiness was meat and drink to Maurice Pialat and his films about sexual tangling and quarreling. Ditto for Bertrand Blier, who jumped onto the same subject with his witty, bizarre fairy tales. Midnight-blue meat and fizzy drink to Jean-Jacques Beineix: style itself.

Japan's representatives of funk and satire include Shohei Imamura — whose most humid sex, struggle, and survival-of-the-fittest movies date from this period — and Juzo Itami, whose snappy, zappy social critiques take on food fads, tax dodgers, and funeral games.

Holland's ironic stylist of sexual politics is Paul Verhoeven, Spain's is Pedro Almodóvar. In Canada, David Cronenberg made horror his own creepy psychological territory, brooding about all the things that can go wrong under your skull and inside your skin.

Elsewhere, skewed views were more tied to cultural traditions. Unlike the second wave of English directors, who filmed books and plays about working-class life, Stephen Frears got down to the real thing, making peripheral characters the center of his films, while directors like Bill Forsyth and Neil Jordan brought, respectively, Scottish quirkiness and updated Irish Catholicism to their movies.

Yugoslavia's Emir Kusturica put his country's off-balance history into every frame of his films. Peter Weir drew on Australian aboriginal concepts for the eerie implications of landscape in both his Australian films and his later American films.

Other recommended titles available on video are:

Percy Adlon: *Bagdad Cafe* (1988)

David Cronenberg: *Rabid* (1977), *The Brood* (1980)

Rainer Werner Fassbinder: *The Bitter Tears of Petra von Kant* (1972), *The Merchant of Four Seasons* (1972), *Fox and His Friends* (1975)

Bill Forsyth: *Comfort and Joy* (1984)

Stephen Frears: *Sammy and Rosie Get Laid* (1987)

Peter Greenaway: *Zed and Two Naughts* (1985)

Werner Herzog: *Stroszek* (1977)

Shohei Imamura: *Vengeance Is Mine* (1979), *The Ballad of Narayama* (1984)

Juzo Itami: *The Funeral* (1984), *The Taxing Woman's Return* (1989)

Paul Verhoeven: *Turkish Delights* (1974), *Keetje Tippel* (English title: *Katie's Passion*) (1975), *Soldier of Orange* (1979), *Spetters* (1981)

Peter Weir: *The Last Wave* (1977)

Percy Adlon

■

CÉLESTE (1981)

From 1914 to 1921, while Marcel Proust lay in his cork-lined bedroom scribbling out his masterpiece about lost time on frayed pieces of loose-leaf paper, a young housekeeper, Céleste Albaret, waited patiently in the kitchen for "Monsieur" to ring. A country girl, the wife of Proust's chauffeur, she would seem to have had little in common with the hypersensitive, hypochondriacal dandy who insisted his sheets be changed every day and whose mail had to be disinfected before he would read it. Yet *Céleste* is a document of mutual devotion, a very special love story. In some instinctive way, this Céleste—whose book about her years with Proust inspired the German filmmaker Percy Adlon to make this gemlike film—understood Proust as few others did, and she served him as mother, child, and collaborator, bringing him information of the outside world that helped him to write *Remembrance of Things Past.* "I rouse his game and—bang!" she exclaims.

Appropriately, Adlon's film begins by making us aware of time itself: the eternally ticking clock and hissing kettle that fill the hours Céleste spends waiting. Adlon works in a spare, meticulous style, but he's a bit of a Proustian himself, leaping back and forth through these eight years from the springboard of Céleste's memories. And what exquisite scenes she remembers: the excited Proust, returning from a dinner party, describing guests such as the outrageous Jean Cocteau, who leapt onto the table in tribute to Proust. Or the night he returned from a male brothel where he witnessed through a peephole a man ecstatically submitting to a whipping. "How can you watch such things?" the upset Céleste cries. "I'd watch worse," he confesses. "Because I lack imagination. I have to collect it all." In one long night of the soul, he even flirts with death, needing the experience for his book.

In its minimalist, sideways way, *Céleste* achieves what so many films have tried, and failed, to portray—a convincing depiction of the artist at work. We see the writer in all his childish posturing and dedicated glory through Céleste's loving eyes—and through the medium of two extraordinary, subtle performers, Eva Mattes and Jürgen Arndt. This is acting calibrated with the delicacy of a fine jeweler. This moving, hypnotically condensed film knows just how huge a statement is contained in the smallest of gestures.

—*David Ansen*

Percy Adlon

■

SUGARBABY (1984)

Some films drown you in action; others choke you with talk. Percy Adlon's *Sugarbaby* gorges you on flesh, food, and honeyed light. It's a very tactile, sensual movie: a film of tastes and touches, a succulent comedy that lingers over its images like a gourmet eyeing a toothsome morsel. Let's pull out an overused word for it: delicious. No recent movie deserves it more.

The premise at first seems strange, even distasteful. Adlon shows us, in lip-smacking detail, the wild infatuation of a 250-pound middle-aged Munich mortuary attendant for a slim young subway conductor. She pursues him relentlessly, woos him with candy bars and a rare old 1965 Peter Kraus hit ("Sugarbaby," of course). Finally, she conquers him; swooning among sweets and sweats in the satiny pleasure pit she's made of her formerly drab, barren flat.

This is one of the oddest, most touching screen couples since Harold met Maude—yet you have no difficulty understanding the conductor's submission. The smitten mortuary attendant—teetering on stiletto heels, face smeared with mascara and longing—is so suffused with love she's honestly beautiful. Why shouldn't he succumb? She's fond, affectionate, unselfishly loving, adventurous, and brave. His wife is a skinny, driven, uptight yuppie harpie, a blond bombshell with the pin pulled.

The lovelorn nibblers—both of whom give naked, unabashed, delightful performances—have the same names as the actors who play them: Marianne Sägebrecht and Eisi Gulp (not a pseudonym). Respectively, in real life they're a famous avant-garde theater producer and a street acrobat–clown.

Adlon's script was inspired by two contrasting images of Sägebrecht at cast parties for his TV "Don Quixote" (in which she played Mrs.

Sancho Panza): first, floating with somnolent heaviness in a fluorescent-lit pool, and later frugging madly to rock 'n' roll. (These two images now open and close the film, obviously symbolizing passivity and passion, repression and hedonism, living death and the pace that kills.)

Adlon up to now has specialized in careful biographies and historical subjects (*Céleste, The Swing*). Here, he performs a little miracle of sumptuous results from slender means.

Sugarbaby is shot mostly in two apartments, the streets, and the subway, and cinematographer Johanna Heer has bathed each scene (sometimes sections of the same scene) in strange floods of light. Sickly greens hang over the mortuary, anxious blues over Marianne's apartment (where she lives in a cul-de-sac of nonstop snacks, TV propped against the bed). At the first view of her Metro Adonis, the screen explodes with white; later, reds and pinks drench their lovemaking, lapping over the bed like lavender waves.

The camerawork is equally audacious: The first shots of Marianne are from a fixed, tight, Teutonic position. When Eros reigns, the camera becomes languorous, almost random — it swings and sways, drifts over tousled sheets, wanders like a lover's hands.

Sugarbaby will not be to everyone's taste. If you are the teensiest bit anorexic, you may see the entire film (and not just the opening) as some kind of horror story. Moralists of every stripe will be equally revulsed; some may demand that the entire company be sent to Weight Watchers.

But there's a fond, foolish, very humane fire illumining *Sugarbaby* — not just the hot pinks of Heer's lighting, but a flush of acceptance, tolerance, generosity. This tale of love within traps is as pure and sweet (yet disturbing) a romantic comedy as we've seen all year. Watching it, you can almost feel your belly tingle, your cheeks flush, and your heart warm. After a while, you may even want a bite.

— *Michael Wilmington*

Pedro Almodóvar

■

RETROSPECTIVE

Mira! (That's Spanish for "Check this out!") Behold pop-eyed Pedro Almodóvar on opening night of the New York Film Festival where his *Women on the Verge of a Nervous Breakdown* enjoys its American debut. With those caterpillar sideburns bracketing his quizzical face like Spanish question marks, the thirty-seven-year-old man of La Mancha lives up to the title of his best-known feature, *What Have I Done to Deserve This?*

Ten years ago he was an obscure phone company employee in Madrid. Tonight Almodóvar is the *tostada* of New York. Dressed in basic black on black, the director of a parti-colored fiesta of a movie strolls onstage at Avery Fisher Hall where the usually withholding first-nighters welcome him giddily, with thunderclaps of applause and lightning laughter. What did Almodóvar do to deserve this? He made a comedy of bad manners.

In a nasal singsong that sounds like Desi Arnaz by way of Woody Allen, Almodóvar graciously greets the enthusiasm from those waiting to see his seventh feature in seven years: "I want to marry you! I want to marry you all!" And then he confides (or does he declaim?): "I am not accustomed to playing the part of the insider. For so many years I have been the outsider looking in."

Applause — and giggles — are constant throughout the picaresque *Women on the Verge,* the saga of saucy Pepa (Carmen Maura), abandoned by her two-timing, four-flusher sweetheart. After Pepa attempts suicide by spiking her gazpacho with Valium, she confronts a suddenly life-affirming problem: Her cigarette has set the bed aflame. Mattress flambé just doesn't go with cold vegetable soup, however spicy. If Pepa can't extinguish the fire in her heart, at least she can put out the conflagration in her boudoir. And she does so, with frazzled élan — and the help of a garden hose.

The film's delirium is contagious. The Lincoln Center audience becomes one with the valiant Pepa, drugged and determined to be wined and dined and ermined. If this was television, you'd think the crowd's roar was a laugh track. Hear this, that rarest of urban sounds: a Manhattan first-night audience actually enjoying itself.

¡Oye, 'mano! (That's Spanish for "Listen, bro'.") Here is Almodóvar, a cult director on the verge of a nervous breakthrough.

According to his autobiographical notes, "Pedro Almodóvar was born in La Mancha along with the decade of the fifties. It was the time of the cold war, the mambo, the big bands, Balenciaga, the death of Stalin, etc., but none of these would make the slightest bit of difference in Calzada de Calatrava, the village where he has born. Almodóvar looked about him and didn't like what he saw. He felt like an astronaut in the court of King Arthur . . ." Madrid was inevitable.

The feature films of Pedro Almodóvar—not to mention his homoerotic Super-8 flicks like *The Fall of Sodom* and *Love Goes; Love Comes*—are studded with irreverent juxtapositions similar to those in his autobiography. These are films about fashion and fascism, about bullfighting students who faint at the sight of blood, about heroin-addicted lesbian nuns. In short, these films cheerfully desecrate Spain's holy trinity of corrida, church, and state.

A good example of his iconoclastic viewpoint is *Dark Habits* (1983), Almodóvar's film about the cuckoo convent where nuns with names like Sister Sin (Carmen Maura) and Sister Manure stage fake miracles to finance their addiction. Or look at *What Have I Done to Deserve This?* (1985), the inglorious life of Gloria (Carmen Maura, of course), a lower-middle-class Madrid housewife who makes ends meet by selling her twelve-year-old son to the dentist and by concocting an ingenious recipe involving a ham bone.

Then there's *Matador* (1986), about the blood-sick bullfighting student and his instructor, whose motto is, "To stop killing is to stop living." Making the bedroom his personal ring, the teacher has taken to substituting women for bulls, killing them at his moment of passion. (Carmen Maura has a supporting role as a police psychiatrist.) Or take *Law of Desire* (1987), a life-imitates-art gag fest about a theater and film playwright-director and his transsexual sister (yes, Carmen Maura) who find themselves actually living through a murder scenario he's been writing.

As you've probably noticed, Almodóvar's leitmotifs are pain and pleasure, sex and death, gender and destiny—and most significant of all, Carmen Maura, the saucer-eyed, bouncy brunette who resembles nothing so much as two coconuts stuffed into a sausage casing. Maura is to Almodóvar what Dietrich was to von Sternberg, what Schygulla was to Fassbinder—but more so. Everything she says is in quotes; everything she does is clownishly exaggerated. How many other actresses could play male-to-female transsexuals, or portray women as though they were female impersonators, and convince you that the gender crisis was protective coloring against predatory machismo? If this sounds campy, you are misunderstanding. This is female picaresque, which some Americans are familiar with in the hilarious manifestos of John Waters and the late, great Charles Ludlam, artists whose misfit heroines were mystified — but rarely defeated — by the assumptions of male prerogative. In Spain it's not only hilarious but also subversive to use feminism as a weapon to satirize — and deflate — the machismo that has ballooned into the patriarchy of corrida, church, and state.

Like his countryman Antonio Gaudí, Almodóvar likes to counterpoise the shapely with the gnarled. Also like Gaudí, Almodóvar creates buildings and interiors that are emotional correlatives. Forget Goethe's icy eulogy that architecture is frozen music; for these Spaniards, architecture and decors are hot cha-cha, a volcanic gush. The gilded clutter of his movies could earn Almodóvar the title of Pedro Gaudy.

Take, for instance, Pepa's bubble-gum-pink penthouse apartment in *Women on the Verge,* with its retro-modern boomerang furniture and its proprietress's scarlet, dress-for-excess suits. Pepa's decor disorder — the seventies suits, sixties color schemes, and fifties furniture — is a symptom of a deadly form of PMS, postmodernism syndrome. Pepa had to live through these official styles sequentially, and now she has to relive them all simultaneously. Pepa's psyche is theatricalized in her decors.

In light of postmodernism syndrome, also consider the role of appliances in Pepa's world: They are really *mis*appliances, symbolic of her misalliance. It's with her Osterizer that Pepa mixes the gazpacho of death. Her telephone answering machine is the only place she hears from her lover, who intones velvet lies on the tape. And Pepa's telephone proves to be a false umbilical cord to the outside world: On the phone she can't really connect with her lovers and friends, so she yanks out this ersatz lifeline. It's not only former National Telephone Company employees like Almodóvar who relish Pepa's rage against this device.

For Pepa (as for Almodóvar, her alter ego), the telephone receiver is a symbol of discredited institutional authority. The telephone in *Women on the Verge* — like Almodóvar's matador's swords, politico-religious scepters, and domestic ham bones — is to be used subversively or discarded. In his cartoonish, utterly original way, Almodóvar aims for nothing short of redefining the phallus.

Mussolini's enemies used to admit that at least the dictator made the Italian trains run on time. Franco's enemies might well concede that the general's repressive policies and institutional pieties made possible the liberating irreverence of this director on the verge. Philosophers more learned than Pedro Almodóvar have pondered the connections between sex and death, pain and pleasure, gender and destiny. But none of them have had such a blast as the manic from La Mancha.

—Carrie Rickey

Jean-Jacques Beineix

■

DIVA (1981)

Nimble and pretty and lighter than air, *Diva* is a delicious little movie, and part of what one loves about it is its Frenchness. The French have not recently given us many films we could love, and perhaps that's surprising, since the pop cultures of America and France were once on such intimate terms. We shared a reverence for detective movies and the French New Wave, for rock 'n' roll and the spirit of May 1968. And then, in the seventies, there was suddenly a sense of cultural divorcement. The New Wave turned either bland (à la Truffaut) or arid (à la Godard), Gallic thought seemed a forbidding thicket of structuralisms and upside-down Marxisms, and the French kept exporting their god-awful adultery comedies. *Diva* comes as a sort of peace offering—in the form of a gorgeous meringue. It's a mad, frothy swirl of French and American fantasies, fetishes, references, and in-jokes, and it's enormously generous. Bursting with disco colors and fashion-magazine poses, *Diva* beckons to its audience. It lets us in on the giddy pleasure it takes in entertaining us.

Like Godard's *Breathless* (1959), the first great film of the French New Wave, *Diva* is about the star-crossed romance of a French man and an American woman. And that romance becomes a metaphor for the pas de deux of French and American sensibilities. But where *Breathless* probed and pricked and tied itself in splendid knots, *Diva* blithely dances; it doesn't pretend to *mean* anything. The first feature directed by thirty-five-year-old Jean-Jacques Beineix (who was once an assistant director for Jerry Lewis), it's a work of prodigious technique and glistening visual beauty, and it borrows wildly from the heavy ruminations of the avant-garde. But it's hardly the second coming of the New Wave. *Diva* is a whirligig, a glamorous joke on moviemaking, half thriller and half whimsy. It has a plot because plots make movies more fun; it's suspenseful because playfulness by itself is boring; its imagery borrows and puns and alludes because catching the references as they fly by is Beineix's idea of a good time.

The central romance is platonic and dreamy; it's a grand and delicate arch, and beneath it the lurid scurryings of killers and pimps and record pirates come to seem stylized and comical, like the gangster-movie ballet that Fred Astaire and Cyd Charisse perform in *The Band Wagon*. Jules (Frédéric Andrei), the eighteen-year-old hero, is a shy, skinny postal messenger in Paris, and the diva he adores is a statuesque black American soprano named Cynthia Hawkins (played by the Philadelphia-born soprano Wilhelmenia Wiggins Fernandez). Sitting in the audience of a crumbling Parisian theater, Jules watches raptly as Cynthia floats onstage, and we do, too. She wears a one-shoulder, pearly gray satin gown, and with her glinting diamond earrings and her gleaming broken teeth, which are like jewels too, she's an incredible vision. She curtsies regally and nods, and as she sings an aria from Catalani's *La Wally,* her full lips offer the words as if they were exquisite morsels; her voice seems magical, heavenly. Jules begins to weep, but there is a Nagra tape recorder in his lap, and as he listens, transported, his hands acquire a life of their own; they're furtively pushing buttons and spinning knobs. After the concert, Jules pushes his way back to Cynthia's dressing room, and, on an impulse, steals that pearly gown. It's not the first time he's violated his beloved, for Cynthia Hawkins has always refused to let her voice be recorded. She is a purist, obsessed with the sanctity of the performer's communion with the audience. And when someone secretly tapes her, she considers it tantamount to a rape.

Of course, Jules wants the tape only for his own pleasure; draping Cynthia's gown across his body, he sits in his cavernous loft and listens to her voice, and dreams. But a pair of elegant Taiwanese record pirates have other ideas: they want to seize the tape and use it to blackmail Cynthia into recording for them. Meanwhile, a second, altogether different tape turns up in the mailbag of Jules's moped. It seems a prostitute has recorded a confession exposing the head of a vast sex-

and-drug ring, and so the police and a pair of hired killers are after Jules, too.

The pirates and cops and thugs all come in twos, and they bounce off one another in patterns. The Taiwanese are ironic incarnations of Fu Manchu inscrutability, hiding beneath their reflecting sunglasses and muttering fortune-cookie pronouncements on the awesome power and patience of the buffalo. The two cops on the case, a horny man and a resistant woman, are a less successful parody of the down-to-earth, blandly chitchatting police types who have dominated American movies and TV for years. And then there are the two deliriously fiendish gangland thugs, a grand joke on the outlandish villains of American B movies. The brainier of the two is a goon called the Spic, who chews gum and slicks his hair back like Bowzer in the rock group Sha Na Na. And the other, Curé, is a brutish skinhead with wrap-around sunglasses and a dolphin's jutting lips. These two are like nightmare rock 'n' rollers, one from the fifties and one from the postpunk new wave, and their conversations become a grunted history of rock aesthetics: the Spic moons over the beauty of garages, whereas Curé's dialogue is an endless list of what he doesn't like: garages, cars, elevators, Beethoven—he doesn't like anything. These thugs kill with ice picks, so that even though they're absurdly overdrawn, they're also genuinely scary; the scariness is part of the movie's daft beauty. Beineix knows he has to keep his whirligig moving, and *Diva* really moves.

At first, Jules is unaware of the skulduggery brewing around him. He meets a young Vietnamese shoplifter named Alba (Thuy An Luu, who was fourteen when the film was made), and she follows him to his loft, which is a sort of pop-culture junkyard full of wrecked cars and expensive stereo equipment and, on the walls, pop-art paintings of cars (one of Jules's friends decorates his apartment similarly, except his fetish isn't cars, it's airplanes; Jules calls him Lindbergh). Alba loves the garish surfaces of Jules's loft, but then she would. Beneath her see-through plastic raincoat, her little minidress is pink, pink, pink, and her clothes emblemize her world: below the shiny surface, more surface. Alba has a wild repertoire of snappy rejoinders and mock-sexual moues, but they're all put-ons; they never really threaten or seduce. She is the heart and spirit of the movie, plastic under plastic. Alba can dazzle you, and yet she thinks of herself as a sort of bauble; she's as innocent and sexy as a doll. And she lives with the movie's version of a superhero: Gorodish (Richard Bohringer), an unshaven Zen nut who stays in an almost empty loft dominated by a lone bathtub and a kinetic sculpture—a thrusting wave captured in a bottle. Gorodish is the movie's Lone Ranger, its king of cool. He saves the day and outwits the baddies, all without the slightest hint of exertion, and he lives in an aerie of metaphor. Everything in his loft is blue, from the neon decorations to the clothes people wear when they visit, and everything is about waves—the sculpture, the blue jigsaw puzzle he's working on; even the blue boxes of Gitanes, with their wavy, streaming design. As a character, Gorodish is a bit remote, but the movie needs him. He's the *deus ex machina* in a white suit, and he sets all the madly spinning elements aright. When he triumphs, the movie returns to its hinges.

Diva is not an avant-garde work, but it has appropriated avant-garde styles. It borrows the jumpy cutting and poster-art colors of Godard and the nutty pulp plotting that Rivette played with in *Celine and Julie Go Boating* and *Paris Belongs to Us,* and the images have the candy-coated colors and off-center compositions one finds in new-wave video tapes. Yet none of this adds up to a statement or even an exploration. It's all flash. *Diva* is a cheery, dilettante movie; it flaunts the vocabulary of cinematic deepthink in a sort of hedonistic celebration of the shallow; it exploits form and laughs at form at the same time. Beineix has concocted characters that seem rich and likable and full-bodied, but they're really little more than collections of amiable traits. Everything they do feels right, but that's because nothing they might do could ever feel wrong; since they're not real characters, they can't do anything that's out of character. The plot lampoons itself every step of the way; it's so improbable that no new twist could *feel* improbable. Even the jokes turn in on themselves. References to movies like *The Seven-Year Itch* and *The Trial* are spoofy throwaways; a young girl stands against the sort of bright yellow wall Godard might have used behind one of his ideologues in a movie like *La Chinoise,* but instead of turning to the camera and spouting Maoist rhetoric, the girl yammers plot details over the phone; it's a B-movie scene painted in Godardian colors. Even a virtuoso chase through a subway becomes a tossed-off gag. Jules, on his motorcycle, flees a cop pursuing him on foot, and the thrill of watching the motorcycle zip down stairs and through snaky corridors is overtaken by our nagging wonderment at how the cop can keep up with him. Then the motorcycle runs out of gas, and Jules abandons it. Naturally, that's when the cop loses him. And where are they? At the Place de l'Opéra, of course.

But in throwing together this haywire, free-associating plot (Beineix and cowriter Jean Van Hamme adapted it from a thriller by Delacorta), Beineix imparts a flavor that's quintessentially French: the flavor of structuralism. *Diva* is like an all-purpose structuralist myth, constructed backwards from the sort of elements structuralists might find when they analyzed it. The kind of chancy rhymes and symmetries that structuralists discover lurking in the legends of South American tribes run through this movie like a glittering filigree. *Diva* throws structure upon structure and rhyme upon rhyme until the references and associations become a starry shower. A shot of bare feet at the end of the film clicks with one at the beginning; a chase through a gorgeous pinball arcade rings off a slick-looking record store, and then off Jules's loft after it's been ransacked. There are curved reflections in sunglasses and in the chrome on elegant white roadsters, and the sunglass images bounce off one another and culminate in a jab-in-the-ribs joke about a blind man. Lofts replicate lofts and classic white cars mirror one another. Even the two tape recordings coexist in a way that's structuralistic and associative, instead of in the usual plotty way that would result in their being switched or confused somewhere along the line. And in setting his whirligig among this constellation of references, Beineix goes beyond fun, to touch the sublime. There's so much to see, so much stuff dancing and bumping around on the screen, that one becomes intoxicated. *Diva* gives us the tang of structure without the analytic aftertaste, the thrill of meaning without its burden. It's like Alba in her cellophane coat: beneath the surface, more surface, and more surface, and more.

The surfaces are marvelous. One of the first things you notice is that the faces in *Diva* are all beautiful, because Beineix and his cinematographer, Philippe Rousselot, have bathed everyone in sweet, rosy light (even the people in the police station look rosy). There are lovely overhead shots and plays of dawn light, and Beineix has hit upon a way of tantalizing us by not quite showing everything; we never do piece together what Jules's loft looks like. The effect is novelistic, literary. We see the chic pop world on the screen, but we also imagine it in a special way, almost as if we were reading about it. That's part of the pleasure Beineix gives us; his images sneak into your consciousness through a door the movies rarely use. And during the romantic sections, Beineix grows calm, almost philosophical. Whenever the aria from *La Wally* plays, the camera begins to waltz and glide, and its vision expands. Jules and Cynthia become friends and soulmates, he with his silent, doting eyes, she with her majestic gait and her charmingly deliberate, Americanized French. Promenading through the Place de la Concorde with a huge white parasol, they're a postcard couple, corny and precious, and yet, against the backdrop of American-movie goons and secret tapes, just right. And in the end, when Jules admits to Cynthia that he has recorded her voice, he insists on playing the tape for her, and she is overwhelmed, enchanted, renewed: she has never heard her voice before. There are those, even among the film's admirers, who accuse *Diva* of being meaningless. And it's true that the movie pretends to meaninglessness, even mocks meaning. But there is meaning in it. Here, in this scene between the French boy and the American woman who has mastered so European an art form, here one catches the whiff of the olive branch. In its parade of American cars and rock 'n' roll thugs and pinball machines, *Diva* brings us news of America, the way *Breathless* did so many years ago. It lets us hear our voice.

—Stephen Schiff

Jean-Jacques Beineix
■
BETTY BLUE (1986)

Betty Blue may be the most explicitly erotic movie ever to be nominated for an Academy Award in the Foreign Film category. The very first frames are taken up with the frantic fornication of an unusually attractive and athletic couple to whom we have not been properly introduced as dramatic characters. One might think that a hardcore porn pic has been put on the cassette by mistake, but as the movie progresses, it becomes clear that an aesthetic calculation of the highest order is at work with color and sound and obsessively romantic narrative. Anglade and Dalle may begin as beautiful figures on a libidinous canvas, but they gradually evolve into compelling protagonists in a quintessentially Gallic tale of *l'amour à la folie* that ends in poignant pathos.

The videocassette version has a few problems with framing Beineix's original widescreen canvas, but, on the whole, enough of this artist's intentions survive to produce the *frissons* of the original. French writer-director Beineix had a big international hit a few years ago with *Diva,* a fanciful blend of punk rock, grand opera, and Cocteaulike fantasy. His second movie, *The Moon in the Gutter,* was a desperately poetical love story—and a complete flop commercially. With *Betty Blue,* Beineix strikes deeper and more sustained notes of emotional involvement amid a very stylized *mise-en-scène.*

His subject is Art itself—and the heavy toll it extracts not only from its practitioners, but also from outsiders caught in its orbit. A failed novelist with a seemingly terminal writer's block is prodded into fulfillment by an uneducated girl with a dangerously free spirit. For a time, her rebellious nature seems comically refreshing. But when her inexplicable depression degenerates into self-mutilation, the picture darkens with a tinkling fatalism that seems to mock the life-giving energy of the opening images of uninhibited lust.

Obviously, *Betty Blue* is not for every taste, least of all the priggish and the squeamish. But for what it is, it is very good indeed. Even the movie's wild overture can be justified artistically inasmuch as it removes the coyness and tease from all subsequent displays of desire.

—*Andrew Sarris*

Bertrand Blier

■

GET OUT YOUR HANDKERCHIEFS (1978)

With utmost gratitude I return to Bertrand Blier's marvelous comedy *Get Out Your Handkerchiefs,* which I first covered in a brief note after a New York Film Festival screening in October 1978. In the interim, this courageous and subversive movie has attracted widespread critical support, including a surprise award as best picture of the year from the National Society of Film Critics. However, many people seem to be circling around the film uneasily. "I hear it's *sexist,"* several friends have said to me, as if this dread possibility placed it beyond the pale. But isn't it time we dropped this naive habit of grading works of art in terms of sexual ideology? (Most of the great art of the past wouldn't stand a chance.) It's depressing to think that thousands of New Yorkers live in mortal fear of coming out on the "wrong" side of a feminist controversy and that perhaps thousands more, exhausted from debating these issues, are avoiding any new provocation. Instead of running to the one movie in town that's completely fresh, they'll probably line up for the latest example of played-out sourness from Neil Simon. No one expects much from Simon, but at least he doesn't cause fights.

After his earlier, cruder efforts at sex comedy (such as *Going Places,* which caused a fair amount of justifiable anger when it played here in 1974), Blier, who both writes and directs, has refined his style considerably. *Handkerchiefs* is consistently charming, even ingratiating, yet there's a mischievous, anarchic spirit under the charm that bothers people. The movie is undoubtedly an offense against the awesome American solemnity about sexual "relationships" — the solemnity that now extends from *Village Voice* to *Reader's Digest* and back again. No, it is definitely not a movie for people who are excessively serious or literal-minded about sex. And it probably won't give pleasure to moviegoers eager for still another conventionally roguish French picture, like *Cousin, Cousine* or *Cat and Mouse* — the kind of picture always described as a "Gallic romp." Blier romps all right, but not in the same playroom with Tacchella and Lelouch.

The movie begins with that staple of boulevard comedy, a cuckold — only this is a cuckold who puts the horns on himself. Gérard Depardieu, the great young French actor with the heavy shoulders and the saddened, homely face of an unsuccessful small-town butcher, is a distraught husband whose heartbreakingly beautiful and delicate wife, played by Carol Laure, has gone into a mysterious funk. She refuses to eat, takes no interest in anything, and faints dead away at the oddest times. What's wrong with her? No one can say, least of all the amiable but rather dense Depardieu, who is so crazy in love with her that he encourages a Mozart-loving teacher whom he meets in a Paris restaurant to go to bed with her and even to get her pregnant. Who knows? Maybe *he* can cheer her up. The teacher, played by Patrick Dewaere as a harmless, self-admiring prig and pseudointellectual (he angrily refuses to listen to any composer other than Mozart), balks at the nutty proposal but eventually gives in, and the three form a comically morose ménage — comic because the sexually compliant wife is completely bored with both of them. There she sits in bed, nude, a muffler around her neck, more sphinx than sex object, while the two useless bumbling lovers — attractive, full-bodied men, accustomed to admiration from women — knock themselves out against the wall of her indifference.

Blier's staging of this is tenderly farcical—only a slight exaggeration of reality—and hauntingly sad. Mozart is really the key to the mood and style here, and he becomes part of the plot: The two men find solace in listening to his music, bully other people into listening as well, and even fantasize offering Laure to the reincarnated composer as a way of repaying their gratitude to him. The movie's language and sexual temperament are playfully coarse, more Henry Miller than Mozart, but there's something unmistakably Mozartian in the sudden, hurting shifts from boundless high spirits to deeply shadowed poignance and loss. At its best, Blier's restrained lyricism—his poetic fancifulness without cloying prettiness and muck—comes within hailing distance of the composer's invincible poise.

It's a pleasingly sensual and sensitive comedy, yet some viewers refuse to be pleased. Apparently, the wife's mysterious withdrawal and lethargy give offense. It's true that Blier doesn't make clear why she hides inside herself or whether she's got much personality to begin with, but we can read Carol Laure's face and make a few guesses. This delicate, quirky woman is probably overwhelmed by her huge, impulsive, well-intentioned but blundering husband, and it's obvious that adding another lug of the same sort to the household only compounds the problem. Her withdrawal is a comic convention that reflects something familiar: Almost every man has had this exasperating experience of a woman's silently checking out, particularly in the years when women were brought up to fight passively without making their feelings and demands explicit.

In any case, Blier makes no pretense of understanding a single thing about women. Ruefully, he limits himself to male experience and male fantasies. So why the angry charges of "misogyny" and "sexism"? When Depardieu and Dewaere talk about women—the usual muttering about "bitches" combined with tender, ethereally silly rhapsodies on female beauty—Blier makes us quite aware that they are painfully out of it, that they really understand only themselves. Even a child could pick that up just by reading the body language: As they run around a corner or down a corridor, Depardieu and Dewaere seem connected by invisible strings. One of *Handkerchiefs'* great joys is this silent-movie poetry of the two big men darting and bobbing and weaving in instinctive harmony. When they approach Carol Laure, however, they look like curators handling a priceless vase from the Ming dynasty (and they break her every time).

Laure finally comes out of it in the rapturously beautiful summer-camp sequence, in which the three adults, counselors for a bunch of teenage brats, meet a thirteen-year-old boy (played by Riton) who has shoulder-length hair, dolorous large eyes, and a brain like Einstein's. Suddenly, magically, Laure straightens up and begins to smile. The movie goes from farce to perverse romanticism. The alarmingly precocious boy (a genius, a scoundrel, an *actual* Mozart) works on Laure's sympathies with wily shrewdness, and what begins for him as an adolescent adventure — peeking under her gown as she sleeps — ends as a full-scale seduction. The men's nutty fantasy of her sleeping with Mozart has been fulfilled, though not in a way that gives them much pleasure.

Banished to boarding school, Riton holds his pals spellbound with his account of what it's like to be inside a woman. His boasting is lyrically precise — awestruck rather than triumphant. We think: Another male conqueror is on his way. Perhaps he'll end up like Depardieu and Dewaere, but at least the cycle has begun. When Laure suddenly enters the dormitory and kisses her lover on the lips (the boys' jaws drop in disbelief), the carnal miracle of their affair is complete. Why does she respond to him? The sex appeal of sheer braininess? Maternal instinct? Again, Blier prefers mystery; an old-fashioned sexual radical, he believes in the possibility of happiness between the most unlikely of partners. There are more surprises — a coda of Buñuelian rigor and cruelty, and a final shot that is one of the cinema's great images of sexual exclusion. *Handkerchiefs* holds in balance the two moods of buoyant comedy and heart-piercing sadness right to the end. It's one of the screen's rare lyric triumphs in recent years.

— *David Denby*

Bertrand Blier

■

BEAU PÈRE (1981)

Remy is a pianist at a Parisian penthouse bar. All night he offers customers dreamy, melancholy cocktail blues, like the Philippe Sarde piece that opens the film. Then he walks home in the shifting blue-violet light between darkness and dawn, unaware that he's moving toward changes that will give *him* the blues.

In the morning, when a low-angle camera makes his hillside home look like the curve of the planet, his wife Martine skids downhill to her death in a traffic accident. "An intersection . . . a truck . . . a wrong reflex," say the police. Then, like a little moon, his stepdaughter comes orbiting over the other side of the hill. At first, it's hard to tell what form of life exists on her gray, androgynous surface: dressed in a sweatsuit, her hair slicked back in a rubber band, she could be young or old, a boy or a girl. Remy is similarly ambiguous. The two new orphans are mirror images: pale faces, cavernous dark eyes and wide, soft mouths that curve upwards like a cat's. Throughout the film they're enveloped in the smoky blues of almost identical shirts and sweaters and surrounded by the evanescent sounds of Remy's music. Everyone and everything in Blier's funny but sad film has the blues, modulating through a series of minor keys that represent states of constant change.

Remy is a rather childlike adult. He's the sort who is always standing around holding a cereal bowl and stooping forward a little to make out what happened. He can't bring himself to tell Marion (Ariel Besse) that her mother has died; instead, he writes the news in a letter and retreats. He has raised her for eight of her fourteen years, but when her biological father comes to claim her, he doesn't have the guts to say that he has become the *real* father. Instead, Marion and her little suitcase disappear over the fateful hill, and Remy mourns for his lost daughter at the local candy store. "Here he consoles himself with comic books," a friend reports to the camera.

Marion, on the other hand, is a rather adult child. She takes things into her own hands. Very late one night, when the pearly, predawn light drifting through the window and the refrains of "Le Lotus Bleu" misting down from his stereo speakers form a pool of melancholy around the lonely Remy, he hears the doorbell ring. Reenter Marion and her suitcases. Soon her tiny figure in a white nightie hovers like a shadow in the background while her father and stepfather trade punches, fighting for her. When the dust settles, she comes forward to kneel and dab their bruises with gauze pads. *"She* decides, not us," they say in homage to the strange angel of their destiny.

More changes are in store. "Your grades are going downhill fast," admonishes Remy as Marion stands in the doorway to his bedroom dressed in a huge man's T-shirt that has taken the place of her nightie.

She comes to sit on his bed as she gives a grave accounting of the trouble: in math class she finds that she's always thinking about him. And during English. And history. What she'd like to do is an independent study—and soon she's laying siege to his bedroom. Her determined little form slips into his bed for study hall (she reads *David Copperfield* while Remy hides behind a copy of *Le Monde*). When he tries to give her a math lesson ("I'm thirty and you're fourteen"), she counters with a quiz ("Can't you sleep with a little girl in your arms?").

The camera and the two characters form planetary alignments during this section of the film. The camera looks over Marion's head to Remy's sensitive, confused face and over his shoulder to her solemn, steady gaze. His cloudiness is no match for her gravity. When her real father takes her off to a ski resort for Christmas, Remy finds himself magnetically drawn to her side. He drives through the night; and in the early morning her form, so bundled in a down jacket and wool cap that she once again looks like a little moon, comes hurling toward him through the pale, frosty air, across the snow and into the bed where, at her insistence, they do finally make love.

As the film evolves, Blier will show the dark side of this romance; but he begins by enveloping Remy and Marion in a dawn, dusk, and moonlight equivalent of the sunshine aura that surrounded the love affair between Carol Laure and the adolescent boy in his earlier film, *Get Out Your Handkerchiefs*. Initially, Blier wants us to feel that his waxing and waning characters are moving between the best parts of childhood and adolescence. Dewaere's face is a strange twilight flower whose shadings constantly shift between genuine responsibility and genuine innocence. And we can see not just innocence, but the dawning of a serious, immovable adult love in Marion's determined back, straight little shoulders, and dead-on gaze.

Blier also makes the first section of the film the most comic. He wants us to think that people who won't admit they're in some strange realm of permanent adolescence are kidding themselves. Marion isn't just a child anymore and it's amusing to see her burdened with such accoutrements of pubescence as *David Copperfield*, which is apparently assigned to every ninth grader in the world. Remy isn't just an adult either; and he's fooling himself when he thinks that the superficial exercise of a parental wisdom, control, and discipline will save him from acting like a teenager. There's nothing funnier than his benign way of beckoning his stepdaughter to come in and "tell Remy what's wrong"—or his useless assumption that he's going to stay out of trouble by holding his hands in the air above her when she slips into bed to give him a hug (as if he were saying, "Look, Ma, no hands on the fourteen-year-old") — or his attempts to enforce the law: "You can stay in this bed for fifteen minutes and then OUT."

It's when Blier transposes his theme to two new settings that the role reversal seems first silly and then sad. Remy's fortunes in real estate, career, and romance begin going downhill at the same time. He quits showing up for work; he gets fired; then he gets evicted. He and Marion move from Martine's hilltop home to an about-to-be condemned apartment on a dead-end street. And talk about not having the discipline to be a good father and provider: Remy doesn't even have the discipline to be a good cocktail pianist. Blier sees a relationship between these things: at the beginning of the film, certain shots place Marion in her nightie and Remy's piano keyboard at angles that form two white wings. In a way, both the girl and the piano are as innocent as angels, and Remy is responsible for both.

At the beginning of the film, we see him behind the piano in a posh lounge. Then we see him underneath the piano that he's moving out of Martine's apartment. Then, from a ladies' tea room, he sings to us in cheesy pop rhymes: "This job is a drag / But it lets me fill the grocery bags / Run the house without snags / And buy Marion a few gladrags."

What could be worse than a tea room? A teenage birthday party. Poor Remy can't even play "Happy Birthday" right. He comes in too late, after everyone has started singing, and stays a few beats behind during the entire song. Then everyone rushes off to disco in the living room while Remy's blurry mug hangs over the piano as he plinks out foxtrots. Man, is he out of it.

That's when we notice that the film's comedy is beginning to separate from its sadder themes. Remy is *so* out of it, he's laughable. But it's also clear that he'll never be able to guide and protect Marion. The morning after the birthday party, they wake up long after she should be in school. The doorbell rings: Marion's real father has decided to pay a visit. When she clambers downstairs in one of those sleeveless men's T-shirts to a tense encounter *à trois,* we suddenly feel that everything is a bit too much. Even those big T-shirts, which had looked nice before, suddenly look ugly. They make her seem much too vulnerable.

That's not because she has grown up too fast, but because the men haven't grown up at all. Posters and photographs of Marion's mother in sweaters or strapless gowns, leaning on one elbow, or smoking a cigarette, have been watching the two orphans throughout the movie. Neither Remy nor Marion makes a move without Mother looking on from the right or left hand corner of the screen. At first you think: wouldn't she feel awful if she knew what was happening to Marion! But, in a way, Marion is fine. She doesn't need a mother because she's ready to be a mother to Remy—and to a future child. She tells him, "When I look at you, I think, 'Maybe one day I can give him a baby. He can't be a stepfather all his life. He should raise his own children.'" She even talks to him in the third person, as if he were some lovable object that needed protection. In fact, *Remy* is the little orphan that Marion's mother Martine should worry about. He needs much more help than someone as young as Marion can give.

One night, Marion is at work earning the "family" income in her usual way: babysitting. When the baby gets sick, she runs for Remy, and they both rush around wondering what to do. Enter Charlotte, the girl's mother. In the bedroom, she lays a soothing hand on the little girl's brow; in the living room, she rests a hand on her grand piano and sinks back into the soft, white armchair that swallows her like a clam. You can almost see the word *SAFETY* written on her forehead. And, as she looks at Remy's permanently melancholy face, her eyes light up like a social worker's spotting a new client.

The next day the camera circles the living room with its creamy wall-to-wall carpeting and matching armchairs—and then moves back to show Remy hurtling out of the elevator doors toward her apartment like an asteroid that has finally found its sun. When she draws him into the living room, he gawks like someone who has just woken up and found himself back in the womb. One nice thing about wombs is that they're very protective—sort of like little padded cells. They can keep you safe from *anything*. Martine was a slightly frazzled model, just past her prime and scared of getting older. For a while, Remy avoided worrying that he was getting older by hanging out with teenagers. Now someone is offering an even easier solution. When you walk into Charlotte's apartment, you feel as if some strong maternal force is tucking you in under the drapes and carpeting. Perhaps Charlotte can even tuck death under the covers and make it seem as safe as the ornamental skull over her mantle.

The last time that we see Remy, Marion has disappeared and Remy is running around town searching for his three missing women. "Marion!" "Martine!" "Charlotte!" he shouts to three vacant rooms. What is he looking for? A daughter! a wife! a mother! Ah, at last: a mother, that was what he wanted all along. When he finally stumbles past Charlotte's living room to her bedroom, her response is warmer than a bowl of chicken soup. "I'll make you lose your blues," Marion has promised him; but Charlotte goes further. She'll even provide Medicare: "I'll cure you!" she says, enfolding him in her arms.

Meanwhile, where is Marion? From the moment that Remy met Charlotte, Marion had known what was going to happen. One day she simply pulls back her hair again into the tight, androgynous little cap we saw at the beginning of the film; packs her suitcases; and, with a bowed head tells Remy, "You have found a new woman; but you have to promise that you will come to see me every now and then." She understands Remy completely and sacrifices herself to do what's best for him. No mother could do more — not even Charlotte. Marion has found the right woman for her boy. Now, at age fourteen, she gets to cry at his wedding.

But that isn't the punch line. The punch line is Charlotte's little six-year-old daughter, who tiptoes in to see her mother hugging her new stepfather and promising to cure him. She is still almost a baby; and the camera, tracking toward her for three repeating close-ups, keeps arriving at her innocent face with its awed, melancholy, uncomprehending blue eyes. For Remy and Marion, the transitions are completed: she will never be a child again and he will never leave the refuge of Charlotte's arms. And, reversing the theme of *Autumn Sonata,* which Blier claims is one of his favorite movies, Remy doesn't suffer because his mother is a better pianist. He has been looking for a mother who is a better pianist. At the end of the film, he decides that he'll never play as well as Charlotte, a concert performer — so he quits altogether. At the end Remy has reached the bottom of the hill and Marion is left stranded half way to the top. But for Charlotte's daughter, the trip is just beginning.

In all of Blier's movies, children and parents are searching for each other; more specifically, sons are looking for mothers. His twin boys Gérard Depardieu and Patrick Dewaere have pursued this quest through several films, to the accompaniment of various musical scores. In *Going Places,* they're two rowdies who rampage through town after town being mischievous: for instance, they pay a new mother to let them nurse at her breasts. Their destructive, open-ended game is set to jazz. In *Get Out Your Handkerchiefs,* Depardieu and Dewaere are the husband and lover who lose Carol Laure to a thirteen-year-old boy: the classical case, according to Blier's mythology. Throughout the film

Mozart and Schubert play in the background while Carol Laure knits; in the end, she has each one of her men sewn up. Depardieu and Dewaere are buried in long sweaters and then dismissed; the thirteen-year-old, enclosed in a neat cocoon, becomes her new husband; and, when we see her last, she's busy knitting little booties for a future baby.

For Blier, this is the essential mother and child reunion. He thinks that women are really married to the idea of their own maternity and that sons are forever in love with their mothers. *Beau Père* repeats this idea to a blues beat. It's tackier because the "son," Remy, is an adult man; and it's sadder, because, for Marion, the process is interrupted halfway. She's left with nothing: no father, no husband, no son.

Nevertheless, *Beau Père* is Blier's gentlest film. Charlotte's daughter is his most innocent character and Marion is his noblest. And, though there's never a moment when Blier isn't making fun of him, even Remy is treated more tenderly than any of the heroes in his other movies. It's true that Remy is a bad father, but he specializes in another gender of parenting. "I am the father," Marion's Dad announces one day when they take her to a doctor's appointment. "And I am the mother!" says Remy, his face lost in a dim glow. No mother could sing a sadder farewell song than Remy does when Marion's father comes to take her away at the beginning of the film. "The little blue suitcase . . ." he croaks mournfully, "Her medical record is in there . . . her polio shot is coming due." Of course, Remy isn't a very competent mother; that's why he needs one of his own. He gives everyone the blues; but at least Remy's blues are full of feeling. He moves through the film under strings of blue Christmas lights, lit by indigo reflections from the departing train that's taking Marion away for awhile, or lost in the gauzy blue-lavender pastels of a phone booth on a foggy night when he's trying to phone Marion at her father's house. These are the emotions that color his life: nostalgia, the pain of separation, the longing for reunion.

The alternative to Remy is Marion's father, who lacks the instinct to be either kind of parent. At the beginning of the film, he seems to have forgotten that Marion exists. He's just as incompetent as Remy, much more insensitive, and a lush to boot. Remy may see everything through a fog, but the father is worse: he sees everything through glasses of cloudy Pernod. Remy may give people the blues, but Marion's father gives people the reds. He runs the King Club, a basement bar that burns in the sooty red glow of its disco music. The jukebox blares "One LOOK / That's all it TOOK / we've got to HOOK / Up together," celebrating the easy pickup and the easy put-down. When she leaves Remy, this is the only kind of love and the only home her father can provide. Against this sort of parenthood, you feel a lot of sympathy for all the film's children — even Remy.

Beau Père is Blier's tenderest movie because it's not about just any children. It's about his concern for his own kids. He has a stepdaughter who is Marion's age, and his own daughter Beatrice is the age of Charlotte's daughter. Like Dewaere, Blier must be less staunch than sensitive. He has invented a story about the hazards his girls will face as daughters, wives, and mothers; and he feels awful that they'll have to put up with fathers, husbands, and sons who might turn out to be just like the men in his own films. I don't know whether this theme will get him an Oscar, but it may qualify him for a different kind of award: Mother of the Year. Blier would appreciate the irony.

— Kathy Schulz Huffhines

Bertrand Blier

■

GOING PLACES (1974)

Bertrand Blier's explosively funny erotic farce is both a celebration and a satire of men's daydreams. It makes you laugh at things that shock you, and some people find its gusto revolting in much the same way that the bursting comic force of the sexual hyperbole in Henry Miller's book *Tropic of Cancer* was thought revolting. The crude energy of the two young roughneck protagonists (Gérard Depardieu and Patrick Dewaere) is overwhelming, grungy, joyous. They're outsiders without jobs or money who want to satisfy their appetites. So they snatch purses, steal cars, swipe things from shops, make passes at almost every woman they get near. It takes a half hour or so before a viewer grasps that the two pals are guileless raw innocents and that almost everything they do backfires on them. They're cavemen who give women what in their exuberant male fantasies women want. Brutal, lyrical slapstick connections get made in this movie. With Brigitte Fossey as the nursing mother on the train; Miou Miou as the scraggly blond waif; Jeanne Moreau as the middle-aged woman, who, after ten years in prison, emerges sex-starved; and Isabelle Huppert as the teenager. The screenplay, by Blier and Philippe Dumarcay, is based on Blier's novel. The cinematography is by Bruno Nuytten; the jazz violin score is by Stephane Grapelli.

— Pauline Kael

David Cronenberg
■

SCANNERS (1981)

Doing justice to a chilling, exhilarating film like *Scanners* is a chancy thing. The picture is a genre classic, a masterpiece in its own spooky way, but saying that evokes visions of elitist projects that delicately scrutinize the human condition. *Scanners* is not like that at all. It is a hard-edge, no-nonsense science fiction thriller, an unpretentious gem that knows its own limits and succeeds brilliantly within them.

The force behind *Scanners* is writer-director David Cronenberg, a thirty-seven-year-old Canadian whose previous features caused *Halloween*'s director, John Carpenter, to say, "Cronenberg is better than all of us combined." Once known for blithely yelling, "More blood!" on the set, Cronenberg has toned down his act considerably here. *Scanners* has two scenes of almost indescribable violence, but they are intrinsic to the director's purpose, the creation of a singularly pervasive sense of skin-crawling disorientation.

Scanners turn out to be freaks of nature, people born with a form of telepathy so intense they can totally control the minds and bodies of others. In its raw form, scanning is a terrible hindrance, and scanners are so overwhelmed by what one calls "the other voices, the ones without lips" that they can barely function. However, with the help of a drug called Ephemerol, scanning can be controlled, its power concentrated. How potent a force does it become? In one jolting sequence in the film's opening minutes, a scanner literally blows another person's head to little tiny bits.

But the immediate shock value of that splattered head, considerable though it is, is only part of its purpose. The deeper objective is to put the audience firmly and forever off balance, tagging *Scanners* as a film in which knowing what will happen next is impossible. The effect is profoundly disturbing, and once Cronenberg establishes it he never relaxes its grip.

The actual plot line of *Scanners* is conventional enough. On one side are the benign scanners, especially our hero, Cameron Vale (Stephen Lack), and his girl (Jennifer O'Neill), on the other the bad ones, led by the menacing Darryl Revok (Michael Ironside), whose aim in life is to "bring the world of normals to its knees." There is also the usual mysterious scientist, Dr. Paul Ruth (Patrick McGoohan), who knows more than he lets on about the inevitable battle between those forces of good and evil.

What is unusual is the expertness of Cronenberg's direction. He has a natural feel for this kind of material, a sureness while handling it, as well as the great good sense to treat the inflammatory components in as low-key a manner as possible. His central conceit, that the best way to physically show telepathic powers is by having the actors grotesquely contort their faces, is a masterful one, and he also has a fine eye for the small details — a bandaged hole in a man's forehead, a mysterious symbol on a miniature bottle, a melting telephone — that are essential to creating and sustaining believability.

While some of the acting is on the weak side, Cronenberg was fortunate in his choice of a bearded Patrick McGoohan. Once the star of the TV series "Secret Agent" and "The Prisoner," he is ideal as Dr. Ruth, biting off his words in a deep, resonant voice fraught with secret teachings. Better yet is Canadian actor Michael Ironside, who uses his death's-head face and demonic grin to turn Darryl Revok into a blood-chilling personification of sheer, unrelenting evil.

Special effects are crucial to a film like this, and again the choices were wise. Gary Zeller, who worked on *Altered States,* coordinated the various fires, crashes, and explosions, and Dick Smith, Hollywood's preeminent makeup artist (the man who made Dustin Hoffman old in *Little Big Man* and Linda Blair ungodly in *The Exorcist*), created *Scanners'* apocalyptic final scene. That episode, an unrelievedly ghoulish battle between two scanners out to literally annihilate each other, is as spectacular as it is difficult to sit through without cringing. Like the rest of *Scanners,* though, it is the very best of its kind to appear in a long, long time.

—Kenneth Turan

David Cronenberg

■

DEAD RINGERS (1988)

David Cronenberg has developed as a moviemaker in ways that scarcely seemed imaginable ten years ago, when his luridly titled horror films — *They Came from Within, Rabid* — were haunting downtown theaters and drive-ins.

Though Cronenberg has always made intensely personal, even obsessive films, he has now acquired the fluency of style, the deep sense of character, and the rhetorical distance necessary to transform his obsessions into art. The forty-five-year-old Canadian has become one of the best filmmakers on this planet.

In his 1986 remake of *The Fly,* Cronenberg brought his perennial themes on the physical manifestations of emotion and his newly honed abilities together to create his first wholly mature film. With its dark insights into sexual and emotional development, played out as a series of harrowing physical transformations, it may even be a masterpiece.

Dead Ringers takes Cronenberg a step further, though it doesn't have *The Fly*'s consummate control. It's almost too rich in ideas for its own good: The sense of concentration and proportion isn't there. But it remains an astonishing, magnetic, devastating piece of work.

It's Cronenberg's *Scenes from a Marriage,* and there are many moments in it, both cinematic and emotional, that are far more gripping than the earlier Ingmar Bergman film.

The marriage here is hardly a conventional one. It exists between two identical twin brothers, Beverly and Elliot Mantle (a brilliant dual performance by Jeremy Irons), who share an interest in reproduction. Brilliant medical students, they have become the leading gynecologists in the city of Toronto, specializing in problems of female fertility.

Elliot is the smooth, assured, outgoing Mantle who handles the grant applications and hospital bureaucrats; Beverly is shy and scholarly, responsible for the research that has given the brothers their reputation. When Claire Niveau (Genevieve Bujold), a movie actress with an interesting reproductive quirk, walks into their office, Elliot initiates a sexual relationship and then turns her over to his uncertain brother. She isn't sure who she is with, and until Cronenberg wants us to know, neither is the audience.

Claire frees up something in Beverly, whose only strong bond has been with his brother; he begins to share her dependency on uppers and downers and, as his emotional and physical needs grow, begins to slide into madness. Elliot tries to rescue him, but can't. They are so tightly linked that he must, inevitably, follow his brother.

Dead Ringers is a departure for Cronenberg in that it no longer relies on bursting special effects and extravagant fantasy. The director has distanced himself from his material, adopting an external point of view: In *Dead Ringers,* the Cronenberg film takes place in Beverly's mind, and we see only its material signs — such as the unspeakable set of "gynecological instruments for mutant women" he commissions from a local sculptor.

The horror may be indirect, but it is also more intense. The film offers no cathartic release for the audience — no opportunity to scream or jump — but rather a constant mounting of strangeness and tension.

On the surface, *Dead Ringers* is smooth and placid, a series of cool, immaculate images, an even, unhurried narrative line. Inside, it seethes.

The brothers' descent is terrifying, but it is Cronenberg's peculiar genius — here, as in *The Fly* — to also find something majestic in it. It is by going too far, in their aspirations or emotions, that Cronenberg's characters fulfill themselves, a fulfillment that lies in a terrible, awesome self-immolation.

In its own way, *Dead Ringers* is the most romantic film of the year. Inseparable, complete in themselves, the Mantles must either destroy the world or leave it.

—Dave Kehr

Rainer Werner Fassbinder

■

THE MARRIAGE OF MARIA BRAUN (1978)

Fait accompli: no matter what the next eleven and a half months may disclose, surely one of the Ten Best Films of 1980 is *The Marriage of Maria Braun.* It is also likely that, in the wit, vividness, and sheer exhilarating beauty of its cinematic realization, it will be the film to sweep aside many of the reservations some filmgoers have harbored about the awesomely prolific West German *Wunderkind,* Rainer Werner Fassbinder. Hailed by Andrew Sarris as "the most important new director of the past decade," first championed hereabouts by the Seattle Film Society, and subsequently represented in every Seattle International Film Festival at the Moore Egyptian, Fassbinder has never had a regular theatrical run in this, ostensibly one of America's hippest movie towns. Such exposure is long overdue; but as long as we've had to wait, *Maria Braun* is probably the best picture to start with.

It begins well. God, does it begin well! A portrait of Adolf Hitler looks out at the audience for a few seconds, then a bomb blast carries it away and we are peering through an impromptu window at a civil marriage ceremony. A uniformed German soldier and his girl are taking their vows as their country is literally blown apart around them. The ceremony completed, the camera backs off and relatives begin to scatter. The civil servant lights out too, but uh-uh, not so fast: the new husband tackles the hapless clerk and pins him to his duty. Lying prone in the rubble, a zany snow of bureaucratic papers falling about them, Hermann and Maria Braun get their marriage contract officially notarized.

The couple spends "half a day and all of one night" together. Then Hermann (Klaus Löwitsch) is off to the Russian front and Maria (Hanna Schygulla) turns to the business of surviving the war and triumphing over the peace. She does so alone; Hermann is among the missing in action. But she continues to be the wife of Hermann Braun. She will not permit her marriage to be abrogated by death or compromised by the vicissitudes of living.

If she takes up with an American soldier (George Byrd)—an avuncular black of sweet and gentle gravity—and comes to care for him tenderly, still she never considers that she might marry him. If she charms, inveigles, and by force of indomitable will and resourceful femininity pushes her way out of society's third-class compartments into the forefront of the renascent German industry and the arms of a wealthy executive (Ivan Desny), nevertheless she looks to the day when Hermann will come back to her and she will have all the blessings of prosperity waiting to bestow upon him.

Even as synopses go, that is a deliberately abbreviated account of the film's storyline. I can't imagine that a more step-by-step recounting of Maria's adventures would serve any purpose but to diminish the prospective viewer's pleasure in the audacious twists of the scenario as it plays out before his eyes. Yet the story of Germany's postwar recovery and lapse into bourgeois complacency, and the specific adventures of the self-proclaimed "Mata Hari of the Economic Miracle," aren't nearly as audacious or aesthetically important as Fassbinder's way of telling the story and Hanna Schygulla's thrilling incarnation of Maria Braun.

To watch this film of Fassbinder's is to realize how carelessly most movies are visualized. There is not a dull shot, not one that fails to catch the eye, provoke the intellect, and remind us what an invigoratingly participatory experience the watching of a film can be. Fassbinder has the ability to frame and impel an event in all its immediacy, at the same time that he comments on the dynamics of the moment. His own self-consciousness as director cues us to that of his characters, who rarely act without seeming to appraise themselves through their own camera eye, checking the strategic advantages that any *mise-en-scène* — of people as well as milieu — may afford. Without forsaking for a moment his sense of dramatic narrative, Fassbinder makes us appreciate that he is photographing ideas in motion.

Motion. *The Marriage of Maria Braun* is about motion. Motion through space, motion through time and history, motion from role to role. Maria Braun shoulders through the crowd at a railway depot hoping that someone will recognize the photograph of Hermann she wears and give her news of him; the camera seems to be her eyes. Later she repeats the journey, the camera again travels and pans through the station — only to surprise us by discovering Maria herself, walking away from the camera position: her identity was not so reliably bound to the camera as we had assumed, and now she has chosen a new course to follow, given up her passive role as a billboard bearing her husband's face and name.

Much later, Maria and her wealthy lover (and employer) are at a party for her mother. Oswald, the lover, stands in a doorway across the room from Maria, looking sad. Maria decides to go to him, but she does not merely cross the space between them — she dances, dances from the arms of one character to the next (mother, mother's boyfriend, sister, sister's husband, grandfather). In doing so, she defines the opportunistic symbiosis at the heart of all relationships in her family and her society at large; and she also somehow transcends the definition, turning the movement into a celebration of her superior comprehension of the moment, her selfhood.

It follows that *Maria Braun* is also about stillness, which serves to heighten and define motion. German cinema has always been marked by an affinity for frames within frames; Fassbinder combines a magisterially fluid camera with a relentless eye for alignments, configurations, visual boxes that give an effect of subliminal freezeframe. Maria's brother-in-law (Gottfried John) returns from the war and assures her that Hermann is indeed dead. She flees from the room where she has heard this and the camera, following the incidental movement of her sister, arrives at a window through which Maria can again be seen — frozen hieratically in space, the determined course of the past few years suddenly arrested.

Her next move is to seek out her devoted black suitor. Cut to the bar where they have met previously. Maria, implacable as a goddess, strides across the dance floor. She meets no obstruction; the dancers clear a path with the precision of a theatrical ensemble, and music and motion stop. The black man rises from his chair. Maria repeats the formal invitation (in English) that first brought them together: "Will you dance with me, Mr. Bill?" His arms go around her; she leans against him. Everyone else is watching. "My man is dead." Bill's head bows over hers. The music begins anew. The dancers resume as if nothing had occurred, and the camera draws away, retracing Maria's line of approach.

The tensions of that moment are exquisite: between Maria's strength and her need for support at this time; Bill's recognition that his opportunity has come, laid against his genuine compassion for the woman; the dancers' apparent recognition of Maria's urgency, and the subsequent suggestion that her arrival occasioned nothing more than a pleasurable variation in the choreography; the theatrical self-consciousness of the staging and behavior, and the consummate perfection of the scene that somehow distills and expresses its full emotional power.

The most productive tension in the film is that between the director and his incandescent star. Fassbinder and Schygulla have worked together since they and several other volatile young players survived the police closure of Munich's Action-Theater in 1968 to found their own *anti-teater* company; their first films were made in 1969 — Fassbinder's present total is near forty — and Schygulla has been featured in most of them.

Their collaboration is complete. Schygulla is the luminous focus of the film's beauty and scathing intelligence; the movie is unimaginable without her. Yet she is as much a compositional element as any feature of the lighting and decor. Time and again Fassbinder directs her into crazily architectonic poses no human being would ever assume naturally, poses that further direct the viewer's eye to the other elements of the shot and sardonically fix their relationships on several levels of action and idea. She dominates and yet she is part of the design — which plays into the final irony in store for Maria: that she imposes her will on every male within range, only to find that a gentlemen's agreement has anticipated and accommodated her freedom-asserting gestures of individuality.

Inevitably one thinks of Sternberg and Dietrich, the puppetmaster and the mannequin who finally seemed mistress of both their destinies. If that irony drove Sternberg into an increasingly cold frenzy as the team progressed from film to film, Fassbinder seems more drolly appreciative of his lot. He appears briefly as a black-marketeer who sells Maria a dress she requires to play bar girl, and also tries to interest her in a set of Kleist. "Books burn too fast," Maria replies; "they don't give enough heat." The scurvy connoisseur of art and beauty smiles at beauty's overriding sense of pragmatism, and daintily kisses her hand.

— *Richard T. Jameson*

Rainer Werner Fassbinder
■

BERLIN ALEXANDERPLATZ (1980)

Inasmuch as Oscar Wilde has defined a cynic as one who knows the price of everything and the value of nothing, my own noncynical view of the videocassette version of the late Rainer Werner Fassbinder's *Berlin Alexanderplatz* is that it is a bargain at $400 for its thirteen sections and epilogue running for fifteen and a half hours on eight videocassettes. Furthermore, video may be the ideal medium for an elongated movie that was originally produced as a television series, but which then achieved a limited cultish vogue at several movie festivals before enjoying a triumphant theatrical release in New York in 1983, and eventually wound up on several ten-best lists, including this reviewer's.

Though it was not Fassbinder's last movie, *Berlin Alexanderplatz* can well serve as his ultimate testament. Fassbinder's relation to Alfred Döblin's well-known but not widely read novel goes much deeper than a one-shot adaptation. In a sense, Fassbinder had been shooting Döblin all his life. Franz Biberkopf, the novel's beleaguered protagonist, was the literary model for Fassbinder's own self-proclaimed persona. Fassbinder enlarged Döblin's characters, giving them more shape and feeling than was possible with the novel's frequent submergence in the inarticulate babble of the street people in the Berlin of 1928.

Though Döblin's technique has been compared to that of James Joyce in *Ulysses* and John Dos Passos in *U.S.A.*, there is something more oppressively *lumpen* and sordid in Döblin's Berliners than is to be found in Joyce's Dubliners and Dos Passos's Amerikans. Through a glass darkly pimps, whores, thieves, soldiers, and low-grade entrepreneurs jockey for position in the bars and gutters of an unfashionable district. Meanwhile Hitler is waiting in the wings to make his monstrous entrance.

Fortunately, Gunter Lamprecht's massive incarnation of Döblin's lower-depths Everyman virtually obliterates the rhetorical barriers between acting and being. He is so undeniably, so ineffably there on the screen that he will ever after spring into vivid life on the printed pages of the novel. For all the movie's cruelties and brutalities, for all the downward spiral into the hell of self-hatred, Fassbinder's treatment of the characters never wavers in its sublime sympathy. The first meeting of Franz Biberkopf and Mieze (Barbara Sukowa) is worthy of Wagner's most soulful musical intimations of innocence regained. Indeed, all the characters are ennobled by the unyielding compassion of Fassbinder's *mise-en-scène*.

As for the acting, Lamprecht's Franz Biberkopf will be the measure by which all future screen acting will be judged, and Sukowa, Hanna Schygulla as Eva, and Gottfried John as Franz's nemesis Reinhold are not to be left behind. All in all, the ensemble of *Berlin Alexanderplatz* is as seamless an expression of life-giving art as has ever graced the screen. And videocassette may be the only way one can properly experience this modern masterpiece. The color, the framing, the titles are more than adequate, and the viewer's ability to regulate the amount of time devoted to any one sitting is worth every penny of the purchase price.

—*Andrew Sarris*

Bill Forsyth

■

LOCAL HERO (1983)

Directors who can wrench a few laughs out of a good script or link a couple of gags together keep the movie business alive. They will all go to Hollywood heaven, and eat together at the great commissary table in the sky, but they're not rare. On the other hand, a director with a comic vision of his own—a way of seeing the world that is funny or odd down to its roots—comes along perhaps once in a decade. Bill Forsyth, the young Scottish writer-director, may be one of those talents. The first film of his to be shown here, *Gregory's Girl,* a very slight comedy about a gangly, lovesick teenage boy in a Scottish "new town," was whimsical and just a little too cuddly-cute, but Forsyth demonstrated that he had a "touch." Again and again, he pulled back from obvious gags while springing mildly subversive satire and casually daft jokes from the most benign contexts. Forsyth's wonderful new movie, *Local Hero,* both expands and fills in the genial atmosphere of *Gregory's Girl.* This director is beginning to create a world that operates according to laws that he alone could give it.

The press notes for the film reveal that *Local Hero* was born when producer David Puttnam read an item in the newspaper about a Scot selling his private North Sea island to an American petrochemical company. Puttnam's idea was a comedy about powerful Texas oilmen and rural Scots; Forsyth took it from there. The first thing that's notable about *Local Hero* is how firmly all the conventional ironies (J. R. dancing in a kilt—that sort of thing) have been avoided. These Texans aren't vulgarians in ten-gallon hats. The head of the company, Felix Happer (Burt Lancaster), imperious and willful in the grandly vague style of men who have been powerful all their lives, is an elderly bachelor whose emotional life is completely caught up in astronomy—constellations, stars, and the comet he dreams of discovering and naming. Like the brilliant, moonstruck Howard Hughes, or J. P. Morgan, who had his theories of history, Happer is the American millionaire as visionary and crank; Burt Lancaster, tensing those still-massive shoulders, brings out the full measure of melancholy that has always lurked under his charging physical power.

Happer sends a lieutenant, MacIntyre, or Mac (Peter Riegert), to buy a Scottish coastal village and turn it into an oil-refinery site. Mac, about thirty, is a bright and successful executive, but his personality begins and ends at his desk. With his glib, confident talk of money and deals and cars, he has the young corporate man's dullness, the utilitarian competence that leaves women unexcited, and Riegert, one of those rare actors who convey intelligence, plays him with an easy manner that nevertheless betrays the way Mac's skill at business covers his depression about himself.

Driving to the small Scottish town with Danny (Peter Capaldi), a very young oil executive — another of Forsyth's loose-limbed, awkward silly-in-love Scots — Mac is overtaken by fog and spends the night in the car. Something mysterious happens here, maybe something magical, for when the two men wake in the morning and drive into the remote village of Ferness, there's definitely been a change in the air. From that point on, everyone is a little pixilated. With its small, neat white houses, Ferness, set on a calm bay surrounded by mountains, is placidly beautiful, and the place is visited by wonders: Shooting stars and the northern lights throb in the sky, and the Atlantic currents wash odd things up onto the shore — crates of oranges, exotic shells from the Caribbean, jovial, capitalist Russians bearing goods. The town's inhabitants — an eccentric, hardworking lot — are so accustomed to the unexpected that they never bat an eyelash.

In his quiet, deadpan style — so measured it could almost be called contemplative — Forsyth piles on the incongruities. Yet he explains nothing, prepares nothing, and never comments on a joke once he's made it. The movie's surface is calm, unruffled, but one bizarre thing after another happens — intelligent mermaids rise from the sea — and finally the incongruities join together for us in a kind of harmony. In this peaceable kingdom, a phantom cyclist roars by Mac every time he comes out of his inn; the minister is a black African with a Highlands accent; and a single punk — a forlorn girl in leathers and blue-green hair — lounges around town, ignored by everyone. The details are arbitrary; there's no reason for any of these things to be so. But in time, lulled by the consistency of Forsyth's errant view, which has just enough bite in it to keep the movie from going soft or coy, we can't see any reason they should *not* be so. Our perception of reality has been gently undermined; we're teased out of rationality.

As Forsyth detonates his shrewd, happy little jokes, the pale-blue northern skies deepen at dusk, the bottles of forty-two-year-old scotch are opened and consumed, and Mac, the buttoned-up-tight American, falls under a spell. Mac is undone, yet Forsyth is sympathetic — he's not about to use the Scots to show up an American. Nor does he turn his countrymen into cloying little darlings. Indeed, the townspeople are more than eager to sell their property, even though an oil refinery would obviously destroy everything wonderful about the town. Their representative, the clever young accountant Gordon (Denis Lawson), who also doubles as innkeeper, knows that putting Mac under a spell is the best way of getting a good deal out of him. Like Steven Spielberg, Forsyth has a strong sense of the comic and spiritual possibilities of goodness. What makes him a filmmaker for adults — and also completely contemporary in feeling — is that he doesn't require the pretense of innocence to make goodness believable.

Forsyth might have turned *Local Hero* into a conventionally satirical study of the effects of money on a town of poor Scotsmen (the Ealing comedies of the fifties had similar themes). Or he might have taken the greening of Mac so far that the young executive would turn against his own company and rally the town to a defense of its paradise. Rather than these clichés, what engages Forsyth is the almost uncanny mood of enchantment and wonder that becomes possible when the will is relaxed and the mind is ready to accept the improbable. *Local Hero* is *Brigadoon* without bagpipes. When the half-mad genius Happer shows up, descending from the sky like his wished-for comet, the triumph of Ferness is complete. For, of course, the visionary Happer belongs there, communing with the shooting stars. Happer's arrival is one of the truly magical moments in recent movies, and Forsyth, unlike Spielberg, creates his magic without resorting to a single special effect. With luck, this director could turn into a splendid maker of oddball comedies — but comedies with a strong center of melancholy and a calm, unhurried sense of beauty.

—*David Denby*

Bill Forsyth

■

GREGORY'S GIRL (1981)

Everything delightfully gentle, quirky, droll, and daft in Bill Forsyth's later movies is right there in his first feature—the story of a gangling teen (Gordon John Sinclair) who's cut from the school soccer team but falls hard for the pretty, coordinated girl goalie (Dee Hepburn) who takes his place. Sinclair is like a sixteen-year-old Big Bird, with stork legs and a sweet, dopey grin. Whether they're snubbing or helping him, every girl knows more than he does—including the little sister who's too young to understand an admirer's praise: "She's only ten, but she has the body of a woman of thirteen."

—*Kathy Schulz Huffhines*

Stephen Frears

■

MY BEAUTIFUL LAUNDRETTE (1985)

My Beautiful Laundrette makes you see why movies like *A Passage to India* and *The Far Pavilions* lumber along so blindly: they're willfully out of touch. While those white-elephant "epics" wallow in nostalgia for the Raj, basking in past glory and picking at old scabs, Stephen Frears's sleek comedy shoots us into mid-eighties London where Asian immigrants are building empires of their own. Fresh, funny, and absolutely contemporary, *My Beautiful Laundrette* is one of the rare breakthrough films of the last decade. It opens up a whole new world to the viewer.

On the face of it, nothing could sound drearier than a film about a South London laundromat owned by a Pakistani—the notion reeks of smoke-grimed highrises and concern for the "little man." But the young screenwriter Hanif Kureishi is an instinctively playful storyteller who skips over the pitfalls of socially conscious filmmaking and concocts a wicked blend of gangster pic, sex comedy, and political melodrama. Rather than getting all sniffly about the plight of the

Asians, he shows us a brave new England whose immigrants see London as a city ripe for conquest. "Compared with everywhere," says one Pakistani, "it's a little heaven here."

Kureishi, himself half-Pakistani and half-English, steers clear of the obvious clichés about Asians and the English, viewing both with a mixture of sympathy and irony. Like Philip Roth in *Goodbye, Columbus,* Kureishi casts an especially sardonic eye on the foibles, ambition, and meanness of an outsider culture—*his* culture—as it seeks money and assimilation. He gives us access to an unfamiliar world where patriarchs struggle to preserve family ties (but prize white mistresses), believe in hard work (on both sides of the law), cock their snoots at the English (whom they reckon deadbeats and losers), and embrace Margaret Thatcher's theory of a "New Enterprise Culture" where race doesn't matter. Says one wealthy entrepreneur: "I'm a profesional businessman, not a professional Pakistani."

Omar (Gordon Warnecke) is an ambitious Pakistani pretty-boy who lives with his father (Roshan Seth), a former left-wing journalist who has drifted into England, disillusionment, and vodka, in roughly that order. Papa believes in the primacy of learning and chastizes his son for betraying his heritage: "They hate us [in England], and all you do is kiss their arses and think of being a good young Britisher." Omar goes to work for his Uncle Nasser (Saeed Jaffrey), a bubbly, low-rent Godfather who has a middle-aged English mistress (Shirley Anne Field) and cuts shady deals with their flashy relative Salim. Unlike Papa, Nasser preaches the gospel of money, teaching Omar "how to squeeze the tits of the system."

When he's given control of his uncle's laundromat, Omar enlists the aid of his white school friend—and lover—Johnny (played with charismatic dash by Daniel Day Lewis). Driven by affection, the desire for honest work, and remorse over his past as a proto-fascist hooligan, Johnny breaks with his old mates, skinheaded "Paki-bashers" (who are portrayed less as thugs than as victims). Yet Johnny also feels uncomfortable with the crooked Pakistanis who employ him. Together, Omar and Johnny transform the dingy laundrette (aptly named Churchill's) into the Las Vegas of laundries, a suds palace complete with neon signs, video games, and a console that pipes in Muzaked waltzes. To keep their business afloat, they learn to "fuck the system"—fornication in all its forms is one of the film's governing metaphors—but their work leads them into massive crises of cultural identity. Pulled by conflicting values and loyalties, they don't know where they fit into the society around them.

My Beautiful Laundrette unfolds Omar and Johnny's story with splendid, almost impudent unpredictability; there's never a dull or moralistic moment (never has gay love been handled more un-self-consciously). Kureishi creates half a dozen juicy characters and salts scene after scene with spontaneous riches: Nasser lolling like a rajah while his daughters massage his feet; his rebellious daughter Tania flashing her breasts to distract Omar from business; Salim primping before a mirror in his shower cap. When Omar lords it over Johnny because he's an Englishman working for a "Paki," we see how the shadow of racial division hangs over even the most intimate relationships. In fact, a sharp political consciousness shines through every scene, but Kureishi never sermonizes, bellyaches, or turns characters into abstractions; instead, their actions dramatize the connections between racism, homosexuality, class hatred, and nationalism. Nor does this movie offer easy answers—it ends indeterminately, giving each character his or her share of the truth. If Salim is right that Asians in England are "nothing without money," Papa is also right that, without education, Omar will remain "an underpants cleaner" and never see clearly *"what* is being done and to *whom."* When Tania lambastes her father's mistress Rachel for living off a married man's money, Rachel answers movingly that the world is open to the wealthy young Tania as it never was to women of her age and class.

At first one fears that the beautified laundrette may become another ponderous metaphor for England, but it's a measure of this film's casual artistry that it wears its symbolism quite lightly. In the world of *My Beautiful Laundrette,* nothing and no one has only one meaning. There are no villains and no heroes; characters constantly reveal new shadings; even the laundrette embodies contradictory values. The new name given it by Omar, "Powders," refers equally to detergent and the drug sales that financed its redecoration. "There's money in muck," Nasser says early on, but the converse proves equally true.

As each new scene redefines this world, Kureishi offers us several thrilling surprises (the heroes' first on-screen kiss is one of the most enjoyable surprises in eighties' film) and creates moments alive with lovely, complex tones. Never does this happen more memorably than opening day at the laundrette, which shifts us between three very different scenes: out on the street, angry punks and laundry-toting housewives crowd around the entrance; in the back room, the gay lovers enjoy a furtive fuck; and in between, Nasser and Rachel dance around the washing machines to classical music laundered by Muzak. Under Frears's perfectly pitched direction, the scene is absurd and beautiful and potentially violent.

Like all of Frears's films (including *Les Liaisons Dangereuses* and *The Grifters*), *My Beautiful Laundrette* is impeccably acted and shows a sneaky visual flair that's miles from the self-conscious flash of such English peers as Adrian Lyne or Alan Parker. Here Frears transforms a sixteen-millimeter TV movie (made for England's Channel Four) into a big-screen success by deft use of color motifs (check out the blues and oranges), cagy camera movements, and witty allusions — including one that makes Johnny into both Marlene Dietrich and Querelle. This last maneuver is vintage Frears, who specializes in taking the raw stuff of melodrama and giving it a quirky, personal spin. (In his undervalued 1970 debut film, *Gumshoe,* he managed to wring genuine feeling from the parodic tale of a Liverpool comedian who dreams of being a hard-boiled detective.) But while *My Beautiful Laundrette* shows off his command of rhythm and tone, it also shows his admirable restraint. Frears doesn't foul things up by trying to outshine material that's already brilliant; what makes the film so pleasurable is the way Frears captures all the wit and poetry Kureishi put into his script. Their collaboration turns a low-budget movie about a laundrette into the most original look at London since *Performance.*

It should come as no surprise that such a cocky, freewheeling story should come from a young, mixed-race writer like Kureishi. In these days of corporate homogenization, all the most energizing new movies seem to come out of the blue. Indeed, in the last few years, only the Spaniard Pedro Almodóvar (*What Have I Done to Deserve This?, Law of Desire*) has done work that seems as startlingly fresh as *My Beautiful Laundrette;* he opens up gay and working-class Madrid in much the same way Kureishi reveals London. In making a virtue of their marginality, Kureishi and Almodóvar are, ironically, part of a century-long trend that has dominated the arts. From jazz to high modernist literature to the movies, the cultural history of the twentieth century is the story of outsiders — the exiled, the disenfranchised, the oppressed, the ignored. Nowhere has this been truer than in England where the insider culture of public schools and Oxbridge has been inbred to the point of imbecility and spiritual chinlessness.

My Beautiful Laundrette escapes the niggling ambition, retrograde vision, and tired-blood emotions that make most English movies about as delectable as English cooking. Kureishi and Frears couldn't care less about the arthritic British themes of repression, lost empire, soldiering on through; they don't spend their time whimpering about being locked behind the walls of Sex, Class, and Race. And like their creators, Omar and Johnny and Uncle Nasser are too busy living to brood over England's tight ass and its wet-blanket soul. *My Beautiful Laundrette* is about what movies *should* be about: politics and screwing, fighting and making money, guilt and anger and love. It's about the juice and the blood that make life worthwhile. Every frame brims with energy and immigrant sass, mocking the lethargy of the dough-faced English, dancing circles around their twee little comedies and chortling like crazy over those overstuffed epics about the Raj. If this film has a flaw, it's that it has too many characters, too many stories, and too much sympathy to fit gracefully into ninety-seven minutes. And that's as it should be. For *My Beautiful Laundrette* is that rarest of things—a movie about *now*.

—*John Powers*

Stephen Frears

■

PRICK UP YOUR EARS (1987)

The opening image in Stephen Frears's fine, damnably intelligent *Prick Up Your Ears* is the burnished, big Buddha's head of Kenneth Halliwell, who has just murdered Joe Orton, his lover and roommate of sixteen years. Lurid and bald-pated, he looks a bit like James Earl Jones's Jack Jefferson, but the murder has knocked out all his ferocity. He's imploring, gentle, bereft; violence has tenderized him. When he goes on to end his own life with an overdose of Nembutal, it's a mercy killing.

Halliwell's face in that scene is an emblem of abject, almost beatific misery, and Frears wants the image to stay with us—as the emblem of the movie. Everything flashes back from this scene; our awareness of the horror to come tinctures even the most larky passages. As in Orton's plays, the shards of smashed taboos litter the fierce frivolity. Even the title *Prick Up Your Ears* carries a shiv of double meaning.

Frears and his screenwriter, Alan Bennett, adapting John Lahr's 1978 Orton biography, have chosen not to make much use of Orton's plays. You don't get a sense of what Orton accomplished as a playwright, what a struggle he had even after he was "discovered," what he meant to the near-moribund British stage in the early sixties. (With plays like *Entertaining Mr. Sloane, Loot,* and his last, the posthumously produced *What the Butler Saw,* Orton was dubbed the Oscar Wilde of Welfare State gentility.) The filmmakers have made a movie about the playwright Joe Orton, but they don't give us the playwright. There's a brazenness to their method. By dealing mostly with Orton's life apart from the stage, they reinforce the notion that Orton's life was the raw, unaltered version of his art; a skeleton's key to his plays and novels and diaries and screenplays. (They also affix a dumb, disposable framing device with Wallace Shawn as John Lahr researching the Orton bio; Lahr's neglected wife/collaborator is supposed to remind us of Halliwell.)

Orton was seventeen when he met Halliwell—seven years older and solidly middle-class—in 1951 as an acting scholarship student at the Royal Academy of Dramatic Art. Orton was raised in drab, monotonous Leicester, in a family leaning toward the lower end of the middle-class; his mother wanted him to be a civil servant. Halliwell's mother was killed by a wasp sting when he was eleven; his father killed himself six years later. Halliwell was orphaned, and Orton considered himself an orphan, too. In the first ten years that they lived together in their cramped Islington bed-sitter, they collaborated on four novels (all unpublished); Halliwell taught Orton the classics and Shakespeare and mythology. They also defaced books in the local library with obscene dustjacket blurbs and scurrilous, reworked covers, decorating their flat with a picture collage of pilfered snippets. For this they were arrested and incarcerated, in separate cells, for six months. (The sentence was absurdly harsh, but the defacements carry a disturbing, porno-Dadaist charge. They may well have been the most creative of the Orton/Halliwell collaborations.)

Away from Halliwell, Orton began to do his own writing. As his plays attracted notoriety, Halliwell was reduced to being Orton's "personal secretary." Orton in public would not acknowledge Halliwell's contributions to his career; Halliwell, in turn, demanded inordinate credit for Orton's successes. (All the plays' titles are his.) No longer Orton's mentor, Halliwell retreated ever further into gloomy bitchiness.

As Orton, Gary Oldman seems exactly right when he says: "Cheap clothes suit me. That's because I'm from the gutter." He wasn't, really, but he fancied himself a guttersnipe. Oldman gives Orton the bearing of a lower-middle-class homosexual cavalier who's trying very hard to be working-class. There's a taunt to his promiscuity; he's always poised for a spree.

As the hulking, prematurely bald Halliwell, Alfred Molina shows us how Orton's promiscuity might have provoked him. There's a wracked, shamed quality to Halliwell's sexual jaunts with other men (all at Orton's instigation). He closes himself off from sympathy. Halliwell is the tortured, preliberated (and pre-AIDS) homosexual archetype. Orton is the priapic, unashamed cruiser — a modern libertine.

Orton's psychological ties to Halliwell lacked a sexual charge — Molina's drear, seething face tells us that. Orton probably stayed with Halliwell precisely *because* he felt no charge. The pairing seems all wrong on the surface, but their neuroses conjoined so perfectly that probably only murder could (and did) release them. (Halliwell showed the dramatic instinct in life that he lacked on the page, or on the stage.)

It's a *folie,* all right, but Frears and Bennett don't quite make it *à deux.* We don't see enough of Orton as Halliwell's callow, unformed acolyte, and so the flip-flop in their relationship when Orton becomes successful doesn't have resonance. Orton the bumbling acting student trying to lose his working-class accent is just an in-joke to us. (And, apparently, to Orton, too. He smirks with foreknowledge.) The characterization of Halliwell as a young man doesn't quite work, either. He's not that far from the twisted, half-mad brooder he became; it's not clear why Orton was drawn to him. (When Halliwell is handed an imaginary cat in acting class, he strangles it, and we in the audience laugh. Even Then He Knew.) We don't see how cowed and daunted Orton must have felt with Halliwell in the beginning, so the unacknowlegment of his debt to him later on doesn't seem like such a big deal. When Orton brings his agent, Peggy Ramsay (Vanessa Redgrave, in a great small performance), as his guest to an awards dinner, leaving Halliwell at home, there should be more cruelty in the mood.

Even so, Oldman and Molina work some minor miracles. For example, it's not clear from the early, flustered sequences with Orton's mother (Julie Walters) why he should be so unmoved at her death. But Oldman, as he also demonstrated in *Sid and Nancy,* has a genius for snarly, free-floating licentiousness. His implacable effrontery seems just right, even if we're not always sure where it comes from. When Orton hands his dead mother's false teeth to a horrified *Loot* cast member as a prop, the moment has a triumphant heartlessness. I think that's because Frears and Bennett don't really condemn Orton. His heartlessness is equated· with his art. The film is saying that to be a writer you have to loot life, and that makes you something of a cur.

It's also saying that it's not enough to have the proper checklist of homosexual/orphan/outcast credentials in order to qualify as an artist. This is Halliwell's great lament at the end of the film, just before he murders. Alfred Molina does it full justice; his eyes sear inward at the brutality of the sick joke life has played on him. The achievement of *Prick Up Your Ears* is that you really feel for Halliwell by the end.

Our responses to Orton are more complicated, and that's as it should be. His homosexuality provided him with his outsider's subversive view: the view of a terrorist farceur. Without missing a beat, he could segue from a swank awards dinner to a public urinal for a pickup. What's disturbing about Orton in *Prick Up Your Ears* is that his actions don't seem to issue from rage or rebellion; as a playwright, Orton wrote in a state of hyperawareness, but in life there was something preconscious about his demolitions. His union with Halliwell was bound to self-destruct, because Halliwell was morbidly over-conscious of every slight, imagined or real. Why did they stick it out so long? Maybe it just proves the dictum: Nothing is as compelling as a bad marriage.

—*Peter Rainer*

Peter Greenaway
■

THE DRAUGHTSMAN'S CONTRACT (1982)

Set in 1694 England, Peter Greenaway's first "big budget" film (it cost half a million dollars) is a snappy, cruel comedy about a draughtsman, Mr. Neville (Anthony Higgins), who agrees to twelve drawings of an estate in exchange for the body of Mrs. Herbert (Janet Suzman), the wife of its owner. As he works, however, Neville discovers that each vista he's depicting contains a discordant element (an empty pair of boots, a misplaced ladder) that may or may not be clues to Mr. Herbert's murder. Frankly, nobody cares if Mr. Herbert has been killed, not even Greenaway, whose theme is not crime but how we understand the world through representations of it, be they Neville's drawings, the contract ("in black and white") between him and Mrs. Herbert, or our own ideas about reality – in a sense, we're all draughts-men. Though hinting that any attempt to understand reality leads us into insoluble mysteries, Greenaway also insists that material power determines which interpretations of the world prevail at any given time; in this case, power lies with Neville's patrons, a coarse and vicious landowning aristocracy which boasts women who joke about pissing like horses and men who gurgle merrily over murdering servants. This class owns the property, hires the draughtsmen to celebrate it, possesses the finished drawings, and ultimately governs the artists, too. This is not a heartening thought and, despite the jokes and painterly lushness of its tableaux, *The Draughtsman's Contract* is not a pleasant movie; like all of Greenaway's work it's charged by a morbidity that verges on the misanthropic. But here anyway, this director's hyperintellectual approach results in more than elaborate pattern-making. "A really intelligent man knows more than he sees," says one of the characters, and these words clearly fit this philosophical mystery story, which doesn't ask whodunnit but how we can be sure we know what we know.

—*John Powers*

Peter Greenaway

■

THE COOK, THE THIEF, HIS WIFE AND HER LOVER (1989)

The Cook, the Thief, His Wife and Her Lover (henceforth abbreviated as *Cook* in my review) is a highly controversial and distinctly original work of cinematic art fashioned by writer-director Greenaway, whose previous works (*The Draughtsman's Contract*, *The Belly of an Architect*) have also been defiantly nonmainstream (and little seen in the U.S.).

His latest, a tale of gruesome Jacobean revenge in a stylized modern setting with seventeenth-century Flemish decor, deliriously *Marienbad*ish camera movements (courtesy of French cinematographer Sacha Vierney), full frontal nudity (male and female), unbridled lust, excremental simulation, sickening physical brutality and mutilation, and a cannibalistic ending to end cannibalistic endings has given pause to many critics and viewers normally far less censorious than Jesse Helms.

Me, I liked it. I put it near the top of my year's ten-best list — in the uncut, unrated, letterboxed version I viewed. Vidmark is also releasing an unrated panned-and-scanned version, and an R-rated version, minus about twenty-three minutes, also panned-and-scanned. Letterboxing is vital to *Cook,* since so much of the formal sweep of the work consists of extended lateral camera movements past sumptuous backgrounds that embellish the lustier-than-life characters.

Gambon's role as "the thief" is probably the most problematic character for audiences, in that he is unrelievedly coarse and brutish and profanely loud, though not entirely devoid of mean-spirited wit. By contrast, Helen Mirren and Alan Howard as the wife and lover break through the barriers of self-conscious unreality to project a deep passion that transcends their lasciviously exposed flesh. Bohringer, a French star, has been cast purposively with his broken English expressing the philosophical grandeur of French cuisine as an elegant exorcism of death.

The final banquet sequence is not for weak stomachs. Nor is this pessimistic allegory of contemporary, anti-intellectual England a happy evening's entertainment for escapism-seeking audiences. But if you're looking for something completely different, in an outrageous sort of way, *Cook* provides one of the most remarkable movie recipes around.

I have not seen the R-rated version — and I don't intend to. After all, the allegedly objectionable aspects of the subject cannot be neatly snipped out with a little cut here and a little cut there. The movie's whole concept is either rotten to the core or the stuff of sublime revenge drama, and I feel adults can judge for themselves. (Children can wait until they become adults who can appreciate a truly grown-up love story of truly horrific dimensions.)

As for charges of the movie reflecting a perverted sensibility, one can never dismiss such charges out of hand. My own opinion is that, at a certain level of aesthetic affect, the excrescences of the flesh are transfigured into the ecstasies of the spirit.

—*Andrew Sarris*

Werner Herzog

■

AGUIRRE, THE WRATH OF GOD (1972)

Werner Herzog once walked six hundred miles from Munich to Paris as a tribute to the German film historian Lotte Eisner, who was in the hospital at the time. Somehow he thought his three-week walk would get her out. That's the kind of man Herzog is, and that's the kind of movies he makes. Dwarfs, the autistic, the blind, prophets, and demagogues — these are the subjects Herzog is drawn to with an obsessional fervor that dovetails ambiguously into the obsessional fervor that is his subject.

From the astounding opening sequence of *Aguirre, The Wrath of God,* one feels a sense of awe that is hard to locate precisely — it's as much at *what* we are seeing as at the fact that someone (Herzog) has actually staged the scene. We are in the Andes. The time is 1560. Through the mist-shrouded mountains we barely discern a line of men, women, animals descending an almost sheer cliff. We move closer and discover Spanish conquistadores in heavy metal armor, Indian slaves bearing cannons and sedan chairs, aristocratic women with fluted collars gingerly treading the mountain path, llamas, pigs, and a Catholic monk. On and on they come, the members of Pizarro's retinue, bearing their symbols of European culture — the cross and the cannon — into the jungle where they hope to find El Dorado.

Running low on supplies, Pizarro dispatches a smaller band of men under Don Pedro de Ursua to find information about the location of El Dorado. If they do not return in a week, he will assume they are lost. Among the band is Don Lope de Aguirre. One look at him and you know you are in the presence of a man possessed by treachery and ambition: his eyes have a murderous visionary glint, he walks with a tilt that sets him at odds with gravity itself. Aguirre is "the great traitor," a malignant overreacher whose lust for power and fame drives him to foment a mutiny against Ursua when Ursua, in the face of Indian attacks and a rising river that washes away their rafts, decides to turn back. Aguirre sets up a pathetic nobleman as the puppet king of their expedition and declares their independence from the Hapsburg crown. It is his aim to conquer a continent—to "produce history the way others produce plays."

Herzog's approach to this adventure is a far cry from the historical pageants we're used to. If the conquistadores had brought a cameraman along with them, instead of a monk to convert the Indians, his footage might have looked like this; it's almost like a home-movie epic. Almost, but not quite. Herzog's images may have the impartiality of a documentary, his dramatic construction may avoid all the rhetorical devices of Hollywood epics, but the distance finally yields a powerfully subjective almost hallucinatory effect. Without sympathizing with Aguirre's obsession, we begin to share it. The sinister silences of the jungle, the eery calm of the river, the sense of being totally adrift from any recognizable signposts of civilization have rarely been conveyed with such tactile immediacy. Clearly Herzog believes these men deserve their doom; just as clearly he commands us to acknowledge the perverse beauty of such *folie de grandeur*.

He conveys this in images that are literally unforgettable. A raft caught in a whirlpool. The blank stare of an Indian playing ancient wood pipes. A hooded horse thrown off the raft by the impetuous nobleman, standing motionless in the jungle, deserted by its masters. A woman, dressed in finery, walking trancelike into the jungle to meet her fate, oblivious to the battle around her. A "savage," having been told that the Bible contains the word of God, holding the book—the first book he has ever seen—to his ear. As food becomes ever more scarce, and more men fall to the poison arrows that fly silently from the riverbank, the men can no longer distinguish between reality and hallucination. In fact, it is all real; it is just that reality has become hallucinatory, a condition of the tropics one finds in the books of Garcia Marquez. A boat rests in the treetops forty feet above ground, a canoe dangling from its stern: could the river have risen that high, or are we dreaming? The men doubt their eyes; we don't. Finally, the denial of reality becomes their last sanctuary. In a scene all the more breathtaking for being pitched on the edge of the absurd, one of the last survivors on the desolate raft gets shot in the leg by an Indian arrow. "That is no arrow. That is not rain. That is no forest," he intones like a chant—the last prayer in a litany of delusion. Though Herzog never milks his story for emotional effect, the final passage of *Aguirre* is a deeply moving meditation on man's deranged lust to imprint himself on history. I have seen it three times now, and each time I broke out in goosebumps. The closing shot alone is worth the price of admission: the grandest, most chilling image of raging solipsism ever filmed.

Herzog is more a poet than a storyteller, and *Aguirre* has a few lapses as a narrative that may throw people off. One of Aguirre's prisoners escapes and we never find out what happens to him. Having made the point that no one can open the captive Ursua's closed fist to discover what he is holding, we expect a fascinating revelation. It never comes. It's not a seamless film, not a particularly subtle one. But that is not the point. Herzog is not a director of nuance. His strokes are broad, his vision is grand, and in *Aguirre* his power is enormous. In another context, the leering, savage performance of Klaus Kinski might seem ludicrously melodramatic; here it is chillingly apt. It may be a knee-jerk response upon hearing the word *Führer* to think of Hitler, but surely we're intended to see him looming behind this fable of a man who dreams of wedding his own daughter and founding "the purest dynasty the world has ever seen." Kinski's Aguirre is both specific and abstract; he's a man who sees himself as a force of nature, "the wrath of God," but it is nature that conquers him.

Finally, one must mention the superb photography of Thomas Mauch, accomplished under the most difficult circumstances, and the simple, hauntingly beautiful choral score by Popol Vuh, which contributes enormously to the impact of the film. *Aguirre, The Wrath of God,* made in 1972, when Herzog was only twenty-nine, is a masterpiece of the New German Cinema and, I suspect, a film for all time.

—*David Ansen*

Werner Herzog

■

THE ENIGMA OF KASPAR HAUSER (1974)

On a morning in 1828, a sixteen year old named Kaspar Hauser was found standing mute and motionless in the central square of Nurem-

berg, Germany. In his hand he held a letter addressed to the comman-
dant of the local military barracks, asking that he become a soldier.

He had never learned to speak and could hardly walk upright. He
had been raised like an animal, apparently chained to the floor of a
windowless stone stable and fed by night by faces he never saw.

Taken in hand by sympathetic townspeople, he learned in five years
to read, write, play the piano, keep a journal, and compose poetry. He
obviously had a good, original, and even visionary mind.

Then, as mysteriously as he had arrived, he was assassinated by a
bullet through his chest. His epitaph calls him "an unknown murdered
by an unknown." The baffling circumstances of his life and his death
have haunted novelists, poets, historians, and psychologists ever since.
More than a thousand books and ten thousand papers are said to have
been written about him.

Now German director Werner Herzog's film, *The Enigma of Kaspar
Hauser,* which was one of the great successes at the 1975 Cannes Film
Festival, has arrived for its first regular commercial engagement. (It has
been shown on local campuses and at Filmex.)

The film, which Herzog also wrote, can only present the enigma,
since history knows no answers. Was he simply the illegitimate child of
a passing, dashing officer and a farm girl? Was he a kidnapped infant or,
as other rumors of the time had it, an embarrassing royal bastard, a son
of Napoleon or the house of Baden?

Herzog opens and closes his film on an undulating meadow of tall
grass, billowing in a strong wind like the face of the sea. It is a perfect
impressionist image — ambiguous, timeless, pastoral, threatening — for
the haunting but often surprisingly funny story. (Hauser was a natural
man, earthy and direct, in one scene demolishing a pompous theological pedant with an incisive stroke of common sense.)

Much of the film's sympathetic power stems from Herzog's inspired
casting of Hauser. He is a nonactor identified only as Bruno S. and his
own story is in its contemporary way as troubling as Hauser's. He is
the illegitimate son of a prostitute who placed him in a mental
institution when he was three, evidently not because he was disturbed
or retarded but because she couldn't take care of him and the asylum
would.

Bruno spent the next twenty-three years in institutions of one kind
and another, including the reform schools he was sent to after
numerous escapes from asylums. He never saw his mother again and
so was almost as victimized by adult society as Hauser himself had

been. He was released back into society in 1958 and was later the subject of a German television documentary where Herzog caught sight of him.

Bruno's biography is not told in the film, but it shows. He has a wide-eyed stare, as if he cannot quite believe the continuing miracles of broad daylight and human kindness. He also has a kind of innocent cunning, the wariness of an animal, or of a child still not quite sure the punishment is over. The speech is blurting, blunt, and unrhythmical, as if learned by rote (yet not as a process of acting). You sense Hauser's earthy wit revisited in a man who more than most could identify with Hauser's lost, dark years.

Herzog makes the gruff and sullen man (Hans Musaus) who delivers Kaspar to civilization the same man who returns to kill him at point blank range. It is as logical an explanation as any: Hauser's increasing articulation and his demonstrated intelligence could well have helped him deduce the solution to his own mystery, to the embarrassment or worse of those who hid him for so long.

Like François Truffaut's *The Wild Child,* also based on an actual occurrence, Herzog's film uses his wild child not only to explore an enigma but also to look at civilization with the fresh and questioning eye of someone experiencing it for the first time, its commonplaces become wonders, its follies looking more foolish than ever.

On his deathbed, Hauser describes a vision he is having of an endless caravan crossing a desert, led by a blind Berber. Like his life and Herzog's movie, it is astonishing, mysterious, sad, and deeply moving.

The Enigma of Kaspar Hauser is a strong and subtle prize from a German cinema speaking with a new and confident voice.

—*Charles Champlin*

Shohei Imamura

■

THE PORNOGRAPHERS (1966)

The kind of aesthete who could fashion a religion out of the old *National Inquirer,* Shohei Imamura has a passion for everything that's kinky, lowlife, or irrational in Japanese culture. He populates his films with murderers, hillbillies, shamans, and prostitutes; incest and voyeurism are his stock-in-trade. Imamura, who began his career as an assistant director to Yasujiro Ozu, is a sort of return of the (national) repressed. Even his plots are like Rorschach blots—there's less a narrative line than a narrative seepage, unevenly spreading in all directions.

The Pornographers is vintage Imamura. This lurid black comedy, which the director adapted in 1966 from Akiyuki Nosaka's prize-winning bestseller (and typically subtitled *An Introduction to Anthropology*), is set in seediest Osaka; affably grotesque, it details the personal and professional trials of one Subuyan Ogata, a minor producer-distributor of eight-millimeter porn films. Perhaps because *The Pornographers* was the first movie Imamura made for his own production company, it's giddy with sympathy for its harried protagonist, a would-be solid citizen whose assistants call him "maestro." (In America, it should be noted, Imamura's own films were treated as exotic porn—a dubbed, recut version of the estimable *Pigs and Battleships* was originally released as *The Dirty Girls* and later as *The Flesh is Hot.*)

Dodging police harassment and yakuza shakedowns, Ogata comes to believe that he and his bizarrely monastic assistants perform a useful social function, comforting the sick and the loveless, alleviating frustration by furnishing clients what society has denied them. (In much the same spirit, Ogata does a bit of pimping on the side, supplying decrepit business tycoons with the "virgin" schoolgirls of their fantasies.) Still, in embellishing the straightforward sleazescape of Nosaka's novel, Imamura gives Ogata a domestic setup more juicily perverse than any of his porn loops. The maestro lives with the widowed Haru, matronly proprietor of a barbershop, but secretly covets Keiko, her frumpy teenage daughter. Haru, for her part, dotes incestuously on her grown son and in her bedroom keeps a live carp she claims to be the reincarnation of her dead husband.

Imamura revels in broad performances and unlikely performers—not forgetting the carp, his actors here are a startling collection of squat, impassive peons, all of whom get at least one chance to run wild through his cramped frames. Locked in a mental hospital, the dying Haru stages a full-fledged freakout that can only be silenced by the blast of Ventures-style rock rising inexorably on the soundtrack. This highly theatrical crack-up aside, *The Pornographers'* set pieces are the making of the fuck films—one-take, two-character jobbies that Ogata hastily shoots with eight-millimeter cameras, all mounted on a board, grinding at once. Each of these productions seems a masterpiece of desperate improvisation: Ogata, his assistants, and their imbecilic "talents" trekking to the remotest part of some Osaka park or squeezing into an impromptu garage studio. ("Is she deaf?" the filmmaker asks, when the suspiciously placid ingenue of a schoolgirl rape epic declines to take direction. "Just a little slow," her partner explains. Not only does the girl turn out to be an idiot, the man she's being filmed with is her father—he keeps her in line by giving her lollipops to crunch.)

Although Imamura includes an occasional audience reaction to Ogata's handiwork, the porn loops themselves are never seen—the better to emphasize the film's quotidian voyeurism. Ogata and Haru's lovemaking is shot from the carp's eye view, while Ogata spends much of the film spying on Keiko. (When he catches her reading one of the strokebooks he sells, he gets hilariously flustered. "That's for stupid adults," he admonishes the girl, as the police burst in and arrest him for smut peddling.) Peeping is built into nearly every scene. Imamura uses the Cinemascope format to make spatial juxtapositions and jolting sight gags: A shot of Ogata selling his wares to a gaggle of overexcited executives is filmed through a window and framed to show the firm's mainly female workers on the other side of the wall. Keiko's graduation is filmed ankle-high, a row of massive teenage calves masking Ogata's tiny, anxious face.

Still, for all Imamura's ribald stylizations, *The Pornographers* is more philosophical than prurient. When not cackling over their creations, Ogata and his assistants spend their time arguing about incest (a divine prerogative in Japanese mythology) or debating the meaning of sex: "No one understands male-female relations. It's complex yet it's vague." (The latter is an equally valid description for the feel of any Imamura flick.) "I'm fascinated by the pathos of being a man," Ogata muses, before Haru's death and Keiko's rejection have rendered him impotent and bitterly misogynistic. After an orgy fails to restore his powers, he takes his colleague's advice and builds a mechanical sex doll, "a mannequin for freedom" modeled upon Haru. A coda set five years later has an avid industrialist visiting one of Osaka's back canals and the boat where Ogata has secluded himself with his creation. "No one is taking my doll to the South Pole, no Martian is touching her!" Ogata screams, turning down a million-yen offer and dumping the guy in the canal.

As anyone who has seen *Eijanaika* or *The Ballad of Narayama* knows, Imamura has a genius for stunning metonymic endings. In the weirdly lyrical finale (one not in the novel, whose unfilmable conclusion has Ogata's lost erection restored when he is fatally struck by a car), the floating laboratory comes unmoored. Alone with his sex doll, he drifts through the harbor and out to sea. According to Ian Buruma, this parodies the denouement of a seventeenth-century classic in which a Japanese Casanova caps a life of debauchery by sailing off for the Island of Women—abruptly, Ogata's "liberation" turns even more reflexive when the image is reduced to the size of flickering eight millimeter. Is Imamura sardonically suggesting that the preceding two hours of frantic hustling and grubby sex have been his version of Ogata's porn? Or is *The Pornographers* the twentieth-century version of the nightlife of the gods?

—J. Hoberman

Shohei Imamura

∎

EIJANAIKA (1981)

Mountainous women wrestle in the nude; a "mountain girl" bites off the head of a snake, and after chewing its fat, spits a stream of fire over an open flame; a pretty girl in a kimono suddenly extends her neck to a height of six or seven feet, the camera rushing upward with her smiling face to catch her tiny giggle of satisfaction when she reaches full length. Welcome to the sideshow of cultural change and ambiguous revolution, as presented by Shohei Imamura in his witty, grotesque, brightly spinning epic of Japan's Edo era, *Eijanaika*.

Though Imamura has been making films since the late 1950s, his reputation wasn't secured in the West until the release of *Vengeance Is Mine* two years ago; with *Eijanaika* following so quickly, Imamura seems clearly established as the most creative filmmaker in Japan today: Next to the willful stasis and curious, cold resignation of Kurosawa's *Kagemusha*, *Eijanaika* places a swirl of action and color; there may not be another director in the world today who can manage so many elements—of design, of theme, of character, of rolling plot structure—on such a large scale, and with such consummate control. Imamura is a political filmmaker—he is interested in the lowest classes of society, in the way they maintain their buzzing vitality despite the weights piled atop them—but he is never a pedant. His imagination glitters, brews; there are enough ideas in *Eijanaika* for half a dozen films, and each is given a full, commanding development.

The title comes from the rallying cry of an 1867 mass movement—which may or may not have been a genuine revolution. The translators render *eijanaika* as "why not?" or, more satisfyingly, as "What the hell?" It is a cry of a dangerous, rock-bottom freedom, of the abrupt realization that traditions are dead, laws arbitrary, society an empty convention. Such was the pass the lower classes of Edo (present-day Tokyo) found themselves in in the middle of the nineteenth century, when the local Shogun clans were battling the emperor for control of the country, inflation was spinning out of sight (a running gag in *Eijanaika* is the price of rice—if a character goes away for a day or two, it's tripled by the time he gets back), and the entire culture was reeling under the opening of the country to the West after two hundred years of enforced isolation. For the poor, there is nothing left—a condition that makes everything possible. Why not wear costumes, dance in the streets, loot stores, tear down buildings? What the hell?

Though *Eijanaika* is based on historical incident, Imamura doesn't have much interest in historical detail (apparently, he even flaunts his indifference—the film is said to be full of unsettling anachronisms that Japanese audiences perceive immediately). The causes of the conflict between the Shogun clans and the emperor are never given (though we assume they're economic) and there's no real attempt made to keep the two sides politically (or even morally) distinct. Instead, Imamura is interested in the *eijanaika* state of mind, which he clearly believes holds clues to modern Japanese life. The subject is approached from two directions, in two different narrative styles. From above, Imamura looks at the political machinations—the briberies, broken alliances, and murders that lead to the breakdown of order—in the style of an action-adventure film (the paranoid drive of these passages, with their insanely complicated plotting, suggests the highly stylized samurai films of Hideo Gosha). And from below, Imamura looks at individual experiences—the gradual erosion of certainty in ordinary lives—in a style of richly ironic character comedy. The two styles blend into something quite original: it's as if Buster Keaton were starring in one of Fritz Lang's Dr. Mabuse films.

The carnival of the opening scene becomes Imamura's ruling metaphor and main staging area. It's actually an entire district, spread out along the riverbank near the Ryogoku bridge (which was rebuilt by the Tokyo government especially for Imamura's film). The area is home to Edo's pickpockets, beggars, prostitutes, and slave dealers—a Times Square with everything but the neon—and the head man is Kinzo (Shigeru Tsuyuguchi), who runs crime and the carnival as two branches of the same business. Kinzo, a practical man if ever, is on the payroll of both the shogunate and the emperor's forces; when the two sides simultaneously order him to start a riot at a silk warehouse and protect it from the mob, he gives both orders to his men without a glimmer of contradiction (and they successfully carry out their mission).

The life-as-a-carnival metaphor isn't a new one—Fellini pretty much holds the patent for movies—but Imamura manages some fresh effects. This carnival isn't the whimsical playground of illusions of the Fellini films: it's a malignant illusion, an institutionalized fraud, recognized by both the people who run it and the people who pay for admission. Yet the need to believe in something is so strong that the carnival has a positive social function: these dreams may be manufactured and ruthlessly peddled, but they are dreams after all—everybody needs something, and not even the show people are exempt. When paper charms begin to float down mysteriously over the carnival—a sign from the sun goddess that she approves of the *eijanaika*—the carnival people pitch in and start distributing their own counterfeits, telling themselves they're helping out the gods. The fraud (which was probably started by some showman in the next district anyway) has a divine origin; the gods can be served and money made simultaneously.

Kinzo's mistress is a country girl named Ine (Kaori Momoi), sold to the carnival by her impoverished parents after her husband disappeared in a shipwreck. She's now the star of an attraction titled "Tickle the Goddess," in which members of the audience take turns trying to blow a paper streamer between her flashing legs; she thinks of herself, unshakably, as an artist. But when Genji (Shigeru Izumiya), her missing husband, suddenly pops up (he'd been rescued by an American ship, and spent six years in the U.S.), she isn't sure what to do—to return to the U.S. with Genji, and start the farm they'd always dreamed of, or stick it out in Edo, where things are getting pretty interesting. Ine is the pivot point between Kinzo's ruthless pragmatism and Genji's money idealism, and pivot she does, betraying both in turn and in increasingly rapid succession. If there's a crisis in the culture, she's living it, unable to choose among the options suddenly and dizzyingly open to her. And, like the *eijanaika*, she's enjoying the crisis, dancing through it with a smile of calculating naïveté.

Ine is also the link between the film's two styles, acting as a willing pawn in Kinzo's political plots, and playing a comic heroine in Genji's misadventures. Genji burns with his new knowledge of America, and wants to share his dream of freedom with Ine; it won't be complete without her. But every time the dream is within reach, Ine lets him down, turning back within sight of the ship that will take them to America, getting herself kidnapped (and not objecting too much) from the farm Genji has managed to secure in the countryside. Is Genji's freedom — abstract, idealized, and pretty hard work — really preferable to the freedom Kinzo offers in his way, the freedom of money and power? Genji sticks with his plan, with a sober determination that is truly Keatonesque, brushing himself off and grimly starting over every time something explodes. But Genji's adversaries aren't Keaton's inanimate objects and natural forces — they're people, and much less predictable.

The unpredictability that dogs Genji is also the principle of Imamura's narrative line — episodes fire off one another with a lightning crackle, as Imamura puts several plot strands in motion at once and leaps between them, jamming them together and yanking them apart. Kinzo plots schemes involving Genji, the political factions plot schemes involving Kinzo, soon it's impossible to say who is controlling whom. Causes and effects are carefully, exuberantly muddled: the complicated plot soon seems to be roaring along on its own, impelled by some internal energy none of the characters can grasp. Meanwhile, Imamura is multiplying the focal points in his images — bright colors compete with sudden movement, individual faces compete with compelling group compositions for our attention. Imamura seems to be shooting lines of energy across the screen; sometimes he'll exploit the hard, sharp lines of Japanese architecture to give the frame an internal, geometric tension; at other times, he'll create a rhythmic tension between foreground and background actions, a contrast that seems to pull the image apart.

Over the course of its two and a half hours, *Eijanaika* has been gathering energy, storing it up. When the *eijanaika* riots finally arrive, the stored energy bursts forth: it's an irresistibly giddy rushing moment. (And it's a tribute to Imamura's intelligent, offbeat timing that, even though we've expected the riots to serve as the climax of his film, they still arrive unexpectedly, spontaneously.) As the dancing, shouting hordes stream out of the riverside carnival, threatening to cross the Ryogoku bridge into forbidden territory, Imamura allows us to feel the crowd's excitement, its sense of mad freedom — yet, by photographing the river-crossing through space-compacting telephoto lenses, he also traps it, pinning it down in a two-dimensional space where the energy of the crowd loses its thrust, its purpose. Though Kinzo has encouraged the riots for practical, political reasons, they are more than political now. The energy created, exploited, and barely contained by the carnival has slipped out, leveling everything before it. It is an energy without cause and without control, fed equally by greed and ideals, dreams and frauds. The politicians can play with it, but they can't keep it down. The cry of *"Eijanaika!"* is innately human. Vital and monstrous, it sounds through every culture.

— Dave Kehr

Juzo Itami

∎

TAMPOPO (1986)

Bravely, the widow and her son cling to their humble homestead, struggling to make a go of it in a harsh and unyielding landscape. Then one dark and stormy night, the tall and taciturn stranger, accompanied, of course, by his comical sidekick, rides up. They seek sustenance and shelter, but taking pity on these good, hard-pressed people, they stay to set things right, even recruiting a magnificent five or six to help them rout evil and restore order to this little Eden before heading off into the sunset.

Ah, yes, the classic western form. Well, not quite. For the setting is not the great American plains in the nineteenth century, but an industrial wasteland in contemporary Japan. The widow's threatened property is not a ranch but a noodle restaurant. Her rescuer, despite his boots, belt, and ten-gallon hat, is not a cowboy, but a very literally westernized truck driver.

Writer-director Itami's satire on a great movie form is sly and subtle and does useful double-duty by providing a solid structure for his film. The relationship that develops between sweet, spunky Tampopo (Nobuko Miyamoto) and rough, naturally noble Goro, her rescuer (Tsutomu Yamazaki), as he puts her through the stern retraining course that will make her not just the fastest but the chicest noodle-slinger in the territory is winsome but unsentimental. Yet neither is truly his subject. Food is. And not just the humble fare of Tampopo's ramen shop.

For man does not live by noodles alone — not nowadays, in the age of the international gourmet movement. Now that the world is our oyster, the oyster (among other formerly exotic viands) has become, for some of us, our world. And so Itami blithely skips away from Tampopo's place whenever his whimsical spirit moves him to show, in vignettes, how the basic drive for nurture has been deliriously distorted. A group of Japanese businessmen all end up ordering the same item from a French menu because they are unable to cope with its intricacies and equally unwilling to admit it; a group of women who might be their wives earnestly take a course in how to eat spaghetti without slurping; a master eater pontificates on the proper method of appreciating a bowl of soup as if it were a great work of music or literature; a sad little boy wanders a park wearing a sign his parents have hung around his neck, warning strangers that he only eats natural foods, and must not be given sweets or other snacks. A vagrant's only joy is to sneak into a kitchen and prepare a perfect rice omelette. A mother is roused from her deathbed to make one last meal for her family before succumbing. Needless to say, this final gift is consumed before mourning is permitted to begin.

A recurring figure in these divertissements is a gangster, elegant in a perfectly cut white suit. He is all too well aware of the connection between food and that other basic drive, sex, and he has a game-for-anything girlfriend who permits him to dine delicately on a seafood treat spread across her tummy and with whom a perfect orgasm is achieved as they pass a raw egg from mouth to mouth. Rubbed out by a rival gang, he dies in her arms, murmuring of pork stuffed with yams.

Outrageous? Not more so than the prose of a typical restaurant critic. Or maunderings of the neighbors down the block, just back from their gourmet tour of the continent. And in its unpretentious acuity, a lot funnier . . . if Itami were a chef he might rank with Escoffier; as a moviemaker he certainly ranks with Preston Sturges as a deflator of middle-class pretensions. Compared to him, most contemporary comedy directors are just staging food fights.

—*Richard Schickel*

Juzo Itami

■

A TAXING WOMAN (1987)

If you think Juzo Itami was tuned into the eighties in *The Funeral* and *Tampopo,* wait until you see the deadpan humor he wrings from the ways that sex and potency and almost everything else are tied to money in his third comedy, *A Taxing Woman.* In a social landscape—specifically Japan, but quite recognizably universal—where money is the new lifeblood, it doesn't come as a surprise to see that one tax miscreant commits ritual suicide not by slashing his wrists, or running himself through with a sword, but by writing the number of a secret bank account in his own blood and handing it to a tax inspector—as a bullhorn-toting gangster bellows, "Violence is obsolete. Today we go to prison for tax evasion."

That's the springboard for Itami's rambunctious comedy of social mores. *A Taxing Woman* is just that, a mousy but relentless tax inspector who beneath her freckles is the Wyatt Earp of the new Japan. If the play on words in the title of the film wasn't so apt, Itami could have called it *Taxbusters.* Essentially, the film places her on a collision course with a devious entrepreneur named Gondo. Ryoko, the tax ferret, is played by Itami's wife, Nobuko Miyamoto, who will be remembered as the all-but-defeated noodle shop owner in *Tampopo.* Tsutomu Yamazaki, her mentor in *Tampopo,* is her antagonist here, the limping, but otherwise fast-lane Gondo, who makes most of his money through his hidden ownership of a lucrative chain of quickie sex hotels.

When Ryoko is promoted from auditor to inspector, after rooting out tax shortfalls in mom-and-pop noodle shops and high-volume pachinko parlors, she trembles at the chance to investigate Gondo, who, her infallible instincts tell her, is a big fish. Itami insists he never intended to make a screwball comedy where financial statements are the new sexual battleground. He says *A Taxing Woman* is a detective story, no more. But just as its satirical elements are wonderfully vivid, so is the sexual tension that develops in an unarticulated manner between the fast-buck Gondo and the woman whose life has become her job.

Their most touching link lies in the fact that both neglect their children. At one point, she interrupts her investigation of Gondo to chase after his teenage son who bolts from the house and clearly can use an understanding ear. Not lost upon her is the fact that she leaves her own kid too long with a sitter while she chain-smokes and insinuates her way into Gondo's life with the aid of a computer and a lot of spying. Her colleagues aren't as restrained in their hounding. At one point, the film seems to turn into a case of "Getting Gondo's Garbage," as their search for evidence of unreported income veers into the odiferous. And when a door is slammed on an investigator's foot, he cheerfully says, pointing to his undented safety shoe, "Even a truck can't crush 'em!"

Any hope that this new kind of chase movie will veer into romance is doomed, however, by the singlemindedness of both pursuer and pursued. But despite his roundhouse swings at the new entrepreneurial aggressiveness that is hurtling Japan into space-age materialism, Itami seems to have a grudging affection for the hard-driving go-getters. Perhaps it's just that he knows that nobody loves the taxman. Or tax woman. Certainly he poses the question of whether Gondo's driving ambition is really more despicable than Ryoko's.

Until the tax army mobilizes and raids Gondo's house on a military scale, Ryoko's diminutiveness had made her the sympathetic character. But the balance shifts when we see how high the odds are against the beleaguered Gondo. As doubtful as he is about Japan's rampaging materialism, Itami is anything but enamored of his country's functionaries, with their martial arts approach to bookkeeping. Having taken on death, food, sex, and now taxes, it'll be interesting to see what Itami can go on to for subject matter of similarly universal reach. Meanwhile, there's a certain rightness about the idea of a samurai money movie from Japan, and it's hard to imagine a more slyly rollicking one than *A Taxing Woman*.

—*Jay Carr*

Neil Jordan

■

MONA LISA (1986)

In Neil Jordan's beautiful and heartbreaking Mona Lisa, Bob Hoskins
has his best role yet—he's the small-time ex-con George, a violent yet
scrupulous and upright man who falls in love with an elegant black
prostitute and becomes her protector, knight, and patsy. Hoskins has
often played softhearted but volatile men, and this time he goes
further than ever before in suggesting the ways brutality can grow out
of moral feeling. The movie is both tender and acrid—a romantic
gangster film. It takes its title as well as much of its mood from the Nat
King Cole fifties standard, which has lush strings and a mood of gentle
yearning. The Irish-born writer-director Neil Jordan conceived the
role for Hoskins, and as you watch Hoskins, who is a poignant figure
from first scene to last, you're beguiled into hearing the song in an
ideal way—not as fifties kitsch but as a troubled expression of romantic
bafflement.

In movies, a stupid hero can be irritating and finally unbearable. But
Hoskins, who is short, barrel-chested, and balding, with a pugnacious
nose and a small mouth that can turn into an oval of rage, has played
men of ordinary, or less than ordinary, intelligence without losing the
audience for an instant. He was Arthur Parker, the sexually frustrated
song salesman in the original, BBC version of *Pennies From Heaven,* the
London gangster losing his grip in *The Long Good Friday,* and the
nattering, affectionate mobster–club owner Owney Madden in *The
Cotton Club.* His characters are men of action who have resources of
feeling denied most of us. Utterly decisive in action, Hoskins becomes
not merely the hero of his movies but an actor who is loved by the
camera—loved, that is, the way Humphrey Bogart and James Cagney
were loved—as a possibility of honor and courage.

Of course, he's a less stylized and impervious actor than either of
those masters—more the sweaty lower-middleclass man, the anxious
striver denied dignity and love. In *Mona Lisa,* returning home to
London after serving a seven-year prison term, George stands dumb-
struck at the door, amazed by the sight of his lovely fifteen-year-old
daughter. Before he can identify himself (she doesn't recognize him),
his wife turns him away. He's homeless, cut off from what he loves,
and when he goes to pay a call on Mortwell (Michael Caine), the

vicious gangster for whom he loyally took the fall seven years earlier, Mortwell is hidden and inaccessible—working somewhere in the labyrinth of sex clubs, whorehouses, and blackmail rackets that he runs and that George can never understand.

George is shunted into a nothing job: He becomes cover and driver for a black tart who has fought her way up from the streets. Now a deluxe call girl, Simone (Cathy Tyson, Cicely's niece) works the Arab millionaires Mortwell sends her to and also, on her own, the West End hotels. As a cover, George is hilariously inadequate—he is so awkward in the lobby of the Ritz that he actually looks like a cheap ponce, and nearly gets them both thrown out. He's a clown and an idiot—an idiot in the Dostoevskian sense of someone too innocent, too unimaginative, to take in the simple facts of evil in the world. That this man has committed violence, and possibly even murder, makes him that much more deluded, but by no means unbelievable.

Simone and George make an odd but satisfying couple. Cathy Tyson, only twenty, is physically astonishing—very tall, straight as an arrow, with the most beautiful mocha skin and thick, abundant hair pulled tight and then sent falling at an acute angle. The outrageous tilt of that hair, combined with the perfect cut of her features gives Tyson the singular, highstrung look of an Asian princess. Most girls who look like her have been trained as models, but Tyson has in fact acted with the Royal Shakespeare Company, and she speaks like a princess, too, in soft, low, yet authoritative tones—a mesmerizing murmur.

George would like to think of Simone as a lady, but she's too straight to entertain that particular illusion. Her candor, in a world of lies, has an almost ironic clarity. Speaking of her clients, she says, "Sometimes they fall for what they think I am." "Which is what?" asks George, who is sure that he knows the answer. "A black whore," she says. Poor George—no wonder he's dazzled! While he's trying to unravel remarks like these, Simone, who has grown genuinely fond of him, presses her face into his and asks a favor. Find a girl, she says, a blonde, Cathy, who has disappeared somewhere in Mortwell's domain.

As George enters the night world of clubs, peep parlors, and S&M dens, the movie grows lusher, darker, and more sinister. Composer Michael Kamen returns to the "Mona Lisa" theme, turning parts of the melody, in his own arrangement, into a threatening, mordant refrain, and Jordan produces a mossy, underwater grotto look—the lighting is orange and pale green. I haven't seen Jordan's *The Company of Wolves* (1985), but on the basis of this movie, I would say that he is a first-rate talent. There are a few whimsical scenes between George and his buddy, Thomas (Robbie Coltrane), who lives in a camper and produces bizarre plastic sculptures, that don't quite come off. But everything else in the movie is expressive and dramatic, and in the spectacle of the man of violence defeated by modern crime methods, there's something rare as well, a mood of poignancy and irony mixed together. Jordan and Hoskins have put us inside George's skin. When he explodes, we're dismayed but not really surprised.

His name may be a nod to the George who slew the dragon and became the patron saint of England, and also, more immediately, to George C. Scott, who played a severe Midwesterner searching the Los Angeles porno underworld for his own daughter, in *Hardcore*. But unlike that grim avenger, Hoskins's George doesn't vent his disgust. He's really too unassuming to judge anyone. When he finds a possible Cathy, a girl no older than his own daughter, he can barely breathe as she comes on to him, and we can see that he's turned on as well as nauseated. This movie isn't priggish the way *Hardcore* was. For Jordan, the porno-prostitution world is death, but is has a lurid power that can't be shaken off. The devils have real magic.

George goes deeper and deeper in his selfless, seemingly gratuitous quest, finally rescuing Cathy, in a great scene, at the mouth of hell. The story ends as it must, in terror and violence. Jordan pulls off the most reckless moves, even the kind of thing that most directors fail at — the moment of despair when George treats Simone, for the first time, as a cheap whore. Of course, George is a hopeless sap, an excluded male, for the genuinely grateful Simone will never reward him the way he wants. There's a wonderful fatalistic pull to the romantic drama in *Mona Lisa* — the music, the photography, Hoskins's moving performance, everything works together. The movie says that the true romantic is always a loser, a baffled man just like the lover in the song, who asks whether his Mona Lisa is warm and real or just a cold, lonely, lovely work of art.

— *David Denby*

Neil Jordan

■

THE COMPANY OF WOLVES (1984)

Irish novelist-filmmaker Neil Jordan's astonishing blend of lyricism and terror. This multileveled retelling of "Little Red Riding Hood" — supposedly through a young girl's feverish nightmares — dredges up every possible mythopoetic, psychosexual connotation and is enacted in a rapturous, dreamily artificial stage setting (by Anton Furst) that recalls Arthur Rackam and Hieronymous Bosch.

—*Michael Wilmington*

Emir Kusturica

■

WHEN FATHER WAS AWAY ON BUSINESS (1985)

Emir Kusturica's *When Father Was Away on Business* opens in a seemingly oblique way, with a laborer singing a Spanish song in a Yugoslavian field. Why a Spanish song? Because, the shrewd laborer explains, it won't get him into political trouble. That sounds like one of those grimly sardonic Eastern European jokes. Yet in a way it quickly conveys the climate of the film. It's a warm, rich, deeply felt, refreshingly imaginative chronicle of a Sarajevo family weathering political and other troubles during the tense years of the Tito-Stalin rupture from 1949 to 1953.

The father (Miki Manojlovic), a jaunty philanderer, seems a seedy Charlie Chaplin with his twitchy mustache, penguin walk, and quickly ignited vitality. Heedlessly, he wisecracks to his jealous mistress about a political cartoon. The next thing he knows, he's being bundled off to a forced labor camp by his sour brother-in-law, a party bigwig who thinks the mistress is just what he needs to get his mind off his ulcer. "Away on business" is a euphemism. It's what families of political detainees reply to queries about the whereabouts of absent menfolk. Yet, as engagingly cocky as the roguish father is, the film really belongs to the baby of the family, chubby six-year-old Malik (Morena D'E Bartolli), who's preoccupied with sleepwalking, soccer, and sex.

It's tempting to think of this child's-eye view of a politically turbulent period as a Yugoslav *Amarcord,* but it has an earthy specificity all its own. It lovingly inscribes the eccentricities of each family member: Grandpa, who detests bathing; Malik's owlish older brother, who hoards scraps of film and dreams of making movies; their wonderfully unsinkable mother (Mirjana Karanovic), who overlooks her husband's unfaithfulness, takes in sewing, and drags the boys to the muddy labor camp as soon as their father is allowed visitors. Kusturica's ability to juggle humor and poignancy reaches its peak when Malik is simultaneously fascinated by what his reunited parents are up to in the next room, and determined to interrupt them and claim his mother's attention.

There's nothing revisionist about the film; Kusturica is content to specify a world and let his fully formed characters fill it with wonderful individuality. *When Father Was Away on Business* seems most itself when, to heal a quarrel, the family spontaneously climbs into bed together and hugs and sings, huddled like puppies. The performances all are so good that we're hardly aware we're watching performances at all. But most impressive is Kusturica's directorial assurance, especially when he leaves heightened naturalism and climbs into poetry every time Malik sleepwalks to free himself from history and the strict social order he inhabits.

The sleepwalking becomes more and more airborne. Eventually, it becomes magical, Chagall-like, as earth tones give way to lunar, otherworldly lighting. Kusturica, thirty, is a director from whom we'll be seeing more. This is only his second film. It deservedly won a Golden Palm at Cannes; his first, *Do You Remember Dolly Bell?* won a Golden Lion at Venice. That film hasn't been shown yet in the United States, but *When Father Was Away on Business* is as impressive a calling card as any young director's in recent years. It has charm, heart, poetry, and style. It's joyful and humane—the up, up, and away film of the year.

—*Jay Carr*

Emir Kusturica

■

TIME OF THE GYPSIES (1989)

Yugoslavian directors have a special gift for the juiciest, fleshiest forms of magical realism. Launching his most recent trip into one of those larger-than-life worlds, Emir Kusturica went beyond the Sarajevo childhood of his prize-winning *When Father Was Away on Business*. *Time of the Gypsies,* which won Kusturica the best director award at 1989's Cannes Film Festival, takes a flying leap into gypsy culture.

The opening plunges over the muddy square of a gypsy shantytown, past flocks of darting geese, into a shack with its TV perched on a cardboard box. That's where grandma lives with her lecherous, ne'er-do-well son; her teenage grandson, Perhan; and her six-year-old granddaughter, Danira.

Grandma — played by a real gypsy in her cheerfully clashing bandanas, shawls, and hoop earrings — is like a big, wrinkled apple the size of the planet, solid and enduring. Danira — born with one leg shorter than the other — is a small round face with huge eyes, watching life from the bed where she's confined. Perhan — with his dark, lyrical, cross-eyed stare and snaggletoothed grin — is the beautiful-and-ugly main character.

All around him, he sees the equally beautiful-and-ugly folktale world where angels and trolls fly through ordinary life, "The world began when Earth was separated from sky," says grandma, explaining the beginnings of gypsy rootlessness. Perhan's special talent, inherited from her, is his way of making spoons, forks, and tin cans scoot along tables, slither up walls, and glide through the air. He and his gift for levitation are a natural part of gypsy life's floating opera.

Simultaneously funny, terrifying, and marvelous, it's the kind of place where Perhan's crazy uncle might hitch up a tractor and pull the roof off their home. Or where the ghost of Perhan's dead mother might fly after her children in the form of a wedding veil. Or where, in the movie's most heart-stoppingly beautiful image, Perhan and his true love, Azra, make love for the first time in a river surrounded by the burning barges and swinging lanterns of an autumn gypsy ceremony.

"Don't let her feet see more sky than earth," Perhan tells his grandma when he leaves Azra under her hawk's eye. A local con man has promised Perhan the money to fix Danira's stunted leg and marry

Azra. But, for better and worse, everyone in the story is fated to see more sky than earth. When he's lured into a ring of thievery, begging, pimping, and baby-selling across the border in Italy, Perhan loses his innocence in a hurry. But the magic stays. The whole movie is like the moment when Perhan, staring hypnotically into the eyes of his ugly, wattled pet turkey, trains it to spread its wings by miming flight with his own skinny arms.

Though messy and sprawling, *Time of the Gypsies* spreads its wings, too. In its rougher gypsy vision of Chagall's flying donkeys and angels, it finds the sense of wonder Hollywood spends millions failing to locate.

—*Kathy Schulz Huffhines*

Maurice Pialat

■

LOULOU (1980)

The most electrifying performers on-screen at Cannes this year were Isabelle Huppert and Gérard Depardieu in Maurice Pialat's *Loulou.* They should have won awards for displaying the full range of their talents from heart-breaking restraint to soul destroying release. In addition, they just happen to be the sexiest couple in the history of the cinema—which means not necessarily the most romantic couple, or the most scintillating individual sex objects. For romance we have Vivien Leigh and Laurence Olivier, Simone Simon or Michele Morgan and Jean Gabin, Arletty and Barrault, Dietrich and Cooper, Garbo and Barrymore, Sullavan and Boyer, Presle and Philipe, Dunne and Grant, Bergman and Bogart, Darrieux and De Sica, Hiller and Livesey. For sex, Fonda and Voight can be cited for one or two scenes in *Coming Home,* an otherwise tedious piece of sermonizing. There is at least one critic who was visibly turned on by the simulated spectacle of Marlon Brando's projecting his Method personality up Maria Schneider's supposedly buttered anus in *Last Tango in Paris,* but that can hardly be described as "coupling." Susannah York, Bibi Andersson, Diane Keaton, Jill Clayburgh, Romy Schneider, Machiko Kyo, Laura Antonelli, Lea Massari, Monica Vitti, Jeanne Moreau, Harriet Andersson, and

Susan George, among many other delectable damsels, have had their moments of simulated ecstasy on screen, but their partners remain dim in the memory.

The first clue to the revolutionary originality of *Loulou* is that the name is the male's rather than the female's. Depardieu plays a socially marginal character who frequents discos and cafes. At first he seems like an ordinary hoodlum because of the low-key realism with which Pialat treats the lurid milieu. When we see Huppert in this world, we immediately assume that she is socially marginal as well, but it turns out that she comes from a richer, more educated class, and that her job and tastes actually place her among the fringe of the intelligentsia. Loulou is more her fantasy sex object than she his. Her lover, who doubles as her employer in a television-ad agency, is, by turns, violently jealous and tenaciously masochistic. The Huppert character falls into bed with the Depardieu character, and gives up just about everything to stay there. "He never stops," she says of Loulou to her ex-lover. Loulou never works either, and that presents problems.

But the audience can never get a grip on the film or its characters because of the disconcerting discrepancy between the subject and the style. French audiences were made uncomfortable by Loulou's arrogance and complacency, and Huppert's downward mobility was therefore dismissed as implausible. Furthermore, Loulou opened on the next-to-last day of the festival during a driving rain that effectively dampened cafe debates. My own first reaction to the film was mixed, but on the road to Aix-en-Provence and Avignon, I found myself returning mentally to the squalid bedrooms in which Huppert and Depardieu sprawled in nude abandon, and I began to feel the force of Pialat's oddly stylized bedroom lyricism. I began to understand why he disdained the facility of a gratuitously violent act that could end the sensual enslavement of this reciprocally magnetic twosome.

This is a film about eroticism, not closet pornography. The audience can never get far enough away from the characters to achieve the moral distancing required for true voyeurs. Nor is the milieu ever inauthentic to the point that the audience can be lulled into wet dreamland. The audience keeps expecting society to wreak some terrible punishment on the characters for their sensual indulgence. After a climactic abortion, one would think the relationship would end. Instead, Huppert and Depardieu lurch away together. All the time that Huppert and Depardieu are on the screen, they radiate the most dangerously anarchic sexuality one can imagine. You have to watch out for this Loulou.

He lives his life as if there were really no tomorrow, only a finite series of tonights. He haunts even my typewriter, and Huppert stands beside him, almost purring with a mysterious contentment. You will have a chance to see *Loulou* at this year's New York Film Festival. Don't miss it. Huppert and Depardieu now belong to the ages.

—Andrew Sarris

Maurice Pialat

■

À NOS AMOURS (1983)

Can anyone else raise temperatures like a promiscuous sixteen-year-old girl? The object of erotic longing, she's also the target of vulgar reproach — simultaneously siren and whore. In his new film, *À Nos Amours,* Maurice Pialat, whose *Loulou* overflowed with torrential female sexuality, fixes his gaze on a teenage nymph. But his fascination lies less in the cooings and couplings of his heroine, Suzanne, than in her dammed-up emotions. Although Suzanne's unhappy circumstances — a middle-class family torn by marital discord and selfishness — are familiar enough to be the stuff of sociological soap opera, Pialat's precise technique enables his characters to emerge from the welter of detail as individual sufferers, not case studies. And Suzanne's bedhopping escape from her family becomes a spiritual pursuit of happiness, intense and single-minded.

Not that she's a romantic heroine ready to sacrifice all for love. We first see her at summer camp, rehearsing a play in which she asks her lover whether he's ready to die for love, but it's not long before we see her giving her real-life lover the heave-ho. Actually, "lover" is too strong a word for Luc, with whom Suzanne shares a virginal adolescent infatuation. In the supersensitive way of young love, Luc senses her waning interest and lets her go. That night, Suzanne makes love for the first time, to an obnoxious American tourist, thereby condemning Luc to her past — as someone she knew when she was innocent.

When fall comes, she's back in her family's combination apartment/furriery, no longer her parents' sweet little girl but a young woman obsessed with completing her sexual education. One night, she returns home late from a date, only to find her father waiting up for her. They share a rare moment of comfortable intimacy during which her father reveals that, fed up with her mother, he's leaving home. Pialat, a hefty teddy bear of a man, plays Suzanne's father with sad eyes and a pursed-mouth exasperation: it's the right complement to the mismatched moods of gentleness and brutality that seem to dictate his behavior. And after he leaves the family, his strong emotions infect the entire household — Suzanne, her mother, and brother Robert, all of whom begin to feed on one another.

Suzanne's mother flies into bouts of hysteria; her brother, intent on a playwriting career, grows increasingly frustrated by suppressed incestuous desire; Suzanne spends more time with her lovers, an expanding list of boys who can take her out of herself. Several times she is asked whether she likes a particular boy; invariably she replies, "I must, or I wouldn't be with him." All her boys are likable, but they're also detachable after use, and ultimately disposable.

This begins to sound like TV docudrama (*Suzanne: Portrait of a Teenage Slut*), and it would be if Pialat's style were any less aggressive. The director shoves his lightweight cameras into the middle of the action, rushing to capture family violence as both Robert and Suzanne's mother try to beat her promiscuity out of her. These scenes have a jagged syncopation: they build and fall without regard to conventional dramatic structure. And Pialat prefers to focus on the moments after volcanic eruptions, in the seconds when his characters regain self-consciousness. He even cuts to an outsider, an employee cutting a coat and smiling in embarrassment as Suzanne gets whacked by Robert. It's always the presence of characters that determines the position of the camera. Pialat is interested in Suzanne not as a phenomenon but as a person making moral choices.

Those choices become more difficult when Suzanne runs into Luc, who's still carrying a torch. He's tried indifference, cruelty, even making love to one of Suzanne's friends; meanwhile Suzanne keeps trying to sort out her feelings. At one point she accuses Luc of wanting to make love to her simply because she's let others do it; finally she tells him, a week before marrying someone else, that she doesn't think she can experience love at all. In running away from her family, whose lack of love has led to violence, she hasn't found love, only emotional dislocation.

But just as she seems to have settled into bourgeois complacency after six months of loveless marriage, her father returns. While

Suzanne and her husband, Robert and his bride and brother-in-law, old friend Michel, and Suzanne's mother are sitting around after a party, in walks father with a prospective buyer for the apartment. Planting himself at the table, he accuses one person after another of hypocrisy and failure, barely averting a violent scene with his wife. Filmed with an intimacy so excruciating it's almost indecent, the scene rips off the family's facade. And Suzanne lets Michel fondle her under the table, practically in front of her husband.

Throughout Pialat avoids cause-and-effect explanations: Suzanne's actions always precede the family crises that might otherwise seem to have prompted them. It's as if the director were shrugging and saying, "Yes, this unhappy girl is driven into a succession of lovers' arms by her family, but she might have ended up there anyway." As Suzanne, Sandrine Bonnaire, who won a César (French Oscar) award for Best Newcomer, is always holding back; she's a still water amid the emotional cascades of her family. As Robert, Dominique Besnehard is a plump, clumsy jumble of ambition and suspicion, never more foolish than when he thinks he's made a success. But even he is sympathetic when he runs around picking up after his hysterical mother.

À Nos Amours is not a "well-made" film. Its compositions are violent, its construction is often as untidy as life's, and its climax resolves none of the issues. But it's a fierce film, brilliantly realistic and tough, and its reticence about right and wrong, its reluctance to judge rather than observe, make it the most wrenchingly honest film about sex to hit the screens since *Luna*.

—*Henry Sheehan*

Maurice Pialat

■

UNDER SATAN'S SUN (1987)

When this film won top prize at Cannes—by a unanimous vote of the jury—the festival audience booed. I can understand both responses because Maurice Pialat's dark, brooding, almost Dostoevskyan movie serves up a peculiar combination of stylistic precision and religious obscurity. It's based on a novel by Georges Bernanos (best known for

Diary of a Country Priest) and, in its way, tackles a similar theme to *The Last Temptation of Christ:* the smothering difficulty of knowing whether one is following God's will, succumbing to the wiles of Satan, or merely suffering from some murky hallucination. The cramped, beefy Gérard Depardieu plays Father Donissan, a priest driven to the hairshirt by his sins and his failings as his parishioners' shepherd. In a set of rigorously staged encounters with a careerist priest (Pialat), a satanic horse trader, a dying child, and a murderess (played by the great Sandrine Bonnaire), Donissan is tempted to stray from the saintly path — if he is actually on it. Although this movie's concern with religious faith may strike some as outmoded, *Under Satan's Sun* is strikingly modern. Bernanos and Pialat confront the viewer with a reality of ineffable opaqueness — the world resists our every attempt to grasp it — and they offer an ultrasophisticated notion of sin: Satan entices Donissan with the chance of knowing the profoundest thoughts of those he meets. The very difficulty of these themes can prove frustrating, especially since Pialat (*À Nos Amours*) has an innate pessimism that turns Donissan's story even bleaker than in the novel: Bernanos believed in God, and Pialat pretty clearly doesn't. Pialat's film will fill up the heads of those who let it. That may be only one person in ten, but that one will think *Under Satan's Sun* a great film.

—*John Powers*

Paolo and Vittorio Taviani

■

PADRE PADRONE (1977)

Thirty years after the dawn of neorealism, the Italian cinema of Fellini, Bertolucci, Wertmuller, and the late Visconti looks more and more like a baroque hall of mirrors, full of sensual splendor, personal fantasy — and a large dose of self-indulgence. Against some of the wilder excesses of recent years, *Padre Padrone,* a film made for Italian television by Paolo and Vittorio Taviani, stands as a stern, welcome rebuke. The Taviani brothers have gone back to the soil broken by Rossellini and De Sica and refertilized it in fresh, surprising ways.

Their film, a work of desolate poetry and harsh physical power, is a gritty tribute to the spirit of survival.

The spirit is that of Gavino Ledda, whose autobiography inspired the film. Until the age of twenty Ledda was an illiterate Sardinian shepherd who had spent most of his life — from the age of six when his father took him away from school to tend the family flock — in the crushing isolation of the craggy Sardinian hillsides. A virtual outcast from humanity, a slave to the brutal authority of his father, Gavino finally escaped Sardinia to join the Italian Army. There he discovered that his illiteracy, and his Sardinian dialect, had made him an outcast from society as well. But the years of silence inspired in him an insatiable hunger for words. While training as a radio technician, he began to learn Italian — then Latin and Greek. Armed with knowledge, he returned to his homeland to battle his intransigent patriarch and come to terms with his past. Now a professor of linguistics and a writer, Ledda himself introduces his story. Taking up the stick with which his father used to beat him, he hands it to the actor (Omero Antonutti) who will play his father.

In outline, Gavino Ledda's story may suggest the pat inspirational symmetry of a Sunday sermon, but this is far from the truth of the movie. There is joy and triumph here, but also a fierce, compacted anger, and an awareness that old battles are always replaced by new ones. The Tavianis tell Gavino's story in a style at once primitively direct and cooly modern, alternately keeping us at a distance and plunging us into the wild, subjective reality of Gavino's world.

Padre Padrone is as much about silence and sound as it is about patriarchal tyranny, and the Tavianis' use of sound is one of the boldest and most exhilarating in recent movies. When an accordion player suddenly appears to Gavino (Saverio Marconi) on the hillside, playing a Strauss waltz, we hear it as a man would who has heard only the rustling of an oak, the braying of goats, and the sound of the wind — not as a lone instrument, but as a blast of joyous orchestral music. It is this music — and the promise of other worlds it contains — that inspires Gavino to defy his father by slaughtering two lambs to trade for the accordion. When six-year-old Gavino (Fabrizio Forte) milks a belligerent goat, we hear not only what the boy is thinking but the goat's reply.

The movie continually abandons realism to capture the Sardinians' subconscious: we eavesdrop, in a sense, on the secret thoughts and dreams of the townsfolk. In one breathtaking and hilarious sequence, the camera cuts from one scene of lust to the next—boys sodomizing mules and masturbating over chickens, parents grappling on a bed, lovers taking each other in passion, while the sounds of their feverish panting join and swell into a cacophony of communal lust. It's a passage unlike any I know of in movies, and it is only one of many in *Padre Padrone*. Indeed, the stylistic flourishes may seem too dazzling at times, a kind of betrayal of the raw power of Gavino's story. Yet the power remains, and out of it the Taviani brothers have made a film that sings with a terrible, moving beauty.

—*David Ansen*

Paolo and Vittorio Taviani

■

THE NIGHT OF THE SHOOTING STARS (1981)

The Night of the Shooting Stars (the original Italian title is *La Notte di San Lorenzo*) is so good it's thrilling. This new film by Vittorio and Paolo Taviani (who made the 1977 *Padre Padrone*) encompasses a vision of the world. Comedy, tragedy, vaudeville, melodrama—they're all here, and inseparable. Except for the framing device, scenes that take place in a blue-lighted, fairy-tale present, *Shooting Stars* is set in a Tuscan village and its environs during a summer week in 1944, when the American troops were rumored to be only days away, and the Germans who had held the area under occupation were preparing to clear out. But this setting is magical, like a Shakespearean forest; it exists in the memory of Cecilia, who is telling the story of what happened that August, when she was a sultry six-year-old hellion (played by Micol Guidelli), and her family was part of a group of a few dozen villagers who had decided to disobey official orders. Convinced that the Germans, who had mined their houses, meant to destroy the whole town—San Martino—that night, they stole out after dark and went to find the Americans. The directors (who also wrote the script, with Giuliani G. De Negri) are great gagmen—they aren't afraid to let Cecilia exaggerate. She remembers herself as a tiny six-year-old who is independent of adults and smarter than life. It doesn't take much stretch of our imaginations to grasp that accidents that befell the child—such as tumbling onto a basket of eggs—have become enlarged. The basket itself has assumed heroic proportions, and, having been blamed for what she couldn't help, the little girl takes a demonic joy in smashing the two eggs that are still intact. The Cecilia we see never complains and always finds ways to amuse herself; when she has witnessed an on-the-run wedding (the groom is AWOL, the bride's pregnancy is close to term) even the hops she takes, out of sheer pixilated excitement, are a bit higher than life. At this rushed wedding, an old man drinks a ceremonial glass of wine and gives a recitation about what happened to Achilles and Hector as if the Trojan War had taken place in his own lifetime. I think you could say that *Shooting Stars* is about how an individual's memories go to form communal folklore, and vice versa, so that we "recall" what we've heard from others as readily as what we've actually seen or heard. And the myth becomes our memory—the story we tell.

The Tavianis' style here is intellectualized, but their effects are unaccountable and gutty. Right at the start, in the chaos of a war that's lost but not yet over, and with army deserters making their way home and hiding out from the Germans and the local Black Shirts, and with families split between resistance fighters and fascists, and nobody sure what the Germans will do before they pull out, San Martino is victimized by a practical joker who plays "Glory, Glory Hallelujah" on his phonograph. It's a marching version, with drums and woodwinds, of the old camp-meeting hymn that became "John Brown's Body" and later the "Battle Hymn of the Republic," and it begins softly, as if John Brown's brigades were at a distance and coming closer, and the townspeople, who have been cowering in their cellars, think that the Americans, their liberators, have arrived, and rush out to greet them. One boy is so sure of it, he sees them.

Galvano (played by Omero Antonutti, the powerful father of *Padre Padrone*) is the leader of the group that sneaks away in the night; at times he's like a theater director. He tells his people to wear dark clothes for camouflage, and the whole troupe scrambles into black coats and coverings at the same time—it's like backstage at the opera, with everyone getting ready for the masquerade scene. And then there's another, quicker routine: the dogs who must be left behind, because their barking would betray the group, bark because they're being left behind. At last, Galvano's villagers are out in the country. They have been told that the Germans will blow up the town at 3:00 A.M., and when it's close to three they stand still and listen. We hear their thoughts, and then, exactly at three, distant shelling can be heard, and we see close-ups of ears, like enlarged details of paintings by Uccello. The villagers listen to the destruction of San Martino — the only world they know — and we see their hands clenching their house keys, and see their expressions. Galvano doffs his hat and weeps for San Martino; a man throws his key away. It's an unostentatiously beautiful passage. The people mourn, but they're too excited to feel crushed: they're out on the road looking for Americans. In the morning, they take off their black clothes. The August landscapes are golden, and Cecilia is proud of her pleated, red print pinafore. It's made of the same material as her mother's sundress; they're wearing matching mother-daughter outfits.

Shooting Stars keeps opening up and compressing as it cuts back and forth between what happens to the group in the hills and what happens to the others, back in San Martino, who believed the authorities when they told them that they'd be safe if they took refuge in the cathedral. The elderly bishop, who has collaborated — has done what he was told — offers bland assurances to everyone while praying to God that he will really be able to protect his flock. (His prayer has a note of apprehensiveness; life is making a skeptic of him.) So many townspeople gather inside that the bishop runs out of wafers, but the people have brought loaves of bread with them and they break these into bits. He consecrates the bread, and everyone is given the Host — the ritual has never seemed more full of meaning. When the crowded cathedral explodes, the door blasts open and smoke pours forth; two priests bring the bishop out, and, dazed he slumps in the square. The pregnant bride had become too ill to go on with the trekkers in the country, and her mother had hauled her back on a litter and taken her into the cathedral; now the mother tries to carry the mortally wounded, unconscious girl out, and the bishop, pulling himself to his feet, helps her. For a minute, they're both slightly bent over, facing each other and tugging at the helpless girl; they're forehead to forehead, and their eyes lock. It's an insane, cartoon effect — "This is what trusting in God and the fascists gets you!" — and it makes the pain of the situation more acute. *Shooting Stars* is so robust that even its most tragic moments can be dizzyingly comic. When Richard Lester attempted black humor on the horrors of war (in the 1967 *How I Won the War*), the scenes were jokey and flat, and the people were no more than puppets. In *Shooting Stars,* black humor is just one tonality among many, and the exhausted mother and the double-crossed bishop aren't diminished by being revealed as dupes; having shared their rock-bottom moment, we feel close to them. Many voices are joined in these memories, and though the people who have headed out for freedom may look more courageous, the film doesn't degrade the ones who stayed behind. They had their reasons — children, old age, fears. In one way or another, they're all like that woman with the pregnant daughter.

Out on the roads, a Sicilian girl who has been shot by German soldiers — who is already dead — flirts and makes small talk with some stray G.I.s, Sicilian-Americans from Brooklyn, before she accepts her death. The only other movie director I know of who could bring off an epiphany like this is the Ukrainian Dovzhenko, the lyrical fantasist of the silent era. The Tavianis present their wildest moments of fantasy in a heightened realistic form; you believe in what you're seeing — but you can't explain why you believe in it. I think that we're eager to swallow it, in the same way that, as children, we put faith in the stories we heard at bedtime, our minds rising to the occasion, because what happened in them was far more real to us than the blurred events of our day. And for the grown woman Cecilia the adventures that she took part in have acquired the brilliance and vitality of legend.

San Martino is probably much like the town of San Miniato, between Pisa and Florence, where the brothers were born (Vittorio in 1929, Paolo in 1931), and which was the site of a massacre carried out by the Germans. (Their first short film — *San Miniato, July 1944,* made in 1954 — was about this massacre.) The full fresco treatment they give the events of that summer in *Shooting Stars* is based partly on wartime incidents that they themselves witnessed when they were adolescents; they have said that everything they show actually happened — that the events they didn't witness they picked up "one by one . . . from all kinds of sources, official and otherwise." It's this teeming, fecund mixture, fermenting in their heads for almost forty years, that produces this film's giddy, hallucinated realism.

The movie is not like anything else — the Taviani brothers' pleasure in the great collection of stories they're telling makes it euphoric. It's as if they had invented a new form. In its feeling and completeness, *Shooting Stars* may be close to the rank of Jean Renoir's bafflingly beautiful *Grand Illusion,* and maybe because it's about the Second World War and Renoir's film was about the First, at times it's like a more deracinated *Grand Illusion.* Trying to pick the name by which he'll be known in the resistance, a man who sings in church decides that he wants to be called Requiem. A married couple who belong to

Galvano's group are out in the middle of nowhere, listening to the sounds of a warplane overhead, and the man holds his wife's compact up so she can see to put on her lipstick. Galvano's hungry people come across a watermelon patch, and the film becomes a bucolic festival; one girl can't wait for a melon to be cut open—she smashes it with her bottom. At night, all of them sleep piled on top of each other in a crater—a shell hole—as if their bodies had been flung there in a game of pick-up-sticks. And the image is so vivid that somehow you don't question it. Was this crater with its groundlings conceived as a secular joke on the seraphic figures floating in the painted domes of churches? You don't boggle at anything in this movie. The Tavianis have the kind of intuition that passes understanding. An era is ending, the society is disintegrating, but they take a few seconds to show us Galvano, who has gone to a stream to bathe, standing still in the water, completely at peace—his mind a blank. It's a transcendent image. He could be anywhere and the water would renew him; he has a sense of balance. Galvano gets to consummate his lifelong dream, but before he goes to bed with the woman he has loved for forty years—the woman who hasn't been accessible until now, because she became part of the landed gentry—they kiss, and he tells her apologetically that his kiss would be better if he hadn't lost three teeth. What he's saying is "Do you know what you've made us miss?"

The film's greatest sequence is hair-raisingly casual—a series of skirmishes in a wheat field. Still looking for the American troops and spotting nothing but Germans, the villagers come to a wheat field and meet up with a group of resistance fighters who need help with the harvest (or the fascists will get it), and the villagers lend a hand. And suddenly all the ideological factions that have been fighting in the country are crawling around in the tall wheat. There's a civil war taking place in the fields, with men who all know each other, who in some cases are brothers or cousins, going at each other with clubs and guns and pitchforks. These are not noble peasants. Two old friends wrestle murderously, each demanding that the other surrender; the gentle bridegroom kills a fifteen-year-old fascist, who is groveling in terror, and the kid's father falls to the earth and scoots in a circle like an animal in agony. Scenes from this battlefield could turn into Anselm Kiefer's huge straw landscapes, which are like windswept, overgrown memorials that have come up out of the past—out of war and mud and destruction. At one chaotic moment, a couple of people who are tending a wounded old woman reach out at arm's length for the flask of water that a couple of other people have just given to a wounded man, and then, realizing that they're enemies, both pairs start shooting at each other — from a distance of about three feet. It's a pure sick joke, like something Godard would have tried in *Les Carabiniers* if he'd thought of it. In *Shooting Stars,* you're never reminded of a filmmaker who isn't a master.

The Taviani brothers say that if there is a theme running through their movies it's "From silence to communication," but they try to spoof their own theme, too. When Cecilia and another little girl meet up with two G.I.s, Cecilia's friend picks the one she likes, and he gives her a chocolate bar, but Cecilia's G.I. indicates that he has nothing to offer her. Silently, she makes funny ugly faces at him, and he replies in kind, and then, wanting to give her some token, he improvises — he blows up a condom as if it were a balloon, and she dances off with her prize. This, like several other scenes in the movie, is reminiscent of Rossellini's 1946 film *Paisan;* the Tavianis, who saw that film when they were university students in Pisa, say that it was *Paisan* that made them decide to become moviemakers. And so maybe this G.I.-condom scene can be passed over — it's effective in the thin, overcooked manner of *Life* journalism in the forties. It's an amusing parody of a whole batch of romantic encounters in wartime movies, but it's also a dismayingly pat little number.

In a sense, everything in *Shooting Stars* is a theatrical routine (but not on that level). The Tavianis' style keeps you conscious of what they're doing, and, yes, the technique is Brechtian, but with a fever that Brecht never had. The Tavianis make stylized unreality work for them in a way that nobody else ever has; in *Shooting Stars* unreality doesn't seem divorced from experience (as it does with Fellini) — it's experience made more intense. They love style, but it hasn't cost them their bite — their willingness to be harsh and basic. During the brief period when a movie is actually being shot, a director often wishes that he had someone to help him — someone who knew what was inside his head. These two do, and that may account for the calm assurance of the film and its steady supply of energy. Every sequence is a flourish, but there's heft in the Tavianis' flourishes, and no two have the same texture or tone. The shaping of the material is much more conscious than we're used to. The movie builds, and it never lets up — it just keeps channeling its energy in different directions. Even when *Shooting Stars* is at its most emotionally expansive, you're aware of the control the directors have. What they're controlling is exaltation. That's the emotional medium they're working in.

They use sound in a deliberately primitive way: the sound here — whether it's from nature or Verdi or the score by Nicola Piovani — makes memories flood back just as odors sometimes bring things back. It's sound of great clarity, set against silence. (A superb fanfare is heard during the film's main title — a fanfare followed by cannon fire and then, for a moment, nothing.) The memories the sound brings back come up out of the muck and are heavily filtered; they're distorted, and polished until they gleam. And the directors' visual techniques — their use of dissolves, especially — keep you conscious of the processes of memory etching in and eroding. The film's impassioned style is steeped in nostalgia. Cecilia's mythicized memories are her legacy to her own child, to whom she is telling this story at bedtime. For the Tavianis, as for Cecilia, the search for the American liberators is the time of their lives. For an American audience, the film stirs warm but tormenting memories of a time when we were beloved and were a hopeful people.

—Pauline Kael

Paul Verhoeven

■

THE FOURTH MAN (1983)

The Fourth Man begins with images of a spider web and a crucifix, then cuts to a disheveled alcoholic writer arising from his grungy bed and murdering his boyfriend — a murder that turns out to be merely a fantasy. At this point the viewer has reason to think he's in for some heavy European gloom and doom, but he isn't. What appears to be a death-obsessed, symbol-laden, dreamlike thriller turns out to be (among other things) a wickedly funny comedy. It's the paranoid writer hero, Gerard Reve (Jeroen Krabbé), not Dutch director Paul Verhoeven, whose mind is cluttered with symbolic dreams. Off to give a lecture in the Dutch seaside town of Flushing, Reve sees an undertaker and automatically assumes the coffin is for him. Even now one isn't sure if this is a tongue-in-cheek parody of *Wild Strawberries* or some attempt at a fancy Borgesian thriller but as the thriller plot thickens, so does Verhoeven's sardonic sense of humor.

With each new movie, Verhoeven, the Netherlands' best-known director (*Soldier of Orange, Spetters*), tries something different. Here, in the guise of a chiller, he's giving us a portrait of the artist as an infantile, lecherous, woman-fearing cad, a victim of his own maniacal imagination. The novelist, who's homosexual, is seduced in Flushing by a blond femme fatale named Christine (Renée Soutendijk). He decides to stay with her after seeing the photograph of her boyfriend, Herman (Thom Hoffman), a young hunk he had tried desperately to pick up in an Amsterdam train station. While scheming to seduce the boyfriend, he discovers that Christine has had three previous young husbands, all of them now dead. He becomes hysterical, convinced that either he or the boyfriend will be her fourth victim. Is he justified, or merely mad? There is evidence to support either view . . . Jeroen Krabbé does a marvelous job revealing this complicated hero's charm, childishness, brilliance, and lust: his daring comic performance has won him several awards. The fascination of Verhoeven's dark and stylish riddle is its ability to work simultaneously as mystery and satire, to enter its hero's obsession and mock it as well. There's not a dull moment in it.

—*David Ansen*

Peter Weir

■

PICNIC AT HANGING ROCK (1975)

We, forty million of us, live hard along the coasts. We're mostly in the cities on the edge of this vast continent. It's just there to be seen if you live there. It affects you even if you're not conscious of it—that great emptiness. You can travel and see nature as it was before the history of man, and you can be days driving from a hamburger joint or something. It doesn't take any imagination at all to feel awed.

—Peter Weir in an interview with *Movietone News*

They told us in grade school that Australia was one of the seven continents, like Africa, Europe, Asia. The information was jarring. A country had no business being a continent, especially if it seemed more like a superisland, a Jules Verne place, a landmass lodged in some separate ocean of its own. Even Antarctica was easier to connect with the imaginative space of lands where normal living goes on. No matter how they built their globes, on the mind's-eye map Australia was more Down Under than anywhere else.

Some measure of that sense of exotic otherness persists today, and has a lot to do with the current interest in Australian cinema. Whereas the New German Cinema stirs excitement through the particular, and very individual, styles of its sharpest directors (Herzog, Fassbinder, Wenders), even an artistically deficient specimen of Australian cinema is worth seeing right now as a vicarious trip through an environment.

By environment I mean several things. The landscape, surely— unspoiled by either industry/technology/progress or excessive cine- matic familiarity; even the cities, indistinguishable from their Western prototypes, become mysterious when seen against an alien backdrop, furnace-baked in a sunlight unfiltered by known atmosphere. Environ- ment also includes climate, an aspect of life largely ignored in other cinemas but ineluctably a presence here. There needn't be black rain or boulder-sized hailstones crashing out of a sunny sky, as in Weir's *The Last Wave;* it is enough that these filmmakers be concerned with communicating the feel of the air in a particular place at a particular time of day, and what this has to do with people's lives.

Most of all, environment in this case also involves a climate of mind, of readiness, of native energy palpably yearning toward defining itself on film. The Australian government is all for this. In 1970 it virtually legislated the new Australian cinema (there were a couple of others, decades ago) into existence—Public Relations joining hands with Art in the candid hope that movies catching the spirit of the country couldn't help but be good for the country, at home and abroad.

And the really intriguing thing is not so much that Australian cinema offers us a lot that is new in subject matter or technique, but rather (in a manner appropriate to a broken-off chunk of a once-great empire), that it gets such distinctive perspectives and moods by adopt- ing, adapting, rediscovering much that is old. It comes at sophistication by way of naïveté. Such an approach can prove reductive: sometimes naive is just naive, and one smiles politely and slips away before the contact becomes a protracted embarrassment. But sometimes the results are very special.

On St. Valentine's Day 1900, two teachers, a coachman, and a party of students from Mrs. Appleyard's college for young ladies went picnicking at Hanging Rock, Victoria. In the drowsy afternoon somebody notices that all watches in the vicinity stopped at midday. Shortly thereafter, three of the girls and one instructor disappeared, in a manner never explained.

The mystery of *Picnic at Hanging Rock* is not confined to the events of the narrative. Joan Lindsay, who wrote the novel in her sixties, would become very upset when pressed about its basis in fact. Surely no one gets through life without wondering, at some point or another, whether it's possible to vanish from the face of the earth without account or trace. How fascinating to encounter a documented case of this — if that's what the tale was. The lady would never quite say; and the fascination grew.

Peter Weir's 1975 film version doesn't "explain" its central mystery either, though viewers of his later *The Last Wave* (released before *Picnic* on these shores) have the benefit of some hefty clues. *The Last Wave* focuses on an apparently unremarkable Sydney lawyer whose involvement with some aborigines accused of tribal murder leads him to startling perceptions about the environment around him, the civilization of which he is a part, and his own identity. Of particular suggestibility with regard to *Picnic at Hanging Rock* is the aboriginal concept of "dream time," a phenomenon somewhere between a parallel universe and an all-encompassing vision of reality. You can physically disappear into dream time. Moreover, the lawyer comes to realize he himself has participated in it all his life, via premonitory hallucinations; he is, as it turns out, quite a special fellow.

I feel obliged to supply that brief gloss from another film by the director — eminently proper critical showboating — at the same time I'm a little uneasy about doing so. You see, I really liked *The Last Wave* until it tied itself up so tidily in the final reel; and I prefer *Picnic at Hanging Rock* because it refuses to tie itself up, because it stands forth — maddeningly, for some viewers — in its own irreducibility as fictional/ historical event, like the Rock itself, and as movie.

One could have a field day cataloguing antimonies the film plays with: the non-dreamtime watch fixed on Mrs. Appleyard's ample but barren breast, versus the soft-spoken announcement by Miranda, most enchanting of the vanished-spirits-to-be, that she no longer wears her own watch because "I couldn't bear it ticking above my heart"; the petite greenhouse on the schoolgrounds, an anti-Eden set against golden-tinted verdure literally a-hum with vitality; the interior of the college, dominated by rigidly framed portraits of departed Appleyards and classical paintings of decorous nudity, as against the million-years-old surface of Hanging Rock, from which a multitude of faces seem to peer, and on which the truant girls slowly strip off their stockings.

Similarly, the detailwork is a literary Freudian's delight: a knife cutting a neat pink gash on St. Valentine's cake, a lizard skittering past a sleeping girl, the starchy Miss McCraw (indispensable "masculine intellect" to Appleyard's tight-bunned widowhood) meditatively peeling a banana. And if that Rock these females are clambering over is supposed to be phallic, why do they keep finding clefts?

Much of the film's technique is self-consciously derivative. There is an academic singlemindedness in the way mirrors are used, German-Expressionist fashion, to anticipate who's going to pass through the Hanging Rock looking-glass, and later to isolate those whose lives and sanity have been most undone by the disappearances (which occur in the first half of the movie, leaving a good deal of time for the rest of the world to register the shock waves). Michael, a young man who happened to be at the Rock the day of the incident, becomes obsessed with the memory of Miranda, whose beauty struck him as swanlike. Among other things, this occasions a Buñuelian deadpan from Michael, awake at night, to a real live swan sitting at the foot of his bed.

All of these image-patterns, symbolic systems, and influences ought to be noted; but if taken in isolation they suggest mere symbolmongering or filmmaking-by-formula, in combination they urge us toward something much more appealing. For *Picnic at Hanging Rock,* though it gravely teases us with echoes of primal appleyards where the race fell into Knowledge, is really about getting beyond symbolism, beyond knowledge, beyond the separation of humankind from the nonconceptualizing rest of the world. And these various systems themselves contribute to the superabundance of texture by which the film seeks to achieve this.

"Love abounds," begins a schoolgirl's "Ode to St. Valentine." As for *Picnic at Hanging Rock,* it simply loves to abound. Its colors are rich, its imagery resplendent; it tantalizes with voluptuous variations on the theme of how life at once lends itself to and confounds the forms of fictionmaking. Isn't it silly to sit around stroking dead-ended Freudianism, for instance, when the movie itself is ravishing?

Anybody with an I.Q. above eighty can supply a symbolical para-phrase of the moment when Miranda unhooks the rusty gate to admit the picnic party to the Hanging Rock area, a flight of startled birds erupts, and Weir imposes the whip-pan of their passage upon a lumi-nous close-up of Miranda turning her head to follow. Someone with a sense of stylistic tradition may refer to the moment in Buñuel's *Belle de Jour* when a diagonal pan of autumn leaves overlapped a vertical caress of the heroine's housefront, then gave way to her calm face behind a rainstreaked window—a distillation of the acquisition of wisdom on a hedonistic pilgrimage toward mortality. Someone with a fixation on production values may note that the labwork is deficient here, and the overlap rather primitively achieved. A formalist will point out that the layered wheeling of that cinematic moment sets up a curvilinear motif of camera motion, the characters' trajectories within the landscape, and choreography for rocks.

But it takes only an eye and a soul to catch the exultation of a movie sensibility in thrall of his medium and the world and the beauty that is uniquely possible when he brings the two together. It remains a mystery, but we can live with it. Indeed, we can't live without it.

—*Richard T. Jameson*

Peter Weir

■

GALLIPOLI (1981)

Two unsuspecting lads discover that war is hell in *Gallipoli* (Para-mount), and while that loss-of-innocence angle won't come as a huge surprise, stay tuned. Despite director Peter Weir's penchant for under-scoring the obvious, here's new proof that Australian cinema is alive and well and buzzing with creativity. *Gallipoli,* with all its failings acknowledged, is an engagingly intimate antiwar epic, generally skip-ping the *Sturm und Drang* of battle to focus on the boys, both competi-tive runners—and both beautifully acted by Mel Gibson and Mark Lee—who run off to find glory by fighting the Turks at Gallipoli in 1915. There's a long touristic stretch of fun and games at an Egyptian training camp that could stand drastic trimming, yet Weir redeems himself with several unforgettable scenes — the lads' encounter in the western Australian desert with a grizzled old prospector, who can scarcely imagine what war is ("I knew a German once . . . how'd it *start?*"), and a homesick officer ruefully whistling his favorite opera on the eve of Armageddon. Best of all is a surreal sequence with a group of skinny-dipping soldiers, shells plopping into the sea all around them as they dive underwater, nude and still playful amid floating bits of shrapnel, until a small crimson cloud reveals that someone's hit. Very few movie moments can top that.

—Bruce Williamson

Wim Wenders
■
RETROSPECTIVE

The New German Cinema, which began with such a bang in the early seventies, ended with a whimper sometime during the early eighties. Its most brilliant filmmaker, Rainer Werner Fassbinder, died (in 1982) like a rock star, of drugs and ugly living; its visionary class clown, Werner Herzog, dribbled into insignificance shortly after the bellyflop of his grandest folly, *Fitzcarraldo* (he still makes movies, but they have grown increasingly fatuous and unwatchable). And that left only Wim Wenders, the third and most enigmatic of the founding triumvirate, to soldier on. His is a career that has been pronounced dead more than once — most spectacularly after he spent four years in Hollywood making the flaccid detective thriller *Hammett.* But in 1988, he released a near-masterpiece, *Wings of Desire,* a movie whose sublime black-and-white images of phlegmatic angels peering into human souls announced that, even if the New German Cinema was dead, its moody metaphysical branch was very much alive and well.

Which might have come as a surprise to those of us familiar with Wenders's early, strenuously metaphysical films: *The Goalie's Anxiety at the Penalty Kick* (1971), *Alice in the Cities* (1974), *Wrong Move* (1975), and *Kings of the Road* (1976) — movies that made him famous in Germany before his eerie thriller *The American Friend* (1977) made his name in America. At first viewing, these films are hopeless: gray, angst-ridden studies of gray, angst-ridden people, lost souls who search for identity against the bleakest of landscapes. Trains and trucks and planes whoosh incessantly along these gloomy horizons, and engines and sirens whoosh incessantly along the sound tracks — engines, sirens, and, everywhere, American rock 'n' roll.

Wenders's early features ignore plot and remain stubbornly reticent about character. And yet, exasperating as they often are, they reward a second viewing. Watching them again, I still fought off annoyance and occasionally sleep, but I also found myself admiring not so much what Wenders had accomplished in them, but the strange beauty of the artistic and moral struggle they convey.

"The Yanks have colonized our subconscious," says one of the German wanderers in *Kings of the Road*, and Wenders's films bear him out. In *The Goalie's Anxiety*, the protagonist, Bloch (Arthur Brauss), commits a meaningless murder and then embarks on an equally meaningless journey; it comes to seem a pilgrimage from one Rock-Ola juke box to the next. The hero of *Kings of the Road* keeps a juke box in the back of his truck, and Tom Ripley (Dennis Hopper), the American friend, has one in his Hamburg bedroom. American rock and American genre movies are the only cultural referents that turn up in these films, except for an occasional nod toward Faulkner or Highsmith, and in the Wenders night, neon signs vie with the moon. The director grew up in a defeated Germany, and much of his generation, appalled at the Nazi past, embraced the lurid culture of the conqueror. And yet Wenders's cinema of alienation is peculiarly Teutonic. His men — and his major characters are almost exclusively men because, as Wenders admits, he doesn't understand women — are outcasts, clutching transistor radios and newspapers to their chests like amulets, toying endlessly with Coke machines and pay phones, trudging dutifully off to the movies, driving aimlessly. They begin sentences without knowing how or even whether they will end them. Here and there they'll mumble a snatch of a Bob Dylan song, chanting the foreign phrase as if it were a prayer. And yet their inability to make contact doesn't torture them, because they can't fathom what contact might mean. Cut off from their families and, like Germany itself, from their pasts, they stumble into friendship reluctantly, fearfully. Isolation is all they know, and they feel safe inside it.

It's always seemed to me that Wenders's method — making alienated movies about alienation — was a perfect example of the imitative fallacy: you don't depict boredom, the wisdom goes, by making a boring movie. And on first viewing, I found most of Wenders's work so ponderous that if someone had suggested a second viewing, I might cheerfully have removed his or her tongue. But years have passed since those first encounters, and I recently ventured a second. In so doing, I experienced a specific kind of alchemy, the kind I've felt during second viewings of films by Robert Bresson and Carl Dreyer. Wenders's pace, his way of looking at things, overrode mine and even admonished it; his placid, unblinking stare replaced my impatient one; and his logy, Germanic sense of humor began to tickle me, the way unexpected incidents tickle you when you've gone too long without sleep.

I don't mean to suggest that Wenders is the equal of Bresson and Dreyer — I doubt he ever could be — or that he has any of their holy fervor. The masochistic alienation that is his central theme strikes me as old hat, and whenever his characters talk about it, his movies begin to sound as bland and insincere as the gospel according to *The 700 Club*. But there *is* something fervid, even religious, in Wenders's sensibility, something his meandering method makes hard to find at first. Wenders is religious in the manner of a solemn fetishist; he's religious about the objects and the sounds he loves, about the stark, painfully beautiful landscapes he's drawn to, and about his quixotic, movie-mad quest to capture on film the things he sees. When Phil (Rüdiger Vogler), the journalist hero of *Alice in the Cities,* returns from a cross-country tour of the United States, he's supposed to have written an article for a German magazine. Instead, all he has to show for his travels is a handful of Polaroids, and a gnawing anxiety that "they never really show what it is you saw." "When you drive across America," he says, "something happens because of the images you see. . . . I lost touch with the world." To which his sullen girlfriend replies, "You did that a long time ago. That's why you always need proof, proof that you experience."

Perhaps that's what excites me now about Wenders's films. Once you enter his peculiar flow, you find yourself immersed in a personal and strangely honorable struggle — not the characters' struggle, which may seem dull, but Wenders's own: his struggle to make the world real. I don't think Wenders is a natural filmmaker; he's not a primitive visionary like Werner Herzog, much less a sophisticated one like Rainer Werner Fassbinder. He doesn't know how to tell a story, and he doesn't much care. And the way he puts his films together is maladroit; if you look closely at his reaction shots, you can see that his actors (principally Rüdiger Vogler, the blond, horse-faced star of most of his movies) have been asked to respond to something they don't quite understand; their expressions are off-key and inappropriate, as the expressions are in science fiction movies where the players have to react to special effects that haven't been filmed yet. Wenders's movies are repetitious and often needlessly obscure (his editor, Peter Przygodda, may be his worst enemy). And yet, for all that, a vision emerges — the vision of an artist who has no special style or knack but has built a cinematic universe, anyway, out of the desire to create and to penetrate the estrangement he feels from the world and its parts. Or, to put it in terms dear to the German heart, out of will.

This feverish desire to create is a theme that runs through all Wenders's work, and it's such a European notion that Americans may not go along with it. In *Wrong Move,* an eccentric update of Goethe's *Wilhelm Meister's Education,* the young Wilhelm (Vogler again) desperately wants to be a writer. "I wish to write, to write," he seethes. "I'd like to write something essential — essential as a house, or an evening glass of wine." But what has he to say? This is Wenders's dilemma, too, and for someone who is not a natural, the only answer may be that there's nothing to say, that civilization is a blank. Contact with others is intolerable but essential, because encounters with others tell us what the world is like, give us something to say. The story of *Wrong Move* resembles the stories in all Wenders's films: a loner meets people, profits by the experience, and then goes on alone — to Create; one can create only in isolation. In *Alice in the Cities,* which is sort of an *Annie* with angst, circumstances leave Phil the destitute guardian of a nine-year-old German girl whose mother has disappeared in New York. Traveling with young Alice, he feels burdened, exasperated, eager to be alone, but by the time they part, after a darkly comical search for her grandmother, he is healed and ready to write again.

And in *Kings of the Road,* at once the most revealing and the most infuriatingly tedious of Wenders's early films, two hollow-souled schlubs bring out each other's artistic urges. Bruno (Vogler), the owner-driver of the truck they live and travel in, makes a living fixing movie projectors in the crumbling towns along the East German border. His passenger, Robert (Hanns Zischler), is a linguist who longs to be published. Riding together opens them both up, but they also grow tired of each other, and finally part ways. Whereupon both find themselves suddenly inspired to fulfill creative dreams: Bruno makes a little movie out of images he splices together at a theater he services; Robert uses his father's printing press to publish a manifesto on his mother's death. Soon enough, they are drawn back together, and once more they exchange lessons, fight, and part, presumably the wiser for their friendship and the soul-searching it's occasioned.

But if this is Wenders's message, it's not what makes sitting through his films worthwhile. The endless shots of blank skies and featureless horizons; the fuzzy, ethereal music; the chilling way each gray city blurs into the next; the fascination with flickering television screens and crumbling, deserted buildings — these effects make Wenders's themes seem less simplistic and sentimental than they are. In the end, though, it's his images that stay with you — or, perhaps more accurately, his battle to produce them. Coming off the street into a theater, we may find them unwatchable: why stare and stare at this pinball machine, this ash tray, and this grim street? There's nothing *interesting* about them. In *The Goalie's Anxiety,* we watch the world through the killer's eyes, and everything looks like Wenders-land; the universe is slow and enigmatic, and each object — an apple, a bridge, a tree, a corpse — has equal emotional weight. Of course, in *Goalie's Anxiety* that way of looking at things is the way of a madman, but in *Alice, Wrong Move, Kings of the Road,* and even *The American Friend,* it becomes ours, and it feels new. Wenders's way of seeing is like the matter-of-fact seeing in Bresson or Ozu, but without emotion, without transcendence or spirituality or joy. Things aren't symbols, they simply are what they are, and if we slow ourselves down enough to look at them, they fill us — just as a car chase or a love scene fills us in a Hollywood movie. In his recent twelve-minute diary film *Reverse Angle: NYC, March '82,* Wenders talks about the "poison ivy" images of American TV, and in *Alice,* Phil says, "All [American TV] shows become a commercial. Not one image leaves you in peace. They all demand something of you." Wenders's unbeautiful, uninspired images demand nothing. At best, his films just represent, the way the Lumière films did, only instead of lasting a few minutes, they go on and on — they're as long and as full of suggestive, meaningless objects as a Robbe-Grillet novel. You get used to it; you live in it for a while. "I can't think in 'plot,'" Wenders has said. "I can only think in 'situations.' Maybe they become a story. If they don't, well, at least I didn't lie." And if they don't, there's nothing to keep track of, no work to do, nothing to follow. You can drift in and out of the atmosphere Wenders creates, watching what you like or watching your likes and dislikes themselves. And watching becomes a kind of breathing.

This sounds like no special achievement until you see Wenders's aggressively boring early shorts, *Same Player Shoots Again* (1968) and *Silver City* (1969), or until you look at the dull, pretentious works of his imitators, movies like *Radio On* and *Permanent Vacation*. Somehow, in the years between 1971 and 1976, Wenders had hit upon just the right form for his undemanding images. And then, with *The American Friend* and, later, *Wings of Desire,* he moved on. These films were breakthroughs for Wenders, and, in the light they shed, I suppose his earlier works seem rather drab. But not insignificant. For those who have the desire—and the stamina—to look, the early Wenders films offer their own richly personal view of one moviemaker's struggle to see.

—*Stephen Schiff*

Wim Wenders
■
WINGS OF DESIRE (1987)

In *Wings of Desire,* Wim Wenders finds love, angelically. Dreamy and seraphic, it's not only the loveliest, most delicate, most original angel movie ever made; it's the kind of metaphysical love story that makes love itself seem daring and miraculous, pushing up from beneath bleak tons of ruin. It moves from a rueful contemplation of humankind by a pair of overcoated angels to a serene but powerful urge on the part of one of them to take the plunge, turn human himself, and give up eternity for the love of a trapeze artist. From start to finish, *Wings of Desire* is a spellbinder that seems blessed, starting with the rapt gentleness in which the film is bathed, continuing with the film's visual language and the spiritual world it captures with such stunning imagination and economy.

Even the plot gimmick of having the angels only able to see in black and white is used to feed the somber yet airborne tone of the film. It begins with a shot of clouds, then an overhead panning shot of Berlin—angel's-eye views in silvery black and white. Only children can see the angels, who glide softly through Berlin, harvesting peoples' thoughts and feelings, suffering with them, occasionally laying a gentle hand on a troubled shoulder or pressing a fevered head. Often, sardonic expressions flicker across the faces of the angels, played by Bruno Ganz and Otto Sander with a keen, sentient purity. Not that everything about them is solemn. Amusingly, they wear the heavy overcoats favored in Berlin. And the film is filled with muted ironies, including the fact that the angels keep their hands in their pockets a lot, even when perched on the large winged statue atop the victory column in the Tiergarten.

Wenders's angels hang out a lot in the municipal library, too, presumably because they're most comfortable around other researchers and gatherers of data. Each of the angels carries a sad—but not wearying—weight of experience in his or her face. If Sander feels a pang of impotence when he's unable to keep a suicide from jumping, Ganz is renewed by the wonder of hearing a schoolboy describe a fern. Observing, testifying, collecting, preserving, the angels aren't permitted to take direct action from the spiritual world. But the miracle of the film is that while it is mostly tender and elegiac, it's also filled with the green shoots of renewal. Even before Ganz happens on the trapeze artist (Solveig Dommartin) practicing in the poignantly small-time one-ring circus where she works, he feels stirrings. He wants to drink coffee, lie through his teeth.

He confesses to his sidekick that he's tired of floating ethereally above it all, that he wants to make contact with the tangible world. On cue, Wenders's camera celebrates the specificity of the mundane—tire marks on pavement, a feather floating on water, raindrops glistening, a discarded newspaper dancing atop a stream of air issuing from a subway grate. It's no longer enough for the angel to glide through the world dispensing sympathetic presence and the very occasional steadying hand or healing touch. Ganz's face with its putty nose, soulful eyes, and little ponytail, is a perfect vehicle for his longings. Although Wenders wrote the screenplay with Peter Handke, it's clear that Handke's trademark isolation is going to yield to Wenders's obvious urge to ally himself to something warm, breathing, mortal, and sensual.

In this case, it's Dommartin, the lonely aerialist. Amusingly, she sports showier wings than the angels, even though hers are only made of chicken feathers. She's pals with her circus chums. But she knows the circus will disband for the winter, and she knows she isn't the world's greatest aerialist. "I fly around the ring like a soup chicken," she sighs, "then I become a waitress again." She's as ready for union as Ganz's discontented angel. The only question is how they'll get together, even when Ganz starts seeing bits of the world in color, like a human. You'll probably think the film turns sentimental if I tell you that Peter Falk, playing himself in Berlin making a movie about the Nazi era, dispenses avuncular encouragement in his streets-of-New York voice.

But he, too, fits in with Wenders's scheme deftly as well as warmly, even when he looks the camera in the eye, speaking as America's angel (and movie) guru, and growls, "I can't see ya, but I know you're here. I can feel ya." When the angel who turns in his wings and the lady on the flying trapeze finally meet, the moment almost gets away from them in a declaration of love that's marked by a startlingly teutonic earnestness. But the bravery of their coming together, and the amazement on Ganz's face keeps the scene aglow. In gesture, facial expression, and especially voice, I don't ever recall an actor able to make yearning seem so velvety.

It isn't only man-woman love that Wenders is celebrating. After his own decade of alienation, he seems to have come to terms with his own German identity, and uses the film to celebrate the survival power of Berlin, bleak and bombed-out and fenced-in as some of its parts remain. Wenders was right to tip his hat to his cinematographer, the veteran Henri Alekan, by naming the little circus after him. *Wings of Desire* owes a lot of its impact to Alekan's pewtery tones, magical lighting, and fluid camera movements. At times, you're ready to believe that the camera can move through walls as easily as the angels. And when Ganz goes over the wall, he goes over the Berlin Wall. *Wings of Desire* shines with several kinds of rightness—moral, spiritual, aesthetic. I'm ready to call it a classic, and I'm ready to see it again and again. It thoroughly justifies its dedication to three of film's angels— Yasujiro Ozu, François Truffaut, and Andrei Tarkovsky.

—Jay Carr

THE NEXT WAVE

It's global village time again, as the Pacific Rim checks in with more than Hondas. In mainland China, interesting films are coming from the so-called Fifth Generation directors, the first class of graduates from the Peking Film Academy to learn moviemaking after the Cultural Revolution. To its fans, state-of-the-art animation means "Japanimation." And magazines like *Cahiers du Cinéma* and *Film Comment* have called the Hong Kong comedy-action movies by direc-

Opposite page: scene from *Red Sorghum*.

tors such as Tsui Hark, Stanley Kwan, and John Woo "the best popular cinema in the world today."

New African directors like Idrissa Ouedraogo of Burkina Faso and Souleymane Cisse of Mali are joining notable members of an earlier generation, such as Senegal's Ousmane Sembene.

Other emerging moviemakers in the wave-to-wave pattern have pushed funkiness to edgy Freudian kinkiness (Jane Campion), social satire to minimalist prole irony (Aki Kaurismäki), style to media stylization as a subject in its own right (Atom Egoyan).

We're still discovering great directors — filmmakers like Theo Angelopoulos, who has made a number of movies respected in Europe but first dawned on the American art-house audience with his *Landscape in the Mist*. Angelopoulos, with his uniquely Greek dovetailing of influences from earlier masters like Bresson and Tarkovsky, is an argument for home-grown products in a foreign film age when financing dictates the international coproductions that seldom knit multiple countries as well as the Russian-Italian pairing of Nikita Mikhalkov and Marcello Mastroianni in *Dark Eyes* or the best-of-two-worlds influences on Harvard-educated Indian director Mira Nair's *Salaam Bombay*.

African Films: Souleymane Cisse
■

YEELEN (BRIGHTNESS) (1987)

Yeelen (*Brightness*), Souleymane Cisse's extraordinarily beautiful and mesmerizing fantasy, is set in the ancient Bambara culture of Mali (formerly French Sudan) long before it was invaded by Morocco in the sixteenth century. A young man (Issiaka Kane) sets out to discover the mysteries of nature (or *komo,* the science of the gods) with the help of his mother and uncle, but his jealous and spiteful father contrives to prevent him from deciphering the elements of the Bambara sacred rites and tries to kill him. In the course of a heroic and magical journey, the hero masters the Bambara initiation rites, takes over the throne, and ultimately confronts the magic of his father. Apart from creating a dense and exciting universe that should make George Lucas green with envy, Cisse has shot breathtaking images in Fujicolor and has accompanied his story with a spare, hypnotic, percussive score. Conceivably the greatest African film ever made, sublimely mixing the matter-of-fact with the uncanny, this wondrous work provides an ideal introduction to a filmmaker who, next to Ousmane Sembene, is probably Africa's greatest director. Winner of the Jury Prize at the 1987 Cannes festival. Not to be missed.

—*Jonathan Rosenbaum*

African Films: Idrissa Ouedraogo

■

YAABA (1989)

News of a film from Burkina Faso like Idrissa Ouedraogo's *Yaaba* probably excites African Americans much less than the announcement of a new mind-numbing Sylvester Stallone epic. The cultural gap that explains this is wider and scarier than the Middle Passage. Hollywood movies corrupt audiences into expecting formulaic plots and blatantly obvious technique. The devices used to make American films into efficient export products that appeal across language barriers have backfired on us, encouraging illiteracy and insensitivity. The noise, the garish sex, the senseless violence, all excite the crudest instincts and, over time, create jaded, debased senses.

Keenan Ivory Wayans wasn't sharp enough to account for this in his Blaxploitation parody, *I'mo Git You Sucka*. He treated the coarsening effect of Hollywood's contemptuous style as a boon to African-American well-being. Even comedian Rudy Ray Moore knew better than that when, back in the seventies, his films *Dolemite* and *The Human Tornado* turned Blaxploitation films ass-up, making the most of the slim opportunity to show some distinctive black American jive and effrontery. In the trash pile, Moore found something organic and authentic, whereas Wayans busied himself polishing tin.

As a result of Hollywood's corrupting influence, black moviegoers have an especially hard time determining types of entertainment that are authentic to their lifestyles, organic to their culture, or edifying to their existence. Like Public Enemy in "Night of the Living Base-heads," we need something to replace what was lost when we were brought here, robbed of our name, robbed of our language, our religion, our culture, our God.

The lack of interest African Americans have in African films is explained partly by the estrangement effected by colonialism (slavery) and the indifference of America's Eurocentric film culture. But Hollywood also has given American viewers a jaded palate. Even an African import filled with dazzling derring-do like *Yeelen* (*Brightness*) would seem wan to those thrilled by *Die Hard* or *Lethal Weapon*.

Filmmakers like Ouedraogo, Souleymane Cisse, Ousmane Sembene, Desiré Ecaré, and others also are burdened by this problem. They must break through the hardened perceptions of action-film fans even in their own countries where the long arm of Hollywood sometimes interferes. It's a poignant dilemma. These pioneering filmmakers train in Europe, but their serious interests lead them to study art films rather than popular hits. When they return home to forge their own national cinemas, their attempts to translate indigenous art forms into movie terms often come out strained in ways that seem inept to us.

The integrity of this method can be maddening—like using calculus to reinvent the wheel—but *Yaaba* is a good sign that the conscientiousness of African filmmakers can pay off with pure artistry. Ouedraogo's simplicity and the extreme effectiveness of his means also may point the way toward saving the souls of the heathenish filmgoers Hollywood has spawned.

Yaaba's gentle tone demands a little patience, like adjusting to the longer forms of Nigerian pop music. The audience that shows this sophistication is the audience that is ready to bridge the oceanic gap between Africa and North America and discover the other sources of their "American" cultural heritage.

Ouedraogo's tale of a prepubescent boy's awakening to the complex of character types in his home on the outskirts of Ouagadougou is like the numerous folktale bildungsromans seen mostly from Eastern Europe like *If I Had a Gun, When Father Was Away on Business,* and *My Little Village.* But Ouedraogo avoids quaintness. He follows wily little Bila (Noufou Ouedraogo) and his demure cousin Nopoko (Roukietou Barry) through the steps toward their future lives together. He shows the kind of deft simplicity of Satyajit Ray's *Pather Panchali*—the artlessness that people mistook for primitivism.

It's gradually apparent that Ouedraogo has organized his action and various shots perfectly to portray the casual life cycle that is revealed when Bila and the villagers face a small, but intense, crisis. Ouedraogo shows a dramatist's instinct and an artist's lyricism. There's not a bland, *National Geographic* moment. Each image, photographed by Matthias Kalin, is charged with fable. The establishing shot of Bila and Nopoko pouring water on her mother's grave has a primal elegance. With Yaaba (Fatimata Sanga) standing in the background, the graceful harmony of the scene says that these people and their habits rise from the earth and will return to it. The tone is spiritual, not anthropological. Bila, Nopoko, and Yaaba share a charmingly contentious relationship. They're discovering the eternal laws that we observe. And Ouedraogo keeps our observation dramatic and sensual. Bila's coming of age is his awakening to the roles of women—his attraction to Nopoko, the balance of power between his parents and the fascination with which he honors Yaaba, the aged woman the villagers have cast out as a witch.

Tall, balding, and slack-breasted, Sanga's Yaaba, a leather-covered skeleton, is a striking figure of female wisdom and mystery. The humane lesson she teaches Bila is sobering rather than sanctimonious. Yaaba's demonstration of virtue and paradox recalls another stern, solitary female figure, Hildur Carlsberg, in Carl Dreyer's 1924 silent classic, *The Parson's Widow*. Either a film student like Ouedraogo is well acquainted with that film or else the patterns of human behavior in Scandinavia also hold true in Africa.

Yaaba makes both connections seem wondrously probable. Certainly Ouedraogo's anecdotal style communicates with an eloquence comparable to Dreyer. The opening and closing shots that conceptualize an African sense of destiny are the most plangent images in any movie this year. **(Video request.)**

—*Armond White*

Theo Angelopoulos

■

RETROSPECTIVE

I remember when I saw Dreyer's Ordet. *I was delirious for three days. I was in shock: as if I were sick, but happily sick . . . How can such perfection exist?*

— Theo Angelopoulos

Each to his own epiphany. In 1989, when I first saw Angelopoulos's *Landscape in the Mist,* I felt something similar. The world settled into a different rhythm, as scene after scene — those chilly-poetic views of roadsides, highways, barren Greek landscapes in the faintly wintry light of late afternoon — rolled ineluctably away.

A lyrical "road" movie about the odyssey of two children across a dreamy and desolate modern topography, *Landscape* suggests Antonioni in the sixties, Wenders, *Au Hasard Balthazar* — while generating its own unique purity and power. The realm it opens up is both real and surreal. Gas stations, roadside cafes, a brutal rape in the back of a lorry: all these suggest the here and now. A bizarrely ecstatic snowfall, a huge stone hand pulled from the sea by a helicopter: these suggest fantasy, the past.

It's a bridge film, long overdue. For *us,* right now, Angelopoulos is one of the cinema's great unsolved mysteries. He's directed two of the most beautiful and profound movies of our time — *Landscape* and the 1975 *The Traveling Players* — yet they're little-known, little-seen.

His voice is unique, even in Greece — where movie lyricists before him (Cacoyannis, Koundouros) seem, by comparison, forced, thin, calculated. It is Angelopoulos's view which, like Ford's of America, Ozu's of Japan, may radically change the way we perceive his country, its past, its dreams.

Being Greek, I am part of Greek cinema, but not in the provincial sense . . .

Angelopoulos gained his vocation in Paris, as one of the movie fanatics who haunted Langlois's Cinémathèque. His political education, he says, came from being struck in the face by a policeman's club in 1964, while a crowd demonstrating for Papandreou was being dispersed. He began under the authoritarian Greek Colonels at the time of *Z,* and, like his brethren in Eastern Europe, Russia, and Franco's Spain, he had to work in a subversive code, sending messages above the censors' heads. But, like any *cinéaste*/cinephile — like Godard, Scorsese, Bertolucci — his revolutionary departures all had precedents.

> *Look, I don't know how younger filmmakers relate to cinema . . . but for us, for my generation — the "rats of the Cinémathèque" — it was not a relation either personal or one of simple expression. . . . It was a feverish symbiosis. The American genres from my youth which influenced me subterraneously were the musicals of Minnelli and Stanley Donen and the American gangster movie in its golden age: with Billy Wilder, Huston and Hawks.*

Much like the Hollywood left-wing directors of the forties, he begins (in 1970), with a black-and-white murder mystery, *The Reconstruction.* His first film shows an *Ossessione*-style crime of passion unraveled in the bleak village of Vista in Epirus by a team of investigators and a film crew (headed by Angelopoulos himself). This homage to *noir* reveals two key obsessions at once: the Greek land, the crimes buried beneath it. Ruminate on the land, the film suggests, and you will discover tragedies below — like the husband's corpse in *The Reconstruction,* buried under a garden row of onions.

In *Days of '36* (1972), he fully discovers his unique style: a way of recording horror by staring at masked images, making the audience aware of what is *not* shown. *Days of '36* re-creates a historical incident, a prison hostage episode, that helped lead to the Metaxas dictatorship. Ordinarily, we would expect to be taken into the cell, the council rooms, kept intimately abreast of plots and counterplots. Instead, in *Days of '36,* we seem always stuck on the periphery — down a corridor, above a courtyard, outside a locked door, off in a field somewhere, following characters who speak laconically or not at all. Everything is cryptic, indirect. Yet everything breathes with menace.

> *The (Greek) dictatorship is embodied in the formal structure of Days of '36. Imposed silence was one of the conditions under which we worked. . . . If I tried to express myself more clearly, I would have been censored. So I made the film in such a way that the spectator realizes that censorship is involved.*

In *Days of '36,* Angelopoulos gives us, as lucidly as possible, the dilemma of discourse in a country where you can't speak freely. Look at the world *very closely,* he suggests. Fixate, meditate, examine every clue. Try to guess what's really going on. His *silence* is eloquent. And that is what he became: the director of eloquent silence — who, instead of concentrating on characters, concentrates on the landscape around them. In his early films, his people are less individuals than groups, less groups than figures of the earth, lost in what surrounds them — the land, the sea, the sky. In *Reconstruction,* the landscape is already almost a hero/villain. From *Days of '36* to *Alexander,* it is protagonist or antagonist. Then, in the last "trilogy," it recedes again, becomes a background — albeit one which dominates its inhabitants. All his later films spring from a meditation on the land. All bend under the unspoken weight of a terrible past.

The early indirection survives into his later, more "psychological" films: *Voyage to Cythera* (1983), *The Beekeeper* (1986), *Landscape in the Mist* (1988). In *Landscape,* he heightens the force of an annihilating rape sequence by again denying us witness: holding his camera on the closed rear of the truck where the rape takes place — the world proceeding heedlessly around it — so that, under the vast sky, by the underpopulated road, the barren field, our *helplessness* becomes as horrible as any violence.

Greek people have grown up caressing dead stones. I've tried to bring mythology down from the heights and directly to the people. . . .

The Traveling Players — perhaps the greatest unseen (in America) film of the seventies — takes place during 1939–52. Its plan is epic (Brecht crossed with Aeschylus and Mizoguchi): to reveal the period's political history while focusing on a group of itinerant actors who spend those fourteen years wandering through provinces and cities, performing — in increasingly threadbare circumstances — a popular Greek folk tale, *Golfo the Shepherdess.* The actors, whose personae all stem from "the House of Atreus," are of varying political hues — ranging from active Nazi collaborators (Aegisthus), to opportunists (Chrysothaeme), to centrist Greek patriots (Agamemnon), to the apolitical (Clytemnestra), to left-wing idealists (Elektra), to Communist guerrillas (Orestes). And they fill these roles as much as the mythic ones of wandering general, faithless wife, betrayer, or vengeful son.

We remember them afterward more as a troupe than as individuals. Historical and mythic patterns enslave them equally. So does time, which keeps looping in on itself. *The Traveling Players* is, notoriously, a four-hour film that contains only eighty separate shots—about one every three minutes. There is little dialogue apart from the stage scenes. Instead, in long, moving, often wordless tableaux, repeated with a hypnotic force and rhythm, we watch street battles from alleys, parades or demonstrations from the side of a road, a disarming army from a courtyard—and, periodically (the film's *leitmotif*), theatrical performances from the pit or wings as they are stopped, harassed, or violently interrupted.

The Traveling Players is about dramas that can never unfold without interference, about governments that fall, revolutions that are aborted, and entire streams of history that are diverted. And, by implication, a movie that cannot be shot (but was, anyway). It's about the world that lies just outside the view of the drama, thwarting or changing it. And it is about the transcendence of time.

Events flow into each other continuously. We begin a walk down a street during a 1952 election campaign and finish it on a square in 1939. A group of reactionary hoods emerge from a dancehall in 1946, march rowdily down the street and, minutes later, join a Conservative election rally, circa 1952. The movie opens—after a touchingly rustic accordion intro—as the actors arrive in a small provincial town in 1952. It finishes when the (much different) troupe arrives at the same village in 1939—heavy with the weight of their own future.

The spectacularly oblique form was, partially, an act of subterfuge. Even the parallels with Aeschylus may be something of a ruse, to secure the authorities' permission for a frankly subversive film. There are three "act" divisions, in which the characters—Agamemnon, Elektra, and Pylades—relate to us crucial off-screen events: the 1922 Asia Minor defeat by the Turks, the 1944 betrayal of the postwar "coalition" and the imprisonment of radicals. But these scenes, shot after the Colonels fell, are almost all we get of direct address. For the rest, we must, like detectives, piece together the truth from the tableaux—while situating ourselves in the "dead spaces and time," as Angelopoulos calls it, of those unbearably yet beautifully protracted pans and tracking shots—lit by his master cinematographer, Giorgos Arvanitis.

I draw techniques from everything I've seen. . . . I continue to love very much the films of Murnau, Mizoguchi, Antonioni. More recently: Tarkovsky's Stalker, *Godard's* Every Man for Himself. *And, of course,* Ordet *. . . But the only specific influences I acknowledge are Orson Welles, for his use of plan-sequence and deep focus, and Mizoguchi, for his use of time and off-camera space.*

Once he discovered his method, Angelopoulos, like any great obsessive, took it to extremes. Throughout *The Traveling Players,* we can feel his excitement. It matters little whether he was forced into it by a partial deficiency, say a difficulty with dialogue. What matters is the way his new style releases so many scenes of astonishing beauty and power: the players' starved, snowy circle around the chicken, the panoply of postliberation banners in an Athens square suddenly put to rout, the interrupted seaside wedding feast, the last weary burst of applause around Orestes's grave. The film is like a cataract pouring forth from barren rock. Everywhere we can sense the weight of oppression; everywhere we can sense it breaking down, disintegrating.

My films are very much about the problems of power — and they are political only insofar as [those] problems are political. Under the Colonels, there was a clear antithesis; there was more coherence on the left, whereas now it is scattered and in disarray. . . .

The Traveling Players, begun under a dictatorship, completed under a democracy, still managed to so offend the new government that the film had to be *smuggled* into Cannes — where it won the Critics' Prize. Angelopoulos's next movie — my least favorite after *The Reconstruction* — was done in the same ultratheatrical epic mode, based on a news item — a 1949 Greek partisan found frozen in the mountains — from which Angelopoulos drew a framework to put Greece's Right symbolically on trial. But, here, he seems to be shadow-boxing, *imposing* censorship rather than circumventing it. And in *Alexander the Great* (1980), an epic tale of a mythical bandit who begins as a liberator and ends as a tyrant, Angelopoulos says he became a tyrant himself, to cast and crew, on their Macedonian mountain location. In his very next work, *Voyage to Cythera,* he creates a plainly self-referential character, a film director obsessed with Greece and politics, and calls him . . . Alexander.

[Seeing a mountain village for the first time] was a discovery . . . of another Greece I did not know. I came across an interior space — what can be called an inside Greece — which was unknown to most people of my generation, people born and raised in the city. . . .

By this time, Angelopoulos has plainly decided to modify the style invented for *The Traveling Players*. Now, working in a failed bourgeois society instead of a repressive fascist state, he will confront malaise directly. He will tell stories almost as artificial, many-layered, symbol-laden, politically dense, and poetically compact. And he will disguise them further as conventional dramas, psychological art films that follow alienated protagonists through modern landscapes. This is the mode of early Godard, of Bergman, of Antonioni — whose scenarist (Tonino Guerra) and star (Marcello Mastroianni) he borrows for *The Beekeeper*.

Now, Angelopoulos will bury his artifice in the film, rather than use it to disorient or mystify his oppressors. *Voyage to Cythera* is about an old man — the country's leftist past — who remains unreconciled to the present. *The Beekeeper* is about an alienated ex-leftist, also trapped between past (his father's world) and present (a sexy young hitch-hiker). *Landscape in the Mist* is about two illegitimate children, a girl and a boy (named Alexander), comforted for years by a myth their mother has invented — their father is in Germany — who try to find him "across the border." Along the way, they run into the Traveling Players, in the throes of dissolution, declaiming on a desolate strip of beach.

The central current in all three films is bleak. The present has become unbearable; the past is a betrayal or myth; the future an enigma that is probably fatal. But is this the cul-de-sac it seems? A weird escape hatch exists in all three films. *Voyage to Cythera* takes place inside a filmmaker's head, Mastroianni's joyless couplings with the hitchhiker occur before an abandoned movie screen, and the misty landscape toward which the children flee may be contained in a scrap of film they find in a street along the way. Perhaps total despair cannot overcome a world which — for all its folly, warfare, bloodshed, treachery, disappointment, and catastrophe — can still produce those images that, like all the other rats of the Cinémathèque, he remembered so long and loved so well?

Art is a significant human adventure. . . . The significance is to be found in whether, from an external adventure, it manages to be transformed into an internal one. . . .

In a better time and place — at least for foreign films on American screens — Theo Angelopoulos would not have gone so unnoticed here for the twenty years of his filmmaking career; he has been a victim of both bad timing and his own intransigent perfectionism. *Landscape in the Mist* — a masterpiece as lovely as *Vertigo, L'Avventura, Sansho Dayu, Stalker,* or *My Darling Clementine* — is, as much as *The Traveling Players,* a summation of all its maker's strengths, poetry, fears, and exaltations. It is a world crystallized in an image or sound: the hand that rises from the sea, the accordion that starts the performance (a performance we know will always be cut short).

Greece is a country where, it is said, common people love and speak its great poetry. Angelopoulos, very uncommonly, finds poetry in corruption, betrayal, and witness: in children estranged from their father, in a country estranged from its heritage, in love's paralysis, the impossibility of art, the mists of death — above all, in the rich and resonant *silence* around him: that silence of history, of the land, of the mountains, ocean, and sky, all viewed with the fixed gaze through which, like Conrad, he finally makes us *see.*

All the Angelopoulos quotes are from interviews by Constantine A. Themelis and Tony Mitchell. **(Video requests.)**

— *Michael Wilmington*

Jane Campion
■
SWEETIE (1989)

In *Sweetie,* Jane Campion's unsettlingly original, macabrely funny first film, the camera seems to capture its images from never-before-seen angles. Everything in the universe Campion has created is just slightly off-kilter, as if the Earth had positioned itself awkwardly beneath your feet. The film's subject is family life, but voices seem to call down from the flowers on the wallpaper, and every crack in the sidewalk threatens danger. It's about family life as Kafka might have viewed it.

From its opening shots on, the film unfolds a mood of enveloping peculiarity. In essence, *Sweetie* is a horror movie; it's about the horror of having relatives who crowd in, wear your clothes, occupy your guest room, and, without the slightest urging, attach their lives to yours.

Deeper down, though, there's another layer, and this is where Campion is happiest. She likes it when family turbulence is repressed and springs out in freaky new shapes. Campion's style isn't articulate; it's based, in fact, on inexpressiveness, on the thoughts that get tangled up and don't quite work themselves to the surface. Her jokes, too, hit you upside the head, like Freudian snowballs zinging in from nowhere.

The movie is slow to bring its own themes to the surface (it never fully does), busying itself instead with laying out its shadowy, suggestive atmosphere. The first section introduces us to a bony Australian named Kay (Karen Colston), who wears her dark hair in bangs that drop like a curtain just above her brow. Peeking out from underneath are a pair of huge, panicky eyes that appear to be on perpetual alert for signs of some invisible menace.

When we first see her, Kay is lounging on her bed above a floral-printed carpet, and the way Campion has shot it, the image might seem idyllic—a sort of dreamy transcendence on a leafy bank of clouds—if, on the soundtrack, she weren't talking about the hidden powers of trees and how, as a little girl, she was afraid that the big ones outside her house had sinister designs and were growing their roots out under the house to get her.

Campion develops the film narrative according to its own dark, neurotic logic. After a visit to a fortune-teller who tells her she is to encounter a man "with a question mark on his face," Kay meets Louis (Tom Lycos), whose front forelock curls down to a mole on his forehead. Having decided that fate has played its hand, the couple immediately set up house, where things go along well enough until Louis plants a scraggly baby arbor in the backyard, rekindling Kay's childhood tree terrors.

The sapling, of course, cannot be allowed to survive, and there's an eerie hilarity in the way Kay yanks it out of the ground in the middle of the night and appears, ever so subtly, to strangle the life out of it. This "death" signals the end of the couple's sex life. Claiming that she has a cold, Kay moves into the room across the hall. But even after the cold has vanished she can't bring herself to move back. And though neither of them is particularly happy about it, every night, just before hitting the hay, the couple kiss good night, like brother and sister, and lock the doors to their separate bedrooms.

At this stage, with the arrival of Kay's sister, Dawn (Genevieve Lemon), the movie shifts gears. Nicknamed *Sweetie,* Dawn is a well-upholstered nightmare with dyed jet black hair, black fingernails, and cradle-born dreams of a glamorous show-biz life. Materializing out of thin air with her boyfriend-producer, Bob (Michael Lake), an upright slug who's either a junkie or a narcoleptic, Sweetie seems to have only one purpose in life and that is to set Kay's teeth on edge. At first, Kay won't even claim her as family. "I didn't have anything to do with her. She was just . . . born."

Like a child star gone to hideous seed, Sweetie is the most wholly unsympathetic screen creation since Dennis Hopper's Frank in *Blue Velvet.* And while watching her, we're aware that Campion is intentionally taking us to the edge of revulsion, daring us to push her character away. Still, even after Gordon (Jon Darling), the girls' father, arrives, all forlorn because his wife has left him to work out West for a bunch of cowboys, and we see how sickly manipulative the family relationships are, our disgust becomes more complicated but perhaps even more urgent.

As skilled a creator of otherworldly moods as Campion is, *Sweetie* doesn't have much narrative drive, and I found it vastly more compelling in the beginning, when Kay was center stage, than after the destabilizing arrival of her sister.

Still, I loved the way Campion and cinematographer Sally Bongers make the natural and the unnatural (human) landscapes appear lush and supersaturated with color, but at the same time barren, minimalist. Also, a scene in which the jackaroos dance a dusty sunset waltz in the cowboy camp has an almost serene eccentricity. The images imprint themselves instantly into your memory. In making her first film, Campion has done thrillingly atmospheric work, and in the process, established herself as perhaps the most perversely gifted young filmmaker to rise up in years.

—*Hal Hinson*

Atom Egoyan

■

SPEAKING PARTS (1989)
FAMILY VIEWING (1987)

Like some permanent closed-circuit system or perpetual hall of mirrors, contemporary movies feed on older ones, electronically and otherwise. For some American directors, the chain is virtually impossible to break. Steven Spielberg's vaunted "grown-up" romance, the appropriately titled *Always,* a remake of the 1943 MGM fantasy *A Guy Named Joe* that is set in a realm so abstract it might as well be another planet, represents the elevation of movies to holy writ. A svelte embodiment of the old Hollywood, Audrey Hepburn, is inscribed as a universal demiurge, while a bumbling swain takes his cues not only from the invisible Richard Dreyfuss but also from a doubly disembodied John Wayne. Dreyfuss's ubiquitous presence as a guardian angel enables Spielberg to equate the pleasures of voyeurism with those of direction, and designate both as sublime.

Scarcely so sanguine is the no less image-obsessed *Speaking Parts,* the third feature by the Cairo-born, British Columbia–raised, Toronto-based Atom Egoyan. Egoyan specializes in bleakly comic family dramas that position people and TV sets in novel, usually erotic entanglements. Not yet thirty, he's widely regarded as the most original Canadian director since David Cronenberg. Indeed, the witty, sinister *Speaking Parts* — chosen to open the Canadian section of Toronto's most recent Festival of Festivals (and distributed here by Zeitgeist Films) — immediately establishes a Cronenbergian sense of dread, crosscutting between a lone mourner in a video-equipped crypt and the ominous impersonality of a high-rise hotel's laundry room.

For Spielberg, the movies are a kind of cheerful religion. For Egoyan, their successor form, video, is at once a phantasm and a commodity, a private hallucination and a nexus of social relations, a *doppelgänger* and an Other, a form of truth and a source of mistaken identity. A clerk in a seedy video store analyzes customers on the basis of their rentals and supplements his income by taping weddings and orgies. A monstrous TV producer is all but omnipotent: "People have always watched what I like to watch," he grandly tells the aspiring actor (and freelance gigolo) Lance. "You have, too, ever since you were a kid." The producer issues his commands and kudos via a closed-circuit vid screen, and later, a doomed, mutually manipulative couple usurps his technology to engage in a more advanced form of telephone sex.

The video monitor is the ruling icon in virtually every one of *Speaking Parts'* interiors. (Egoyan may be a self-conscious outsider, given his background, but he belongs to a specifically Canadian tradition—namely, the Marshall McLuhan/*Videodrome*/SCTV sense of TV as All.) Lisa, a disturbed hotel chambermaid, uses a home VCR to literally play out her obsession with coworker Lance. The video recorder is a shrine on which she runs and reruns the wildly disparate movies in which he appears as an extra. True, Lance has never had a speaking part. But as Lisa defensively tells the clerk in the video store she haunts, "He's on the screen. There is nothing so special about words." Lance, however, is not quite so complacent. He tries to elevate his career to another plateau by pursuing an affair with the screenwriter Clara.

Although no article on Egoyan fails to invoke the title *sex, lies, and videotape,* these obsessions were already amply apparent in his previous film, *Family Viewing.* At once stilted and slapdash (but filled with ideas nonetheless), *Family Viewing* makes elaborate use of surveillance TV and technology-enhanced sex to recount an Oedipal struggle in an incestuous nuclear family. (Among other things, the young hero has to prevent his father from erasing his childhood home videos—Dad wants to use them to make pornographic movies.) Shown at the 1987 Montreal International Festival of New Cinema and Video, *Family Viewing* inspired a gesture that would reverberate throughout the film world: acknowledging a new generation, Wim Wenders turned over his $5,000 prize (in Canadian currency) for *Wings of Desire* to the hitherto unknown Egoyan.

An overlapping cast and kindred themes link *Speaking Parts* to *Family Viewing,* but the new film is far more technically polished—if not more conventionally structured. As a director, Egoyan thrives on urban anxiety and excels at scenes based on the deadpan staging of a single monstrous gag. *Speaking Parts* has a languorous, seductive quality and a free-floating science-fiction ambience. (According to the maker, it's set "about five years in the future.") But although Egoyan has supported himself as a freelance TV director, he is not primarily a narrative filmmaker. The lapses in continuity and relative absence of street life or connecting shots subvert *Speaking Parts'* sleek, generic look. Similarly, Egoyan's creatures are far too off-puttingly narcissistic and creepily selfish to allow for easy audience identification. Lisa has a particular genius for inappropriate behavior. Assisting the video clerk in taping a wedding, she reduces the bride to tears with her interview technique. "What do you see in Ronnie?" she asks with dumb insistence. "When you look at him, what are you looking at?"

What are you looking at, indeed. This disconcerting effect has impressed even the film's detractors. *Speaking Parts'* "fundamental emptiness never prevents it from developing momentum," *New York Times*'s Janet Maslin noted when the movie was screened at last year's New York Film Festival. "It is moved along by some form of postmodern peristalsis rather than by dramatic urgency." In fact, *Speaking Parts* is fueled by its characters' desperate attempts to use image constructions to improve their mysteriously impoverished lives. Lisa is fixated on Lance. Clara's script is based on her own story, and she becomes increasingly hysterical when the malevolent producer changes the story line to eliminate her role.

The plight of Lisa and Clara, as well as the movie's overall lack of narrative resolution, heightens its intimation of an image of underclass breeding in the barrios of the North American metropolis. No less than Spielberg, Egoyan lives in a society that is overwhelmed and dominated by synthetic images. The difference is that Egoyan understands the class distinction between those who make images and those millions more who only consume them.

—*J. Hoberman*

Fifth Generation Chinese Films:
Tian Zhuangzhuang

■

THE HORSE THIEF (1987)

If the two aesthetically richest decades in the history of cinema have been the 1920s and the 1960s, it is in no small part due to the fact that it was during these two golden ages that film came closest to becoming a universal language. Some recent film theorists, arguing that film images are dependent on linguistic structures, have denied the claims for silent film's universality. But the fact remains that the consolidation and purification of silent film language in the twenties coincided with an international film culture where cross-pollination seemed almost the rule rather than the exception.

The same impulse toward internationalism that led to shop signs in Esperanto and a virtual absence of intertitles in the very influential *The Last Laugh* (1924) also turned most of the giants of the period — Chaplin, Dreyer, Eisenstein, Flaherty, Griffith, Lubitsch, Murnau, Sternberg, and Stroheim, among others — into a race of globe-trotters. "Fair exchange isn't robbery," Art Blakey pointed out at the Chicago Jazz Festival, referring to the mutual education that passed between him and his various sidemen over the years. The same could be said of those periods in film history when countries are most open to ideas from abroad.

The second golden age came about largely through the efforts of a new generation of directors to reapply some of the ideas of the twenties and forge another international film culture. Films as diverse as *Hiroshima, Mon Amour* and *Hatari, Breathless, Blow-Up, The Savage Innocents, Fahrenheit 451, 2001: A Space Odyssey, Playtime, Contempt,* and *The Rise of Louis XIV* were virtually defined by their multinational elements and sentiments; and for the first time since the twenties — barring perhaps only the impact of Italian neorealism in the forties — Hollywood styles of filmmaking were fundamentally overturned by new developments from abroad. Some of the most banal tropes of current movies — such as ending a film with a freeze frame — can be traced back directly to the innovations of this period.

If one adopts a cyclical theory of film history, the next golden age of internationalism will be the first decade of the next century. Director Tian Zhuangzhuang has said that he made *The Horse Thief* for the twenty-first century, and one wonders if he might have had some of this internationalism in mind. For the power of this breathtaking spectacle from the People's Republic of China is to a large extent its capacity to communicate directly beyond the immediate trappings of its regionalism and culture, not to mention its nationality and its period. The relatively small role played by dialogue and story line and the striking uses of composition and superimposition make it evocative of certain films of the twenties, although it is anything but a silent film: the chants, percussion, and bells of Buddhist rituals and the beautiful musical score that accompanies them form an essential part of its texture. And the film's bold uses of color and a rectangular 'Scope format, as well as its mesmerizing camera movements and very eclectic style of editing, make it more readily identifiable with movies made in the sixties.

Set in the remote wilds of Tibet with a cast consisting entirely of Tibetan nonprofessionals, *The Horse Thief* concerns a man named Norbu, an occasional horse thief who is eventually expelled from his clan for stealing temple offerings. Living in isolation with his wife Dolma and his little boy Tashi, he periodically returns to the tribe's temple to pray and appears to be genuinely remorseful about his crime, particularly after his son dies. But after two more harsh winters and the birth of another son, he finds it necessary to steal again in order to keep his family alive, and even kills a scared ram. After he is told by an old woman of the clan, who may or may not be his grandmother, that his wife and child can return, but that he is "a river ghost, full of evil," he steals another couple of horses and sends his family back to the clan on one of them.

Tian is a member of China's so-called fifth generation of film-makers — those who entered the Beijing Film Academy after the end of the Cultural Revolution and began to have access to a wide range of films from abroad. According to Alan Stanbrook of *Sight and Sound*, Tian and his former classmates — including Chen Kaige (*Yellow Earth*), Huang Jianxin (*The Black Cannon Incident*), and Zhang Yimou (*Red Sorghum, Ju Dou*) — were "weaned on directors like Godard, Antonioni, Truffaut, and Fassbinder."

Before being released, *The Horse Thief* suffered two kinds of censor-ship at the hands of government authorities. One of these was an addition rather than a subtraction — the date 1923, which flashes on the screen before the first image, thus locating the action in a specific period rather than making it more timeless, which was the director's intention. The other form of censorship was the elimination of corpses from the first of three separate "sky burials" in the film, when human bodies are fed to carrion crows. We do, in fact, see these birds feeding on flesh, but evidently the original version was more explicit.

All three of Tian's features to date are concerned with minority cultures in China. The difference between isolation and community is obviously part of what *The Horse Thief* is about, but even this concern seems often dwarfed by his characters' positions in the visual, auditory background of the landscape and the sounds of the Buddhist rituals. (In this respect it is worlds apart from Nicholas Ray's *The Savage Innocents,* about Eskimo life, in spite of certain visual and behavioral resemblances.) Composed mainly of short sequences connected to one another by quick fade-outs or slow lap dissolves, the film offers itself almost entirely as spectacle, and as such seems to be structured more on musical terms than on narrative ones; in this framework, Norbu figures less as a theme than as a solo instrument that occasionally rises above the ensemble passages—plaintive in the isolation, yet never divorced from the surrounding musical context.

The musical sensibility is apparent in the recurrence of certain locations, sounds, and camera setups; in the lightning-quick shot of the collapse of a tent, effected by Norbu's accomplice in the first horse theft that we see; in a remarkable sequence devoted to Norbu's extended praying and prostrations, which hypnotically combines camera movements and superimpositions with a use of other human figures that ambiguously alerts our sense of his isolation; in the slow drip of water from melting snow that Norbu catches in a jug to bring to his ailing child; in the intricately structured sequence showing the clan's westward migration, as fine a piece of epic poetry as some of the grander collective movements in Ford; and, above all, in the depictions of the Buddhist ceremonies and rituals, which are themselves patterned like musical structures. And despite the highly formalized nature of Tian's visual style and rhythm, the flow of a given sequence never becomes predictable: an unexpected low or tilted camera angle, all the more jarring in a 'Scope format, will suddenly veer a scene's progress in a different direction; or an unforeseeable shift in the camera's distance from a subject will bring about a similar reorientation.

In short, the relative paucity of plot is never experienced as an absence because virtually every shot becomes an event in itself. As in *2001,* the overall movement of *The Horse Thief* is toward revelation. The film's environmental and ecological mysticism, while inextricably tied to Tibetan Buddhist ceremonies, has little of the heavy cultural baggage one associates with the mysticism of Andrei Tarkovsky, or even with the more folkloric mysticism of Alexander Dovzhenko or Sergei Paradjanov, which it more clearly resembles. Perhaps where it most sharply distinguishes itself from other films is in its ambiguous juxtaposition of human figures with landscapes; without ever proposing an antihumanistic or even nonhumanistic vision, it nevertheless situates the human in a different relationship to nature. Partaking of some of the universal language imparted to us by the silent cinema of the twenties in its compositional boldness and simplicity, and by the eclectic cinema of the sixties in its awareness and development of this cinematic past, *The Horse Thief* is a film of the future in more ways than one.

—*Jonathan Rosenbaum*

Fifth Generation Chinese Films: Zhang Yimou

■

RED SORGHUM (1988)

During 1989's fiftieth anniversary of the great 1939 films, a lot of people have wondered: Where are our grand, sweeping visions of the world, our movies that once raised terrific entertainment to the level of art? In China, that's where. Director Zhang Yimou's *Red Sorghum*—funny, funky, lusty, and rip-roaring—turns love and sorrow, peace and war into a story so powerful it virtually boils out of the celluloid.

Based on a semiautobiographical short story by young writer Mo Yan, the movie begins with the author's voice-over: "This is a story about my grandma and grandpa—with, maybe, a little stretching of facts." Immediately, we see the world the way his grandma saw it at eighteen. A poor man's daughter betrothed to a leprous old winery owner in exchange for a mule, Gong Li has a red silk marriage cloth thrown over her head as her future husband's workers cart her in a crimson-covered sedan chair to her new home. She's the kind of proud-spirited girl who'd steal a pair of her dad's scissors to kill herself rather than go through with the marriage arrangement, and she isn't above casting an appreciative eye on the strapping, bare back of Jiang Wen's young sedan-bearer whenever her flapping layers of red cloth are blown aside.

The eight carriers purposely jolt her, gossip about her ("Don't let the old goat touch ya, honey"), and sing her a raunchy wedding night song: "When her husband lifts the veil, he'll find a pockmarked face and a chicken neck." But as they pass through the local sorghum field, a well-known hideout for bandits, they're in for a big surprise. The masked outlaw who stages a holdup pulls Gong Li out of her cloth coverings, and, to their shock, she's beautiful.

The whole film is a series of surprises, of veils suddenly removed to reveal that life is never what you expect it to be. Packing every frame and making every sequence bristle with energy, director Zhang Yimou punches home a story that's like the repeating but changing stanzas of a folk song. If Gong Li's first abduction into the sorghum field leads to a murder, her second abduction leads to the birth of a child.

If we first see an overwhelming image of the tall, red, plumy sorghum trampled down in lust, we'll eventually see an equally overwhelming image of the same fields crushed by the Japanese army's pre–World War II invasion. No other current director is capable of the bold, robust, intoxicating, frightening personal stamp Zhang Yimou puts on every frame. Give him the weeds that would be anyone else's sow's ear, and he'll turn them into a silk purse: a startling, brilliantly colored, deeply felt vision of the shifting forces of life and death.

The plot and performances do the same. The horrible husband Gong Li has imagined suddenly turns into the mate who's much more to her liking. The slavery she expected at the winery suddenly turns into mastery. And vice versa. The life bursting from her fields and household can turn into destruction. The red wine joyfully sloshed over everything and everyone — and virtually slung into the camera lens — can suddenly turn into scenes drenched in blood. The "Wine Song" sung for the new harvest can turn into a grim anthem of war, and the courtship song "Press On Bravely, Darling" can turn into an elegy.

American audiences may be slightly unsettled by Gong Li as the nice girl who greets bandits and abductions with quietly pleased or openly thrilled grins. They'll be much more unsettled by Jiang Wen's wild and crazy, bawdy and brutal, funny and solid hero.

We should be unsettled. In our media-saturated culture, life and death have been turned into a TV commercial's jump-cuts and sound bites. In movies like *9¹/₂ Weeks* and *Rambo,* sex and violence have been turned into magazine ads and comic books. When, in the end, a red veil of fate descends over this film's human figures, they stand in a sorghum field bent to the ground under a strong wind. And what would be a bummer ending from any other director becomes, with Zhang Yimou, one of the decade's most powerful images of life's tragic but epic grandeur.

— *Kathy Schulz Huffhines*

PEKING OPERA BLUES (1986)

The power-pop triumph of the past few years, *Peking Opera Blues* lures you in with its pounding, crazy beat. The very first image is a close-up of an elaborately made-up Chinese opera performer staring down the camera and howling with laughter. His stylized gaiety is infectious; it dares the viewer to remain aloof. This action comedy by Hong Kong director Tsui Hark is a breathlessly choreographed jape that's almost irresistible.

Like much recent HK fare, *Peking Opera Blues* is a period piece that reflects the Crown Colony's anxiety vis-à-vis reunification with the People's Republic. Hark has described the movie as a satire on the Chinese "ignorance of democracy," but it seems equally a fantasy about the breakdown of an established social order. Set in 1913, two years after the fall of the last emperor, the film is the sort of tangled narrative thicket in which unscrupulous warlords engage in sinister conspiracies, while adventurous gold diggers search for hidden jewels amid frequent bouts of stylized make-believe. As the title suggests, theater rules: Hark's cubistic backstage is a vortex of entertainment, greed, and intrigue wherein three attractive heroines—a comic gold digger, a would-be actress, and a general's daughter, who for no particular reason (and not very convincingly), has disguised herself as a boy—join forces to pursue their separate agendas. Typically, the aspiring actress is the most "sincere" character.

Peking Opera Blues is like an action film built around the Bangles—a glitzy, ironic pajama party in which the stars almost never stop role-playing, their antics punctuated by all manner of reversals, sight gags, and subversively gender-bending pratfalls. (Women were not permitted to appear in the Peking Opera, something addressed here with a vengeance.) The whole movie has a knowing quality that hovers over, and ultimately supersedes, the perfunctory plot. With its kick fights and chases egged on by the gongs and clicks of James Wong's keening, twanging score, the film is a continual coming attraction for itself—the action as accelerated in Hark's bang-bang editing as it is amplified by his performers' exaggerated reactions, continual hide-and-seek, and frequent disguises. (The most frequently asked question: "How come you are here?")

In its insouciant, breakneck pace, *Peking Opera Blues* owes something to the Spielberg/Lucas *Indiana Jones* films, but it's less overweening and more deliberately flimsy (not to mention wholly immune from ethnocentric Indy-imperialism). The mode is self-aware rather than self-conscious. As blatantly two-dimensional as the movie is, it engages the entire spectrum of popular amusement East and West. When Hark travesties a traditional opera by having a pair of (disguised) characters turn up onstage in identical costumes, he combines the consternation of two of the most celebrated Marx brothers routines. But at the same time that *Peking Opera Blues* parodies its source, it derives the most spectacular acrobatic stunts organically, from the rich soil of the opera's form.

How does one get to be the world's wittiest action director? Born in Vietnam, transplanted to Hong Kong during the war, Hark attended film school in Texas, codirected a documentary (with Third World Newsreel's Chris Choy) in New York's Chinatown, then returned to HK to make his reputation in television. Clearly this thirty-seven-year-old director/producer/sometime actor, who has been twisting local genres since his thriller, *The Butterfly Murders,* appeared in 1979, knows something about the relative nature of cultural values and the instability of ruling forms.

Hark suggests a comic Eisenstein. It's not just his machine-gun editing, but his use of typage, his analysis of circus attractions, his fascination with signs, and his interest in political upheaval that link him to the Soviet master. If Hark belongs to the Internationale of commercial entertainment, it may be because the era of revolutionary heroism is long since over. Like Eisenstein's, Hark's movies seem to flow from some preideological wellspring: For all its pow, *Peking Opera Blues* has an unexpected backbeat of melancholy and loss — it's the boat person's *Battleship Potemkin*.

—J. Hoberman

Hong Kong Films: Stanley Kwan

■

ROUGE (1987)

The glory of Hong Kong cinema is that it's genuinely popular — its best work shares the tastes and enthusiasms of ordinary filmgoers. No recent movie proves this more pleasurably than this elegant ghost story by Stanley Kwan (at thirty-three one of the best young filmmakers anywhere). The scene is 1987 Hong Kong. A young man encounters a beautiful woman dressed like a courtesan of the 1930s: melancholy and desperate, she reveals that she's a ghost looking to meet up with her lover, with whom she committed a double suicide half a century earlier. The young man takes her home, much to the initial wrath of his girlfriend, a career woman who's every bit as independent as the ghost is dependent. Soon, however, this eighties yuppie couple are working together to help their forlorn guest, who can't cope with a Hong Kong that has become unrecognizable to her. Where are all the brothels, opium dens, ruby-bright theaters? Where the operatic passion of Hong Kong's glorious past? As this old-fashioned ghost story unfolds forward and flashes back — building to a climax both magical and pungent — it gradually becomes clear that *Rouge* is a sneaky-smart piece of entertainment. It's a movie about romance and calculation, the myth-laced past and the hyperrational present. A portrait of modern city, and an ancient civilization, forever haunted by ghosts.

—*John Powers*

Hong Kong Films: John Woo

■

A BETTER TOMORROW (1986)

At a time when much Hollywood storytelling has been sapped by self-consciousness, Hong Kong keeps turning out stories with astonishing energy and *joie de vivre*. This gangster pic by John Woo was a box-office smash, and it's easy to see why: it's all operatic emotions, breakneck pacing, Peckinpah-style violence, and stylish, movie-star performances that HK's teenage viewers are certain to emulate when they hit the streets. The story itself is a packet of clichés about crime and redemption, focusing on two brothers—one a cop (Leslie Cheung) and one a gangster (Ti Lung)—whose "careers" lead them into life-and-death conflict. But the film's real star is Chow Yuen Fat, whose exuberant portrait of a grinning, swaggering gunslinger dominates the film from the start—he embodies the ideals of love, loyalty, and conquest that give the tale its fire. At times, there's more fire than artistry at work in this movie, which has some clumsy patches and several different visual styles. (I've been told that Woo didn't actually direct all the scenes.) Yet even when *A Better Tomorrow* gets raggedy, it never stops being deliriously entertaining: this is popular filmmaking with a vengeance. And, as an added attraction, it offers the funniest subtitles imaginable.

—*John Powers*

International Coproductions: Nikita Mikhalkov
■

DARK EYES (1987)

Magical is the word for *Dark Eyes,* Nikita Mikhalkov's gorgeously rueful, elegantly funny comedy of weakness. From start to finish, it's one of those charmed and charming enterprises that can do no wrong, setting Marcello Mastroianni in motion as an amiable turn-of-the-century lapdog named Romano whose response to a crisis at the bank run by his wife is to bolt to a spa. There, after some decorous hanky-panky, he falls in love with a softly willowy Russian (Elena Sofonova). His idleness is as much a spur to their romance as her freshness and modesty. Besides, she's the only one who takes his nonsense seriously. He begins the film mocking his own buffoonery, tiptoeing exaggeratedly through a lawn party, then snoring through a musicale that unfolds in a drawing room as his wife frantically puts on a brave front, fighting disaster.

You'll gather that this is the kind of role that Mastroianni has made a specialty of over the years. Indeed, if you regard his career as a meal, this particular role is the dessert. He's got it all covered—effortlessly, stylishly, wrapping his gentle charm around his character's uselessness, wearing it like a badge of perverse honor. An aristocrat by marriage, he's even more of an aristocrat by manner, gracefully crumbling into self-made ruin, suggesting along the way that success on any level would be unspeakably vulgar. His big problem is that he finds himself stuck with a grandly impetuous gesture he unfurls at the spa — after unsuccessfully chasing the Russian visitor, he overwhelms her by marching with studied nonchalance in his white suit into a mud bath to retrieve her windblown hat.

He's smart enough to realize that he's touched not by her, but by her reaction to him. Although he's surrounded by women who treat him with generosity and affection (his wife, Silvana Mangano, and his mistress, inscribed with delightfully saucy worldliness by Marthe Keller), the Russian woman's naive belief in him is so intoxicating that he hurtles off to Russia after her. The rueful yet compassionate view of human weakness is recognizably Chekhov's — "The Lady with the Dog" is one of the stories that serves as the film's source. But the miracle of Mikhalkov's film is that he's been able to avoid having the film's Russian and Italian accents cancel each other out. Each enhances the other. The film is at once quintessentially Italian, especially when Mikhalkov evokes the richness of Visconti in the family mansion and the surrealistic comic exuberance of Fellini at the spa, and utterly Russian once the wayward lover gypsies across that country's border.

The comedy is as delicious as any in ages, quite apart from the film's exhilarating pictorial verve. Wheelchair races and costly hypochondria are satirized with proud Fellinian sumptuousness at the spa. As a fat soprano belts out Rossini, Mastroianni turns giddy with delight upon discovering that falling in love with the Russian woman is yet another way of falling in love with himself. Making inspired fun of narcissism, *Dark Eyes* plays like Fellini reborn when it's in Italy. But as soon as it gets to Russia, it's transformed into sublimely comical Chekhov. The first big Russian joke is the paralysis of the Imperial bureaucracy, none of whose gold-braided civil servants wants to take the responsibility of signing the permit that would let the visitor go to the backwater where the woman lives lovelessly with the provincial governor.

Finally, using his cover story of wishing to build an unbreakable glass factory, he makes it. Alighting from the modest side of the train, he thinks he's playing to an audience of a peasant woman and her cow. He's startled to find, however, that the whole town has turned out to greet him. Before he knows it, he's being hugged and kissed effusively to the strains of a military band, swallowing vodka at an alarming rate, and importuned by a Chekhovian doctor who fears for the ecology. Eventually, he penetrates the governor's mansion (the pompous governor is played with a hilariously teetering self-importance by the great Innokenty Smoktunovski) and is reunited with his love object. No sooner does he hustle her out of the suffocating mansion, than they're making love surrounded by feathers in a chicken house.

Then comes the showdown. Will the aristocrat, who hates the idea of hurting anybody, have the follow-through to back up his grand gesture? The outcome of the story-within-a-story aboard an ocean liner will surprise nobody. Yet it isn't the plot that carries *Dark Eyes*, or even Mastroianni's career-capping portrayal of the charming mediocrity at its center. It's Mikhalkov's ability to make each culture seem to spend itself prodigally in turning Fellini and Chekhov into movie soulmates. In *Dark Eyes*, Russia and Italy bring out the best in each other. Most multicultural productions — *The Sicilian* is the most recent, most woeful example — yield a Tower of Babel mishmash. But in *Dark Eyes*, the chemistry is heavenly.

—Jay Carr

Japanimation: Hiroaki Yoshida

■

TWILIGHT OF THE COCKROACHES (1987)

Mavens call the technique "Japanimation," a startling overlay of cartoon imagery onto live-action sequences. Nothing quite prepares you for its effect in *Twilight of the Cockroaches*, a seriously funny cartoon saga about an impending roach holocaust in a Tokyo apartment complex — as told from the bugs' point of view. You've heard of underground movies? Well, this one's a ground-level epic.

In this uniquely witty film, written and directed by Hiroaki Yoshida, the animated roaches are heroes and the live-action humans are villains, wielding bug bombs the way madmen deploy those of the nuclear variety. Slated for extermination are dainty Naomi, a comely roachling in a blue strapless sheath and go-go boots; her handsome fiancé, Ichiro, and Hans, the mysterious stranger to whom Naomi finds herself powerfully drawn.

Naomi and Ichiro live in what he calls "up-market" bliss. That is, in the apartment of Mr. Saito (Kaoru Kobayashi), a sloppy bachelor whose dirty dishes and messy flat are cockroach heaven. A gourmand, Saito cooks a different kind of cuisine every night, and the residue of his meals enables Naomi and Ichiro (and their legion of relatives) to "eat Italian" one night and Chinese the next. Since Saito never cleans his apartment, Naomi and Ichiro sleep in splendor inside one of his Nikes, although when they get married, they plan to move somewhere more upscale, perhaps to a corner of the Saito apartment with a window.

All this is shown from the roaches' perspective, and Saito looks like a sullen grotesque the size of a redwood. When he walks, it seems to Naomi that the earth moves. However, he's the perfect host for his insect houseguests, permitting them a Roman holiday without apparent end. Unaware of the plight of other roaches, Naomi's people call Saito's apartment "the Homeland."

While Ichiro has never left his native "country," Naomi — who in animation terms is something of a cross between Natalie Wood and Nancy Kwan — is comparatively well traveled. She has been across the courtyard — in cockroach distance, that's like crossing the Pacific — where she met Hans, warrior roach. Hans's view of humans is apocalyptic. You see, the apartment where he lives is that of Saito's "Lady Neighbor" (Setsuko Karasumaru), a neatness freak who lives to kill all roaches.

Intuitively, Naomi knows that she and Ichiro live in a fool's paradise and that Hans's world view is more realistic. Her intuitions are borne out when Saito and the Lady Neighbor become involved. Quicker than you can say "Raid," the fastidious woman turns Saito's flat into a militarized zone. Boric-acid bombs burst where marinara sauce once dribbled. Roach motels replace the four-star digs formerly enjoyed by Saito's itty-bitty guests. In order to save her species, must peace-loving Naomi become a kamikaze cockroach?

The marvel of Yoshida's movie is that it completely involves humans in identifying with our historical enemy, the roach. Yoshida achieves this in hilarious juxtapositions of scale: A fingernail seems as big as the Ritz, and a human proportionally more colossal. In *Twilight*, speck-sized cockroaches cower in the skyscraper shadows of humans, household fixtures are magnified. When toilet seats (where licentious roaches hang out) and soup bowls become the size of the Colosseum,

Twilight has the spatial imagination of Claes Oldenburg. Yoshida's movie succeeds in making roaches human-scaled and humanoid.

(Yoshida has just completed shooting his American feature debut, *Iron Maze,* in Braddock, Pennsylvania. Even if it is just a fraction as imaginative as *Twilight,* it will be one of the more compelling films of 1991.)

Whether viewed as a diverting action film or as an allegory of genocide, *Twilight of the Cockroaches* is the most original picture of the year. With its subtle allusions to Hiroshima and Dachau, this comedy has unexpected resonance. You will think twice before getting out that can of Blockade. **(Video request.)**

—*Carrie Rickey*

Aki Kaurismäki
•
RETROSPECTIVE

For journalists and programmers, an international film festival is a frantic network of hot lines and hot tips that within a matter of hours can make a hitherto unknown movie or director the subject of intense, buzzing word of mouth. Festivals live for the buzz, and the buzz became a roar last February in Berlin during the packed press screening of *Ariel,* the movie *Variety* later termed "the insider hit of the festival," the most recent feature by a young Finnish director with the mellifluous name, Aki Kaurismäki.

Aki who? A thirty-two-year-old former film critic and sometime scriptwriter, Kaurismäki broke into production with the 1981 rockumentary *The Saimaa Gesture,* which he codirected with his older brother, Mika; Aki has since made five features. Drawing on European literature, American popular culture, Scandinavian *weltschmerz,* and a sense of irony that befits life spent on the border between East and West, Aki Kaurismäki's productions are supercool, sometimes cruel black comedies of contemporary Finland, featuring aggressively ordinary-looking types living lives of unquiet desperation.

So far, Kaurismäki films have appeared in the United States only in the context of fraternal retrospectives. If Mika's films are less dis-

tinctively hardboiled and more blandly romantic than Aki's, together
the brothers are something of a phenomenon: they're responsible not
only for more than a third of the output of the entire Finnish film
industry, but as founders of the ultrahip Midnight Sun Film Festival
(held over four twenty-four-hour days each June at Sodankylä, one
hundred miles north of the Arctic Circle), they have successfully
plugged themselves (and Finland) into the international film scene.

Still, it's Aki who seems the more driven of the two. For his first solo
film, the younger Kaurismäki audaciously tackled Dostoyevsky. The
antihero of *Crime and Punishment* (1983) works in a slaughterhouse and
murders not a moneylender but the man who three years before killed
his fiancée in a drunken hit-and-run accident. Uncharacteristically
turgid (the only Aki Kaurismäki feature to run more than ninety
minutes) and totally distanced (the director proclaimed it an "homage
to those golden years when one murder was sufficient for one crime
film"), *Crime and Punishment* at least got the lead out of Kaurismäki's
system. He followed up with the more absurdist and abstractly violent
Calamari Union (1985).

The premise of this mock *noir*—an exercise in attitude, populated by
fatal women and driven by a fifties-rock score—has seventeen hipster
thugs, all named Frank, attempting to leave their working-class
Helsinki neighborhood for the seaside suburb of Eira. Shot in impeccable black and white, with more than one scene musing upon the sci-
fi perfection of the Helsinki subway, this sullen odyssey is interpolated
with all manner of Russian movies, video-game landscapes, even a
totally unmotivated rock performance at which all the Franks sing
about what "bad boys" they are. By the end of the movie, fifteen
Franks have been killed or forced to take menial jobs; two survive and
row to Soviet Estonia, the mythical happy-ending land (!) of more than
one Kaurismäki opus.

While *Calamari Union* marked the birth of a Finnish enfant terrible,
Shadows in Paradise (1986) was the first Aki Kaurismäki film to get
much attention south of Helsinki. To view Kaurismäki's head-on
compositions of humorously taciturn characters in an iconic, over-
bright environment, it's evident that he's taken a long look at Rainer
Fassbinder's 1972 breakthrough film, *The Merchant of the Four Seasons*.
The story of a romance between a wide-eyed, inexpressive garbage-
man and a sullen supermarket cashier played out against a backdrop of
entropic bingo parlors, dreary discos, and cold little beaches is at once
ridiculously trite and touchingly epic: "The terrifying mouth of a

garbage collector, the sea crashing upon the shore, a few kisses . . . the tragicomic life in a metropolis." (Fassbinderesque, too, is the laconic dialogue. Describing her aunt's trip to Florida, the heroine remarks that "all she saw was some Finns and Donald Duck.")

Although *Shadows in Paradise* doesn't manage to pay off its debt to the German wunderkind, Kaurismäki took on another sort of classic in *Hamlet Goes Business,* one of the surprise hits of the 1988 Berlin Film Festival. Here, Shakespeare isn't desecrated so much as rematerialized in gleaming black and white, the action transposed to a gloomy corporate landscape where beefy guys in loud sport coats attempt to corner the world market in rubber ducks. ("Hardly ever before has the poetry of Shakespeare been respected to such an extent that it has remained untouched after the adaptation into another art form," Kaurismäki riffed. "No wonder Ophelia is crying bitterly in the corner of her bathroom.") Petulantly porcine, with slicked-back blond hair and a penchant for rockabilly, the erstwhile Prince of Denmark is played by Pirkka-Pekka Petelius, the most popular TV comic in Finland, as an overage punk—bugging his business associates and drawing comic strips during board meetings.

Confidently post-Fassbinder in its *noir*ish angles and deadpan detachment, *Hamlet* is periodically interrupted by surges of rock 'n' roll energy. (Rock, which provides Kaurismäki characters with more pleasure than anything else does—sex included—continues to be a touchstone of his work. He made three music videos in 1986 and recently served as executive producer of *From Russia with Rock,* a Finnish report on the Soviet music scene.) According to one Finnish critic, *Hamlet's* "visual references hark back to the grandiloquent Finnish crime films of the forties and fifties," and the movie is one of the most elegant *noir* pastiches of recent years. Still, Kaurismäki cautioned viewers not to "be fooled by the plastic beauty of this movie: the question is about money—a matter of life and death."

In his latest film, Kaurismäki has returned to his naturalistic (or "naturalistic") mode: *Ariel* reiterates the themes of *Shadows in Paradise* with greater sureness and skill. The film has a balladic compression and a lyricism that's both affecting and sour. The hero of this admirably terse seventy-four-minute drama is a young Lapland miner who, laid off when the mine closes, drives to Helsinki in his antique white Cadillac convertible, teams up with a disaffected meter maid, and falls into a life of crime. Effortlessly shifting gears from road film to worker drama to prison story (or rather, the ideas of these), Kaurismäki's deadpan saga is filled with oblique sight (and sound) gags: a successful jailbreak is indicated by a street sign crashing through a men's-clothing-store window; worker solidarity is reduced to a broken music box that tinkles the opening bars of the "Internationale" ("Arise, ye prisoners of starvation").

Trafficking as it does in proletarian realism, the longing for escape, the lower depths, violence, and betrayal, *Ariel* suggests the modern equivalent of a 1940s Warner Brothers B film. (Indeed, the movie knowingly quotes *High Sierra* in its continual interplay of Finnish and American pop.) And, as with Kaurismäki's previous movies, it's beautifully made. Cinematographer Timo Salminen proves as masterful at shooting color as he is with black and white; the action is set against a succession of ravishingly bleak urban landscapes. I haven't seen so unostentatiously pictorial a film since Robert Frank and Rudy Wurlitzer's similarly autumnal *Candy Mountain*.

Although Kaurismäki has yet to find an American distributor, his European reputation continues to build. (*Ariel* emerged from Berlin with Austrian, Canadian, West German, French, British, Dutch, Swiss, Swedish, Spanish, and Portuguese distribution deals.)

By summer, Kaurismäki will have finished *A Match Factory Girl*, the third film of the trilogy begun with *Shadows in Paradise*, continued with *Ariel*, and "dedicated to the memory of Finnish reality." Next is *I Hired a Contract Killer*, promoted as "an Ealing Studio–style B movie about a man who wants to die but is too 'yellow' to end his suffering," to be made in London. (As Kaurismäki jumps from genre to genre — mixing and matching, suffusing each with a mixture of Nordic angst and sardonic hipsterism — he begins to suggest less a Finnish disciple of Fassbinder and Wenders than a postmodern Ingmar Bergman.)

This month's Cannes Film Festival should see the premiere of *Leningrad Cowboys Go America*, a rock 'n' roll road movie featuring the Finnish band Sleepy Sleepers (distinguished in publicity photos by their alarming, pointed Woody Woodpecker pompadours) and shot in the U.S. Since Kaurismäki's Finland suggests an exotic version of the American Midwest, it should be interesting to see what he does with our landscape. "Somewhere in the tundra, in no-man's-land, lives the worst rock 'n' roll band in the world, an outfit with no audience and absolutely no commercial potential," he explains. "And so they decide to bury their national identity and go to the United States, where people will eat any kind of shit. This film is the story of their journey over the ocean and through the continent, a story of seamy bars and honest folk in the backyards of the Hamburger Nation. Ugly actors, good feelings. Yeah." Here's a voice for the nineties: the beat goes on. (**Available on video:** *Ariel* and *Leningrad Cowboys Go America.*)

—*J. Hoberman*

Mira Nair

∎

SALAAM BOMBAY (1988)

The rich, saturated colors of *Salaam Bombay* often illuminate dark compositions. The images are brimming with hue and with humanity. This is the special vision that director Mira Nair brings to her first fiction feature, after a preparatory background of making documentaries.

Nair and her cinematographer Sandi Sissle have an uncommon appreciation of visual beauty: They combine a refined, aestheticized sensibility with a respect for truth. Imagination is used to transform reality, making the squalor of contemporary Bombay, where the underworld of poverty and drugs is on the surface, intoxicatingly vivid.

In a style that recalls the ethnographic filmmaker Robert Gardner, Nair looks at the street life of Bombay as though discovering the complexity of nature and ritual. It's a form of exoticism, but without condescension. Nair is thrilled by the world she sees, curious about the personal exchanges that take place between ragamuffins, pimps, and prostitutes.

The understanding Nair elicits is the result of strenuously maintained intelligence and pride. It's conceivable that an ordinary Indian filmmaker would give in to the pathetic, sociological stereotypes about the Third World, as Hector Babenco did in the Brazilian *Pixote*. But Nair tells the story of Krishna (Shafiz Syed), a ten-year-old boy abandoned by the circus he works for, as a way of representing an open response to modern urban India.

Krishna's plan to scrounge enough money to return home to his family puts him in the innocent-victim role of Dickens's Oliver Twist. It's plain that Nair utilizes this literary association as a way of conveying clearly the truths of her ethnic world. She combines European consciousness and formality with a personal sense of commitment and identification.

A lot of what happens in the plot of *Salaam Bombay* conforms to previous tales of street youth scuffling and wonderment, like Truffaut's *The 400 Blows,* Satyajit Ray's *Aparajito.* Many observations that would seem pathological in other contexts—such as the induction of a young girl (Chandra Sharma) into a brothel; the haggling network of drug-addict guttersnipes led by Chillum (Raghubir Yadav); the unorthodox, fractured family of a pimp-prostitute and daughter—take a poetic shape and effect. The excellent performances help, but Nair's trained appreciation for the truth makes it all cohere. You can see the awesome vistas of the crowded city as the factual foundation for Nair's foreground projection of irresistibly sympathetic emotions: Krishna's alert, wide-eyed wonder recalls a brown Rita Tushingham, and Nana Patekar as Baba the pimp suggests a muscular, debauched Prince.

Nair shows affection and understanding for all her characters, not just the children. This links the film to Renoir's own India-set *The River,* while the teeming street scenes suggest *Black Orpheus* and the ever-present threat of hostility and violence resembles the grotesqueries of *Los Olvidados* and the poignancy of *Shoeshine.*

All these films mix, subconsciously, with the experience of watching *Salaam Bombay.* It's the emotional and political work of film-literate women—Nair, Sissle, and the screenwriter, Sooni Taraporevala. They have filtered their ethnic backgrounds through their cultural education. One can feel all the great European social fictions these women have been exposed to as well as their passionate sense of social responsibility. The high contrasts of intelligence and emotion, education and nature, fiction and documentary, are as vivid and startling as the film's chromatic scale. It's an extraordinary film with a miscegenated look and feel. The film's final reference to *Children of Paradise* is meant as rueful cross-cultural irony.

—*Armond White*

RECOMMENDED FROM ENGLAND

What's happening in recent British movies? Channel Four is happening—the innovative network that helped fund more than half the films in this chapter and almost all of the directors at one point or another in their careers. Channel Four is particularly sold on the spunk and poetry of working-class life—the spunk of *Wish You Were Here,* the poetry of *Distant Voices, Still Lives.*

Opposite page: scene from *The Krays.*

It supported the early careers of filmmakers Pat O'Connor and Chris Menges, whose best political films based in class and family are *Cal* and *A World Apart*. It has funded the traditional British strengths: the writing and acting of playwright-directors like David Hare (*Wetherby*), actor-directors like Kenneth Branagh (*Henry V*), and such writing-directing teams as Dennis Potter and Jon Amiel (*The Singing Detective*). Its spirit supports the attitude: who needs American punks and gangsters if we can have our own in *Sid and Nancy*, *The Krays*, and *The Long Good Friday?*

Jon Amiel

■

THE SINGING DETECTIVE (1986)

It's easy to understand why *The Singing Detective,* now being released as a film, was such a TV milestone on the BBC in 1986 and on PBS the following year. Most TV is linear, two-dimensional, naturalistic. Dennis Potter's partly autobiographical six-hour miniseries is richly layered as few entertainments are. It braids noir pastiche, psychodrama, flashbacks, parody, autobiography, tough hospital comedy, and a complex rendering of the problematic nature of existence. There's singing—lots of forties tunes, with "Peg O' My Heart" the theme song, and a team of doctors dropping their professional postures to launch into a zany chorus of "Dry Bones" during a consultation in a ward. There's also detective work, but not the kind you'd expect. Most of it takes place inside the protagonist's head.

Just as the songs are never employed for facile nostalgia, the detecting is more than the usual gumshoe-in-a-trenchcoat-under-a-streetlight stuff. It's tied to a hospital patient's journey to wholeness. It necessitates the peeling away of layers of immobilizing guilt and aborted identities by a writer of cheap detective fiction named, wickedly, Philip Marlow. He lies in a ward, crippled by psoriasis, trying to stay sane by plotting another caper for his fictional alter ego, a private eye who also sings with a dance band. The real and imagined characters collide with hallucinatory exuberance in his head, as he sorts himself out, coming to grips with his miserable boyhood in a village near the Welsh border, where his usual way of spending time was to sit high up in a tree vowing to put things right when he was an adult and a detective.

Guilt, rage, pain, paranoia, and yeasty imagination as a tough, playful saving grace rifle the lexicon of pop imagery and at times loathe it as they haunt the writer, especially one image of a nude female corpse being hauled out of the Thames over the side of a boat under the Hammersmith Bridge. As anyone who saw Potter's *Pennies from Heaven* (the BBC miniseries, not the Hollywood film) and *Dreamchild* knows, he's an expert at invoking pop icons, then turning them on their heads. Here, they trigger pain, not nostalgia; and one is keenly aware of how much of *The Singing Detective* is delivered through the aching eyes of the magnificent Michael Gambon in the haunted, haunting title role.

Marlow's trapped, suffering, acid-tongued presence is of course much more involving on the large screen, and so is the use made of darkness by Potter and his excellent director, Jon Amiel. The supporting cast is almost uniformly excellent, too, especially Lyndon Davies as Marlow's dewy, affecting ten-year-old self. The proof of the power of *The Singing Detective* is that only the first part, when most long pieces come on strong, requires work to sit through. Once you've cottoned on to its disjointedness, though, it becomes increasingly involving. Except for boxy sound, the production values can more than bear the increased scrutiny invited by big-screen exposure. If anything, the increased depth of field, color, and texture enhance them.

In the end, *The Singing Detective* is about the mystery of self, the way we make our own world minute by minute, the way we learn, along with Marlow, that the world consists, in Potter's words, "of all clues, no solutions." At first, Marlow's stricken eyes, unable to block the eruptions of memory and anguish, are almost unbearable, scrambling frantically for release from a body that seems a cruel prison of red, scaly, inert flesh. His ultimate liberation, when it comes, seems satisfyingly earned. The makeup work here is, by the way, expert. It's not for the faint of heart. But then *The Singing Detective* is not for the dim of wit. It's as impressively multilayered as anything on any size screen during the eighties. It's one of the reasons TV is making the film world nervous.

—*Jay Carr*

Kenneth Branagh

■

HENRY V (1989)

No Shakespearean play has been served so well on film as *Henry V,* which has twice been masterfully adapted to the screen by superb British actors making memorable directorial debuts.

Kenneth Branagh's 1989 version and Laurence Olivier's 1944 production are more than good re-creations of theatrical experiences: They're great movies, intelligent spectacles with action, humor, and drama. Although they share a common source, the movies differ profoundly in look, style, and interpretation. Having just watched them back-to-back, I can recommend them as a fascinating double bill.

Henry V is the story of a young British king proving his mettle—and his right to rule—against overwhelming odds on the battlefields of fifteenth-century France. In the decisive—and incredible—engagement on the field of Agincourt, 10,000 French were slain and only twenty-nine British were killed, according to Shakespeare. (The actual numbers were, historically, not far off.) It was one of those epochal moments, a last gasp of medieval warfare: The clumsy, armored knights were no match for Henry's mobile archers. And the muddy field was sloppy and treacherous, so the French troops who slipped and fell were trampled by the onrushing horde behind them.

Olivier's film, shot on the eve of the Allied invasion of Nazi-occupied France, was conceived as a morale booster. It is a celebration of patriotism and British valor dedicated to the pilots of the RAF, who fought the Battle of Britain in the air before the United States entered the war. Branagh's version, reflecting contemporary attitudes, is a grim, antiwar film.

Neither movie is merely war propaganda. Their attitude toward war colors—literally—the vision of both Olivier and Branagh. Olivier's *Henry V* is shot in glorious Technicolor, which emphasizes the medieval pageantry of the French and British courts and rituals of combat. Branagh's version has colors so muted it often looks monochromatic.

Olivier was thirty-six, a graceful and sophisticated matinee idol, a flier with the Naval Air Arm, newly sobered and matured by war. Stylistically, his movie acknowledged its theater roots—yet is not a filmed record of a performance.

It reminds its audience of the continuity of the British empire during the glory days. Olivier begins his movie with an aerial view of Elizabethan London (an evocative set, in miniature), then zooms in on a production of the play at the Globe Theater. When Henry and his troops set sail for Calais, the watching-a-play mode is abandoned and the movie shifts smoothly into conventional drama.

Branagh, like Olivier, uses an actor—the Chorus—to set the scene and comment on the action when necessary. His *Henry V* opens with the Chorus hurrying past movie gear on a darkened sound stage. But Branagh gets these preliminaries over with quickly; he intends his film to be realistic. Branagh's battle of Agincourt is fought, as was the real one, in rain and mud. And, at twenty-seven, Branagh looks like Henry must have, a feisty young man finessed by hotheads and opportunists into going to war, an instrument as well as a wielder of power.

There's a psychotic intensity in Branagh's performance that keeps us, and his courtiers, on edge. His voice is steely, and he speaks low and naturally, rather than mellifluously, like Olivier. And his filmmaking mirrors his performance: There's a nervous, edgy momentum to the camera movement, editing, and music.

The self-serving bishops who persuade young Henry to go to war to reclaim his hereditary throne are Machiavellian scoundrels, not clowns whose maneuverings are so transparent that the groundlings guffaw at them in Olivier's version. In Branagh's somber film, not even the comic characters are true clowns but are weary, tragic figures; and the French king is sad and fatalistic, but not ridiculous and feeble, as he is in the Olivier version.

Both versions conclude by doing justice to the play's abrupt and seemingly tacked-on romantic ending, in which the victorious warrior king woos the king of France's daughter. It's a charming, amusing scene: The macho Henry suddenly stops grinding his teeth at his enemies and making pep talks to his army and speaks of love to the spunky Katharine. It's a scene from out of the blue, but Shakespeare knew what he was doing: The violence ends with a kiss, a reconciliation, and hope.

In these two films, you'll find astonishing displays of how ideology can transform the same basic material into radically different experiences. Each version is a vivid demonstration of the influence of the time and the context in which it was made.

—*Joseph Gelmis*

Alex Cox
■

SID AND NANCY (1986)

Given the subject matter of *Sid and Nancy,* Alex Cox's rock-and-roll tragicomedy about Sex Pistol Sid Vicious and his American-groupie girlfriend Nancy Spungen, whom he almost certainly stabbed to death in their room in the Chelsea Hotel on October 12, 1978, what's startling about the movie is how much fun it is. Oh, the last chapter is harrowing, all right, and Cox pulls no punches when it comes to depicting the pair's heroin addiction or the scuzzy desperation that just about defined their lives. Though no one was actually there to see if Sid killed Nancy, the film makes it more than plausible that the stabbing was, in some ghastly way, the culmination of their love affair, a last-ditch act of compassion that sent her to a place where she'd be happier. (A few months later, Sid, while out on bail, died of a heroin overdose following a failed suicide attempt.) Yet I don't think *Sid and Nancy* would mean much to us if it were just the story of two clinging junkie lovers who fulfilled their destiny by dragging each other into the grave. The movie shows us how the couple's cracked self-destruction grew out of their immersion in the London punk scene of the mid to late seventies, a scene that negated everything—politics, sex, "feelings," perhaps life itself—yet offered a dark catharsis to those who gave themselves up to it. And the beauty of the movie is that it lets us revel in the abrasive, fuck-everything exuberance of punk even as it shows Sid and Nancy's lives sliding into the gutter. With its inhumanly quick rhythms and terminal nihilism, punk (at least in its early, safety-pin-through-the-cheek days) was the first school of rock whose participants declared war not just on authority but on themselves. *Sid and Nancy* is the first postmodernist rock-rebellion fable, a movie in which rock's long-standing credo—the flaunting of youth's elemental passions—has turned in on itself, becoming maniacally destructive yet exhilarating in a gonzo new way. Alex Cox's triumph is having captured both punk's freedom and its decadence, and by the end of the movie you're convinced the two are inseparable.

Of course, many serious-minded music fans (and, for that matter, Cox himself) regard Sid Vicious as having been a degraded aberration within the punk world. In a sense they're right. Yet I think Cox's showbiz intuition goes deeper than that. On some level, he understood that to make a true punk movie, one had to confront not simply the angry, moralistic, I-am-an-anarchist part of the culture but the Sids and Nancys, the goofball anarchists who were really just selfish, pissed-off kids, who pushed nihilism to the edge, who were to the rest of punk what punk was to the rest of society. Sid and Nancy incarnated one side of the punk spirit in all its infantile, body-hating fury. They went too far, and punk was about going Too Far, about shattering the codes of society and of rock and roll itself. It was about lust and fear and hatred and apathy in forms that weren't "redeemable." Sid Vicious was warped, maybe a little crazy, but saying he didn't embody the essence of the punk spirit is like saying Gary Gilmore didn't embody the essence of armed robbery. Like Gilmore, Vicious tugs at our imagination because he trashed the boundaries of the way even a bad boy was supposed to behave.

Sid and Nancy is dark, all right, but it's also a bristling youth comedy, and Cox (who wrote the screenplay with Abbe Wool) moves it to a jacked-up tempo that's like a cinematic equivalent of punk's forced rhythms. Sid (Gary Oldman), a tall, gangly carouser, stands with a permanent, flaccid tilt that makes the sheer act of his walking around unexpectedly graceful. His spiky black hair, which explodes atop a pale-white, handsome face, isn't just another ugly punk 'do — it's fitting somehow, as if he were a teenager from Hell. Nancy (Chloe Webb), a middle-class Jewish girl from New Jersey, is an aggressively tawdry peroxide blonde with good legs and a permanently congested voice — part wheeze, part whine — that's essentially the voice of an overindulged seven year old wailing to her mother that she wants her candy *now;* she sounds like a more scabrously sarcastic version of Gilda Radner's Lisa Leupner after one too many 'ludes.

From the opening scene, Cox's refusal to let these characters be too ingratiating gives the film its subversive comic charge. Here are Sid and his buddy Johnny Rotten (Drew Schofield) stomping through the London streets and smashing the front window of a Rolls-Royce. Here's Johnny the professional scourge popping his zits in the mirror in the midst of a social gathering or trying to squash Nancy's groupie ambitions by sneering, "None of us fuck, see? None of your free-hippie-love shit here!" Here's Sid carrying on dart wars in the pub, spray-painting the hallway of an apartment building he happens to be sauntering through, smashing a journalist over the head with his bass guitar, or carving into his own chest with a razor blade. Here's Nancy bringing Sid around to meet her grandparents in the States ("Don't swear, Nancy," scolds her grandmother; "Fuck you, grandma!" comes the reply), the wasted Sid slurping from a bottle of peppermint schnapps at the dinner table. And here are the Sex Pistols, performing their blistering gigs — sadomasochistic rock rituals in which the musicians spit beer on their fans, who return their affection by giving them the finger.

Most rock movies invite us to live vicariously through their rule-flouting characters. Cox stages these vintage punk antics with so much authenticity that we share the mad, iconoclastic thrill of it all yet also stand back, aghast. Nothing is sugar-coated or made too innocent; there's always some feral skinhead bashing something in the background, and we get a heady jolt of how nasty — and funny — the original punks were, how their behavior was shocking and ticklish at the same time. What attracts you to Sid is that he's so utterly . . . himself; he's so genuine — that is, unpremeditated — in his stuporous narcissism and his willingness to destroy anything in his vicinity, notably his own body, that there's something almost pure about him. The British theater actor Gary Oldman looks the part. His face has the same angular planes as Vicious's, the same thin, goofy-protruding lips, and he gives Sid a blankly happy stare that neither lets much out nor takes much in. The phrase "out-of-control" is such a cliché that it's rare to see a character who truly is. Robert De Niro's Johnny Boy was one; Oldman's Sid is another. His beautifully intuitive performance establishes that Sid isn't so much angry or cretinous as lacking some essential moral-cerebral center that censors out random destructive impulses. He's like a kid without a superego, and since he's utterly indifferent to pain, it's understandable that Nancy would be drawn to him; her life has clearly been one long self-hating wallow. They first get together after some joker in a pub tosses a glass of beer in her face and sends her scurrying out in tears. Cox is ingenious. The way he stages this moment, it's not just another bit of random rowdiness — Nancy's bitter humiliation is the first unguarded emotion he's let seep into the movie. Sid runs out to talk to her, and she's in misery, clawing a brick wall with her fingernails. When he asks if her hand hurts, and she says yes, he says, "So does this," and calmly whams his forehead into a brick wall, bouncing off it like a rubber mallet. The exchange is like a ten-second encapsulation of the punk ethos: genuine frustration and anger transmogrified into head-slamming rebellion — into theater. From that moment on, we know these two are going to get along.

Nancy, who turns Sid on to smack practically the day they meet, isn't treated as a corrupting influence; he's already an alcoholic, and he's the one who first asks her to buy drugs for him. The first hour of the movie weaves their relationship into a furiously compact overview of the Sex Pistols' career, and though the scenes zip by at a pace better suited to viewers in the know, Cox gets in pretty much everything: the early London gigs; the delirious riot-concert aboard a boat on the Thames the day of the Jubilee celebration, complete with bobbies cracking heads; the semidisastrous tour of the American hinterlands, which finished off the band. The concert scenes, which the actors performed live under the supervision of former Sex Pistols bassist Glen Matlock, feature most of the songs off *Never Mind The Bollocks Here's The Sex Pistols* (which is to say, some of the greatest rock and roll ever recorded), and the music helps give the film its thrilling, headlong pulse. Sid may not know how to play his bass, but he's an inspired spotlight-grabber, and his career with the Pistols comes off as the most ludicrously speedy star-is-born saga in history. It seems over before it's begun, which is exactly what it felt like in 1977 — and, with hindsight, what the Sex Pistols' career ought to have felt like.

Cox gets in delicious satirical digs along the way, whether at the smiling, cowboy-attired audiences who showed up to see the Pistols as a freak-show novelty act or at a seventies-hippie record executive who sits next to Rotten on the tour bus and offers to sing him the "punk" song he's written. (It's a measure of how much Cox gets you on the punk wavelength that when this doofus starts singing about how "I wanna job, I wanna job, I wanna *good* job . . . one that satisfies my artistic needs," you want to be Johnny Rotten for a moment just to flash him the look of loathing he deserves.) As Rotten, Drew Schofield gives a more than serviceable performance, and he's quite good in the concert scenes, but I couldn't help feeling there was something miss-ing in his impersonation. His nastiness is too conventional — he lacks Rotten's calculation, his post-Warholian, malevolent gleam. David Hayman, on the other hand, contributes a masterful turn as the Sex Pistols' creator/manager, Malcolm McLaren, who stands in the back-ground like a fatherly evil genius, supervising the band's gripe sessions or discreetly encouraging Sid to vomit in public, for the cameras — all the while beaming a self-satisfied grin, as though the whole business were just terribly *amusing*. Cox understands how it took a savvier, older promoter like McLaren to see Sid's potential as "a fabulous disaster" and then exploit the hell out of it, or how it took the quintessentially stuffy BBC to goad the Sex Pistols into swearing on the air—a national psychodrama gone suddenly public.

Sid and Nancy's feelings for each other may have mingled disastrously with their heroin addiction, but what they had, at bottom (at least as Cox portrays it), was a conventionally obsessive love/hate relationship, and that's exactly what's moving about it. Without being sentimental, the film says that beneath the dope and despair and the whining selfishness, Sid and Nancy were all too human—that love is love, period. And since they found each other amid the hateful trappings of the punk world, in which the image of the dominatrix hovers as a kind of hellish sex goddess, the affair's underlying normality seems almost courageous; we can witness their self-destruction without feeling smothered by it. There's a stirring equality to the relationship: when Sid and Nancy are making out in an empty recording studio and she asks him to "kiss my toes," it's a dominatrix command, yet she purrs it out like a loving little girl—and Sid's compliance is a sign that she's not just a groupie to him. Nancy starts out as a wheedling, simpering joke of a character, yet Chloe Webb's performance slowly grows in emotional stature, much as Holly Woodlawn's did in *Trash*. The transatlantic phone call she makes to her mother, in which she begs for money as a "wedding" present to her and Sid (actually, she just needs it to buy drugs), is a classic scene. It says everything there is to say about the way burnt-out runaway kids despise their parents yet never get over them. Nancy the eager-beaver groupie tries to be manipulative, but she's really more inept than anything, and Webb plays her as a kind of dilapidated good-time girl. Sid and Nancy are soulmates; beneath their delinquent bravado, they move to the same slurry-voiced rhythm. When Nancy tries to keep Sid awake on the last night before the U.S. tour and he gets steamed and stalks out of the room, she sits there on the bed, desolate, and wails, "What about the farewell drugs?!" It's a priceless moment, at once hilarious and romantic. She really means it—she had her teenage heart set on shooting up together one last time.

The couple's downward slide parallels Sid's descent as a solo performer. He films the legendary "My Way" clip (which Oldman imitates to the letter, right down to Sid's brilliantly scary, eyeballs-into-the-forehead parody of high sentimentality) and then tries to launch a concert career managed by Nancy, who's a lot more enthusiastic about the whole business than he is. Although the movie suggests that Sid had some charisma as a singer (the scene in which he does "Something

Else" at Max's Kansas City is an electric little performance), he's too wasted to pursue it; soon he's crawling around on stage barely able to form the words, until everyone in the joint (including Johnny Rotten) has walked out on him. By now, Sid and Nancy have moved into a dingy little room at the Chelsea, and Cox both slows the movie down and bleeds the comedy out of it, a daring move that pays off. Sid and Nancy reach their druggy point of no return when the curtains go up in flames and they just lie there in bed, too zonked to care; punk's militant disregard for self-preservation has become a form of slow suicide. And as the two sit in that pathetic, darkened gray-green room, trying to recall the last time they screwed or scraping up money for their cheerfully sinister dealer, who pops in from time to time like a messenger from the Twilight Zone, we're hit by the realization that Nancy is slowly goading Sid into doing her in — her need to leave this world is almost sexual. (At the time, there were rumors of a love-suicide pact.) Sid and Nancy are busy destroying their bodies, but in another sense they simply lie around until there's nothing left to do but die.

As hopelessly grim as all this sounds, *Sid and Nancy* is one of the most liberating movies in years. It's a cautionary tale in the best sense, in that it offers the spectacle of two people succumbing to their worst impulses (in this case, *very* bad impulses) yet refrains from passing judgment; watching the film, we share in the very downward-spiraling fantasy of punk imperviousness that led to their dead end. Sid and Nancy may not have known better than to trash themselves, but they were nobody's victims, and it's our investment in the most squalid aspects of their lives that finally redeems them for us. The two start out as jokes; they end as tragedies — but human ones. And in the film's concluding scene, an epiphany that dares to place both characters on the side of the angels, we can look at these two blasted remnants of a punked-out society and see that, yes, they loved each other, and that was enough. In all likelihood, it was more than either of them ever asked for.

— *Owen Gleiberman*

Terrence Davies

■

DISTANT VOICES, STILL LIVES (1988)

An autobiographical film about growing up in a Catholic working-class family in Liverpool in the forties and fifties. Achronological glimpses of a traumatic family life, with particular emphasis on a funeral and two weddings. A collection of radio shows and nostalgic songs sung at parties and pub gatherings. A highly condensed, triple-distilled family album of faces and feelings organized around a few key locations. A series of emotional and visceral jolts whose brute power and intensity could not be conveyed by a conventional linear story. A seamless block of passionate memories defined by the beauty and terror of the everyday.

The problem with all these descriptions of *Distant Voices, Still Lives* is that though each is partially accurate, they only dance around the periphery of what is a primal experience; that they represent the shards of my attempts to describe the essence of a masterpiece that reinvents filmgoing itself.

The movie opens with the sound of thunder and rain followed by a radio announcer giving a weather report; then we see a frontal shot of the Davies house in the rain, and the mother (Freda Dowie) opens the front door to collect three bottles of milk. In a closer frontal shot inside the house, she calls up the front stairway to her three children to come down to breakfast ("It's seven o'clock"), then returns a moment later to call them again. The camera remains fixed on the empty stairway, though we hear the footsteps and voices of the children descending. A woman's off-screen, unaccompanied voice begins to sing "I Get the Blues When It's Raining" as the camera slowly moves forward, then turns right and makes a 180-degree pan to the closed front door, and the sound of the rain outside starts up again.

There's a dissolve to the same front door, now open to clear weather; a hearse slowly pulls up in front (as we soon discover, it's about ten years later), and another off-screen unaccompanied female voice begins to sing "There's a Man Goin' Round Takin' Names." This continues over a dissolve to the children, now grown — standing with their mother as if posing for a portrait in front of the photograph of the father, which the camera slowly approaches as the figures in the foreground step away.

Another shot shows the four remaining members of the family entering the hearse, followed by a dissolve to the same family posing again, in the same spot, this time for Eileen's wedding. Over the sound of rain again, Eileen says, "I wish me dad was here," to which Maisie replies, "*I* don't." There's an off-screen aural flashback to the quarrel between Maisie and her father about wanting to go to a dance, a quarrel that a moment later we see as well as hear. Maisie is scrubbing the floor in the cellar, and the brief scene ends abruptly with the father tossing coins on the floor and then beating her with a broom.

Nothing in the above summary can convey the weight, the flow, or the impact of these sounds and images; they create a world of their own that is so self-sufficient and distinct from other film experiences that it is impossible to say whether this sequence — or any subsequent ones in the film — is proceeding quickly or slowly. We all know that "real time" and "film time" aren't the same thing, but the emotional time of recollection that this film works with is so singular that it doesn't seem to bear much relation to what we ordinarily mean by either of these temporal registers. The film as a whole lasts only eighty-five minutes, but the density that it conveys is closer to that of a three-hour epic.

English kitchen-sink realism is not a mode for which I have much affection, and while there might be some academic relationship between *Distant Voices, Still Lives* and such hallmarks as *This Sporting Life, Saturday Night and Sunday Morning, The Loneliness of the Long Distance Runner, A Taste of Honey,* and *Georgy Girl,* I think that much of the comparison winds up confusing a lot more than it clarifies. "Technically" speaking, Davies's film is closer to avant-garde, and its emotional impact bears more relationship to the films of directors like John Ford, Yasujiro Ozu, Robert Bresson, Charlie Chaplin (whose *Limelight* theme is a played by Tony on the harmonica), Kenji Mizoguchi, and Leo McCarey.

It isn't surprising, however, to learn that Davies loves Hollywood musicals, and that a shot of black umbrellas in the rain in front of a movie theater is included as a specific reference to *Singin' in the Rain,* the first film he ever saw. (The same shot pans up to posters advertising *Love Is a Many Splendored Thing* and *Guys and Dolls,* and the following shot is a pan across a large audience watching the former — the tearjerking theme song is heard off-screen — that finally settles on the weirdly lit figures of Maisie and Eileen sobbing uncontrollably.) Though an independent British feature, *Distant Voices, Still Lives* ultimately harks back to an era in Hollywood filmmaking when strong emotions could both be expressed and elicited more directly, without shame, and the role of music throughout the film remains firmly within this tradition. Indeed, not only the off-screen songs cited above but also countless tunes sung by major characters, at parties and in the local pub, command a surprisingly yet justifiably large amount of the film's attention.

For this reason I strongly disagree with several critics who have tried to draw a parallel between Davies's use of period pop songs and the ironic musical excursions in works by Dennis Potter such as the miniseries "The Singing Detective" and the movie and series *Pennies from Heaven,* which use these touchstones in an antithetical way. Potter treats these songs as lies, and he uses them to point up their falsity in relation to the wretched lives of his characters. The bitterness and defeatism of his vision are not very far from the positions assumed toward soap opera by Douglas Sirk in the fifties and by Rainer Werner Fassbinder in the seventies—a form of cynicism that can only deal with strong emotions and sentimentality by placing them (implicitly in Sirk, explicitly in Fassbinder) inside quotation marks.

Davies, like Chaplin and McCarey, regards strong emotions and sentimentality as authentic and even indispensable tools for understanding and dealing with life. This can be seen in the sequence when Davies's use of pop music is superficially closest to Potter's. One of the daughters, as a little girl, is watching her mother, seated on a second-story windowsill, wash the outside of the window. A cut to a reverse angle shows the mother washing the same panes from inside the house, and as the camera slowly tracks toward her, we hear Ella Fitzgerald singing her dreamy version of "Taking a Chance on Love." The song continues over an abrupt jump-cut to a different scene downstairs, in which the father grabs the mother, dragging her and beating her to the floor (out of frame), repeatedly screaming "Shut up!" in response to her cries of pain. Then, as the song continues to the end of the chorus, another jump-cut shows the mother's bruised face in profile, followed by a slow pan down to her bruised arm as she polishes the furniture.

If the same action and the same recording were used in a Potter film, it seems likely that the Ella Fitzgerald record would be heard only after the mother's beating and that the mother would lip-synch the lyrics— that is, the ironic truth of the song's lyrics ("Here I go again . . .") would be used to ridicule both the pathos of the mother's predicament and the inadequacy of those lyrics in dealing with that predicament. Davies, on the other hand, clearly loves both the song and his mother, and uses the record as a hymn to her courage and endurance — a hymn that in no way reduces the unbearable harshness of the beating; it allows us to hear the song's lyrics in an ironic fashion without leading us to feel any contempt for them or for feelings they represent. It is an extraordinary moment, and without trying to suggest that this comparison necessarily invalidates Potter's gallows humor when he uses similar materials, I think it can be argued that the sheer rawness and power of the emotions expressed here by Davies are outside of Potter's range entirely.

In general, Davies's sympathy and empathy rest more with the women in the film than with the men. This becomes particularly apparent in the pub scenes in *Still Lives,* when the marriages of Eileen, Maisie, and their friend Mickey (Debi Jones) register as tragic curtailments of their solidarity with one another and of their innocence, which is represented by many of the songs that they sing together, including not only such white-bread standbys as "Buttons and Bows," "That Old Gang of Mine," and "Bye, Bye, Blackbird," but also such ethnic favorites as "My Yiddisher Mama" and "Brown-Skinned Girl." Implicitly the husbands of Eileen, Maisie, and their friends are perceived as somewhat muted variations of their father. ("They're all the same," Mickey remarks at one point. "When they're not usin' the big stick, they're fartin'.")

There's nothing intellectual about Davies's approach to his characters, and no analytical grids are placed over them, although the restriction of the action to a handful of recurring locations — mainly the front of the Davies house, the stairway, the living room, the children's upstairs bedroom, the stable where the father works, a hospital ward, the local Catholic church, and the nearby pub — circumscribes our glimpses of the characters to only a few special areas, which intensifies the film's highly elliptical manner.

The film's emotional continuity grants Davies an enormous stylistic freedom, and he takes full advantage of it without ever compromising his vision. The awesome strength of *Distant Voices, Still Lives* as a whole is that it makes every moment necessary and indelible as well as beautiful. I have every reason to believe that years from now when practically all the other new movies playing are long forgotten, it will be remembered and treasured as one of the greatest of all English films.

—*Jonathan Rosenbaum*

David Hare

■

WETHERBY (1985)

A man kills himself among strangers. They never knew who he was, and they do not know why he chose to die. A man dying among strangers is like a tree falling unobserved in the forest. Death, especially suicide, requires resonance from those who knew the living person before it can be assigned its proper meaning. That is why *Wetherby* is such a haunting film, because it dares to suggest that the death of the stranger is important to everyone it touches—because it forces them to decide how alive they really are.

The movie begins with a woman who is living a sort of dead life. Her name is Jean Travers (played by Vanessa Redgrave); she was once in love with a young man who went off to fight the war and was killed. He was not killed gloriously, but stupidly, while getting involved in someone else's drunken quarrel, but he was dead all the same. As the movie opens, Jean has been teaching school in the small town of Wetherby, where her life is on hold. She doesn't walk around in a state of depression, she does have friends, she is a good teacher, but she is not engaged in life because she put all of her passion into the boy who died so many years ago.

One night she throws a small dinner party. Everyone drinks wine and sits around late, talking. One of the men at the table, John Morgan, sits mute all evening and finally makes a short speech about pain and love and honesty that sounds as if every word were written with his own bitter tears. The next day, John Morgan comes back to Jean's house, sits down for a cup of tea, and kills himself. A funny thing comes out in the investigation: John Morgan was not known to any of the people at the dinner party. Apparently he invited himself.

The film moves from this beginning into an examination of the people who were touched by the death. In addition to Jean, there are the Pilboroughs (Ian Holm and Judi Dench), the local constable (Tom Wilkinson), and a young woman (Suzanna Hamilton) who knew the dead man. Some small suspense develops for a while when it appears that Jean spent some time upstairs with John Morgan during the evening of her party—but that, and many other things, seem to be dead ends.

The movie flashes back into events in Jean's youth, and she is played as a young girl by Joely Richardson, Redgrave's daughter. There is an innocence and tenderness in those early scenes, as young Jean and her boyfriend kiss and neck and make promises, and as Jean gradually realizes that she is looking forward to marriage but he is much more excited by the prospect of putting on a uniform and going overseas. He goes overseas, and in some ways this movie is about the fact that Jean has become a middle-aged woman still waiting for him to come back.

Wetherby was written and directed by David Hare, who also wrote the film *Plenty*. Both films are about women who were never able to fully live their lives after what happened to them during the war. I admire both films, but I found *Wetherby* more moving, because the heroine of *Plenty* was essentially a disturbed woman using her war memories as a crutch, and Jean Travers is a whole and healthy woman who only needs to give herself the permission to live. I left the movie thinking that was the lesson she learned from John Morgan. Hoping so, anyway.

— Roger Ebert

David Leland

■

WISH YOU WERE HERE (1987)

In the town on the southern coast of England in which David Leland's *Wish You Were Here* is set, the grayness of the sky and the sea and the weathered storefronts seems more than simply an attribute of weather. The people seem grayed-out, too, as if a sprinkling of ash had settled over them.

The only splash of color is Lynda (Emily Lloyd), a robustly perverse teenager who's the daughter of the local barber (Geoffrey Hutchings). In contrast to her surroundings, everything about Lynda is bright, vivid, alive. When we first see her she's flying down the boardwalk along the beach on her bike, wind in her hair, the hem of her skirt stuffed up into her underwear so that a generous portion of leg is displayed. The color of the skirt—a cotton-candy pink that matches her lipstick—is perfect. It brings out the glow in her cheeks and makes her look lusciously ripe, like a peach about to fall from its branch. Whizzing about, she seems winged, untamable.

On the handlebars of Lynda's bike is a periwinkle-colored pinwheel, spinning freely as she breezes along, and that's her symbol. Set in 1951, the movie is about a young girl who uses sex to shock, and how these shocks, liberally administered, keep her spirit alive. As Lynda, Lloyd is a raging malcontent — an angry young brat. But her anger doesn't manifest itself in conventional ways. (Nothing in her personality does.) Instead of fevered rants, Lynda peppers her targets with a nonstop barrage of hilarious obscenities. These blistering attacks aren't contrived; they just bubble out of her, and it seems never to have crossed her mind that she might censor herself. Not censoring herself, in fact, is what keeps her going; it's what keeps the pink in her cheeks.

Lynda has a genius for the profane mot, and she uses it indiscriminately. And as we learn from flashbacks, she started early. On the day her father returned from service in World War II, she shocked him and his guests by whispering a pungent aside to her little sister, who dutifully reported it to the others in the room. (This is after greeting him on the front steps wearing a gas mask.)

But Leland establishes a deep empathy with his heroine, and, seeing through the little girl's eyes the look of suffocating boredom on her mother's face as she portions out the tea and biscuits, we can immediately see the purpose served by her rebellious, briny outbursts. The mother died when Lynda was only eleven, and it's to this lost parent, the one who might have been able to understand her and help her through her troubles, that the film's title is addressed. And Leland never lets us forget that there's something broken rattling around inside Lynda, and that this, in part, is what's making all the noise.

Leland is particularly shrewd about this aspect of Lynda's character. He doesn't attempt to rationalize her behavior or categorize her problems. And when she wags her bum at the doctor and her father, or perches on top of an office desk in the bus depot where she works to give the workers a look at her new knickers, he doesn't attempt to romanticize her into a symbol of liberated nonconformity. That he leaves open the possibility that there may be more than a touch of pathology in Lynda's behavior, that her free-spiritedness is not only the mark of a rebel but also a sign of deep resentments and anger, gives her greater dimension. Making her a heroine would diminish her, so Leland gives her to us straight — mixed-up, antagonistic, self-centered, captivating.

Leland never loses his comic footing either. He has a real talent for sexual slapstick. In common parlance, Lynda might be called a problem child. Her father, not knowing how to deal with her sexual frankness, thinks there's something wrong with her, that she's genuinely afflicted. This assumption gives occasion to the film's funniest scene, a visit to a wild-haired psychiatrist who questions her, in a modulated, dispassionate manner—the manner of a biologist inspecting a slide—about her filthy mouth. Nervously chain-smoking and trying desperately to retain the upper hand, the doctor prods her to run through the alphabet, starting with A ("best place"), listing all the dirty words she knows. Appearing to take the bait, Lynda complies, but quickly turns the tables on him, and the scene escalates into a sublime bit of psycho-burlesque, a sort of Freudian "Who's on First."

Wish You Were Here is really Lloyd's movie, and the prospect of finding a performance like the one she gives here is one of the main reasons why people still get excited about going to the movies. As Lynda, Lloyd is so fresh that she seems almost downy, newly hatched. This is her first movie role—she was just sixteen when the film was made—but she's so sassy and unaffected that you'd think she's been acting for years.

Lloyd's features are open and inquisitive and just slightly unformed; she hasn't quite grown into her face yet, and that makes her perfect to play Lynda. Lloyd has an instinctual vivacity on screen, a natural glow.

Everything about Lynda is rooted in sex, but without being overtly sexual. At sixteen, Lynda is still a mere chick, but already she appears to have taken in a lot. In the actual sense, Lynda has almost no experience of sex. But she's an eager initiate. Too impatient to wait for a boy she's interested in to ask her out, she skips the usual courtship protocol and tells him, flat-out, she fancies him and does the asking herself, flashing a bit of thigh as enticement.

Still, though she's clear-eyed about sex, everything seems brand new to her. Just walking along in spiky heels and seamed stockings, she's swept away by the sensations she feels, and the idea that she can provoke men by twitching her hips makes her nearly dizzy with excitement. She's revved up about life, about sex, about whatever's around the next corner, and she can't wait to get started.

Lynda's got energy to burn, but there's no outlet for it in her musty, provincial hometown. Her naughty high jinks are her only form of self-expression, and one night in the back yard, filled with profane abandon, she improvises a bawdy dance set to the music of her favorite obscenity, and fully unfurled, she seems truly inspired — the Isadora Duncan of smutty outrage.

It's Lynda's rambunctious, self-destructive exuberance — the sense that she's a genuine misfit — that makes this more than a routine coming-of-age story. Lynda is a rich, spirited creation, and Leland's work here, as both screenwriter and director, is sharp and evocative. This is his first time out as a director — he's been known previously as the screenwriter on *Mona Lisa* and *Personal Services* — but he shows here as he did in his earlier scripts that he knows how to make sexual tension funny.

In addition, in the scenes involving Eric (Tom Bell), a bookie and the operator of the local cinema, Leland shows a talent for capturing the pathos in squalor. When the older man — Bell is in his fifties — seduces Lynda, the movie turns abruptly down a darker, creepier road, but Leland retains control, and he shows how Eric's bluish stubble, his slitted, blurry eyes, and the slummy disarray of his flat above the movie theater combine to form a picture of a rake come to ruin.

The moody second half of the film, though, isn't as compelling or original as the first. For a good portion of it, Lynda plays Lolita to Eric's Humbert, but though it's clear that she is impatient with her younger, less experienced partners and could use a more practiced hand, it's not immediately obvious what this spectacular girl sees in her seedy scarecrow lover.

The ending, too, which presents Lynda as a triumphant heroine in the style of the postwar movie stars whose stories she watched at the local theater, is not entirely satisfying. Not that you want to see her come to a bad end. But as it stands, the finish is too conventional, too pat.

These are quibbles, though. *Wish You Were Here* is an impudently sexy comedy, and both the director and his young star have made auspicious debuts. Even the neatness of the ending doesn't really throw you off much. For this film, Leland has used some of the details from the early life of Cynthia Payne, the famous madam who served as his model for *Personal Services,* and you want her to prevail, to cut loose. It would be too much of a letdown to leave Lynda grounded and sorrowful; after watching her crash rudely, blithely about, upsetting tea rooms and scandalizing stuffy matrons, the last thing you want is for her to pay for her eccentricity.

— *Hal Hinson*

John Mackenzie

■

THE LONG GOOD FRIDAY (1980)

The Long Good Friday is a rabidly engaging British gangster movie, brimming over with moxie. It presents a radical vision of the Western world governed by an unholy trinity of Money, Lust, and Murder. This violently hyperbolic film mixes the iconography of Christianity and the underworld, and in so doing makes the extraordinary suggestion that dying capitalist societies can only be saved through the economic adventurism of criminal overlords.

Harold Shand, the East End London crime boss at the center of the movie, is more than the antihero; he's the anti-Christ, uniting barbarians and bourgeoisie in a Pox Britannica. Surrounded by "legitimate" help, from cops to city councillors, Shand single-handedly controls a criminal empire built on casinos and prostitution. His "gun moll" is a vision of class, aptly named Victoria, who once played lacrosse with Princess Anne. Shand plans to buy up the moribund London dockyards and renovate them for the 1988 Olympics. His call for the "new London" wickedly echoes the New Testament's call for the "new Jerusalem." Yet on the very Good Friday that Shand is trying to seal a financial partnership with the American mafia, somebody kills one of his right-hand men, attempts to murder his mother and blasts one of his businesses to smithereens.

Classic gangster heroes, like Little Caesar, fought their way out of the faceless mob only to be punished in the end for their brutal ambition. In forties and fifties *film noir* like *The Killers,* the absurd dangers of a godless universe forced criminals to make perilous, often fatal existential choices. The case of Harold Shand is different. Throughout the movie, he struggles to control his animal urges and personal prejudices, acting like a proper, civic-minded businessman. (His clear distaste for drugs stems from their social destructiveness.) In his own left-handed way, Shand runs a well-lubricated system of conglomerate capitalism. If he's doomed, it's because in the modern world of volatile social expectations and terrorism, the system has broken down. In an ironic sense, Harold Shand becomes a sacrificial lamb for all our Western sins: after Shand, the apocalypse.

The movie is viciously funny and enthralling—except when director John Mackenzie and writer Barrie Keeffe underline their points with a thick Magic Marker. Shand's gang has such obvious fascist potential that it's overkill to have him brag about his syndicate as "the best organization since Hitler put a swastika on his jock-strap." More damaging is the moviemakers' deliberate obfuscation of the double-dealings, presumably to indicate how fragile the laws of cause and effect are in today's chaotic societies. Their narrative puzzles are fatiguing even when they're comprehensible.

But Mackenzie, Keeffe, and the cast blast right through their own pretensions: scene by scene, this is by far the most brillant British movie since *The Duellists.* The film never allows us to exult in Shand's violence. There's a shocking, blasphemous edge to the imagery, even when it *doesn't* involve a car being blown up in a church courtyard or a security guard's hands being nailed to the floor. As Shand's civilized facade succumbs to the beast within, the sting is satiric as well as visceral. When Harry hangs key underworld associates upside-down from meat hooks in an abattoir hoping to find a traitor in his ranks, he could be conducting his own parody of crucifixions.

In Harold Shand, the moviemakers create a completely charismatic character. He is more than a natural force: he's *un*naturally forceful—a nuclear dynamo. In his introductory shot, Shand blasts through an airport terminal like a guided missile. Shand is an infuriating, admirable, uproarious mixture of born leader and organization man, bigot and progressive industrialist, enforcer and behemoth. He's caught between his atavistic reflexes and his messianic aspirations. Surprising a black pimp in bed with a white prostitute, he sneers, "beauty and the beast," but a few minutes later, he laments the decrepit ghetto streets because "these people deserve something better."

Though Shand wants to integrate England into contemporary Europe, the man himself remains as obdurately cockney as fish and chips. The filmmakers refuse to dilute their native culture and in the process bring to the screen both corrosive visual textures (I loved a pub called the Lion and the Unicorn) and an argot full of poetic panache. Happily, the film opens with a glossary: the whispering word *grass* means *informer,* the penile *ponce* means *pimp.* The faces in the cast have none of the usual "Masterpiece Theatre" pallor: the film is filled with scene stealers, including comedian Dave King as an obsequious, crooked cop; P. H. Moriarty as the scarily scarred thug called Razors; and super-smooth Paul Freeman (Belloq in *Raiders of the Lost Ark*) as one of Shand's most hedonistic henchmen. Even that aging cult actor

Eddie Constantine brings the right touch of dinosaur conviction to the role of the chief mafia envoy.

But the make-or-break part is Harold Shand, and Bob Hoskins goes all the way with it. Known to American audiences only from the original BBC miniseries "Pennies from Heaven" and from small roles in films like *Zulu Dawn,* Hoskins has a beefy, dark, intense physicality that in England has made him "everybody's favorite cockney actor" (to quote London's entertainment guide *Time Out*). Hoskins is built like a bowling pin and has a voice like a pinsetter's, a perpetual soft growl with a sandpaper roughness, even at its most tender. Hoskins can do more with his cheeks and jowls than Richard Nixon: he can make the curve of his teeth look as ominous as a crossbow, and he uses his eyes as gun sights. Hoskins has the gift usually attributed to American, not English, actors—of getting so far inside a character's skin that we seem to be witnessing vivid behavior rather than bravura performance.

When I spoke to Hoskins by phone during his brief publicity trip to New York, he said that he and writer Keeffe had worked together to base Harold Shand on a "real heavy mob type." Director John Mackenzie, he said, always insisted on authenticity: "In that scene when Shand gives out the guns, a lot of those guys are the real thing. I started shouting at some of me mates in one scene, and the gangsters told me to stop shouting. 'These guys *know* who you are,' they told me.

"What we wanted to make," Hoskins continued, "was a *really* British gangster film. There've been a lot of attempts, but they usually end up as impersonations of American films. It was the same with the French—they had to develop their own personalities, first with Gabin, then with Delon and Belmondo. Anyhow, we didn't want to do an impersonation. That's why we spent so much time with real gangsters."

Financed by Lord Lew Grade, *The Long Good Friday* was produced without interference. But once it was completed, said Hoskins, "all these executives and producers starting telling Lord Grade that if he released this film, he'd lose his knighthood." When Lord Grade tried to recut the film and sell it to television, producer Barry Hanson rebelled and started showing it on the sly to critics and industry reporters. Hoskins takes partial credit for the film's eventual release: "I met Eric Idle at a party and thought he must have a pot of money after *Life of Brian,* so I got him to take a look at our picture." The Monty Python-George Harrison organization, Hand Made Films, acquired the movie from Lord Grade, and it was an immediate critical and popular success.

In his famous essay, "The Gangster as Tragic Hero," critic Robert Warshow observed that most crime films present "a steady upward progress followed by a very precipitate fall." But according to Hoskins, the creators of *The Long Good Friday* consciously wanted to reverse the structure. "Our guy *starts out* as a tycoon," says Hoskins, "but we carefully worked out his progression in reverse, so that the character reverts to the way he was when he was working his way up there. I mean, by the end, I'm actually whacking around me bird!"

Shand's "bird," Victoria, is played by the sensual Helen Mirren, who in no small performing feat manages to control most of her big mug's detonations and even, in a wrestling feint, calm him to a standstill. "I've known Helen for years," said Hoskins. "The great thing was, she had as much control over the gangsters on the set as she did over me!"

Surprisingly, there's been little backlash to the film's violence and irreverence. "Any conservative pressure would have come from Lord Grade," explained Hoskins, "and he's made such a fool out of himself, he was in no position to put the pressure on. You've got to remember the British film industry nearly *sank* when Lord Grade spent $40 million making *Raise the Titanic!* That movie just went under, but we took off as soon as we got into the theaters. Anyone who would have tried to bugger us up would have looked very foolish."

—*Michael Sragow*

Peter Medak

■

THE KRAYS (1990)

"Shall I tell you my dream?" asks the hushed voice of a mother telling a bedtime story. "I dreamed I was a white swan. And I had a beautiful egg. And inside it there were children's voices. And they were mine. And they were wonderful. And they were perfect."

At the beginning and end of *The Krays*, Ma Kray (Billie Whitelaw, in a magnificent performance) tells us this dream of how her twin boys might change her from an ugly duckling into a beautiful swan. We see her vision of the white swan that's graceful, beautiful, wonderful, and perfect.

Her boys did not turn out to be wonderful and perfect. They turned out to be Ron and Reggie Kray, notoriously sadistic gangsters who ruled London's East End during the sixties. What's wonderful is this film's way of turning their true-life story into an eerie, touching, weirdly funny, ultimately tragic fable about parenthood.

Like all parents, Ma Kray is determined to make her children repeat what went right in her life and not what went wrong. She's not fond of her layabout husband and bad provider dad, and she's not alone in that opinion. The twins' Aunty Rose (Susan Fleetwood), Aunty May (Charlotte Cornwall), and Grandma (Avis Bunnage) are always sitting in the kitchen bad-mouthing men. They're like four huge, formidable, matriarchal Mack trucks.

Ma has another son, Charlie (Roger Monk), but she's most mesmerized by the twins. It gives her a strange thrill that they don't just mirror her hopes, they mirror each other. When young Ron takes sick and doctors foolishly insist on putting him in the hospital, all four of the family's women march in to pluck him back. "'E's pinin'," they explain. "'E needs Reg."

Obviously, no good will come of all this. When the movie cuts from the twins as children to the twins as adults, they're taking over the East End's protection rackets. To prove they're better men than their dad and grandpa, they do their dirty deeds with unusual weapons: three-foot sabers. How far should they go when it comes to gangland terror? Looking into each other's narcissistic stares, their mutual answer is: all the way. Real brothers Gary and Martin Kemp of the pop group Spandau Ballet were cast as the adult Krays. Playing Ron, the psychopathic bro, Gary uses his flat cobra head to suggest that his character really enjoys carving a bloody smile in someone's face. Though he likes slapping his male moll for leaving clothes on the bedroom floor or playing with his pet snake, he's happiest when he's with Reg.

That's why he's not thrilled when Reg marries timid, pretty Frances (Kate Hardie). Playing Reg, the gentler bro, Martin Kemp softens his pudgy python jaws whenever he casts adoring looks at his new wife. He fills their home with 365 beautiful dresses, one for every day of the year, and can't understand why she isn't happy. He gives her everything his mother hoped for and never got from her husband and father. And he can't understand why her response is a shrieking nervous breakdown when she's caught on a staircase between the twin wall-to-wall mirrors that trap her in the cage of her own infinitely repeating images.

Equally original and compelling is the film's way of trapping Ron and Reg inside the frame of their mother's dreams for them. It's a frame that says: The more you love your children, the more you may turn them into hateful people. The more you want them to repeat what you think is good, the more they may repeat something worse than you can imagine.

In their well-known Piranha Brothers sketch based on the Krays, Monty Python milked sardonic wit from the twins' despicable behavior. Screenwriter Philip Ridley and director Peter Medak begin there, but go much further. There's ironic humor, bitter fairy-tale justice, and a full sense of tragic fate when, at different points in the story, Ridley and Medak offer condolences to Ma Kray's dream. Their twin offerings — each twenty feet high, each the best money can buy — are two floral funeral arrangements spelling out in soft, white chrysanthemums the words *FRANCES* and *MOTHER*.

— *Kathy Schulz Huffhines*

Chris Menges
■
A WORLD APART (1988)

A World Apart, which is set in Johannesburg in 1963, is one of the most vibrantly intelligent political films I've ever seen. The director, Chris Menges, refuses to melodramatize. He denies us the familiar satisfaction of conspiracies unveiled and heroes in triumph, and so the movie doesn't provide the primal narrative pleasures of thrillers like *Z* or *All the President's Men* or *Silkwood*. It's subtler and harder-hitting. And after a while, I began to feel almost grateful for the lack of melodrama — began to realize, in fact, that the hollow "uplift" of just about every leftist political film of the past twenty years has generated its own form of complacency. Beneath the swift, glancing surface of *A World Apart,* one senses a finely controlled anger, anger at an injustice so vast that merely to describe it is to court frustration and defeat. Yet the film's outrage comes through in a special way. It's less about the struggle against evil than it is about the contours of evil—about the way a system like apartheid actually works, and about how it shreds the lives of everyone caught in its machinery.

The film is based on the true story of Ruth First, a white upper-middle-class journalist who, along with her husband, Joe Slovo, became deeply involved in the antiapartheid movement. Slovo, who was wanted by the government because of his activities in the outlawed Communist party, went into exile, and First was arrested and incarcerated under the Ninety-Day Detention Act, the infamous measure that allows the regime to imprison anyone in the country for three months without trial. Many of the blacks detained under this act never made it out of prison alive. Ruth First, on the other hand, was subjected to abusive interrogations and threats, let out, imprisoned again, and finally released. She wrote a book about her experience, entitled *One Hundred and Seventeen Days* (the amount of time she spent locked up), and then moved her family to London.

A World Apart is her story, and it's also her daughter's story. The daughter, Shawn Slovo, who was thirteen when all this happened, wrote the screenplay; and the film, on the surface at least, is about how her mother's imprisonment tore the family apart. It's about Slovo's own confusion and fear and resentment, and how she came to understand and accept her mother's devotion to the antiapartheid movement, in part by realizing she herself wanted to join the struggle. Yet if the film were merely concerned with the relationship between a driven, courageous white woman and her teenage daughter (they're called Diana and Molly Roth here, and played by Barbara Hershey and Jodhi May), it might not have much resonance. With riveting detail, *A World Apart* shows us the link between what happens to the Roths and the systematic oppression of South African blacks. For the way Diana Roth's family comes apart is a direct echo of what the South African government has done to blacks, tearing husbands from wives, parents from children. The film doesn't pretend the indignities suffered by the two races are morally equivalent—something the clunky, miscalculated *Cry Freedom* came close to suggesting. Instead, it dramatizes how a regime like South Africa's rules not simply through intimidation and murder, but by insinuating itself into the fabric of daily life.

Menges, the gifted British cinematographer (*Local Hero, The Killing Fields, The Mission*) making his directorial debut here, has a background in documentaries, and he's drawn on it extensively. *A World Apart* doesn't look or feel like other movies. It has a clean, objective surface, with the point of view shifting at a moment's notice. The effect is almost pointillistic, and I think I know exactly why Menges chose it. He's made a political movie in which nothing has "symbolic" value, in which everything, from Diana's clenched-jaw determination to the oppressive tactics of the Afrikaners, comes in three dimensions. His visual style, which is so naturalistic it's dazzling, allows us to feel we're eavesdropping on actual lives — to feel (in a way most political movies don't allow us to) that these could be our living rooms, our fears.

Diana Roth's whole activist personality — tight, self-righteous, obsessive — isn't explained, and it doesn't need to be. The antiapartheid movement isn't something you dabble in. Anyone more serene couldn't take the pressure, and indeed, Diana has an ulcer, and not much energy for her children. Yet she isn't closed off to them. She and her husband have said almost nothing about their work, because their daughters are too young to understand. And that's where the tension between Diana and the thirteen-year-old Molly develops. Molly is no longer too young. She's starting to think like an adult, to realize that the bits and pieces of liberal-humanist thinking she's assimilated from her parents have become the basis of her own outlook. Yet she's still living in a child's pampered, insulated universe. And so she resents her mother for not being there. She's too sensitive not to realize the political struggle is a valiant one, yet what she really feels is, "How could this mean so much to you? How could anything be more important than *me?*" By letting us see Diana Roth through her daughter's confused, even embittered eyes, the film divorces her activism from nobility, makes it seem less than noble, yet necessary.

The film shows us the subtlety of the South African regime — how it has tentacles that reach everywhere, with the participation of many of the leading citizens. Early on, the police burst into a birthday party Diana has thrown for herself. They're searching for her husband, who's already left the country, and though the blacks at the party quickly get rid of their drinks (it's illegal for whites to serve them alcohol), the way Menges shoots the scene you sense the obscene, unbridled strength of these policemen with their growling dogs. Later, the oppression becomes more personalized. Molly goes to visit her best friend, whose father has decided he doesn't want his girl playing with the daughter of a known communist. In a harrowing scene, he grabs Molly, forces her into his car, and takes her back home. The violence of his outburst suggests the primitive, patriarchal undercurrents of the whole regime.

So do the patronizing reassurances of Diana's interrogators, who tell her, "We happen to have respect for women in this country!" Gradually, we're given more and more drastic sensations of violation and claustrophobia. That's the film's theme: the way a fascist government disrupts private life — both literally (it can put anyone it wants to in prison) and spiritually (the mere threat of imprisonment casts a pall of impotence over everyone in the country).

At first, Diana seems to endure her detention quite well. She faces questioners defiantly, refusing to name names of resistance fighters, implying she's too strong to crack. But they know how to get to her. The police are hostile as a matter of course; even their Afrikaans accents sound repressed, inhuman — no sympathy in those dry, cracked vowels. Muller (David Suchet), a manipulative officer who tries to win Diana's trust, brings her a couple of books. Her cramped cell had been getting to her, and she grasps the books as though they were magical objects. Then, after another uncooperative interview, the books are taken away, and Diana throws her cot all over the cell in frustration. By putting us inside her semideranged state, the film begins to get at the horrid power of a regime like South Africa's: that what it brings out in those it oppresses (mostly blacks, but some whites, too) are feelings of denial and injustice so intense they become a quiet form of madness. Authors like Ralph Ellison and James Baldwin have conjured such feelings, but few movies have touched them, and A World Apart begins to provoke a slow, empathetic anger.

There are scenes Menges stages with the purity of a master. Early on, the Roths' longtime housekeeper, a black woman named Elsie (Linda Mvusi), sits next to Molly's bed and teaches her the black national anthem. The scene sounds corny, yet Menges uses it to establish the warmth that exists between these two, to highlight their intimacy and their differences; it's all done with a beautiful quietude. The black characters aren't on screen as much as Diana or Molly, but they're fleshed out, and they stay with you. As Solomon, Elsie's activist brother, Albee Lesotho has a gap-toothed radiance. When he stands in a church, reminding the parishioners that they didn't always live in shantytowns, his wounded pride stings. And later, when Elsie receives word that Solomon has been killed by the police, Linda Mvusi has one scene that's a tour de force. She reacts with a sorrow so complete that no consolation is possible, yet this never belies her absolute lack of surprise in hearing the news. The scene is really about the inevitability of tragedy for black South Africans, and their awareness of that.

Barbara Hershey is somewhat limited by the filmmakers' conception of the character. We see Diana's workaholic, rabble-rousing side, but not a lot more. And when Hershey speaks to the children, the actress is gentle (and strong) enough to let us see that she could have given the character other dimensions. Still, her singlemindedness is part of the point, and Hershey makes Diana's very toughness—her lack of fear—enthralling. As Molly, Jodhi May seems to capture the most private moments of a sensitive teenager. This is the kind of smart, cautious young character who can't help wearing her feelings on the outside. The most impressive thing about May's performance is that she stays true to Molly's sulky narcissism, even as she shows you the innocence behind it. In form, *A World Apart* is a coming-of-age movie in which Molly learns that having beliefs and actually living by them are two different things. It's a deceptively simple lesson, and what gives it its power is that the characters must call on resources most of us will never have to think about using. In the final frames, Menges leaves us with raw, existential images of rock-hurling rioters, and the film makes explicit what it's been saying through the character of Diana Roth all along: that the cry for human freedom is a primitive, instinctive one—a "cause" that subsumes all others.

—*Owen Gleiberman*

Pat O'Connor

■

CAL (1984)

Inarticulate and furtive, skinny Cal (John Lynch) and his thickset father crouch over cigarettes in the Belfast home where they're the only Catholics on a Protestant street. On the sliver of Lynch's face, the shards of their broken-off conversations, and the lives of one man and one woman, director Pat O'Connor builds a moving, ironic story about Ireland's entrapping circles of guilt and death. It's the best movie yet about the Troubles because it's the only one that turns the big political issues into a human story as personal and intimately scaled as an expiring sigh.

Nineteen-year-old Cal's own troubles begin when he lets himself be pushed by bullying IRA friends into driving the car when they shoot a Protestant policeman in his home. Then, when he runs into the victim's wife Marcella (Helen Mirren) at the town's library, he slowly, even unknowingly makes her the center of his life. He acts from a need that's as mute, dumb, and blindly insistent as a plant trying to root itself. All he knows is that he needs to be where Marcella is—watching her, following her. Eventually he becomes her friend and lover as she offers him first her dead husband's clothes, then his wife's body. Inch by inch, Cal is pushing himself toward a new life, hardly realizing that he's trying to understand his guilt in Marcella's loss by learning how to love Marcella herself.

He does this in a darkening landscape, heavy with irony. In the book that's the basis of his adapted screenplay, novelist Bernard McLaverty openly despises and satirizes both the Protestant gang that burns down Cal's father's house and the IRA crowd that loves violence for its own sake. More insidiously, McLaverty shows how generations of hatred have deadened personal feelings. There's the dulled routine of Cal's unloving life with his father. Then, there's Cal's discovery that Marcella had ceased caring for her indifferent policeman husband: even his guilt turns out to be hollow. Finally, there's the deadly joke of Cal's fate—walking into the trap of his IRA connections by simply walking into the town library.

O'Connor, in his first feature film, improves on the novel. Creating quietly realistic scenes between Cal and his father (Donal McCann) and adding drama to the final tangle with the IRA, O'Connor gives the story a satisfying emotional flow. He's attentive to the sad solidity of his Irish landscape—something McLaverty tended to see in terms of dirt and muck. And his director's eye is apparent in every frame—each locked in darkness but lit by the inner glow of a lamp, a face, a flash of water.

Most of all, though, it's O'Connor's way of drawing performances from his actors that counters irony by illuminating feeling and emotionally weighting the darkness. British actress Mirren is affecting as Marcella, a woman filled with tension and depth, imprisoned in drabness, in love with life. But first-time actor Lynch is the marvel. He's a curtain of lank hair and a pair of yearning, hurt eyes in a hollowed, knife-edged face. Lynch's floridly shifting yet realistic performance enlarges emotion while making it seem burdened and stifled as Cal stumbles toward his fate, in love with his own pointless guilt.

—*Kathy Schulz Huffhines*

RECOMMENDED FROM FRANCE

Beyond *Breathless* and *The 400 Blows,* France is the home of great documentarists: Chris Marker, Marcel Ophuls, and Claude Lanzmann. As everyone knows, it's a country that has been consistently good at finding all the threads in the sexual tapestries of charming pop entertainments like *Cousin, Cousine* or the pictures of more offbeat relationships in *Entre Nous* and *Monsieur Hire.* With *Jean de Florette* and *Cyrano,* French filmmakers are currently

Opposite page: scene from *Monsieur Hire.*

reaching broader audiences by making epics with the stars who can carry them and directors who take the time to make them work.

Claude Berri

■

JEAN DE FLORETTE (1986)

Shrewd, grasping, rich old Cesar Soubeyran (Yves Montand) and his simpleton nephew Ugolin (Daniel Anteuil) covet their neighbor's land. Each has his reasons, but they are not good enough. Not good enough, that is, to justify their terrible plot to force decent, innocent, intelligent Jean de Florette (Gérard Depardieu), his patient wife, and lovely child to sell their holdings at a distressed price. The idea is simple: the Soubeyrans stop up their well. Its execution is grim and protracted; they must silently stand by, offering sympathy but no practical assistance as Jean descends first to exhaustion, then to madness, finally to death as he tries to fight an extended drought with the few gallons of water he can painfully haul from a spring that is miles away over rugged mountain trails.

The time is some sixty years ago. The place is equally distant; primitive Provence in the south of France. And the questions are: why do the machinations of these villains grip us so vividly? Why does the fate of Jean and his family move us so deeply? Above all, by what means does this cruel tale of victimization — there is probably no other great movie that so relentlessly documents the meanness of the human spirit in action — manage to release in us, of all ironies, such a spirit of joyous welcome?

Partly it is a matter of emotional scale. This is not a movie of half-way measures. The wicked are irredeemably wicked. The good are unalterably good. And both qualities are played full-out. No one is permitted to slip into anything a little more comfortable and up-to-date, like ambiguity or absurdism. And no one is permitted to palely loiter among his half-formed thoughts.

Take Montand's Cesar, for example. His stride, his gesture, his voice bespeak implacable authority. Even his moustache reinforces the mes-- sage. It is not the adornment of routine villainy, crimped, primped, and striving for respectability. It is an ample, well-rooted assertion of masculine self-sufficiency, of immunity to the judgments, the hesitations of the common run of men. He possesses himself as confidently as he possesses his wealth and standing in the community. His antagonist, Jean, has toiled since birth under the curse of a hunchback. He knows all about burdens, yet even so, his endurance under the new ones heaped upon him by the Soubeyrans is almost unbearable to witness. When, at last, he cracks and curses God, Depardieu makes us feel not just the ground shifting under his feet, but under our own as well. As for Anteuil, bound to his uncle by blood, drawn to de Florette by compassion, he gives perhaps the most intelligent performance of obtuseness on record. And the most suspenseful. He is always taking his character up to the edge of understanding, then falling back into confusion.

So acting on the grand scale compounds our relief at slipping free of our postmodernist bonds, of regressing happily back to a time when our serious fictions were both sure and energetic in their morality. But such works require time and space to grow properly. Compression is an invitation to contrivance, forced coincidence, and melodrama. And director-adapter-producer Berri was not going to reduce this film to that level. Intending to do justice to the two-volume novel by Marcel Pagnol (which was itself a reworking of material he used in a commercially failed film), Berri pursued the rights to a book he loved for six years before Pagnol's widow relented to him. Determined to make a separate film of each portion of the novel simultaneously, and equally determined to show the passing of the seasons and the years, and their effects on his characters, he ended with the most expensive ($18 million) project in French film history.

The money, above all, bought him amplitude. His people are almost never isolated in a close-up that would falsely psychologize them or force-feed the audience's emotions. They are most of the time at some distance from the camera, framed against, dwarfed by, the abrupt Provençal landscape that formed them. The measured classicism of Berri's editing matches his camerawork. It creates a powerful illusion that we are watching them absorbing, internalizing, their region's changing light, weathers, and seasons in the same way they take in its harsh geology. Not one shot ever implies that they achieve even momentary dominance over this country and climate. Quite the contrary. Even when they are sheltered from its wayward tempers their comforts — even Cesar's — are at once crude and fragile.

The spaciousness of Berri's style is, of course, "old-fashioned," so much so that it strikes us with the force of the new. But its most important function is to link his films with two currently disused narrative traditions. One is that of the naturalistic novel, in which the insistence on locating characters within a detailed rendering of their world forces the reader to recognize that the seemingly minor incidents of ordinary life bespeak the workings of vast, elemental forces. The other, astonishingly enough, is Greek drama, in which the establishment of psychological intimacy with a character is irrelevant, since their destinies are determined not by themselves but by the circuitous workings of blind fate. Though naturalism is the controlling mode of *Jean de Florette,* audiences should bear the Greek model in mind when they see the story's conclusion, *Manon des Sources.* In it the eerily beautiful Emmanuelle Béart plays Jean's daughter, now grown up, and ready to take vengeance on her father's tormentors. To be prepared for it is one more reason to see *Jean de Florette.* But none are needed. It is a complete achievement in itself, a towering yet completely approachable accomplishment of the contemporary cinema.

—*Richard Schickel*

Claire Denis

■

CHOCOLAT (1988)

Chocolat barely has a plot—it's all theme. What makes it an impressive film is that the writer-director Claire Denis is devoted to thematics. She expresses the subject of racial difference photographically if not dramatically, sensually if not politically.

In the setup, a white French woman recalls her childhood friendship with the black African servant at her family's home in Mindif, Cameroon, in the 1950s. This memoir form accounts for Denis's enigmatic exposition; a great deal is unclear or misunderstood about the characters' encounters. This isn't a movie to teach the masses about brotherhood. The one thing that the protagonist—and Denis—is sure of is that a level of communication is missing between whites and blacks. That's why this emotionally hazy film is photographed and directed with such keen, piercing clarity. Its simplicity is a form of innocent recall.

The political fact of Equal But Different becomes Denis's aesthetic rule. The sensual, erotic tension keeps this political scheme from being insultingly effete. The first exchange between the girl France and the servant Protee (Issac de Bankole) is a cultural orientation: He spices her snack of buttered bread with black ants then relaxes in the sun while watching her eat it.

That scene demonstrates trust and power as the unconscious terms of the relationship. Unlike Shirley Temple and Bill "Bojangles" Robinson, France and Protee's relationship has not been rendered "natural" (or neuter) by social convention. It could be the first meeting of the races, like Robert Colescott describes in the margins of his "historical" paintings, where anything could happen and the balance of power might shift.

Throughout *Chocolat* (the press book says the title is French slang for "to be had"), Denis plays on the black-white, power-trust dualities in ways that test a viewer's allegiance to its characters. The imagery is full of contrast without bias: white stones line a road at night; a fade-out shot of Protee imperceptibly engulfs the viewer in darkness; and daytime shots keep the landscapes sharply defined. Cinematographer Robert Alazraki brings a moral simplicity to the color. Beauty is not charged up or romanticized like in *Out of Africa*. One perceives beauty through the serene plainness of things.

Certainly Denis's observation of racial conflict lacks urgency, but I don't think this is as terrible as the patronizing attitude of more violently aggressive films by liberal zealots. Her perceptions can be shrewd and complex as when a crazed ex-seminarian who visits France's family first taunts the white adults about their racial attitudes and then accosts Protee's servile complacency. Some in the audience cheered Protee's attack on his tormentor but I think they missed the point. Denis sees where even the accusation against Protee makes sense. She reads Protee's self-denying acquiescence. He's affixed himself to the white colonial household as none of the other Africans have. Protee is misaligned, deluded, the opposite of the group of black men who we see involved in a surreptitious meeting when France's father searches for a doctor during an emergency. There's a whole other world of black-African consciousness that Protee does not embody.

In *A Passage to India* the whites' relation to the colored colonies was expressed in exoticism and sexual arousal. Denis's passage to Africa has a highly sexual subtext (de Bankole moves with an actor's grace and confidence but he is also a strongly erotic figure) yet she mutes that old-fashioned, repressed "ethnography." She understands the sexualizing of the Other as a parasitism no different from economic exploitation. Denis underplays it so as not to overvalue it.

Denis's remoteness can be frustrating—she may have spent too much time in apprenticeship to Wim Wenders and Jim Jarmusch. One suspects that if she were more forthcoming about her feelings on racial conflict she might well seem banal—griping about the failure of interracial communication when she's really disturbed by thwarted miscegenation. So far she seems to have discovered her own very ponderable niche.

The adult France carries a scar burned into her palms years ago when Protee, feeling humiliated and hurt, failed to protect her. The scar that emblemizes her naïveté also shares Protee's pain. It's a mark of racism's two-edged sword.

—*Armond White*

Diane Kurys

■

ENTRE NOUS (1983)

The first impressive release of 1984, the French import *Entre Nous,* should establish itself as a strong contender for the Academy Award as best foreign language film. It should also elevate the young writer-director Diane Kurys, thirty-five, to the highest echelon of the profession. She's achieved remarkable assurance and impact across a broad range of dramatic challenges, from the evocation of elaborate historical and social settings to a painfully close, acute observation of the dynamics of family life, sexual intimacy, and marital misunderstanding. *Entre Nous* dredges up emotions and touches nerves as vulnerable as those agitated in the course of recent films like *Shoot the Moon* and *Smash Palace,* but it has an unpredictably novel, haunting account of incompatibility and alienated affections to tell. In addition, Kurys's narrative style and outlook seem distinctively revealing, witty, and intriguing, the reflection of powers of observation concentrated with exceptional clarity and sardonic ambivalence on feminine modes of longing, evasion, and duplicity.

Entre Nous is Kurys's third feature, and all have evidently drawn to a considerable extent on autobiographical material. Indeed, the impact of the fadeout is enhanced by a printed epilogue which suggests that the story grew out of traumatic, or at least perplexing, childhood memories, a little girl's witness of scenes of conflict and estrangement that ultimately separated her parents forever. However, since it's impossible to determine how much of the content represents effectively transformed autobiography and how much effectively interwoven fiction the first-person note doesn't so much authenticate the tangled, unhappy lives we've been following as add a stunning kicker. True or false, it's a peculiarly effective, wrenching way to sign off.

The original title, which may still be retained in France, was *Coup de Foudre,* which could be translated as "thunderclap" or "bolt from the blue" but also has the colloquial meaning "love at first sight," all of these possibilities being exquisitely appropriate to the subject matter. The chronicle of a marital mismatch that gradually unravels when one partner becomes romantically attached to someone else, *Entre Nous* proves a unique variation on this familiar theme. The obviously unconventional aspect is that the marriage-wrecking attachment develops between two women and seems undeniably lesbian, although it suits Kurys's purposes to portray the relationship as a bond of intimacy always lingering on the threshold of downright carnal affirmation. What's even more surprising in the long run is the highly individualized nature of the romantic triangle — a case so specific and detailed that it defies easy, clichéd exploitation as a touchstone of sexual perversity, betrayal, and ambiguity. Though certainly compelling and suggestive, the course of events depicted in *Entre Nous* doesn't follow the pattern of any other romantic triangle that springs readily to mind or confirm "typical" notions of even inverted infatuation. Kurys seems to have uncovered a love affair singular enough to transcend or at least confound generalizations about the characters.

The story begins with the arrival of Isabelle Huppert as Lena, a young Belgian refugee, at a concentration camp in the Vichy jurisdiction in 1942. She reluctantly and rather passively avails herself of an escape route offered by a young man, a recently demobilized French Legionnaire named Michel (Guy Marchand), who is attracted to Lena while serving on the chow line. He passes her a note proposing marriage, and Lena nods assent after a few moments of reflection, perhaps reassured by the remark of another inmate who advises her, "Phony marriages don't count—you won't have to stay together."

Lena receives an unexpected shock at the ceremony when she discovers that Michel is a Jew (so is she, evidently, but this point may be obscured until much later when we discover her mother's tombstone in a Jewish cemetery) and may offer less protection than she presumed. However, he assures her that as a French national, he's in no danger of deportation. She relents, invites him into bed, and they contrive to survive after the Vichy collapse by escaping over the Pyrenees to Italy, Michel heroically carrying Lena on his back during part of the trek.

Simultaneously, we're introduced to a second young bride destined to become an emotional casualty of the war—Miou Miou as Madeline, a glowing bundle of good humor and affection at her wedding. She's plunged into shock and despair soon afterwards when the groom, whom she seems to idolize, is caught in a sudden outbreak of fighting in the courtyard of their art school. He dies in Madeline's arms, and the young widow takes refuge with her parents.

The timeframe is advanced to the early 1950s, bridged by a beautifully looping, panoramic camera movement, and we rediscover both women in Lyon, where their paths cross at a school pageant. Lena and Michel have two daughters, Florence and Sophie, and have begun to prosper modestly on the strength of Michel's proprietorship of a garage. Madeline has remarried, fecklessly, uniting herself with a handsome bum of an actor named Costa (Jean-Pierre Bacri) who scrambles to make a living as a petty chiseler. They have a son, René, enrolled in the same school with Lena and Michel's girls, and he appears doomed to some kind of hideously neurotic future, the heritage of parents too narcissistic to treat him with anything but impatience and vexation.

It's evident from the outset that Madeline and Costa are users. Anxious to keep an appointment elsewhere, he presumes on Lena to keep an eye on René during the pageant. She's still considerably lingering there after everyone else has gone when Madeline finally shows up to claim her son—and indicate an immediate, peculiarly insinuating interest in the other woman. Miou Miou's performance suggests that something vital and spontaneous perished in Madeline when her young husband died, leaving this strangely subdued, calculating emotional predator to carry on an idle, amoral search for some kind of distraction or compensation. Always a bit of a sleepwalker herself and grateful rather than devoted to her husband, a hard-working vulgarian innocent of any pretensions of refinement, Lena responds to Madeline's overtures and cultivates a friendship so rich in feminine confidentiality and exclusivity that it eventually transcends her marital obligations and loyalties.

In a way it scarcely matters if Lena and Madeline get around to consummating their affair physically, because it's clear that they place loyalty to each other above any other considerations. On one occasion they're so wrapped up in thoughts of a mutual business venture that they lose track of little Sophie, who turns up hours later at Michel's garage, prompting him to fly into a baffled rage at his wife. On the evening the couples meet socially for the first time, Madeline whispers to Lena upon parting, "You're not made for each other," and the implication is pretty plain that there's now a nature worthy of Lena's devotion in the vicinity. Ultimately, the women collaborate in a number of little deceits to keep the menfolk conveniently oblivious, including an ingenious scheme that obliges Lena to steal from Michel to pay back a debt Costa can't make good.

There's an element of absurdity about these women that Kurys is keenly aware of and perfectly willing to satirize. They don't really have the means to cultivate the voluptuously feminine culture, revolving around a dilettantish absorption in fashion and "art" and sensual anticipation, that appeals to their mutually susceptible vanities. Madeline's pretensions are subsidized mostly by her doting parents and Lena's by her oblivious husband — at least until he sees the writing on the wall so plainly that he trashes the symbol of their alliance, a dress shop, and becomes the odd man out once and for all.

The encounters between Miou Miou and Huppert are suffused with hints of erotic anticipation that the characters never quite consummate. They aren't above deceiving their husbands with other men and then trading impressions of these adventures, but their own physical contact remains oddly teasing and tentative, an imitation of the clingy, touchy suggestiveness of the fashion magazines. Since it's difficult to believe that a filmmaker as modern as Kurys would choose to be coy on this point, it appears that the teasing behavior is integral to the conception, another sign of the peculiarly arrested emotional development of Lena and Madeline. Evidently, it also suits their pretensions to linger in a state of latent lesbian commitment.

It's unusual, to put it mildly, to find such a devious, hermetic feminine relationship being scrutinized by a perceptive woman filmmaker. Although Kurys doesn't spare the oblivious, foolish men from equally funny, clinical scrutiny, there's a fresh note of partiality in her eventual conviction that Michel is the most injured party in this squalid triangle. Even if Kurys believes that the mother has her reasons and can't help betraying her husband in this particular set of circumstances, her heart goes out to the abandoned, uncomprehending male—in short, to her father, if one can trust the autobiographical intimations.

This inclination is reinforced by Guy Marchand's performance, easily the most direct and sympathetic in the film. It's the embodiment of an intellectually and spiritually limited man who nonetheless operates on a nakedly exposed, sincere level of feeling. In part he's deceived by the nature of his wife's estrangement because of its sheer feminine elusiveness and delicacy—what working stiff can begin to account for such mysterious, irrational shifts of feeling? It's greatly to Diane Kurys's credit that she seems to appreciate how inexplicable and maddening such shifts can be and how much emotional grief they can provoke. *Entre Nous* explores previously unexplored terrain in the no-man's land that often separates male and female notions of love, honor, and duty. It appears to be an unusually compassionate but also tough-minded daughter's attempt to make sense of the terrible fact that her parents were ultimately irreconcilable strangers.

—*Gary Arnold*

Claude Lanzmann

■

SHOAH (1985)

Claude Lanzmann's *Shoah* is not simply the most ambitious film ever attempted on the extermination of the Jews, it's a work that treats the problem of representation so scrupulously it could have been inspired by the Old Testament injunction against graven images. "The Holocaust is unique in that it creates a circle of flames around itself, a limit which cannot be crossed because a certain absolute horror cannot be transmitted," Lanzmann wrote in a 1979 essay, ostensibly about the miniseries "Holocaust." "Pretending to cross that line is a grave transgression."

Shoah, which takes its title from the Hebrew word for "annihilation," doesn't cross that line, it defines it. For much of its nine and a half hours, the film seems formless and repetitive. Moving back and forth from the general to the specific, circling around certain themes, *Shoah* overwhelms the audience with details. For those who demand linear progression, Lanzmann's method may seem perverse—the film's development is not a temporal one. "The six million Jews did not die in their own time, and that is why any work that today wants to render justice to the Holocaust must take as its first principle the fracturing of chronology," Lanzmann has written. Although *Shoah* is structured by internal corroborations, in the end you have to supply the connections yourself. This film throws you upon your own resources. It compels you to imagine the unimaginable.

Length aside, *Shoah* is notable for the rigor of Lanzmann's method: the eschewing of archival footage and narration in favor of contemporary landscapes and long interviews (shown mainly in real time) with those who, in one form or another, experienced the Holocaust. "The film had to be made from traces of traces of traces," Lanzmann told one interviewer. Like the Swedish *Chaim Rumkowski and the Jews of Lodz* or the Hungarian *Package Tour,* two recent documentaries with less global perspectives on the war against the Jews, *Shoah* embodies a powerful and principled restraint. Like Syberberg's *Hitler, a Film from Germany,* it refuses to "reconstruct" the past, thus thwarting a conventional response and directing one to the source of one's own fascination.

Lanzmann, however, is scarcely as theatrical as Syberberg. In some respects, his strategy resembles that employed by Jean-Marie Straub and Danièle Huillet. The Straubs' 1976 *Fortini-Cani,* for example, punctuates readings by the Italian-Jewish-communist poet Franco Fortini with long ruminations upon sylvan vistas where, thirty-odd years earlier, the Nazis massacred a group of Italian partisans. Lanzmann shares the same conviction that the past surrounds us, that history is inscribed (if only through its erasure) on the present. In his "Holocaust" piece, he approvingly quotes the philosopher Emil Fackenheim: "The European Jews massacred are not just of the past, they are the *presence of an absence.*" This is why, while the vast Auschwitz complex has come to epitomize the Nazi death machine, *Shoah* emphasizes Treblinka—a camp built solely to exterminate Jews, a backcountry site razed and plowed under by the Nazis themselves in an attempt to conceal all physical evidence of eight hundred thousand murders.

The landscapes in *Shoah* are no less tranquil than those of *Fortini-Cani,* but they are haunted beyond the mind's capacity to take them in: Piney woods and marshy fields cover mass graves, a brackish lake is silted with the ashes of hundreds of thousands of victims. The camera gazes at the overgrown railroad tracks, end of the line, site of a ramp where a quarter of a million Jews were unloaded then hurried along with whips to their doom; it considers the postcard town of Chelmno where, one day after Pearl Harbor, the first Jews were gassed in mobile vans, using engine exhaust. What can be more peaceful than the ruins of Birkenau's snow-covered cremos and gas chambers? Of course, not every vista is so scenic. In one unforgettable camera movement, Lanzmann slowly pans down to the brown winter grass covering the rusty spoons and personal detritus that still constitute the soil of Auschwitz.

What binds these landscapes together are the trains that chug through Europe bound for Poland and the east. Lanzmann even managed to find an engineer who drove the Jewish transports. One of the film's recurring images is that of a train crossing the Polish countryside or pulling up in Treblinka station, with this very engineer, now wizened and bony as some medieval Death, looking back toward his invisible freight. In the argument of *Shoah,* these trains underscore the extent of bureaucratic organization needed to commit genocide, the blatant obviousness of the transports, and, finally, the existential terror of the journey. While the Jews were systematically deprived of water, the railroad crew was plied with drink. Through a translator, the former engineer tells Lanzmann the run was so harrowing the Germans were forced to pay a bonus in vodka. "He drank every drop he got because without liquor he couldn't stand the stench," the translator explains. "They even bought more liquor on their own . . ."

If landscapes give *Shoah* its weight, interviews provide its drama. Over and against these images of present-day Poland and Germany is the testimony of witnesses ranging from Jewish survivors to Polish onlookers to Nazi commandants. But the film is as filled with silence as with talk. Nine hours' worth of subtitles barely make a comfortably margined two-hundred-page book. Pauses, hesitations, are often more eloquent than words. The evident torment with which Jan Karski, a onetime courier for the Polish government, recalls two clandestine tours of the Warsaw ghetto carries an expressive charge far beyond his pained, halting description. Indeed, his face gray with agony, Karski breaks down and bolts off camera before he can even start.

Moreover, words are belied by expressions. Among the most scandalous aspects of *Shoah* are Lanzmann's interviews with the Polish residents of Chelmno and Treblinka. Although there are exceptions, their blandly volunteered memories and perfunctorily offered concern ("It was sad to watch—nothing to be cheery about") are almost more damning than the casual antisemitism ("All Poland was in the Jews' hands") the interviewer has little difficulty in provoking. Real malice only surfaces in tales of "fat" foreign Jews "dressed in white shirts" riding to their death in passenger cars where "they could drink and walk around" and even play cards. "We'd gesture that they'd be killed," one peasant adds, passing his finger across his throat in demonstration. His buddies assent, as if this macabre signal was itself an act of guerrilla warfare directed at the Germans.

If the sequence induces the unbearable mental image of trains run by drunken crews, packed to overflowing with a dazed, weeping human cargo, careering through a countryside areek with the stench of gas and burning bodies, jeered at by peasants standing by the tracks, this and more are corroborated by the surviving Jews: "Most of the people, not only the majority, but 99 percent of the Polish people when they saw the train going through—we looked really like animals in the wagon, just our eyes looked outside—they were laughing, they had a joy, because they took the Jewish people away."

As for the Nazis, it's hard to know which is worse, the pathetic evasions of the avuncular Franz Grassler, onetime deputy comissioner of the Warsaw ghetto, insisting that the Jews knew more about the final solution than did their jailers, or the affable, expansive Franz Suchomel, an S.S. *Unterscharführer* at Treblinka, expressing a grotesque camaraderie with the people he was killing. Among other things, *Shoah* precisely details the means by which the Jews were compelled to participate in their own destruction. Meanwhile, the testimony of Suchomel and others, such as the former head of Reich Railways Department 33, demonstrates that genocide—by which the Nazis proposed to have the Jews vanish *without a trace*—posed incredible logistical difficulties, solvable only by a modern, mobilized bureaucracy. It is here that the language of problem solving takes on a hallucinative unreality. Suchomel allows that at its peak, Treblinka "processed" twelve thousand to fifteen thousand Jews each day ("We had to spend half the night at it"), a train-load of victims going "up the funnel" in two or three hours. Unlike at Auschwitz, prisoners at Treblinka were gassed with engine exhaust. "Auschwitz was a factory!" Suchomel explains. "Treblinka was a primitive but efficient production line of death."

You watch this in a state of moral nausea so strong it makes your head swim. Nor does Lanzmann ease you into the flow. *Shoah* opens at the site of the Chelmno death camp, with one of the film's few narrative voice-overs observing that of the four hundred thousand Jews who were sent there only two survived. (Later we meet them.) The film's second part begins with another sort of horror, Suchomel singing the Treblinka anthem:

> *Looking squarely ahead, brave and joyous,*
> *At the world,*
> *The squads march to work.*
> *All that matters to us now is Treblinka.*
> *It is our destiny.*
> *That's why we've become one with Treblinka*
> *In no time at all.*
> *We know only the word of our commander,*
> *We know only obedience and duty,*
> *We want to serve, to go on serving,*
> *Until a little luck ends it all.*
>   *Hurray!*

Each morning, he explains, the newly arrived Jews selected for slave labor were taught the song: "By evening they had to be able to sing along with it." (Even now I can't get this idiotic martial melody out of my head. In Jean-François Steiner's *Treblinka,* it is reported that, after the day's work, Jewish laborers were compelled to stand at attention and repeat these words for hours — as well as sing the anthem as they marched.)

Lanzmann's most detailed interviews are with former members of the *Sondercommando* — the Jews who were kept alive at Treblinka and Auschwitz to stoke the annihilation machine. "We were the workers in the Treblinka factory, and our lives depended on the whole manufacturing process, that is, the slaughtering process at Treblinka," one explains. Only the naive or the pitiless can call them collaborators. In a sense, these men hyperbolize the dilemma of Jewish survivors in general — it is one of the Holocaust's cruelties that every Jew who survived is somehow tainted. One woman who managed to weather the war hiding in Berlin describes her feelings on the day that the last Jews in the city were rounded up for deportation: "I felt very guilty that I didn't go myself and I tried to escape fate that the others could not escape. There was no more warmth around, no more soul . . . [only] this feeling of being terribly alone. . . . What made us do this? To escape [the] fate that was really our destiny or the destiny of our people." A terrible fate, an absolute isolation are ideas that recur in *Shoah* again and again.

If the Nazis are all too human, the survivors are as mysterious as extraterrestials. What is one to make of the urbane, ironic Rudolf Vrba smiling as he describes cleaning the bodies out of the gas chamber, or the beseeching eyes of Filip Müller, survivor of five liquidations of the Auschwitz special detail? (His relentless discourse — an account of undressing corpses, shoveling them into the cremo, witnessing the last moments of thousands of Jews, some knowing, some not — is delivered in a tone of perpetual amazement, as though always for the first time: "It was like a blow on the head, as if I'd been stunned.") Unlike other accounts of the Holocaust, *Shoah* deliberately minimizes acts of individual heroism — to have been a Jew in Hitler's Europe was to have had the most appalling kind of heroism thrust upon you. "I began drinking after the war," the grim, noble-looking Itzhak Zuckerman, second-in-command of the Warsaw ghetto's Jewish Combat Organization, tells Lanzmann. "It was difficult. Claude, you asked for my impression. If you could lick my heart, it would poison you."

People have been asking me, with a guilty curiosity I can well understand, whether *Shoah* really has to be seen. A sense of moral obligation is unavoidably attached to such a film. Who knows if *Shoah* is good for you? (One hopes, probably in vain, that reviewers will declare a moratorium on the already debased currency of movie-ad hype.) There were many times during the screening that I regarded it as a chore and yet, weeks later, I find myself still mulling over landscapes, facial expressions, vocal inflections — the very stuff of cinema — and even wanting to see it again. The published text can in no way substitute for the film itself; the "text" of *Shoah* can only be experienced on the screen. On the other hand, the book is quite helpful in grasping Lanzmann's structure. For, if at first, *Shoah* seems porous and inflated, this is a film that expands in one's memory, its intricate cross-references and monumental form only gradually becoming apparent. One resists regarding *Shoah* as art — and, as artful as it is, one should.

Shoah transfixes you, it numbs you, and finally — with infinite tenderness and solicitude — it scars you. There are moments in this film when you simply can't bear to look at another human being, it is something you must experience alone. *Shoah* teaches us the meaning of the word *inconsolable*. The film ends in Israel (as it has to) with a member of the Jewish Combat Organization describing his fantasy, while searching the empty ruins of the Warsaw ghetto, of being "the last Jew." (After he finishes comes a coda of trains rolling implacably on. . . .)

Leaving the theater, you may recall one survivor's account of a secret trip to "Aryan" Warsaw on the eve of the ghetto uprising: "We suddenly emerged into a street in broad daylight, stunned to find ourselves among normal people. [It was as if] we'd come from another planet." The horror of it is, that planet is ours.

—*J. Hoberman*

Patrice Leconte
■

MONSIEUR HIRE (1989)

Although wrenching in its climax, Patrice Leconte's *Monsieur Hire* is an oddly optimistic film, plumping for the eternal nature of love and the individual's ability to respond and change according to his own feelings, even at the most desperate, inconsolable hour. *Monsieur Hire* moves easily from the peculiarities of its characters to the generalities of its observations, despite the fact that its title character is so very peculiar and, at first glance at least, so remote. As a matter of fact, this masterpiece's first, and maybe greatest, virtue, is Michel Blanc's sublime performance. Playing a man of preternatural reserve, Blanc, without recourse to anecdotal background, portrays a man who has always found it difficult to love and perhaps impossible to be loved, a tailor who moves as unobtrusively as he can, clad in black, buttoned-up suit and coat, using an excessively correct appearance and manner as a blind to any display of feeling, his own or anybody else's.

Yet, M. Hire is no monster, and Blanc communicates his humanity through sparsely seeded gestures, minutely graded shifts in his features, and a carefully modulated voice that fairly seethes with self-control. When we first see him, he is applying a folk remedy to a little girl, holding the back of her head as they count to thirty, his friendly act unimbued with any sense of warmth. It is that underlying detachment that strikes as heavy a chord as his friendliness — which seems partly ominous, even sinister — and, as if sensing that, the child is one of a pack that spend their time playing pranks on Hire.

However, pranks are the least of Hire's problems. A young woman has been murdered in the neighborhood, and the frankly unsocial Hire has been targeted as a suspect by the local policeman, Inspector Maigret (Andre Wilms). Of course, Georges Simenon's Maigret is the least typical of policemen, and Leconte, in this adaptation of Simenon's *Les Fiançailles de Monsieur Hire* (which was made into *Panique* by Julien Duvivier), has gone even further in stressing the purely unofficial nature of policing. In fact, Maigret is a fairly minor character here, and his motivation appears personal, a result of some private anguish he feels over the murder, a treatment that emphasizes the social nature of Hire's aloof solitude.

For Hire's suitability as a suspect seems more a function of his cold reserve than of the paltry circumstantial evidence arrayed against him. Yet, Hire's own frank admission of his isolation clashes with his infatuation with Alice (Sandrine Bonnaire), the young woman who lives in the apartment across from his. Satisfied with gazing at her from the darkness of his flat, he discovers his splendid isolation is forever smashed when a bolt of lightning suddenly illuminates his face, first terrifying Alice, but eventually bringing them into tentative contact with one another.

Leconte films this action in evocative widescreen compositions that beautifully depict not only the successive moments of loneliness and company, but the way these moments can coexist at the same moment and in the same place. Alice has a boyfriend, Emile (Luc Thiller), with whom she is deeply in love, but her feelings for Hire grow undeniably stronger. Leconte not only shows a surreptitious union among the three, occurring to Emile's apparent ignorance on a subway train, but, in a brilliant sequence at a boxing match, offers glimpses of private passion amid public exposure that lend concrete finality to his dourly hopeful vision of momentary romance.

The film's typically dark and shadowy frames offer only indistinct backgrounds, highlighting the foregrounded characters so that they seem to float away from their surroundings. Leconte has also gone to great lengths to make the urban surroundings as nonspecific as possible; you cannot say with assurance, for example, whether the action unfolds in Paris or not. Yet, there the film still refuses to flatten out its environment into a safely reassuring thematic mirror. You may not be able to tell what city the action occurs in, for example, but it is very much a city, with recognizable people doing recognizably human things. Hire's character refuses to collapse into a tidy, antisocial package; in fact, he is a star at a local bowling alley, performing stunts for an appreciative crowd of regulars.

This air of unpredictability is crucial, not just to the plausibility of the film's assertions, but to the very nature of its plot. For all its concentration on character, the film is remarkably successful as a mystery, and though the press kit warns the unwary reviewer not to give away the plot, I found the entire parade of reversals and twists so consistently surprising and pleasurable, that I am going to refrain from any further description of the plot altogether.

Yet, these twists are, to use a sadly overworked word, organic, rather than mechanical. Like Hire's own stubbornly individual traits, they grow out of a faith in human possibilities that, no matter how unhappily stunted, form the essence of *Monsieur Hire*'s convictions. And it is that faith that makes this film a lofty and brilliant work.

—*Henry Sheehan*

Chris Marker

■

SANS SOLEIL (1982)

The images are of an award ceremony in a small African country. The president, a former freedom fighter, is decorating his ex-guerrilla comrades, who now make up the army's senior officer corps, and one general cries, as the medals are attached to his uniform. A voice on the soundtrack interrupts the subsequent moving embrace. The general, this voice tells us, is not crying out of sentiment; he's angry that he hasn't been raised higher than his brother officers. A year later, to rectify the error, he will overthrow his old friend, Luis Cabral of Guinea-Bissau, sending him into exile.

The image is only partial; it requires the soundtrack to complete the circle of understanding. And that is part of the program of Chris Marker's *Sans Soleil,* a fictional documentary that questions our ideas of appearance, memory, and history. Marker is not after glib solutions; he's not here just to state that appearances are deceiving. For the narrator of his own movie is a fictional newscaster reading letters from a cinematographer who doesn't exist. The images are real, the soundtrack is created. Each tells its own truth.

An elusive figure to Americans, Chris Marker was one of the seminal figures of the French New Wave, a Left Bank intellectual who helped create the climate that nurtured Godard, Rohmer, and the other enfants terribles. He's primarily a documentarian, but the basis of his aesthetic is the power of montage, and to serve it he's made films that are nothing more than compilations of stills, including a science-fiction movie about the destruction of Paris (*La Jetée,* 1963). He's also a committed leftist who in the late sixties became part of a filmmakers' collective that, unusually enough, survived to become a real workers' film group.

Marker the intellectual, the theorist of montage, and the leftist are all evident in *Sans Soleil,* whose intellectual breadth seems ostentatious at first but eventually coheres. The film opens with the voice of a woman who's reading the letters she's received from the fictional Sandor Krasna, the continent-hopping cinematographer who has supposedly shot the footage we'll be watching. She punctuates her reading often with "He said" or "He went on" but makes no comments of her own — she's the vessel of another consciousness, one that's warning us to beware of every separate and detached subjectivity. As she talks, the film's first images appear on the screen: we see children playing. She reads from a letter that describes this as Sandor's perfect image of happiness, and the film then takes a circuitous route to fulfill that image. Her voice continues to accompany each shot, describing, anticipating, or explaining.

Krasna begins by confessing his failure to invest the image with any feeling that might communicate itself to an audience. He talks about trying to combine it with other images (a deliberately clichéd shot of American militarism), about surrounding it with black film leader ("So if they don't see the image, at least they'll see the black"), but nothing has worked. This is the setup for the parade of images to come—images that resemble a random amalgam of documentary and touristy footage, images that concern themselves with rituals and, increasingly, with other images.

Krasna is repeatedly drawn to Japan. His travels there give him a feeling of the excitement of returning home; for him, the unseen shaper of the film, Japan lives through images and rituals that not only obscure cultural realities but also hold the key to them. In the early footage, Krasna finds the symbols that echo throughout the film. At a shrine for cats, a couple pray for their pet, not dead but lost—someone must pray for it now so that it will find its way to the afterlife when it does die. Their prayers, to the god who lives among the shrine's feline figurines, cross space and time, as does, later, the image of another cat. This one is on a rooftop in an Icelandic town that has been covered by the ashes of a volcano. It's a friend's film of a town Krasna had visited before the eruption (though we see none of the photographs he says he took there); these "objective" images, with spires and roofs that have barely escaped being covered, have replaced his own more subjective memories. His letter comments, "It's as if the year '65 had disappeared."

A film in which coups and cats jostle for space must be the product of a peculiar mind. Marker is using these images not to reflect but to fashion a mind, the fictional Krasna's. The first part of the film, Krasna's collection of visual memories, prepares for the second, which examines the value of those memories, the ability of memory to plumb appearances and write history. Marker's creation of an invisible character becomes a profound examination of how we store the past.

As one of Krasna's shots picks up a right-wing speaker atop a truck outside a Tokyo department store, he is reminded of when he first saw the speaker, at a demonstration protesting the construction of a new airport during the sixties. He shows some of the footage of the violence at that demonstration and then, in the present, a memorial demonstration at the same site. Later, a video artist, a friend of Sandor, runs these images through a machine that distorts them, colors them, so that they are only momentarily recognizable. Yet the swinging of police truncheons is clear and unmistakable. The machine offers a way to make the artist's subjectivity concrete, and yet the image retains its essential integrity. The machine lets "every image construct its own legend."

When Krasna see the strange Icelandic landscape created by the volcano, he imagines it as the scene of a science-fiction movie he will create, *Sunless,* in which a man from the fortieth century returns to earth to discover the history of some songs by Mussorgsky, the "Sunless" songs. These still exist in the visitor's time, but nobody knows what they mean anymore, so he has been sent into the past to unlock their secrets. The people of the future have no common ground with the music. They hope their explorer can do for them what Krasna's friend's machine can do: supply the subjectivity that allows a viewer (or a listener) to connect directly with an objective image (or song).

It would take a book to unravel all the strands of Marker's work. He's a master editor, and his images and sequences rush by propulsively, often with playful connections: Japanese girls dancing; rituals for the repose of the souls of broken dolls and later for broken scraps of things; prayers for departed animals at a Tokyo zoo followed by a giraffe being clumsily shot in Africa; Krasna attempting to get women of some African islands to gaze back at his camera as he records them; a sequence of faces that stare out at the viewer from Japanese television. In one spectacular sequence, Marker edits footage of a Japanese train, a cartoon of a train, and video-treated images of samurai, horror, and sex films that isn't just a virtuoso display but a key to Krasna's perceptions.

Sans Soleil ends almost where it begins, with Krasna's happy children. Yet now it's no longer a clichéd image but a bond between an audience and a filmmaker. Marker ends his film a little after Krasna ends his. As Krasna's final images are treated by the video machine, the soundtrack pronounces him "free of the lie that had prolonged the existence of those images." Just then there is a shot of a hand pulling a plug out of a console; the screen goes blank. Marker may be free of these images, but he's not finished. **(Video request.)**

—*Henry Sheehan*

Marcel Ophuls

■

HOTEL TERMINUS: THE LIFE AND TIMES OF KLAUS BARBIE (1987)

Do you really want to pack a lunch and see four and a half hours of film about a middle-rank Nazi? How indispensable is Marcel Ophuls's *Hotel Terminus: The Life and Times of Klaus Barbie?* Seeking an answer, you turn to *The Nation,* only to learn that the magazine's editor instigated the project and that the former publisher is a producer of the film. Moreover, this reviewer spent New Year's Eve 1985 watching Part I of *Shoah.* You are about to get advice from a certified fun guy, who is in the pay of the film's backers. And I tell you with all my heart: See *Hotel Terminus.*

If I belabor my own partisanship and the magazine's, it is for reasons intimately connected with the meanings of this film. About one hundred people voice their opinions in the picture, from a farmer in Barbie's native village to the attorneys at his 1987 trial in Lyons. Along the way, one encounters former resistance leaders, an unrepentant veteran of the S.S., several retired American spies, some journalists and filmmakers, the one-time president of Bolivia, and Günter Grass—as big and varied a cast as one could imagine. Few disagree about what Barbie did. Even the slippery Jacques Vergès, who defended Barbie at his trial, acknowledges facts by his avoidance of them. But everyone, depending on his or her situation, puts a different construction on Barbie's actions. You can state with little fear of contradiction that Barbie, as the Gestapo chief of Lyons, tortured people and sent forty-four innocent children to Auschwitz. But if you go one step further and call his actions a crime—indeed, if you try to call attention to Barbie at all—you have taken a position in a bitter, multi-sided debate. It's not just the Nazis and their apologists who befog judgment in *Hotel Terminus.* It's also the resistance veterans, replaying the movement's old conflicts; the former collaborators, who insist that they, too, were part of the resistance; the prosecutor in Lyons, sidestepping some of the most damning evidence against Barbie; the French wire service reporter, who casually accuses Serge and Beate Klarsfeld of getting rich off Nazi-hunting. Each side has its version of Barbie and its use for him; and that, more than the record of his actions, is the theme of *Hotel Terminus.*

Ophuls leaves you in no doubt about his own feelings. He is appalled that we should see every moral and political question as if in a row of funhouse mirrors. But since he has no choice except to live in the funhouse, he also feels free to laugh. While he goes about examining the misrepresentations of Barbie and establishing a faithful image of his own, Ophuls regularly interrupts the investigation with outbursts of mockery and low humor. He cheerfully drops in unannounced on former Gestapo agents to wish them a merry Christmas, intercuts some Mack Sennett footage to illustrate U.S. intelligence-gathering methods, and with a broad smile teases the interview subjects he dislikes. With one of his assistant directors, he even performs a high-spirited sketch about prospective interviewees suddenly losing their memory at the mention of Barbie's name.

This is not to say that *Hotel Terminus* is a laugh riot, even though it *is* one of the few films about Nazis since *The Producers* with any truly funny moments. But I do see significance in Ophuls's incidental humor: It is an assertion of strength. Comedy, according to one standard definition, consists in the eruption of vitality through deadening social constraints. In *Hotel Terminus,* society could hardly be any deadlier; and yet truth comes out and a villain receives his punishment. As he leads the audience through the sometimes muddled, sometimes outrageous interpretations of Barbie's career, Ophuls guides as much through his robust self-confidence as by careful analysis and research. And, given the nature of the tale, the audience needs all the confidence it can get.

For this is the story of a man who was useful to many people besides the Nazis, right up to the present. At the end of the war, U.S. military intelligence listed Barbie as its third-most-wanted man; and when it found him, it hired him. The cold war already had begun, and the United States was pleased to work with anyone — even Barbie — who claimed to have agents in Moscow. The French, meanwhile, wanted to put Barbie on trial for his role in killing the resistance leader Jean Moulin. Yet French intelligence, on an anticommunist crusade of its own, seems deliberately to have bungled every attempt to locate Barbie. His trial would have strengthened public support for those resistance leaders who had made common cause with the communists; and so the French looked for him, though not too hard, while the Americans, sensing that Barbie might eventually prove an embarrassment, severed their relationship with him, though not too strictly. Barbie and his entire family escaped to Peru, aided by a quasi-official underground that operated with agents from the Catholic Church. And once in Peru, Barbie again found high-level protectors. A man experienced in interrogation and torture was useful in South America, too.

Barbie was identified in 1971 (earlier, according to some) yet was too well protected to be brought back to France. He moved to Bolivia, where he dabbled in corporate larceny and gunrunning in addition to his usual political activities. His extradition had to be put off until 1983, when a coup left him momentarily exposed. Even then, jailed and awaiting trial, he continued to serve a purpose. Albert Rosset, a National Front politician in Lyons, blandly remarks that *they* — meaning the Jews — got Kurt Waldheim elected president of Austria, thanks to their hounding of Barbie. So it's the Jews' own fault, Ophuls replies. Rosset shrugs, with the nonchalance of a man whose party has been doing nicely in the polls. Barbie's mere presence in France has been enough to help him, just as it opened an opportunity for Jacques Vergès. At the trial, Vergès did not so much defend Barbie as use the occasion to indict an ill-defined but suspiciously Hebraic-seeming political establishment. Toward the end of *Hotel Terminus,* the writer Alain Finkielkraut observes that Vergès, who is Eurasian, had called on a black man and an Arab to help defend a Nazi. At the war's end, Finkielkraut says, who would have foreseen that three representatives of the "inferior" races would someday join forces with a soldier of the master race? But then, these people, too, have a political agenda, in which Barbie, even aged and infirm, can play a role.

Who is this man, who has served so many people so well? From the farmer in his native village, who still calls him "Sonny," we learn that Barbie was the child of schoolteachers. The father, claims the farmer, was a great teacher, when he was sober. When drunk, he would "grab a ruler and lash out at anyone." The mother, though, was a saint — "all she did was pray." This is all we learn of Barbie's childhood; it is enough. By adolescence, Barbie was pious, scholarly, but not so much of a teacher's pet as to alienate his classmates. He was a leader in his school, able to command respect. And he was the first kid on the block to put on a Nazi uniform.

This was the man who turned the Hôtel Terminus in Lyons into a torture chamber: a man who took pleasure in beating people, but who gave the impression of being a *petit bonhomme.* Barbie maintained an air of bourgeois contentment even in the midst of his torture sessions.

Lise Lesèvre, a resistance fighter, remembers awakening after being beaten unconscious and finding herself in an elegant salon decorated with a vase holding a single rose, where a pianist was playing Chopin. Barbie, ever the gentleman, offered her a cordial. She does not tell us whether this was before or after Barbie fractured her spine. We do know that the American spymasters who handled him thought Barbie was an honest man. When Eugene Kolb, his controller, was told to investigate the war crimes charges against Barbie, he did not set up an interrogation. He invited Barbie to the *Bierstube* for some good bratwurst and an informal chat. Later, in South America, Barbie's associates knew he was being sought by the authorities but did not cooperate with them. Klaus, after all, was a friend, a good fellow, a fun guy.

Once more, we are confronted with the normality of evil; not its banality — Barbie's habits were too bizarre for that — but its cloak of everydayness, lent to it by people who don't want to see anything out of the ordinary. Barbie's daughter, who now works as a librarian in Austria, characterizes him only as a very good father. And his Nazism? She doesn't know exactly what National Socialism was, she says. Her response is typical. A good many of Ophuls's interviewees, German and French alike, say that whatever Barbie did, it happened forty years ago. Who can think be bothered to think back forty years? And so people celebrate their holidays — the film is full of scenes decorated for Christmas — and remind Ophuls, whenever he gets on their nerves, that he is filming on private property. Some things are inviolable.

No wonder Ophuls laughs. But his laughter is more than the rattle of despair. It is also a note of triumph. The villains of *Hotel Terminus* may be everywhere; but so are its heroes and heroines, from the witty and elegant resistance leaders Lucie and Raymond Aubrac to the old farmhand Julien Favet, who witnessed the arrest of the children at Izieu and is too stubbornly honest to shut up about it. And, finally, there is the woman to whom *Hotel Terminus* is dedicated, even though she never appears and we do not know her full name.

At the end of the film, the Auschwitz survivor Simone Lagrange shows us the apartment house where she was arrested as a child. When the Gestapo came, she says, all the neighbors hid — all except Mme. Bontout, who tried to pull Simone into the safety of her apartment. *Hotel Terminus,* Ophuls concludes, is dedicated to all the Mme. Bontouts. The best thing I can say about the film is that it leaves you feeling the Mme. Bontouts will eventually win.

— Stuart Klawans

Jean-Paul Rappeneau

■

CYRANO DE BERGERAC (1990)

Gérard Depardieu revitalizes a warhorse of a part in *Cyrano de Bergerac,* a lavish ($17 million) and lengthy (but not overlong at 135 minutes) film version of the Edmond Rostand play about the brilliant poet and swordsman of seventeenth-century Paris who allows his oversize nose to crush his courage in love. Cyrano sees himself as a freak, so he must pour out his feelings to his beloved Roxane (Anne Brochet) in letters she thinks are written by the handsome Christian (Vincent Perez).

A classic to some, *Cyrano* is sentimental drool to others, especially those who've endured amateur productions or the stagy 1950 film version—relieved only by the vigor of Oscar winner José Ferrer in the title role. Steve Martin's update in *Roxanne* (1987) poked fun at the old conventions by having Roxanne dump her dumb jock and hop in the sack with Cyrano. But the antique charms of the story can still seduce us when well done, and director Jean-Paul Rappeneau, who freely adapted the play with Jean-Claude Carrière, knows how to fashion a sumptuously beautiful, hugely entertaining spectacle that also stays alert to the cadences of the heart.

You may be thrown at first by the rhyming subtitles, a translation by Anthony Burgess of the original text's alexandrine couplets. During the famous duel between the Vicomte de Valvert (Philippe Volter) and Cyrano, who provides a witty assault on his own nose ("a monument, a peninsula") to match every thrust and parry, it's hard to keep your eyes on both the action and the subtitles without looking like you've entered an apple-bobbing contest. But the powerful images soon take hold.

Shooting on location in France and Hungary, cinematographer Pierre Lhomme approaches everything from the intimate balcony scene to the raging battle of Arras with a painter's eye for light and shading. And Rappeneau does wonders with the actors. Brochet brings welcome spark to the usually doltish Roxane, while Perez is impressive as the inarticulate but not unsympathetic Christian. Roland Bertin bursts with comic energy as Ragueneau, the pastry maker who feeds the starving poets of Paris in return for a few lines of verse. And Jacques Weber is outstanding as Comte de Guiche, the vengeful aristocrat who proves himself a man of honor in war.

Above all there is Depardieu. Now forty-two, he has acted in more than sixty French films since he made his debut in 1965. He scored his breakthrough as a lewd petty thief in Bertrand Blier's *Going Places* (1974) and went on to win raves for richly varied roles in such films as *The Last Metro, Jean de Florette, Get Out Your Handkerchiefs, Camille Claudel,* and *Too Beautiful for You. Cyrano,* for which he won the best-actor prize at Cannes, is Depardieu at his peak. Beefy and barrel-chested, he is the most unconventional looking of all international male sex symbols. But his oddball appearance only seems to enhance his charm. And Depardieu makes that work for the movie. The Cyrano nose that Michele Burke has designed is oversize but not overstated. He doesn't look freakish. Depardieu's Cyrano is a man whose ugliness is in his own mind. It's not Roxane's romantic ideal he can't live up to; it's his. That's his tragedy.

Cyrano is more than a career culmination for Depardieu; it's a startling surprise. You expect his verbal and physical dexterity, but Depardieu's Cyrano is most memorable in stillness and silence. The play is a constant barrage of verse, but Rappeneau's film takes the time to catch Cyrano watching Roxane out of the corner of his eye or tidying a room in expectation of her arrival or sitting rapt and tongue-tied in her presence. There is something unexpectedly touching in the sight of this hulking warrior lost in love. Other actors have given more flamboyant interpretations of the role, but Depardieu is the definitive romantic Cyrano. He makes you ache with him. As an actor, he has found the confidence to do less. It's a towering performance, magnificent and moving, that does just what any honest telling of the Cyrano legend should strive to do: set us all dreaming.

—Peter Travers

Jean-Charles Tacchella
■

COUSIN, COUSINE (1975)

Violence is one of the strands that braid movie history together. But romance is another, and it is a nice warming jog through the past to count how many among movies you would be happiest to see again had at their center the love of a man and a woman. Including, of course, Claude Lelouch's *A Man and a Woman* and his ingeniously constructed love story *And Now My Love,* in which the audience watched enchanted while destiny drew the couple toward a meeting that could only be incandescently splendid.

The two Lelouch films come first to mind as you watch *Cousin, Cousine* by Jean-Charles Tacchella. It is the most engaging love story since *And Now My Love,* involving another greatly attractive and interesting couple, Marie-Christine Barrault and Victor Lanoux.

She, beautiful and intelligent in equal abundant measures, is the niece of the great actor-mime Jean-Louis Barrault and was the younger woman in Eric Rohmer's *My Night at Maud's.* He is a former mechanic who edged into show business doing cabaret sketches with Pierre Richard (*The Tall Blond Man with One Black Shoe*). Tall, black-haired, and soft-spoken, he suggests a kind of rumpled and relaxed Gregory Peck.

In Tacchella's story, they are cousins by marriage, meeting at a vast family wedding, each bringing unhappiness along with other gifts. She is married to a compulsive and unsubtle chaser (Guy Marchand). He is married to an equally compulsive flirt (Marie-France Piser) whose life is also a nonstop self-indulgent grand tour of the latest emotional therapies.

Given the circumstances, there is almost no way they could not fall in love. Given their attractiveness, watching it happen is as pleasurable in its own way as watching the steam rise in Katharine Hepburn and Humphrey Bogart in *The African Queen.*

He is a combination of free spirit and traditional romantic who rides a motorbike and allows himself no more than three years to a career, lest he grow too tethered. He has been a jazz musician and a naturalist and is currently giving dance lessons.

At first they mean to keep it platonic, a test of good will. But a temptation you can resist is hardly worth having and in all events the gravitational pull of a deepening love is irresistible anyway. The romance is joyous, guilt-free, defiantly open. Thanks to the provocations Tachella has created through the errant spouses, the kissing cousins feel no need to skulk about.

For all the wonders of the love story, it has been clear from the start that Tacchella is not the average spinner of sentimental romantic tales. He has in fact a rather nastily satiric eye for the niceties of bourgeois conventions, and there is a curious tension in the film between the attractiveness of the lovers and the tackiness of their world. It even seems possible that the casting proved so luminously inspired as to make a dark comedy play light. (Mme. Barrault is the wife of the director-general of Gaumont, which made the film, and never has the relative been so absolute a triumph.)

The romance takes place within the family in every sense. The wedding feasts are patchworks of quarrels, overdrinking, fist-fights, unsubtle seductions, exhibitionism, and other symptoms of middle-class decay. Much of it is amusing in a shocky way, but it reveals its calculations in different terms from the exuberant imaginings of the lovers together.

The family relationships are a bit tricky but there is a subplot involving a possible romance between the woman's widowed mother and the man's widower father. It doesn't work out, and Tacchella seems to be saying that conventional tidiness exists neither in life nor in his fictions; some things happen and others don't indeed work out.

The last family gathering is a monster Christmas Eve party, with Barrault and Lanoux scandalizing the group by conducting their own ceremonies privately. Here, I think, the darkness of Tacchella's vision and the grace of his principals clash unattractively. Deserting the group for a private romp becomes not a defiance of some stifling convention but an affront and an embarrassment which plays as psychologically unlikely, given the nature of the two people as we've been shown them. There is a difference between hypocritical convention and simple civility and our friends, in the glow of a new love, are likeliest of all to know it and to be of a mind to embrace the world as well as each other.

The ending as much as anything else suggests that the charm and interest of the stars took over the film and that the audiences, starved for a love story to care about, are choosing to revel in the glow of the romance and to ignore the rather naughty things Tacchella has to say in passing.

Cousin, Cousine has been the sleeper of the year in New York, opening unheralded to small audiences and building, mostly by word of mouth, to hit status. It seems almost certain to find success, because it is literate, expert, witty, and handsome, and because it touches again the romantic strand without which the movies do not long endure.

—*Charles Champlin*

RECOMMENDED FROM ELSEWHERE IN WEST AND EAST EUROPE

The biggest recent art-house successes have come from Scandinavia, Germany, and Italy. Denmark backed Gabriel Axel's *Babette's Feast* and Bille August's *Pelle the Conqueror,* the panoramic follow-up to August's coming-of-age movies, *Zappa* and *Twist and Shout* (the latter available on cassette). Sweden's Lasse Hallstrom had an even bigger worldwide hit with *My Life as a Dog.*

These traditional art-house movies were tickets to Hollywood opportunity, and that was even truer of the big German successes, *Das*

Opposite page: scene from *Pelle the Conqueror.*

Boot and *Men* . . . , two movies that brought a uniquely claustrophobic setting and witty postfeminism to action and romantic comedy. *Heimat* added even deeper shadings to another pop genre, the TV miniseries.

Italy's most successful recent film export is *Cinema Paradiso*. During the seventies, their RAI-TV, like England's Channel Four, unearthed the poetry of working class life. Some of the decade's best films were the ones rooted in Italian soil, wholly or partly supported by Italian TV: Francesco Rosi's *Christ Stopped at Eboli* (reviewed on page 222); the Tavianis' *Padre Padrone* and *Night of the Shooting Stars* (reviewed on page 332); and Ermanno Olmi's *The Tree of Wooden Clogs*.

Some of the best films reviewed in this chapter are by directors whose psychopolitics culminated in one particular outstanding film — from Greece, Costa-Gavras's *Z;* from Poland, Jerzy Skolimowski's *Moonlighting;* from Spain, Victor Erice's *The Spirit of the Beehive;* from Hungary, Istvan Szabo's *Mephisto.* Other recommendations on cassette: Costa-Gavras's *State of Siege* (1973), Skolimowski's *Hands Up* (1967–81), Szabo's *Father* (1966) and *25 Fireman's Street* (1973).

Bille August

■

PELLE THE CONQUEROR (1987)

Finely wrought as Danish director Bille August's *Zappa* and *Twist and Shout* were, nothing in those exemplary coming-of-age films prepares you for the breadth, depth, and fullness of his *Pelle the Conqueror.* Imagine a Scandinavian Dickens novel, brought to the screen with its detail, richness of character, and passion for social reform reimagined in sweeping, urgent visual terms, and you'll have an idea of the epic amplitude of *Pelle.* Grand, deep-breathing, profoundly humanistic, *Pelle* is a magnificent achievement — the kind of work that keeps you going to the movies.

In fact, August adapted only the first part of Martin Anderson Nexo's four-volume novel about Pelle, the son of Lasse, an aging Swedish widower. They emigrate to a Danish island in search of a better life. "We'll eat roast pork and raisins," the grizzled Lasse promises the boy. What they get is oily herring from a common bowl, an occasional boiled potato, and a life of virtual slavery at a place aptly named Stone Farm. They don't even share the rickety workers' quarters, but are brusquely ordered to shack up in a henhouse next to a cowshed. Less because he's old than because he looks so weary, Lasse is put to work not as a farmworker, but as a stablehand.

Soon, young Pelle overcomes his shyness and avidly begins soaking up the particulars of his new Danish world, populated by a marvelously detailed, vividly inscribed cast of characters — among them the brutal overseer, the philandering estate owner, his sad alcoholic wife, a beautiful farm girl who pays dearly for falling in love with a local rich boy, a retarded boy who joins a circus and delights that he's found a home, and the laborer who becomes Pelle's friend when he defends the boy after it becomes humiliatingly apparent that Lasse is too worn out to.

Not that Max von Sydow, as the bent and stubbled Lasse, is a pile of ashes. One of the things that gives the film its power and beauty is its symmetry. As Pelle's life is beginning (the novel describes his evolution into a labor leader), Lasse's is grinding to a halt. But if his courage is ebbing, he still grows excited when Pelle opens a gift, and he's torn with agony as Pelle stumbles through a school recitation. As Pelle grows, it dawns on us that Lasse is more the child of the two. For all that August does with the landscape, his supreme achievement here lies in leading von Sydow to the performance of his career.

The face of von Sydow's Lasse fills the screen, becomes a human landscape, with lined, leathery features bespeaking a lifetime of slow collapse under a weight of hard labor. But while Lasse has been worn down by his circumstances, he isn't defeated by them. What keeps him alive, keeps him dignified through the humiliations he must bear, is his love for his son, love he knows is reciprocated. After a poignant grab for happiness with a widow, he sinks back, consoled by the knowledge that his struggle will be carried on by the next generation.

You've got to see von Sydow in this role. He's dealt with struggle before, having faced angst, war, God's silence, and death in Ingmar Bergman's films. But in all those films, there was an abstract quality about the characters he played. Von Sydow's pale, elongated appearance reinforced the notion that he was playing the mind of Bergman, grappling with the director's demons. In *Pelle,* he plays the heart of Anderson and August. It's a large, elemental role, made larger by the selflessness in this simple man, and von Sydow fills it beautifully. Lasse is an earth father who has passed on to his son a capacity for endurance.

If August draws a performance of greatness from von Sydow, he no less remarkably or unstintingly elicits freshness from hungry-eyed young Pelle Hvenegaard in the title role. The interaction between August and his young star accounts for much of the film's impact, too. It's more than just making us feel we often are seeing things through the boy's eyes, wondrously. More, even, than a matter of paralleling life, death, hope, and despair to larger seasonal images of nature. August knows when to draw back to let us feel lives tied to big, impersonal forces. He's at his trenchant, subtle, imaginative best when he keeps sending Pelle to the shoreline. Sometimes it's an icebound realm of frigid death. But sometimes its foggy indefiniteness beckons invitingly, with enticing mystery. It's when Pelle's world seems most drained of color that it seems most filled with solace from an oppressive present and promise of a future rich in possibility.

—*Jay Carr*

Gabriel Axel
■

BABETTE'S FEAST (1987)

What does an artist require of life? Quite simple things, really. The time and solitude necessary to temper talent and vision. A little money for supplies. The emotional support of kindly and patient friends. And, finally, the right historical moment to present his or her work and a sympathetic critical champion, gently guiding an audience to proper appreciation of the gifts being bestowed upon it.

Simple things. But how hard they are to come by, how much luck is required in the quest, and how rarely artists themselves confront these difficulties in an engaging spirit. The whine of self-pity, the bombast of self-aggrandizement, the low moan of tragedy are the notes most often heard in their accounts of creative lives. Movies, of course, have always been the most ludicrous offenders in this regard, constantly trying to turn the stealth and cunning by which most artists survive into confrontational melodrama.

How marvelous, then, to find a film that comes at this subject from the right direction—obliquely, metaphorically—and in the right mood, that of delicate and gallant irony. Indeed, despite her name's presence in the title of this adaptation of an Isak Dinesen story, Babette Hersant (Stéphane Audran) does not appear in the film until it is almost half over, and then, as it were, in disguise. She is presented merely as a French woman rendered homeless and penniless by the Communard uprising of 1871 in Paris, seeking refuge in a remote village in Jutland, on Denmark's wild west coast. If there is something extraordinary in her bearing, its source—an extraordinary talent—is not hinted at. For fourteen years she toils unpaid, uncomplaining, almost unspeaking, as cook and servant, for the spinster sisters, Marina and Phillipa, who grant her shelter.

They are the sweetly pious daughters of a visionary, schismatic preacher. While he lives, they sacrifice their lives to this faintly absurd work. After he dies they devote themselves to his memory by keeping his dwindling, aging, increasingly fractious flock together. Their story, stretching over many years, is told with deft economy and quiet wit by writer-director Gabriel Axel, who builds an uncannily rich texture out of the simplest materials. Still, one cannot help but wonder what relevance all this has in movie called *Babette's Feast*. Where is Babette? Where is her feast?

Waiting. Serenely waiting. For fate to do its stuff. For it turns out that the seemingly irrelevant history of the spinsters' lives, the lovers they long ago rejected, their eccentric religious community are utterly essential preconditions for Babette's apotheosis. The revelation of her true identity—she was once Paris's premier chef—comes as no surprise once she starts preparations for her triumph. But the intricate ways in which her benefactresses' past provides her with an occasion, a crowd at once tough to conquer yet starving for a masterpiece, even, alas, that necessary critical voice leading them from dubiety to joyous surrender, are wonderfully surprising. "Righteousness and bliss," that voice pompously summarizes their experience. But he is right. In all of movies there is no happier ending than this one: an artist achieving transcendence, her audience learning for the first (and possibly last) time the transforming power of art. Maybe it is not a miracle, but it is a foretaste of the paradise for which they have prayed all their pinched and gloomy lives. And Axel is an altogether worthy *saucier's* apprentice. His orchestration of this perfect little parable matches her culinary skills in subtlety, verve, and perfect taste. From soup to cognac *Babette's Feast* is delicious, a meal memory will forever savor.

—*Richard Schickel*

Costa-Gavras
■

Z (1969)

The question of how to make the "unconverted" sit still for some of the unpleasant truths of our time is brilliantly answered by *Z*, a ruthless and powerful film that stands without peer both as document and thriller. Sit still? Converted and unconverted alike will be riveted to their seats by the impact of this finest foreign language film of the year, a fiercely passionate and coolly detailed story of political assassination and of the death of virtue.

This French film is crime fiction that insists at the outset that similarities to persons living and dead are intentional, just as the Vassili Vassilikos novel on which it is closely based clearly intended similarity to the story of Gregorios Lambrakis, called *Z* in the novel, a Greek deputy whose murder in 1963 led to an abortive political scandal. Lambrakis, a doctor and humanist aligned with peace groups, was a target of rightists, and his assassination, designed by the police, was to be put down as nothing more than "a regrettable traffic accident." What happened thereafter is the stuff of detective thrillers, political manifestos, and classic tragedy, involving the fall of kings and the death of heroes. Suffice it that in the present Greek state [at the time this review was written] not only is the novel *Z* banned (and its author in exile) but the letter *Z* itself is banned, since in Greek it means "he is still alive."

At the core of the film, then, there is the news event, the viciousness of organized violence, the horror of inverted moralities, the terror of the brute heel of authority stamping out humanity on sunny streets in the name of righteous nationalism. And around it the creators have woven a suspenseful tapestry of men from all walks of life, each with his private motivations, each with his own concept of justice. And with step-by-step detailing, they lead to one resolution, snap us into another, and come up with the bitterness of the ultimate devastating truth.

The creators have their own view of the truth. The director and coscenarist, Costa-Gavras, an Athenian in Paris since 1952 who first gave us *The Sleeping Car Murders,* sees his film as "an indictment against a system that calls itself revolutionary but in which everything is a parody, including justice." Jorge Semprun, a deportee from Madrid, coscenarist and author of the dialogue, who wrote screenplay and dialogue for Resnais's *La Guerre Est Finie,* sees its "universal truth — of the mechanisms of corruption, the traps of universal stupidities, the larger universality of hapless courage." And he adds, "Let's not try to reassure ourselves: this type of thing doesn't only happen elsewhere, it happens everywhere."

Clearly, then, this is a "message" film, but much in the manner of *La Guerre Est Finie,* its creators are artists and theirs is primarily an extraordinary and gripping document-drama, a *policier* beautifully balanced on the tiptoe of suspense, its revelations delicately interlocking to solve the puzzle of the murder, its characters rounded out into the individualism of the criminals. Taut, tense, terse, it makes one wince with the blows and writhe with the torture, seethe at the impassivity of the investigator, weep with widow's desolation, rise with the triumph of one man's courage — and crash into the agonizing despair of the final truth. This is the art and artistry of Costa-Gavras, his crowds growling with the animal hatreds of the pack, his officials functioning with the prosaic rituals of reality. Not since *The Battle of Algiers* has there been so textured a recreation of a recent public experience; how phony his creations make the *cinéma vérité* of something like *Medium Cool* seem!

The casting is as inspired as the performances. Yves Montand, as the doctor-deputy who is assassinated, gives so succinct and penetrating a portrait of a man of inspiring convictions that his presence permeates the entire film, though he appears only at the outset. And much in the same way, Irene Papas, her classic deep-eyed beauty exuding the eternal woman, makes an indelible mark in her minor role as the wife. And throughout, Jean-Louis Trintignant, as the investigating judge, gives us a triumphantly enigmatic performance as the impartial seeker after fact, the noncommittal interrogator who does not allow his eyes to flicker even behind dark glasses, whose ultimate actions come as an astonishment — and yet an inevitable conclusion. And these stars are matched by others — Charles Denner, Bernard Fresson, and Jean Bouise as the deputy's supporters; Marcel Bozzufi and Renato Salvatori as the fool and the corrupt fanatic who are the ideal hatchet men, the assassins of all nations; Jacques Perrin, as the crusading reporter without ideals; Georges Geret as the "good" man whose motives are scarcely selfless; Pierre Dux as the general who both heads and embodies the police state.

It is Dux who triumphs in a moment—and there are so many of these perfect moments throughout the work—that epitomizes the forces of the right. One of the reporters besieging him when he is brought to book demands, "General—are you a victim—like Dreyfus?" "Dreyfus was guilty!" the General snarls and strides away.

Mikis Theodorakis, the patriot-composer who lives under house arrest in the Peloponnese, created the score, which was smuggled to France for the film. Raoul Coutard's color photography is, as always, exquisite, but the perfection of Costa-Gavras's direction is that he eschews trickery for its own effect. All is to a purpose and thus *Z* becomes a dual-level work, an absorbing suspense story and a vital outcry for justice. You cannot afford to miss it on either count.

—*Judith Crist*

Doris Dörrie

■

MEN . . . (1985)

Men . . . is a male buddy movie directed by a woman. It is about yuppies in midlife crisis. It is a German comedy.

All this may sound like the stuff of a ninety-nine-minute groan—but it isn't. Far from it. This quick-witted romp brings to mind what movie comedy could be in the days of Billy Wilder and Ernst Lubitsch, before every sparkling trinket had to be encumbered with over-wrought plot and overdone "production values."

Working fast on a slim budget—the movie was shot in twenty-four days and cost $400,000—the thirty-one-year-old director Doris Dörrie has put together a nifty comic gem where the giggles erupt from Serious Questions: selling out, marriage, the relations between men and women.

Ms. Dörrie's "hero" is Julius (Heiner Lautherbach), a self-satisfied advertising executive with two kids, expensive Italian suits, a secretary who provides midday sex, a pretty wife, and a Maserati. His life, he thinks, is just about perfect until on his wife's birthday he discovers — when he sees a hickey on her neck — that she is having an affair.

What really bothers him is the hickey, that sign of youthful passion. "My God," he wails. "Like teenagers."

Julius becomes obsessed with his wife's lover, more because his pride's been wounded than because he's lost her affection. He decides to find out his rival's secret by moving in with him.

At first they seem to be a contrast in types; Julius has smooth, boyish good looks while Stefan (Uwe Ochsenknecht), the lover — an aging hippie artist — radiates a kind of sulky sensuality. But at heart they are the same, Ms. Dörrie seems to be saying. They are perpetual boys perplexed by women and eager to succeed. They are men.

Now being a man in Ms. Dörrie's postfeminist universe is not the bad thing you might suspect. Julius and Stefan are appealing characters, even when they say such things as, "Women can always be talked into being unhappy." They are just as confused about their own identities.

Ms. Dörrie speaks flawless English and has a stylishly punky California look; that is, she's got short blond hair, a long tan body, and wears a small earring in her nose and studded leather straps around her wrist and her bright minidress.

She got the idea for *Men . . .* a few years ago when she was living with a former hippie about five years her senior. His pals — rebellious students grown up into a dentist, a retailer, a film distributor — would come over and discuss world politics, why they were wearing suits instead of blue jeans. Ms. Dörrie wasn't included, but while she cooked for them she eavesdropped, and overheard many of the funny lines that ended up in her movie.

Except for the subtitles, *Men . . .* shouldn't seem very foreign to American audiences. The characters and their settings have the familiar trappings of our own contemporary lives: husbands and wives who remember reading Fromm together once, answering machines, an overblown sense of our early idealism.

Ms. Dörrie, who once worked in a German McDonald's, acknowledges she — and her generation — was greatly influenced by American culture, more so than younger Germans. "To us, America was the land of John Ford and grand images. Today it's the land of Madonna and video clips. It isn't a myth anymore. When I was a kid no one could afford to visit America. Now high-school kids go there on vacation. It isn't a dream anymore."

Though *Men . . .* is Ms. Dörrie's eleventh film, it is her first comedy and her first hit. Since opening nationwide in Germany in January, the picture has been seen by six million people — or ten percent of the population. That makes it Germany's biggest box-office draw since World War II, bigger than *Rambo* or any other American film.

—*Julie Salamon*

Victor Erice
■

THE SPIRIT OF THE BEEHIVE (1976)

You enter *The Spirit of the Beehive* as you enter another country: the magical, terrifying world of childhood. It's a closed, private world, where mystery is legion and nothing is accidental. The child's mind makes patterns out of happenstance, omens out of the ordinary, faith out of ignorance. To everything there is a design, a drama, a meaning, and if you are a young girl like eight-year-old Ana, with an imagination as limitless as the vast plains of her homeland, you follow the magic drama of your mind to a place that is literally out of this world.

In fact, we are in a remote Castilian village in 1940, shortly after the end of the Spanish Civil War. But even the real world has taken on the spare intensity of a dream. The war has pared life down to essentials: only children and the old remain. If there are young men, they are framed in glass: in photographs, or behind the windows of passing trains taking them off to battle. The town has become a haunted playground. There's a void where its heart should be, and too much space for fantasy.

Ana's mother, in exile from a more cosmopolitan life, sits in her vast underfurnished house writing letters to a lover she may never again see alive. She bicycles alone through deserted streets to post her letters at the railroad station. Locked in his own solitary, misanthropic space, her older husband tends his bees, searching for a pattern in their activity that corresponds to his own bleak expectations. At night under his painting of St. Jerome, alone with his journal and his wireless, he tries to set his vision of life's furious, meaningless drone into words before falling asleep at his desk. Upstairs, his wife listens to the train whistle, a cruel reminder of the man she wants and doesn't have.

It is only the children who have the power to make their fantasies real. One day the movie *Frankenstein* comes to town. For Ana and her ten-year-old sister Isabel it is a turning point in their lives, a glimpse into a world of death and divinity. Whispering between beds after the movie, the wide-eyed Ana asks her wiser, more devious sister why the townsfolk killed the monster. The movie lied, Isabel tells her. The monster is alive, a spirit, and she has seen him. "If you're a friend of his you can speak to him." She takes Ana to a deserted farmhouse outside of town where her imaginary spirit resides, and where Ana discovers a giant footprint that embeds itself eternally in her mind. Isabel's mischievous game becomes a kind of spiritual quest for Ana, as her search for the "monster" takes her deeper and deeper into a dangerous, wondrous realm where visions supersede reality.

Though *The Spirit of the Beehive* doesn't depend on a thriller's plot devices, it would not be fair to tell too much more of the story. The chills and surprises are meant to be discovered with a fresh eye, like a child's. Yet they are revealed to us by director Victor Erice with the utmost sophistication and control. His film is like a haunting prose poem, in which every image counts. Erice has a poet's eye for detail, and he leaves nothing to chance: each image and sound reverberates, gaining new meanings with every variation. Bees, mushrooms, cats, fires, railroads, a typewriter: these objects take on the large, almost magical significance that the very young are privileged to see, though we see them through adult eyes as well. Like Ana's world, the movie's world is closed: nothing seems to exist beyond the edge of the frame.

The Spirit of the Beehive unfolds like a fable, but it is a fable smart enough not to tie itself down to a single meaning. One can easily read into this tale of repression and release a parable about the stifling nature of Franco's Spain, but it's unwise to carry this too far. The political implications, like the Freudian ones (the monster as surrogate father) are undeniably there, in the soil of Erice's imagination, but what blossoms from them is something else again. In a general sense, Erice is addressing himself to the consequences of solipsism, to a cultural and private alienation that gives rise to the need for transcendence, whether in the form of the mother's romantic dreams, the father's philosophical overview, or the child's mystical desire for communion with a spirit. Informing the movie is the image of the beehive, a metaphor that works in several ways. The patterns of the village and of the hive are equated in such shots as those of children swarming into the schoolhouse each morning or in the yellow glow that permeates the interiors of the family's house, but one essential distinction remains: whereas the bees are united in a common purpose, all the humans are lost in their separate pursuits, and only Ana's brush with tragedy can jolt the family members out of their respective self-immersions. How long their bond can last is a question Erice leaves unanswered.

It would be a shame if this elegant, chilling, drum-tight film gets lost in the shuffle. It's easily one of the best 1977 has had to offer (it was made in 1973, which tells us something about the sorry state of foreign film distribution). The remarkable performances of the two children — the dark, luminously intense Ana Torrent and the fair, disquietingly changeable Isabel Telleria — are in themselves ample reasons to see *The Spirit of the Beehive*. Erice's art can take us just so far, but without the conviction these two gifted actresses bring to their roles, his fable could not come alive. Neither of them makes a false move. In dealing with parents, however, Erice may be too cryptic for his own good. He parcels out only the smallest scraps of information about them, and while it's remarkable how much these few images convey, next to the children they seem like literary conceptions, not altogether convincing. There are times as well when the director's passion for imagistic symmetry becomes too pat, and artfulness threatens to become artiness. Such a moment occurs when the political fugitive whom Ana takes to be an incarnation of the Frankenstein monster is killed, and his body is laid out beneath the movie screen where *Frankenstein* was shown. It's a life/art parallel that's a little too neat to be swallowed.

But these are minor lapses in a movie that achieves a lyric, spellbinding intensity. On the basis of this one film alone, Victor Erice reveals himself as a director of meticulous craftsmanship and impressive confidence. At a time when most movies assault us with the unmodulated shock tactics of advertising, Erice reminds us of the virtues of the slow build. His elliptical, deliberate style demands an unusual attentiveness from the audience, but we are rewarded many times over. Like the children carried away by *Frankenstein,* we are caught up in Erice's myth. Nor is it an accident that a movie triggers the plot of *The Spirit of the Beehive:* along with the rest, we are watching a director's testament to his art. And in Ana, he has given us a portrait of the artist as an eight-year-old dreamer.

—*David Ansen*

Lasse Hallstrom
■

MY LIFE AS A DOG (1985)

How has Swedish director Lasse Hallstrom remembered so precisely that knife edge between pain and delight that is childhood? In *My Life as a Dog* he has caught it all, in a sterling film whose style sits between the light moments of his compatriot, Ingmar Bergman, and the darker moments of François Truffaut's childhood films. With freshness in such short supply that it's nearly endangered, *My Life as a Dog* should be cherished.

The film's twelve-year-old hero, Ingemar, is frightened and unsettled when his thoughtful and beautiful photographer-mother contracts tuberculosis and is ordered to bed. But like most children, his concern has wild fluctuations. (He is played by Anton Glanzelius in an uncanny performance which is in turn exuberant and introspective. The portrayal won him the Swedish Oscar equivalent as Best Actor, while the film won Best Picture.)

Ingemar tries to do things that made his mother laugh before; he quite consciously saves up funny stories and does pratfalls for her amusement. (You might think that just one look at her younger son, with his elfish triangular grin, his hair a warring series of cowlicks, his young fox's eyes, would lift her spirits.) But with no father at hand, the clattering fights between Ingemar and his always-superior teenage brother rattle their cheap railroad flat and push their mother into terrifying rages.

So, during this summer in the late 1950s, the boys are sent off to different relatives. Ingemar is also separated from the gray, scruffy mongrel Sickum, his closest friend. (Immune to doggy breath, Ingemar spends patient hours arranging Sickum's mouth into a semblance of a smile.)

In a reverse of the expected, his young Uncle Gunnar (Tomas von Bromssen) and Aunt Ulla (Kicki Rundgren), who take in their rambunctious nephew, are wonderful, and the tiny country town itself is idyllic—a Swedish version of Menzel's sweet little Czech village, bursting with bucolic sex, affection, and eccentricity in equal proportions.

Ingemar is also edging his way through preadolescence, and although sex is well down on his list of interests, it is passing like a perfumed breeze though the minds of many of his girl classmates. He seems to be safe with the exquisite Saga (Melinda Kinnaman) who, after all, is the best soccer player in town and a not-so-bad boxer either. Ingemar is among the select few who know that the lean, boyish Saga is a girl. Unfortunately, she can turn as jealous and possessive as his other bewildering female classmates, leaving Ingemar decidedly unsettled.

And the shadow of his mother's illness never leaves his mind. While willing her to be better, he also tries to defend himself against his worst fears by putting her illness into a sort of cosmic perspective: It's not as bad, he says thoughtfully, as the brave little dog Laika, sent up in Sputnik with only food enough for five months; she starved to death for science. "It's important to have things like that to compare it to."

He begins to collect other bizarre examples of life's fatal inequities, the filler pieces without which no newspaper could exist ("Man Crossing Sports Arena Struck by Javelin") and he uses them as a sort of dreadful solace.

It's this dark undertone that keeps *My Life as a Dog* from becoming too sweet or too small. Hallstrom, who adapted the film (along with Reidar Jonsson, Brasse Brannstrom, and Per Berglund) from a novel by Jonsson, has an uncanny knowledge of the spells and rituals with which children try to protect themselves. To see Ingemar clamping his hands on and off his ears to distort the sound of his mother's fury is to be struck with an unmistakable jolt of memory.

Ingemar's "dog life" comes from several sources, including his passion for Sickum. But it's reinforced one evening when his uncle, playfully nuzzling his wife, goes down on all fours and begins barking at her. Ingemar delightedly joins him—here are adults given leave to behave foolishly—but when their bedroom door closes him out, he is pained and reminded of his abandonment again. The barking dog is all that's left of Ingemar's playful mood and he will revert to it, almost uncontrollably, again and again that summer—holding the world at bay with his snaps and snarls. Yet it is that uncle, in all his faint foolishness, who will be Ingemar's bridge to surviving that summer's loss. A rumpled, curly-headed, patient man who works at a glassblowing factory, Uncle Gunnar is Hallstrom's proof of the world's simple, sturdy goodness, and *My Life as a Dog* is ours.

— Sheila Benson

Ermanno Olmi

■

THE TREE OF WOODEN CLOGS (1978)

Ermanno Olmi's *The Tree of Wooden Clogs* towers over the contemporary cinema with its testament of Christian love, devotion, and humility in the midst of heart-rending injustice, but it is great also as a fully articulated work of cinematic art. This should not come as a complete surprise. After all, the film did win the coveted Golden Palm at last year's Cannes Film Festival. Unfortunately, I arrived at Cannes too late to catch it, and it had kept eluding me until very recently. But let's face it: I was not particularly anxious to spend three hours of my dwindling life with nonprofessionals in the roles of peasants in turn-of-the-century Bergamo. I knew I'd have to see the film sooner or later, but better later than sooner, I thought. I bring up this matter of my instinctive reluctance only because I suspect that many of my readers may choose to ignore even rave reviews for a project that seems so far off the beaten summer-entertainment track.

For myself, I've always been suspicious of well-intentioned movies about poor peasants. At the very least, filmmakers tend to look down on the subject from such a dizzying social, economic, and cultural height, that there is a danger that what is supposed to be flesh-and-blood human beings will be perceived instead as pitiable insects crushed by an unjust system. The resulting treatment may run the gamut from slobbering sentimentality to Grand Guignol. Poverty is often exploited as the handmaiden of depravity and inequality as the midwife of violence — all in the name of opening our eyes to the wrongs of the world. Another approach consists of idealizing the peasants in terms of the sincerity and authenticity denied to us inescapably alienated city dwellers. The peasant is presumably closer to the rhythms and roots of nature, the cycle of the seasons, and the ultimate secrets of existence. Ho-hum, I'll take *Manhattan,* or so I thought as I trudged off a few weeks ago for an early morning screening of *The Tree of Wooden Clogs,* a screening, incidentally, which I needed at the time like a hole in the head. There I was, exhausted by my preparations to attend this year's Cannes Film Festival, and I had to spend three irreplaceable hours catching up with the winner of *last* year's festival.

But after only a few minutes of the film, I felt myself magically transported to the realm of sublimely expressed feelings. That exultation, of which only the most magnificent art is capable, awakened me from a near stupor and made me proud to be a humble artisan in the vineyard of cinema. *The Tree of Wooden Clogs* is incomparable. Forget the facile antipapa melodrama, *Padre Padrone;* the glossy, kinky theatrics of *1900;* the sour-spirited satire of *Bread and Chocolate;* forget even the laborious stop-motion rituals of *Farrebique;* and the play-acting of Pagnol. The Renoir of *Toni* and *The River* may be closer to the mark as far as the privileged moments are concerned, but not even Renoir has come close to Olmi's sustained formal perfection here. For example, there is a boat voyage to Milan that equals in its evocativeness the best of Murnau and Mizoguchi. What is truly miraculous about *The Tree of Wooden Clogs* is its fusion of the highest art with the humblest milieu.

The plot, such as it is, rotates among four families on a homestead on Lombardy. The families work as sharecroppers for a landowner who provides them with a house, stalls, and a designated portion of their livestock and equipment in return for two-thirds of their harvest. The land and trees, of course, belong to the owner, who has delegated many of his duties to a foreman. These arrangements are never discussed or debated within the film, but are summarized in a brief foreword. The peasants of this place and period were not yet politically aroused by the ferment in nearby Milan. They go about their work with a deep, unquestioning faith in God and with fond love for their families.

In effect, the spectacle consists in the demonstration of this faith and this love in a series of sacramental acts. Slowly at first, but with increasing emotional intensity, a widow is seen washing laundry by a riverbank to support her six children; a grandfather, showing his granddaughter how to grow tomatoes early in the season; and the widow's fifteen-year-old boy, toiling in a mill to keep the family together. We see touches of madness and stinginess as well. There is a courtship and a marriage and a wondrous trip to Milan where a couple adopts a baby from a nunnery. Finally and climactically, a gifted peasant child breaks his wooden clog on his long walk home from school, which he has been privileged to attend despite his lowly status. His father, beset by money problems, realizes that his son cannot walk barefoot to school. He slips out in the dead of night to chop down one of the landowner's young poplar trees, in order to make a new pair of clogs for his son. As he labors all night on the wooden clogs, the images of toil are transfigured into the holiest of images of transcendent love known to the human spirit.

The act of ecological desecration is discovered a few days later, and the entire family is expelled from the farmstead. The other sharecroppers wait fearfully in their own kitchens until the cart moves off into the distance, with a light dangling by a wheel. Then they come outside to watch the light disappear in the growing darkness. The utter helplessness of the poor has never been depicted with such unbearable irony, and yet this is not what the picture is about. Olmi shows instead that love is unconditional and that it can flourish blessedly even in the most difficult circumstances.

I do not know how Olmi obtained performances of such unyielding dignity and sobriety. I do not believe that this film will ever serve as a model of anything else. I remember asking the late Roberto Rossellini about Olmi. It had struck me that *Il Posto* and *The Fiancés,* for all their virtuosity, seemed to partake of a certain snideness. "No," Rossellini assured me, "Olmi is completely sincere, even naive." Rossellini's words came back to me as I watched the cinematic miracle that is entitled *The Tree of Wooden Clogs.* To see it is to be stirred to the depths of one's soul.

—Andrew Sarris

Wolfgang Petersen

■

DAS BOOT (1981)

Genre, a perceptive man said, is just another word for stealing. But there is stealing and there is stealing, petty larceny as well as the grandest of theft, and into that enticing latter category falls *Das Boot* (The Boat). This story of men at war under the sea has hardly a newly minted plot device or character trait to its name, yet rarely has familiar material been put together with such verve and dash. A very traditional war movie done with the most rigorous attention to both physical and psychological realism, *Das Boot* is the submarine movie to end all submarine movies, a genre film that, like a child thriving under discipline, makes more out of its inherent limitations than less restricted movies manage with all the freedom in the world.

Based on Lothar-Gunther Buchheim's widely read, semi-autobiographical novel about a journalist's experiences on German U-boat 96 cruising the North Atlantic in the autumn of 1941, *Das Boot*'s most obvious departure from the norm for American audiences is that it makes do with Them instead of Us as heroes. But except for a single shot of drowning English-speaking sailors—done in by one of the U-96's torpedoes—we are never aware of the sub's crew, who are mostly apolitical or anti-Nazi to begin with, as the enemy. How could we be? The brave, enigmatic captain, his loyal No. 2, the psycho in the engine room, the shared terror of attack by pesky depth charges, and enough male bonding and hearty camaraderie to fill a year's worth of *Boy's Life*—it's all so familiar from all those American and British films with pleasantly poetic titles like *Run Silent, Run Deep, Above Us the Waves,* and *The Enemy Below* that the switch in nationality is hardly noticeable. What really separates this film from its predecessors is not country of origin but a pair of creative decisions—one distinctly European, the other traditionally American—made by the film's German producers to give their conventional material as high a gloss as it could stand.

The American approach is, to be blunt, the spending of money without shame. *Das Boot* cost more than $12 million, not eye-catching by domestic standards but enough to make it the most expensive German film ever made. And that sum was not spent on star salaries but in persuit of verisimilitude, to purchase the kind of technical skill that used to be the exlusive domain of Hollywood. In addition to two full-size submarines, for instance (one used for exteriors, the other for interiors), three fully detailed scale models were built, including a thirty-five-foot oceangoing job that could cruise as well as dive on remote-control command. The result is a series of vivid outdoor action sequences that will deceive even the sharpest eye.

Most of the money, however, was spent on the creation from scratch of that U-boat interior. While movie submarines have invariably looked like hotel rooms with periscopes in the middle, this one is fanatically authentic, down to the last rivet. And though the boat was constructed so that its walls could be pulled back to allow, in director Wolfgang Petersen's words, "someone to sit back comfortably in a chair with a cigar in his mouth and say, 'Action,'" he insisted on shooting in the enclosed space to ensure reality. "I wanted to force the cameraman to shoot the whole film in this tube — I wanted the audience not to see this as decoration but to feel that we are all totally in this boat for months and months."

Hiring someone like Wolfgang Petersen to direct *Das Boot* is the European factor. Though he's had experience with logistically complex TV movies, his feature background is largely in intense character studies like *The Consequence* and *Black and White as Days and Nights,* and picking him to direct the biggest budget, mass-audience film in his country's history is a bit like choosing John Cassavetes to direct *Jaws.* Yet *Das Boot* is elevated above the usual by nothing so much as that choice; it is Petersen's abilities as a director of actors, his insistence on crushing realism, both mental and physical, that underlie the film's success.

U-boat 96 is 150 feet long and 10 feet wide; a man with outstretched arms could almost touch both sides. In this cigar tube, where the concept of "bath" exists only as a word in a crossword puzzle, forty-three men live for months on end, sharing a single toilet, sleeping in shifts for lack of space, and trying not to go crazy from the alternating boredom of pointless cruising and the chaos of sudden attack. Petersen and director of photography Jost Vocano, who shot more than 90 percent of the film with a hand-held camera rigged with a special steadying gyroscopic mount, so immerse us in the oppressiveness of this tiny tin that we are practically overcome by the fetid stink of the ripe salamis hanging from the walls. Except for Jürgen Prochnow as the captain, a Clint Eastwood type with the face of a suffering Christ, the actors are largely unfamiliar even to German audiences, and director Petersen went so far as to cast people off the streets if they looked right. And he did the nine months of filming in sequence, so that by the finale those faces reflect the toll of living and working in that terribly cramped space.

Petersen has also been a sensitive enough director to emphasize the plain and ordinary humanity of the crew members, using letters, photographs, snatches of music, bits of dialogue, so that when they find themselves in danger we care very much about their survival. And the perils U-96 encounters would mortify John Wayne — depth charges are the merest beginning for this lot, and each time the boat survives an ominous threat it is only to confront another one even more potentially deadly.

Petersen is especially good at building tension in these traumatic episodes and in capturing the hellish, apocalyptic, almost unimaginable chaos of a submarine under intense attack. There has been talk of *Das Boot* being an antiwar film because of the way it details the horrors of that claustrophopic maelstrom, but that is a bit much. *Das Boot* succeeds because it is classic filmmaking with a vengeance, its appeal the timeworn one of storybook heroism, albeit in a realistic frame and for a cause even the heroes seem to despise. It is a film that plays it straight, taking care not to betray our expectations with coyly modernistic plot twists, and it teaches the pleasant lesson that even the most melodramatic material is susceptible to quality control.

—*Kenneth Turan*

Edgar Reitz

∎

HEIMAT (1983)

Edgar Reitz's *Heimat* is probably the first great original film-novel, a work of extraordinary range and ambition. If most films today are so morally and artistically shabby that they depress you, this one is elating: It stretches your ideas of what movies can achieve and can be.

Heimat — which runs fifteen and a half hours and covers sixty-four years (1918–1982) in a fictional German village called Shabbach — has a novel's plentitude of character and event, heightened by a great film's visual and dramatic resources. It is Reitz's attempt to reclaim his country's history, prompted by his anger at the television miniseries "Holocaust" (whose characters he found "Americanized" and distorted). Perhaps that reaction flaws it slightly; there's an irony and discretion used in portraying the Nazis that will alienate some viewers.

But Reitz assumes we all grasp the evils of Hitler's regime. He's after the story we usually don't get: not of tyrants or victims, but of ordinary people, bystanders who allowed themselves to be blinded — and then, mostly, tried to blot out the memories after the war. It's the flip side of the devastating reality Claude Lanzmann reveals in *Shoah:* the montrous truths all these people sealed off.

Heimat is in eleven sections, and though it's the linkage and progression that dazzle you, any one of the eleven taken alone is better than most films you'll see this year. There's something heroically profuse about *Heimat* — prodigal, Bruegelian, a vast, Balzacian beehive of a story. More than two dozen major characters appear, with many minor ones drifting in and out, and they're all drawn by Reitz and his phenomenally gifted cast — professionals and amateurs — with superb intimacy and thoroughness.

The story centers on two village families, the Simons and the Weigands, joined together after World War I with marriage of Paul and Maria (a towering performance, running through the entire film, by Marita Breuer). The crux of *Heimat* — taken, like much else, from Reitz's own family history — occurs at the climax of the first part: Paul succumbs to wanderlust, abandons his family, and walks off down the road. Most films would follow the wanderer, the Odysseus. This one even begins with the classic image, his return home after the war. But *Heimat* instead is Penelope's saga: It's about all those who stayed. The title translates roughly as "homeland," suggesting both a matrix of nostalgic feelings and a heavy sentimental German film genre (one such, also called *Heimat,* is seen by Maria at the beginning of Part 5). The town itself becomes a protagonist, inexorably changing.

There's an excitement about watching this movie — particularly in the eight-hour theatrical chunks the director finds preferable — that far outweighs its daunting length.

We meet most of the characters in their youth, sometimes even in infancy, and follow them to old age and death; every action, every lovingly observed village ritual echoes and reverberates. Two lovers tumble in a sylvan embrace in the twenties, and we can project forward to the lives of their children, and grandchildren, half a century later.

Actions and events, bits of the landscape, begin to take on almost mystical significance; we can never tell how they'll return or recur, as the years roll on.

Reitz and cinematographer Gernot Roll make a rainbow of innovation, dryly rapturous, or shot with a near-Fordian mixture of spontaneity and reverie. They do something that seems odd at first, alternating between color and monochrome, sometimes within sequences or single shots. But besides any conscious pattern, there's a sense that they're using whichever stock fits a given moment, an idea revolutionary in its simplicity. Reitz's writing sometimes suggests Böll, and there's even a trace of Joyce (those peculiar little epiphanies of the everyday in *Dubliners*); Reitz's cinematic style is so eclectic that it variously recalls the Tavianis, Herzog, Tarkovsky, Welles, Lang, and Fellini. But the influences are totally subsumed: He's a true original.

Heimat accomplishes that magical task all art aspires to: It alters your perceptions, steeps you in its own created reality. It's a really stunning achievement of the imagination. Days after seeing it, you may find images of Shabbach and its villagers in your mind's eyes—the lush fields, distant mountains, Maria's knowing smile, the rheumy eyes of her brother Eduard (an amiable dolt who marries a whore and becomes the Nazi mayor), and the ferretlike features of the perpetual gladfly, Glasisch (Kurt Wagner), who loved Maria in youth and survives almost to the end. It's a lyrical film, but a knowing one; celebrating families and probing the forces that rend them, painting a ravishing countryside while showing, beneath, the demons that ravaged it. Watching *Heimat* we get a pleasure like that of a great nineteenth-century novel: Reitz hews up a piece of the earth and gives it to us, rich and teeming with life. Life buoyant and tragic; life in its nakedness, dreams, and disguises, life caught with a fullness and sympathy that few filmmakers can give us: a song of blood and earth—of home, and all that's hidden there.

—*Michael Wilmington*

Jerzy Skolimowski

■

MOONLIGHTING (1982)

The Polish director Jerzy Skolimowski once described himself as "laughing through clenched teeth." That phrase perfectly captures the spirit of *Moonlighting,* probably the wiliest film ever made about the collision of East and West. Hilarious and claustrophobic—like an unholy cross between Joseph Conrad and Samuel Beckett—it's an extended Polack joke with a punch line that could hardly be bleaker.

Moonlighting takes place in the winter of 1981, near the end of Solidarity's first bid to take control of Poland. Four Polish laborers go off to London with their tools, pretending to be on holiday; actually, they've been illegally hired to redo a flat owned by "the Boss" back in Warsaw. It seems a wonderfully fair arrangement. In a month, they'll make a year's wages back home, and the Boss has to pay only a quarter the cost of British labor. At first, workers Banaszak, Wolksi, and Kudaj (all Solidarity members) come off as the Warsaw road company of the Three Stooges. Potato-fed and potato-faced, they lurch about, take numerous pratfalls, and grumblingly follow the orders of their leader, Nowak (Jeremy Irons, in his first memorable screen performance). Nowak, who narrates the film, is the only one of the four to speak English—he's the others' connection to the outside world.

He's also the emotional weak link, an empty man haunted by his fear of failure and what the Boss may be up to with his wife Anna back home. Attempting to call her on December 13, Nowak discovers that martial law has just been declared. Not a member of Solidarity himself, he's torn by indecision: Should he tell the men, or will they stop working if he does? Seized by the logic of his position as foreman—and his desire to do something right for once—he chooses to keep them in the dark. Ashamed of this, and worried about the lack of money for materials, Nowak starts stealing to keep his men in food and underwear. (Since shoplifting is probably the movie's most nerve-wracking crime—everything the thief does is so visible—we writhe each time Nowak enters the neighborhood grocery.)

Yet even as he convinces himself he's working for the collective cause, he becomes just a bush-league version of General Jaruzelski, the man who cracked down on Solidarity. To keep his men ignorant (and working), Nowak bans them from church, burns their already state-censored mail, and orders them to stay in the flat; at one point, he even rips down a Solidarity poster on the street, lest it somehow put ideas in their heads. Bit by bit, the Boss's unfinished flat becomes a metaphor for the imprisoning Polish state, with Nowak an unhappy dictator who enforces even his most personal quirks (he won't let the men smoke). The others keep on working, but they hate him.

Moonlighting offers an obvious allegory of Polish life under the Party, with its bosses who live high, its beleaguered functionaries who try to hold things together, its oafish-seeming workers who do all the hard labor and get nothing for it. Yet, Skolimowski's angle on this is characteristically oblique. He gets us to identify with the neurotic Nowak, who's more like the average Western film viewer than the other workers (he speaks a language that alienates him from his fellows). For a while, anyway, we laugh at the other three because they have dumb faces and do things like shock themselves on light sockets; we share Nowak's derision. Yet however much sympathy we feel for him, he remains an oppressor who lies to his men even as he underestimates them. Though often buffoonish and by no means heroic, Banaszak, Wolksi, and Kudaj actually make the confining flat beautiful—they produce something. And their ultimate anger at Nowak's thieving and manipulation confers upon them a new dignity; it justifies their solidarity against their foreman. Skolimowski doesn't glorify these men (he obviously finds them clownish, too, a lot of the time). Nor does he want us to hate Nowak, a man condemned by his own weakness to a desperate loneliness.

The usual critical Cold Warriors seized on *Moonlighting* when it came out in 1982, using it as further proof of how horrible life is in Eastern Europe. Unfortunately, they seemed not to notice that Skolimowski's vision of the West is hardly more positive. In the Polish "police state" it's normal to leave your bicycle unchained outside a store, but the first time Nowak does it in London, the whole audience groans—we know what will happen. And, of course, it does. Nowak's a quick study, though, and soon knows the ways of the West; he simply steals somebody else's bike for himself. From start to finish, *Moonlighting* treats the Free World as little more than a supermarket whose consumer objects constantly tempt you while security cameras monitor your progress to the checkout line—where you're greeted by workers every bit as alienated as the Poles in the flat. In this consumerist jungle, whose only flash of green is the unnatural color of money, the once-innocent Nowak becomes far more deeply corrupted than he ever would have guessed. His final theft isn't food for the men — it's a luxury item for himself. Skolimowski is aware of all the ways you can lose your freedom.

On one of his forays, Nowak passes a Wrangler shop and sees a typical English advertisement, a model jutting her rear end into the camera to show off her skintight jeans. He enters the store with a crude black-and-white snapshot of Anna, a vaguely pretty, sulky-looking woman wearing a sweatshirt with "Wrangler" written on it. To the surprise of the shopgirl, he tries to convince her that this photo should be used on a poster. Such naïveté is sweet and we laugh — poor, silly Polack to think *that*. But the joke is also on our own Western sophistication. We've become so attuned to market values that it seems foolish, even unnatural, to use an ordinary woman in an advertisement for everyday wear.

Not everything in *Moonlighting* is so sneakily pointed. When a bunch of children come caroling, the workers pop the door open and, together for once, begin serenading them in Polish — a comic moment that's charged with a strange, poignant lyricism. This whole movie is built on sequences that have the effortless, almost casual subversiveness of Buñuel; Skolimowski never seems to be straining for Art. Yet there's not a wasted shot in the full ninety-seven minutes. Even bits that look like simple comic throwaways — Londoners filling other people's trash cans on the sly — serve Skolimowski's larger notions about East and West, about the absurd, selfish deeds people perform by moonlight.

Back in Poland, where he was an early collaborator with Roman Polanski, Skolimowski had a reputation as a master improviser who liked to work fast. Inspired by the clampdown on Solidarity, *Moonlighting* was shot in a little over three weeks, and the finished film shows that Skolimowski's methods have remained spontaneous enough to incorporate happy accidents. At one point, Nowak pedals past a man walking a poodle. While filming this shot, a cat unexpectedly walked on camera and arched its back at the dog in warning; the two animals eyed each other warily. In this chance encounter, Skolimowski found a natural metaphor for all the film's tensions.

Tensions of which he's well aware. As an émigré artist who's lived in London and Los Angeles, he knows what it means to be stranded between two worlds; Nowak is, in part, Skolimowski's surrogate. The original idea for the film came, in fact, when he invited Polish workers to fix up his West Kensington house in return for being taken to strip shows and the like. The military crackdown gave this idea a new political resonance and allowed the director — the most uncompromising of the Polish filmmakers to emerge in the sixties — to express his own grief and rage at what had been done, once again, to his country. And, I suspect, it let him assuage his own guilt at living so well in the West when things were so bleak in Poland. (With typical irony, Skolimowski gives himself a cameo as the Boss.)

Moonlighting was a box-office flop in the United States, and it's easy to see why. At a time when the West was eager to sentimentalize Solidarity, Skolimowski showed a bunch of apparently bumbling workers led to disaster by an angst-riddled betrayer who wins no redemption. Nor did he give American audiences the easy satisfactions of, say, *Moscow on the Hudson,* which suggested that, despite everything, the West really is the Free World. For all the wit and grace of this movie (and of all his best work), Jerzy Skolimowski remains one of the most pessimistic of all filmmakers — a man who cut his teeth on the rubble of post-World War II Warsaw. Laughing and clenching, he knows that we spend our lives in endless bouts of gridlock, headbutting, and pain. He knows there are no Free Worlds to be found.

—John Powers

Istvan Szabo

■

MEPHISTO (1981)

Istvan Szabo's *Mephisto* — an adaptation of the long-suppressed novel by Thomas Mann's son, Klaus — is an almost magnetically powerful indictment of political opportunism in the arts. Its hero, Hendrik, begins as a provincial actor in pre-Hitler Germany, erupting with demons of ambition, drive, energy. When we first see him backstage at a frilly, opulent musical show he seems on the verge of exploding: a volcano with its peak momentarily capped. Gradually, he climbs to the top, marrying the daughter of a prominent artistic family, assuming greater and greater parts, appearing at rallies for the Communist party, moving in "society," and finally staging his greatest triumph: as Mephistopheles in Goethe's *Faust.*

But this is only the prelude. Coincident with Hendrik's rise is Hitler's. Most of Hendrik's old allies are driven underground or out of the country. With consummate opportunism, he switches sides—joins his fortunes to the favors of a sadistic minister and general (a thinly disguised portrait of Hermann Goering) and becomes director of the German state theater. He plays Mephistopheles once again, but in a safer, stodgier production suited to the tastes of his overlords. It goes without saying that the real-life roles have been switched; it is Mephisto—Hendrik—who has sold his soul to the Devil, and Mephisto who must give it up when the forces of hell call in their chips.

The original *Mephisto* was a *roman à clef* and the subject of the longest libel suit in German history. (Klaus Mann, who wrote the book in 1936 and died in 1949, never lived to see it published in his native land; thirty years later, it is still tied up by the courts.) Hendrik was based on the German actor and state theater director Gustaf Grundgens, who had once been married to Klaus's sister, Erika, and whom Goering later championed. Grundgens, too, was famous for his Mephistopheles, and his heirs saw to it that this devastating portrait of their father was unpublishable in the fatherland.

Now, ironically, Szabo's film, made in Hungary, has made the novel world famous; it won the foreign-film Oscar in April 1982 over the formidable competition of Andrzej Wajda's Cannes winner and hymn to the Solidarity movement, *Man of Iron*. And the violently critical picture of Grundgens becomes—in Karl Maria Brandauer's brilliant portrayal of Hendrik—perhaps the screen's quintessential portrait of the artist as weak-willed, slimy opportunist, prostituting, corrupting, and destroying himself by inches as he toadies to a fascist regime. In Brandauer's hands Grundgens has posthumously won an evil immortality.

Not that Hendrik is unattractive or unsympathetic. One of the great qualities of Szabo's film is that it makes us see the sympathetic side of Hendrik—his attempts to use his influence to help his friends, to administer "justly" as part of a fascist bureaucracy—and the real power and brilliance of his acting. He isn't an easy target for ridicule or contempt. To a degree, we can follow the justifications and sophistries he falls into—that he must preserve his art in the face of everything; that it can stay untouched by the bloodshed and chaos around him.

Brandauer, at the beginning, gives Hendrik an almost impish quality, both demonic and childish. There's a wonderful, long erotic scene between Hendrik and his black dancer-mistress in which his lovemaking seems tender and spastic and violent all at once. Hendrik is like many artists — a big child. He preserves that child within him — the un-self-consciousness, the spontaneity, the sense of wonder — for his acting, but turns devious and corrupt in the outside world to promote his career. He hides his mistress, marries women he doesn't love, adopts philosophies he doesn't believe whenever it suits him, whenever another path to success seems about to open. On the stage, through his consummate artifice, he becomes the incarnation of power, of evil, of cunning and corruption. Offstage, he is a weakling with a dash of genius, never really evil, only pathetic.

The real evil is in the Goering character, played with equal bravura by Rolf Hoppe. Hoppe paints him full of magnificent contrasts: a fat, bullet-headed, brutal-looking man with a cold, aristocratic gaze and sensual lips; a sadist who speaks mildly and with studied cultivation but who becomes merciless when aroused. In real life, Goering was a genuine war hero with a Byzantine sex life and some artistic pretensions: he pillaged French museums of their best art, and one of his favorite movies, amazingly, was Renoir's *Grand Illusion*. He also sponsored Grundgens's career, at the behest of his movie-actress wife. Hoppe, like Brandauer, imparts equal measures of irony and lucid, terrifying insight to this role; he becomes the inverse of Hendrik — faintly ludicrous on the surface, terrifying underneath.

But *Mephisto* is not simply a superb psychological drama or a wounding political parable. Its real genius comes from Szabo's deep penetration into the world of theater — all its charm, all its artifice — and the soul of the actor — quicksilver, mercurial — and its exposure of both of them to the pitiless light of social brutalities. *Mephisto* has many of the same themes and ideas as Truffaut's recent *The Last Métro;* the difference lies in the brilliant elaboration of detail with which Szabo recreates that darkling, incandescent backstage world. Brandauer's Hendrik convinces us on two levels: as a superb actor and as a reprehensible, pitiable man. The performance is stunning, but, as *Mephisto* reminds us continually, a performance never arises in a vacuum. Around it, and within it, are turbulence and chaos. The final hell of Mephisto comes as searchlights stab at him in a dark, empty stadium — the man at last without his masks, helpless, undisguised, trembling in the raw light as darkness surrounds him.

—*Michael Wilmington*

Giuseppe Tornatore

■

CINEMA PARADISO (1988)

There's magic, romance, and fun in Italy's entry for the best Foreign Film Oscar, which has already received the Grand Jury Prize at Cannes. This is only the second feature for writer-director Giuseppe Tornatore, known for documentaries and TV films, but he has plugged into something vital about the hold movies have on us. Set in a small village in postwar Sicily—before TVs and VCRs—the film re-creates a time when people gathered in shoe-box theaters, like this little village's Cinema Paradiso, to watch flickering images that could conjure up the whole world.

Tornatore tells his story through the eyes of a fatherless eight-year-old boy named Salvatore, played by Salvatore Cascio, who persuades Alfredo (Philippe Noiret), the Paradiso's gruff projectionist, to take him on as an assistant. Noiret's beautifully modulated performance blends perfectly with Cascio's exuberance; they are both superb. For Salvatore, the outmoded projector, the frames of celluloid, and the posters are all holy relics. Alfredo even permits his protégé to see uncut films before the village priest orders the excision of any glimpse of *amore*.

Later, Alfredo urges the adolescent Salvatore (Marco Leonardi) to find a new life outside the confining village. The boy does so, and he never looks back. When the adult Salvatore (Jaques Perrin), now a film director in Rome, returns for Alfredo's funeral, the Paradiso is about to be razed to make way for a parking lot. Movies and the ways of seeing them have changed, and so has Salvatore, who seems detached until he receives Alfredo's legacy—a gift too surprising to reveal—which finally allows Salvatore to weep for his loss. Tornatore's sublime film makes it tough not to join Salvatore. Movie lovers will lose their hearts to *Cinema Paradiso,* not out of nostalgia, but for Tornatore's vigorous demonstration of the enduring power of dreams.

—*Peter Travers*

RECOMMENDED FROM THE SOVIET UNION

Aside from the most prominent directors, the history of interesting Russian filmmaking from the 1960s to the 1990s is the history of the "shelvies" and the post-*glasnost* movies. The best of the films censored and "shelved" by government authorities are *Repentance* and *My Friend Ivan Lapshin*. Since then, new opportunities to take a direct look at contemporary Soviet upheaval have offered, in the three best-known cases, the kitchen-sink realism of *Little Vera* and *Taxi Blues* — and, in the most poetic of the

Opposite page: scene from *Little Vera*.

post-*glasnost* films, Vitaly Kanevski's tale of 4,000 blows, *Freeze, Die, Come to Life*.

Tengiz Abuladze

■

REPENTANCE (1987)

The savagely brilliant *Repentance,* set in a small city in Soviet Georgia, may come as shock to Americans on more than one level. Since it surfaced at Cannes and then at Telluride and Toronto, the talk has been about the film's anti-Stalinism, possibly leading American audiences to expect a dark and dry polemic.

If so, they overlooked the fact that the director, Tengiz Abuladze, is a Georgian and, in the words of Jay Leyda, scholar of the Soviet film, "It is nearly impossible for a Georgian to make an ordinary movie."

And so, for all its thinly veiled allegory, *Repentance,* and particularly its first third, is lit with bursts of satiric humor, with music, bits of opera, and great flights of surreal imagery, which only serve to intensify its growing horror. And it is never less than physically gorgeous.

The film is a story within a story, opening and closing in the cluttered, folksy kitchen of a beautiful sad-eyed woman, Ketevan (nicknamed Keti), who is making cake after cake, all in the shapes of small village churches. Her visitor is a sort of Saroyanesque comic relief: a mustachioed soldier absently munching the steeples off her cakes. He's shocked by the newspaper's front page: Varlam Aravidze, the city's last, great mayor, his own personal friend, has died. As we move into Varlam's funeral and what follows, we are also moving into Keti's reverie of the recent past.

The funeral's bombastic excesses, punctuated by the little soldier's eye-rolling and gnat-catching, are nice enough for silent film comedy, but what follows is pure Buñuel — or Abuladze. To the increasing consternation of his adult son, Avel, daughter-in-law Guliko, and grandson Tornike, Varlam will not stayed buried.

Dawn after the funeral finds his bulky figure, arms folded, propped up against a tree in Avel's courtyard. Reburied, he appears again and again. Finally, his "persecutor" is caught. It is a woman who will admit the deed but not her guilt: As long as she lives, she says with defiant dignity, the tyrant Varlam Aravidze will not lie decently buried.

And as she explains why, we move back in time to see the woman as the beautiful eight-year-old Keti, blowing soap bubbles from the window of her artist-father's house on the day Varlam was elected mayor.

(In this superlative cast, an actor of stunning range, Avtandil Makharadze, plays Varlam and Avel: Varlam, histrionic, cunning, operatic; Avel, naturalistic and contemporary. They are such extraordinarily different characterizations that apparently even Soviet audiences had trouble realizing that this was a dual role.)

Our first glimpse of Varlam alive and at his prime is chilling. As he stands on a balcony, with his Fuehrer's mustache, his Mussolini black skirt strapped by leather suspenders, his Stalin-like shock of hair and his pince-nez glinting in the sun, Varlam is a kind of composite dictator. (It is not lost on Soviet audiences that Joseph Stalin and his notorious secret police chief, Lavrenti Beria, were both from Georgia. And no one from any culture will miss the Edward Gorey–like raven, gibbet, and noose, just to Varlam's right.)

Abuladze keeps his touch lightly wicked during Varlam's first political address, packs it with silent-film slapstick touches, with a pinky-comic floating cherub wearing a Varlam mustache, but the comic moments are winding to a close.

Varlam enters as a heavily flirtatious, opera-loving fool, enchanted by Keti's entire, beautiful family — her chestnut-bearded and Christlike father, Sandor, and her exquisite, exotic mother, Nina (played by Abuladze's own daughter). But soon Varlam hides his dangerous side less and less, his contempt for art, religion, humanistic values. As his detractors begin to disappear, guards in medieval armor begin to stalk the city, their arrival a stomach-clutching signal of despair.

This reign of terror is given great images: Nina's dream in which she and a fleeing Sandor try to hide among clods of dirt, only their beautiful, eggshell-fragile faces above ground, while Varlam's mounted knights thunder past their ears.

Most searing of all is a sequence that Abuladze has taken from a true incident: Some of the women of missing men hear that trees carved with the names of exiled prisoners have turned up at a logging camp. Wading in water, the black-clothed women move from log to log, finding their husbands' and sons' names among them, caressing the truth within the wood. As Keti and Nina search for Sandor's name, the logs are split and cut; the truth is reduced to toothpicks and then to sawdust.

It is the film's most terrible moment, worthy of Andrei Tarkovsky. Not all of *Repentance's* controlled fury has this power; some of the heavy-laden symbolism remains opaque and baffling, and there is nearly a quarter more story to come, the part dealing with the legacy of the adult Avel and his tortured teenage son, Tornick.

Yet the questions of conscience with which Tornick assaults his father are crucial to Abuladze's rigorous moral conclusion, since the director clearly considers Avel an even greater villain than his father. (Abuladze was co-writer of the screenplay, with Nana Djanedlidze and Rezo Kveselava.) Most likely these are the most troubling moments for Soviet audiences as well, which have apparently greeted the film with minutes of standing applause as well as stunned astonishment at its close. In truth, they are more melodramatically staged than any other section of the film.

Yet *Repentance,* for all its occasional allegorical mysteries, is coherent and powerful, and unswerving in its persistence that Stalinist evil not remain below ground. The fact that *Repentance* has been chosen as the official Soviet entry in the Best Foreign Film category at the Academy Awards is only part of the heartening aura that attends its arrival.

— *Sheila Benson*

Alexei Gherman
■

MY FRIEND IVAN LAPSHIN (1986)

Once-banned Soviet director Alexei Gherman's *My Friend Ivan Lapshin* is like a bitter aperitif—strange and hard to swallow. Its subtle political references to the Soviet Union of fifty years ago may leave you confused or even cross; they did me, at first. You could call its plot anecdotal or even irrelevant and no one would argue with you.

Yet the film is haunting; having seen it, I want to look again. And like a difficult piece of literature, its obliqueness is provoking; I want to learn how to understand it.

Withheld from release for almost three years, *Ivan Lapshin* begins as a "sad tale, a declaration of love" from a middle-aged writer in present-day Russia to the people he lived with as a seven-year-old boy in a small port town on the Volga in 1935. Moving back in time smoothly, we see them as he did.

They are Lapshin, the town's police chief, a lean, interesting-looking career officer in the NKVD (precursor of the KGB); three of his men, including the narrator's father; the boy himself; and other house-holders in this rude, communal flat. (The subtitles never hint at the whereabouts of this seven-year-old's mother.)

Shortly after Lapshin's fortieth birthday celebration, a journalist-friend, Khanin, despondent over his wife's sudden death from diph-theria, moves in with them. The chaotic opening action, as the men prowl the flat restlessly, seems as wildly random as its camera angles, yet none of it is.

What narrative there is concerns a third-rate theatrical troupe that has come to town. In a diffident, almost schoolboy fashion, Lapshin develops a crush on Natasha, the most ardent and untalented of the actresses. (He provides the troupe with almost-impossible-to-get firewood as a sign of his affection.) Though Natasha would deny it with her last crying/laughing breath, she is a quintessential Chekhov fascinator.

Lapshin's glancing relationship with Natasha—inevitably in love with someone else, the married Khanin—occurs at the same time that Lapshin finally tracks down a long-sought murderer, the dangerous Solovyov, in a sort of grand, *cinéma vérité* police raid at the film's end. (Shot in inky blacks and grays, it still has more authority than most criminal actions in films.)

Plot, most assuredly, is not the point of the film. Background is, and a swirling sense of recollection that is its dreamlike attraction. Gher-man's talent is in his method: the minute re-creation of this miserable period, in a camera that is never still, moving sensuously, sometimes through mists or haze. Characters sometimes glance into its lens, startled but accommodating its presence.

Gherman, with cinematographer Valery Fedosov, has shot this memory piece, based on a novel of his father's, in tints like faded photographs, ochers and smoky grays. And not even his aesthetic is clear-cut; just when we decide that it is the present only which appears in color, a color sequence invades the past.

What American audiences must also struggle with is its possibly unfamiliar political background. There are no overt references to Stalin; only at the movie's end, his portrait appears at the head of a trolley that rattles through town, pulling yet another of the town's bands ("One for everybody here," Natasha complains wildly), this one ominously militaristic. It is like a reference to another filmic trolley, the famous one at the end of *Slave of Love,* which carries its heroine uncertainly toward a postrevolutionary future.

Yet 1935 was a watershed year for the Soviets. After the forceful collectivization of the peasantry, Stalin's Great Terror began in December of 1934, with the assassination of a Leningrad party secretary, Sergei Kirov. And we are told that it is from Leningrad that Lapshin has been transferred.

Gherman has explained in interviews that Lapshin "has unshakable faith in Stalin, but at night he weeps. There is something ominous in the air." Papa Yuri Gherman's novels were part of a huge outpouring of Soviet literature that attempted to make its long black leather-coated cops, the forerunners of the KGB, into dashing figures like the Canadian Mounties.

His forty-nine-year-old filmmaker son, whose career, like that of Elem Klimov and Serge Paradjanov, has finally been released with the thaw of Gorbachev's *glasnost* (openness), seems more concerned with the general misery of provincial life where shortages of almost everything — gasoline, sugar, firewood — are the order of the day.

If Lapshin is a romanticized figure, it is through the casting of Andrei Boltnev, a lanky Henry Fonda–esque actor, in the role. We see that Lapshin, although given to the nightmares and solitude of conscience, has enormously dangerous powers. He jokes almost offhandedly "about putting someone in his place." That place is, increasingly, the work camp. We learn that the plain, stringy-haired prostitute whom Lapshin has obligingly provided for Natasha to study as a model for her role at the theater, has been sent off to one, after she has turned on Natasha like a spitting cat.

And near the theater, where earnest Soviet Boy Scouts proudly tend a science project where the fox and chickens live together in harmony, there is disaster. "The predator's instinct just flared up," and the fox has eaten his pen mates. No wonder the idealistic Lapshin broods at night.

Because *My Friend Ivan Lapshin* is not an overtly anti-Stalinist portrait of one of his most early murderous eras, it may be seen in some quarters as a whitewash. It might seem that you don't need corpses piling up like cordwood to sense the dangers and the disillusion that are beginning to seep into its characters' very bones, like the mists and mysteries of this disturbing film. **(Video Request.)**

—*Sheila Benson*

Vitaly Kanevski

■

FREEZE, DIE, COME TO LIFE (1990)

Here's the post-*glasnost* Soviet film that's more than a post-*glasnost* film. Vasily Pichul's *Little Vera* and Pavel Lounguine's *Taxi Blues,* movies by brave directors, say: "This country is in a mess." *Freeze, Die, Come to Life* is from a poetic director who turns the same point into a work of art.

Vitaly Kanevski won 1990's Best First Film prize at the Cannes Film Festival with this movie named for the freeze tag game he played as a kid in an east Russian mining town. He's the Truffaut of the Gulag, retelling his own story in the life of his hero, ten-year-old Valerka. With no father and a barmaid mother who answers suggestions that she marry by saying, "Tramps like me sell it cheap," Valerka's landscape is even bleaker than the one faced by Truffaut's hero in *The 400 Blows.*

In summer, the boy's town is an expanse of mud and puddles. In winter, it's frozen mud and ice—the kind of place Stalin would consider a promising site for two grim camps: one for Japanese POWs, one for resettled or politically dissident nationals. Like kids everywhere, though, the hero and his remarkable friend Galiya know how to take the frozen world around them and make it come to life.

Galiya is a little older and much smarter than Valerka, but she likes his spunky spirit enough to teach him what's what. When he copies her marketplace business selling hot tea, you can tell from her cheerfully watchful turnip face that she thinks he has possibilities. She decides to pal around with him even though he pushes his own product by loudly claiming her pot has cockroaches. When someone steals the skates he's bought with his tea proceeds, she figures out how to spring him from school and steal the skates back.

Prowling the railroad tracks, they may bump into a great adventure or into evidence of Soviet poverty and Stalin's cruelty. Of the two prisoner groups, the Japanese have the better deal. Valerka and Galiya never know when they'll step into the shed where a fifteen-year-old girl at the labor camp is begging a miner to impregnate her so she'll be sent home. Or when a Moscow intellectual in the flour line will go stark, raving mad and wander off to mix his flour with mud and eat it while the circle of town kids who expected to taunt him fall silent at this horror more incomprehensible than the ones they've already seen.

In an image as deeply felt as anything in the greatest early Soviet films, Kanevski holds his camera on the gaunt El Greco face of the Moscow man whose crazy eyes seem to be looking beyond earth for salvation. But these images of frozen life are always balanced by images of the kids' softly radiant resistance. In alternating scenes, Kanevski makes you see his desolate train-stop town first as a muddy pit, then as a track of light.

Even after *glasnost,* worried producers gave him money to film only the first ten minutes of his controversial movie. He used it to buy out-of-date film stock and shoot the entire story, inventing a way to make the old stock work for the tarnished, "dirty marble" look he had in mind: "Like marble steps walked on in the snow," he said during a Cannes interview, "soiled but very beautiful."

Every image works just that way, with the grays, stark whites, and smoky blacks reflecting his story's combination of harsh, luminous experience. Even his camera seems eager for everything good or bad life can offer as it presses up against faces or pushes right into the frenzy of the flour line. In one of Valerka's tricks, he throws yeast into the school latrine, then plays innocent when the principal insists that kids march through the muck singing an anthem to Stalin: "Ebullient, mighty, no one more powerful. . . ." Throughout the movie, yeasty humor is always part of Kanevski's brew of horror and lyricism.

During its last half hour, the story's journey with the kid pursued by cops and exploited by thieves gets a bit bumpy, and the concluding image meant to represent social insanity falls far short of Kanevski's intentions. But of the new films from the Soviet Union, this is the one I'd most strongly recommend. The first feature by a fifty-five-year-old director who spent eight years in a labor camp, this is the post-*glasnost* debut that makes me look forward to a sequel. **(Video request.)**

—Kathy Schulz Huffhines

Pavel Lounguine

■

TAXI BLUES (1990)

Pavel Lounguine's *Taxi Blues* is *glasnost*'s first morning-after film. It's chaos buzzing over the dregs of *glasnost*'s extinguished binge, so up to date that it points the way toward the sobering possibility that *glasnost* may turn out to be the briefest of summers before a long winter of civil war and reaction. Crude, vital, immediate, propelled by hurtling energy, it sends a Russian taxi driver and Jewish saxophonist chasing after each other in a landscape spinning with disorientation. It's surrounded by demoralization, but high on its own energy. Yet energy-worship, as anyone with a long memory knows, is one of the preludes to fascism. What's most ironic about this comedy of chaos is that it reveals the same old Russian malaises ready to pounce — class warfare, antisemitism, nihilism, dead souls.

The film begins with working-class Ivan stoically planted behind the wheel of his taxi, hauling a bunch of late-night partygoers led by manic Lyosha. One by one, the revelers drop away until only Lyosha and Ivan remain. Then Lyosha takes off, stiffing Ivan for seventy rubles on the meter. After an angry Ivan comes looking for Lyosha, and finds him all too willing to be beat up, as if he's done this many times before, a perverse kind of bonding ensues. First, Ivan shoves Lyosha into a toilet stall and impounds his saxophone. Then, when he finds it's valuable, he has another idea. He goes back and takes Lyosha's passport instead and turns him into an indentured servant — making him scrub the taxi, tote customers' baggage, and perform other menial tasks, giving Lyosha a piece of floor to sleep on in his own apartment until the debt is paid. What he wants, in his anti-intelligentsia, antisemitic way, is respect. Ivan wants Lyosha to apologize, to respect his dignity.

The plan backfires, though, in a couple of ways. First, Lyosha lets the tub overflow while he's off hunting cologne to drink, causing four hundred rubles damage. Then, the stoical Ivan, given to taking out his rage by lifting weights when not indulging in violent clinches with his pork-butcher girlfirend, starts to change. The overflowing water rather obviously symbolizes what Lyosha comes to mean to Ivan, just as the slaughterhouse where he has become a familiar represents the life he had been leading. After stripping Lyosha of his Western clothes and writing him off as a hopeless drunk, Ivan is amazed to see Lyosha canonized by appearing on television. In the end, he finds that the drunken folksinging of the slaughterhouse no longer satisfies him, and he goes to a rock-jazz concert and cries.

But it costs him. Surprisingly, the film's dark subtext argues, like Plato, that art brings even greater ruin to the working classes than drink—of which there is plenty. Everybody is either selling bootleg vodka in alleys or garages or queueing up to buy it. The Russia they stumble through doesn't seem liberated so much as uprooted. Late in the film, when Ivan lands hard on a smart-mouth kid and rips off the American flag sewn on the sleeve of the kid's T-shirt, we understand what's happening, why Ivan is lashing back at the symbolic source of the new and confusing frustration with which freedom is buffeting him. One of the things that imparts immediacy to Lounguine's messy but compelling film is its sudden eruptions of brutality of several sorts.

What's shocking about the pervasive antisemitism is the casualness with which it's expressed, as if its lies blaming Russia's ills on the Jews are a given. And yet the film belongs more to Piotr Zaitchenko's working-class Ivan than to Piotr Mamonov's nouveau-Dostoyevsky member of the intelligentsia. For all his limitations, Ivan has heart, whereas we only hear Lyosha's genius and deep soul proclaimed; we never believe in it. Ivan's rage seems to be based on something; Lyosha's—which he turns on himself—isn't. But we do believe in the deep-rootedness and virulence of the class warfare they're caught up in, and how resistant to change it is. It's going to take more than relabeling to reduce the load of misery under which Russia once again seems to be groaning in *Taxi Blues*. Even if, paradoxically, Lounguine inscribes it with enormous gusto. One can easily understand why Russians feel uneasy about this film being exported. It strikes that old Russian nerve—the fear of being regarded as uncultured. But it also strikes home. **(Video request.)**

—*Jay Carr*

Vasily Pichul

■

LITTLE VERA (1988)

Orson Welles once predicted that a film might someday change the world—though it wouldn't necessarily be a *good* film. He did not foresee that the movie itself might prove unnecessary.

Such is the case with *Little Vera,* the first Soviet film to be promoted in *Playboy.* Following in the tradition of Marilyn, Jayne, and Mamie van Doren, Natalya Negoda now makes her appearance on the newsstands and in the sock drawers of America. Even as I write, an arc of erotic energy is rising from our continent, jetting over a Great Circle Route to descend on Moscow in a pacific haze. I interrupt the healing flow only to bring the harmless, incidental news that *Little Vera* is actually pretty good.

Rough-edged, alert, and frequently very funny, the film is the work of director Vasily Pichul, writer Maria Khmelik, and an excellent cast headed by Negoda, whose talents go well beyond her willingness to spread *glasnost.* Already fifty million Soviet citizens have seen *Little Vera,* according to the American distributor. No doubt the film's two brief nude scenes account for part of that success; though they might seem negligible in America, where *Playboy* gives better value for your money, the scenes must be a real provocation in the Motherland. But they are only a small part of the film's challenges, which turn out to involve even the choice of location.

Set in Soviet Ukraine, in an industrial landscape full of smokestacks, railyards, and docks, *Little Vera* takes place in a city named for the postwar era's chief censor of the arts, Zhdanov. There, in an apartment you can all but smell, lives Vera. Her parents harbor illusions that she might go to college, but that seems unlikely, unless they've started giving lessons in hair streaking, gum chewing, and staring into space. Vera labors as a telephone operator but works only at hanging out, usually with the sort of people who get a cold eye from the cops. She's among them at an open-air disco, complete with gang fights and bad rock music, when she meets Sergei (Andrei Sokolov).

He looks like the star of *Alexander Nevsky,* Nikolai Cherkassov, trying to imitate James Dean. No sooner have he and Vera exchanged their first cigarette than they retire to his pit of a dormitory, to make love beneath AIDS posters warning against casual sex. By this point, even the slowest-witted viewer will have gathered that these young people qualify for the label of hooligans. But it also should be obvious that Vera and Sergei are thoroughly, astonishingly innocent. "Do you love me?" Vera asks, rising from his bed. "Of course," Sergei replies. And, for the rest of the film, they stick to their word.

To a degree that is remarkable in any feature film, Soviet or otherwise, *Little Vera* refuses to schematize its characters. Vera's father is a hopeless alcoholic, but he also holds his job steadfastly and truly loves his children. The mother is tired and bitter, but she still contrives a lavish luncheon for Vera and Sergei, at which she performs with relentless optimism. Vera's brother, a doctor who lives in Moscow, is a pompous, arrogant, pill-pushing young twit who nevertheless makes the long trip to Zhdanov whenever his family needs him. These are all people who have managed to make a mess of their lives, as people often will; and the film does not blame them for it. It follows closely and sympathetically instead, putting the viewer into the middle of this disorderly family while allowing enough distance for the audience to think, and to laugh.

Shot with frequent recourse to a hand-held camera, which stays on top of the actors yet doesn't seem to crowd them, *Little Vera* is full of improvisatory moments and small gestures that turn out to be just right. When the police break up a fight at the disco, you see one of them smile for just a moment as he shoves a young man into the van. When Vera's father is in his cups late at night, his drink of choice turns out to be not Soviet vodka but Beefeater's gin. A delicate negotiation between Vera and her mother is interrupted when the brother casually walks into the scene; oblivious, he stands between the two women, yawning, then playfully clamps a clothespin onto Vera's sleeve before exiting. A dressmaking session with Vera and her best friend turns into a combination drinking binge, crying jag, and yoga demonstration; a visit to police headquarters, where Vera has to give a deposition, turns into a painfully funny exercise in bureaucratic slapstick. If there is a lesson to be learned from all this, political or moral, then it has escaped me. All I got from the film was the pleasure of seeing the crowded, irrational, sweaty texture of the characters' lives.

And that's why Andrei Zhdanov, in his time, would have made the filmmakers fear for their lives. Few figures in the history of the arts have so richly deserved to be pissed on; and I am happy to think that the persecutor of Akhmatova and Shostakovich, however he turns in his grave, must now be getting wet from *Little Vera*. It's a fine enough irony that his name will be linked forever with that of the first Soviet citizen to pose naked for an American girlie magazine. But, better than that, the city of Zhdanov is the scene of the following exchange.

"Do you have a goal in life?" Sergei asks Vera, as the two lay entwined on a beach. "We have a common goal," she replies solemnly: "Communism." With those words, played for laughs before fifty million Soviet citizens, the world indeed changed.

—*Stuart Klawans*

RECOMMENDED

FROM

SOUTH

AMERICA

Like the carioca, almost all movies from Brazil are rambunctiously sexy and tuneful, with bass rhythms critiquing Brazilian society. If you want a good time — and more — call *Dona Flor and Her Two Husbands, Opera do Malandro, Hour of the Star,* or *Bye Bye Brazil.* For a film in the unsparing yet poetic tradition of *Los Olvidados,* see *Pixote.*

Once the dictatorship lid was off, Argentina became the South American country exporting the most important films in the mid-

Opposite page: scene from *Sugar Cane Alley.*

eighties: Luis Puenzo's *The Official Story* and Maria-Luisa Bemberg's *Camila*. Directors Gregory Nava and Euzhan Palcy brought important Central American and Caribbean stories to the screen by tapping American Playhouse funds for *El Norte* and international financial backing for *Sugar Cane Alley*.

Suzana Amaral

■

HOUR OF THE STAR (1985)

"I am a typist, a virgin, and I like Coca-Cola." So says Macabea, the ugly duckling heroine of this excellent Brazilian film based on a novella by Clarice Lispector. What Macabea *doesn't* say—but what director Suzana Amaral, a mother of nine, shows with humor and poignancy—is that she's also doomed. Doomed by her background (she's an ignorant peasant from the sticks). Doomed by her circumstances (she's lost in the cruel city of São Paolo). Doomed by her society (Brazil pays no heed to poor women). And doomed by her dreams (she imagines herself as a glamorous film queen). Yet through all this doom, Macabea succeeds in becoming one of the most endearing heroines in years. Whether scarfing chicken as she sits on the toilet or falling for a popinjay who's bound to treat her badly, she always incarnates a peculiar state of grace (perfectly caught by actress Marcelia Cartaxo). Often funny and never patronizing, this small gem of a film lives up to the strange beauty of its heroine's ill-starred life.

—*John Powers*

Hector Babenco

■

PIXOTE (1981)

There are three million abandoned children in Brazil—swarms of scavenging, thieving street kids. Unwanted—many of them children of prostitutes or unmarried mothers—they're born into vagrancy; turned loose by parents who can't feed them or send them to school, they learn to pick pockets and grab purses and hustle. It's their only way of surviving. In the Brazilian movie *Pixote* (pronounced roughly "pee-*shoat*"), a judge has been murdered on a street in São Paulo, and the police have to take some action, so they routinely round up dozens of these kids, including ten-year-old Pixote (Portuguese slang for "Peewee"), and throw them in a reformatory. There, behind rotting walls, Pixote (Fernando Ramos da Silva) watches as several of the larger boys gang-rape a kid not much older than he is. He sees boys beaten and killed, and he learns to say nothing when the guards and officials come around and ask questions. A bully spits in his milk and he drinks it down, because if he doesn't he'll be in trouble with one group or another. He stares as if he weren't there—his round eyes go dead, and his truculent baby face is indifferent. But he's a little camera taking it all in, and he's quick—he learns how to maneuver.

A group of boys, including Pixote, break out, and he and three others stick together like a family; they snatch enough purses and wallets to make their way to Rio de Janeiro and begin dealing cocaine. Outsmarted by the adult criminals, the kids buy an aging, drunken prostitute from a pimp and go into business with her: she brings men home and they rob them, at gunpoint. When you see children who are treated as an urban infestation—who *are* an urban infestation—you recognize the enormous difference between countries where kids get an education and countries where large numbers of them don't. (The slum children who were recruited to act in this movie can't read or write.) As the director, Hector Babenco, sees it, there's something essential missing in Pixote: no one has ever made him feel that his life had any value. He's a snub-nosed infant asserting his wants, and when they're denied his mouth turns down and he changes into a baby gangster—a runt Scarface. He kills innocently, in the sense that he doesn't understand the enormity of the crime.

When the boys are on the grayish beach in Rio, Babenco isn't doing travel poster shots of Sugar Loaf. *Pixote* has its own look—a very distinctive pinkish glow, as if the film stock were infused with the colors of dawn—and there are lovely pale-salmon tones and grays and browns. The incidents don't appear to be set up for the camera—things just seem to be happening and every image is expressive. (Well, maybe not every one: when the whore brings an American back to her fleabag, he's such a crude, swag-bellied gringo that the picture seems, fleetingly, to be pandering to audience hostility.) What goes on in this movie is different from what goes on in American movies. The imagination at work is both romantic and antiromantic, and the mixture has the intensity that reaches back at least as far as *Don Quixote*. (Babenco, who wrote the script with Jorge Duran, from the novel *Infância dos Mortos,* by José Louzeiro, may have chosen the film title for its ironic echo of Quixote.) Brazil is steeped in poverty and paganism and Christianity and Pop; starving teenage transvestites— Indian and Negro—put on wigs and call themselves Marilyn. Babenco's imagery is realistic, but his point of view is shockingly lyrical. South American writers, such as Gabriel García Márquez, seem to be in perfect, poetic control of madness, and Babenco has some of this gift, too. South American artists have to have it, in order to express the texture of everyday insanity. In Colombia a few years ago, I saw soldiers stationed on street corners who wore gold-spiked helmets and carried machine guns; they didn't look down as a shriveled little girl of perhaps eight, bent over parallel to the pavement from the weight of a huge bundle of wood on her back, passed by at their feet. The little girl, who will undoubtedly be deformed, walked past buildings with enormous billboards advertising American action movies; Yul Brynner, Burt Lancaster, and other stars are giant deities looming over the cities.

When Pixote and his pals mug somebody, the camera pulls back so that we have a view of the whole area: we get the social picture, and we see them dart in, score, and run off. It's fast teamwork, like a football scrimmage; each mugging has its own choreographic plan. But most of the incidents in the film aren't so distinctly shaped. They're loose and sometimes a little blobby. (When kids and the whore, Sueli, lock one of her customers in the trunk of his car and drive off to celebrate—they park, turn up the car radio, and dance—we're distracted by wondering what happening to the poor guy in the trunk. In other scenes, we wonder what happens to the fresh corpses.) Throughout the film, though, even when the acting is minimal there are no wrong notes in it. (Babenco says that the children themselves "guided" him, and came up with ideas that changed perhaps 40 percent of the script.) And the lighting is extraordinary: in the second half, and particularly after Sueli appears, the tones shift from the pastels to bright pinks and reds, and at night a boy's Afro acquires an orange aureole from the light reflected from the neon signs. But Babenco doesn't build the film rhythmically, and you don't feel the dramatic intensification that you do when a structure is beautifully worked out. (There's a particularly confusing episode in which the guards pack some of the boys into a van and send them to a prison.) *Pixote* doesn't have the purity of *Shoeshine* or the surgical precision of *Los Olvidados*. It's effective cumulatively, and, because of the strength of feeling that Babenco has put into it, it becomes more and more devastating. Babenco is only a first-generation South American (his parents — Russian and Polish Jews — left Europe in the midthirties and went to Argentina), but he's not afraid to be florid, and his excesses are some of his finest moments.

At its best, *Pixote* isn't a political film, except in a larger sense in which films such as Vigo's *Zero for Conduct* and Jean Genet's *Un Chant d'Amour* are political films. I think *Pixote* has some relation to those two pictures — certainly it shares their feeling for the ecstatic — and it may also relate to several Fellini movies. It has a fairly obvious thesis: when you see the handsome Babenco in the prologue and then meet Pixote, the child resembles the director so startlingly that it's almost as if Babenco were saying, "This could have happened to me or to you or to anybody who was deprived of minimal care and affection." The film is too pat and predictable when the kids start being destroyed by their contact with adults. And it's too clever when Pixote sits on Sueli's bed staring at the TV, then at Sueli and one of his pals going at it, and back to the TV; you register that the kids are making another attempt — a grotesque attempt — to construct the family they never had. Babenco is wildly ambitious, in the manner of gifted young artists: he's attempting to be a poet while making points for us to process. But the richer characters — Lilica (Jorge Julião), a seventeen-year-old transvestite homosexual, and the whore Sueli (Marília Pera) — transcend the demonstration. Jorge Julião, who hasn't acted before, and Marília Pera, who is a leading Brazilian stage actress, give such full performances that they take the picture to the ecstatic levels that Babenco hoped for.

The swanlike Lilica, who has a classic transvestite look, is in terror of his next birthday. (In Brazil, children under eighteen can't be prosecuted for criminal acts; they're merely sent to reform schools, like the ones we've seen.) Lilica is a soft creature, flamingly nelly—an imitation of a young girl without parody. Emotionally, he's the most courageous kid of the bunch. The brutality he has seen inflicted on others hasn't made him callous; it has deepened his understanding and made him more loving. Pixote's soul hasn't been awakened; Lilica seems all soul. He's like a male version of the Giulietta Masina character in *Nights of Cabiria,* except that he's smarter and funnier, and much younger. He suffers romantic tragedies, but he doesn't go long without falling in love again.

Sueli is the whoriest whore imaginable. When we first see her, she has just given herself an abortion; she's feverish and full of hate. Pixote is frightened by the sight of the bloody fetus, and she cruelly, vindictively forces him to understand what it is. In the scenes with her, as she begins to have a swell time with the kids, dancing and drinking and coupling, the movie achieves a raw, garish splendor. Sueli is alive in the most brutal sense. When Pixote, who has accidentally killed one of the other kids while trying to help him, vomits, she takes him in her arms and consoles him. He puts his mouth to her breast and hangs on, suckling. He won't let go. What he's doing is perhaps too overtly Oedipal and symbolic, but it's an amazing scene, because of Sueli's violent response. She's repelled by his attempt to become her child; she pulls him off her and throws him out. This sick, broken-down streetwalker may have cradled him in her arms for a minute, but she doesn't want the burden of this child any more than she wanted the fetus she threw in the waste can.

After I saw *Pixote,* I had an opportunity to speak to Babenco, and since the street kids in the movie are all boys, I asked, "What of the girls?" His answer was "Their lives are ten thousand times as bad." I was left wondering whether his two women characters—a treacherous drug dealer, Debora, also aging, who kills one of the four boys, and Sueli, who takes Lilica's young lover away from him and destroys the remnants of the family—are supposed to be an indication of how poisoned the girls' lives are, or are a part of a melodramatic myth. The film is apparently nonjudgmental, but at a deeper level, it's judgmental as hell.

No matter what act of horror Sueli has participated in, she's elated—ready for a high time. She takes a savage's delight in the spoils. She may suddenly weep, even as she's dancing, but the tears are strictly for herself. Sueli needs Pixote and the other kids to make a party out of the horror of her life; horror *is* her party, and after some gullible john has been robbed she dances as if at a tribal celebration. She's a mother who thrusts children away or takes them as lovers. Babenco must have intended her to be the opposite of what he intended the children to be. (The kids do horrible things, but they don't rejoice in them.) Lilica's is the most sexual presence in the movie; he represents tenderness, love. Sueli represents annihilation — and the uglier her deeds are, the more hauntingly beautiful she becomes. (That's where Babenco shows class, and a genuine feeling for the mythic.) Marília Pera, who appeared in the first of Babenco's two earlier features, is best known as a comedienne. Playing Sueli must have been a deliverance for her; dusky and aquiline-faced, she has an Anna Magnani–like presence — horrifying and great. Babenco is too didactic about Pixote's blank slate; the sociological component of this film doesn't get at much that we don't know, and what the camera is going to find in most of the boys' faces has been predetermined. But Marília Pera's face registers the immediacy of the moment. Her Sueli is like a raging sun; when the inexpressive kids revolve around her and feel they own her, it's almost as if she were their only chance to learn what can be in a face.

It's not the boys' innocence that the movie seems to be about but their innocence in relation to the camera. Pixote sits still and the camera gets nothing from his impassive face; we may halfway accept Babenco's notion that he's so young that there's nothing written on it yet, and that his impassivity is his survival technique. But isn't it really that he's a blank because he's not an actor? Sueli darts around and the camera picks up everything she feels. The picture comes to life with Sueli, because she's the whore spawned out of men's darkest imagining, in the way that Medea and Clytemnestra and Lady Macbeth and Jocasta and Euripides's fierce Helen of Troy were spawned, and because the actress is so sharply and completely there.

The picture isn't quite great, maybe because you can see it struggling to be, and the end (a lyric, ironic switch on the *Vitelloni* ending) is awfully portentous, with the rejected Pixote, gun in pocket, kicking a can as he walks down the railroad tracks — a baby bandit on his way. You know it's supposed to make you think. But what I thought about was a male fantasy of barbaric, rejecting females, and an actress whose display of passion wiped the little nonactor kids off the screen. *Pixote* is good enough to touch greatness; it restores your excitement about the confusing pleasures that movies can give.

— *Pauline Kael*

Bruno Barreto

■

DONA FLOR AND HER TWO HUSBANDS (1977)

Dona Flor and Her Two Husbands, a classic erotic comedy by Brazil's Bruno Barreto, establishes the twenty-three-year-old director as the latest international filmmaking prodigy.

The film, made when Barreto was twenty-two — an improbable age for such an achievement — reflects a joyously humorous and sensuous temperament, and the pleasure of discovering him is enhanced by the exuberance and geniality of his style.

Dona Flor has the pleasurable clarity and familiarity of a folk tale. In fact, folklorists could probably identify variations of the same fanciful triangle in the sexual myths, fables, and jokes of many cultures.

This blithe Brazilian story, adapted by Barreto from a prominent novel by Jorge Amador, is set in Bahia in the late thirties and early forties. The story begins with a prologue commemorating the day in 1943 when the heroine, a beautiful and affectionate treasure named Dona Flor, becomes a widow. The morning after an all-night Carnival revel, Dona Flor's dissolute but beloved husband Vadinho finally carouses himself into an early grave, collapsing on the street while dancing with mad abandon in an aggressively lewd costume — blouse and skirt, with a grotesque artificial phallus flopping beneath the skirt.

As the stricken Dona Flor embraces her dead husband, the credits roll and we hear the first rendition of Chico Buarque's swirling, insinuating theme song, "What Could It Be?", in which metaphors about the mystery and perversity of romantic love multiply so rapidly and rapturously that they seem to overflow the haunting melody. With Buarque's invaluable assistance, Barreto creates a heady romantic comedy mood and never loses it.

In flashback we discover why the respectable, long-suffering Dona Flor adored her disreputable, incorrigible Vadinho. Although he abused her, stole from her, cheated on her, he also thrilled her in a way she could not resist. The fable requires one to accept Vadinho as a drunken lout and erotic genius at one and the same time.

After a prolonged period of mourning. Dona Flor finds "widow's migraine" less and less bearable. She enters into a second marital union with a man totally unlike Vadinho. Her second husband, the neighborhood pharmicist Teodoro, is kind, generous, and faithful. Teodoro and

Dona Flor are even sexually compatible. But there's a slight catch: Teodoro is a completely conventional lover. Dona Flor isn't dissatisfied, but there are times when she feels an overwhelming desire for the talents of the wild, unpredictable Vadinho. With the help of a little imagination, she contrives to achieve a happy reconciliation between her nice and naughty selves.

Dona Flor may be psychologically dubious, another case of men projecting their fantasies of a woman's desire onto a female protagonist. But who can say for certain? *Dona Flor* proves sublimely effective for the transient purposes of stylized romantic gratification. Even if Amado and Barreto deceive themselves about the nature of Dona Flor's desires, the fact remains that some forms of romantic projection are more flattering, gallant, and affectionate than others.

The film is free of the nasty undertones detectable in Buñuel's *Belle de Jour,* where the filmmaker can't help gloating about the dirty thoughts he perceives behind the heroine's chaste facade. The motives behind the suggestiveness of *Dona Flor* appear sincerely loving. Amado and Barreto take pleasure in the thought of their heroine's pleasure.

As Dona Flor, Sonia Braga is such an appealing and responsive actress that her performance would have captivated moviegoers even if Amado and Barreto had failed to clarify their feelings. It will be a terrible deprivation to the public if Braga somehow fails to become an international star of the magnitude of Sophia Loren, Jeanne Moreau, and Liv Ullmann. A screen beauty with earthy attributes and a thrillingly expressive face, Braga creates that peculiarly satisfying illusion of attainable loveliness.

Jose Wilker makes Vadinho an amusing reprobate. Not at all an impressive physical specimen, Wilker portrays Vadinho's sexiness as a complacent, lecherous presumption. He's ruled completely by his appetites, and these give him a maniacal, irresistible determination. He seems barely human, a point that is exploited for ironic humor in the latter stages of the story. Vadinho is closer to an imp, a personification of Libido. Mauro Mendonca contributes an equally witty performance in a totally different vein as the upstanding Teodoro.

Barreto's technique is admirably deft at every crucial turn. A precocious romantic sophisticate, he blends sheer technical facility with a magnanimous, sensual outlook. Even the grainy, thickly textured color, which may strike some American eyes as excessive or amateurish, serves an expressive purpose by reinforcing the primitive wit of the story and exoticism of the settings. Barreto uses Dona Flor's skill as a cook to link culinary and sexual pleasure in perhaps the wittiest visual terms since *Tom Jones*. His lust for life seems as strong as Vadinho's but humanely refined by his artistic sensibility. Barreto can express lust with class, and it's an exhilarating, civilized gift.

—*Gary Arnold*

Maria-Luisa Bemberg

■

CAMILA (1984)

Argentine Maria-Luisa Bemberg's historical romance *Camila* is a torrid love triangle among a man, woman, and God—an unusually erotic and ecstatic film about an 1847 Buenos Aires socialite, Camila O'Gorman, who elopes with her confessor, Ladislao Gutierrez, a Jesuit priest.

With her gracefully dancing camera, Bemberg breathtakingly depicts Camila's and Ladislao's fandango of passion and piety. Her movie is unlike any other, a fervid combination of *The Thorn Birds* and *Kasper Hauser*. If you can imagine a melodrama not dripping with sentiment but gripping, with earned emotion, then you can begin to anticipate *Camila*'s power.

Though Ladislao and Camila are popularly known as the "Romeo and Juliet of the Pampas," Bemberg's portrait of the two is not as star-crossed lovers but as spirited pioneers of a moral and sexual revolution that threatens both church and state.

Camila and Ladislao each resist the tyrannical regime of Juan Manuel de Rosas, a law-and-order despot whose image is enthroned on the high altar next to Jesus's. (Because of its complicity with the church, the Rosas regime is known as "The Holy Federation.")

When the Mazorca, Rosas's secret police, execute partisans of the free press, Ladislao deplores it from his pulpit and Camila protests at the dinner table, where her father summarily dispatches his willful daughter to her room. Though engaged to Buenos Aires's richest and most eligible bachelor, Camila has eyes only for Ladislao, confiding to her sisters, "I want to love someone about whom I can feel proud!" Bemberg might be the first director to make a movie where moral desirability is sexier than physical charm.

She establishes her heroine as an outspoken free-thinker, unlike most of the submissive Buenos Aires women of her day. Camila, however, is very much like her grandmother, a political radical who lives Miss Havisham–style, among her souvenirs — under house arrest on the O'Gorman plantation. (And played by the still-radiant Mona Maris, a starlet of thirties and forties films.)

In the shimmering, haloed light of *Camila,* love is blind — and blindfolded. Thinking she's confessing an erotic dream to the family priest, Camila is startled to hear Ladislao's unfamiliar, heart-stirring voice recommend penance. Playing blindman's bluff later at a family fiesta, Camila lovingly caresses the face that goes along with her new confessor's voice — surprised at his sensuous appeal and its effect on her nervous system.

(As Camila, Susu Pecoraro resembles a willowy Natalie Wood. Though conventionally pretty, Pecoraro clenches her tormented intelligence in a determined jaw, transforming her character into an unconventional beauty and powerhouse.)

The last thing devout Camila or pious Ladislao want is to violate law or order. But each is emboldened by the other's courage in speaking out against Rosas's hypocrisy. Beneath their moral attraction to each other simmers carnal desire — which reaches an inexorable boil despite Ladislao's repeated mortification of flesh.

As Ladislao, Spanish heartthrob Imanol Arias is certainly the handsomest creature ever seen in a cassock — not to mention an actor of stunning subtlety. Ladislao's soul says "No, no," but there's "Yes, yes" in his heart — a mind/body split the dusky actor makes palpably urgent. And a split well illustrated by Bemberg with her moody, chiaroscuro lighting.

Though implied rather than graphic, Bemberg's depiction of Camila's and Ladislao's passion is hot enough to melt the polar cap. "What am I to do with you?" the smitten priest asks his lovely parishioner. "Whatever you want," replies Camila, fearless in her ardor.

Camila's father warns her, "A single woman is a disorder of nature, like anarchy." Her mother extends his metaphor, ironically describing matrimony and nationalism as patriarchal prisons: "Sometimes the best jails are those you cannot see." In eloping with Ladislao, Camila acts on her mother's secret wish for free love while perversely fulfilling her father's command for marriage.

Immediately the elders of church and state denounce Camila's and Ladislao's flight as "the most atrocious act ever committed in our country." Rosas demands their execution for sacrilege against God and country, and his secret police sniff out the illicit lovers — now schoolteachers in a frontier village.

Bemberg's remarkable film explores the intersections of church and state, priest and God, man and woman — a story as resonant now as it was in 1847 when the priest and woman living as man and wife rocked the foundations of the Rosas regime. It's a brilliant illustration of how expressing personal freedom disrupts the political order.

And it's also a brilliant love story. In their final days together, Camila tremulously confesses to Ladislao, "When I see you pray, I'm jealous." Though she ultimately loses her man to God, she gains a strength that comes only from believing in herself as passionately as she believes in her Ladislao and her Lord.

—Carrie Rickey

Carlos Diegues
■

BYE BYE BRAZIL (1980)

It's rare to come across truly great movie images, and we share them like treasured souvenirs — images like Jack Nicholson in the football helmet in *Easy Rider,* the bone turning into a spaceship in *2001,* the peacock spreading its feathers in the snow in *Amarcord,* and the helicopter assault in *Apocalypse Now.*

To the short list of great images, a film named *Bye Bye Brazil* adds one more. A small, raggedy troupe of traveling entertainers is putting on a show in a provincial Brazilian town. The townspeople sit packed together in a sweaty, smoky room, while the magician creates for brief moments the illusion that both he and his audience are more sophisticated than they are. It is time for the climax of his act, and he springs a completely unexpected image on his audience, and on us: Bing Crosby sings "White Christmas" while it snows on his amazed patrons.

That moment provides more than an image. It provides a neatly summarized little statement about *Bye Bye Brazil,* a film which exists exactly on the fault line between Brazil's modern civilization and the simple backwaters of its provinces. The film sees Brazil as a nation where half-assimilated Western culture (in the form of Bing Crosby, public address systems, and politicians) coexists with poverty, superstition, simple good nature, and the permanent fact of the rain forest.

The movie is about the small troupe of entertainers, who travel the backroads in a truck that contains living quarters, a generator, and the props for their nightly shows. The troupe is led by Lord Gypsy, a young man who is half-hippie, half-nineteenth-century medicine show huckster. At his side is Salome, a damply sultry beauty who is his assistant but also has a tendency to do business on her own. Swallow, a strongman, doubles as crew and supporting act.

These three pick up two hitchhikers, a young accordion player and his pregnant wife. And then *Bye Bye Brazil* tells the story of the changing relationships among the five people, and their checkered success with roadshow vaudeville.

Having said that, I've conveyed almost no notion of this movie's special charms. It shows us a society that most American audiences never have seen in the movies, the world of very old, very small Brazilian towns perched precariously along the roads that link them to faraway, half-understood cities.

Television has not come to most of these towns. Electricity is uncertain. The traveling entertainers provide more than music and magic; they provide a link with style that is more fascinating to the audiences than the magician's tricks. People do not pay to see the show, so much as to wonder at these strange performers who speak the same language but could be from another planet.

—*Roger Ebert*

Ruy Guerra

■

OPERA DO MALANDRO (1986)

In *Opera do Malandro,* writer-director Ruy Guerra has a fascinating idea: making a Brazilian *Threepenny Opera,* transplanting the old Brecht-Weill ambiance to Rio de Janeiro and the malandros underworld of the early forties.

The original *Threepenny* invented a kind of socialist cabaret; for cinema novo filmmaker Guerra, it's a cultural touchstone. Guerra wants the juice, dash, insolence, and melody of a great cynical popular show—like Bob Fosse's *Cabaret,* whose lithe choreographic swagger and smoky, tawdry-rainbow decor are often mimicked here. But he also wants, like Brecht, to bring out social themes, analyze both the glittery surface and dark soul of a tempestuous period. He gets more glitter than darkness, but it's occasionally a dazzling try.

The film's source is a 1978 stage play by one of Brazil's most popular singer-composers, Chico Buarque (*Bye Bye Brazil*). Guerra films it opulently. He drenches the movie in hothouse studio artificiality, calls up memories of Minnelli, Donen, and Charles Vidor, and swirls his camera through a misty, neon wonderland of stylized crime and nightlife. This film has an impudent glitter; even when it's not quite working, it makes you smile.

Buarque and Guerra choose a time of maximum ferment—when Brazil's pro-Hitler Vargas dictatorship was about to falter and when American culture (MGM musicals and Warners gangster movies)—had begun to sweep Rio, entrancing, among others, the young Ruy Guerra. In the movie, and in life, the malandros were antiwork Rio lowlifes: a melange of bums, artists, singers, hookers, gamblers, and gangsters—much like the London ne'er-do-wells of *Threepenny Opera.*

As layabouts, they were also automatic enemies of the work-oriented, militaristic Vargas tyranny; they were defiantly anti-Nazi and pro-American. America furnished their dreams. Its musicals floated in a perfumed haze of Technicolor bliss; its gangsters gave the pimps their style. (Guerra, in slightly mocking homage, opens *Opera* with a screening of Hawks's *Scarface.*) For Buarque and Guerra, the malandros have two sides: heroes at first, later—as American culture overwhelms Brazil's—they become villains.

Chico Buarque's score isn't a great one, but it's catchy, melodic. Sometimes it soars; sometimes it sounds like a one-note samba; sometimes it summons up memories of Michel Legrand's Cherbourg umbrellas. It's best when Guerra gets a particularly dynamic performance (as he does from fiery Elba Ramalho, as Max's girl Margot). Guerra also has a truly raving beauty, Claudia Ohana of *Erendira,* as Lu, his sly, materialistic little heroine. Ohana's dark, preening, lovely face draws your eyes anywhere in the frame.

Intermittently successful, *Opera do Malandro* is still a thinking-person's musical, with lots of plush delights. The film doesn't need to hit all those gleaming targets for us to enjoy it.

—*Michael Wilmington*

Gregory Nava

■

EL NORTE (1983)

In a remote village in Guatemala, a woman speaks about the wonders of "the North." "In the United States, even the poorest people have toilets," she informs her family. "There's a lot of money there."

After ten years of poring over tattered copies of *Good Housekeeping* magazine, this Guatemalan Indian is firmly convinced that America is a land of suburban housing tracts where Cadillacs cruise down tree-lined streets and every front lawn has a sprinkler.

As shown in Gregory Nava's remarkably lush, lyrical epic, *El Norte,* this particular Guatemalan village looks far more idyllic than any suburban tract house. The houses may be rustic in appearance, but they are painted in bright, cheerful colors that make them seem terribly inviting. The women wear traditional Mayan costumes, which add a false note of gaiety.

For the tranquil picture-postcard beauty of the village is deceptive. The atmosphere is filled with tension for it seems that the men in the village have grown tired of working for the rich, tyrannical landlords and they are planning some sort of armed protest. "For the rich, the peasants are just a pair of arms," one of them explains to his teenage son, Enrique (David Villalpando). "We're trying to show we have hearts and souls. We feel."

Enrique soon has an opportunity to prove he is "a man with a heart and soul" when his parents are killed during the insurrection by government soldiers, and he and his sister, Rosa (Zaide Silvia Gutierrez) decide that their only hope is to make the perilous journey north.

In the second segment of this most impressive three-part movie, which is an American Playhouse production and, as such, will eventually be shown on public television, Enrique and Rosa arrive in

Tijuana which, in contrast to their vibrant homeland, is a dismal "lost city" where instant cardboard shacks provide temporary refuge for the thousands of Latin Americans who struggle to reach "the promised land" on the other side of the border.

They finally find "a coyote," someone who, for a price, guides illegal immigrants across what amounts to a war zone, who insists that the safest way to make the illegal border crossing is to crawl through a rat-infested sewage tunnel. In the movie's most dramatic scene they finally succeed in reaching the end of the tunnel where a magical sight awaits them — the glittering lights of San Diego.

The third and final segment of the movie is not only the liveliest, it contains some gentle satiric jabs at the *gringos* whose behavior understandably mystifies Enrique and Rosa. Pleased with their dingy L.A. efficiency apartment because it has "a flush toilet," and one electric light, they learn that the best way to deal with these strange "North Americans" is to "just smile and say yes" to anything they say.

The sweet-natured Rosa simply does the wash by hand rather than offend her insensitive employer who automatically assumes she can read all the absurdly complicated instruction on her washing machine. Enrique quickly ingratiates himself by working hard in a posh restaurant where the menu is entirely in French and the kitchen employees are mainly Spanish-speaking "illegals."

Nava, with the help of his producer, cowriter, and wife, Anna Thomas, has created a warmly sympathetic movie about the tragic plight of the illegal immigrants, and a haunting visual poem. Through the efforts of cinematographer James Clennon, Nava has nearly matched the unique style of Latin American writers like Gabriel García Márquez, whose tales are a vibrant mixture of fantasy and reality.

—Kathleen Carroll

Euzhan Palcy
■
SUGAR CANE ALLEY (1983)

Sugar Cane Alley is the free translation of *Rue Cases Nègres* — "Black Shack Alley," which was slang for the tumbledown collection of huts where Martinique's black agricultural wage slaves lived in the 1930s. Although slavery had long been abolished, the blacks forced to toil in Caribbean sugar-cane fields were in some ways worse off than their forebears. Free of any obligation to care for their employees, the French neocolonialists who owned the fields could maintain their own standard of living by letting the global depression trickle down on their impoverished field hands. So you'd expect a film set in that world of exploitation and suffering to be a bleak one. But Euzhan Palcy's movie shines like the warm summer days of childhood; it captures a youngster's confusing passage into adulthood, his dawning awareness of the world that stretches beyond his poor home village. There's the humiliation of life under the overseer's whip, but there's also the discovery of surprising joys by resilient people.

Although *Sugar Cane Alley* opens with the disorganized bustle of a small village awakening to a day's backbreaking work, the film soon leaves the departing workers to concentrate on the mayhem wreaked by the unattended children—an unusual choice that not only introduces us to the village population but also establishes a high-spirited tone. The children may be "deprived" from birth, but they're not burdened; to them, the world is still a big tropical playground. *Sugar Cane Alley* focuses on José (Garry Cadenat), who is saved from a life in the cane fields by his fierce, elderly stepmother, Amantine; she propels him from village to regional school and, finally, to an academy for prize pupils in the island's capital, Fort-de-France. Although this reads like an ordinary rags-to-riches plot, Palcy presents José's story as a series of vignettes unified more by tone than by narrative. José's school days are refracted through a memory that bathes them in the colors of a child's mind; the triumph of a good day in class is tempered by the abuse of a calculating landlady. Thus *Sugar Cane Alley* becomes a film about memory. The events of the film take on the size and importance a child would give them, and so they become the key to a child's emotional life.

Many of the characters have a familiar, self-consciously folkloric look, but Palcy prevents the film from falling into stereotypes. One of José's teachers is his village's storyteller, an old man named Mebouze. It's a tricky part—in an American film you could easily imagine its being played by Burl Ives. But Mebouze's recounting of imperialism and racism ensures that we'll see him as larger than life but not sentimental. At first Palcy depicts Mebouze mostly through the eyes of José: when Mebouze tells the child a story he tells us too. But Palcy also wants us to feel what José is feeling. After Mebouze dies of exhaustion in the cane fields, José discovers him at night, at the foot of a hill. The boy calls for his fellow villagers, and when they appear, we see the light of their torches descending the hillside like a funeral procession. It's an organic, mystical moment — one of several that imbue the film with transcendent beauty. And the funeral itself is a strange combination of religiosity and irreverence presided over by a sassy, improvising villager — a confusing (Palcy doesn't fall into the trap of overexplaining) but beguiling mixture of African, French, and island culture with a bit of New Orleans funeral parade thrown in.

The end credits accord special thanks to Jean Rouch, the French anthropologist-filmmaker who, in movies like *Chronicle of a Summer,* sought the personal in the cultural. Palcy is an apt disciple of Rouch, and some of his film's best scenes compress joy and sorrow in an epiphany of ritual. Throughout *Sugar Cane Alley,* old Amantine is in failing health; her one hope is that she'll live long enough to see José saved from her own fate as a field hand. The boy and the old woman are as close as any natural mother and son, and when Amantine finally dies, José is alone as never before. But rather than succumbing to bathos, Palcy shows us José giving Amantine a sacramental washing. Lingering on the young hands wiping the final traces of dirt from the old, worn feet, *Sugar Cane Alley* escapes from mere poignance to ineffable depths of loss and remembrance; in its poetic use of visual detail, it creates a moment that belongs uniquely to cinema.

— *Henry Sheehan*

Luis Puenzo

▪

THE OFFICIAL STORY (1985)

It is a normal evening: two old school chums are getting together after seven years, catching up on each other's news. Alicia (Norma Aleandro) is particularly eager for Ana (Chunchuna Villafañe) to meet Gaby, the five-year-old girl she and her husband adopted when she was an infant. Late that night the two women sit gossiping and getting tiddly on eggnogs when, without at first modulating her tone, Ana explains why she left Argentina so suddenly without saying goodbye to anyone. It is a tale of midnight abduction, a blow to her head—and waking up naked, tied to a table prepared for torture.

The scene is a great one, awesomely played by the two actresses. The way terror can suddenly appear in the midst of banality, the basic irony that is the source of most modern horror fiction whether it be crude slasher pic or elegant Hitchcock classic has never been more eloquently or economically stated. For Ana, at least, there is relief in hysterically speaking at last of what has been, for her, unspeakable. For Alicia, however, the friend's nightmare only hints at the one she herself is to face. Under the terror imposed by the junta, which ruled Argentina until 1983, Ana has observed, many of the babies born in prison were put up for adoption. It is possible that Alicia's Gaby may be a child of *desaparecidos,* the "missing ones" (there were more than nine thousand of them) who simply vanished without a trace during the state's infamous "dirty war" on alleged subversives.

Alicia, who does not inquire too deeply into how her husband Roberto (the excellent Héctor Alterio) happens to be doing so well in business, finds herself compelled to look more carefully into her child's background. Frustration with the utter lack of documentation—obviously it was in the state's interest not to keep records—leads to obsession. And obsession leads to a belated political awakening, including recognition that she would not have this child were Roberto not so involved with an evil regime. It also brings her, at last, into contact with a woman who is probably Gaby's grandmother and her only living relative.

How these good women resolve their anguish *The Official Story* wisely does not state. There is no Solomonic wisdom applicable to this situation. In any event, the film's business is not to unwind a plot but to frame a parable about the individual's relationship to totalitarianism. And that is subtly written on the lovely face of Aleandro as she descends from serenity and self-possession to a final, harrowing acknowledgment that her privileged life was based on willed blindness, that her future is as an emotional *desaparecido.* Hers is a performance that one knows will not be forgotten, much as one would like to try to erase it, and all that it stands for, from memory.

—*Richard Schickel*

RECOMMENDED

FROM

AUSTRALIA

During the 1970s and early 1980s, the Australian government was the world's most generous in sponsoring serious films. This opened the door for the down-under point of view of Peter Weir (listed in the second chapter, "The Second Wave"); Fred Schepisi (his films *The Chant of Jimmie Blacksmith* and *Barbarosa* were reviewed in our earlier book, *Produced and Abandoned*); Gillian Armstrong (whose *High Tide* was also reviewed there); and Bruce Beresford, whose feeling for character and landscape are evident

---

Opposite page: scene from *The Road Warrior*.

in *Breaker Morant*—and in *Don's Party* (1976), *The Getting of Wisdom* (1977), and *The Fringe Dwellers* (1987), all available on video.

All four directors went on to Hollywood projects, turning their talent for character and setting to, for instance, Schepisi's *A Cry in the Dark,* Weir's *Witness,* Armstrong's *Mrs. Soffel,* Beresford's *Tender Mercies* and *Driving Miss Daisy.*

Paul Cox and Carl Schultz, who emigrated to Australia from Holland and Hungary, respectively, make Euro-Australian films about relationships that are less sunny. Beyond pioneer directors like Schepisi, Weir, Armstrong, and Beresford and the darker eighties films by Shultz and Cox, there are the distinctively Aussie contributions to popular genres—Nadia Tass's comedy *Malcolm,* and mad-to-the-max George Miller's best film, *The Road Warrior.*

Bruce Beresford
■

BREAKER MORANT (1980)

What Hollywood has forgotten, Australia remembers. While the major studios busy themselves packaging trendy performers (*Stir Crazy, Nine to Five*), capitalizing on presold properties (*Flash Gordon, Popeye*) and dreaming up can't-miss projects (Neil Diamond *is The Jazz Singer*), down in Australia they are making movies. Movies that are about character and incident, movies that started because someone had a story he felt impelled to tell, not a deal he was dying to make. Movies like *The Chant of Jimmie Blacksmith, My Brilliant Career* and *The Getting of Wisdom* are, despite all the fuss made over them, extremely conventional at heart, but they know how to capture and hold an audience, a technique that seems to have become something of a lost art in this part of the world.

Breaker Morant is the most successful film in Australia's history. Directed by Bruce Beresford, who did *The Getting of Wisdom,* it took ten Australian Film Institute awards, that country's Oscars. Traditional and well-made above all else, *Breaker Morant* stuns not with originality but with expertise, a brisk, bracing film with more bite to it than anything the major studios have released in months.

Harry "Breaker" Morant was a historical figure who's become quite the folk hero in Australia. A self-exiled Englishman, an expert horse breaker as well as a poet, he was an officer in the Bushveldt Carbineers, a primarily Australian unit of the British Army that was organized during the Boer War to fight behind the lines against commandos.

A man of impetuous temper, Morant at the film's opening becomes enraged by the mutilation and death of a friend and goes on a revenge tear, capturing and killing a handful of Boers. Because the British feel the need to make an example of their justice both to keep the Germans out of the war and to convince the Boers that their peace feelers are legitimate, Morant and two fellow lieutenants are arrested and charged with murder.

As with *Jimmie Blacksmith,* there is a sense of inevitability here, the sureness that Morant and company will be found guilty. There is also the familiarity of this kind of story, the courtroom drama military style done brilliantly by Stanley Kubrick in *Paths of Glory.* Yet *Breaker Morant* is completely engrossing because director Beresford, who also gets partial credit for the screenplay, has made a film in which everything is functional, everything works. The dialogue has a sharpness, a toughness to it, the use of dramatic close-ups and quick cutting in the courtroom scenes is precise and effective, and the acting, especially Edward Woodward as the ironically fatalistic Morant, and Jack Thompson as the inexperienced but impassioned lawyer who defends him, is excellent. Beresford has also done the material the great service of not whitewashing it, not diluting its unpalatable edges. Morant was a hothead and an egotist—one of his men says sotto voce, "Soon he'll be on the other side. He's a big enough bore, isn't he?"—and his compatriots were in some ways worse. The decision not to turn them into paragons makes their case even more interesting.

What *Breaker Morant* does is shed a small light on the way war affects those who fight it, who get entangled in the pull of history. What, the film asks, is customary behavior during wartime? *Breaker Morant* returns again and again to the point that the Boer War marked the end of genteel fighting between gentlemen, that it was "a new kind of war for a new century," and it is chilling to realize that the arguments Major Thomas, Morant's lawyer, used could be applied to defend Lieutenant William Calley's part in the massacre at My Lai. "The tragedy of war," Thomas says, "is that its horrors are committed by normal men in abnormal situations." As devastating as the slaughter is for the victims, *Breaker Morant* reminds us that its effect on the living dare not be forgotten.

—*Kenneth Turan*

Paul Cox

■

MAN OF FLOWERS (1984)

Paul Cox's *Man of Flowers* begins with a painting and a striptease. In the case of the former (which appears behind the opening credits), the camera eye is at first focused in tight, on the refined profile of a Renaissance nobleman and, to his left, a pale forest of organ pipes. An actual forest is visible in the distance—to be precise, part of a meticulously landscaped park of which the gentleman seems to be taking survey from a balcony. Still inventorying the details of the painting—patterns of shrubs and trees, the statue of a satyr—the camera drifts rightward and then starts to withdraw slowly, so that we begin to perceive the composition entire. The last element we become aware of is a naked woman, alabaster and robust, a curving landscape unto herself and the real focus of the man's transfixed (we now recognize) gaze.

The striptease which almost immediately follows recapitulates, but also revises, the dynamics of this aesthetic movement. This time we open on a closeup of a woman, a saucy working-class gamine (Alyson Best) who proceeds to remove article after article of her clothing, to the "Love Duet" from *Lucia di Lammermoor,* for the delectation of a well-to-do client. The camera pulls back slowly so that eventually we are watching from somewhere behind this seated gentleman's left shoulder. As with the painting, the shot contains a good deal more information. The setting for the striptease, a room in the man's house, is as meticulously and symbolically composed as the environment of the painting. In fact, the young woman stands in front of another painting, modern, abstract, a complex of curved and thrusting shapes evocative of human genitalia, male and female at once. The space surrounding her is replete with statuary, objets d'art—and vegetation. Whereas the painting behind the main title is by definition frozen in time, a snapshot of erotic potentiality, Cox's "action painting" of another erotic moment not only suggests the Renaissance painting become movie, but also indexes the particular sensibility of Charles Bremer (Norman Kaye), the watcher/artist seated at right who has willed the moment into being.

Like the Norman Kaye character in Cox's earlier *Lonely Hearts,* Charles Bremer is a lonely middleaged man with some quirks. Recently left a considerable fortune by his late mother, he has the freedom to indulge tastes which had heretofore seemed impossible to fulfill. Those Wednesday-afternoon stripteases, for instance, are followed not by any fleshly consummation, but rather by scurrying across the road to a nearby church where he coaxes passionate chords from the organ. He attends figure-study classes where, to the despair of the dogmatic instructress, he insists on superimposing nonexistent flowers over the outline of the nude. He tends to ignore practical realities like the gas bills the postman brings, but never fails to write daily letters to departed Mother, keeping her up to date on his curious progress toward contentment.

Technically, Charles is undoubtedly quite mad. Eventually we learn that he has spent time in a sanitarium (he obtained release principally because he was able to give the doctor "a big check—he said I was a good man and could see him any time"). As a child, he was considered retarded because his direct responsiveness to the world of sensations led him to lay a hand on his aunt's lush cleavage, and to follow her around the parlor with his nose pressed to her aromatic back. Yet his madness is as felicitous as it is benign. Charles collects and cherishes singular, beautiful things—artworks, people, memories, most especially flowers—in which he discovers still more beauty by combining them into a new aesthetic whole. He is an artist of the beautiful who composes within the frame of reality.

Let there be no assuming here that Paul Cox has added to the sappy/happy tradition of sainted-fool movies (e.g., most egregiously *King of Hearts*), in which filmmaker and audience revel endlessly in the facile conviction that lunacy is wisdom and rationality a destructive dead end. As both man and artist-figure, Charles Bremer strives hard and conscientiously after whatever consolation and understanding he achieves. Rather than simply stringing together a series of bittersweet comic encounters between this quixotic pilgrim and an often out-of-joint world, Cox has devised a narrative which in its very form embodies Charles's talent for seeing, and making existential and artistic sense of what he sees.

Consider the flashes of childhood memory—pale, flickering, home-movie-like scenes—periodically cut into the present-tense narrative. Young Charles and his parents walking in a park; a formative early linking of affection, aestheticized beauty, and a flower; enigmatic glimpses of familial disruption—these roil with primal yet seemingly accidental images. The deliberate technical "imperfection" of the photography, the blunt, ragged handheld camerawork, enhance the suggestiveness with which, say, enormous red lips in close-up become a billboard image of terror and desire, a fleshy flower with teeth. ("Herzogian," the viewer may register, recalling comparable home-movie passages in *The Mystery of Kaspar Hauser*—and then one realizes that Werner Herzog himself has been cast as the Teutonic razor-cropped father!) These interludes probe the roots of Charles's neuroses, but without the insistent neatness of clinical diagnosis. They are simply the most direct and elemental representations of experience as apprehended and interpreted by two artists at different planes of aesthetic remove—present-tense character Charles Bremer remembering and stylizing his own past, and writer-director Paul Cox subsuming Bremer's own perceptions within yet another frame.

Kostas (1979) and *Lonely Hearts* (1982), the other Cox films we've had a chance to see, evocatively explore sensuality and loneliness as primary themes of the human condition. All along Cox has displayed a talent for drawing sympathetic characters so richly imagined that their efforts to make contact provoke reciprocal commitment from the audience. *Man of Flowers* likewise boasts vividly idiosyncratic individuals who invariably come off as knowable people, not just collections of usefully entertaining shticks (the Wednesday-afternoon stripper, for example, has a well-developed life and history apart from Charles's patronage). But the film also marks a quantum leap on Cox's part in terms of formal and conceptual ambitiousness, and visual mastery as well. *Kostas* and *Lonely Hearts* seemed the work of a good writer and sympathetic director; *Man of Flowers* is the work of a complex writer whose direction fully realizes his literary ideas. Paul Cox is currently being hailed as the most worldly *auteur* to emerge from the New Australian Cinema, one who, unlike such willfully esoteric film-makers as Peter Weir and Fred Schepisi with their quasi-aboriginal mystiques, locates the marvelous in the mundane. If you haven't made his acquaintance already, this is a good time.

—*Richard T. Jameson (with Kathleen Murphy)*

George Miller

■

THE ROAD WARRIOR (1981)

If you write about movies, you get used to being asked certain questions, like ferinstance: "What do you look for in a really good movie?" I try to answer that one in terms as elemental as possible: "In a really good movie, everything matters. No shot is wasted. At any given point, you look at the screen and you feel that what you're seeing had to be seen, and couldn't have been visualized any other way. The film brings a world to life; even if it's zany or bizarre, that world is reality for the duration of the movie, and every movement, every tone, is indispensable to that reality."

Elementally speaking, *The Road Warrior* is one of the best, and certainly most exciting, movies I've seen in years. It's an epic action film, maybe the first great one since *The Wild Bunch*. It's also the high-octane adventure movie *Raiders of the Lost Ark* was widely mistaken for. But the film's genre is only coincidental with its success. As so many films and TV shows of the past decade have demonstrated, car chases can be as boring as watching grass grow. The "action" and "excitement" that count in *The Road Warrior* are essentially matters of how, not what; of storytelling rather than the type of story told.

The story *is* good, though. Indeed, it's been good for thousands of years. A wanderer in the wasteland, expert at defending himself in a hostile world and long habituated to being a loner, happens upon a small, beleaguered community. The particular wasteland he wanders is set a few decades in the future, a post–world war environment where gasoline ("juice") is essential to mobility and survival. The wanderer, Max (Mel Gibson), is an ex–highway cop whose souped-up Interceptor, "the last of the V-8s," is also the last vestige of the life he once held dear. "A burnt-out, desolate man," Max goes to the aid of the afore-mentioned community only because they have something he needs: they're operating a petroleum refinery in the desert, trying to amass enough fuel to make the journey north to a fabled paradise. They're good people, the noblest remnants of civilization, and they're besieged by a motley outlaw army, grotesque, punky avatars of the worst that history has to offer. Max does not, cannot, belong to either group, but he becomes the agent of their ultimate confrontation.

Max was introduced in a 1978 Australian film called *Mad Max,* which dealt with a decaying, though still preapocalyptic, world "a few years from now." *Mad Max* also introduced a new director, George Miller, whose genius for quicksilver action sequences and cartoonish wit was immediately apparent. The script was rather formulaic in its atrocity-revenge, atrocity-revenge progressions, and the film's U.S. distributor increased its unfortunate resemblance to Roger Corman–style exploitation fare by redubbing the dialogue with flat American accents and dumping the movie into the drive-ins. *Mad Max* flopped in the States but scored a runaway hit elsewhere; grossing $100 million internationally, it was the greatest popular success of the New Australian Cinema.

Mad Max was a good picture and a very promising first film, but *The Road Warrior* is light years beyond, so much so that one scarcely thinks of it as a sequel. (Not to worry if you haven't seen the earlier film: a prologue tells you all you need to know.) Miller had more money — a few million dollars instead of a few hundred thousand — and he and his partner, producer Byron Kennedy, have made every cent count. More crucially, Miller has purified his narrative, transcending the exploitation-film formulae of *Mad Max* (by assimilating the lessons of, among other models, the mythic studies of Joseph Campbell!); and he's sharpened the lucidity and concentration of the style that was already so impressive in his debut film.

There are moments in *The Road Warrior* that leave the inveterate moviegoer blissful with gratitude. Max is led to a hilltop by a wonderfully screwball character called The Gyro Captain (played by Bruce Spence, who looks about seven feet tall and seven inches wide); the camera cranes up behind them and the refinery breaks into view for the first time; in the valley below and to widescreen-right, long, parallel flumes of dust mark the relentless advance of the bikes, dune buggies, and hotrod vehicles of the outlaw army, moving to reinforce the patrols already circling the fragile fortress. It's the kind of shot the mind's eye supplies when reading adventure tales, and the sort of precise, evocative, integral visualization filmmakers almost never bother trying for in an era when the responsibility for visual coups is lazily farmed out to the special-effects boys.

Few other images in *The Road Warrior* are as grand as that one, but none is perfunctory, none lacks for a wealth of specific interest and the capacity to surprise. The story is always in progress in the images and the recognition shocks they contain. Miller never dotes on his effects.

The Road Warrior feels as chock-full, as exhaustively detailed, as an entire epic cycle, but it's barely more than ninety minutes in length. One marvels at the proliferation of invention in incident, characterization, costuming, landscape, props. Something happens, BLINK!!, it's gone and something else is happening; the effect is not of a desperate, catchall scamper from one discrete effect to the next, but of an accumulating pattern of information and sensation. Miller gives the viewer credit for being observant, and also judiciously self-aware. There's a strong satiric bent to his vision that subtly softens us up to accept the most preposterous of his conceits (e.g., the leader of the outlaw band, a desert Darth Vader who styles himself "The Humungus"; or a fur-wearing, tunnel-crawling, boomerang-wielding dervish blithely identified as "The Feral Kid"). Miraculously, this does not undercut, but rather enhances, the ozone-snap spirit of high adventurism.

Only one factor seriously compromises *The Road Warrior*'s claim to a place of honor up there with *Seven Samurai* and *The Wild Bunch*: it's populated with caricatures and character types rather than great flesh and blood characters. But they're vivid caricatures, strong and distinctively etched types. Mel Gibson's Max has darkened into a much more compelling fellow than he was in the earlier film (though local viewers will be more apt to recognize him as the slightly more worldly of the two lads in Peter Weir's *Gallipoli*); although he can't have more than a dozen lines of dialogue, and by definition must conduct himself as a man practiced at keeping his deepest feelings secret, even from himself, Gibson manages to make Max much more than a monolithic stick-figure. Bruce Spence creates a unique, and giddily memorable, variant on the galoot who appoints himself the hero's sidekick— though it must be insisted that he has invincible competition from *the* greatest mongrel dog in the history of the cinema. As Pappagallo, the visionary leader of the endangered society, Mike Preston contributes an enigmatic presence to an underwritten role (he reminds me of a blond Robby Robertson). But the face and form people are never going to forget belong to Vernon Wells, a massive warrior in punk-Mohawk hairdo and centurion leather, who conceives a passionate hatred for Max, and at several points fairly launches himself right off the screen with such ferocity that he'll lodge in our nightmares forever.

—*Richard T. Jameson*

Carl Schultz

■

CAREFUL, HE MIGHT HEAR YOU (1983)

If you were wondering whether Australian films might be losing their momentum, don't. Director Carl Schultz's brilliant American debut film, *Careful, He Might Hear You,* about a custody fight between a kind poor aunt and a cold rich one over their six-year-old nephew in Depression-era Sydney, immediately places him on an equal footing with such celebrated compatriots as Bruce Beresford, Peter Weir, and Fred Schepisi. One almost hesitates to add that *Careful, He Might Hear You* is based on Sumner Locke Elliott's autobiographical novel. It might lead you to believe that the film is more confessional than it is. Elliott was quite objective about his fictionalized younger self, and Schultz, a transplanted Hungarian, takes Elliott's novel even farther into pictorial, emotional, and even mythic richness.

The film's title comes from the whispered words of the boy's benevolent guardians, his mother's sister Lila, and Lila's good-hearted husband, George. They strive to conceal unpleasantness from the boy, which of course only increases his anxiety. They never refer to the boy's dead mother, a bohemian novelist, by name. To them, she's "Dear One." They won't say she's dead, only that she "slipped away." For that matter, nobody ever uses the boy's real name, William. He's called P.S. because his mother once said he was a postscript to her ridiculous life. Slippery words that explode in his face are constantly interposed between the boy and the world he uneasily inhabits.

The boy's problems are compounded when another aunt materializes. Cool, elegant, high-handed Vanessa, who arrives from London on an ocean liner as exotic as a spaceship, is slender as a lily and jagged with chic. She means to haul P.S. off to her stone mansion and remake him in her genteel image. But the boy doesn't immediately learn of the bitter tug-of-war between the two sisters. Caught between the ineffectual kindness of one aunt and the cruel barrenness of the other, and lied to by both, he grows confused, unable to locate his own feelings. When he hears them hiss at one another, he throws up. One of the things that makes the film so unswervingly powerful is that it makes us share the boy's dread at his paralyzing helplessness and endless entrapment in the adult infighting.

But P.S., miserable as he is with his rich aunt and his piano lessons, and his tormented existence in a cruel private school, finds he isn't helpless despite a court's steamrolling of Lila and George in favor of Vanessa. Beneath her chilly poise, the repressed Vanessa has her weaknesses. He first learns of them when she has hysterics during a middle-of-the-night thunderstorm and joins him in his bed. The scene, bathed in icy, blue light, is Gothic in a satisfying nineteenth-century way. He also learns that Vanessa is using him as a stand-in for his roguish drifter of a father, whom she loved and then hated for marrying her sister. Young P.S. finds a way to fight back.

John Hargreaves perfectly projects the father's ne'er-do-well charm; we can believe he heartens P.S. during their single brief visit. Robyn Nevin and Peter Whitford are touchingly decent as poor asthmatic Lila and George, her unemployed trade-unionist husband. And young Nicholas Gledhill is uncannily convincing as the victimized P.S. But the film's most haunting element is Wendy Hughes's high-strung, almost ectoplasmic Vanessa. Not since Dominic Guard in *The Go-Between* has a young actor generated the evocative power Gledhill projects. But Hughes, in a complete turnabout from her plain-Jane in *Lonely Hearts,* is the linchpin of this extraordinary film. She's as eerily compelling as the madly autocratic Miss Havisham in *Great Expectations.* She piles guilt and Oedipal conflict of almost unbearable proportions on the boy's head. Her remarkable achievement, and Schultz's, arises in part from the way they charge the hothouse atmosphere with unstated, but powerful, erotic undercurrents. And with mystery. *Careful, He Might Hear You* could easily have been mere sumptuous soap opera, on the order of *Kramer vs. Kramer.* Schultz turns it into something far more primal. It's a film that will stay with me for years.

—*Jay Carr*

Nadia Tass

■

MALCOLM (1986)

Too infrequently a small movie arrives from left field, taking its audience by surprise, riding on a word-of-mouth high — a *Choose Me, Arthur, Stand By Me* kind of discovery.

Now from Australia we have just such a delight — *Malcolm*, a dazzling inventive, tender, utterly unpretentious comedy. If you can't remember the last time you laughed out loud at a movie; if the great Ealing comedies of character are still your standard of excellence, then *Malcolm* is your cuppa, mate.

Malcolm has hardly gone unheralded on its home ground. Over the weekend, it became Australia's Cinderella story. A family affair and a first feature for its director and writer, made for the equivalent of $650,000, it won eight Australian Film Institute Awards (their Oscars): best picture, director, actor, supporting actor and actress, editing, screenplay, and sound. The win for director Nadia Tass marks the first time a woman has gotten that honor in Australia; her husband, David Parker, was *Malcolm*'s writer, coproducer, and cinematographer. And the character of Malcolm was loosely based on John Tassopoulos, the director's younger brother, who died in 1983 at the age of twenty-five.

In a way, a passel of awards almost creates problems for a movie this modest. *Malcolm* isn't *Dr. Zhivago*. Or *Lawrence of Arabia*. It's small, deadpan witty, almost a visualization of its music by the splendidly irreverent Penguin Cafe Orchestra. Mostly it sneaks up on you. Like Malcolm (played by the thatch-haired, piercingly blue-eyed and splendid Colin Friels).

His thumb held protectively inside his fist, Malcolm walks leaning ever so slightly into an imaginary wind and crosses the street rather than pass in front of a small dog or children at play. He is, at the same time, a mechanical genius and what the world thinks of as "slow." Living alone since his mother's recent death, Malcolm has held a job, working around his beloved railway trams, until a too-clever invention of his gets him sacked.

At this point, it's the consensus of the neighbors and shopkeepers in his little Melbourne community that Malcolm should get a boarder. Enter Frank (John Hargreaves), an ex-con, and, in very short order,

Frank's lady love, Judith (Lindy Davies) a cheerful, handsome woman *d'un certain mileage.*

The two settle into Malcolm's Victorian gingerbread bungalow, with its comforting, dark interior. (This is one of the few comedies to be celebrated in rich, dark tones.) The house is crammed with Malcolm's ingenious inventions: toy trams, a little motor-driven pickup truck he sends halfway up the street for his morning milk, even a thingamabob that exercises his cockatoo.

His new "friends" are racy and disreputable, and layabout Frank is clearly up to no good, but they please Malcolm down to his socks. They also bring him out into the world, even if it's a world of hot TV sets and elaborately planned heists.

Fascinated by what he's seen (and overheard), Malcolm throws himself into a frenzy of creation. In his garage workshop, he begins building devices that—it seems to him—have been needed for the stickups and getaways he's watched on television, and if you think I'm going to describe a single one, you're badly mistaken. The Bond gadgeteers had better pack it all in and hire Malcolm. His brain-children have the pure joy of an animated cartoon (and the gurgle and musical rhythm of one too, thanks to the Penguin Cafe score).

The filmmakers build this unlikely trio with economy and out-rageous, silent-movie sight gags. But something deeper has been building as well. From the beginning, as we watch an idea make its uncertain way behind Frank's eyes and out his mouth, it's clear that this lodger, who can think of Malcolm as a "moron," is a pretty dim bulb himself. He's simply functional in the outside world—and only there on its fringes.

Malcolm's sterling qualities are not lost on Judith, however. Nor on us, from the unveiling of his very first invention. (Judith is also the movie's voice of moral outrage at a babe like Malcolm being pulled into some very dark woods.) What remains is for Frank to move, with the greatest reluctance, over to our side, a journey that is fully half the film's fun.

Hargreaves, Davies, and Friel are simply marvelous. It's hard to recognize the anguished, golden-bearded intellectual of *My First Wife* in Hargreaves's Frank, the chain-smoking tough with the short fuse. Davies's Jude is a marvelous creation: casually sensual, generous, motherly; most herself around men but the sort of woman who genuinely likes other women as well.

A character like Malcolm's, the world's pure innocent, is a magnet for actors, usually in moist little television dramas. The classically trained Friels steers clear of the role's obvious pitfalls; this is not Lenny or Charly, but a sturdy, open, engaging *naif*, let loose to practice his arts in an astonished world. (Malcolm's reponse to the *Grand Guignol* story from Frank's past is the summing-up of his character—and the film-makers' unsentimentality.)

You'll also find a hilarious bit by Chris Haywood, as Frank's partner in crime. (He was the sleazy painter who came to such a memorably bad end in *Man of Flowers*.)

Are these criminal machinations all vaguely immoral? Absolutely, in the best tradition of *The Lavender Hill Mob*. And somehow, with *Malcolm*'s down under earthiness and complexity of character, even more fun.

—Sheila Benson

ABOUT THE CONTRIBUTORS

David Ansen is a movie critic and senior writer at *Newsweek*. He wrote the documentary *The Divine Garbo*, which appeared on TNT in 1990, and *The One and Only . . . Groucho* for HBO in 1991. He has won three Page One awards from the Newspaper Guild of New York. He was formerly the movie critic at *The Real Paper*.

Gary Arnold has been senior movie critic of *The Washington Times* since March 1989. He was the movie critic of the *Washington Post* from April 1969 to September 1984, and he has contributed movie reviews and essays on popular culture to many other publications.

Sheila Benson was the *Los Angeles Times* film critic from 1981 to 1991. Since April 1991 she has been the *Los Angeles Times* critic-at-large. From 1974 to 1981 she was one of the two film critics for the *Pacific Sun* in Marin County.

Jay Carr is *The Boston Globe*'s film critic. He was previously the theater and music critic for the *Detroit News* and won the 1971–72 George Jean Nathan Award for Dramatic Criticism.

Kathleen Carroll is movie critic for the *New York Daily News*. She has been chairperson of the New York Critics Circle three times. She was formerly associate professor in the Communication Arts Division of St. John's University. She ran a program at Toronto's Festival of Festivals, while regularly reporting on the Cannes Film Festival.

Charles Champlin was principal film critic for the *Los Angeles Times* from 1967 to 1980 and retired as arts editor and critic-at-large columnist in April 1991. He presently hosts "Champlin on Film" and "The Great Directors" series on Bravo cable.

Richard Corliss is a film critic for *Time* magazine and contributing editor of *Film Comment.* He is the author of *Talking Pictures.*

Judith Crist, an adjunct professor at the Columbia Graduate School of Journalism, began her career in film criticism at the *New York Herald Tribune* and has reviewed movies for a variety of publications and on television. She is the author of *The Private Eye, The Cowboy and the Very Naked Girl, Judith Crist's TV Guide to the Movies,* and *Take 22: Moviemakers on Moviemaking,* now in paperback.

David Denby is film critic of *New York* magazine and writes the "Rear Window" column for *Premiere.* His articles and reviews have also appeared in *The New Republic, The Atlantic,* and *The New York Review of Books.*

Morris Dickstein's film criticism has appeared in *American Film, Chaplin, The Bennington Review, In These Times, Grand Street, The Nation,* and *Partisan Review,* of which he is currently a contributing editor. He teaches literature and film at Queens College, CUNY, and is the author of *Gates of Eden* (Penguin). With Leo Braudy, he edited *Great Film Directors: A Critical Anthology* (Oxford).

Roger Ebert is the Pulitzer Prize–winning film critic of the *Chicago Sun-Times,* co-host of television's "Siskel & Ebert," and author of *Roger Ebert's Movie Home Companion* and *Two Weeks in the Midday Sun,* a journal of the Cannes film festival.

Joseph Gelmis has reviewed movies for *Newsday* since 1964. His articles on films and filmmakers are syndicated to publications in the United States and Britain by the Los Angeles Times/Washington Post News Wire. He has taught at the State University of New York at Stony Brook, hosted a weekly radio show on WBAI FM, and is the author of *The Film Director as Superstar.*

Owen Gleiberman is the movie critic for *Entertainment Weekly.* He reviewed movies for the *Boston Phoenix* from 1981 to 1989. He has also written for *Premiere* and is heard on National Public Radio's "Fresh Air."

Hal Hinson is a film critic for *The Washington Post.*

J. Hoberman has reviewed movies for *The Village Voice* since 1978. He is a contributing writer to *Premiere* and has a regular column in *Artforum.* He is the coauthor (with Jonathan Rosenbaum) of *Midnight Movies* and the author of *Bridge of Light,* a history of the Yiddish-language cinema, published by the Museum of Modern Art and Schocken Books in 1991. He is also the author of *Vulgar Modernism,* a collection of pieces written in the eighties from *The Village Voice* and elsewhere.

Richard T. Jameson has written for the *Seattle Weekly, Pacific Northwest,* and *7 Days* and edited the Seattle Film Society's journal, *Movietone News,* from 1971 to 1981. He has been the editor of *Film Comment* since the beginning of 1990.

Pauline Kael began reviewing movies for *The New Yorker* in 1967. Since then, her work has been compiled in *Going Steady, Deeper into Movies* (National Book Award Winner, 1973), *Reeling, When the Lights Go Down, 5001 Nights at the Movies, Taking It All In, State of the Art, Hooked* (a 1991 expanded version of *5001 Nights at the Movies*), and *Movie Love.* Her first two collections, *I Lost It at the Movies* and *Kiss Kiss Bang Bang,* include essays and reviews written for *Partisan Review, Sight and Sound, Film Quarterly,* and *The Atlantic,* as well as *The New Yorker. The Citizen Kane Book* contains her long essay "Raising Kane," and she also wrote the introduction to *Three Screen Comedies by Samson Raphaelson.*

Dave Kehr has been the movie critic of the *Chicago Tribune* since 1986. From 1975 to 1986, he was the movie critic of the *Chicago Reader.*

Stuart Klawans reviews films for *The Nation* and WBAI radio. His commentaries and fiction have appeared in *The Village Voice, Grand Street, The Threepenny Review, Entertainment Weekly,* and the *Times Literary Supplement.*

John Powers is a film critic for the *L.A. Weekly* and writes a regular Hollywood column for *Sight and Sound.* He is currently at work on a book about mosquitoes and history.

Terrence Rafferty reviews books and films for *The New Yorker.* His movie writing has also appeared in *The Nation, Sight and Sound, The Atlantic, The Threepenny Review,* and *Film Quarterly.*

Peter Rainer, the current chairman of the National Society of Film Critics, writes film criticism and commentary for the *Los Angeles Times* and writes regularly on film for *American Film*. From 1981 until its demise in 1989, he was film critic for the *Los Angeles Herald Examiner*. Rainer's writing has also appeared in *The New York Times Magazine, Vogue, GQ, Newsday, Premiere, Mademoiselle,* and *Connoisseur,* where he was film critic from 1974 to 1984. Rainer has appeared as a film commentator on such television shows as "Nightline," "ABC World News Tonight," and "CBS Morning News." He has also taught film criticism at the USC Graduate Film School.

Carrie Rickey is a film critic for *The Philadelphia Inquirer*. She was previously the film critic for the *Boston Herald* and *The Village Voice*.

Jonathan Rosenbaum has written for over fifty periodicals, including the *Chicago Reader* (where he has been film critic since 1987), *Cahiers du Cinéma, Elle, Film Comment, Sight and Sound,* and *Tikkun*. His books include *Moving Places: A Life at the Movies* and *Film: The Front Line 1983*. He edited Orson Welles's *The Big Brass Ring* and *The Cradle Will Rock* and Peter Bogdanovich's *Conversations with Orson Welles* (the latter two forthcoming in 1992).

Julie Salamon is the film critic for *The Wall Street Journal*. She is the author of the novel *White Lies* and the book *The Devil's Candy: The Bonfire of the Vanities Goes to Hollywood*.

Andrew Sarris is film critic for the *New York Observer* and professor of film at the School of the Arts at Columbia University. He is also the author of ten books, including *The American Cinema, Confessions of a Cultist, The John Ford Movie Mystery,* and *Politics and Cinema*. He was a movie reviewer for twenty-nine years at *The Village Voice*.

Richard Schickel has reviewed movies for *Time* magazine since 1972; before that he was *Life's* film critic. He is the author of many books, most notably *The Disney Version, His Picture in the Papers, D.W. Griffith: An American Life, Intimate Strangers: The Culture of Celebrity, Schickel on Film,* and his latest, *Marlon Brando: A Life in Our Times*. He is also a producer-writer-director of television documentaries, the latest of which, *Barbara Stanwyck: Fire and Desire,* appeared in summer 1991 on

TNT. He has held a Guggenheim Fellowship and has won the British Film Institute book prize.

Stephen Schiff is critic-at-large of *Vanity Fair* and a film critic on National Public Radio. A former correspondent on CBS-TV's "West 57th," and a Pulitzer Prize finalist in 1983, he has written film criticism for *The Atlantic*, the *Boston Phoenix*, *Film Comment*, *Glamour*, and *American Film*.

Henry Sheehan is the film critic of *L.A. Style* and a contributing critic to *The Hollywood Reporter* and the *L.A. Weekly*. From 1986 to 1991 he was film critic of the *Los Angeles Reader*. He has written on film and related subjects for *Film Comment*, *Sight and Sound*, *The Boston Globe*, the *Boston Phoenix*, *Premiere*, and *The New York Times Book Review*.

Michael Sragow was the editor of *Produced and Abandoned: The Best Films You've Never Seen*, the first in this National Society of Film Critics series. He has been the movie critic for the *San Francisco Examiner* since 1985 and also contributes movie notes to *The New Yorker*. He was previously movie critic for the *Boston Phoenix*, the *Los Angeles Herald Examiner*, and *Rolling Stone* magazine. His book, television, and movie criticism has appeared in *Esquire*, *The Atlantic*, *Mother Jones*, *Harper's*, *The Nation*, *The New Republic*, *New York* magazine, *Film Comment*, *American Film*, and *Sight and Sound*.

Kevin Thomas has been the movie critic of the *Los Angeles Times* since 1962. He has served on the juries of the Tokyo, Chicago, Berlin, Montreal, and Tehran film festivals. A fourth-generation California newspaperman and native Angeleno, he was named a chevalier in France's Order of Arts and Letters for his "contributions to French cinema."

Peter Travers is the film critic for *Rolling Stone* magazine.

Kenneth Turan is the chief film critic for the *Los Angeles Times*. He has been a staff writer for *The Washington Post* and *TV Guide* and film critic for *GQ* and National Public Radio's "All Things Considered." He is the coauthor of *Call Me Anna: The Autobiography of Patty Duke*. He is on the board of directors of the National Yiddish Book Center.

Armond White is the film critic and arts editor of the Brooklyn-based weekly, the *City Sun*. He is the author of the forthcoming Brian De Palma study, *Total Illumination*.

Bruce Williamson has been *Playboy*'s movie critic (and a contributing editor there) for more than two decades. He was a former chairman of the New York Film Critics Circle, a movie critic at *Time* magazine from 1963 to 1967, and, for a brief period, a movie-media critic for *Life*.

Michael Wilmington has been a movie reviewer for the *Los Angeles Times* since 1984. He contributes regularly to *L.A. Style, Film Comment,* and *Sight and Sound,* and was formerly a film editor at *L.A. Weekly*. He is coauthor of *John Ford* (British Film Institute, 1973) and has won five Milwaukee Press Awards for art criticism while working at *Isthmus*.

MAIL-ORDER VIDEO RENTAL AND SALES COMPANIES

Beta Library
836224 Promenade Station
Richardson, TX 75083
214–385–2382

Beta Library deals in sales and mail-order of Beta-format tapes. Although it primarily offers domestic films, of its 500-plus titles, 82 are foreign. All titles are priced at $19.95. Beta Library buys and swaps tapes. Free catalog and an update of new stock every six months.

Captain Bijou
PO Box 87
Toney, AL 35773
205–852–0198

This "video store–plus" offers "everything that is worth watching or that does not cost that much." Captain Bijou is a "shopping mall" of obscure films on video, a mix of foreign, cult, westerns, animation, and B-movies. Also sells movie-related paraphernalia: posters, comic books, calendars, scripts. Catalog $3.00

Discount Video Tapes, Inc.
PO Box 7122
Burbank, CA 91510
818–843–3821
Toll-free fax 800–253–9612

This discount sales company carries about 200 foreign titles along with other rare and unusual finds: comedies, westerns, serials, documentaries, and silent films. Owner Woody Wise recommends the foreign flick, *The Sheep Has Five Legs*. Deals with public-domain material. Sales only. Free catalog.

Evergreen Video Society
213 West 35th St., 2nd floor
New York, NY 10001–4042
800–225–7783 or 212–691–7362

Evergreen specializes in its 2,000 foreign film titles and boasts 5,000 titles overall. Sales and rentals across the country. Free catalog by request.

Facets Video
1517 West Fullerton Avenue
Chicago, IL 60614
800–331–6197 or 312–281–9075
Fax 312–929–5437

One-third of Facets Video's extensive catalog is dedicated to a selection of over 2,000 foreign releases spanning thirty-five countries. Also provides a selection of independent American films, documentaries, "wacky cult films," science-fiction, silent, instructional, travel, and fine arts tapes, including five versions of *Magic Flute* and six versions of *Romeo and Juliet*. Catalog is $7.95 for nonmembers and $5.45 for members with discounts on rentals. Deals both in rentals and sales.

Festival Films
2841 Irving Avenue South
Minneapolis, MN 55408
612–870–4744
Fax 612–874–8520

Festival carries 1,000 foreign film titles, offering a list of silent films, classics, and animation as well. Sales only. Free catalog.

Home Film Festival
PO Box 2032
Scranton, PA 18501
800–258–3456 (national)

Home Film's video collection includes 1,200 recent and classic foreign film titles, along with a selection of independent works, documentaries, and Hollywood classics. A comprehensive catalog is available with membership. Free information kit and film list. Deals in both rentals and sales.

Marshall Discount Video Service
3130 Edsel Drive, #328
Trenton, MI 48183
313–671–5483

Currently stocks all the major distributors of foreign film cassettes and plans to include the entire range of independent distributors by the end of 1992 in its extensive collection of 50,000 titles. Dave Marshall claims his catalog is the "most complete and gigantic" available for $10.00. Laser list is $7.00.

Movies Unlimited
6736 Castor Avenue
Philadelphia, PA 19149
800–523–0823 or 215–722–8398
Fax 215–725–3683

This mail-order/phone-order company supplies "everything available on video," including hundreds of foreign films. The catalog is over 600 pages, listing 20,000 titles. Customers send $7.95 plus $3.00 shipping for the catalog and receive a $5.00 credit voucher on a first order of $25.00 or more. Sales only.

PBS VideoFinders
1–900–860–9301

Operators available 6 A.M. to 5 P.M. Pacific Standard Time. Video-Finders is a paid telephone search service that locates video copies of 2,500 PBS programs and about 58,000 entertainment titles including foreign films. VideoFinders answers inquiries about availability, cost, and distributor, and often will place special orders. The call is $2.00 for the first minute, $1.00 for each additional minute. Customers should have the film title ready to ensure prompt service.

Tamarelle's International Films
7900 Hickman Road
Des Moines, IA 50322
800–356–3577 or 916–895–3429
Fax 515–254–7021

Tamarelle's is the foreign film division of Commtron, offering a selection of 1,500 recent and classic foreign film titles. An annual catalog is available along with semiquarterly updates. Sales only.

Video Yesteryear
Box C
Sandy Hook, CT 06482
800–243–0987 or 203–426–2574

Yesteryear's collection of 1,200 titles includes several hundred foreign films as well as documentaries, westerns, television shows, and a "fine selection" of silent films. All tapes come from the company's own source material. Send $2.50 for the most recent 240-page catalog. Sales only.

Whole Toon Catalog
PO Box 369
Issaquah, WA 98027
206–391–8747

Whole Toon lists 17,000 titles of animation videos, including hundreds of foreign animation films from Japan, France, Hungary, and other countries. Also sells books, posters, and cartoon memorabilia. Free catalog (for first class mail delivery, allow $2.00 shipping). Sales only.

PERMISSIONS

Every effort has been made to identify the holders of copyright of previously published materials included in this book. This process was complicated by the sudden death of editor Kathy Schulz Huffhines and the loss of some of her work. The publisher apologizes for any oversights that may have occurred; any errors that may have been made will be corrected in subsequent printings upon notification to publisher.

Grateful acknowledgment is made to the following for permission to reprint copyrighted material:

David Ansen: for his *Real Paper* reviews of *The Spirit of Beehive* (April 30, 1977), *Judex* (1975), and *Aguirre, the Wrath of God* (1977).

Boston Globe: for Jay Carr's reviews of *A Taxing Woman* (May 18, 1988), *When Father Was Away on Business* (May 1, 1985), *Wings of Desire* (June 24, 1988), *Dark Eyes* (October 30, 1987), *The Singing Detective* (April 21, 1989), *Pelle the Conquerer* (February 10, 1989), *Taxi Blues* (February 22, 1991), *Careful, He Might Hear You* (July 27, 1984), *Repentance* (February 19, 1989), and for his retrospective of Andrei Tarkovsky (January 1, 1987). Reprinted courtesy of the *Boston Globe*.

Boston Herald: for Carrie Rickey's review of *Camila* (April 12, 1985). Reprinted with permission of the *Boston Herald*.

Boston Phoenix: for Owen Gleiberman's reviews of *Sid and Nancy* (November 11, 1986) and *A World Apart* (July 15, 1989); for Stephen Schiff's reviews of *Bob le Flambeur* (September 28, 1982), *Man of Marble* (March 3, 1981), *Diva* (June 8, 1982), and for his retrospective of Wim Wenders (September 14, 1982); for Michael Sragow's reviews of *The Leopard* (January 17, 1984) and *The Machioka Sisters* (June 4, 1985); for

Henry Sheehan's reviews of *Sugar Cane Alley* (May 22, 1984), *À Nos Amours* (February 26, 1985), *Sans Soleil,* and *La Jetée* (October 9, 1985).

Cambridge Express: for Kathy Schulz Huffhines's review of *Beau Père.*

Jay Carr: for his reviews of *Pandora's Box, Carmen,* and his retrospective of Jean Renoir.

Chaplin film magazine: for Morris Dickstein's review of *The Silence* and *Persona* (1988).

Chicago Reader: for Dave Kehr's reviews of *The Seven Samurai* (February 4, 1983), *Once Upon a Time in the West* (February 4, 1983), *The Good, the Bad, and the Ugly* (capsule), *Coup de Torchon* (April 8, 1983), and *Eijanaika* (February 4, 1983); for Jonathan Rosenbaum's reviews of *Red Desert* (capsule), *Parade* (December 1, 1989), *Brightness* (capsule), *The Horse Thief* (September 18, 1987), and *Distant Voices, Still Lives* (August 18, 1989). Copyright © 1983, 1987, 1989, *The Chicago Reader.* Reprinted by permission.

Chicago Tribune: for Dave Kehr's reviews of *The Nun* (November 30, 1990) and *Dead Ringers* (September 23, 1988).

City Paper: for John Power's review of *Moonlighting* (February 1983).

Judith Crist: for her *New York Herald* reviews of *This Sporting Life* (July 17, 1963), *Loves of a Blonde* (September 13, 1966), *Billy Liar* (December 7, 1963), and for her *New York* magazine review of *Z* (December 8, 1969).

Detroit Free Press: for Kathy Schulz Huffhines's reviews of *Cal, Le Doulos, The Krays, Life and Nothing But, Three Brothers, Time of the Gypsies,* and *Red Sorghum.*

Morris Dickstein: for his reviews of *Metropolis, M, La Strada,* and *Kagemusha* (*Bennington Review,* April 1981).

Roger Ebert: for his *Chicago Sun-Times* reviews of *Wetherby* (December 27, 1985) and *Bye Bye Brazil* (August 11, 1981).

Fame magazine: for Carrie Rickey's retrospective of Pedro Almodóvar.

Film Comment: for Richard Corliss's retrospective of Ingmar Bergman (March/April 1983).

Kathy Schulz Huffhines: for her reviews of *Alexander Nevsky, Gregory's Girl,* and *Freeze, Die, Come to Life.*

In These Times: for Morris Dickstein's retrospective of Luis Buñuel (August 24–September 6, 1983).

Richard T. Jameson: for his *Seattle Weekly* reviews of *Cria!* (September 28, 1977), *The Marriage of Maria Braun* (January 16, 1980), *Picnic at Hanging Rock* (July 11, 1979), *Providence* (August 31, 1977), *Man of Flowers* (November 21, 1984), and *The Road Warrior* (July 27, 1982).

Pauline Kael: for reviews, from her book *5001 Nights at the Movies* (Henry Holt & Co., New York, 1991), of *À Nous la Liberté, Aparajito, The Conformist, The Baker's Wife, The Blue Angel, The Cabinet of Dr. Caligari, Children of Paradise, Cleo from 5 to 7, Earth, General della Rovere, La Terra Trema, Last Tango in Paris, The Lavendar Hill Mob, Les Enfants Terribles, Mother, Paisan, Pather Panchali, Pépé le Moko, Nosferatu, Open City, Sunday Bloody Sunday, Zazie dans le Métro, The World of Apu, Ugetsu,* and *Vampyr;* for her reviews in *The New Yorker* of *Night of the Shooting Stars* (February 7, 1983), and *Pixote* (November 9, 1981); for reviews, from her book *I Lost It at the Movies* (Atlantic-Little Brown, Boston, 1965), of *The Earrings of Madame de . . . , L'Avventura, Shoeshine, Odd Obsession,* and *Les Cousins.*

Los Angeles Herald Examiner: for Peter Rainer's reviews of *Bizarre, Bizarre* (October 24, 1978), *The Last Emperor* (November 20, 1987), *Au Revoir les Enfants* (December 16, 1987), *The Home and the World* (July 10, 1985), and *Prick Up Your Ears* (May 1, 1987).

Los Angeles Times: for Sheila Benson's reviews of *An Unfinished Piece for a Player Piano* (May 26, 1982), *My Life as a Dog* (May 14, 1987), *My Friend Ivan Lapshin* (May 22, 1987), and *Malcolm* (November 5, 1986); for Charles Champlin's reviews of *Accident* (May 5, 1967), *The Enigma of Kaspar Hauser* (December 8, 1976), and *Cousin, Cousine* (October 31, 1989); for Kevin Thomas's reviews of *Stray Dog* (August 30, 1963), *High and Low,* (February 25, 1964), *Landru* (March 6, 1964), and *Night and Fog* (October 15, 1965).

Monthly Film Bulletin: for Jonathan Rosenbaum's review of *The Life of Oharu* (March 1975).

The Nation: for Stuart Klawans's reviews of *Little Vera* (May 15, 1989) and *Hotel Terminus: The Life and Times of Klaus Barbie* (November 7, 1988).

Newsday: for Joseph Gelmis's review of *Henry V* (December 7, 1990).

Newsweek: for David Ansen's reviews of *Celeste* (November 11, 1982), *Padre Padrone* (January 16, 1978), *The Fourth Man* (June 18, 1984), *The Decline of the American Empire* (November 17, 1986), and *Hope and Glory.*

New York magazine: for David Denby's reviews of *Get Out Your Handkerchiefs* (January 22, 1979), *Local Hero* (March 1983), and *Mona Lisa* (April 16, 1986).

New York Daily News: for Kathleen Carroll's review of *El Norte* (January 11, 1984).

The New Yorker: for Michael Sragow's reviews of *Sabotage* (July 30, 1990), *Hobson's Choice* and *Oliver Twist* (October 23, 1989), *The Fallen Idol* (September 17, 1990), *Orpheus* (September 10, 1990), *Sansho the Bailiff* (May 28, 1990), *Knife in the Water* (August 7, 1989), *Christ Stopped at Eboli* (August 27, 1990), *Umberto D.* (August 31, 1990), *The Raven,* and *The Wages of Fear.*

New York Observer: for Andrew Sarris's review of *The Cook, the Thief, His Wife and Her Lover* (April 30, 1990).

The Philadelphia Inquirer: for Carrie Rickey's retrospective of Michael Powell (February 25, 1990) and her review of *Twilight of the Cockroaches* (August 31, 1990).

Playboy: for Bruce Williamson's review of *Gallipoli.*

John Powers: for his *Los Angeles Weekly* reviews of *My Beautiful Laundrette* (March 1986), *Under Satan's Sun* (1988), and *Point Blank;* and for his reviews of *Hour of the Star, A Better Tomorrow, Rouge, Zéro de Conduite, The Passenger, The Tokyo Story, The Draughtsman's Contract,* and *The Time to Live and the Time to Die.*

Premiere: for J. Hoberman's review of *Speaking Parts* and *Family Viewing* (April 1990) and his retrospective of Aki Kaurismäki (June 1989).

Terrence Rafferty: for his *New Yorker* reviews of *L'Atalante* (November 5, 1990), *Boyfriends and Girlfriends* (July 25, 1988), and his retrospective of François Truffaut (December 31, 1984).

Rolling Stone: for Michael Sragow's review of *The Long Good Friday* (May 27, 1982); for Peter Travers's reviews of *Cyrano* (November 29, 1990) and *Cinema Pardiso.*

Jonathan Rosenbaum: for his review of *Paris Belongs to Us* and for his retrospectives of Sergei Paradjanov and Pier Paolo Pasolini.

Julie Salamon: for her *Wall Street Journal* reviews of *Vagabond* (May 22, 1986) and *Men . . .* (July 29, 1986).

San Francisco Examiner: for Mike Sragow's reviews of *Murmur of the Heart* (April 7, 1989) and *The Entertainer* (September 8, 1989).

Andrew Sarris: for his reviews, from his book *Confessions of a Cultist* (Simon and Schuster, New York, 1970), of *Gertrud* (*The Village Voice,* April 2, 1966), Italy's Big Four (*Showbill,* January 1961), *Nights of Cabiria* (*Film Culture,* January 1958), *The Servant* (*The Village Voice,* March 26, 1964), and his retrospective of Carl Dreyer (*New York Times,* March 31, 1968).

Second Sight: for Richard Schickel's reviews of *If* (February 28, 1969) and *My Night at Maud's* (June 19, 1970).

Henry Sheehan: for his *Los Angeles Reader* reviews of *Diary of a Country Priest, Mouchette, Story of Women,* and *Monsieur Hire.*

■

For use of the photographs, grateful acknowledgment is made to the following:

International Film Exchange Ltd.: for the scene from *Little Vera*.

Janus Films: for the scene from *Jules and Jim*.

Miramax Films: for the scenes from *The Krays* and *Pelle the Conquerer*.

New Line Cinema: for the scene from *Get Out Your Handkerchiefs*.

New Yorker Films: for the scenes from *L'Atalante* and *Red Sorghum*.

Orion Pictures Corp.: for the scene from *Monsieur Hire*.

Public Broadcasting System: for the scene from *Sugar Cane Alley*.

Warner Brothers: for the scene from *The Road Warrior*.

INDEX OF DIRECTORS

Abuladze, Tengiz, 482–484
Adlon, Percy, 258, 259–261
Allen, Woody, 109, 113, 174, 262
Almodóvar, Pedro, xvii–xviii, 258, 262–265, 297
Altman, Robert, 161
Amaral, Suzana, 496
Amiel, Jon, 390–391
Anderson, Lindsay, 15, 122, 123–127
Angelopoulos, Theo, 354, 358–364
Antonioni, Michelangelo, 2, 3, 40, 41, 42–43, 43–47, 173, 358, 362, 363, 371
Armstrong, Gillian, 515, 516
Attenborough, Richard, 7
August, Bille, xviii, 451, 452–454
Axel, Gabriel, 451, 454–456
Babenco, Hector, 386, 497–501
Barreto, Bruno, 502–504
Bartlett, Hall, 126
Becker, Jacques, 237
Beineix, Jean-Jacques, 258, 265–271
Bemberg, Maria-Luisa, 496, 504–506
Beresford, Bruce, 515–516, 516–518, 524
Berger, Ludwig, 8
Bergman, Ingmar, xvii, 37, 57, 108–119, 204, 223, 230, 284, 363, 385, 453, 463
Berri, Claude, xviii, 422–424
Bertolucci, Bernardo, 122, 127–139, 176, 192, 330, 359
Blier, Bertrand, 271–282, 447
Boorman, John, 122, 139–142, 205
Branagh, Kenneth, 390, 392–393
Brassai, —, 183
Bresson, Robert, 4, 43, 79, 92, 113, 122, 142–147, 183, 230, 346, 348, 354, 401
Breuer, Marita, 471
Brooks, Mel, 237

Browning, Tod, 4
Buñuel, Luis, xvii, xviii, 2, 4, 42, 43, 99–107, 114, 230, 274, 342, 343, 475, 482, 503
Cacoyannis, —, 358
Campion, Jane, xviii, 354, 364–366
Carné, Marcel, 2, 26–29, 133
Carpenter, John, 282
Cassavetes, John, 469
Chabrol, Claude, 10, 121, 122, 147–156, 184, 211, 213
Chaplin, Charles, 30, 35, 42, 47, 131, 151, 180, 370, 401, 402
Chen Kaige, 371
Choy, Chris, 376
Cisse, Souleymane, 354–355, 356
Clair, René, 1, 2, 28, 29–30, 35
Clement, Dick, 237
Clouzot, Henri-Georges, 1–2, 30–31
Cocteau, Jean, 2, 6, 31–32, 33, 41, 183, 188, 259, 271
Coppola, Francis Ford, 9
Corman, Roger, 522
Costa-Gavras, 452, 456–458
Cox, Alex, 394–399
Cox, Paul, 516, 518–520
Crichton, Charles, 2, 10
Cronenberg, David, 258, 282–285, 367
Dali, Salvador, 99
Davies, Terrence, 400–403
Demy, Jacques, 126
Denis, Claire, 424–426
De Sica, Vittorio, 2, 3, 40–41, 50, 63–66, 81–82, 330
Diegues, Carlos, 506–507
Disney, Walt, 76, 109, 207
Donen, Stanley, 359, 508
Dörrie, Doris, 458–460

Dovzhenko, Alexander, 2, 3, 98, 230, 335, 372
Dreyer, Carl Theodor, 4–6, 92, 113, 162, 346, 357, 358, 370
Dupont, E. A., 110
Duvivier, Julien, 2, 32, 437
Ealing, –, 293, 385, 526
Ecaré, Desiré, 356
Egoyan, Atom, 354, 367–369
Eisenstein, Sergei, 2, 3, 4, 39, 93–97, 137, 191, 370, 376
Erice, Victor, 223, 452, 460–463
Fassbinder, Rainer Werner, 257, 258, 263, 285–291, 340, 344, 346, 371, 383, 384, 385, 402
Fellini, Federico, 2, 3, 40, 41, 42, 43–44, 47–54, 55, 187, 193, 204–205, 313, 330, 337, 379, 380, 472, 499
Feuillade, Louis, 33
Feydeau, Georges, 28
Feyder, Jacques, 28
Flaherty, –, 370
Ford, John, 75, 77, 109, 165, 358, 372, 401, 459, 472
Forman, Milos, 157–158
Forsyth, Bill, 258, 291–294
Fosse, Bob, 508
Franju, Georges, 2, 33
Frank, Robert, 385
Frears, Stephen, 258, 294–301
Gance, Abel, 244–245
Gardner, Robert, 386
Gaudí, Antonio, 264
Genet, Jean, 499
Gherman, Alexei, 484–487
Godard, Jean-Luc, 4, 37, 43, 89, 103, 105, 107, 121, 126, 133, 139, 159–163, 184, 185, 187, 205, 211, 212, 250, 265, 268, 337, 359, 362, 363, 371, 439
Gosha, Hideo, 75, 307–308
Greenaway, Peter, 258, 301–304
Griffith, D. W., 40, 97, 215, 370
Guerra, Ruy, 507–509
Hallstrom, Lasse, 451, 463–465
Hare, David, 390, 404–405
Hark, Tsui, 354, 375–376
Hawks, Howard, 77, 109, 237, 359, 508
Herzog, Werner, 37, 257, 258, 304–308, 340, 344, 346, 472, 520
Hitchcock, Alfred, 2, 7, 10–11, 42, 100, 110, 150, 244, 245, 246, 513
Hou Hsiao-hsien, 353

Huang Jianxin, 371
Huillet, Danièle, 431
Huston, John, 57, 359
Ichikawa, Kon, 3, 66–74
Idle, Eric, 411
Imamura, Shohei, 258, 308–315
Itami, Juzo, 258, 315–318
Ivens, Joris, 236
Jancso, Miklos, 251
Jarmusch, Jim, 426
Johnson, Lamont, 57
Jordan, Neil, 258, 319–322
Kanevski, Vitaly, 482, 487–488
Kaurismäki, Aki, 354, 382–386
Kaurismäki, Mika, 382–383
Keaton, Buster, 100
Klimov, Elem, 486
Korda, Alexander, 7–8
Koundouros, –, 358
Kubrick, Stanley, 161, 517
Kurosawa, Akira, xvii, 2, 3, 75–84, 85, 95, 230, 311
Kurtzman, Harvey, 109
Kurys, Diane, 426–430
Kusturica, Emir, 258, 322–325
Kwan, Stanley, 354, 377
Lang, Fritz, 2, 3, 19, 34–36, 40, 99, 213, 312, 472
Lanzmann, Claude, 236, 421, 430–436, 471
Lattuada, Alberto, 43
Lean, David, 2, 7, 11–12
Leconte, Patrice, 436–438
Leland, David, 405–408
Lelouch, Claude, 272, 448
Leone, Sergio, 77, 122, 164–169
Lester, Richard, 181, 334
Lewis, Jerry, 265–266
Loridan, Marceline, 236
Losey, Joseph, 122, 169–174
Lounguine, Pavel, 487, 489–490
Lubitsch, Ernst, 108, 109, 370, 458
Lucas, George, 9, 354, 376
Ludlam, Charles, 264
Lumière, –, 348
Lyne, Adrian, 297
McBain, Ed, 83
McCarey, Leo, 401, 402
Mackenzie, John, 409–412
Mailer, Norman, 130, 131, 132
Malaparte, Curzio, 40
Malle, Louis, 57, 121, 123, 174–181
Marker, Chris, 203, 239, 421, 438–441

Mazursky, Paul, 19
Medak, Peter, 412–414
Melville, Jean-Pierre, 121, 181–188
Menges, Chris, 414–418
Mieville, Annie-Marie, 162
Mikhalkov, Nikita, 122, 123, 188–191, 354, 378–380
Miller, George, 516, 521–523
Minnelli, Vincente, 359, 508
Mizoguchi, Kenji, 3, 41, 84–88, 212, 230, 360, 362, 402, 466
Monty Python, 109, 411–412, 414
Moore, Rudy May, 355
Murnau, F. W., 2, 3, 36–37, 40, 86, 161, 362, 370, 466
Nair, Mira, 354, 386–387
Nava, Gregory, 496, 509–510
O'Connor, Pat, 390, 418–420
Olivier, Laurence, 392–393
Olmi, Ermanno, 220, 452, 465–467
Ophuls, Marcel, 421, 442–445
Ophuls, Max, 3, 13–16, 28, 41, 133, 190
Ouedraogo, Idrissa, 354, 355–357
Ozu, Yasujiro, xviii, 3, 89–93, 309, 348, 351, 358, 401
Pabst, G. W., 2, 3, 37–38, 40
Pagnol, Marcel, xviii, 2, 3, 33, 423, 466
Palcy, Euzhan, 496, 510–512
Paradjanov, Sergei, 122, 191–192, 372, 486
Parker, Alan, 297
Pasolini, Pier Paolo, 192–194
Peckinpah, Sam, 57, 89, 164, 377
Petersen, Wolfgang, 468–470
Pialat, Maurice, 145, 258, 325–330
Pichul, Vasily, 487, 491–493
Polanski, Roman, 122, 123, 194–196, 475
Potter, Dennis, 402–403
Powell, Michael, 2, 7–9
Pressburger, Emeric, 7–9
Pudovkin, Vsevolod, 2, 3, 93–94, 98
Puenzo, Luis, 496, 512–513
Rappeneau, Jean-Paul, 446–447
Ray, Nicholas, 371–372
Ray, Satyajit, 122, 123, 196–201, 356, 387
Reed, Carol, 2, 11, 12
Reitz, Edgar, 470–472
Renoir, Jean, xvii, 16–21, 43, 60, 133, 154, 162, 171, 198–199, 244, 246, 335, 387, 466, 478

Resnais, Alain, 42, 43, 121, 123, 181, 202–206, 457
Richard, Pierre, 448
Richardson, Tony, 122, 123, 207–211
Rivette, Jacques, 20, 26, 121, 211–213, 236, 268
Rohmer, Eric, 10, 121, 123, 214–219, 439, 448
Romand, Françoise, 236
Romero, George, 237
Rosi, Francesco, 63, 122, 123, 219–222, 452
Rossellini, Roberto, xvii, 2, 3, 40, 41–42, 43–44, 50, 54–56, 83, 330, 337, 467
Rouch, Jean, 512
Saura, Carlos, 122, 123, 223–225, 251
Schepisi, Fred, 515, 516, 520, 524
Schlesinger, John, 122, 123, 225–228
Schlöndorff, Volker, 184
Schultz, Carl, 516, 524–525
Scorsese, Martin, 7, 9, 359
Scott, Ridley, 161
Sembene, Ousmane, 354, 355, 356
Sennett, Mack, 28, 181, 443
Sirk, Douglas, 402
Skolimowski, Jerzy, 452, 473–476
Spielberg, Steven, 244, 293, 367, 369, 376
Sternberg, Josef von, 2, 3, 38–39, 133, 263, 289, 370
Straub, Jean-Marie, 431
Stroheim, Erich von, 4, 17, 85, 370
Sturges, John, 77
Sturges, Preston, 316–317
Syberberg, —, 431
Szabo, Istvan, 452, 476–478
Tacchella, Jean-Charles, 272, 447–449
Tarkovsky, Andrei, 122, 228–230, 351, 354, 362, 372, 472, 484
Tass, Nadia, 516, 526–528
Tati, Jacques, 122, 231–237
Tavernier, Bertrand, 121, 123, 237–243
Taviani, Paolo, 220, 330–338, 452, 472
Taviani, Vittorio, 220, 330–338, 452, 472
Thompson, Peter, 236
Thornton, Leslie, 236
Tian Zhuangzhuang, 369–373
Tornatore, Giuseppe, 479

Truffaut, François, xviii, 10, 43, 110, 121, 122, 184, 204–205, 211, 213, 243–248, 265, 308, 351, 371, 387, 463, 478, 487
Vadim, Roger, 6
Varda, Agnès, 121, 249–251
Verhoeven, Paul, 258, 338–339
Vidor, Charles, 508
Vigo, Jean, xviii, 21–26, 133, 499
Visconti, Luchino, 2, 3, 40–41, 42, 43–44, 56–63, 133, 330, 379
von Sternberg, Josef. *See* Sternberg, Joseph von
von Stroheim, Erich. See Stroheim, Erich von
Wajda, Andrzej, 122, 123, 251–255, 477
Warhol, Andy, 240
Waters, John, 264
Wayans, Keenan Ivory, 355

Weir, Peter, 258, 339–344, 515, 516, 523, 524
Welles, Orson, xviii, 21, 33, 52, 64, 236, 252, 362, 472, 491
Wenders, Wim, xvii, 257, 340, 344–351, 358, 368, 385, 426
Wertmuller, Lina, 330
Whale, James, 4
Whelan, Tim, 8
Wiene, Robert, 2, 39
Wilder, Billy, 359, 458
Wise, Robert, 184
Woo, John, 354, 377–378
Wurlitzer, Rudy, 385
Wyler, William, 184
Yoshida, Hiroaki, 380–382
Zeffrelli, Franco, 63
Zhang Yimou, 371, 373–374

INDEX OF ACTORS

Abuladze, (daughter of Tengiz Abuladze), 483
Adjani, Isabelle, 247
Albers, Hans, 38–39
Aleandro, Norma, 512, 513
Allegret, Catherine, 133
Alterio, Héctor, 513
Andersson, Bibi, 108, 111, 112, 115, 325
Andersson, Harriet, 110, 111, 112, 223, 325
Andrei, Frédéric, 266
Angelopoulos, Theo, 359
Anteuil, Daniel, 422, 423
Antonelli, Laura, 325
Antonutti, Omero, 331, 333
Arias, Imanol, 505
Arkell, Marie-Monique, 144
Arletty, 29, 325
Arnaz, Desi, 262
Arndt, Jürgen, 259
Arnoul, Françoise, 21
Ashcroft, Peggy, 228
Astaire, Fred, 266
Audran, Stéphane, 104, 107, 152, 238, 455
Aumont, Jean-Pierre, 27
Awaji, Keiko, 82
Azema, Sabine, 242, 243
Bacri, Jean-Pierre, 428
Baker, Stanley, 173
Balin, Mireille, 32
Banerjee, Victor, 197, 198
Bannen, Ian, 140
Banzie, Brenda de, 12
Baranovskaya, Vera, 98
Bardot, Brigitte, 161, 162
Barrault, Jean-Louis, 27, 28, 29, 325, 443

Barrault, Marie-Christine, 215, 448, 449
Barry, Roukietou, 356
Barrymore, Lionel, 325
Bartolli, Morena D'E, 323
Basehart, Richard, 53
Bass, Alfie, 10
Batalov, Nikolai, 98
Bates, Alan, 209
Battisti, Carlo, 65
Beart, Emmanuelle, 424
Bell, Tom, 408
Belmondo, Jean-Paul, 159, 160, 184, 185, 187, 411
Bergman, Ingrid, 21, 42, 325
Bernard, Jacques, 188
Berry, Jules, 19
Bertheau, Julien, 106
Bertin, Roland, 446
Besnehard, Dominique, 329
Besse, Ariel, 275
Best, Alyson, 518
Blain, Gérard, 148, 149
Blair, Linda, 283
Blanc,
Blanck, Dorothée, 251
Bogarde, Dirk, 170, 171, 173, 205, 206
Bogart, Humphrey, 57, 139, 160, 174, 182, 183, 184, 185, 187, 319, 325, 448
Bogatyrev, Yuri, 189
Bohringer, Richard, 267, 303
Bolger, Ray, 207
Boltnev, Andrei, 486
Bonnaire, Sandrine, 249, 250, 329, 330, 437
Botti, Laura, 193
Bouise, Jean, 457
Bourseiller, Antoine, 251
Boyer, Charles, 14, 32, 325

Bozzufi, Marcel, 457–458
Braga, Sonia, 503
Branagh, Kenneth, 390, 393
Brandauer, Karl Maria, 477, 478
Brando, Marlon, 124, 127, 128, 129, 130,
    131–133, 134, 136, 174, 325
Brasseur, Pierre, 29
Brauss, Arthur, 345
Brialy, Jean-Claude, 148, 149, 213
Britton, Tony, 228
Brochet, Anne, 446
Bromssen, Tomas von, 464
Bronson, Charles, 165
Brooks, Louise, 37, 38
Brynner, Yul, 498
Bujold, Genevieve, 284
Bunnage, Avis, 413
Burstyn, Ellen, 206
Burton, Richard, 211
Byrd, George, 286
Cadenat, Garry, 511
Cagney, James, 319
Caine, Michael, 319
Calamai, Clara, 41
Callas, Maria, 193
Capaldi, Peter, 292
Cardinale, Claudia, 59, 165
Caron, Leslie, 134
Cartaxo, Marcelia, 496
Casarès, Maria, 29, 31
Cascio, Salvatore, 479
Cassel, Jean-Pierre, 104
Cauchy, Daniel, 182
Chabrol, Claude, 213
Chaplin, Charles, 12, 322
Chaplin, Geraldine, 223, 224
Charisse, Cyd, 266
Charpin, 32, 33
Chatterjee, Soumitra, 197, 198, 201
Chatterjee, Swatilekha, 197, 198
Chaulet, Emmanuelle, 217
Chen, Joan, 136
Cherkassov, Nikolai, 94, 137, 491
Cheung, Leslie, 378
Chiaki, Minoru, 76
Chow Yuen Fat, 378
Christie, Julie, 227
Chunibala, 200
Clayburgh, Jill, 325
Clémenti, Pierre, 139
Cluzet, François, 153
Colston, Karen, 365
Coltrane, Robbie, 321

Connery, Sean, 141
Constantine, Eddie, 161, 410–411
Cooper, Gary, 253, 325
Cordy, Raymond, 29
Corey, Isabelle, 185
Cornwall, Charlotte, 413
Cosima, Renée, 188
Courtenay, Tom, 226
Craig, Wendy, 171
Dagover, Lil, 39
Dahlbeck, Eva, 111, 112
Dalio, Marcel, 20, 32
Darc, Mireille, 163
Darling, Jon, 366
Darrieux, Danielle, 13–14, 151, 325
Dasté, Jean, 23
Davies, John Howard, 11
Davies, Lindy, 527
Davies, Lyndon, 391
Davis, Sammi, 139, 140
Davoli, Ninetto, 193
Davray, Dominique, 251
Déa, Marie, 31
Dean, James, 491
de Bankole, Issac, 425, 426
DeBanzie, Brenda, 208, 210
Decomble, Guy, 186
Del Dol, Laura, 225
Delon, Alain, 59, 184, 186, 411
Demongeot, Catherine, 181
Demy, Jacques, 213
Dench, Judi, 404
Denham, Maurice, 228
De Niro, Robert, 396
Denner, Charles, 151, 457
Depardieu, Gérard, 253, 272, 273, 274,
    279–280, 281, 325, 326–327, 330,
    422, 423, 446, 447
Dermithe, Edouard, 188
De Sica, Vittorio, 14, 42, 55, 325
Desny, Ivan, 286
Dewaere, Patrick, 272, 273, 274, 276,
    279–280, 281
Diamond, Neil, 516
Dickinson, Angie, 142
Dietrich, Marlene, 37, 38, 263, 289,
    297, 325
Dommartin, Solveig, 350
Douglas, Kirk, 57
Dowie, Freda, 400
Dresdel, Sonia, 12
Dreyfuss, Richard, 367

Duchesne, Roger, 182, 185
Dumont, Margaret, 28
Dunne, Irene, 112, 325
Dux, Pierre, 458
Eastwood, Clint, 167, 169, 469
Edwards, Sebastian Rice, 139, 140
Elam, Jack, 167
Esposito, Gianni, 213
Fabien, François, 215
Fabre, Saturnin, 32
Fabrizi, Aldo, 54
Falconetti, Marie, 4, 162
Falk, Peter, 351
Fassbinder, Rainer Werner, 289
Feher, Friedrich, 39
Fejto, Raphael, 178
Fernandez, Wilhelmenia Wiggins, 266
Ferrer, José, 446
Ferreux, Benoit, 175
Ferreux, Fabien, 175
Ferzetti, Gabriele, 5, 166
Field, Shirley Anne, 209, 295
Finch, Peter, 227
Finney, Albert, 209, 210
Fleetwood, Susan, 413
Fonda, Henry, 75, 165, 486
Fonda, Jane, 134, 254, 325
Fonda, Peter, 164
Forte, Fabrizio, 331
Fossey, Brigitte, 281
Fox, James, 170, 171
Frankeur, Paul, 104
Fraser, Helen, 226–227
Fraser, John, 195
Freeman, Paul, 410
Fresnay, Pierre, 20, 30
Fresson, Bernard, 457
Friels, Colin, 526, 527, 528
Furneaux, Yvonne, 195
Gabin, Jean, 19, 20, 32, 325, 411
Gabrio, Gabriel, 32
Gambon, Michael, 303, 391
Ganz, Bruno, 350, 351
Garbo, Greta, 325
Garet, André, 185
Gelin, Daniel, 175
Gendron, François-Eric, 217
George, Susan, 326
Gérard, Henriette, 6
Geret, Georges, 458
Gibson, Mel, 343, 521, 523
Gielgud, John, 206
Girardot, Annie, 41

Girotti, Massimo, 132, 133, 193
Glanzelius, Anton, 463
Gledhill, Nicholas, 525
Glushenko, Eugenia, 189
Godard, Jean-Luc, 213
Gong Li, 373, 374
Goya, Chantal, 162
Granger, Farley, 150
Grant, Cary, 243, 325
Gray, Dorian, 49
Gray, Joel, 208
Greenwood, Joan, 171
Griffies, Mona, 226
Guard, Dominic, 525
Guidelli, Micol, 332
Guinness, Alec, 10, 11
Gulp, Eisi, 260
Gunzburg, Nicolas de. See West, Julian
Gutierrez, Zaide Silvia, 509
Hamilton, Suzanna, 404
Hara, Setsuko, 90
Hardie, Kate, 413
Hargreaves, John, 525, 526, 527
Harris, Richard, 46, 123–124
Hayman, David, 139, 397
Haywood, Chris, 528
Head, Murray, 227
Helm, Brigitte, 35
Henrey, Bobby, 12
Hepburn, Audrey, 10, 367
Hepburn, Dee, 294
Hepburn, Katharine, 243, 448
Herrand, Marcel, 29
Hershey, Barbara, 415, 418
Hessling, Catherine, xvii, 17, 18, 162
Higashiyama, Chiyeko, 90
Higgins, Anthony, 301
Hiller, Wendy, 8, 325
Hoffman, Dustin, 283
Hoffman, Thom, 339
Holloway, Stanley, 10
Holm, Ian, 404
Homolka, Oscar, 10
Hoppe, Rolf, 478
Hopper, Dennis, 164, 345, 366
Hoskins, Bob, 319, 321, 411, 412
Howard, Alan, 303
Howard, Trevor, 124
Hoyos, Christina, 225
Hughes, Wendy, 525
Hunter, Kim, 8–9
Huppert, Isabelle, 153, 238, 282, 325, 326–327, 427, 429

Hutchings, Geoffrey, 405
Hvenegaard, Pelle, 454
Inaa, Yoshio, 76
Interlenghi, Franco, 64
Irons, Jeremy, 284, 473
Ironside, Michael, 283
Ishizaka, Koji, 69
Itami, Juzo, 69
Ives, Burl, 511
Izumiya, Shigeru, 313
Jackson, Glenda, 227
Jaffrey, Saeed, 295
James, Gerald, 140
James, Sidney, 10
Janda, Krystyna, 252, 254
Jannings, Emil, 38, 100
Jiang Wen, 373, 374
John, Gottfried, 288, 290
Johnson, Dots M., 55
Jones, Debi, 403
Jouvet, Louis, 27, 28
Julião, Jorge, 499
Kalaigin, Alexander, 189
Kane, Issiaka, 354
Karanovic, Mirjana, 323
Karasumaru, Setsuko, 381
Karina, Anna, 161, 162, 212
Kato, Daisuke, 76
Kaye, Norman, 519
Keaton, Buster, 312, 314
Keaton, Diane, 325
Keller, Marthe, 379
Kemp, Gary, 413
Kemp, Martin, 413
Kerr, Deborah, 8, 9
Kimura, Ko, 76
King, Dave, 410
Kinnaman, Melinda, 464
Kinski, Klaus, 306
Kishi, Keiko, 69
Klein-Rogge, Rudolf, 34, 35
Kobayashi, Kaoru, 381
Kotegawa, Yuko, 69
Krabbé, Jeroen, 338, 339
Krauss, Werner, 39
Kwan, Nancy, 381
Kyo, Machiko, 66, 67, 68, 69, 87, 325
Lack, Stephen, 283
Lacoste, Philippe, 163
Ladd, Alan, 183
Ladmiral, Nicole, 144
Lake, Michael, 366
Lamarr, Hedy, 32

Lamprecht, Gunter, 290
Lancaster, Burt, 56–57, 58, 61, 62, 291,
    292, 498
Lang, Fritz, 162
Lanoux, Victor, 448, 449
Laughton, Charles, 11–12
Laure, Carol, 272, 273–274, 276, 279–
    280
Lautherbach, Heiner, 459
Lawson, Denis, 293
Laydu, Claude, 143
Léaud, Jean-Pierre, 128, 133, 162
Leclerc, Ginette, 33
Lee, Mark, 343
Lefèvre, Louis, 23
Legrand, Michel, 251
Leigh, Vivien, 325
Lemon, Genevieve, 366
Leonardi, Marco, 479
Lesotho, Albee, 417
Lewis, Daniel Day, 295
Lindblom, Gunnel, 111, 112, 116
Livesey, Roger, 8, 208, 210, 325
Lloyd, Emily, 405, 406, 407
Loder, John, 11
Lone, John, 137
Loren, Sophia, 503
Lorre, Peter, 35–36
Löwitsch, Klaus, 286
Lulli, Folco, 30
Lycos, Tom, 365
Lynch, John, 418–419, 419–420
Lys, Lya, 99
McCann, Donal, 419
McGoohan, Patrick, 283
Magnani, Anna, 21, 41, 42, 54, 497
Makharadze, Avtandil, 483
Malanowicz, Zygmunt, 196
Malberg, Stanislas Carre de, 178
Mamonov, Piotr, 490
Mandel, Rena, 6
Manesse, Gaspard, 178, 179–180
Mangano, Silvano, 193, 379
Manojlovic, Miki, 322
Mansfield, Jayne, 491
Marais, Jean, 31
Marchand, Corinne, 251
Marchand, Guy, 239, 427, 430, 448
Marchand, Henri, 29
Marconi, Saverio, 331
Marese, Janie, 18
Marielle, Jean-Pierre, 238
Maris, Mona, 505

Martin, Steve, 208, 446
Marvin, Lee, 141, 205
Marx Brothers, 376
Masina, Giulietta, 47–48, 49–50, 53, 500
Mason, James, 14
Massari, Lea, 175, 176, 325
Mastroianni, Marcello, 354, 363, 378–379, 380
Mattes, Eva, 259
Maura, Carmen, 262, 263–264
Maurey, Nicole, 144
May, Jodhi, 415, 418
Mayniel, Juliette, 148, 149
Melville, Jean-Pierre, 184, 188
Mendonca, Mauro, 503
Merchant, Vivien, 173
Messemer, Hannes, 56
Mezogiorno, Vittorio, 219
Michi, Maria, 54, 55, 133
Mifune, Toshiro, 76, 82, 83
Mikhalkov, Nikita, 189
Miles, Sarah, 139, 140, 171
Mills, John, 12
Milo, Sandra, 56
Miou, Miou, 281, 428, 429
Mirren, Helen, 303, 412, 419
Mitchell, Eddy, 238
Miyaguchi, Seiji, 76
Miyamoto, Nobuko, 316, 317
Modot, Gaston, 32
Molina, Alfred, 300, 301
Momoi, Kaori, 313
Monk, Roger, 413
Monroe, Marilyn, 491, 498
Montand, Yves, 30, 422, 457
Moore, Gar, 55
Moreau, Jeanne, 281–282, 325, 503
Morgan, Michele (French actress), 149, 151, 325
Morgan, Michelle (British actress), 12
Mori, Masayuki, 69, 87
Moriarty, P. H., 410
Morier-Genoud, Philippe, 180
Morlacchi, Lucilla, 60
Moschin, Gastone, 139
Moulin, Charles, 33
Muir, Geraldine, 140
Mulock, Al, 167
Musaus, Hans, 308
Mvusi, Linda, 417
Nazzari, Amadeo, 49
Neff, Hildegarde, 152

Negoda, Natalya, 491
Nevin, Robyn, 525
Newley, Anthony, 11
Newton, Robert, 11
Nicholson, Jack, 46–47, 506
Niemczyk, Leon, 196
Niven, David, 8
Noiret, Philippe, 181, 219, 238, 239, 241, 242, 479
Noro, Line, 32
Nortier, Nadine, 145
O'Connor, Carroll, 142
O'Connor, Derrick, 139
Ochsenknecht, Uwe, 459
Ogier, Bulle, 104, 107
Ohana, Claudia, 508
Oldman, Gary, 300–301, 395, 396, 398
Olivier, Laurence, 207, 209, 210, 325, 392
O'Neill, Jennifer, 283
Ophuls, Marcel, 443
O'Toole, Peter, 136
Ouedraogo, Noufou, 356
Palance, Jack, 161
Papas, Irene, 222, 457
Parlo, Dita, 23
Patekar, Nana, 387
Peck, Gregory, 448
Pecoraro, Susu, 505
Pera, Marília, 499, 501
Perez, Vincent, 446
Périer, François, 31, 51
Perrin, Jacques, 458, 479
Petelius, Pirkka-Pekka, 384
Philipe, Gérard, 325
Pialat, Maurice, 328, 330
Piccoli, Michel, 161, 162
Pickles, Vivian, 228
Pinter, Harold, 173
Pisier, Marie-France, 448
Plowright, Joan, 209
Presle, —, 325
Preston, Mike, 523
Prevost, Françoise, 213
Prince, 387
Prochnow, Jürgen, 469
Quinn, Anthony, 53
Radner, Gilda, 395
Radziwilowicz, Jerzy, 253
Raimu, 33
Ralli, Giovanna, 56
Ramalho, Elba, 508
Redgrave, Vanessa, 300, 404, 405

Renoir, Pierre, 19, 29
Renoir, Sophie, 217
Rey, Fernando, 104, 107
Richardson, Joely, 405
Richardson, Ralph, 12
Riegert, Peter, 292
Riton, 274
Rivette, Jacques, 213
Riveyre, Jean, 144
Rivière, Marie, 218
Robards, Jason, 165
Roberts, Rachel, 125
Robinson, Bill "Bojangles," 425
Robinson, Edward G., 19
Rode, Thierry, 163
Rosay, Françoise, 27, 28
Rossiter, Leonard, 226
Roussel, Myriem, 163
Rouvel, Catherine, 151
Rundgren, Kicki, 464
Ryu, Chishu, 89, 90
S., Bruno, 307–308
Sagebrecht, Marianne, 260–261
Sakuma, Yoshiko, 69
Salou, Louis, 29
Salvatori, Renato, 457–458
Sanda, Dominique, 134, 139
Sander, Otto, 350
Sandrelli, Stefania, 139
Sanga, Fatimata, 357
Sassard, Jacqueline, 173
Schell, Maria, 41
Schmitz, Sybille, 6
Schneider, Betty, 213
Schneider, Maria, 47, 127, 134, 325
Schneider, Romy, 325
Schofield, Drew, 395, 397
Schreck, Max, 37
Schygulla, Hanna, 263, 286, 287, 288–289, 290
Scott, George C., 321
Seberg, Jean, 159, 160, 184
Seth, Roshan, 295
Seyrig, Delphine, 104, 107
Sharma, Chandra, 387
Shawn, Wallace, 299
Shcherbuk, Pavel, 189
Shearer, Moira, 9
Shimura, Takashi, 76, 82
Shuranova, Antonia, 189
Sidney, Sylvia, 10
Signoret, Simone, 133
Silva, Fernando Ramos da, 497

Simon, Michel, 18, 19, 23, 24, 27, 28, 133
Simon, Simone, 325
Sinclair, Gordon John, 294
Sjöström, Victor, 111
Skolimowski, Jerzy, 476
Sleepy Sleepers (rock band), 385
Smoktunovski, Innokenty, 380
Smordoni, Rinaldo, 64
Sofonova, Elena, 378
Sokolov, Andrei, 491
Solovei, Elena, 189
Soublette, Andrès José Cruz, 193
Soutendjik, Renée, 339
Spence, Bruce, 522, 523
Stallone, Sylvester, 355
Stamp, Terrence, 193
Stéphane, Nicole, 188
Stoppa, Paolo, 59
Strode, Woody, 167
Stroheim, Erich von, 19, 20
Suchet, David, 417
Sukowa, Barbara, 290
Sullavan, Margaret, 325
Suzman, Janet, 301
Sydow, Max von. See von Sydow, Max
Syed, Shafiz, 386
Tabakov, Oleg, 189
Tagore, Sharmila, 201
Tanaka, Kinuyo, 85, 87, 88
Tarascio, Enzo, 139
Tarkovsky, Arseny, 230
Tati, Jacques, 235, 236
Tavernier, Nils, 153
Telleria, Isabel, 462
Temple, Shirley, 425
Tester, Desmond, 10
Thiller, Luc, 437
Thompson, Jack, 517
Thulin, Ingrid, 111, 112, 114, 116
Thuy An Luu, 267
Ti Lung, 378
Torrent, Ana, 223, 224–225, 462
Toto, 193
Trintignant, Jean-Louis, 136, 138–139, 214, 215, 457
Truffaut, François, 244, 247
Tsuyuguchi, Shigeru, 313
Tushingham, Rita, 387
Tyson, Cathy, 320
Tyson, Cicely, 320
Ullmann, Liv, 108, 111–112, 114, 115, 503
Umecka, Jolanta, 196

Valli, Alida, 41
van Cleef, Lee, 169
van Doren, Mamie, 491
Vanel, Charles, 30, 220, 221
Van Eyck, Peter, 30
Veidt, Conrad, 39
Vernon, Anne, 56
Vernon, John, 142
Viellard, Eric, 217
Vignal, Pascale, 242
Villafañe, Chunchuna, 512
Villalpando, David, 509
Vitez, Antoine, 215
Vitti, Monica, 5, 46, 325
Vogler, Rüdiger, 346, 347
Voight, John, 325
Volonte, Gian-Maria, 222
Volter, Philippe, 446
von Stroheim, Erich. *See* Stroheim,
  Erich von
von Sydow, Max, 453–454
Wagner, Kurt, 472
Walbrook, Anton, 8
Walker, Robert, 150
Wallach, Eli, 169
Walters, Julie, 300
Warnecke, Gordon, 295
Warner, David, 206
Washbourne, Mona, 226

Watts, Gwendolyn, 227
Wayne, John, 164, 165, 367, 470
Webb, Chloe, 395, 398
Weber, Jacques, 446
Wells, Vernon, 523
Werner, François, 177
West, Julian, 6
Whitelaw, Billie, 412
Whitford, Peter, 525
Wiazemsky, Anne, 193
Wilker, Jose, 503
Wilkinson, Tom, 404
Wilms, Andre, 437
Winocourt, Marc, 175
Wood, Natalie, 381, 505
Woodlawn, Holly, 398
Woodward, Edward, 517
Wooldridge, Susan, 140
Wymark, Patrick, 195
Wynn, Keenan, 142
Yadav, Raghubir, 387
Yamazaki, Tsutomu, 316, 317
Yanne, Jean, 163
York, Michael, 173
York, Susannah, 325
Yoshinaga, Sayuri, 69
Zaitchenko, Piotr, 490
Zischler, Hanns, 347

INDEX OF FILMS

Foreign-language titles are alphabetized by the first word, whether or not it is an article. English-language titles beginning with an article are alphabetized by the second word, while retaining the article in its anterior position.

Above Us the Waves, 468
Accatone (The Scrounger), 193
Accident, 122, 172–174
An Actor's Revenge, 73
The African Queen, 448
Aguirre, the Wrath of God, 304–306
Alexander Nevsky, 93–96, 491
Alexander the Great, 360, 362
Algiers, 32
Alice in the Cities, 344, 346, 347, 348
All the President's Men, 414
All These Women, 108, 111
Alphaville, 37, 161
Altered States, 283
Always, 367
Amarcord, 323, 506
The American Friend, 344, 345, 348, 349
An American in Paris, 134
Anatahan, 3
And Now My Love, 448
Andrei Rublev, 229
Annie, 347
Annie Hall, 91
À Nos Amours, 327–329, 330
À Nous la Liberté, 29–30, 35
Antoine Doinel series, 244, 246
Aparajito, 200, 201, 387
Apocalypse Now, 506
À Propos de Nice, 3
Apur Sansar. *See* The World of Apu (Apur Sansar)
Apu Trilogy, 122, 200, 201
Arabian Nights, 194
Architects of Our Happiness, 253, 254

Ariel, 382, 384–385
Arthur, 526
Ashes and Diamonds, 123, 252
Atlantic City, 57, 123
Au Hasard, Balthazar, 102, 358
Au Revoir les Enfants, 177–180
Autumn Sonata, 279
The Aviator's Wife, 217
Awakenings, 92
Babette's Feast, 451, 454–456
Bad Girls. *See* Les Biches (Bad Girls)
The Bad Sleep Well, 82
Bagdad Cage, 258
The Baker's Wife, 33
The Ballad of Narayama, 258, 311
Bandits vs. Samurai Squadron, 75
Band of Outsiders, 160
The Band Wagon, 266
Barbarella, 134
Barbarosa, 515
The Battle of Algiers, 457
Battleship Potemkin. *See* Potemkin
Beaches, 92
Beau Père, 274–281
Beauty and the Beast, 2
Bed and Board, 244
The Beekeeper, 360, 363
Before the Revolution, 122
Belle de Jour, 101, 103, 107, 343, 503
Bellissima, 3, 41
The Belly of an Architect, 302
Berlin Alexanderplatz, 289–291
A Better Tomorrow, 377–378
Betty Blue, 270–271
Beyond the Law, 130

Bezhin Meadow, 94
The Bicycle Thief, 40–41, 50, 65, 81–82
Billy Liar, 122, 225–227
Birch Wood, 123
Birth of a Nation, 40
The Bitter Tears of Petra von Kant, 258
Bizarre, Bizarre, 26–28
Bizet's Carmen, 123, 225
Black and White as Days and Nights,
    469
The Black Cannon Incident, 371
Black Narcissus, 7, 9
Black Orpheus, 149–150, 387
Black Peter, 158
Blade Runner, 161
Blood and Roses, 6
Blood of a Poet, 2, 5
Blood Wedding, 123
Blow-Up, 3, 370
The Blue Angel, 38–39
Bluebeard. See Landru
Blue Velvet, 366
The Boat. See Das Boot
Bob le Flambeur, 181–187
Bonnie and Clyde, 159
The Book of Mary, 162
Boudu Saved from Drowning, xvii, 19
Boyfriends and Girlfriends (L'Ami de
    Mon Amie), 216–219
The Boy with Green Hair, 122
Bread and Chocolate, 466
Breaker Morant, 515–516, 516–518
Breathless, 44, 159–160, 184–185, 187,
    188, 250, 265, 270, 370, 421
The Bride of Frankenstein, 34–35
The Bride Wore Black, 245
Brightness. See Yeelen (Brightness)
Brink of Life, 111
Broadcast News, 91
Broken Blossoms, 27
The Brood, 258
The Burmese Harp, 3, 67
The Butterfly Murders, 376
Bye Bye, Brazil, 495, 506–507, 508
Cabaret, 208, 508
The Cabinet of Dr. Caligari, 39
Cabiria. See Nights of Cabiria (Le
    Notti di Cabiria).
Cal, 390, 418–420
Calamari Union, 383
Camila, 496, 504–506
Camille Claudel, 447
Candy Mountain, 385

Canterbury Tales, 194
Careful, He Might Hear You, 524–525
Carmen. See Bizet's Carmen
Casque d'Or, 133
Caste, 7
Cat and Mouse, 272
Catherine, 17
Cattle Annie and Little Britches, 57
Caught, 16
Céleste, 259–260, 261
Celine and Julie Go Boating, 212, 268
Cesar, 3
Chaim Rumkowski and the Jews of
    Lodz, 431
Changes, 126
The Chant of Jimmie Blacksmith, 515,
    516, 517
The Charleston, xvii, 17
Chikamatsu Monogatari, 85
Children of Paradise, 28, 29, 240, 387
Chinatown, 123, 159
Chloe in the Afternoon, 123
Chocolat, 424–426
Choose Me, 526
Christ Stopped at Eboli, 220, 222, 452
Chronicle of a Summer, 512
Cinema Paradiso, 452, 479
Citizen Kane, xviii, 21, 252, 253
Claire's Knee, 123
Cleo from 5 to 7, 251
Cleopatra, 58
The Clockmaker, 123, 239
Close Encounters of the Third Kind,
    244
Clowns' Twilight. See The Naked
    Night
College, 100
Comfort and Joy, 258
Coming Home, 325
The Company of Wolves, 320, 322
The Conformist, 128, 133, 136, 138–139
Confusion, 233
The Consequence, 469
Contempt, 161–162, 370
The Cook, the Thief, His Wife and
    Her Lover, 302–304
The Cotton Club, 319
A Countess from Hong Kong, 131
Coup de Foudre. See Entre Nous
Coup de Torchon, 237–241
Cousin, Cousine, 219, 272, 421, 447–
    449
The Cousins, 44, 147–151, 152

Cria!, 122, 223–225
Cries and Whispers, 112, 223
Crime and Punishment, 383
The Crime of Monsieur Lange. *See* La
  Crime de Monsieur Lange
Cronaca de un Amore, 42
Cry Freedom, 415
A Cry in the Dark, 516
Cul de Sac, 123
Cyrano de Bergerac, 421, 441–443
The Dance of Death, 134
Dangerous Liaisons (Les Liaisons Dan-
  gereuses), 297
Danton, 123
Dark Eyes, 354, 378–380
Dark Habits, 263
Darling, 123
Das Boot, 451–452, 468–470
Dawn of the Dead, 237
Day for Night, 244, 246
A Day in the Country, xvii
Days of '36, 359–360
Days of Wrath, 4
Dead Ringers, 284–285
Death in Venice, 3
Death Watch, 238, 239
Decameron, 194
Deliverance, 140
Detective, 161, 163
Devi, 123
The Devil's Eye, 108
Diabolique, 2
Diary of a Country Priest (Journal d'un
  Curé de Campagne), 142–145, 148
Diary of a Lost Girl, 3
Die Hard, 356
The Dirty Girls. *See* Pigs and
  Battleships
Dirty Little Billy, 165
The Discreet Charm of the Bour-
  geoisie (Le Charme Discret de la
  Bourgeoisie), 2, 101, 102–107
Distant Thunder, 123
Distant Voices, Still Lives, 389, 400–
  403
Diva, 265–270, 271
Docks of New York, 3
Dr. Mabuse, the Gambler, 3, 35
Dr. Mabuse series, 312
Dr. Zhivago, 526
Dolemite, 355
Dona Flor and Her Two Husbands,
  495, 502–504

Don's Party, 516
Double Indemnity, 66
Dov'É La Liberta, 42
Down and Out in Beverly Hills, 19
Do You Remember Dolly Bell?, 323
Dracula, 4
The Draughtsman's Contract, 301–302
Dreamchild, 391
Driving Miss Daisy, 516
Drôle de Drame. *See* Bizarre, Bizarre
Drugstore Cowboy, 159
The Duellists, 410
Early Summer, 3, 89
The Earrings of Madame de . . ., 13–16
Earth, 98
Easy Rider, 164, 506
Eclipse (L'Eclisse), 3, 46
Edge of the World, 7
8½, 3
Eijanaika, 311–315
El, 101
El Amor Brujo, 123
Elena and Her Men, xvii, 21
Elevator to the Gallows, 123
Elmer Gantry, 57
El Norte, 496, 509–510
The Elusive Corporal, xvii
The Emerald Forest, 140
End of St. Petersburg, 3
The End of Summer, 89
The Enemy Below, 468
The Enigma of Kaspar Hauser, 306–
  308, 504, 520
Enjo, 67
The Entertainer, 122, 207–210
Entre Nous, 421, 426–430
Era Notte a Roma, 42
Erendira, 508
Eroica, 44
Europa 51 (The Greatest Love), 42
Every Day Except Christmas, 15
Every Man for Himself, 362
Excalibur, 140
The Exorcist, 283
The Exterminating Angel, 101, 106
Eyes without a Face, 2, 33
Face to Face, 112
Fahrenheit 451, 370
The Fallen Idol, 12
The Fall of Sodom, 263
Family Viewing, 368
Fanny, 3
Fanny and Alexander, 109, 112–113

The Far Country, 186
The Far Pavilions, 294
Farrebique, 466
The Fat and the Lean, 123
Father, 452
Faust, 3
Fear, 42
F for Fake, 236
The Fiancés, 467
The Fireman's Ball, 158
Fires on the Plain, 3, 72
First Name: Carmen, 163
A Fistful of Dollars, 122
Fitzcarraldo, 344
The Flame and the Arrow, 57
Flash Gordon, 516
Flatliners, 31
The Flesh is Hot. See Pigs and
    Battleships
Floating Weeds, 93
Flowers of St. Francis, 42
The Fly, 284, 285
Foolish Wives, 17, 19
Fortini-Cani, 432
The 49th Parallel, 8
The 400 Blows, 122, 162, 244, 245, 246,
    387, 421, 487
The Fourth Man, 338–339
Fox and His Friends, 258
Frankenstein, 4, 461, 462
Frantic. See Elevator to the Gallows
Freeze, Die, Come to Life, 482, 487–
    488
French Can-Can, xvii, 19, 20, 21
The French Connection, 107
The Fringe Dwellers, 516
From Here to Eternity, 57
From Russia with Rock, 384
Full Moon in Paris, 217
The Funeral, 258, 317
Gallipoli, 343–344, 523
Gandhi, 109
Gang of Four, 212
The Garden of Delights, 123
The Garden of the Finzi-Continis, 3
General Della Rovere, 42, 55–56
Georgy Girl, 401
Germany Year Zero, 3, 41
Gertrud, 4–5, 5–6
Get Out Your Handkerchiefs, 271–274,
    276, 279–280, 447
The Getting of Wisdom, 516
Ghost, 31

Gigi, 151
The Goalie's Anxiety at the Penalty
    Kick, 344, 345, 348
The Go-Between, 525
Going Places, 272, 279, 281–282, 447
The Golden Coach, xvii, 20–21
Gone With the Wind, 70
The Good, the Bad, and the Ugly, 169
The Gospel According to St. Matthew,
    193
Goupi Mains Rouges, 237
Grand Illusion. See La Grande Illusion
Great Expectations, 48
Greed, 102
The Green Bay Tree, 169
The Green Room, 244, 247, 248
Gregory's Girl, 291, 294
The Grifters, 297
Gumshoe, 297
A Guy Named Joe, 367
Guys and Dolls, 401
Hail, Mary!, 159, 162, 163
Halloween, 282
Hamlet Goes Business, 384
Hammett, 344
Hands Up, 452
Hardcore, 321
Harold and Maude, 260
Harvest, 3
Hatari, 370
Hawks and Sparrows, 193
Heaven Can Wait, 108
Heimat, 452, 470–472
Henry V, 390, 392–393
The Hidden Fortress, 3
High and Low, 82, 83
High Sierra, 385
High Tide, 515
Hiroshima, Mon Amour, 202, 203–204,
    205, 370
Hitler, a Film from Germany, 431
Hobson's Choice, 11–12
Holocaust (TV miniseries), 430, 471
The Home and the World, 196–200
The Hoodlum Priest, 148–149
Hope and Glory, 122, 139–141
The Horror Chamber of Doctor
    Faustus. See Eyes without a Face
The Horse Thief, 369–373
Hotel Splendide, 7
Hotel Terminus: The Life and Times
    of Klaus Barbie, 442–445
Hour of the Star, 496

Hour of the Wolf, 112
How I Won the War, 334
The Human Tornado, 355
The Human Voice, 41
If . . ., 122, 125–127
If I Had a Gun, 356
I Hired a Contract Killer, 385
Ikiru, 3, 83
I Know Where I'm Going, 8
Il Bidone, 48
Il Grido, 3, 42
Il Posto, 467
The Immigrant, 180
I'mo Get You Sucka, 355
India, 42
Indiana Jones, 376
The Infernal Machine, 41
Iron Maze, 382
The Italian Straw Hat, 2, 30
Ivanhoe, 79
Ivan the Terrible, 3, 137
I Vinti, 42
I Vitelloni, 3, 43, 48, 52, 53, 501
I Was Born But . . ., 91
Jaws, 469
The Jazz Singer, 516
Jean de Florette, xviii, 421, 422–424,
   447
Joan at the Stake, 42
Jour de Fête, 232
Journal d'un Curé de Campagne. See
   Diary of a Country Priest (Journal
   d'un Curé de Campagne)
Joyless Street, 3
Judex, 33
The Judge and the Assassin, 238, 239
Ju Dou, 371
Jules and Jim, 243, 245–246, 247, 248
Juste avant la Nuit, 152
Kagemusha, 2, 75, 79–81, 311
Kagi (Odd Obsession), 44, 66–69, 72
Kameradschaft, 3
Kanal, 252, 255
Katie's Passion. See Keetje Tippel
   (Katie's Passion)
Keetje Tippel (Katie's Passion), 258
The Killers, 57, 409
The Killing Fields, 415
Kind Hearts and Coronets, 151
Kind Lady, 169
A Kind of Loving, 123
King Lear, 161
King of Hearts, 519

Kings of the Road, 344, 345, 347, 348
King's Ransom, 83
Knife in the Water, 194, 196
Knights of the Round Table, 79
Kostas, 520
Kramer vs. Kramer, 525
The Krays, 390, 412–414
La Bête Humaine, xvii, 133
La Chienne, xvii, 18–19, 133
La Chinoise, 268
Lacombe, Lucien, 178
La Crime de Monsieur Lange, xvii, 19
La Dolce Vita, 3, 43, 45, 181
La Femme Infidèle, 107, 152
La Fille de l'Eau, 17
L'Age d'Or, 99, 102, 103, 105
La Grande Illusion, xvii, 19–20, 335,
   478
La Guerre Est Finie, 457
La Jetée, 439
La Marseillaise, xvii
L'Ami de Mon Amie. See Boyfriends
   and Girlfriends (L'Ami de Mon
   Amie)
L'Amour Fou, 107
La Nave Bianca, 41
Lancelot of the Lake, 79
Landru, 151–152
Landscape in the Mist, 354, 358, 360,
   363, 364
La Notte, 43, 46
La Notte di San Lorenzo. See The
   Night of the Shooting Stars (La
   Notte di San Lorenzo)
La Règle du Jeu, 102, 106
L'Argent, 142
L'Armée des Ombres, 184
La Ronde, 3, 13, 16
La Rupture, 152
Las Hurdes, 102
La Signora Senza Camelia, 42
The Last Command, 38
The Last Emperor, 135–138
The Last Laugh, 3, 370
The Last Métro, 245, 447, 478
La Strada, 43, 48, 50, 52, 53–54
Last Tango in Paris, 47, 127–135, 136,
   159, 325
The Last Temptation of Christ, 330
The Last Wave, 258, 340, 341
Last Year at Marienbad, 106, 107, 123,
   202, 205, 206, 303
L'Atalante, 21–25, 133

La Terra Trema, 40, 58, 62–63
Late Spring, 3, 89
The Lavender Hill Mob, 10, 528
La Voie Lactée, 103
L'Avventura, 5, 42, 43, 44–45, 46, 67, 101, 135, 364
Law of Desire, 263, 297
Lawrence of Arabia, 57, 526
Le Amiche, 42–43
Le Beau Serge, 122
Le Boucher, 152
Le Chaland Qui Passe. *See* L'Atalante
Le Charme Discret de la Bourgeoisie. *See* The Discreet Charm of the Bourgeoisie (Le Charme Discret de la Bourgeoisie)
L'Eclisse. *See* Eclipse (L'Eclisse)
Le Deuxième Souffle, 184
Le Doulos (The Stoolie), 184, 187
The Legend of Suram Fortress, 192
Le Journal d'une Femme de Chambre, 103, 107
Le Jour se Lève, 2, 28
Le Million, 2, 30
Lemmy Caution serials, 161
Leningrad Cowboys Go America, 385–386
Le Notti di Cabiria. *See* Nights of Cabiria (Le Notti di Cabiria)
The Leopard, 56–62
Le Petit Theatre de Jean Renoir (The Little Theater of Jean Renoir), xvii, 18
Le Plaisir, 3, 13
Le Rayon Vert. *See* Summer (Le Rayon Vert)
Les Affaires Publiques, 142
Le Samourai, 184, 186
Les Anges du Peche, 142
Les Biches (Bad Girls), 122, 152
Les Bonnes Femmes, 87, 152, 155
Les Carabiniers, 337
Les Enfants Terribles, 183–184, 188
Le Silence de la Mer, 182, 183
Les Liaisons Dangereuses. *See* Dangerous Liaisons (Les Liaisons Dangereuses)
Les Visiteurs du Soir, 2, 28
Lethal Weapon, 356
Let Joy Reign Supreme, 239
Letters from an Unknown Woman, 16
Liebelei, 3, 15

The Life and Death of Colonel Blimp, 8
Life and Nothing But, 241–243
Life of Brian, 411
The Life of Oharu, 84–87
Limelight, 401
Little Big Man, 165, 283
The Little Match Girl, xvii, 17, 18
The Little Theater of Jean Renoir. *See* Le Petit Theatre de Jean Renoir (The Little Theater of Jean Renoir)
Little Vera, 481, 487, 491–493
Local Hero, 8, 291–293, 415
Lola Montès, 3, 41
The Loneliness of the Long Distance Runner, 401
Lonely Hearts, 519, 520, 525
The Long Goodbye, 161
The Long Good Friday, 319, 390, 409–412
Look Back in Anger, 211
Los Olvidados, 99, 103, 105, 387, 499
Loulou, 325–327
Love at Twenty, 244
Love Goes; Love Comes, 263
Love Is a Many Splendored Thing, 401
Love on the Run, 244
The Lovers, 123, 181
Loves of a Blonde, 157–158
Lucky Luciano, 123
Luna, 329
L'Uomo Della Croce, 41
M, 35–36
Madame Bovary, xvii
Made in USA, 105, 160
Mad Max, 522
The Magician, 37, 111, 113, 114
The Magnificent Ambersons, 21, 102
The Magnificent Seven, 77
Maidstone, 130
The Makioka Sisters, 69–74
Malcolm, 516, 526–528
Mammals, 123
A Man and a Woman, 448
Manhattan, 466
Man of Flowers, 518–520, 528
Man of Iron, 477
Man of Marble, 251–255
Manon, 2
Manon des Sources, 424
Manon of the Spring, xviii
The Man Who Shot Liberty Valance, 165

Marius, 3
The Marriage of Maria Braun, 285–289
Masculine-Feminine, 162
Matador, 263
A Match Factory Girl, 385
Mayerling, 14
Medea, 193
Medium Cool, 457
Men . . ., 452, 458–460
Mephisto, 452, 476–478
The Merchant of Four Seasons, 258, 383
Metropolis, 34–35, 36, 213
Mexican Bus Ride, 100–101
Midnight Cowboy, 123
The Miracle, 41, 50
Miracle in Milan, 3
The Mirror, 229, 230
The Mission, 415
Mississippi Mermaid, 245
Mr. Hulot's Holiday, 232
Mix-Up, 236
The Model Shop, 126
Modern Times, 30, 35
Mona Lisa, 319–321, 408
Mon Oncle, 232
Mon Oncle d'Amérique, 123
Monsieur Hire, 421, 436–438
Monsieur Verdoux, 151
Monty Python's The Meaning of Life, 109
The Moon in the Gutter, 271
Moonlighting, 452, 473–476
Morgan!, 206
Morocco, 3
Moscow on the Hudson, 476
Mother, 98
Mouchette, 143, 145–147
Mrs. Soffel, 516
Murderer among Us. See M
Muriel, 123, 203
Murmur of the Heart, 174–177, 178
My Beautiful Laundrette, 294–298
My Brilliant Career, 516
My Darling Clementine, 75, 165, 364
My First Wife, 527
My Friend Ivan Lapshin, 481, 484–487
My Life as a Dog, 451, 463–465
My Life to Live, 4, 162–163
My Little Village, 356
My Name is Ivan, 228, 229
My Night at Maud's, 214–215, 217, 448

The Mystery of Kaspar Hauser. See The Enigma of Kaspar Hauser
The Naked Night, 110
Nana, 17, 162
New York Stories, 174
Night and Fog, 202–203
Night at the Crossroads, 19
The Night of the Shooting Stars (La Notte di San Lorenzo), 332–338, 452
Nights of Cabiria. (Le Notti di Cabiria), 43, 47–53, 193, 500
9 1/2 Weeks, 374
1900, 137, 466
Nine to Five, 516
Nosferatu, 36–37, 161
Nosferatu the Vampyre, 37
Nostalgia, 229–230
Notes for an African Oresteia, 193
Nouvelle Vague, 161
The Nun, 211–213
Oblomov, 123, 189
October, 4
Odd Obsession. See Kagi (Odd Obsession)
Oedipus Rex, 193
Oedipus Wrecks, 174
The Official Story, 496, 512–513
Oliver Twist, 11
O Lucky Man, 122
Once Upon a Time in America, 122
Once Upon a Time in the West, 164–169
One from the Heart, 9
On Purge Bébé, 16
Open City, 40, 41, 42, 54, 55, 56, 133
Opera do Malandro, 495, 507–509
Ordet, 4, 358, 362
Orpheus, 31–32
Ossessione, 3, 40, 41, 133, 359
Out of Africa, 425
Out 1, 236
Package Tour, 431
Padre Padrone, 220, 330–332, 333, 452, 466
Paisan, 40, 41, 42, 55, 337
Pandora's Box, 37–38
Panique, 2, 437
Parade, 231–237
Paradis Perdu, 244–245, 246
Paris Belongs to Us, 213, 268
The Parson's Widow, 357
Partner, 136
A Passage to India, 198, 294, 425

The Passenger, 46–47
Passion, 163
The Passion of Anna, 112
The Passion of Beatrice, 123
The Passion of Joan of Arc, 4
Pather Panchali, 198, 200, 201, 356
Paths of Glory, 517
Pauline at the Beach, 123, 217
Peeping Tom, 8
Peking Opera Blues, 375–376
Pelle the Conqueror, xviii, 451, 452–454
Pennies from Heaven (BBC miniseries), 319, 391, 402, 411
Pennies from Heaven (Hollywood film), 208, 402
Pépé le Moko, 32
Performance, 142, 297
Permanent Vacation, 349
Persona, 108, 111, 112, 114–116, 117–119
Personal Services, 408
Pickpocket, 122
Picnic at Hanging Rock, 339–343
Picnic on the Grass, xvii
Pigs and Battleships, 309
Pixote, 386, 495, 497–501
Playtime, 232, 233, 234, 237, 370
Plenty, 405
Poil de Carotte, 2
Point Blank, 122, 141–142, 205
Popeye, 516
The Pornographers, 308–311
Port of Shadows, 28, 149
The Postman Always Rings Twice, 133
Potemkin, 4, 93, 94, 97, 376
Pretty Poison, 159
Prick Up Your Ears, 298–301
The Producers, 443
Providence, 204–206
Psycho, 194
Queen Christina, 87
Rabid, 258, 284
Radio On, 349
Raging Bull, 9
Raiders of the Lost Ark, 410, 521
The Rainmaker, 57
Raise the Titanic, 412
Rambo, 374, 460
Ran, 3
Rashomon, 85, 87
The Raven, 30, 31
Rear Window, 102
The Reckless Moment, 16

The Reconstruction, 359, 360, 362
Red Desert, 46
The Red Shoes, 9
Red Sorghum, 371, 373–374
Repentance, 481, 482–484
Repulsion, 194–195
Reverse Angle: NYC, March '82, 348
Ride the High Country, 185–186
Rififi, 185
Rio Bravo, 77
The Rise of Louis XIV, 370
Risky Business, 177
The River, xvii, 17–18, 387, 466
The Road Warrior, 516, 521–522
Rocco and His Brothers, 41, 58, 62
Room at the Top, 124
Rouge, 377
Roxanne, 446
Rue Cases Nègres. See Sugar Cane Alley (Rue Cases Nègres)
The Rules of the Game, xvii, 16–17, 18, 20, 21, 171
Run Silent, Run Deep, 468
Sabotage, 10–11
The Sacrifice, 228–229, 230
The Saimaa Gesture, 382
Salaam, Bombay, 354, 386–387
Salo, 194
Salvatore Giuliano, 122
Same Player Shoots Again, 349
Sammy and Rosie Get Laid, 258
San Miniato, July 1944, 335
Sansho Dayu, 102, 364
Sansho the Bailiff, 88
Sans Soleil, 239, 438–441
Saturday Night and Sunday Morning, 124, 401
Sauve Qui Peut/La Vie, 162, 163
The Savage Innocents, 370, 371–372
Sawdust and Tinsel. See The Naked Night
Sayat Nova, 191–192
Scanners, 282–283
Scarface, 32, 237, 497, 508
Scarlet Street, 19
Scenes from a Marriage, 111, 112, 284
The Scrounger. See Accatone (The Scrounger)
The Searchers, 186
Senso, 3, 41, 133
The Serpent's Egg, 112
The Servant, 122, 169–171, 173
The Seven Deadly Sins, 42

The Seven Samurai, 2, 75–79, 523
The Seventh Seal, 44, 108, 111, 113, 114
The Seven-Year Itch, 268
A Severed Head, 237
sex, lies, and videotape, 368
Shadows in Paradise, 383–384, 385
Shadows of Our Forgotten Ancestors, 191
Shame, 112
Shoah, 236, 430–436, 442, 471
Shoeshine, 40, 44–45, 63–64, 387, 499
Shoot the Moon, 426
The Sicilian, 380
Sid and Nancy, 300, 390, 394–399
The Silence, 108, 110, 111, 114–115, 116–117
Silkwood, 414
Silver City, 349
The Singing Detective (film), 390–391
The Singing Detective (TV miniseries), 402
Singin' in the Rain, 401
The Sisters of the Gion, 3
Slave of Love, 189, 191, 486
The Sleeping Car Murder, 457
Smash Palace, 426
Smiles of a Summer Night, 44, 108, 110, 111
Solaris, 229
Soldier Blue, 165
Soldier of Orange, 258, 339
Sous les Toits de Paris, 2
Speaking Parts, 367, 368–369
Spetters, 258, 339
Spiders, 3
The Spider's Stratagem, 122
Spies, 3, 35
Spirit of the Beehive, 223, 452, 460–463
Spoiled Children, 238, 239, 241
The Spy in Black, 8
Stairway to Heaven, 8–9
Stalker, 229, 362, 364
Stand By Me, 526
State of Siege, 452
Stir Crazy, 516
Stolen Kisses, 244
The Stoolie. See Le Doulos
The Story of Adèle H., 243, 245, 246–247
The Story of the Last Chry-santhemum, 3
A Story of the Wind, 236

Story of Women, 152–156
Strange Deception, 40
Strangers, 42
Strangers on a Train, 150
Stranger Than Paradise, 159
Stray Dog, 81–82, 83
Strike, 3
Stromboli, 3, 42
Stroszek, 258
Sugarbaby, 260–261
Sugar Cane Alley (Rue Cases Nègres), 496, 510–512
Summer (Le Rayon Vert), 217–218
Summer with Monika, 110
Sunday Bloody Sunday, 227–228
A Sunday in the Country, 123, 241, 242, 243
Sunrise, 3, 86
Sweetie, xviii, 364–366
The Swing, 261
Tabu, 3
The Tales of Hoffman, 9
The Tall Blond Man with One Black Shoe, 448
Tampopo, 315–317
A Ts2ste of Honey, 401
Taxi Blues, 481, 487, 489–490
A Taxing Woman, 317–318
The Taxing Woman's Return, 258
Ten Days That Shook the World, 3
Tender Mercies, 516
Teorema (Theorem), 193–194
The Texas Chainsaw Massacre, 237
That Obscure Object of Desire, 101
They Came from Within, 284
The Thief of Baghdad, 7, 8
This Man Must Die, 152
This Sporting Life, 123–125, 401
The Thorn Birds, 504
Three Brothers, 219–221
The Threepenny Opera, 3, 507–508
Through a Glass, Darkly, 108, 111, 112, 113
Time of the Gypsies, 324–325
The Time to Live and the Time to Die, 353
The Tin Star, 186
Tokyo Olympiad, 3
The Tokyo Story, xviii, 89–93
Tom Jones, 123, 504
Toni, 466
Too Beautiful for You, 447
Tootsie, 108

The Touch, 111
Traffic, 233, 237
Trash, 398
The Traveling Players, 358, 360–362, 363, 364
Tree of Wooden Clogs, 220, 452, 465–467
The Trial, 268
True Grit, 164
Turkish Delights, 258
25 Fireman's Street, 452
Twilight of the Cockroaches, 380–382
Twist and Shout, 451, 452
Two Daughters, 123
Two Men and a Wardrobe, 123
Two People, 4
2001: A Space Odyssey, 161, 370, 372, 506
Ugetsu, 41, 69, 87
Umberto D., 45, 65–66
Umbrellas of Cherbourg, 194, 508
Un Chant d'Amour, 499
Un Chien Andalou, xviii, 99, 102
Under Satan's Sun (Under the Sun of Satan), 145, 329–330
Une Partie de Plaisir, 152
Une Vie Sans Joie, 17
An Unfinished Piece for a Piano Player, 188–191
Un Pilote Ritorna, 41
Vagabond, 249–250
Vampyr, 4, 6
Vanina Vanini, 42
Variety, 110
Variety Lights, 43
Vendetta, 16
Vengeance Is Mine, 258, 311
Vertigo, 364
Vingt-quatre Heures de la Vie d'un Clown, 183
Violette, 152
The Virgin Spring, 113
Viridiana, 43, 100, 101, 103
Vitelloni. See I Vitelloni

Viva Italia!, 42
Voyage to Cythera, 360, 362–363
The Wages of Fear, 30, 31
We Are the Women, 42
Wedding in Blood, 122, 152
Weekend, 103, 163
A Week's Vacation, 239, 241
The Well-Digger's Daughter, 3
Wetherby, 390, 404–405
What Have I Done to Deserve This?, 262, 263, 297
When Father Was Away on Business, 322–323, 324, 356
White Nights, 41
The White Sheik, 3, 43, 48, 52
The Wild Bunch, 164, 186, 521, 523
The Wild Child, 243, 244, 245, 247–248, 308
Wild 90, 130
Wild Strawberries, 111, 113, 338
Wings of Desire, 344, 349–351, 368
Winter Light, 108, 111, 113
Wish You Were Here, 389, 405–408
Witness, 516
A Woman Alone. See Sabotage
The Woman Next Door, 245
Women on the Verge of a Nervous Breakdown, xviii, 262, 264
A World Apart, 390, 414–418
The World of Apu (Apur Sansar), 200, 201
Wrong Move, 344, 347, 348
Yaaba, 355–357
Yeelen (Brightness), 354–355, 356
Yellow Earth, 371
Yojimbo, 3
Z, 359, 414, 452, 456–458
Zappa, 451, 452
Zazie dans le Métro, 181
Zed and Two Noughts, 258
Zéro de Conduite, xviii, 21, 22–23, 26, 499
Zulu Dawn, 411
Zvenigora, 3

ABOUT THE EDITOR

Both Mercury House and the National Society of Film Critics were shocked and saddened by Kathy Huffhines's death shortly before this book went to press. It stands as a testament to her dedication, intelligence, and talent.

Born in Akron, Ohio, on June 16, 1943, Kathy Huffhines studied English and education at Stanford and Harvard Universities. She lectured at Tufts University and Boston College before landing her first reviewing job at *The Real Paper* in Boston. She went on to review films for the *Boston Phoenix* and the *Boston Herald,* and from 1987 until her death she was the film critic for the *Detroit Free Press.*

Known in the film community for her enthusiasm, artistic judgment, and crisp style, Kathy was nominated for a Pulitzer Prize in criticism in 1990 by the executive editor of the *Detroit Free Press,* Heath J. Meriwether. Meriwether said that at the *Free Press* Kathy "blossomed as a new and interesting critical voice in the forest of motion picture critics. . . . When you talked to Kathy, you could just feel her exuberance about movies — and life, really. That came through vividly in her writing. We'll all miss her hugely."